Dreams
and
Inward
Journeys

Dreams *and* Inward Journeys

A Rhetoric and Reader for Writers

Third Edition

Marjorie Ford
Stanford University

Jon Ford
College of Alameda

 LONGMAN

An imprint of Addison Wesley Longman, Inc.

New York • Reading, Massachusetts • Menlo Park, California • Harlow, England
Don Mills, Ontario • Sydney • Mexico City • Madrid • Amsterdam

Publishing Partner: Anne Elizabeth Smith
Project Coordination and Text Design: Ruttle, Shaw & Wetherill, Inc.
Cover Designer: Antonina Colbert
Cover Illustration: "The Dream Tree" by Daniel Nevins. Superstock
Electronic Production Manager: Christine Pearson
Manufacturing Manager: Willie Lane
Electronic Page Makeup: Ruttle, Shaw & Wetherill, Inc.
Printer and Binder: Maple-Vail
Cover Printer: Coral Graphic Services, Inc.

For permission to use copyrighted material, grateful acknowledgment is made to the copyright holders on pages 543–547, which are hereby made part of this copyright page.

Library of Congress Cataloging-in-Publication Data

Ford, Marjorie (Marjorie A.)
    Dreams and inward journeys : a rhetoric and reader for writers /
Marjorie Ford, Jon Ford. — 3rd ed.
        p.   cm.
    Includes bibliographical references and index.
    ISBN 0–321–01126–0
    1. College readers.   2. English language—Rhetoric.   I. Ford,
Jon.   II. Title.
    PE1417.F63   1997
808'.0427—dc21   97-257
                                                                  CIP

ISBN 0–321–01126–0

12345678910—MA—00999897

Contents

Prereading/Early Reading   57 | Personal and Interpretive
Response   57 | Critical and Evaluative Response   58

Student Writing

Thematic Introduction   426

Readings examine the impact of political propaganda and the mass media on our dreams, fantasies, myths, and self-concepts.

Readings

CONTENTS BY STRATEGIES AND MODES

Comparison and Contrast

Classification

Definition

Cause and Effect Analysis

Interpretation and Evaluation

Argument

Myths & Tales

TO THE INSTRUCTOR

Why have many of our greatest writers found inspiration or solved problems in their dreams? What can individuals learn from their dreams that will make their waking lives more rewarding? How does the unconscious mind inform the conscious mind using writing or dreams as a medium? In what ways is the writing process like a dream? These are questions that we have been exploring in our writing classes for almost ten years now. And still they remain as signposts; our search for these answers only grows more compelling.

Throughout this past year, as we have written and revised the Third Edition of *Dreams and Inward Journeys,* we have felt very fortunate to have the opportunity to follow our dream. In this new edition we have built on the pedagogical foundation put in place by the First and Second Editions. We continue to support a creative approach to teaching writing and reading that acknowledges the role and importance of the unconscious mind, of dreams, of the imagination, of the heart connected to the reasoning mind. Also fundamental to our approach to teaching writing is the value of integrating rather than isolating the teaching of literature and exposition. We have seen our students' writing develop as they have experimented with different writing projects and genres, from dream journals to arguments and short stories, from practice with the traditional modes such as comparison, causal analysis, and definition to essays that are based on personal experiences or are primarily reflections.

Once again we have enjoyed applying these assumptions in shaping the text around the theme of dreams, a topic that is intriguing, revealing, and challenging. *Dreams and Inward Journeys* presents a rich mixture of essays, stories, poems, and student writings thematically focused on dream-related topics such as writing, reading, memory, myths, obsessions, the double, sexuality, gender roles, technology, popular culture, and visions of the future. Each chapter has an essay of advice on strategies for writing and thinking. All of the selections were chosen because they have personal and social implications that encourage students to read and to write while providing them with new ways of seeing and thinking about themselves in relationships to fundamental social issues as well as universal human concerns.

Some of the **special features** of the third edition include:

- A rhetorical advice section that opens each chapter and provides students with strategies for organizing their thinking and writing.
- Thirty-six new readings that are relevant to the thematic concept of the text, many of which present an understanding of or sensitivity to students who come from minority or immigrant communities.
- Information on keeping a dream journal as well as journal writing prompts before each reading to encourage informal writing that helps students to respond spontaneously and expressively.
- The introduction of drawing as a prewriting activity with examples of our students' black and white pictures to illustrate how this approach works.
- Two or three poems and at least one short story per chapter to introduce the chapter's issues in a concrete, expressive, and literary form.
- Two student essays in each chapter with one cast as a creative or personal response to the chapter concerns while the second is expository or argumentative. Three of the essays in the book are documented research papers.
- Traditional study questions and suggestions after each selection for extended writing projects that invite students to build on their initial reading responses.
- Writing assignments at the end of each chapter that provide opportunities for students to develop connections between selections and also suggest thematically relevant films.

Acknowledgments

In designing this edition we were guided by the excellent advice we received from reviewers around the country. We thank:

Dale Alan Bailes, Moorpark College; Virginia Dumont-Poston, Lander University; Glenda Hicks, Midland College; Kathleen McHale, Nassau Community College; Lorraine Mund, Nassau Community College; and Cathy Sheeley, Penn Valley Community College.

At Longman we want to thank the following dedicated people: Anne Smith, our editor, who fostered the creative vision of the book and kept the project on schedule; Rebecca Gilpin, Administrative Editorial Assistant, who was thoughtful, patient, and thorough; and Janet Nuciforo, our project editor, who brought her creative support and careful review to the final version of this Third Edition.

We are grateful to all of our students in the day and evening programs who have encouraged us through their enthusiasm for the concept as well as through the development of their writing. We extend particular appreciation to those students who submitted essays, stories, or drawings for this edition. In the Writing and Critical Thinking program at Stanford we thank Dolores

Rainer and Professor Carolyn Ross. We salute the fabulous crew in Stanford's Multi-Media Curriculum Development Lab for Education: Lois Brooks, Greg Chalfin, Kathy Fehrn, Charles Kerns, Kristie Lu Stout, Ed McGuigin, Makoto Tsuchitani, Amy Tzon, and Rachel Wilson—their encouragement as well as their technical and creative support were crucial in helping us develop new teaching strategies for application in Stanford's innovative flexible classroom.

Marjorie takes great pleasure in acknowledging her jazz dance instructor, Annie Zane, along with her many friends in dance classes—especially Debbie Hales and Lisa Maurizio—for helping to punctuate the many days when the writing and revising took long hours. Their commitment to music, to dance, to our physical and mental well-being will always be a reminder of the importance of our dreams.

Finally we thank our children, Michael and Maya, for their support of this book project since 1988 and for creating inspiring dreams for their own lives.

Marjorie Ford
Jon Ford

*T*O THE
STUDENT

Nothing said to us, nothing we can learn from others, reaches us so deep as that which we find in ourselves.

THEODORE REIK

dream: 1. a sequence of sensations, images, thoughts . . . passing through a sleeping person's mind 2. A fanciful vision . . . day-dream; fantasy; reverie . . . 3. a fond hope or aspiration 4. anything so lovely, charming, transitory . . . as to seem dreamlike . . . 5. to imagine as possible . . . 6. to conceive of or devise, as by giving free rein to the imagination.

ADAPTED FROM WEBSTER'S
NEW WORLD DICTIONARY

As you can see from the complexity of the definition above, the concept of the dream involves much more than the images that come into our minds while we sleep. The lyrics of popular songs, the plots of movies and novels, advertisements and travel literature—all speak of the power of dreams and promise fulfillment of fantasies of romance, success, or peace of mind. Just as everyone dreams while sleeping, each person has a personal dream or vision that guides his or her waking life. Perhaps it is a dream that one is just starting to explore, a dream that one has been working to accomplish, or a dream that has just "come true."

We have designed this text using the concept of the dream as a common meeting ground, one that we hope will encourage you to better understand yourself, your family, friends, college and professional acquaintances—and the world in which we all live. Dreams and the insights they bring from the inner self, with the universality of their patterns, imagery, and meaning, also provide a central metaphor for the writing process as an inward journey that involves the imagination, creativity, and vision.

Dreams and Inward Journeys: A Reader for Writers, Third Edition, is composed of nine chapters. Each chapter presents an aspect of the book's theme as well as a writing strategy that we think will help you to understand yourself and your world while improving your writing fluency and skills. The earlier chapters ask you to reflect on your personal experiences as a reader and as a writer. As you progress through the book, you will be asked to relate your personal and imaginative experiences to the social and cultural realities that also help to shape your identity and values. In Chapter 1, "Discovering Ourselves in Writing," writing is presented as an often chaotic but powerful and rewarding process that helps the writer to understand himself or herself better and to clarify thoughts and feelings. The writing techniques explained will help you to overcome writing-related anxieties and fears and to get started on your writing. The dream journal project introduced in this chapter will provide you with the opportunity to discover the similarities between the writing process and dreaming—to discover the concerns of your unconscious mind.

In Chapter 2, "Discovering Ourselves in Reading," you will explore the ways in which reading is an active process that encourages a reader to understand and clarify his or her inner resources and values in relation to the values and experiences that have been recorded in a text. Each selection in this chapter presents a unique perspective on the reading process and reflects on the relationships among dreaming, reading, language, and the imagination. The reading strategies introduced discuss techniques for activating and enriching your reading and language experiences while emphasizing how reading is closely related to the process of writing.

The readings in Chapter 3, "Memories from Childhood," explore how childhood experiences and memories, especially those inner experiences that are rooted in dreams, fantasies, or even obsessions, influence our sense of self. The readings included in this section also suggest that the stories created and remembered from our childhood shape our personal myths. In this chapter we discuss creative strategies for writing effective description and narratives. These strategies will help you when you write about your childhood dreams and memories.

Chapter 4, "Dreams, Myths, and Fairy Tales," begins to put your inward journey into a broader cultural perspective, helping you to see new meanings in your life experiences by suggesting how your self-concept and values have been influenced by ancient and popular myths and fairy tales. Some of the readings in this chapter discuss the similarities and relationships between dreams and myths. Because you will be asked to compare different versions of fairy tales, to contrast an early memory of a favorite childhood book with a more recent reading of that book, or to create and evaluate a personal myth, in this chapter we discuss techniques used in comparison writing as well as approaches to making clear evaluative statements.

The readings included in Chapter 5, "Nightmares and Obsessions," reveal situations in which the writer or the main character is overwhelmed by a submerged part of his or her self. Although in some selections the unconscious need is transformed positively into greater self-understanding, several of the obsessions presented in the essays and stories are self-destructive. The thinking and writing strategies presented in this chapter will help you to define and draw distinctions among complex concepts such as those presented in this text: dream, myth, fantasy, fairy tale. We also discuss some common misuses of words and barriers to clear communication as well as the difference between the private and public meanings and associations of words.

Chapter 6, "Journeys in Sexuality and Gender," explores issues of gender and sexuality in both fiction and nonfiction works as they influence an individual's self-concept and role in society. The readings also examine the ways that sexuality is reflected in dreams and emotional life, as well as the way that sexual feelings are channeled through myths and rituals. The writing and thinking strategy presented in this chapter, causal analysis, will help you to analyze and interpret the readings and will provide you with a structure for composing the essays you will be asked to write in response to the readings.

Chapter 7, "The Double/The Other," begins with a discussion of the dual nature of the human personality and presents readings, including a variety of classic stories, many of which are based on dreams or fantasies. These stories reflect different forms of the dualistic struggle within the human mind: the good self as opposed to the evil self, the rational self as opposed to the irrational self. The writing strategies in this chapter focus on how to create a balanced argument through exploring opposing viewpoints, empathizing with your audience, making decisions, and taking a final position of your own.

To what extent have your self-concept and self-image been influenced by the dreams of our mass culture or the prevailing political ideology? What happens to those people who don't choose to fit into, or who feel excluded from, the predominant "dream" of their society? These are some of the questions that are considered in the readings included in Chapter 8, "Society's Dreams." The writing strategies covered will help you to analyze social issues and to think critically about outside sources of opinion while maintaining your own personal perspective and sense of voice in research-oriented writing.

The finest quality of dreams is that they can become visions; they can help us to reshape and rebuild our personal, social, and spiritual worlds. We have chosen essays and stories that speak of visions of the future and visions born of dreams for "Dreams of Vision and Prophecy," the final chapter of the text. And for a final writing project you might decide to create your own vision of the future, imagining a utopian society or developing an ideal program for improving a serious social problem. Synthesis and problem solving, the writing strategies presented in this chapter, will help to reinforce your understanding of the chapter's readings and guide you in structuring your final essay.

Our experiences as writing teachers continue to confirm the importance of giving students many opportunities to share their writing with their peers. We have included student essays for you to share in class and hope that you find these student essays both helpful and inspiring. You can use them as a point of departure for class discussion of student writing. We hope, too, that you begin to share your own writing. We believe that you can gain confidence and motivation when you work on your writing with your peers and your instructor.

Although writing is a demanding and challenging activity, it can be a valuable and meaningful experience when you feel that you are writing about something vital, something that engages your mind and your feelings. We have worked to provide opportunities for this type of engagement through the materials and activities included in this text. We hope that this text will guide and help you to uncover and understand more fully some of your personal and public dreams.

Marjorie Ford
Jon Ford

Discovering Ourselves in Writing

1

Writing itself is one of the great, free human activities. . . . For the person who follows with trust and forgiveness what occurs to him, the world remains always ready and deep, an inexhaustible environment, with the combined vividness of an actuality and flexibility of a dream.
WILLIAM STAFFORD
The Way of Writing

I think that dreams are a way that people's minds illustrate the nature of their problems. Or maybe even illustrate the answers to their problems in symbolic language.
STEPHEN KING
The Symbolic Language of Dreams

. . . [A] writer is someone entranced by the power of language to create a magic show of the imagination, to make the dead sit up and talk, to shine light into the darkness of the great human mysteries.
TIM O'BRIEN
The Magic Show

The Writing Process and Self-Discovery

William Stafford has said that "writing itself is one of the great, free human activities. There is scope for individuality, and elation, and discovery, in writing." At the same time, a good writer is also a patient craftsperson. Writing makes demands on both the creative and the rational sides of the mind. From the creative and intuitive mind it summons forth details, images, memories, dreams, and feelings; from the rational and logical mind it demands planning, development, evidence, rereading, rethinking, and revision.

Perhaps it is this basic duality associated with the act of writing that can sometimes make it feel like a complex and overwhelming task. Practicing and studying particular writing strategies such as those presented in each chapter of *Dreams and Inward Journeys,* along with drafting, revising, and sharing your writing with your peers and instructor, will help you to develop

1

your self-confidence as a writer. As a writer you need to be aware of the feelings and fears of your unconscious self as well as the expectations of your rational mind. Balancing these two sides of your mind—knowing when, for example, to give your creative mind license to explore while controlling and quieting your critical mind—is an important part of the challenge of developing self-confidence and learning to write well.

Stages of the Writing Process

Most professional and student writers benefit from perceiving writing as a process with a number of stages. Although these stages do not need to be rigidly separated, an awareness of the different quality of thoughts and feelings that usually occur in each of the stages of writing is useful and will help you to create a finished piece of writing that speaks clearly about your own concerns, values, and opinions. The stages of the writing process include the prewriting phase, the drafting phase, and the revision phase. As you become a more experienced and skillful writer, you may find that you want to adapt this process to your own goals, perhaps by spending more time in preliminary reading to collect background information for research essays or possibly by spending less time prewriting if you are working on an essay that must be written in a shorter time frame or during an in-class exam.

As preparation for writing the initial draft of an essay, prewriting allows you to pursue a variety of playful, creative activities that will help you to generate ideas and understand what you want to say about your subject. Drafting is your rapid first "take" on your topic and should be done after you have concentrated on the subject matter of your paper and thought about the thesis or core concept around which you want to center the ideas and examples of your essay. You may find, however, that as you write your first draft, your thesis and focus shift or even change dramatically. Don't be concerned if this happens to you. Many professional writers have learned that although they begin the drafting phase feeling that they have a focus and thesis, the actual process of writing the draft changes their initial plan. Rewriting is a natural part of the writing process. As you keep returning to your draft and continue to work to shape your thoughts into clear sentences, they will capture your inner feelings and ideas.

While you will need to rewrite to clarify your thinking and ideas, the process of revision can also be approached in stages. They include revising for your paper's overall shape and meaning, which may involve outlining the rough draft; rearranging whole paragraphs or ideas and examples; developing and cutting redundancy within paragraphs; refining and clarifying sentences and individual words; and, finally, proofreading for grammar, spelling, and punctuation.

Strategies for Prewriting

The prewriting stage of writing is particularly exciting for those who enjoy creative expression. If you are apprehensive about writing and don't see yourself as a "creative thinker," prewriting activities may help you to discover new or forgotten images, memories, and ideas, as well as to make connections you may never have anticipated. You may find yourself liberating a creative spirit hidden in the recesses of your mind. Only you read and evaluate your prewriting; at this stage you determine what seems interesting and relevant. Prewriting makes the writing of later drafts easier because it helps you to clarify and organize your thoughts before they are put into a formal format. Drawing, freewriting, invisible writing, brainstorming, clustering, and journal keeping are all effective prewriting techniques that will help you to discover what you really want and need to say.

Drawing Drawing a picture in response to a topic can help you begin to understand what you think and feel. In the first example of drawings in response to a topic included in this text, students Lori Sunamoto and Cori Nelson used a computer program to capture their writing processes. Following each drawing, originally completed in color, is the student's explanation of her drawing and writing process.

Cori Nelson

I was trying to show how I collect my letters and words from vastly different areas—in writing, I try to bring together the different pieces of my life. I try to bring all the different colors and textures around me together into sentences and paragraphs. I spelled out the word bird because birds inspire a lot of my writing. (This drawing was originally done in color, not in black and white as reproduced here.)

Lori Sunamoto

This picture represents my writing process. I think of my mind as being as open as a midnight sky. And sometimes the clouds that swirl around in my brain part for just a moment, allowing me to see the stars and the infinite night. This is when ideas come to me, or perhaps it is more appropriate to say that this is when I am allowed to catch a glimpse of all that is "out there." Writing is almost like trying to pluck the stars from the sky and hold them in your hand.

A number of professional writers have spoken of the value of drawing as a way to develop ideas or understand a new text. In *The Nature and Aim of Fiction* Flannery O'Connor maintains, "Any discipline can help your writing . . . particularly drawing. Anything that helps you to see, anything that makes you look." While drawing an image from a complex text you are reading, you will be able to focus your thoughts on the details that may have already unconsciously captured your imagination. This process of drawing about a piece of writing will increase your engagement with it and help you to clarify your response as you make that response more tangible. In this edition of *Dreams and Inward Journeys* we have included examples of drawings that students completed after reading a poem about which they were to later write a formal paper. You can also try this drawing exercise after reading the essays and stories included in this text. The first drawing about a poem is included after "The Waking" by Theodore Roethke.

Freewriting   A freewriting can start anywhere and usually lasts from five to fifteen minutes. During these brief writing sessions, it is important to continue to write and not to censor any idea or feeling that comes to your mind. If you seem to run out of thoughts, just write, "I have no more to say" or anything you wish until a new thought emerges. After ten minutes of freewriting, read what you have produced and try to sum up the central idea or feeling of the piece. You can then proceed to another freewriting, using the summary statement as a new starting point. Writers often do several freewrites before they decide on how to focus their thoughts.

Invisible Writing   With invisible writing, the writer creates "invisible" words, or words that can't be seen while the writer is working. Some writers never even look at the words generated in an invisible writing exercise but instead use the exercise as a rehearsal, a building of mental pathways that will make the actual writing of their paper less halting and painful. Many writers find new insights in their thoughts that were produced invisibly. Invisible writing can be done by writing on the back of a piece of carbon paper onto a piece of notebook paper or with a dimmed computer screen. While you are freewriting and invisible writing, do not consciously pay attention to central ideas, relationships between ideas, organizational patterns, or grammatical or spelling errors of any kind; concentrate instead on getting your ideas and feelings out in words.

Brainstorming   Brainstorming, which can be done effectively in groups or individually, involves writing a list of all the words, phrases, ideas, descriptions, thoughts, and questions that come to your mind in response to a topic or issue. As in freewriting, it is essential not to stop to censor, judge, or correct any idea or feelings. The process of listing will, itself, bring up new ideas and associations. Ideas will build on one another, leading to thoughts that are original and fresh, while creating a list will help you to see relationships between ideas that may have previously seemed disconnected. When your list is complete, normally in fifteen to twenty minutes, go back to find patterns of thought or main ideas that you have uncovered. Bracketing or circling related ideas and details may help you to form an organizational plan. Through brainstorming you can begin to formulate a rough outline for your essay that will guide you in the drafting phase of writing.

Clustering   Clustering or mapping closely reflects the way in which the mind functions in making nonlinear connections between ideas. Combined with brainstorming or freewriting, clustering can also help you to perceive clearer relationships between ideas. Start your cluster by placing the topic to be explored in the center of the page. Draw a circle around it, and then draw lines out from your central circle in different directions to connect it with other circles containing additional ideas, phrases, or clues to experiences. The words in these circles will naturally develop their own offshoots as new associations emerge. The pattern being created by the clustering process continually changes in complex ways because any new idea will relate to all of the ideas already recorded. As in freewriting, clustering should be done without stopping. Once the cluster feels completed to you, write for a few minutes about what you have discovered through your clustering. Completing a cluster and a related freewrite can help you to understand how you want to focus your topic and help you to organize the major relationships between ideas, examples, and details.

Journal Keeping   Daily writing in a notebook or journal will help you to develop a record of your thoughts and feelings. Keeping a journal is similar to the type of prewriting assignments we have just discussed in that it allows you freedom to explore parts of your inner world, knowing that your writing will not be evaluated. Keeping a journal of your responses to the journal topics and study questions in this text is one of the most effective ways to develop your confidence and skills as a writer. Both of the student essays included in this chapter were developed from journal entries that focused on strong inner experiences and images that initially seemed very private but that were clarified and made public through drafting, revising, peer sharing, and more revision.

The Dream Journal   Because this text has been developed around the theme of dreams, and because the process of understanding your dreams may lead you to new insights and images that you may find useful in more formal writing, we recommend that you extend your journal-keeping activity into the night world by writing down your dreams. Through keeping a dream journal you can improve your ability to recall dreams and you can begin to capture unconscious images that intrigue or possibly disturb you. Perhaps, too, you will begin to notice more similarities between your dream images and some of the dreamlike stories in this text. Your appreciation of metaphors and symbols will increase.

By keeping your dream journal, you will also begin to realize how understanding your writing process is similar to understanding your dreams. The first written draft of your dream is like a prewriting of an essay: a set of strong, if chaotic, images that you can work with thoughtfully and creatively. As you bring form and meaning to a dream through analysis and interpretation, you bring form and meaning to an essay through drafting and revising those first generative ideas that begin the process of writing an essay, a story, or a poem.

Keep your dream journal at your bedside along with a pen or dark pencil. The best time to write in your dream journal is in the early morning or immediately on awaking from a vivid dream. Some students have even used a tape recorder to capture their "dream voice," its sounds and rhythms. Try to write in your dream journal three or four times a week, even if you have only a dim or fleeting image or impression to record. Write down all the details you can remember, indicating a shift, jump in time, or unclear portion of the dream with a question mark or ellipsis. Try not to censor or "clean up" the dream imagery, even if the thinking seems illogical, chaotic, or even embarrassing to you. Avoid interpreting your dream as you are recording it, although you might list in the margins any associations that immediately come to mind in relation to the images as you record them. Later, as you reread your dream journal entries over a period of several days, you may see patterns and more complex associations emerging and you may want to write about them.

Prewriting strategies are more frequently used in the generative stage of the writing process, but we encourage you to use these techniques whenever you feel yourself getting "blocked." During the drafting stage of writing, or even after an instructor has returned your paper to you with corrections on it, the exercises discussed here can continue to help you get in touch with what you really want to say, with your own inner voice.

T H E M A T I C   I N T R O D U C T I O N

 Writing can be described as an inward journey. The process of discovering what resides within your mind and your spirit begins anew each time you start a writing project. Many people find it difficult to begin, wondering, perhaps, how they will be able to untangle all of their thoughts and feelings, how they will finally decide on the most accurate words and sentence patterns to make their statement clear and compelling. You may feel overwhelmed by the possibilities of all that is waiting to be discovered within you, and at the same time you may feel a sense of wonder and excitement, anticipating pleasures and rewards of uncovering and expressing new parts of your mind, imagination, and spirit.

The complex feelings often experienced at this stage of the writing process have been eloquently described by many authors whose language, images, and ideas can serve as your guides. They experience writing as a process of self-discovery and self-understanding rooted in the experiences of the unconscious and conscious mind, in the experiences of dreams and of childhood memories, and in everyday events and goals.

This chapter's readings begin with Langston Hughes's poem, "Theme for English B." The poem's speaker, a young African American, questions his white writing instructor's assignment and assumptions about the simplicity of telling the truth: "Go home and write / a page tonight. / And let that page come out of you — / Then, it will be true." The speaker, like many writers from minority or immigrant cultures, realizes that it is not simple to create an identity that acknowledges mainstream American culture and language traditions without diminishing the importance of his unique culture and language.

Poets and teachers, novelists and essayists have offered advice about writing that may have helped the speaker in Hughes's poem. Poet and teacher William Stafford asks writers to trust themselves in the next selection, "A Way of Writing." He believes that if writers are receptive to their minds, allowing themselves time to "fish" for ideas in their unconscious minds and if they do not evaluate their work as it is being produced, they will find an inexhaustible source of ideas and experiences to explore through writing. In "Teaching Two Kinds of Thinking by Teaching Writing," writer and English professor Peter Elbow presents an approach to writing that helps the creative, intuitive unconscious mind to work separately but supportively with the logical, critical mind.

Some writers turn specifically to their dreams for guidance. In "Aim for the Chopping Block," essayist and poet Annie Dillard explains how a dream that taught her how to chop wood also helped her to make her vision of a book into a reality. In the next selection, based on an interview, "The Symbolic Language of Dreams," Stephen King discusses the ways in which his dreams have helped him to solve problems that he has had writing. He compares his writing process to a dream state: "Part of my function as a writer is to dream awake."

Many writers take a similar position on the dreamlike state of the writer's mind. In the next selection, "The Magic Show," Tim O'Brien claims, "When I am writing well, invoking well, there is a dreamlike sense of gazing through the page as if it were the thinnest onionskin parchment, watching the spirits beyond, . . . This is the sensation I get — both physical and emotional — as a waking dream unfolds into words. . . ." Casting the writer into the role of magician of the imagination, O'Brien believes that writers shine ". . . light into the darkness of the great human mysteries."

The meanings of language, like the meanings of life, are not always immediately and simply apparent. In "Mother Tongue," the final essay written by a professional writer selected for this chapter, Amy Tan is critical of achievement tests and the conventional skills approach to teaching writing that she encountered in her high school. She claims that she developed her talents by incorporating all that she and her mother, a non–native speaker, knew about language and about life: ". . . what language ability tests can never reveal: her [mother's] intent, her passion, her imagery, the rhythms of her speech and the nature of her thoughts."

Just as Tan learned to write as she journeyed through life, so too does the speaker in the poem "The Waking" by Theodore Roethke. The speaker's spirit rings as a refrain throughout the poem, reminding us of his unique way of seeing his life journey, of seeing the connections between his conscious and unconscious mind: "I wake to sleep, and take my waking slow / I learn by going where I have to go." This chapter's final poem, "The Thought-Fox" by Ted Hughes, set in the loneliness of midnight, symbolically captures his mysterious and dreamlike process of creating a poem.

The two student essays that conclude this chapter give further insights into how writing shapes an individual's inner growth and identity. In her essay "Who Am I When I Write?" Susan Helfter explores the ways in which creating images in writing helped her to uncover and better understand previously hidden sides of her personality. Joyce Chang, in her essay "Drive Becarefully," discusses her changing feelings about her mother's English. Chang identifies with Amy Tan's conclusions in "Mother Tongue." Like Tan, after much inner struggle she has come to accept and delight in her mother's language as fundamental to both of their identities, even if it is not perfectly correct textbook English.

As you read the selections that follow we think that you will come to better understand how writing is a process of self-discovery, an inward journey, a way of uncovering, creating, and clarifying your relationship to your inner world and with the people and communities around you.

Langston Hughes

Theme for English B

A native of Missouri, Langston Hughes (1902–1967) received his B.A. from Lincoln University in Pennsylvania in 1929. Hughes, who wrote many plays, stories, and poems, was a leading interpreter of the African American experience in the United States during the 1930s and 1940s. His work combines verse form with the rhythms of spirituals and blues. Collections of his poetry include Shakespeare in Harlem *(1941),* Montage of a Dream Deferred *(1951), and* Ask Your Mama *(1961). In the following poem Hughes explores the difficulty of writing openly about feelings and experiences for an audience outside his own culture.*

JOURNAL

Explore your feelings about writing papers for your English instructors.

The instructor said,

Go home and write
a page tonight.
And let that page come out of you—
5 *Then, it will be true.*

I wonder if it's that simple?
I am twenty-two, colored, born in Winston-Salem.
I went to school there, then Durham, then here
to this college on the hill above Harlem.
10 I am the only colored student in my class.
The steps from the hill lead down into Harlem,
through a park, then I cross St. Nicholas,
Eighth Avenue, Seventh, and I come to the Y,
the Harlem Branch Y, where I take the elevator
15 up to my room, sit down, and write this page:

It's not easy to know what is true for you or me
at twenty-two, my age. But I guess I'm what
I feel and see and hear, Harlem, I hear you:
hear you, hear me—we two—you, me, talk on this page.
20 (I hear New York, too.) Me—who?
Well, I like to eat, sleep, drink, and be in love.
I like to work, read, learn, and understand life.
I like a pipe for a Christmas present.
or records—Bessie, bop, or Bach.

25 I guess being colored doesn't make me *not* like
    the same things other folks like who are other races.
    So will my page be colored that I write?
    Being me, it will not be white.
    But it will be
30 a part of you, instructor.
    You are white—
    yet a part of me, as I am a part of you.
    That's American.
    Sometimes perhaps you don't want to be a part of me.
35 Nor do I often want to be a part of you.
    But we are, that's true!
    As I learn from you,
    I guess you learn from me—

Questions for Discussion

1. Although the speaker in the poem is writing for his English instructor, what audience is Langston Hughes addressing? If you think he has more than one audience in mind, describe his potential readers.
2. Why is the speaker in the poem critical of his instructor's assumption that a page that comes "out of you . . . will be true"? Do you agree with the speaker's perspective on his instructor's assignment? Why or why not?
3. How does the speaker's identity as a student of color influence his identity as a student and a writer?
4. What does the speaker reveal about his identity through his writing?
5. What lines in the poem suggest that the relationship between the writer and the audience is reciprocal and collaborative? In what way does the speaker's response suggest that the relationship between himself and his instructor may be unequal and not true to the authentic spirit of artistic expression?
6. Would Hughes agree with the concept that writing is an inward journey? Explain your response.

Ideas for Writing

1. Write an essay in which you reflect on the insights into the writer's relationship with his or her audience and the writing process that the poem presents. In what ways has reading Hughes's poem helped you to better understand why writing for an instructor can be difficult as well as rewarding?
2. Write a poem or an essay to your instructor or to your class that expresses how you feel about writing and the writing process. Or, draw a picture of your writing process and then write an explanation of your picture.

William Stafford

A Way of Writing

William Stafford (1914–1993) was born and raised in Kansas, where he worked on farms and in oil refineries and, as a conscientious objector, served time in work camps during World War II. He earned his B.A. and M.A. at the University of Kansas and his Ph.D. at the University of Iowa. Stafford has taught creative writing at the University of Iowa and at Lewis and Clark University in Oregon. Stafford won the National Book Award for Traveling through the Dark *(1963) and has also written nonfiction, including* Writing the Australian Crawl: Views of the Writer's Vocation *(1978). Stafford kept a daily journal, considered competitiveness corrupting, and retained his belief in pacifism as a way of life. He is best known for his personal lyric poetry, which is complex in its perceptions of how inner feelings can be balanced with the social and environmental concerns of rural America. His most recent publication,* Passwords, *a collection of poetry, was published in 1991. Stafford's "A Way of Writing," which originally appeared in the Spring 1970 issue of the literary magazine* Field, *expresses Stafford's views on the need for receptivity to and trust of one's inner world during the act of writing.*

JOURNAL

Develop an image or draw a picture that captures your creative process as a writer, a painter, a dancer, or a musician. Discuss the form of creativity that you find most rewarding.

1   A writer is not so much someone who has something to say as he is someone who has found a process that will bring about new things he would not have thought of if he had not started to say them. That is, he does not draw on a reservoir; instead, he engages in an activity that brings to him a whole succession of unforeseen stories, poems, essays, plays, laws, philosophies, religions, or—but wait!

2   Back in school, from the first when I began to try to write things, I felt this richness. One thing would lead to another; the world would give and give. Now, after twenty years or so of trying, I live by that certain richness, an idea hard to pin, difficult to say, and perhaps offensive to some. For there are strange implications in it.

3   One implication is the importance of just plain receptivity. When I write, I like to have an interval before me when I am not likely to be interrupted. For me, this means usually the early morning, before others are awake. I get pen and paper, take a glance out of the window (often it is dark out there), and wait. It is like fishing. But I do not wait very long, for there is always a nibble—and this is where receptivity comes in. To get started I will accept anything that occurs to me.

Something always occurs, of course, to any of us. We can't keep from thinking. Maybe I have to settle for an immediate impression: it's cold, or hot, or dark, or bright, or in between! Or—well, the possibilities are endless. If I put down something, that thing will help the next thing come, and I'm off. If I let the process go on, things will occur to me that were not at all in my mind when I started. These things, odd or trivial as they may be, are somehow connected. And if I let them string out, surprising things will happen.

4   If I let them string out. . . . Along with initial receptivity, then, there is another readiness: I must be willing to fail. If I am to keep on writing, I cannot bother to insist on high standards. I must get into action and not let anything stop me, or even slow me much. By "standards" I do not mean "correctness"—spelling, punctuation, and so on. These details become mechanical for anyone who writes for a while. I am thinking about such matters as social significance, positive values, consistency, etc. I resolutely disregard these. Something better, greater, is happening! I am following a process that leads so wildly and originally into new territory that no judgment can at the moment be made about values, significance, and so on. I am making something new, something that has not been judged before. Later others—and maybe I myself—will make judgments. Now, I am headlong to discover. Any distraction may harm the creating.

5   So, receptive, careless of failure, I spin out things on the page. And a wonderful freedom comes. If something occurs to me, it is all right to accept it. It has one justification: it occurs to me. No one else can guide me. I must follow my own weak, wandering, diffident impulses.

6   A strange bonus happens. At times, without my insisting on it, my writings become coherent; the successive elements that occur to me are clearly related. They lead by themselves to new connections. Sometimes the language, even the syllables that happen along, may start a trend. Sometimes the materials alert me to something waiting in my mind, ready for sustained attention. At such times, I allow myself to be eloquent, or intentional, or for great swoops (Treacherous! Not to be trusted!) reasonable. But I do not insist on any of that; for I know that back of my activity there will be the coherence of my self, and that indulgence of my impulses will bring recurrent patterns and meanings again.

7   This attitude toward the process of writing creatively suggests a problem for me, in terms of what others say. They talk about "skills" in writing. Without denying that I do have experience, wide reading, automatic orthodoxies and maneuvers of various kinds, I still must insist that I am often baffled about what "skill" has to do with the precious little area of confusion when I do not know what I am going to say and then I find out what I am going to say. That precious interval I am unable to bridge by skill. What can I witness about it? It remains mysterious, just as all of us must feel puzzled about how we are so inventive as to be able to talk along through complexities with our friends, not needing to plan what we are going to say, but never stalled for long in our confident forward progress. Skill? If so, it is the skill we all have, something we must have learned before the age of three or four.

8   A writer is one who has become accustomed to trusting that grace, or luck, or—skill.

9   Yet another attitude I find necessary: most of what I write, like most of what I say in casual conversation, will not amount to much. Even I will realize, and even at the time, that it is not negotiable. It will be like practice. In conversation I allow myself random remarks—in fact, as I recall, that is the way I learned to talk—so in writing I launch many expendable efforts. A result of this free way of writing is that I am not writing for others, mostly; they will not see the product at all unless the activity eventuates in something that later appears to be worthy. My guide is the self, and its adventuring in the language brings about communication.

10   This process-rather-than-substance view of writing invites a final, dual reflection:

1. Writers may not be special—sensitive or talented in any usual sense. They are simply engaged in sustained use of a language skill we all have. Their "creations" come about through confident reliance on stray impulses that will, with trust, find occasional patterns that are satisfying.

2. But writing itself is one of the great, free human activities. There is scope for individuality, and elation, and discovery, in writing. For the person who follows with trust and forgiveness what occurs to him, the world remains always ready and deep, an inexhaustible environment, with the combined vividness of an actuality and flexibility of a dream. Working back and forth between experience and thought, writers have more than space and time can offer. They have the whole unexplored realm of human vision.

Questions for Discussion

1. What do you think Stafford means when he says that a writer must be receptive? What image does he use to help the reader understand his concept of the creative process?

2. Is it difficult for you to allow yourself to write down your thoughts and feelings without censoring them as they flow through your mind? How often do you give yourself the time to reflect and write alone in a peaceful place?

3. Have you ever used prewriting activities such as freewriting or invisible writing to encourage or allow yourself to write without editing? If you have tried such activities, what was their effect on your writing?

4. Why does Stafford feel that it is important for a writer to be willing to fail? Do you agree with him on this point? Is it hard for you to accept the imperfection and unpredictability of your early drafts? If you have ever experienced writer's block or felt frustrated with your writing, do you think that reading Stafford's essay will help you?

5. Although Stafford's writing advice comes out of his experiences as a poet, why do you think that his advice will be useful to you in an expository writing course?

6. Stafford says, "Writing itself is one of the great, free human activities. There is scope for individuality, and elation, and discovery, in writing."

Do you agree with his assertion? Develop several examples to support your point of view.

Ideas for Writing

1. Write an essay that describes your writing process and discusses the internal barriers that make writing difficult for you. Discuss the strategies that have helped you to overcome writing blocks.
2. Develop an essay that uses comparisons or metaphors, such as Stafford does with his metaphor of writing as fishing, to describe your own writing process.

 ## Peter Elbow

Teaching Two Kinds of Thinking by Teaching Writing

Peter Elbow (b. 1935) was raised in New York. He earned his first B.A. at Williams College (1957) and a second B.A. from Exter College, Oxford (1959). He then did graduate work at Harvard University and completed his Ph.D. at Brandeis University (1969). Elbow, who has taught at a number of universities including the Massachusetts Institute of Technology, Evergreen State College in Olympia, Washington, and the State University of New York at Stony Brook, is currently a professor of English at the University of Massachusetts at Amherst. He has been writing books about writing for over twenty years, including Writing without Teachers *(1973),* Writing with Power *(1981),* Embracing Contraries: Explorations in Learning and Teaching *(1986), and most recently* A Community of Writers *(1988, 1994). Elbow, who has contributed articles on the teaching of writing to national English teacher's journals for almost thirty years, also speaks at many national conferences for teachers of writing. His work has had a significant impact on the way writing is taught at colleges and universities throughout the United States.*

JOURNAL

Discuss activities and attitudes that help you to come up with new ideas and to be creative.

1 When I celebrate freewriting and fast exploratory writing on first drafts—the postponing of vigilance and control during the early stages of writing—it seems to many listeners as though I'm celebrating *holidays* from thinking. Some

say, "Yes, good, we all need holidays from thinking." Others say, "Horrors! Their vigilance muscles will get flabby and they'll lose their ability to think critically." But I insist that I'm teaching thinking.

2   Of course it's not the only way I teach thinking through writing. I also teach it by teaching careful, conscious, critical revising. Thus I teach two kinds of thinking. I'll call them first-order thinking and second-order thinking.

3   First-order thinking is intuitive and creative and doesn't strive for conscious direction or control. We use it when we get hunches or see gestalts. We use it when we sense analogies or ride on metaphors or arrange the pieces in a collage. We use it when we write fast without censoring and let the words lead us to associations and intuitions we hadn't foreseen. Second-order thinking is conscious, directed, controlled thinking. We steer; we scrutinize each link in the chain. Second-order thinking is committed to accuracy and strives for logic and control: we examine our premises and assess the validity of each inference. Second-order thinking is what most people have in mind when they talk about "critical thinking."

4   Each kind of thinking has its own characteristic strengths and weaknesses. I like to emphasize how second-order thinking often brings out people's worst thinking. If you want to get people to seem dumber than they are, try asking them a hard question and then saying, "Now think carefully." Thinking carefully means trying to examine your thinking while using it too—trying to think about thinking while also thinking about something else—which often leads people to foolishness. This is one of the main reasons why shrewd and sensible students often write essays asserting things they don't really believe and defending them with wooden reasoning they wouldn't dream of using if they were just talking thoughtfully with a friend.

5   First-order thinking, on the other hand, often heightens intelligence. If you want to get people to be remarkably insightful, try asking them the hard question and then saying, "Don't do any careful thinking yet, just write three or four stories or incidents that come to mind in connection with that question; and then do some fast exploratory freewriting." It turns out that such unplanned narrative and descriptive exploratory writing (or speaking) will almost invariably lead the person spontaneously to formulate *conceptual* insights that are remarkably shrewd. These are fresh insights which are rooted in experience and thus they usually get around the person's prejudices, stock responses, or desires for mere consistency; they are usually shrewder than the person's long-held convictions. (See "The Loop Writing Process" in my *Writing With Power*.) In addition (to bring up a writerly concern), these insights are usually expressed in lively, human, and experienced language. In short, to use Polanyi's terms, we know more tacitly than we do focally. Finally (to raise another writerly concern), when someone really gets going in a sustained piece of generative writing and manages, as it were, to stand out of the way and relinquish planning and control—when someone manages to let the words and images and ideas choose more words, images, and ideas—a more elegant shape or organization often emerges, one more integral to the material than careful outlining or conscious planning can produce. It's not that the rough draft writing will itself be well organized in its totality—though that occasionally

happens. What's more common is that the exploratory zigzagging leads finally to a click where the writer suddenly sees, "Yes, that's the right handle for this whole issue, now I've got the right point of view, and now I see the right organization or progression of parts. I couldn't find it when I just tried to think, plan, and outline."

6   Yet despite my fascination with the conceptual power of creative intuitive thinking—of what might seem to some like "careless thinking"—I have learned not to forget to tell the other side of the story. That is, we are also likely to be *fooled* by first-order thinking. In first-order thinking we don't reflect on what we are doing and hence we are more likely to be steered by our unaware assumptions, our unconscious prejudices, our unexamined point of view. And often enough, no shape or organization emerges at all—just randomly ordered thoughts. We cannot *count on* first-order thinking to give us something valuable.

7   Thus the two kinds of thinking have the opposite virtues and vices. Second-order thinking is a way to check our thinking, to be more aware, to steer instead of being steered. In particular, we must not trust the fruits of intuitive and experiential first-order thinking unless we have carefully assessed them with second-order critical thinking. Yet we probably won't *have* enough interesting ideas or hypotheses to assess if we use only our assessing muscles: we need first-order thinking to generate a rich array of insights. And first-order thinking doesn't just give us more; it is faster too. Our early steps in second-order thinking (or our early steps at a higher level of second-order thinking than we are practiced at) are often slow backward steps into wrong-headedness (Bruner, 1966). Yet this is no argument against the need for second-order thinking. Indeed I suspect that the way we enlarge the penumbra of our tacit knowledge is by searching harder and further with the beam of our focal knowledge.

8   We are in the habit—in the academic culture anyway—of assuming that thinking is not thinking unless it is wholly logical or critically aware of itself at every step. But I cannot resist calling first-order thinking a bona fide kind of thinking because it is a process of making sense and figuring out: though not consciously steered or controlled, it is nevertheless purposive and skillful.

9   There is an obvious link between the writing process and these two kinds of thinking. I link first-order intuitive or creative thinking with freewriting and first-draft exploratory writing in which one defers planning, control, organizing, and censoring. I link second-order thinking with slow, thoughtful rewriting or revising where one constantly subjects everything to critical scrutiny.

10   But I'm not content merely to assert a link. The two writing processes enhance the two thinking processes.

11   It is obvious how careful revising enhances second-order thinking. If having any language at all (any "second signaling system") gives us more power over our thinking, it is obvious that a *written* language vastly increases that power. By writing down our thoughts we can put them aside and come back to them with renewed critical energy and a fresh point of view. We can criticize better because writing helps us achieve the perennially difficult task of standing outside our own

thinking. Thus outlines are more helpful while revising than at the start of the writing process because finally there's something rich and interesting to outline. Revising is when I use the "X-ray" or "skeleton" exercise—asking both the writer and her readers to isolate the central core of inference in a paper: What is the assertion and what premises and reasons does it rest on? This is the best practice for critical thinking, because instead of being a canned exercise with artificial ingredients unconnected to the student, it is an exercise in assessing and strengthening the thinking which is embodied in one's own or someone else's live discourse. Since we are trying for the tricky goal of thinking about our subject but at the same time thinking about our thinking about it, putting our thoughts on paper gives us a fighting chance. But notice that what most heightens this critical awareness is not so much the writing down of words in the first place, though of course that helps, but the *coming back* to a text and re-seeing it from the outside (in space) instead of just hearing it from the inside (in time).

12   But does freewriting or uncensored, generative writing really enhance creative first-order thinking? You might say that speaking is a better way to enhance creative thinking—either through brainstorming or through the back and forth of discussion or debate. But that only works if we *have* other people available, people we trust, and people skilled at enhancing our creative thinking. Free exploratory writing, on the other hand, though we must learn to use it, is always available. And since the goal in creative thinking is to harness intuition—to get the imagination to take the reins in its own hands—solitary writing for no audience is often more productive than speaking. Speaking is almost invariably to an audience, and an audience puts pressure on us to make sense and avoid inferences we cannot explain.

13   You might also argue that intuitive thinking is better enhanced by silent musing; or going for a walk or sleeping on it or any of a host of other ways to push a question away from focal attention back to the preconscious. But such attempts at nonlinguistic processing often merely postpone thinking instead of actually enriching it. Freewriting and exploratory writing, on the other hand, are almost invariably productive because they exploit the autonomous generative powers of language and syntax themselves. Once you manage to get yourself writing in an exploratory but uncensored fashion, the ongoing string of language and syntax itself becomes a lively and surprising force for generation. Words call up words, ideas call up more ideas. A momentum of language and thinking develops and one learns to nurture it by keeping the pen moving. With a bit of practice, you can usually bring yourself to the place where you can stop and say, "Look at that! I've been led by this unrolling string of words to an insight or connection or structure that I had no premonition of. I could never have proposed it if I were just musing or making an outline. I wasn't steering, I was being taken for a ride." Heuristic prewriting techniques that involve only list-making or diagram-making tend to lack the generative force that comes from the use of actual syntax— speech on paper.

14   I'm not trying to disparage spoken discourse or nonverbal back-burner work. They can be wonderful. But they are not as reliable as writing for enhancing first-order thinking.

15   "Taken for a ride." The metaphor evokes what's good but also what's fearful about first-order thinking and uncensored writing. It is dangerous to be taken for a ride, literally by a horse or metaphorically by a shark. "Eternal vigilance." But the goal of first-order thinking or writing is to *relax* vigilance and be taken on as many rides as possible: *as long as* we remember that this is only half the process. We must assess the results with second-order thinking or revising. In short, by using the writing process in this two-sided way, I can foster contraries: our ability to let go and be taken on surprising rides; yet also our ability critically to assess the resulting views.

Practical Consequences

16   I am not concluding from all this that there is only one right way to think or write. We all know too many good thinkers or writers who contradict each other and even themselves in their methods. But this notion of opposite extremes gives a constructive and specific picture of what we're looking for in good thinking and writing. That is, even though there are many good ways to think and write, it seems clear that excellence must involve finding *some* way to be both abundantly inventive yet toughmindedly critical. Indeed this model of conflicting goals suggests why good writers and thinkers are so various in their technique: if they are managing to harness opposites—in particular, opposites that tend to interfere with each other—they are doing something mysterious. Success is liable to take many forms, some of them surprising.

17   As a teacher, it helps me to have these two clear goals in mind when I come across a student about whom I must say, "She clearly *is* a smart person, but why is she so often wrong?" Or "She clearly thinks hard and carefully, but why is she so characteristically uninteresting or unproductive in her work?" I can ask of any person or performance, "Is there enough rich material to build from?" and, "Is there a careful and critical enough assessment of the material?"

18   If I am careful to acknowledge to my students that things are complex and that there is no single best way to think or write—and that excellence in these realms is a mystery that can be mastered in surprising ways—then I may justifiably turn around and stress simplicity by harping on two practical rules of thumb.

19   First, since creative and critical thinking are opposite and involve mentalities that tend to conflict with each other, it helps most people to learn to work on them separately or one at a time by moving back and forth between them. If we are trying to think creatively or write generatively, it usually hinders us if we try at the same time to think critically or to revise it: it makes us reject what we are engaged in thinking before we've really worked it out at all—or to cross out what we've written before we've finished the sentence or paragraph and allowed something to develop. But if we hold off criticism or revising for a while, we can build a safe place for generative thinking or writing. Similarly, if we devote certain times to wholehearted critical thinking or revising, we can be more acute and powerful in our critical assessment.

20   For one of the main things that holds us back from being as creative as we could be is fear of looking silly or being wrong. But that worry dissipates when we know we will soon turn to wholehearted criticism and revising and weed out what

is foolish. Similarly, one of the main things that holds us back from being as critical as we could be is fear that we'll have to reject everything and be left with nothing at all. But that worry also dissipates when we know we've already generated an
extremely rich set of materials to work on (or if we haven't, we know we can do so
quickly whenever we turn to wholehearted generating). In short, even though
creative and critical thinking can magically coalesce in the hands of masters and
at certain special moments when the rest of us are at our best, it usually helps us to
work on them separately so they can flourish yet reinforce each other.

21   Second rule of thumb. It usually helps to *start with* creative thinking and exploratory writing and then engage in critical assessment and revision afterward—
after we have gotten ourselves going and there is already lots to assess. It's not that
we should necessarily try to force our writing into two self-contained steps
(though I aim for this when all goes smoothly). Often I cannot finish all generating or all first-order thinking before I need to do some revising or criticizing—
which will sometimes force a new burst of generating. We are never finished with
generating—and having generated, we always need to criticize and revise. I used
to think that I should try to finish getting my students good at creative generating
before I went on to work on revising and being critical. But I've discovered that
some students won't let go and allow themselves to be creative till after we do
some hard work on critical thinking and revising. They don't feel safe relaxing
their vigilance till I demonstrate that I'm also teaching heightened vigilance.
Sometimes, early in the semester, I ask students to rethink and revise a paper in
order to prove to them that they are not stuck with what they put down in early
drafts, and that careful critical thinking can make a big difference.

22   But the fact remains that most people get more and better thinking—and less
time-wasting—if they start off generating. My main agenda for the beginning of a
semester is always to enforce generating and brainstorming and the deferral of
criticism in order to build students' confidence and show them that they can
quickly learn to come up with a great quantity of words and ideas. Then gradually
we progress to a back-and-forth movement between generating and criticizing. I
find I help my own writing and thinking and that of my students by consciously
training ourselves to start with first-order thinking and generating and to take it
on longer and longer rides—to hold off longer and longer the transition to criticizing and logic. Back and forth, yes, but in longer spells so that each mentality has
more time to flourish before we move on to its opposite.

Mutual Reinforcement

23 Because the history of our culture is often experienced as a battle between reason
and feeling, between rationality and irrationality, between logic and impulse—
and because intuitive first-order thinking is indissolubly mixed up with feeling, irrationality, and impulse—we end up with disciplined critical thinking and uncensored creative thinking dug into opposed trenches with their guns trained on each
other. Logic and reason have won the battle to be our standard for thinking, but
not the battle for hearts and minds, and therefore champions of logic and reason
understandably criticize all relaxations of critical vigilance. Similarly, champions
of creative first-order thinking sometimes feel they must criticize critical thinking

if only to win some legitimacy for themselves. But this is an unfortunate historical and developmental accident. If we would see clearly how it really is with thinking and writing, we would see that the situation isn't either/or, it's both/and: the more first-order thinking, the more second-order thinking; the more generative uncensored writing, the more critical revising; and vice versa. It's a matter of learning to work on opposites one at a time in a generous spirit of mutual reinforcement rather than in a spirit of restrictive combat.

Questions for Discussion

1. Why does Elbow teach "two kinds of thinking"? Why does he consider the intuitive and creative mode "first order" and the critical mode "second order"?
2. Elbow gives examples of each kind of thinking. Discuss other examples for each mode? Why does Elbow think that we need to engage in both kinds of thinking to produce good writing? Explain why you agree or disagree with him.
3. According to Elbow why is freewriting preferable to brainstorming aloud or "silent musing" as a way to generate ideas? Explain why you agree or disagree with Elbow?
4. Discuss the meaning of the metaphor "taken for a ride" in relationship to the two kinds of thinking.
5. What does Elbow expect when he asks us to "work on opposites one at a time in a generous spirit of mutual reinforcement"? Provide an example from your own writing process that supports his expectation.
6. What parts of Elbow's approach are new to you? Which of his ideas will be most useful? Why?

Ideas for Writing

1. Using recent writing projects as examples, describe the ways in which you have attempted to create a positive interaction between the two kinds of thinking in your own work. Discuss both your successes and the problems that you have experienced.
2. Write a response to Elbow's approach to thinking and writing. Discuss the reasons why you agree and/or disagree with him. Develop supportive examples and evidence for all your major points.

 # Annie Dillard

Aim for the Chopping Block

Poet, essayist, and naturalist Annie Dillard (b. 1945) was raised in Pittsburgh, Pennsylvania. She received an M.A. in 1968 from Hollins College in Virginia. Dillard has worked as an editor and college teacher and has written many essays and books, including Pilgrim at Tinker Creek *(1974), for which she received a Pulitzer Prize. She is the author of an autobiography of her early years,* An American Childhood *(1987).* Mornings Like These: Found Poems *(1995) is her most recent collection. Dillard has also written several collections of criticisms and essays about nature. Although she is a prolific writer, Dillard often finds writing a painful experience, "hard, conscious, . . . frustrating." The following selection is excerpted from her book* The Writing Life *(1989).*

JOURNAL

Write about how dreaming or meditation has helped you to develop your skill and confidence in a creative activity such as writing, dancing, cooking, or playing a sport.

1   Once, in order to finish a book I was writing and yet not live in the same room with it, I begged a cabin to use as a study. I finished the book there, wrote some other things, and learned to split wood. All this was on a remote and sparsely populated island on Haro Strait, where I moved when I left Virginia. The island was in northern Puget Sound, Washington State, across the water from Canadian islands.

2   The cabin was a single small room near the water. Its walls were shrunken planks, not insulated; in January, February, and March, it was cold. There were two small metal beds in the room, two cupboards, some shelves over a little counter, a wood stove, and a table under a window, where I wrote. The window looked out on a bit of sandflat overgrown with thick, varicolored mosses; there were a few small firs where the sandflat met the cobble beach; and there was the water: Puget Sound, and all the sky over it and all the other wild islands in the distance under the sky. It was very grand. But you get used to it. I don't much care where I work. I don't notice things. The door used to blow open and startle me witless. I did, however, notice the cold.

3   I tried to heat the cabin with the wood stove and a kerosene heater, but I never was warm. I used to work wearing a wool cap, long wool tights, sweaters, a down jacket, and a scarf. I was too lazy to stick a damper in the wood stove chimney; I kept putting off the task for a warm day. Thoreau said that his firewood warmed him twice—because he labored to cut his own. Mine froze me twice, for the same reason. After I learned to split wood, in a manner I am shortly to relate—after I learned to split wood, I stepped out into the brute northeaster and split just enough alder to last me through working hours, which was not enough splitting to warm me. Then I came in and kindled a fire in the stove, all the heat of which vanished up the chimney.

4   At first, in the good old days, I did not know how to split wood. I set a chunk of alder on the chopping block and harassed it, at enormous exertion, into tiny wedges that flew all over the sandflat and lost themselves. What I did was less like splitting wood than chipping flints. After a few whacks my alder chunk still stood

serene and unmoved, its base untouched, its tip a thorn. And then I actually tried to turn the sorry thing over and balance it on its wee head while I tried to chop its feet off before it fell over. God save us.

5   All this was a very warm process. I removed my down jacket, my wool hat and scarf. Alas, those early wood-splitting days, when I truly warmed myself, didn't last long. I lost the knack.

6   I did not know it at the time, but during those first weeks when I attacked my wood every morning, I was collecting a crowd—or what passed on the island for a crowd. At the sound of my ax, Doe and Bob—real islanders, proper, wood-splitting islanders—paused in their activities and mustered, unseen, across the sand-flat, under the firs. They were watching me (oh, the idleness) try to split wood. It must have been a largely silent comedy. Later, when they confessed, and I railed at them, Bob said innocently that the single remark he had ever permitted himself had been, "I love to watch Annie split wood."

7   One night, while all this had been going on, I had a dream in which I was given to understand, by the powers that be, how to split wood. You aim, said the dream—of course!—at the chopping block. It is true. You aim at the chopping block, not at the wood; then you split the wood, instead of chipping it. You cannot do the job cleanly unless you treat the wood as the transparent means to an end, by aiming past it. But then, alas, you easily split your day's wood in a few minutes, in the freezing cold, without working up any heat; then you utterly forfeit your only chance of getting warm.

8   The knack of splitting wood was the only useful thing I had ever learned from any dream, and my attitude toward the powers that be was not entirely grateful. The island comedy was over; everybody had to go back to work; and I never did get warm.

9   Here is a fairly sober version of what happens in the small room between the writer and the work itself. It is similar to what happens between a painter and the canvas.

10   First you shape the vision of what the projected work of art will be. The vision, I stress, is no marvelous thing: it is the work's intellectual structure and aesthetic surface. It is a chip of mind, a pleasing intellectual object. It is a vision of the work, not of the world. It is a glowing thing, a blurred thing of beauty. Its structure is at once luminous and translucent; you can see the world through it. After you receive the initial charge of this imaginary object, you add to it at once several aspects, and incubate it most gingerly as it grows into itself.

11   Many aspects of the work are still uncertain, of course; you know that. You know that if you proceed you will change things and learn things, that the form will grow under your hands and develop new and richer lights. But that change will not alter the vision or its deep structures; it will only enrich it. You know that, and you are right.

12   But you are wrong if you think that in the actual writing, or in the actual painting, you are filling in the vision. You cannot fill in the vision. You cannot even bring the vision to light. You are wrong if you think that you can in any way take the vision and tame it to the page. The page is jealous and tyrannical; the page is

made of time and matter; the page always wins. The vision is not so much destroyed, exactly, as it is, by the time you have finished, forgotten. It has been replaced by this changeling, this bastard, this opaque lightless chunky ruinous work.

13   Here is how it happens. The vision is, *sub specie aeternitatis*, a set of mental relationships, a coherent series of formal possibilities. In the actual rooms of time, however, it is a page or two of legal paper filled with words and questions; it is a terrible diagram, a few books' names in a margin, an ambiguous doodle, a corner folded down in a library book. These are memos from the thinking brain to witless hope.

14   Nevertheless, ignoring the provisional and pathetic nature of these scraps, and bearing the vision itself in mind—having it before your sights like the very Grail—you begin to scratch out the first faint marks on the canvas, on the page. You begin the work proper. Now you have gone and done it. Now the thing is no longer a vision: it is paper.

15   Words lead to other words and down the garden path. You adjust the paints' values and hues not to the world, not to the vision, but to the rest of the paint. The materials are stubborn and rigid; push is always coming to shove. You can fly—you can fly higher than you thought possible—but you can never get off the page. After every passage another passage follows, more sentences, more everything on drearily down. Time and materials hound the work; the vision recedes ever farther into the dim realms.

16   And so you continue the work, and finish it. Probably by now you have been forced to toss the most essential part of the vision. But this is a concern for mere nostalgia now: for before your eyes, and stealing your heart, is this fighting and frail finished product, entirely opaque. You can see nothing through it. It is only itself, a series of well-known passages, some colored paint. Its relationship to the vision that impelled it is the relationship between any energy and any work, anything unchanging to anything temporal.

17   The work is not the vision itself, certainly. It is not the vision filled in, as if it had been a coloring book. It is not the vision reproduced in time; that were impossible. It is rather a simulacrum and a replacement. It is a golem. You try—you try every time—to reproduce the vision, to let your light so shine before men. But you can only come along with your bushel and hide it.

18   Who will teach me to write? a reader wanted to know.

19   The page, the page, that eternal blankness, the blankness of eternity which you cover slowly, affirming time's scrawl as a right and your daring as necessity; the page, which you cover woodenly, ruining it, but asserting your freedom and power to act, acknowledging that you ruin everything you touch but touching it nevertheless, because acting is better than being here in mere opacity; the page, which you cover slowly with the crabbed thread of your gut; the page in the purity of its possibilities; the page of your death, against which you pit such flawed excellences as you can muster with all your life's strength: that page will teach you to write.

20   There is another way of saying this. Aim for the chopping block. If you aim for the wood, you will have nothing. Aim past the wood, aim through the wood; aim for the chopping block.

Questions for Discussion

1. Why does Annie Dillard write in a cabin? Where do you prefer to write? In what ways does your writing place affect your creativity and your ability to write well?
2. How does Dillard learn to split wood? Do you think many skills can be learned the way Dillard learns this skill? What does her "learning process" suggest about the way a person learns to write?
3. How does Dillard understand the relationship between the vision of the work of art and the work as it takes shape on paper or canvas? Does your writing follow a similar process?
4. What does Dillard mean when she says that the blank page "will teach you to write"? Do you agree?
5. Explain the meaning of Dillard's conclusion. Why does she return again to the image of the chopping block after her discussion of vision? Do you think that the chopping block is an effective metaphor for the writing process? Why or why not?
6. Which of Dillard's writing techniques would you be most likely to practice in your own writing? Why?

Ideas for Writing

1. Develop your journal entry into an essay in which you explain a creative process that you enhanced or mastered through dreaming or meditation.
2. Based on your own experience of writing, discuss Dillard's view of the writing process, particularly of the initial "vision" of a piece and its relationship to the finished work. Begin by explaining how you understand Dillard's writing process; then discuss how her process is relevant to you as a writer. Develop examples from the ways that you have used prewriting strategies, outlines, drafts, and revising in the past and/or refer to other writers in this chapter to support your ideas.

 ## Stephen King

The Symbolic Language of Dreams

Stephen King (b. 1947) was raised in Portland, Maine. After graduating from the University of Maine in 1970 with a B.A. in English, King taught high school and worked at odd jobs, finding time to write short fiction only at night. King's first book, Carrie *(1974), a story of the supernatural and of the cruelty of adolescence, was an immediate best seller. Stephen King has continued to be one of the most popular writers of gothic horror novels. Some of his best known works include* 'Salem's Lot *(1975),* The Shining *(1977; film version 1980),* The Dead

Zone (1979; *film version 1983*), Firestarter (1980; *film version 1984*), Christine (1983; *film version 1983*), It (1986), Misery (1987; *film version 1990*),
The Dark Half (1989) Rosa Madden (1995), *and* Desperation (1996).
Stephen King lives in Bangor, Maine, with his wife and their three children. In the
following interview you will learn about the various ways in which King's dreams
have helped him with his writing.

Write about a time when a dream or intuition helped you to solve a writing
problem or to understand an issue in your waking life.

1   One of the things that I've been able to use dreams for in my stories is to show
things in a symbolic way that I wouldn't want to come right out and say directly. I've always used dreams the way you'd use mirrors to look at something you
couldn't see head-on—the way that you use a mirror to look at your hair in the
back. To me that's what dreams are supposed to do. I think that dreams are a way
that people's minds illustrate the nature of their problems. Or maybe even illustrate the answers to their problems in symbolic language.

2   When we look back on our dreams, a lot of times they decompose as soon as
the light hits them. So, you can have a dream, and you can remember very vividly
what it's about, but ten or fifteen minutes later, unless it's an extraordinarily vivid
dream or an extraordinarily good dream, it's gone. It's like the mind is this hard
rubber and you really have to hit it hard to leave an impression that won't eventually just erase.

3   One of the things that we're all familiar with in dreams is the sense that familiar or prosaic objects are being put in very bizarre circumstances or situations. And
since that's what I write about, the use of dreams is an obvious way to create that
feeling of weirdness in the real world. I guess probably the most striking example
of using a dream in my fiction was connected to the writing of 'Salem's Lot.

4   Now, I can think of only maybe five or six really horrible nightmares in the
course of my life—which isn't bad when you think that that life stretches over
forty-four years—but I can remember having an extremely bad dream when I was
probably nine or ten years old.

5   It was a dream where I came up a hill and there was a gallows on top of this hill
with birds all flying around it. There was a hangman there. He had died, not by
having his neck broken, but by strangulation. I could tell because his face was all
puffy and purple. And as I came close to him he opened his eyes, reached his
hands out and grabbed me.

6   I woke up in my bed, sitting bolt upright, screaming. I was hot and cold at the
same time and covered with goosebumps. And not only was I unable to go back to
sleep for hours after that, but I was really afraid to turn out the lights for weeks. I
can still see it as clearly now as when it happened.

7   Years later I began to work on *'Salem's Lot*. Now, I knew that the story was going to be about a vampire that came from abroad to the United States and I
wanted to put him in a spooky old house. I got about that far in my thinking and,
by whatever way it is that your mind connects things, as I was looking around for a
spooky house, a guy who works in the creative department of my brain said, Well
what about that nightmare you had when you were eight or nine years old? Will
that work? And I remembered the nightmare and I thought, Yes, it's perfect.

8   I turned the dead man into a guy named Hubie Marston who owned a bad
house and pretty much repeated the story of the dream in terms of the way he
died.

9   In the story, Hubie Marston hangs himself. He's some sort of black artist of the
Aleister Crowley kind—some sort of a dark magician—and I kind of combined
him with a stock character in American tabloidism—the wealthy guy who lives
and dies in squalor.

10   For me, once the actual act of creation starts, writing is like this high-speed
version of the flip books you have when you're a kid, where you mix and match.
The cover of the book will say, "You Can Make Thousands of Faces!" You can put
maybe six or seven different eyes with different noses. Except that there aren't just
thousands of faces, there are literally billions of different events, personalities and
things that you can flip together. And it happens at a very rapid rate. Dreams are
just one of those flip strips that you can flip in there. But they also work in terms
of advancing the story.

11   Sometimes when I write I can use dreams to have a sort of precognitive effect
on the story. Precognitive dreams are a staple of our supernatural folklore. You
know, the person who dreamed that flight 17 was going to crash and changed his
reservation and sure enough, flight 17 crashed. But it's like those urban fairy tales:
you always hear somebody say, "I have a friend that this happened to." I've never
actually heard anyone say, "This happened to *me*."

12   The closest that I can come to a precognitive experience is that I can be in a
situation where a really strong feeling of déjà vu washes over me. I'm sure that I've
been there before. A lot of times I make the association that, at some point, I had
a dream about this place and this series of actions, and forgot it with my conscious
mind when I awoke.

13   Every now and then dreams can come in handy. When I was working on *It*—
which was this really long book—a dream made a difference.

14   I had a lot of time and a lot of my sense of craft invested in the idea of being
able to finish this huge, long book. Now, when I'm working on something, I see
books, completed books. And in some fashion that thing is already there. I'm not
really making it so much as I am digging it up, the way that you would an artifact,
out of the sand. The trick is to get as much of that object as you possibly can, to
get the whole thing out, so it's usable, without breaking it. You always break it
somewhat—I mean you never get a complete thing—but if you're really careful
and if you're really lucky, you can get most of it.

15   When I'm working I never know what the end is going to be or how things are
going to come out. I've got an idea what direction I want the story to go in, or

hope it will go in, but mostly I feel like the tail on a kite. I don't feel like the kite itself, or like the wind that blows on the kite—I'm just the tail of it. And if I know when I sit down what's happening or what's going to happen, that day and the next day and the day after, I'm happy. But with *It* I got to a point where I couldn't see ahead any more. And every day I got closer to the place where this young girl, who was one of my people—I don't think of them as good people or bad people, just my people—was going to be and they were going to find her.

16   I didn't know what was going to happen to her. And that made me extremely nervous. Because that's the way books don't get done. All at once you just get to a point where there is no more. It's like pulling a little string out of a hole and all at once it's broken and you don't get whatever prize there was on the end of it.

17   So I had seven, eight hundred pages and I just couldn't stand it. I remember going to bed one night saying, I've got to have an idea. I've got to have an idea! I fell asleep and dreamed that I was in a junk yard, which was where this part of the story was set.

18   Apparently, I was the girl. There was no girl in the dream. There was just me. And there were all these discarded refrigerators in this dump. I opened one of them and there were these things inside, hanging from the various rusty shelves. They looked like macaroni shells and they were all just sort of trembling in a breeze. Then one of them opened up these wings, flew out and landed on the back of my hand. There was a sensation of warmth, almost like when you get a subcutaneous shot of Novocain or something, and this thing started to turn from white to red. I realized it had anesthetized my hand and it was sucking my blood out. Then they all started to fly out of this refrigerator and to land on me. They were these leeches that looked like macaroni shells. And they were swelling up.

19   I woke up and I was very frightened. But I was also very happy. Because then I knew what was going to happen. I just took the dream as it was and put it in the book. Dropped it in. I didn't change anything.

20   In the story "The Body," there's an incident where several boys find themselves covered with leeches. That was something that actually happened to me. There's a lot of stuff in "The Body" that's just simply history that's been tarted up a little bit. These friends and I all went into this pond about a mile and a half from the house where I grew up and when we came out we were just covered with those babies. It was awful. I don't remember that I had nightmares about the incident then but of course I had this leech dream years later.

21   I really think what happened with this dream was that I went to sleep and the subconscious went right on working and finally sent up this dream the way that you would send somebody an interoffice message in a pneumatic tube.

22   In the Freudian sense I don't think there is any subconscious, any unconscious where things are going on. I think that consciousness is like an ocean. Whether you're an inch below the surface or whether you're down a mile and half deep, it's all water. All H_2O.

23   I think that our minds are the same nutrient bath all the way down to the bottom and different things live at different levels. Some of them are a little bit

harder to see because we don't get down that deep. But whatever's going on in our daily lives, our daily thoughts, the things that the surface of our minds are concerned with eddy down—trickle down—and then they have some sort of an influence down there. And the messages that we get a lot of times are nothing more than symbolic reworkings of the things that we're concerned with. I don't think they're very prophetic or anything like that. I think a lot of times dreams are nothing more than a kind of mental or spiritual flatulence. They're a way of relieving pressure.

24   One way of looking at this water metaphor might be to talk about jumbo shrimp, everybody's favorite oxymoron. They're the big shrimp that nobody ate in restaurants until 1955 or 1960 because, until then, nobody thought of going shrimping after dark. They were there all the time, living their prosaic shrimp lives, but nobody caught them. So when they finally caught them it was, "Hello! Look at this. This is something entirely new." And if the shrimp could talk they'd say, "Shit, we're not new. We've been around for a couple of thousand years. You were just too dumb to look for us."

25   A slightly different way of looking at this is that there are certain fish that we get used to looking at. There are carp, goldfish, catfish, shad, cod—they're fish that are more or less surface fish. They go down to a depth of maybe fifty, sixty or a hundred feet. People catch them, and we get used to seeing them. Not only do we see them in aquariums or as pictures in books, we see them on our plates. We cook them. We see them in the supermarket in the fish case. Whereas if you go down in a bathysphere, if you go down real deep, you see all these bright fluorescent, weird, strange things with membranous umbrellas and weird skirts that flare out from their bodies. Those are creatures that we don't see very often because they explode if we bring them up close to the surface. They are to surface fish what dreams are to our surface thoughts. Deep fish are like dreams of surface fish. They change shape, they change form.

26   There are dreams and there are deep dreams. There are dreams where you're able to tap sources that are a lot deeper. I'm sure that if you wanted to extend this metaphor you could say that within the human psyche, within human thought, there really are Mindanao trenches, places that are very very deep, where there are probably some extremely strange things floating around. And what the conscious mind brings up may be the equivalent of an exploded fish. It may just be a mess. It may be something that's gorgeous in its own habitat but when it gets up to the sun it just dries out. And then it's very gray and dull.

27   I remember about six months ago having this really vivid dream.

28   I was in some sort of an apartment building, a cheesy little apartment building. The front door was open and I could see all these black people going back and forth. They were talking and having a wonderful time. Somebody was playing music somewhere. And then the door shut.

29   In the dream I went back and got into bed. I think I must have shut the door myself. My brother was in bed with me, behind me, and he started to strangle me. My brother had gone crazy. It was awful!

30   I remember saying, with the last of my breath, "I think there's somebody out there." And he got up from the bed and went out. As soon as he was out I went up and closed the door and locked it. And then I went back to bed. That is, I started to lie down in this dream.

31   Then I began to worry that I hadn't really locked the door. This is the sort of thing that I'm always afraid of in real life. Did I turn off the burners on the stove? Did I leave a light on when I left the house? So, I got up to check the door and sure enough it was unlocked. I realized that he was still in there with me. Somewhere.

32   I screamed in the dream, "He's still in the house." I screamed so loud I woke myself up. Except I wasn't screaming when I woke up. I was just sort of muttering it over and over again, He's in the house, he's in the house. I was terrified.

33   Now, I keep a glass of ice water beside the bed where I sleep and the ice cubes hadn't melted yet, so it had happened almost immediately after I fell asleep. That's usually when I have the dreams that I remember most vividly.

34   Part of my function as a writer is to dream awake. And that usually happens. If I sit down to write in the morning, in the beginning of that writing session and the ending of that session, I'm aware that I'm writing. I'm aware of my surroundings. It's like shallow sleep on both ends, when you go to bed and when you wake up. But in the middle, the world is gone and I'm able to see better.

35   Creative imaging and dreaming are just so similar that they've got to be related.

36   In a story like "The Body" or *It*, which is set around the late fifties or the early sixties, I'm literally able to regress so that I can remember things that I'd forgotten. Time goes by and events pile up on the surface of your mind like snow, and it covers all these other previous layers. But if you're able to put yourself into that sort of semidreaming state—whether you're dreaming or whether you're writing creatively the brainwaves are apparently interchangeable—you're able to get a lot of that stuff back. That might be deep dreaming.

37   I'm aware, particularly in recent years, how precious that state is, I mean the ability to go in there when one is awake. I'm also aware, as an adult, of the vividness of my sleeping dreams when I have them. But I don't have any way of stacking up the number of dreams that I have as opposed to anybody else. My sense is I probably dream a little bit less at night because I'm taking off some of the pressure in the daytime. But I don't have any inherent proof of that.

38   I can remember finding that state for the first time and being delighted. It's a little bit like finding a secret door in a room but not knowing exactly how you got in. I can't remember exactly how I first found that state except that I would sit down to write every day and I would pretty much do that whether the work went well or the work went badly. And after doing that for a while it was a little bit like having a posthypnotic suggestion.

39   I know that there are certain things that I do if I sit down to write: I have a glass of water or I have a cup of tea. There's a certain time I sit down around eight o'clock—or 8:15 or 8:30—somewhere within that half hour every morning. I have my vitamin pill; I have my music; I have my same seat; and the papers are all

arranged in the same places. It's a series of things. The cumulative purpose of doing those things the same way every day seems to be a way of saying to the mind: you're going to be dreaming soon.

40   It's not really any different than a bedtime routine. Do you go to bed a different way every night? Is there a certain side that you sleep on? I mean I brush my teeth. I wash my hands. Why would anybody wash their hands before they go to bed? I don't know. And the pillows: the pillows are supposed to be pointed a certain way. The open side of the pillowcase is supposed to be pointed *in* toward the other side of the bed. I don't know why.

41   And the sleeping position is the same: turn to the right, turn to the left. I think it's a way of your mind saying to your body, or your body saying to your mind—maybe they're communicating with each other saying—we're gonna go to sleep now. And probably dreaming follows the same pattern if you don't interrupt it with things like drug use, alcohol or whatever.

42   The dreams that I remember most clearly are almost always early dreams. And they're not always bad dreams. I don't want to give you that impression. I can remember one very clearly. It was a flying dream. I was over the turnpike and I was flying along wearing a pair of pajama bottoms. I didn't have any shirt on. I'm just buzzing along under overpasses—*kazipp*—and I'm reminding myself in the dream to stay high enough so that I don't get disemboweled by car antennas sticking up from the cars. That's a fairly mechanistic detail but when I woke up from this dream my feeling was not fear or loathing but just real exhilaration, pleasure and happiness.

43   It wasn't an out of control flying dream. I can remember as a kid, having a lot of falling dreams but this is the only flying dream that I can remember in detail.

44   I don't have a lot of repetitive dreams but I do have an anxiety dream: I'm working very hard in a little hot room—it seems to be the room where I lived as a teenager—and I'm aware that there's a madwoman in the attic. There's a little tiny door under the eave that goes to the attic and I have to finish my work. I have to get that work done or she'll come out and get me. At some point in the dream that door always bursts open and this hideous woman—with all this white hair stuck up around her head like a gone-to-seed dandelion—jumps out with a scalpel.

45   And I wake up.

46   I still have that dream when I'm backed up on my work and trying to fill all these ridiculous commitments I've made for myself.

Questions for Discussion

1. King says, "I think that dreams are a way that people's minds illustrate the nature of their problems. Or maybe even illustrate the answers to their problems in symbolic language." Explain why you agree or disagree with King through reference to your own experiences and the experiences of people who are close to you or whom you respect.

2. Discuss several ways in which King uses his dreams in his writing. Have you used your dreams to help you with your writing? How? If this is a new idea for you, how do you think you might try to use dreams in your writing?

3. King gives us a good sense of the types of dreams that he has, of the impact that his dreams have had on him, and of the detailed fabric of his dreams. Compare and contrast your dreams to King's dreams. What does this comparison and contrast suggest to you about how your dreams might have a significant impact on your waking life?

4. What conclusions about the way in which the mind functions does King develop through his metaphors of the mind as an ocean, as a nutrient bath, as water? What different roles do the jumbo shrimp and the fish play in his explanations?

5. What relationship does King find between his process of writing and his process of dreaming? Why does King believe that "Creative imaging and dreaming are just so similar that they've got to be related"? Explain why you agree or disagree with King.

6. Write an essay that analyzes the meaning of several of your dreams and explores how you have made them a part of your waking life.

Ideas for Writing

1. Write down a dream or nightmare that is vivid in your mind but that has never been recorded in words. Then write an analysis of the dream. What do you think it is telling you?

 # Tim O'Brien

The Magic Show

Tim O'Brien (b. 1947) was raised in Austin, Minnesota. He earned his B.A. at Macalester College and did graduate work at Harvard University. In 1968 he was drafted and sent to Vietnam, where he served two years in the infantry and received a Purple Heart. After returning home, O'Brien worked as a reporter for the Washington Post. *His first book, the memoir* If I Die in a Combat Zone *(1973), explores his Vietnam experiences, as does most of his subsequent fiction. O'Brien's first two novels were* Northern Lights *(1975) and* Going After Cacciato *(1978). His third novel,* The Nuclear Age *(1985), tells of a Vietnam-era radical and draft evader who builds a bomb shelter in his back yard many years after the war. O'Brien's most highly praised work is* The Things They Carried *(1990), a collection of related war stories. His most recent novel is* The Lake in the Woods *(1994). In the essay that follows, O'Brien discusses some of the magical and mysterious ways of a storyteller.*

What memories and feelings do you have about magic shows? Have you ever thought of a writer as a magician? Discuss.

---

1   As a kid, through grade school and into high school, my hobby was magic. I enjoyed the power; I liked making miracles happen. In the basement, where I practiced in front of a stand-up mirror, I caused my mother's silk scarves to change color. I used scissors to cut my father's best tie in half, displaying the pieces, and then restored it whole. I placed a penny in the palm of my hand, made my hand into a fist, made the penny into a white mouse. This was not true magic. It was trickery. But I sometimes pretended otherwise, because I was a kid then, and because pretending was the thrill of magic, and because for a time what seemed to happen became a happening in itself. I was a dreamer. I liked watching my hands in the mirror, imagining how someday I might perform much grander magic, tigers becoming giraffes, beautiful girls levitating like angels in the high yellow spotlights, naked maybe, no wires or strings, just floating.

2   It was illusion, of course—the creation of a new and improved reality. What I enjoyed about this peculiar hobby, at least in part, was the craft of it: learning the techniques of magic and then practicing those techniques, alone in the basement, for many hours and days. That was another thing about magic. I liked the aloneness, as God and other miracle makers must also like it—not lonely, just alone. I liked shaping the universe around me. I liked the power. I liked the tension and suspense when, for example, the magician displays a guillotine to the audience, demonstrating its cutting power by slicing a carrot in half; the edgy delight when a member of the audience is asked to place his hand in the guillotine hole; the hollow silence when, very slowly, the magician raises up the blade. Believe me, *there* is drama. And when the blade slams down, if it's *your* hand in the hole, you have no choice but to believe in miracles.

3   When practiced well, however, magic goes beyond a mere sequence of illusions. It becomes art. In the art of magic, as opposed to just doing tricks, there is a sense of theater and drama and continuity and beauty and wholeness. Take an example. Someone in the audience randomly selects a card from a shuffled deck—the Ace of Diamonds. The card is made to vanish, then a rabbit is pulled out of a hat, and the hat collapses into a fan, and the magician uses the fan to fan the rabbit, and the rabbit is transformed into a white dove, and the dove flies into the spotlights and returns a moment later with a playing card in its beak—the Ace of Diamonds. With such unity and flow, with each element contributing as both cause and effect, individual tricks are blended into something whole and unified, something indivisible, which is the nature of true art.

4   Beyond anything, though, what appealed to me about this hobby was the abiding mystery at its heart. Mystery everywhere—permeating mystery—even in the most ordinary objects of the world: a penny becomes a white mouse. The universe seemed both infinite and inexplicable. Anything was possible. The old rules were

no longer binding, the old truths no longer true. If my father's tie could be restored whole, why not someday use my wand to wake up the dead?

5   It's pretty clear, I suppose, where all this is headed. I stopped doing magic—at least of that sort. I took up a new hobby, writing stories. But without straining too much, I can suggest that the fundamentals seemed very much the same. Writing fiction is a solitary endeavor. You shape your own universe. You practice all the time, then practice some more. You pay attention to craft. You aim for tension and suspense, a sense of drama, displaying in concrete terms the actions and reactions of human beings contesting problems of the heart. You try to make art. You strive for wholeness, seeking continuity and flow, each element performing both as cause and effect, always hoping to create, or to re-create, the great illusions of life.

6   Above all, writing fiction involves a desire to enter the mystery of things: that human craving to know what cannot be known. In the ordinary world, for instance, we have no direct access to the thoughts of other human beings—we cannot *hear* those thoughts—yet even in the most "realistic" piece of fiction we listen as if through a stethoscope to the innermost musings of Anna Karenina and Lord Jim and Huck Finn. We know, in these stories, what cannot be known. It's a trick, of course. (And the tricks in these stories have been elevated into art.) In the ordinary sense, there *is* no Huck Finn, and yet in the extraordinary sense, which is the sense of magic, there most certainly *is* a Huck Finn and always will be. When writing or reading a work of fiction, we are seeking access to a kind of enigmatic "otherness"—other people and places, other worlds, other sciences, other souls. We give ourselves over to what is by nature mysterious, imagining the unknowable, and then miraculously knowing by virtue of what is imagined. There are new standards of knowing, new standards of reality. (Is Huck Finn real? No, we would say, by ordinary standards. Yes, by extraordinary standards.) For a writer, and for a reader, the process of imaginative knowing does not depend upon the scientific method. Fictional characters are not constructed of flesh and blood, but rather of words, and those words serve as explicit incantations that invite us into and guide us through the universe of the imagination. Language is the apparatus—the magic dust—by which a writer performs his miracles. Words are uttered: "By and by," Huck says, and we hear him. Words are uttered: "We went tip-toeing along the path amongst the trees," and we see it. Beyond anything, I think, a writer is someone entranced by the power of language to create a magic show of the imagination, to make the dead sit up and talk, to shine light into the darkness of the great human mysteries.

7   In many cultures, including our own, the magician and the storyteller are often embodied in a single person. This seems most obvious, I suppose, in religion, which seeks to penetrate into the greatest mysteries of all. The healer, or the miracle worker, is also the teller of stories about prior miracles, or about miracles still to come. In Christianity, the personage of Jesus is presented as a doer of both earthly miracles and the ultimate heavenly miracle of salvation. At the same time Jesus is a teller of miraculous stories—the parables, for instance, or the larger story

about damnation and redemption. The performance of miracles and the telling of stories become part of a whole. One aspect serves the other. In the culture of the North American Kiowa tribes, the shaman or witch doctor was believed to have access to an unseen world, a world of demons and gods and ancestral spirits, and these spirits were invoked in rites of healing and exorcism and divine intervention. But the shaman also told stories *about* those spirits: their wars, their loves, their treacheries, their defeats, their victories. The shaman's earthly claims upon his people were at once validated and legitimized by heavenly stories.

8   My point, of course, has to do with the interpenetration of magic and stories. In part, at least, storytelling involves the conjuring up of spirits—Huck Finn or Lord Jim. And those spirits, in turn, make implicit moral claims on us, serving as models of a sort, suggesting by implication how we might or might not lead our own lives. Stories encourage and discourage. Stories affirm and negate. In the tales of the Kiowa shaman, as in those of the modern New York novelist, spirits of virtue struggle against spirits of evil, heroes go up against villains, antiheroes confront antivillains, and in the course of the narrative a spirit's spirit is both defined and refined in moral terms. But these terms are not absolute. Stories are rooted in particulars—this village, this time, this character—and it strikes me that storytelling represents one form of what we now call situational ethics. The spirits in a story cast moral shadow and moral light. By example, through drama, stories display our own potential for good and evil: the range of moral possibility is extended.

9   There is also, I think, an incorporeal but nonetheless genuine "aliveness" to the characters, or ghosts, that are conjured up by good stories. In *The Sun Also Rises*, Jake Barnes and Brett Ashley and Bill Gorton and Mike Campbell are identities—spirits of a sort—that live between the covers of that book. They are not embodied, of course, and never were. They have no flesh and never did. Yet these characters live in the way spirits live, in the memory and imagination of the reader, as a dead father lives in the memory of his son or in the imagination of his daughter. The storyteller evokes, and invokes, this spirit world not with potions or pixie dust, but, as I suggested earlier, with the magic of language—those potent nouns, those levitating verbs, those tricky little adverbs, those amazing conjunctions, the whole spectacular show of clauses becoming sentences and sentences becoming paragraphs and paragraphs becoming stories. The Kiowa shaman achieves a similar effect by inducing in his tribe a trancelike state, summoning a collective dream with the language of incantation and narrative drama. The writer of fiction, like the shaman, serves as a medium of sorts between two different worlds—the world of ordinary reality and the extraordinary world of the imagination. In this capacity, the writer often enters a trancelike state of his own. Certainly this is my own experience. When I am writing well, invoking well, there is a dreamlike sense of gazing through the page as if it were the thinnest onionskin parchment, watching the spirits beyond, quietly looking on as the various characters go about their peculiar business. This is the sensation I get—both physical and emotional—as a waking dream unfolds into words and as the words unfold into a piece of fiction. Half in the embodied world, half in a world where bodies

are superfluous. I realize, as this semitrance occurs, that the page before me is only paper, the typescript only ink, and yet there is also a powerful awareness of those ghostly characters in motion just behind the page, just beyond the boundaries of the mundane. Whatever we call this process—imagination, fantasy, self-hypnosis, creativity—I know from my own life that it is both magical and real. And I think other writers of fiction would offer similar testimony. In any case, to complete the parallel with which I began, it is reported that the Kiowa shaman, too, enters the trance of his own dream, partly as a way of inducing that dream in his tribe, partly to serve as a guide into and through the other, fictional world. The more I write and the more I dream, the more I accept this notion of the writer as a medium between two planes of being—the ordinary and the extraordinary—the embodied world of flesh, the disembodied world of idea and morality and spirit.

10   In this sense, then, I must also believe that writing is essentially an act of faith. Faith in the heuristic power of the imagination. Faith in the fertility of dream. Faith that as writers we might discover that which cannot be known through empirical means. (The notions of right and wrong, for instance. Good and evil. Ugliness and beauty.) Faith in story itself. Faith that a story will lead, in some way, to epiphany or understanding or enlightenment. In the most practical sense, just to *begin* a story involves a great leap of faith that the first imagined event will somehow lead to the next, that chapter two will somehow follow upon chapter one. Faith that language will continue to serve us from day to day. Faith that a story will take us somewhere—in the plot sense, in the thematic sense—and that the destination will be worth the journey. And just as faith seems essential to me as a writer, and maybe to all of us, it seems also true that crises of faith are common to the vocation of the storyteller: writer's block, lapses of confidence, the terror of aesthetic subjectivity as the final arbiter of excellence. For all of us, I would guess, there is, at least on occasion, a terrible sense of howling in the dark. I would suppose that many of us have experienced more than one crisis of faith—in our talents, in our lives—and yet because we are still at work, still writing, I would also suppose that we have at some point undergone a renewal of that faith.

11   So far I've been discussing, in a less than systematic way, a set of "mysteries" inherent in the *process* of writing fiction. But it seems to me that the fiction itself—the story, the novel—must ultimately represent and explore those same mysteries. Or to say it bluntly: it is my view that good storytelling involves, in a substantive sense, a plunge into mystery of the grandest order. Briefly, almost in summary form, I want to examine this notion through two different windows of craft—plot and character.

12   It is my belief that plot revolves around certain mysteries of fact, or what a story represents as fact. What happened? What will happen? Huck and Jim hop on a raft (fact) and embark on a journey (fact) and numerous events occur along the way (facts). On the level of plot, this narrative appeals to our curiosity about where the various facts will lead. As readers, we wonder and worry about what may befall these two human beings as they float down a river in violation of the ordinary social conventions. We are curious about facts still to come. In this sense, plot involves the inherent and riveting mystery of the *future*. What next? What

are the coming facts? By its very nature, the future compels and intrigues us—it holds promise, it holds terror—and plot relies for its power on the essential cloudiness of things to come. We don't know. We want to know.

13   In a magic act, as in a story, there is the reporting (or purporting) of certain facts. The guillotine *is* sharp, it *does* cut the carrot, the man's hand *does* enter the guillotine's hole, the blade *does* slam down. For an audience, the mystery has entirely to do with future facts. What will become of this poor man? Will he lose his hand? Will he weep? Will the stump bleed as stumps tend to do?

14   Without some concept of the future, these questions would be both impossible and irrelevant. It is the mystery of the future, at least in part, that compels us to turn the pages of a novel, or of a story, or of our own lives. Unlike the animals, we conceive of tomorrow. And tomorrow fascinates us. Tomorrow matters—maybe too much—and we spend a great portion of our lives adjusting the present in hope of shaping the future. In any case, we are driven to care and to be curious about questions of fate and destiny: we can't help it, we're human.

15   On one level, then, I am arguing in defense of old-fashioned plot—or in defense of plot in general—which is so often discredited as a sop to some unsophisticated and base human instinct. But I see nothing base in the question, "What will happen next?" I'm suggesting that plot is grounded in a high—even noble—human craving to *know*, a craving to push into the mystery of tomorrow.

16   This is not to argue, however, that plot need give an impression of finality. A good plot does not tie up the loose ends of the future in a tidy little knot. The plot of my own life has not often, so far as I can tell, resolved itself in any neat and final way. Death itself, when it comes, dissolves into enigma. Maybe this, maybe that. But who knows? Who really *knows*? The plot mystery of life—what will happen to us, to all of us, to the human race—is unresolved and must remain that way if it is to endure as a compelling story. As a species, I believe, we are beguiled by uncertainty. It is both a gift and a burden. We crave knowledge, yes, but we also crave its absence, for the absence alone makes possible the joy of discovery. Once the factual curtain falls—for instance, if we were to know beyond doubt that Lee Harvey Oswald acted on his own to assassinate President Kennedy—that ticklish sense of uncertainty vanishes and the puzzle no longer puzzles and the story is both finished and boring. Nothing remains to ignite curiosity. Nothing beckons, nothing tantalizes. As Edmund Wilson suggests in his famous comment, "Who cares who killed Cock Robin," there is something both false and trivial about a story that arrives at absolute closure. With closure, the facts of today have no bearing on the facts of tomorrow. (It seems ironic that most so-called mystery stories conclude with no mystery whatsoever. The killer's methods and motives are exposed. Ah, we think, no *wonder*. All is explicable, all is settled. The case is closed.) A satisfying plot, I believe, involves not a diminution of mystery but rather a fundamental enlargement. As in scientific endeavor, the solution to one set of problems must open out into another and even greater set. The future must still matter. The unknown must still issue its call. One tomorrow must imply the next.

17   About real people, we sometimes say: "Well, she's a mystery to me," or "I wonder what makes him tick." Such comments represent, I think, a deep and specific

desire for the miraculous: to enter another human soul, to read other minds and hearts, to find access to what is by nature inaccessible. A person lives in his own skin. All else is other, and otherness is suspect. If we see a man laugh, for instance, we might guess that he is experiencing elation or giddiness or joy of some sort. But perhaps not. Maybe it's ironic laughter, or nervous laughter, or the laughter of the insane. Again, who knows? In a story called *The Lady With the Pet Dog*, Chekhov has one of his characters muse as follows: "Judging others by himself, he did not believe what he saw, and always fancied that every man led his real, most interesting life under cover of secrecy as under cover of night." It is easy to sympathize with this view. Like Chekhov's character, we can "judge others by ourselves," but we cannot directly experience their loves and pains and joys. We know our own thoughts—we know by the act of thinking—but we cannot think those "other" thoughts. The mystery of otherness seems permanent and binding, a law of the universe, and yet *because* it is a mystery, *because* it binds, we find ourselves clawing at the darkness of human nature in an effort to know what cannot be known. "I love you," someone says, and we begin to wonder. "Well, how much?" we say, and when the answer comes, "With my whole heart," we then wonder about the wholeness of that heart. We probe and probe again. Along with Chekhov, we fancy that there is some secret lodged inside a human personality, hidden as if under cover of night, and that if light could be cast into the darkness of another's heart, we would find there the "real" human being. Such curiosity seems to me both inevitable and misdirected. Judging from what I know of myself, the human "character," if there is such a thing, seems far too complex and fluid and contradictory ever to pin down with much solidity or specificity. To really know a human character, to expose a single "secret," strikes me as beyond reach. In a sense, we "know" human character—maybe even our own—in the same way we know black holes: by their effects on the external world. The source of the light is sucked up by the nature of nature.

18   My focus here is on the construction of literary character, and my general argument is that characterization is achieved not through a "pinning down" process but rather through a process that opens up and releases mysteries of the human spirit. The object is not to "solve" a character—to expose some hidden secret—but instead to deepen and enlarge the riddle itself. Too often, I believe, characterization fails precisely *because* it attempts to characterize. It narrows; it pins down; it explicates; it solves. The nasty miser is actually quite sweet and generous. The harlot has a heart of gold. The gunfighter is a peaceable guy who yearns to own a small cattle ranch. The failure here is twofold. For me, at least, such solutions do not square with my sense of the immense complexity of man's spirit. The human life seems cheapened. Beyond that, however, this sort of characterization has the effect of diminishing the very mystery that makes us care so passionately about other human beings. There is false and arbitrary closure. A "solved" character ceases to be mysterious, hence becomes less than human. As with plot, I believe that successful characterization requires an enhancement of mystery: not shrinkage, but expansion. To beguile, to bewitch, to cause lasting wonder—these are the aims of characterization. Think of Kurtz in *Heart of Darkness*. He has witnessed

profound savagery, has immersed himself in it, and as he lies dying, we hear him whisper, "The horror, the horror." There is no solution here. Rather, the reverse. The heart *is* dark. We gape into the tangle of this man's soul, which has the quality of a huge black hole, ever widening, ever mysterious, its gravity sucking us back into the book itself. What intrigues us, ultimately, is not what we know but what we do not know and yearn to discover.

19   The magician's credo is this: don't give away your secrets. Once a trick is explained—once a secret is divulged—the world moves from the magical to the mechanical. Similarly, with plot and character, the depletion of mystery robs a story of the very quality that brings us to pursue fiction in the first place. We might admire the cleverness of the writer. But we forget the story. Because there is no miracle to remember. The object of storytelling, like the object of magic, is not to explain or to resolve, but rather to create and to perform miracles of the imagination. To extend the boundaries of the mysterious. To push into the unknown in pursuit of still other unknowns. To reach into one's own heart, down into that place where the stories are, bringing up the mystery of oneself.

Questions for Discussion

1. Why did Tim O'Brien enjoy performing magic shows as a child? What comparisons does he make between performing magic and writing stories? Does his analogy make sense to you? Explain.
2. Explain why O'Brien believes that language is "magic dust." Do you agree or disagree with him? Support your point of view through reference to your own experiences as a reader and a writer.
3. According to O'Brien, why do religions make healers into storytellers? Can you provide evidence of your own to support O'Brien's perspective?
4. In what sense do stories provide situational ethics? Suggest examples from your own reading to show how you interpret O'Brien's claim.
5. Why does O'Brien argue that the purpose of character and plot must be to heighten the riddles and mysteries of life? Do you agree or disagree with him? Why do characters from a novel seem to be alive?
6. "The more I write and the more I dream, the more I accept this notion of the writer as a medium between two planes of being—the ordinary and the extraordinary—the embodied world of flesh, the disembodied world of idea and morality and spirit." Explain why you agree or disagree with O'Brien. Refer to your own reading and writing experiences.

Ideas for Writing

1. Have you ever thought of a writer as a magician? Has this essay changed your understanding of the storyteller's (writer's) role and his or her craft? In what ways? Develop an essay in which you explain how you can apply O'Brien's concept of the writer as magician to your own thinking, reading, and writing processes.
2. Develop item 3 or 6 under Questions for Discussion into an essay.

✦ Amy Tan

Mother Tongue

Born in Oakland, California, in 1952 to immigrant parents, Amy Tan received an M.A. (1974) from San Jose State University, where she studied linguistics. Her first bestselling novel, The Joy Luck Club (1989), was inspired by the stories told by Chinese-American women of her mother's generation. Tan has written two other novels, The Kitchen God's Wife (1991) and The One Hundred Secret Senses (1995), as well as a number of essays in which she explores cultural and linguistic issues. As you read the following essay, notice how Tan uses her experiences growing up bilingual in a Chinese-American family to challenge the traditional expectations of academic writing achievement tests.

JOURNAL

In her essay Amy Tan states that she is "fascinated by language in daily life." Discuss examples of odd, striking, or creative uses of language that you have noticed in everyday life or conversation.

1   I am not a scholar of English or literature. I cannot give you much more than personal opinions on the English language and its variations in this country or others.

2   I am a writer. And by that definition, I am someone who has always loved language. I am fascinated by language in daily life. I spend a great deal of my time thinking about the power of language—the way it can evoke an emotion, a visual image, a complex idea, or a simple truth. Language is the tool of my trade. And I use them all—all the Englishes I grew up with.

3   Recently, I was made keenly aware of the different Englishes I do use. I was giving a talk to a large group of people, the same talk I had already given to half a dozen other groups. The nature of the talk was about my writing, my life, and my book, *The Joy Luck Club.* The talk was going alone well enough, until I remembered one major difference that made the whole talk sound wrong. My mother was in the room. And it was perhaps the first time she had heard me give a lengthy speech, using the kind of English I have never used with her. I was saying things like, "The intersection of memory upon imagination" and "There is an aspect of my fiction that relates to thus-and-thus"—a speech filled with carefully wrought grammatical phrases, burdened, it suddenly seemed to me, with nominalized forms, past perfect tenses, conditional phrases, all the forms of standard English that I had learned in school and through books, the forms of English I did not use at home with my mother.

4   Just last week, I was walking down the street with my mother, and I again found myself conscious of the English I was using, the English I do use with her.

We were talking about the price of new and used furniture and I heard myself saying this: "Not waste money that way." My husband was with us as well, and he didn't notice any switch in my English. And then I realized why. It's because over the twenty years we've been together I've often used that same kind of English with him, and sometimes he even uses it with me. It has become our language of intimacy, a different sort of English that relates to family talk, the language I grew up with.

5   So you'll have some idea of what this family talk I heard sounds like, I'll quote what my mother said during a recent conversation which I videotaped and then transcribed. During this conversation, my mother was talking about a political gangster in Shanghai who had the same last name as her family's, Du, and how the gangster in his early years wanted to be adopted by her family, which was rich by comparison. Later, the gangster became more powerful, far richer than my mother's family, and one day showed up at my mother's wedding to pay his respects. Here's what she said in part:

6   "Du Yusong having business like fruit stand. Like off the street kind. He is Du like Du Zong—but not Tsung-ming Island people. The local people call putong, the river east side, he belong to that side local people. That man want to ask Du Zong father take him in like become own family. Du Zong father wasn't look down on him, but didn't take seriously, until that man big like become a mafia. Now important person, very hard to inviting him. Chinese way, came only to show respect, don't stay for dinner. Respect for making big celebration, he shows up. Mean gives lots of respect. Chinese custom. Chinese social life that way. If too important won't have to stay too long. He come to my wedding. I didn't see, I heard it. I gone to boy's side, they have YMCA dinner. Chinese age I was nineteen."

7   You should know that my mother's expressive command of English belies how much she actually understands. She reads the *Forbes* report, listens to *Wall Street Week*, converses daily with her stockbroker, reads all of Shirley MacLaine's books with ease—all kinds of things I can't begin to understand. Yet some of my friends tell me they understand 50 percent of what my mother says. Some say they understand 80 to 90 percent. Some say they understand none of it, as if she were speaking pure Chinese. But to me, my mother's English is perfectly clear, perfectly natural. It's my mother tongue. Her language, as I hear it, is vivid, direct, full of observation and imagery. That was the language that helped shape the way I saw things, expressed things, made sense of the world.

8   Lately, I've been giving more thought to the kind of English my mother speaks. Like others, I have described it to people as "broken" or "fractured" English. But I wince when I say that. It has always bothered me that I can think of no way to describe it other than "broken," as if it were damaged and needed to be fixed, as if it lacked a certain wholeness and soundness. I've heard other terms used, "limited English," for example. But they seem just as bad, as if everything is limited, including people's perceptions of the limited English speaker.

9   I know this for a fact, because when I was growing up, my mother's "limited" English limited *my* perception of her. I was ashamed of her English. I believed that

her English reflected the quality of what she had to say. That is, because she expressed them imperfectly her thoughts were imperfect. And I had plenty of empirical evidence to support me: the fact that people in department stores, at banks, and at restaurants did not take her seriously, did not give her good service, pretended not to understand her, or even acted as if they did not hear her.

10   My mother had long realized the limitations of her English as well. When I was fifteen, she used to have me call people on the phone to pretend I was she. In this guise, I was forced to ask for information or even to complain and yell at people who had been rude to her. One time it was a call to her stockbroker in New York. She had cashed out her small portfolio and it just so happened we were going to go to New York the next week, our very first trip outside California. I had to get on the phone and say in an adolescent voice that was not very convincing, "This is Mrs. Tan."

11   And my mother was standing in the back whispering loudly, "Why he don't send me check, already two weeks late. So mad he lie to me, losing me money."

12   And then I said in perfect English, "Yes, I'm getting rather concerned. You had agreed to send the check two weeks ago, but it hasn't arrived."

13   Then she began to talk more loudly. "What he want, I come to New York tell him front of his boss, you cheating me?" And I was trying to calm her down, make her be quiet, while telling the stockbroker, "I can't tolerate any more excuses. If I don't receive the check immediately, I am going to have to speak to your manager when I'm in New York next week." And sure enough, the following week there we were in front of this astonished stockbroker, and I was sitting there red-faced and quiet, and my mother, the real Mrs. Tan, was shouting at his boss in her impeccable broken English.

14   We used a similar routine just five days ago, for a situation that was far less humorous. My mother had gone to the hospital for an appointment, to find out about a benign brain tumor a CAT scan had revealed a month ago. She said she had spoken very good English, her best English, no mistakes. Still, she said, the hospital did not apologize when they said they had lost the CAT scan and she had come for nothing. She said they did not seem to have any sympathy when she told them she was anxious to know the exact diagnosis, since her husband and son had both died of brain tumors. She said they would not give her any more information until the next time and she would have to make another appointment for that. So she said she would not leave until the doctor called her daughter. She wouldn't budge. And when the doctor finally called her daughter, me, who spoke in perfect English—lo and behold—we had assurances the CAT scan would be found, promises that a conference call on Monday would be held, and apologies for any suffering my mother had gone through for a most regrettable mistake.

15   I think my mother's English almost had an effect on limiting my possibilities in life as well. Sociologists and linguists probably will tell you that a person's developing language skills are more influenced by peers. But I do think that the language spoken in the family, especially in immigrant families which are more insular, plays a large role in shaping the language of the child. And I believe that it affected my results on achievement tests, IQ tests, and the SAT. While my English skills were never judged as poor, compared to math, English could not be con-

sidered my strong suit. In grade school I did moderately well, getting perhaps B's, sometimes B-pluses, in English and scoring perhaps in the sixtieth or seventieth percentile on achievement tests. But those scores were not good enough to override the opinion that my true abilities lay in math and science, because in those areas I achieved A's and scored in the ninetieth percentile or higher.

16   This was understandable. Math is precise; there is only one correct answer. Whereas, for me at least, the answers on English tests were always a judgment call, a matter of opinion and personal experience. Those tests were constructed around items like fill-in-the-blank sentence completion, such as "Even though Tom was _____, Mary thought he was _____." And the correct answer always seemed to be the most bland combinations of thoughts, for example, "Even though Tom was shy, Mary thought he was charming," with the grammatical structure "even though" limiting the correct answer to some sort of semantic opposites, so you wouldn't get answers like, "Even though Tom was foolish, Mary thought he was ridiculous." Well, according to my mother, there were very few limitations as to what Tom could have been and what Mary might have thought of him. So I never did well on tests like that.

17   The same was true with word analogies, pairs of words in which you were supposed to find some sort of logical, semantic relationship—for example, "*Sunset* is to *nightfall* as _____ is to _____." And here you would be presented with a list of four possible pairs, one of which showed the same kind of relationship: *red* is to *stoplight*, *bus* is to *arrival*, *chills* is to *fever*, *yawn* is to *boring*. Well, I could never think that way. I knew what the tests were asking, but I could not block out of my mind the images already created by the first pair, "*sunset* is to *nightfall*"—and I would see a burst of colors against a darkening sky, the moon rising, the lowering of a curtain of stars. And all the other pairs of words—red, bus, stoplight, boring—just threw up a mass of confusing images, making it impossible for me to sort out something as logical as saying: "A sunset precedes nightfall" is the same as "a chill precedes a fever." The only way I would have gotten that answer right would have been to imagine an associative situation, for example, my being disobedient and staying out past sunset, catching a chill at night, which turns into feverish pneumonia as punishment, which indeed did happen to me.

18   I have been thinking about all this lately, about my mother's English, about achievement tests. Because lately I've been asked, as a writer, why there are not more Asian Americans represented in American literature. Why are there few Asian Americans enrolled in creative writing programs? Why do so many Chinese students go into engineering? Well, these are broad sociological questions I can't begin to answer. But I have noticed in surveys—in fact, just last week—that Asian students, as a whole, always do significantly better on math achievement tests than in English. And this makes me think that there are other Asian-American students whose English spoken in the home might also be described as "broken" or "limited." And perhaps they also have teachers who are steering them away from writing and into math and science, which is what happened to me.

19   Fortunately, I happen to be rebellious in nature and enjoy the challenge of disproving assumptions made about me. I became an English major my first year in

college, after being enrolled as pre-med. I started writing nonfiction as a freelancer the week after I was told by my former boss that writing was my worst skill and I should hone my talents toward account management.

20   But it wasn't until 1985 that I finally began to write fiction. And at first I wrote using what I thought to be wittily crafted sentences, sentences that would finally prove I had mastery over the English language. Here's an example from the first draft of a story that later made its way into *The Joy Luck Club,* but without this line: "That was my mental quandary in its nascent state." A terrible line, which I can barely pronounce.

21   Fortunately, for reasons I won't get into today, I later decided I should envision a reader for the stories I would write. And the reader I decided upon was my mother, because these were stories about mothers. So with this reader in mind— and in fact she did read my early drafts—I began to write stories using all the Englishes I grew up with: the English I spoke to my mother, which for lack of a better term might be described as "simple"; the English she used with me, which for lack of a better term might be described as "broken"; my translation of her Chinese, which could certainly be described as "watered down"; and what I imagined to be her translation of her Chinese if she could speak in perfect English, her internal language, and for that I sought to preserve the essence, but neither an English nor a Chinese structure. I wanted to capture what language ability tests can never reveal: her intent, her passion, her imagery, the rhythms of her speech and the nature of her thoughts.

22   Apart from what any critic had to say about my writing, I knew I had succeeded where it counted when my mother finished reading my book and gave me her verdict: "So easy to read."

Questions for Discussion

1. Amy Tan discusses her awareness of using language differently when speaking with different audiences and on different occasions. How often are you aware of consciously choosing your words to communicate effectively and expressively with your particular audience? As an experiment, keep a log for several days that records the situations when you switch the way you use English for a specific group of friends, for teachers, for relatives, or for a work situation. Share your observations and conclusions with your classmates.

2. Why is Tan critical of the descriptive term "limited English"? How did this term influence her perception of her own mother?

3. Why is the article entitled "Mother Tongue"? What do Tan's examples about how she would often speak for her mother suggest?

4. Why is Amy Tan critical of the achievement tests she was given as an adolescent? Do you agree or disagree with her point of view and conclusions?

5. Why does Tan believe that high school teachers encourage Asian students to study math and science? How does Tan explain her success as a

writer in spite of the guidance and advice provided by her teachers and boss?

6. According to Tan, what is the real test of a writer? What advice does Tan offer to the person who aspires to be a successful writer?

Ideas for Writing

1. "I am a writer. And by definition, I am someone who has always loved language. I am fascinated by language in daily life." Develop Amy Tan's idea that language is fascinating into an essay, using personal experiences and examples from your reading that illustrate language's complexity and power.

2. Write an essay in which you discuss how your rebellion against a cultural or social myth helped you to develop a skill and talent that is both useful and rewarding.

 # Theodore Roethke

The Waking

Theodore Roethke (1908–1963) grew up in Saginaw, Michigan, where he spent much of his time in his father's large commercial greenhouses. Even as a young man, Roethke had a sense that he would become a poet; he began to write and study the craft of poetry before attending the University of Michigan and Harvard. For most of his life Roethke supported himself and his family as a teacher of creative writing at the University of Washington. Roethke's poetry often celebrates his students, about whom he cared deeply. His intense and emotional nature is also reflected in his love for nature and his interest in understanding the spiritual world. Commenting on his first volume of poems, Open House *(1941), Roethke shared his "intention to use himself as the material for his art." Roethke explores his inner world and reflects on the natural mysteries of life in volumes such as* The Lost Son *(1948) and* Words for the Wind *(1957).* On the Poet and His Selected Prose *(1966) gives readers insight into his writing process. In the poem that follows, Roethke explores his thoughts and feelings about the powers of the natural world and about the relationship between conscious intention and fate, between sleeping and waking dreams.*

JOURNAL

What connections have you discovered between your waking life and your dreams?

I wake to sleep, and take my waking slow.
I feel my fate in what I cannot fear.
I learn by going where I have to go.

We think by feeling. What is there to know?
5 I hear my being dance from ear to ear.
I wake to sleep, and take my waking slow.

Of those so close beside me, which are you?
God bless the Ground! I shall walk softly there,
And learn by going where I have to go.

10 Light takes the Tree; but who can tell us how?
The lowly worm climbs up a winding stair;
I wake to sleep, and take my waking slow.

Great Nature has another thing to do
To you and me; so take the lively air,
15 And, lovely, learn by going where to go.

This shaking keeps me steady. I should know.
What falls away is always. And is near.
I wake to sleep, and take my waking slow.
I learn by going where I have to go.

Questions for Discussion

1. "I wake to sleep, and take my waking slow." What do you think the speaker of the poem means in this refrain?
2. What mood do the rhythms and refrains of the sentences establish in the poem?
3. In the context of the poem, what is the meaning of the refrain "I learn by going where I have to go"? Can you apply this statement to your own life?
4. What are the mysterious ways of nature as revealed in this poem?
5. What does the poem imply about the role of sleep and dreams in our waking life?
6. The poem's speaker states, "We think by feeling. What is there to know?" Do you agree with the narrator's claim? How would you answer the question that follows the claim?

Ideas for Writing

1. Begin by drawing an image or images from the poem. Then write an interpretation of the poem and apply its meaning to your own life experiences.
2. Write an essay in which you discuss the relationship between one's waking and sleeping life. When appropriate, refer to your own experiences and to those of other writers in this text.

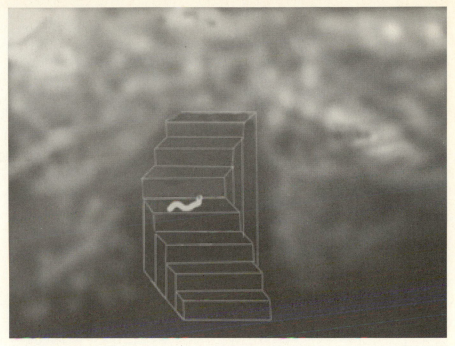

Alfredo Soto

"The lowly worm climbs up a winding stair."

As I drew my picture I contemplated what the meaning of that line was in Theodore Roethke's poem titled "The Waking." The image of the worm remained in me when I finished the poem. Puzzled, I decided to try to decipher its cryptic meaning. Despite drawing it, I was unclear about why the author used the image of a worm climbing stairs. Then, I had a thought. I began to think that the author, like the worm climbing the stairs, woke up in the poem unable to see what lies ahead of him but went on nonetheless. The use of the worm also shows the difficulty of the journey. Like Roethke says in the poem, he learns by "going where [he has] to go." The worm knows nothing about what is above him nor what awaits him at the top of the stairs, so it too must learn about where it's going as it goes. So the worm was used as a subtle analogy.

 Ted Hughes

The Thought-Fox

Ted Hughes (b. 1930) was raised in England. Although his father was a carpenter and his mother a housewife, they encouraged Hughes to attend the university at Cambridge. Hughes has earned an international reputation as a poet, publishing over thirty volumes of poetry from The Hawk in the Rain *(1957) to more recent collections such as* New Selected Poems 1957–1981, Wolfwatching *(1989),*

and Moortown Diary *(1989). Hughes has also written many children's stories*
and has published collections of prose, the most recent of which is Winter Pollen:
Occasional Prose *(1994). Hughes was the Poet Laureate of England in 1984.*
After the tragic suicide of his wife, Sylvia Plath, the confessional poet and the
mother of their two young children, Hughes has helped to collect and edit her
work. His own writing always reflects a profound interest in capturing the rhythms
of nature and animals, as you will see in his poem "The Thought-Fox."

JOURNAL

What is the best time of day for you to write? Why? Do you ever think of yourself as a type of natural creature when you are writing? Which creature?

I imagine this midnight moment's forest:
Something else is alive
Beside the clock's loneliness
And this blank page where my fingers move.

5 Through the window I see no star:
Something more near
Though deeper within darkness
Is entering the loneliness:

Cold, delicately as the dark snow
10 A fox's nose touches twig, leaf;
Two eyes serve a movement, that now
And again now, and now, and now

Sets neat prints into the snow
Between trees, and warily a lame
15 Shadow lags by stump and in hollow
Of a body that is bold to come

Across clearings, an eye,
A widening deepening greenness,
Brilliantly, concentratedly,
20 Coming about its own business

Till, with a sudden sharp hot stink of fox,
It enters the dark hole of the head.
The window is starless still; the clock ticks,
The page is printed.

Questions for Discussion

1. What is the poem's speaker imagining as his "fingers move" on the "blank page"?
2. Why doesn't the speaker see a star in the night sky?
3. How does the poem's speaker reveal the process through which he perceives the fox and then writes about it?
4. Why does the speaker see his creativity in the form of a fox? How does his presentation of the fox's action reveal the process of creativity?
5. What is the relationship between the fox and the speaker of the poem?
6. What does the poem suggest about inspiration and the creative process?

Ideas for Writing

1. Write an essay about the inspiration and the creative process involved in a piece of your writing that you are proud of. How did you use physical experiences, memories, imagination, and problem solving to finish your writing?
2. Develop a poem or story about inspiration and the creative process through the use of a symbol or symbols.

 ## Susan Helfter

Who Am I When I Write?

Susan Helfter, who wrote this essay for the first assignment in her Freshman Composition course, values her writing process as it helps her to capture, understand, and express her ideas and feelings. While your feelings about the writing process may be different from Susan Helfter's, thinking about her essay may help you to begin to clarify your own motivations and reasons for writing.

JOURNAL

Discuss what you feel is mysterious or even frightening about the writing process. How does writing help you to get in touch with your unconscious mind?

Hesitantly she drew back the curtains, peering into the dust-shrouded room. Trying very hard not to break the stillness, she carefully stepped over the sill and into the room. With a slow sigh she let out her breath, feeling like an intruder upon the house's solemn stillness. But she couldn't be helped. The magic of the place called to her, begged her to discover its secrets. Once this place contained life in abundance. Now even though the people were gone, bits of their past remained scattered throughout the house, ready to tell their story to anyone who had the courage to listen.

1   When I write, I feel like the little girl in this story who has uncertainly ventured into an unknown, forbidden realm. There is something about writing that calls me, just as the mysterious old dwelling called to the girl. Taking the first step into a writing project requires the same kind of courage from me that the girl needed to climb over the window sill and into the house. Once I have taken the initial plunge and committed myself to a project, I still feel a little scared, often not knowing where the words will lead me. This parallels the way the little girl feels when she finally stands in the midst of the dust-filled furniture and memories. There is so much to explore through writing that it is intriguing, overwhelming, and terrifying all at once.

2   Taking the first step past the overwhelming feelings is definitely the hardest part. But after I find the first few words, writing stimulates a spontaneity in me which conversation lacks. In conversation each person gets a chance to voice part of an opinion, but must then allow the other person or persons to speak. Listening carefully to others is an essential and beneficial part of learning, but it sometimes restrains the listener from blurting sudden inspirations on the spur of the moment. When I'm writing, I can shift gears whenever I want. This can be seen in the poetry I doodle in private. One poem I wrote started out with a doodle-dee-dum phrase, progressed into a rap beat, and ended up being a story about God creating people as toys. These loosely connected leaps of imagination would have been impossible to contemplate during casual conversation. That's the beauty of writing. It allows me to ask questions, to answer them, and to create bridges to related topics.

3   Although writing facilitates random brainstorming, it also shapes dreamy ideas into the more solid and lasting substance of words. Reflective writing forces me to create concrete images that I might otherwise avoid. It's relaxing to let my mind drift in self-reflective thought, but much more constructive to examine my feelings and motives on paper. The classic example of reflective writing would have to be the diary. Diaries are like a collection of letters to a friend that you never have to worry about mailing. No guilt is involved in being late to the post office or missing a week of writing. If I feel like recording my thoughts in my diary, I do so; if I don't, no one is being let down. While not demanding in any sense, reflective writing helps me to capture my questions and intentions on paper.

4   But writing is much more than just recording words and thoughts on paper. Writing becomes a channel which brings my deepest emotions to the surface. The old saying, "Give them a piece of your mind," is often difficult to carry out face to face, but occurs naturally through writing. Whenever I feel angry at the world or at myself, I examine and absolve my frustrations by writing myself a ten-page letter. I also express my deepest loves and joys in poetry or letters. In this way, writing creates a physical representation of my inner self. That is what writing is all about for me: finding the real feeling inside me and the best way to express it.

5   As I continue to write, I hope to discover new composition styles that will help me to more clearly convey my emotions and thoughts. I want to blend the curiosity and emotion of the child within me with the maturity that my adult experiences bring. In this way, my writing will grow as I grow, but never lose the charm

of imagination which makes it uniquely me. Perhaps a part of me will always be like the little girl peering into a secret and forbidden realm, a dust-filled, memory laden room; fortunately, a stronger part of me has the courage to face the secrets, believing in the power that words have to express the real me.

Questions for Discussion

1. Susan Helfter compares her writing process to a little girl "peering into a secret and forbidden realm, a dust-filled, memory laden room." How does this comparison help you to better understand her writing process, with its special challenges and rewards?
2. Contrast Helfter's writing process and her attitude toward writing to your own process and attitudes.
3. Which of the images that Helfter develops do you think is most effective? Why? Do you often use images to help express your ideas?
4. Like Helfter, create and explain an image that conveys what the writing process means to you.

 ## Joyce Chang

Drive Becarefully

Joyce Chang (b. 1975) was raised in northern California. Living in a predominantly white neighborhood and growing up in a traditional, close-knit Asian family, Chang struggled to integrate her Chinese heritage with mainstream American culture. In the essay that follows, she explores the problem of coming to terms with her mother's broken English, in light of reading Amy Tan's essay, "Mother Tongue."

JOURNAL

Write about what you have learned about language and/or communication from your parents.

1 " . . . my mother's 'limited' English limited my perception of her. I was ashamed of her English." Amy Tan's self-evaluation in her essay, "Mother Tongue," clung to my conscience as I continued reading. I could have said those words myself. I have definitely thought those words a million times. Like Tan, I too used to be ashamed of my mother's English. I used to shudder whenever I heard an incorrect verb tense, misplaced adverb, or incorrect pronoun come from her lips. Like many people, I couldn't look beyond my mother's incorrect grammar to see the intent and beauty behind her words.

2   My mother immigrated to the United States in the 1970s, speaking only a few words of English. As time went on, she gradually learned more and more words, although her sentence structure remained very basic. As a young working woman and mother of two, my mother didn't have much of a chance to improve her grammar. Taking ESL courses was not one of her immediate concerns—trying to beat rush hour Chicago traffic to get home in time to make dinner was what she worried about. So my mother went on using phrases like "He go to the store."

3   Since I had the advantage of being born and raised in the United States, my English abilities quickly surpassed those of my mother by the time I was in grade school. I knew all about auxiliary verbs, the subjunctive, and plurals—my mother didn't. I could form sentences like "He treated her as if she were still a child." For my mother to convey that same idea, she could only say "He treat her like child."

4   My mother's comprehension of the English language was comparable to her speaking abilities. When I was with her, I learned early on not to try any of the complicated, flowery, descriptive sentences that I had been praised for in school. Anything beyond a simple subject-verb-object construction was poorly received. When I was very young I did not think much about having to use a different English with my mother. The two Englishes in my life were just different—one was not better than the other. However, that feeling quickly changed in third grade.

5   My young mind could not always switch between the two Englishes with ease. I usually knew which English belonged in which world, but sometimes my Englishes crossed over. I remember one day in third grade when I was supposed to bring something for a "cultural show-and-tell." It must have been sometime in winter— around Chinese New Year. My mother had given me a "red bag" for show-and-tell. A "red bag" is an envelope that contains money. Chinese people give and receive these envelopes of money as gifts for the new year. As my mother described it to me, "The bag for good fortune . . . you rich for New Year." When I tried to explain the meaning of the red envelope to my class, I used my mother's words, "The bag for good fortune. . . . " I do not think my classmates noticed my grammatical shortcomings, or maybe they did notice but chose not to comment. In any case, my teacher had an alarmed look on her face and sharply demanded, "What did you say?" She seemed to be in complete bewilderment at how one of her students who spoke "good English" could suddenly speak "bad English." Thinking that she just didn't hear me the first time, I innocently repeated the exact same phrase I had said before.

6   "Where did you learn *that* English?" she questioned. "It's wrong! Please speak correctly!" she commanded.

7   After her admonishment it took me a while to continue speaking. When I finally opened my mouth to utter my first word, all I could think of was "I hope this is correct." I was relieved when I finished with no further interruptions.

8   Hearing my teacher say that my mother's English was wrong had a lasting impression on me. When I went home that day, all I could think about when my mother spoke was the "wrongness" of her English, and the "wrongness" of her as a person. I took her awkward phrases, sentence fragments, and other incorrect phrases as a sign that she somehow was "incorrect." I became irritated with her

when she made grammatical mistakes at home. I became ashamed of her when she made those same mistakes outside of the house.

9   By the time I entered high school I was tired of being ashamed of my mother's English. I thought I would do her a favor and take on a mission to improve her English. The mission turned out to be a lot more difficult than I thought it would be. No matter how many times I would tell her something that she said was wrong, she would still say the same phrase over and over again. For example, whenever I left the house, my mother would say, "Drive becarefully." After the first time she said that, I told her it was wrong. I would then add, "The correct way to say that is 'drive carefully' or 'be careful driving.'" She would then nod and say good-bye. However, the next day as I headed out the door, mother would come up to me and say "drive becarefully" again. I would get incredibly frustrated because she never seemed to learn. I was glad, however, that at least I was the only one to hear such an "incorrect" statement.

10   One day, however, a friend of mine was with me as we headed out the door. As usual my mother screamed out "drive becarefully" as we walked toward the car. I immediately rolled my eyes and muttered, "It's 'drive carefully.' Get it right."

11   Later, as I drove my friend back home, she asked me a question that I will never forget. "Is it your mom who wants to improve her English or is it you who wants to 'improve' her?" I was stunned at first by my friend's question. I had no response. After a lot of thinking, I realized my friend was right. My mom was satisfied with her English. She could convey her thoughts and didn't care that she did it in a way that was different from the standard. She had no problem with her use of language—I did.

12   After that conversation, I began to accept the idea that there are many different Englishes and one is not necessarily better than the other. As long as a person is understood, it is not necessary to speak textbook perfect English. Presently, I am very concerned with how people treat others who speak "limited" English. I understand how easy it is to misperceive and mistreat people. In her essay "Mother Tongue," Tan also writes about how people are perceived differently just because of their "limited" English. She describes the problems her mother encounters day to day, "people in department stores, at banks, and at restaurants did not take her seriously, did not give her good service, pretended not to understand her, or even acted as if they did not hear her." Although I am very angry when I read about how a person with "limited" English is mistreated, I still understand how it is all too easy for a person not to take someone seriously when he/she does not speak the same English as that person. It is also easy to assume a person who speaks "broken" English wants someone to help him "fix" it.

13   Now, when I find myself talking with people who speak "another" English, I try to look for the meaning and the intent of what they say, and ignore the perhaps awkward structure of their statements. Also when I encounter someone who speaks an English different from my own, I try not to assume that he or she wants to "improve" it.

14   As Tan concludes her essay, the importance of what is spoken lies in a person's ". . . intent, . . . passion, . . . imagery, . . . and nature of . . . thoughts." These are

the things I now look for when someone speaks to me. Incorrect verb tenses, misplaced adverbs, and incorrect pronouns are less significant issues. As I begin to realize this more, I feel more comfortable with not only my mom's different English but my own. My mom's English is the one I grew up with at home. It is one of the Englishes I speak.

15   The other day I went home to help my mom run errands.

16   "Go to store," she said.

17   "Buy what?" I asked.

18   "Juice and eggs. Drive becarefully!" my mom warned.

19   I couldn't help but to smile. I like hearing that now.

Questions for Discussion

1. When does Chang begin to think about her mother's English? Why is the example that Chang develops to illustrate how her attitude was changed especially effective?

2. Could you identify with any aspects of Chang's feelings and attitudes about her mother's English or with her struggle to accept her mother for who she is rather than "fix her"?

3. Do you agree or disagree with Chang's teacher's attitude and her definition of correct English? Explain your point of view.

4. Do you agree or disagree with Chang's conclusion, "As long as a person is understood, it is not necessary to speak textbook perfect English."

Chapter Writing Topics

1. Drawing on your own experiences and on evidence from selections in this chapter, discuss the importance and role of dreams and the unconscious mind in the writing process.

2. The authors in this chapter discuss ways in which they have been influenced to become writers. Write an essay in which you explore the ways experiences, people, and personal goals have helped you to develop your writing.

3. Tim O'Brien, William Stafford, Stephen King, and other writers included in *Dreams and Inward Journeys* experience and value writing as a process of self-discovery and healing. Write an essay in which you explore this perspective on writing.

4. Develop an essay based on one or two metaphors or comparisons that illustrate the uniqueness of your writing process. Refer to specific writing projects or rituals whenever possible to make your essay concrete and persuasive. Or, draw a picture that expresses your writing process and then write an explanation of your picture.

5. Did the writing in this chapter give you new insights into the creative potential of the human imagination, the nature of creativity, and the

creative process? Explain your new insights and how particular selections helped you to understand and formulate these insights.

6. A number of writers and scientists have attributed creative functions of the mind to the right side and logical functions to the left side of the brain. Write an essay or a dialogue that explores how you understand and work with the conflicts between the creative and the problem-solving aspects of your mind. Or, write a dialogue between your right and left brain to explore and analyze an important decision that you are having difficulty making.

7. See one of the following films, either by yourself or with several of your classmates. Write an individual or collaborative review that discusses the ways in which the film explores the inner world of the writer: Suggestions for films include:

The Postman, Dreamchild, Naked Lunch, Anne Frank Remembered, Misery, The Color Purple

2

Discovering Ourselves in Reading

A dream which is not understood is like a letter which is not opened.

> The Talmud

Looking back, it's clear to me that I was reading as a creator, bringing myself . . . to a collaboration with the writer in the invention of an alternate world. These books were not collections of abstract symbols called words, printed on paper; they were real events that had happened to me.

> PETE HAMILL
> *D'Artagnan on Ninth Street: A Brooklyn Boy at the Library*

The imagination, which may appear to bear such individual fruit, is rooted in a compost of forgotten books.

> ELIZABETH BOWEN
> *Out of a Book*

Responding to Reading Through Writing

When people read, they are concerned with self-discovery just as they are when they write and when they explore their dreams. Reading is a complex process that a reader controls consciously and also experiences unconsciously. In the act of reading, as in a conversation, a dialogue takes place between the voice of the inner self and the voice of the text that is being read. A good conversation with a text can lead to the development and clarification of the reader's values and ideas. At the same time, reading requires a more formal understanding of literary conventions and language codes.

Once absorbed in this complex mental process, a reader often identifies with the characters, the ideas, the emotions, and the cultural and social assumptions of the text. Readers then are able to experience new and different realities vicariously; these encounters can contribute to the reader's personal growth as they present new intellectual and emotional experiences that help readers to build their inner resources. As a person becomes a better reader and develops a richer life through reading, his or her writing may also become more fluent and varied, by way of the reader's becoming more conscious of public values, opinions, and cultures that are different from his or her personal experiences.

One of the most valuable ways to respond to what you read is through responsive writing of journals, essays, stories, and poems. Writing about what you read will help you to articulate and clarify your responses and will improve your own writing as you develop your own writer's voice through connecting to the words and thoughts of others. As with any form of writing, responses to reading can move through a series of phases or stages, each one building upon the next, moving gradually from prereading strategies to interpretation and evaluation.

Prereading/Early Reading

In the "prereading" phase you read "around" what you plan to read more carefully, browsing through titles, subheadings, noting epigraphs, topic sentences, headnotes and footnotes, just as you probably did when you first picked up this textbook. Prereading can be a very helpful process if you combine it with writing down basic questions that you have during this initial "browsing" stage. Does this work seem like fact or fiction? Was it written recently or in the distant past? Is its style experimental or traditional? Is the writer American or is he or she from a different culture and country? Is the writer male or female? Is the subject a familiar one? Do you need more background knowledge to understand the subject? Asking and answering such questions can help you to become involved with the text and can help to put you into a receptive frame of mind.

After previewing the work, proceed to the second part of the first stage in reading, the "early reading" phase, in which, as in writing a first draft, you simply "plunge in," reading the work quickly to get an overall sense of its meaning, perhaps noting a few key passages or putting a question mark by an idea or detail that seems unfamiliar or confusing. At this stage of reading avoid negative preconceptions about the content of the reading; don't tell yourself, "This is an essay or story about a subject in which I have absolutely no interest"; try instead to be open to the reading. Avoid evaluating the text before you give yourself a chance to become engaged with it.

Personal and Interpretive Response

In this second stage, the interpretive response phase, put the reading aside for a moment and write down a few immediate, personal reactions: Is this piece what I expected it to be? Did it make me angry? sad? elated? How did the piece challenge me? What didn't I understand after the first reading? Reread your notes and questions before attempting another reading. This second time read more slowly and reflectively. Try to answer some of your initial questions as well as to move toward an overview and interpretation of the piece as a whole: its "meaning," or your view of its meaning at this stage in your reading.

Look for those patterns that support an interpretation or view of the work: metaphors, plot and subplot, character relationships and conflicts, point of view, evolving persona, or narrative voice. Mark your book, placing circles around and drawing lines to connect ideas and images that you believe form a pattern of meaning. Ask yourself how much of the work is meant to be responded to literally, and how much is meant to be considered as ironic or symbolic. Record responses to this stage of the reading process in writing, including some particular quotations and references to the text. Also compare your reactions at this stage of reading with your written responses to the first reading of the text. You will probably find that your ideas have deepened considerably and that you have a more complete and interpretive view of the work than you did initially.

Critical and Evaluative Response

For the third stage in your reading/writing process, the "critical" phase, reread the story again more rapidly, after reviewing your second written response and your textual references. Now write a final response, clarifying how this reading confirms, expands on, or causes you to question or revise your earlier readings. Using particular elements in the text that you noticed in your earlier readings as evidence, try to draw some larger evaluative conclusions about the work and your response to it: Is your overall response to the values, ideas, and emotions in the work positive or negative? How do you feel about the unity of the piece, its quality as writing? How do the values of this selection reflect or illuminate issues of concern to you and to your community? Was there something new and special about the experience of reading this work? Did it remind you of or seem to build upon other, similar works with which you are familiar? After finishing the text, did you want to read more by this writer or learn more about the theme of the work by reading related works by other writers? Would you recommend the work to other readers?

In reading and writing about the essays, stories, and poems selected for this textbook, try to practice the slow, three-stage reading and written response process outlined above, taking time to write down questions and responses in your notebook and in the margins of the text. Give yourself enough time to absorb and think about what you have read.

THEMATIC INTRODUCTION

Reading can be an extremely active, intriguing, and creative process. While reading a text, you may notice omitted scenes and transitions or open-ended questions left unanswered by the author. While answering these questions, you are also writing your own text mentally, side by side with the author. As you become a more sophisticated reader, you may begin to use the questions raised by the texts you read as points of departure for your own interpretations of a work. As you continue to read and to reread a text, you will begin to see it from different perspectives, identifying with different characters and ideas, perceiving different elements as more important or dominant. The varying ways in which you respond to what you are reading reflects your growing process of understanding the text and yourself as a reader.

Each of the selections in this chapter presents a unique perspective on the way people read and interpret texts; each reflects on the ways that reading plays a part in the development of the reader's inner life and imagination. In the first selection, a meditative poem by Wallace Stevens, "The House Was Quiet and the World Was Calm," the speaker focuses on how a reader with a calm mind can come to feel like a part of a book that he or she is reading, suggesting too that meditation is essential to learning from a text. Pete Hamill, in "D'Artagnan on Ninth Street," recounts his imaginative childhood adventures in reading at the Brooklyn library, adventures that stimulated his lifelong quest for knowledge, experience, and the pleasures of language. Richard Wright, in "The Library Card," also shares his passion for reading; he speaks of his inner awakening through the knowledge he uncovers in the books of great social writers of his time. Unlike the other writers in this chapter, Wright found that his struggle to find himself through reading was intensified and shaped by the fact that as a Southern Negro he had to lie even to be able to check books out from the library.

The next two selections focus on the importance of reading in a child's life. In "Reading Blind" Margaret Atwood discusses the lifelong effects of reading aloud to children and of telling stories. Atwood believes that stories live through our voices and endure because they capture our attention. Like many authors Atwood knows that a good reader develops himself or herself through reading, listening, and deciding from within what makes a piece of writing succeed or fail. Like Atwood, Elizabeth Bowen in "Out of a Book" emphasizes that a love of reading is born in childhood when parents and relatives share stories with their children. Bowen emphasizes the ongoing benefits of a love of reading developed in childhood: the deep significance of the inner resources that books provide for children and the role that memories of books can have. Bowen concludes that most creative writers loved to read as children. Following these essays on the effects of reading is Jorge Luis Borges's postmodernist short story, "The Book of Sand." In this story the main character's obsession with the infinite and mysterious, the monstrous "Book of Sand," leads the reader to wonder about the nature of truth and reality as they have been accumulated and told through written words. Borges's narrator leaves us wondering if knowledge in books is like the sand of our imaginations.

The final two poems in the chapter explore the relationships between reading, imagination, interpretation, and creativity. Denise Levertov's poem, "The Secret," reflects on the trusting, intimate, and loving relationship between the reader and the poet, showing how the words in a poem may produce ideas and feelings in the reader that the writer may not have consciously intended. Next is Samuel Taylor Coleridge's classic poem "Kubla Khan: or, a Vision in a Dream," which is a "fragment" that came to him in a dream after he had been reading about the Mongolian Empire of Genghis Khan. Through its vision, the poem comments on the nature of the creative process.

The two student essays that are included in this chapter offer responses to the readings. In "The Book Store" Maria Pitcher explores some of the concepts about the long-lasting effects of reading on an individual's character that Elizabeth Bowen presented in "Out of a Book." Lissy Goralink in "The Sandstorm of Time and Knowledge" argues that Borges's story is about an inner journey to self-knowledge, which "is the most important goal in life, and should drive us to read, to search, to journey, to converse, and to look in the mirror."

We hope that your journey through the readings in this chapter will be an adventure for your mind, your imagination, and your spirit.

 ## Wallace Stevens

The House Was Quiet and the World Was Calm

One of America's foremost poets of ideas, Wallace Stevens (1879–1955) was educated at Harvard University as a lawyer and spent most of his life working as an executive of the Hartford Accident and Indemnity Company. Stevens published his poetry in reviews, and his first book of poems, Harmonium, *came out in 1923. He received national acclaim when he was awarded the Pulitzer Prize for his* Collected Poems *in 1954. Much of Stevens's poetry present his attempt to impose order on the world through the structured visions provided by art and po-*

etry. As you read Stevens's poem, try to create in yourself the kind of calm, yet at-
tentive mental state that the poem evokes.

Describe the particular place or type of place where you feel the most comfortable reading.

The house was quiet and the world was calm.
The reader became the book; and summer night

Was like the conscious being of the book.
The house was quiet and the world was calm.

5 The words were spoken as if there was no book,
Except that the reader leaned above the page,

Wanted to lean, wanted much most to be
The scholar to whom his book is true, to whom

The summer night is like a perfection of thought.
10 The house was quiet because it had to be.

The quiet was part of the meaning, part of the mind:
The access of perfection to the page.

And the world was calm. The truth in a calm world,
In which there is no other meaning, itself

15 Is calm, itself is summer and night, itself
Is the reader leaning late and reading there.

Questions for Discussion

1. How are the "quiet" and the "calm" a part of the meaning of the book
   being read in the poem? For example, if it had been "noisy," would the
   book have had a different meaning or would it have been read differently?
2. What is Stevens saying in the poem about the relationship between
   reading and truth? Does Stevens seem to believe there is any absolute

truth to be derived from reading, or does he believe that truth through the poem is subjective, changeable?

3. Why is the summer night portrayed in the poem "like perfection of thought"? Have you ever thought a quiet summer night in this way?

4. In line 5 the speaker of the poem says: "The words were spoken as if there was no book." Have you ever had the feeling that the words you read are "coming off the page," that they have begun to take on a life of their own?

5. Poems often contain ambiguities, that is, words, phrases, and lines that can be read in more than one way and which invite the reader to interpret them personally and imaginatively. Give examples of words, phrases, and lines in the poem that you consider ambiguous. Indicate some of the possible meanings you find in them, and discuss how the poem's ambiguity contributes to the comment it is making about the act of reading.

Ideas for Writing

1. Have you ever read a book in the way that Stevens describes in his poem? Write a short paper in which you describe your experience of reading a particular text.

2. Argue for a very different view of the reading experience than Stevens does. Is reading ever an active, noisy, jarring, imperfect, and tentative process?

 ## Pete Hamill

D'Artagnan on Ninth Street: A Brooklyn Boy at the Library

Born in Brooklyn, New York, Pete Hamill has had a varied writing career as the author of essays, novels, scripts for film and television, and short stories. He is best known as a reporter, particularly for his realistic, observant pieces on life in New York City, which have appeared in major newspapers and in such periodicals as Playboy *and* Life. *Hamill has written many novels, most recently* Women: A Novel of the Fifties. *His short stories have been collected in* Invisible City *(1980), and his essays and columns can be found in many collections including Irrational Ravings (1971) and* Piecework *(1996). The following essay, a recollection of childhood days spent at the Brooklyn Public Library in Prospect Park, is an example of Hamill's personal and imaginative style of journalism.*

Describe a significant experience in your childhood or adolescence that in-volved books and reading.

1   The library was on Sixth Avenue and Ninth Street on the south slopes of the Brooklyn hills and for a long time in my young life it was the true center of the world.

2   The formal name, back then, was the Prospect Branch of the Brooklyn Public Library, but to me it was always just The Library and it remains that way in mem-ory. I seem always to have gone there on Saturday mornings, following the same route each time, hurrying past the grocery stores, bakeries, drugstores and bars of Seventh Avenue. At the corner of Ninth Street, I turned left and the broad street dropped away into the distant jumble of the waterfront. On clear mornings, I could see past the elevated tracks of the IND subway and glimpse the Statue of Liberty in the harbor and the vertical smudge of the skyline of Manhattan. But usually I ignored the view. I was locked into a sensuous, almost religious ritual, with the holy sanctuary of the library drawing me like an iron filing to a magnet.

3   I can feel now the way my blood quickened as I crossed the trolley tracks, passed the stately brownstones and the small synagogue and saw ahead the wild gloomy garden behind the library. As a gesture of support, I would run a finger along the menacing iron pickets of the garden's fence. I wanted that fence to stand forever, holding back the jungle; each spring, the riot of weeds and nameless plants seemed to grow more menacing. I sometimes imagined it spilling into the streets, marching steadily forward to link with Prospect Park. Or it would turn to the nearest target: the library itself. The vengeful blind force of untamed nature would climb those granite walls, seep under the windows and assault the books, those sheaves of murdered trees, sucking them back to the dark earth.

4   But then I would glance through the immense windows, relieved: the books were still there. Turning at Sixth Avenue, I would look up, feel momentarily dwarfed by the majesty of the mock Corinthian columns that framed the en-trance. Then I would take the wide granite steps two at a time. Into my second home. I was 10 the first time I took that journey alone; I kept taking it until I was 17 and went off to the Navy.

5   Inside, behind walls as thick as any true fortress, I always felt safe. The high-roofed building was warm in winter and cool in summer, and although it seemed built to last forever, and the sense of space was unlike anything I knew except the lobbies of movie houses, the attraction was not merely shelter. I was there on a more exciting mission: the discovery of the world.

6   In those years during and after the war, I was a citizen of a hamlet we all simply called "the neighborhood" (now cynically renamed the South Slope by real estate developers). There were strict rules (Pay Your Debts, Don't Cross Picket Lines, Don't Squeal to the Cops, Honor the Old) and powerful institutions (the church, the police station and Rattigan's Bar and Grill). There was wisdom in the hamlet,

of course, and honor, and the safety of the familiar. But within the boundaries of this working-class parish there were also men who gave it a dangerous edge: sallow-faced characters with gray fedoras and pinkie rings who carried guns under their coats; youth gangs called the Tigers and the South Brooklyn Boys, who wore pegged pants and rolled through the streets with the swagger of victorious armies. There were homeless rummies too, and deranged vets still fighting Tarawa or the Hürtgen Forest, and cops on the take and brawling dock wallopers and apprentice wise guys. As a boy, I was afraid of them, a condition that went beyond the normal fears of childhood. But I knew one big thing: none of them ever came to the library.

7   So, in one important way, the library was a fortified oasis. At the same time, it alarmed me. The books seemed to look down upon me with a wintry disdain. Most certainly they were adult, and I stood before them as an ignorant child. They knew what I did not know; they were, in some ways, the epitome of the unknowable, full of mystery and challenge and the most scary thing of all, *doubt*. The harder I worked at cracking their codes, the more certain I was that the task was impossible. I will carry that awe before the printed word to my grave.

8   At first, in my tentative probes of the Caliph's palace, I was condemned to the children's room. I liked the bound volumes of a magazine called St. Nicholas, full of intricate pen drawings and the cheery innocence of the 19th century. I read through most of Robert Louis Stevenson (enthralled by "Treasure Island" and "Kidnapped," disturbed by "Dr. Jekyll and Mr. Hyde," defeated by "The Weir of Hermiston"); Dumas *père* thrilled me with "The Count of Monte Cristo" and "The Three Musketeers"; I consumed "Howard Pyle's Book of Pirates." But the rest of the books meant nothing to me; they all seemed to be about kids living in idyllic country glades, rabbits who talked and an elephant named Babar who had adventures in Africa. Outside the library, I was already traveling through the Africa of Burne Hogarth's comic-strip version of "Tarzan" and plunging into the South American forests of Bomba the Jungle Boy. When I read "The Count of Monte Cristo," I began to think of the children's room as another version of the Château d'If.

9   But even in that brightly lit cell, a peculiar process had begun. On the street, I consumed the artifacts of what is now called popular culture: comics, movie serials at the Minerva and the Globe, boys' books that were not in the library (Bomba, the Buddy series, Tom Swift, even G. A. Henty) and radio serials about Captain Midnight, the Green Hornet, Captain Silver and the Sea Hound. Out there, I was swept away by the primary colors of melodrama.

10 The library took that instinct for the lurid and refined it. The books that were talked about in schoolyards and on rooftops gave me a need for narrative, for removal from the dailiness of my life. But they stood in relation to the books in the library as the raw does to the cooked.

11 At first, I didn't know one writer from another. It didn't even occur to me that books were actually written by a lone man or woman sitting somewhere at a desk. They were there on the shelf and you took them down and opened them and be-

gan to read. To this day, I don't remember learning to read any more than I remember learning how to breathe. And in those years, I read books with a joyous innocence I've only rarely felt in all the years that followed. I had not begun to read, as I do now, as a writer; that is to say (in Stevenson's phrase), I was not reading as a predator.

12   Looking back, it's clear to me that I was reading as a creator, bringing myself (and comics, radio, movies, the street) to a collaboration with the writer in the invention of an alternate world. These books were not collections of abstract symbols called words, printed on paper; they were real events that had happened to *me*. So I was Jim Hawkins. I was Edmond Dantès. I was D'Artagnan. I hid from Blind Pew. I discovered the hidden grotto. I fought duels with the henchmen of the evil Milady. But alas, I also discovered early that telling these tales to my friends could sometimes provoke boredom or scorn; the stories then became part of my buried private history, another solitary vice.

13   When I escaped at last from the children's room, I felt like an explorer who had been handed a map written in invisible ink. As in life, one thing always led to another. At 14, I was trying to understand Latin at Regis High School. In the stacks at the library, this led me to Stevenson's "Virginibus Puerisque," which I still read for pleasure and reward; to Cyril Connolly's "Unquiet Grave" (the byline read "by Palinurus"), and though I surely understood virtually nothing it said, and skipped all the passages in French, I was consumed for a week by its mood of romantic loss. I pored over a translation of Cicero's accounts of murder trials. I took home a book called "Daily Life of the Romans" and copied most of the line drawings of free men and slaves. None of this helped me much with Latin, but the journey did take me to the meditations of Marcus Aurelius, and that splendid book was to help me through the brief anguish of losing all faith in religion.

14   Other books provoked similar journeys. The Bomba books led me to the geography section of the library, to volumes about South America, to a biography of Simón Bolívar and the fevered discovery of the existence of the great Chilean Bernardo O'Higgins, as Irish as I was, the liberator of his country. In that time, I often rode through the Andes of my imagination, a member of a revolutionary army, about to charge hard upon the hated viceroys in the capital; or I was an old man, seeing the revolution betrayed, saying (with Bolívar): "I have ploughed the seas." These were wars, conflicts, tragedies in the real world, but they were not taught in our schoolbooks, and so they became (I arrogantly thought) my own private discovery. If you lived in Brooklyn in those years, you said words like Caracas and Lima, Cartegena and Bogotá, the Amazon and the Orinoco, as if they were digits on a secular rosary. Years later, I would travel this private tributary to school in Mexico City, to Diego Rivera, David Alfaro Siqueiros and José Clemente Orozco, to Carlos Fuentes and Octavio Paz, Luis Buñuel and José Luis Cuevas, Jorge Luis Borges and Julio Cortázar, the granite of Neruda and the magical groves of Macondo.

15   The library taught me one other thing that has survived and expanded through the course of my life: the love of books themselves as *objects*. I came to love the feeling of a well-made book, the look of type on fine paper, the leathery

worked splendor of certain bindings. I even loved the aroma of certain books, the smell of drying paper, the moldy fragrance of the past. This also has a context. I grew up as the oldest son of seven children of Irish immigrants; we were, I suppose, poor; there were always books in the house but none of them were very fancy. The library allowed me to borrow the first beautiful things I ever took home. When I was not reading them, I would place them on tables, on the mantelpiece, against a window, just to be able to see them, to turn from dinner and glance at them in the next room. I hated to bring them back, and often borrowed some books three or four times a year, just to have them around. There are 10,000 books in my library, and it will keep growing until I die. This has exasperated my daughters, amused my friends and baffled my accountant. If I had not picked up this habit in the library long ago, I would have more money in the bank today; I would be richer.

16   In short, the library was a place where most of the things I came to value as an adult had their beginnings. Art was there, poetry, history and words. Millions of words. Trillions. Politicians have come and gone since many of them were written, empires have risen to temporal glory and collapsed into decay. But those words remain as powerful as they were when I was a boy and will be there long after I'm gone. I went to the library in a different time, of course, during the last years before the arrival of the great obliterating force of television. I went to the library in search of entertainment and discovered the world.

17   Today, kids don't seem to embark on that exhilarating journey as often as they did when I was young. Politicians keep chiseling away at the branch libraries, truncating their hours, reducing their staffs. The dumb forces of darkness still riot in the garden. But there, through the windows, you can still see the shelves. The books stand in eternal wintry challenge, full of wonder, fear, certainty and doubt, just waiting to be opened. Hey, young man, hurrying by, a Walkman plugged into your skull: pause a moment, mount those steps and enter. The world awaits you.

Questions for Discussion

1. Why does Hamill refer to his experiences and feelings about the library as comparable to a "sensuous, almost religious ritual"? What aspects of sensuousness and ritual behavior are explored in the essay? Do you have similar associations with spending time at the library? Why or why not?

2. Hamill describes a childhood fantasy of the fence of the library as "holding back the jungle" of untamed, natural vegetation that somehow menaces the world of the books inside, and compares the library itself to a "fortress." What does this fantasy suggest about the place of books and reading in the culture and imagination of a child?

3. Hamill feels that his true mission in the library was "the discovery of the world." What examples does he provide in his essay of discoveries

that came to him at the library? How does he contrast those discoveries with the world of his neighborhood in Brooklyn?

4. How does Hamill relate the "lurid" materials he consumed from popular culture to the books he reads at the library? How does his reference to "the raw [and] the cooked" help to explain the relationship?

5. In what sense was Hamill "reading as a creator" during his childhood days at the library? Do you think this is a common response to the world of reading? Have you ever had a similar experience as a reader?

6. Hamill gives examples of imaginative, vicarious, and inward journeys inspired by his childhood reading. How did those journeys help him to obtain a wider, more complete view of the world than what he was taught in the classroom?

Ideas for Writing

1. Write an essay about an experience you recall from your childhood in which you felt that new imaginative vistas were opened to you through the world of reading.

2. Hamill concludes his essay by lamenting that young people today do not spend as much time at the library as when he was a child; instead, they acquire knowledge of the world through television and recorded music. Do you agree with Hamill that young people who are mass media consumers but not avid readers lose out on an important dimension of life? Write an essay in which you take a position on this issue, providing support and examples from your own experiences and observations.

  Richard Wright

The Library Card

Richard Wright (1908–1960) grew up in an impoverished area of rural Mississippi. He moved to Chicago, then to New York, and eventually left the United States to live and write in France. Wright, who is best known for his novel Native Son *(1940), was considered the leading black author in the United States after its publication. He influenced James Baldwin and other black writers coming of age in the 1950s. His autobiography,* Black Boy *(1945), tells the story of his childhood in the segregated South of the 1920s and 1930s. In "The Library Card," a selection from his autobiography, Wright recounts his struggles to educate himself through reading books from the public library, to which he was denied access because of the color of*

*his skin. As you read about how Wright's life was changed by books, think about
which of your reading experiences have significantly influenced your life.*

JOURNAL

Write about a book that influenced your life.

1   One morning I arrived early at work and went into the bank lobby where the
Negro porter was mopping. I stood at a counter and picked up the Memphis
Commercial Appeal and began my free reading of the press. I came finally to the editorial page and saw an article dealing with one H. L. Mencken. I knew by hearsay
that he was the editor of the *American Mercury*, but aside from that I knew nothing about him. The article was a furious denunciation of Mencken, concluding
with one, hot, short sentence: Mencken is a fool.

2   I wondered what on earth this Mencken had done to call down upon him the
scorn of the South. The only people I had ever heard denounced in the South
were Negroes, and this man was not a Negro. Then what ideas did Mencken hold
that made a newspaper like the *Commercial Appeal* castigate him publicly? Undoubtedly he must be advocating ideas that the South did not like. Were there,
then, people other than Negroes who criticized the South? I knew that during the
Civil War the South had hated northern whites, but I had not encountered such
hate during my life. Knowing no more of Mencken than I did at that moment, I
felt a vague sympathy for him. Had not the South, which had assigned me the role
of a non-man, cast at him its hardest words?

3   Now, how could I find out about this Mencken? There was a huge library near
the riverfront, but I knew that Negroes were not allowed to patronize its shelves
any more than they were the parks and playgrounds of the city. I had gone into
the library several times to get books for the white men on the job. Which of
them would now help me to get books? And how could I read them without causing concern to the white men with whom I worked? I had so far been successful in
hiding my thoughts and feelings from them, but I knew that I would create hostility if I went about the business of reading in a clumsy way.

4   That afternoon I addressed myself to forging a note. Now, what were the names
of books written by H. L. Mencken? I did not know any of them. I finally wrote
what I thought would be a foolproof note: *Dear Madam: Will you please let this nigger boy*—I used the word "nigger" to make the librarian feel that I could not possibly be the author of the note—*have some books by H. L. Mencken?* I forged the
white man's name.

5   I entered the library as I had always done when on errands for whites, but I felt
that I would somehow slip up and betray myself. I doffed my hat, stood a respectful
distance from the desk, looked as unbookish as possible, and waited for the white

patrons to be taken care of. When the desk was clear of people, I still waited. The white librarian looked at me.

6   "What do you want, boy?"

7   As though I did not possess the power of speech, I stepped forward and simply handed her the forged note, not parting my lips.

8   "What books by Mencken does he want?" she asked.

9   "I don't know, ma'am," I said, avoiding her eyes.

10   "Who gave you this card?"

11   "Mr. Falk," I said.

12   "Where is he?"

13   "He's at work, at the M—Optical Company," I said. "I've been in here for him before."

14   "I remember," the woman said. "But he never wrote notes like this."

15   Oh, God, she's suspicious. Perhaps she would not let me have the books? If she had turned her back at that moment, I would have ducked out the door and never gone back. Then I thought of a bold idea.

16   "You can call him up, ma'am," I said, my heart pounding.

17   "You're not using these books, are you?" she asked pointedly.

18   "Oh, no, ma'am. I can't read."

19   "I don't know what he wants by Mencken," she said under her breath.

20   I knew now that I had won; she was thinking of other things and the race question had gone out of her mind. She went to the shelves. Once or twice she looked over her shoulder at me, as though she was still doubtful. Finally she came forward with two books in her hands.

21   "I'm sending him two books," she said. "But tell Mr. Falk to come in next time, or send me the names of the books he wants. I don't know what he wants to read."

22   I said nothing. She stamped the card and handed me the books. Not daring to glance at them, I went out of the library, fearing that that woman would call me back for further questioning. A block away from the library I opened one of the books and read a title: *A Book of Prefaces*. I was nearing my nineteenth birthday and I did not know how to pronounce the word "preface." I thumbed the pages and saw strange words and strange names. I shook my head, disappointed, looked at the other book; it was called *Prejudices*. I knew what that word meant; I had heard it all my life. And right off I was on guard against Mencken's books. Why would a man want to call a book *Prejudices?* The word was so stained with all my memories of racial hate that I could not conceive of anybody using it for a title. Perhaps I had made a mistake about Mencken? A man who had prejudices must be wrong.

23   When I showed the books to Mr. Falk, he looked at me and frowned.

24   "That librarian might telephone you," I warned him.

25   "That's all right," he said. "But when you're through reading those books, I want you to tell me what you get out of them."

26   That night in my rented room, while letting the hot water run over my can of pork and beans in the sink, I opened *A Book of Prefaces* and began to read. I was

jarred and shocked by the style, the clear, clean, sweeping sentences. Why did he write like that? And how did one write like that? I pictured the man as a raging demon, slashing with his pen, consumed with hate, denouncing everything American, extolling everything European or German, laughing at the weaknesses of people, mocking God, authority. What was this? I stood up, trying to realize what reality lay behind the meaning of the words . . . Yes, this man was fighting, fighting with words. He was using words as a weapon, using them as one would use a club. Could words be weapons? Well, yes, for here they were. Then, maybe, perhaps, I could use them as a weapon? No. It frightened me. I read on and what amazed me was not what he said, but how on earth anybody had the courage to say it.

27   Occasionally I glanced up to reassure myself that I was alone in the room. Who were these men about whom Mencken was talking so passionately? Who was Anatole France? Joseph Conrad? Sinclair Lewis, Sherwood Anderson, Dostoevski, George Moore, Gustave Flaubert, Maupassant, Tolstoy, Frank Harris, Mark Twain, Thomas Hardy, Arnold Bennett, Stephen Crane, Zola, Norris, Gorky, Bergson, Ibsen, Balzac, Bernard Shaw, Dumas, Poe, Thomas Mann, O. Henry, Dreiser, H. G. Wells, Gogol, T. S. Eliot, Gide, Baudelaire, Edgar Lee Masters, Stendhal, Turgenev, Huneker, Nietzsche, and scores of others? Were these men real? Did they exist or had they existed? And how did one pronounce their names?

28   I ran across many words whose meanings I did not know, and I either looked them up in a dictionary or, before I had a chance to do that, encountered the word in a context that made its meaning clear. But what strange world was this? I concluded the book with the conviction that I had somehow overlooked something terribly important in life. I had once tried to write, had once reveled in feeling, had let my crude imagination roam, but the impulse to dream had been slowly beaten out of me by experience. Now it surged up again and I hungered for books, new ways of looking and seeing. It was not a matter of believing or disbelieving what I read, but of feeling something new, of being affected by something that made the look of the world different.

29   As dawn broke I ate my pork and beans, feeling dopey, sleepy. I went to work, but the mood of the book would not die; it lingered, coloring everything I saw, heard, did. I now felt that I knew what the white men were feeling. Merely because I had read a book that had spoken of how they lived and thought, I identified myself with that book. I felt vaguely guilty. Would I, filled with bookish notions, act in a manner that would make the whites dislike me?

30   I forged more notes and my trips to the library became frequent. Reading grew into a passion. My first serious novel was Sinclair Lewis's *Main Street*. It made me see my boss, Mr. Gerald, and identify him as an American type. I would smile when I saw him lugging his golf bags into the office. I had always felt a vast distance separating me from the boss, and now I felt closer to him, though still distant. I felt now that I knew him, that I could feel the very limits of his narrow life. And this had happened because I had read a novel about a mythical man called George F. Babbitt.

31   The plots and stories in the novels did not interest me so much as the point of view revealed. I gave myself over to each novel without reserve, without trying to criticize it; it was enough for me to see and feel something different. And for me, everything was something different. Reading was like a drug, a dope. The novels created moods in which I lived for days. But I could not conquer my sense of guilt, my feeling that the white men around me knew that I was changing, that I had begun to regard them differently.

32   Whenever I brought a book to the job, I wrapped it in newspaper—a habit that was to persist for years in other cities and under other circumstances. But some of the white men pried into my packages when I was absent and they questioned me.

33   "Boy, what are you reading those books for?"

34   "Oh, I don't know, sir."

35   "That's deep stuff you're reading, boy."

36   "I'm just killing time, sir."

37   "You'll addle your brains if you don't watch out."

38   I read Dreiser's *Jennie Gerhardt* and *Sister Carrie* and they revived in me a vivid sense of my mother's suffering; I was overwhelmed. I grew silent, wondering about the life around me. It would have been impossible for me to have told anyone what I derived from these novels, for it was nothing less than a sense of life itself. All my life had shaped me for the realism, the naturalism of the modern novel, and I could not read enough of them.

39   Steeped in new moods and ideas, I bought a ream of paper and tried to write; but nothing would come, or what did come was flat beyond telling. I discovered that more than desire and feeling were necessary to write and I dropped the idea. Yet I still wondered how it was possible to know people sufficiently to write about them? Could I ever learn about life and people? To me, with my vast ignorance, my Jim Crow station in life, it seemed a task impossible of achievement. I now knew what being a Negro meant. I could endure the hunger. I had learned to live with hate. But to feel that there were feelings denied me, that the very breath of life itself was beyond my reach, that more than anything else hurt, wounded me. I had a new hunger.

40   In buoying me up, reading also cast me down, made me see what was possible, what I had missed. My tension returned, new, terrible, bitter, surging, almost too great to be contained. I no longer *felt* that the world about me was hostile, killing; I *knew* it. A million times I asked myself what I could do to save myself, and there were no answers. I seemed forever condemned, ringed by walls.

41   I knew of no Negroes who read the books I liked and I wondered if any Negroes ever thought of them. I knew that there were Negro doctors, lawyers, newspapermen, but I never saw any of them. When I read a Negro newspaper I never caught the faintest echo of my preoccupation in its pages. I felt trapped and occasionally, for a few days, I would stop reading. But a vague hunger would come over me for books, books that opened up new avenues of feeling and seeing, and again I would forge another note to the white librarian. Again I would read and wonder as only the naïve and unlettered can read and wonder, feeling that I carried a secret, criminal burden about with me each day.

Questions for Discussion

1. Why does Wright want to learn about Mencken? When Wright finally reads Mencken, how is he affected? What does he learn about words and about courage from reading Mencken? How does reading Mencken change his day-to-day life?

2. How would you feel if, like Wright, you were not allowed to check books out of the public library? How does Wright manage to check out books despite the restrictions?

3. As Wright gets more involved in reading, how is his understanding of himself, of his friends and supervisors, of the world in which he lives, changed? Does he seem to be more accepting or less accepting of his life? Why does Wright find reading satisfying?

4. What effect does Wright's reading have on his desire to write? Why is it difficult for him to write, despite the "new ideas and moods" he is exposed to?

5. What is the nature of the "secret criminal burden" that Wright feels he carries around as a result of his reading? What do you think it would take for Wright to ease his burden?

6. Describe the work of a writer whom you felt was "fighting with words . . . using words as a weapon." How did you feel about his or her style?

Ideas for Writing

1. Discuss a writer whose work has had an important impact on your changing self-concept and values.

2. Have you ever found that gaining new insights from reading has made you feel alienated from the people and community around you? What were you reading? How did you integrate this new awareness into your lifestyle and way of thinking? Write about these experiences.

  Margaret Atwood

Reading Blind

Margaret Atwood was born in Ottawa, Canada, in 1939 and spent her childhood in rural areas of Canada. She received a B.A. from the University of Toronto and an M.A. from Radcliffe. Atwood has written poems, stories, essays, and popular novels such as Surfacing *(1972),* The Handmaid's Tale *(1986),* Cat's Eye *(1989),* The Robber Bride *(1994), and* Alias Grace *(1996), as well as a book of criticism about the literature of her homeland:* Survival: A Thematic Guide to Canadian Literature *(1972). Her short story collections include* Dancing Girls, Bluebeard's Egg, Wilderness Tips, *and* Murder in the Dark. *Atwood is a strong advocate of Canadian independence. As a champion of the rights of women, her writing often focuses on political issues and the inner lives of women. "Reading Blind" was first published as the introduction to* The Best Short Stories of 1989. *As you read it, contrast your early childhood reading experiences to Atwood's opinions.*

How do you judge the quality and value of something that you have read?

1   Whenever I'm asked to talk about what constitutes a "good" story, or what makes one well-written story "better" than another, I begin to feel very uncomfortable. Once you start making lists or devising rules for stories, or for any other kind of writing, some writer will be sure to happen along and casually break every abstract rule you or anyone else has ever thought up, and take your breath away in the process. The word *should* is a dangerous one to use when speaking of writing. It's a kind of challenge to the deviousness and inventiveness and audacity and perversity of the creative spirit. Sooner or later, anyone who has been too free with it will be liable to end up wearing it like a dunce's cap. We don't judge good stories by the application to them of some set of external measurements, as we judge giant pumpkins at the Fall Fair. We judge them by the way they strike us. And that will depend on a great many subjective imponderables, which we lump together under the general heading of taste. . . .

2   I've spoken of "the voice of the story," which has become a sort of catchall phrase; but by it I intend something more specific: a speaking voice, like the singing voice in music, that moves not across space, across the page, but through time. Surely every written story is, in the final analysis, a score for voice. Those little black marks on the page mean nothing without their retranslation into sound. Even when we read silently, we read with the ear, unless we are reading bank statements.

3   Perhaps, by abolishing the Victorian practice of family reading and by removing from our school curricula those old standbys, the set memory piece and the recitation, we've deprived both writers and readers of something essential to stories. We've led them to believe that prose comes in visual blocks, not in rhythms and cadences; that its texture should be flat because a page is flat; that written emotion should not be immediate, like a drumbeat, but more remote, like a painted landscape: something to be contemplated. But understatement can be overdone, plainsong can get too plain. When I asked a group of young writers, earlier this year, how many of them ever read their own work aloud, not one of them said she did.

4   I'm not arguing for the abolition of the eye, merely for the reinstatement of the voice, and for an appreciation of the way it carries the listener along with it at the pace of the story. (Incidentally, reading aloud disallows cheating; when you're reading aloud, you can't skip ahead.)

5   Our first stories come to us through the air. We hear voices.

6   Children in oral societies grow up within a web of stories; but so do all children. We listen before we can read. Some of our listening is more like listening in, to the calamitous or seductive voices of the adult world, on the radio or the television or in our daily lives. Often it's an overhearing of things we aren't supposed to hear, eavesdropping on scandalous gossip or family secrets. From all these scraps of voices, from the whispers and shouts that surround us, even from the ominous silences, the unfilled gaps in meaning, we patch together for ourselves an order of events, a plot or plots; these, then, are the things that happen, these are the people they happen to, this is the forbidden knowledge.

7   We have all been little pitchers with big ears, shooed out of the kitchen when the unspoken is being spoken, and we have probably all been tale-bearers, blurters at the dinner table, unwitting violators of adult rules of censorship. Perhaps this is what writers are: those who never kicked the habit. We remained tale-bearers. We learned to keep our eyes open, but not to keep our mouths shut.

8   If we're lucky, we may also be given stories meant for our ears, stories intended for us. These may be children's Bible stories, tidied up and simplified and with the vicious bits left out. They may be fairy tales, similarly sugared, although if we are very lucky it will be the straight stuff in both instances, with the slaughters, thunderbolts, and red-hot shoes left in. In any case, these tales will have deliberate, molded shapes, unlike the stories we have patched together for ourselves. They will contain mountains, deserts, talking donkeys, dragons; and, unlike the kitchen stories, they will have definite endings. We are likely to accept these stories as being on the same level of reality as the kitchen stories. It's only when we are older that we are taught to regard one kind of story as real and the other kind as mere invention. This is about the same time we're taught to believe that dentists are useful, and writers are not.

9   Traditionally, both the kitchen gossips and the readers-out-loud have been mothers or grandmothers, native languages have been mother tongues, and the kinds of stories that are told to children have been called nursery tales or old wives' tales. It struck me as no great coincidence when I learned recently that, when a great number of prominent writers were asked to write about the family member who had had the greatest influence on their literary careers, almost all of them, male as well as female, had picked their mothers. Perhaps this reflects the extent to which North American children have been deprived of their grandfathers, those other great repositories of story; perhaps it will come to change if men come to share in early child care, and we will have old husbands' tales. But as things are, language, including the language of our earliest-learned stories, is a verbal matrix, not a verbal patrix. . . .

10   Two kinds of stories we first encounter—the shaped tale, the overheard impromptu narrative we piece together—form our idea of what a story is and color the expectations we bring to stories later. Perhaps it's from the collisions between these two kinds of stories—what is often called "real life" (and which writers greedily think of as their "material") and what is sometimes dismissed as "mere literature" or "the kinds of things that happen only in stories"—that original and living writing is generated. A writer with nothing but a formal sense will produce

dead work, but so will one whose only excuse for what is on the page is that it really happened. Anyone who has been trapped in a bus beside a nonstop talker graced with no narrative skill or sense of timing can testify to that. Or, as Raymond Chandler says in "The Simple Art of Murder": "All language begins with speech, and the speech of common men at that, but when it develops to the point of becoming a literary medium it only looks like speech."

11   Expressing yourself is not nearly enough. You must express the story. . . .

12   Perhaps all I want from a good story is what children want when they listen to tales both told and overheard—which turns out to be a good deal.

13   They want their attention held, and so do I. I always read to the end, out of some puritanical, and adult, sense of duty owed; but if I start to fidget and skip pages, and wonder if conscience demands I go back and read the middle, it's a sign that the story has lost me, or I have lost it.

14   They want to feel they are in safe hands, that they can trust the teller. With children this may mean simply that they know the speaker will not betray them by closing the book in the middle, or mixing up the heroes and the villains. With adult readers it's more complicated than that, and involves many dimensions, but there's the same element of keeping faith. Faith must be kept with the language— even if the story is funny, its language must be taken seriously—with the concrete details of locale, mannerism, clothing; with the shape of the story itself. A good story may tease, as long as this activity is foreplay and not used as an end in itself. If there's a promise held out, it must be honored. Whatever is hidden behind the curtain must be revealed at last, and it must be at one and the same time completely unexpected and inevitable. It's in this last respect that the story (as distinct from the novel) comes closest to resembling two of its oral predecessors, the riddle and the joke. Both, or all three, require the same mystifying buildup, the same surprising twist, the same impeccable sense of timing. If we guess the riddle at once, or if we can't guess it because the answer makes no sense—if we see the joke coming, or if the point is lost because the teller gets it muddled—there is failure. Stories can fail in the same way.

15   But anyone who has ever told, or tried to tell, a story to children will know that there is one thing without which none of the rest is any good. Young children have little sense of dutifulness or of delaying anticipation. They are longing to hear a story, but only if you are longing to tell one. They will not put up with your lassitude or boredom: If you want their full attention, you must give them yours. You must hold them with your glittering eye or suffer the pinches and whispering. You need the Ancient Mariner element, the Scheherazade element: a sense of urgency. *This is the story I must tell; this is the story you must hear.*

16   Urgency does not mean frenzy. The story can be a quiet story, a story about dismay or missed chances or a wordless revelation. But it must be urgently told. It must be told with as much intentness as if the teller's life depended on it. And, if you are a writer, so it does, because your life as the writer of each particular story is only as long, and as good, as the story itself. Most of those who hear it or read it will never know you, but they will know the story. Their act of listening is its reincarnation. . . .

17   From listening to the stories of others, we learn to tell our own.

Questions for Discussion

1. Why does Atwood believe that criteria or lists designed to determine what makes a good piece of writing will inevitably make the judge feel like a fool? How does Atwood think that people decide whether a piece of writing is good? Do you agree or disagree with her? Why?
2. What does Atwood mean by "the voice of the story"?
3. Why does Atwood believe that reading aloud is a crucial aspect of a piece of writing? What does she think that our culture has lost by not emphasizing reading aloud to children, to family members, to friends and colleagues? When was the last time that you heard someone read a poem or a story, an essay or lecture? How was your response to the piece's content affected by its oral delivery?
4. How does Atwood think children come to value stories? Why does she think that some people become writers?
5. Does Atwood believe that stories of dragons and talking donkeys are any less real than the stories we heard in our mother's kitchen or the realistic stories we read about in newspapers? Explain her point of view and why you agree or disagree with it.
6. Why does Atwood argue that language is taught by mothers? Do you agree or disagree with her?
7. Why does Atwood believe that the writer must keep the reader's faith? Why does Atwood think of holding the attention of children first when defining what makes for a good story?

Ideas for Writing

1. Atwood concludes, "From listening to the stories of others, we learn to tell our own." Write an essay that explains why you agree or disagree with Atwood. Refer to your own experiences and to the ideas of writers in this text to support your point of view.
2. Develop a two-week plan for your family or friends that will involve you in more "blind reading" of literature such as stories, poems, plays, or lectures. Keep a journal that records and reflects on the impact of these events. Then write an essay that discusses what you have learned about the value of "reading blind."

 # Elizabeth Bowen

Out of a Book

The Irish writer Elizabeth Bowen (1899–1973) was born in Dublin. She worked in a hospital in Ireland during World War I and at the British Ministry of Information during World War II. Bowen's long career as a writer began with the novel The Hotel *in 1927. Her final novel was* Eva Trout *(1968). Her stories have been collected in several volumes; Bowen has also published nonfiction. Labeled as a psychological realist, Bowen acknowledges this aim: "Characters pre-exist. They are found. They reveal themselves slowly to the novelist's perception as might fellow-travelers seated opposite one in a very dimly lit railway carriage." In the selection that follows Bowen shows how a child's love for reading that blossoms early will continue to grow throughout adulthood.*

JOURNAL

Did you enjoy reading as a child? Did you enjoy listening to stories? Write about a memory you have of a favorite book or of a special time you remember listening to a story.

1   I know that I have in my make-up layers of synthetic experience, and that the most powerful of my memories are only half-true.

2   Reduced to the minimum, to the what did happen, my life would be unrecognizable by me. Those layers of fictitious memory densify as they go deeper down. And this surely must be the case with everyone else who reads deeply, ravenously, unthinkingly, sensuously, as a child. The over-lapping and haunting of life by fiction began, of course, before there was anything to be got from the printed page; it began from the day one was old enough to be told a story or shown a picture book. It went on up to the age when a bookish attitude towards books began to be inculcated by education. The young person is then thrown out of Eden; for evermore his brain is to stand posted between his self and the story. Appreciation of literature is the end of magic: in place of the virgin susceptibility to what is written he is given taste, something to be refined and trained.

3   Happily, the Eden, like a natal climate, can be unconsciously remembered, and the magic stored up in those years goes on secreting under today's chosen sensations and calculated thoughts. What entered the system during childhood remains, and remains indistinguishable from the life of those years because it was the greater part of the life. Probably children, if they said what they thought, would be much franker about the insufficiency of so-called real life to the requirements of those who demand to be really alive. Nothing but the story can meet the untried nature's need and capacity for the whole. Of course one cannot narrow down children to the reading child; but I could not as a child, and I cannot now, conceive what the non-reading child must be like inside. Outdoor children were incomprehensible to me when I was their age, and I still find them dull; I could not, and cannot, find out what makes them do what they do, or why they like what they like; and of such children now they are grown up I can only say that I cannot conceive what they remember, if they do remember—for how can even the senses carry imprints when there was no story? The non-reading active children were not stupid; they had their senses. Nor was it the clever children who

read most, or who were at any rate the ones who inhaled fiction—quite apart there were always the horrible little students, future grown-ups, who pursued knowledge. The light-headed reading child and the outdoor child had more in common (in fact, the life of sensation) than either had with the student. Readers of my kind were the heady ones, the sensationalists—recognizing one another at sight we were banded together inside a climate of our own. Landscapes or insides of houses or streets or gardens, outings or even fatigue duties all took the cast of the book we were circulating at the time; and the reading made of us an electric ring. Books were story or story-poetry books: we were unaware that there could be any others.

4   Some of the heady group remained wonderfully proof against education: having never graduated these are the disreputable grown-ups who snap up shiny magazines and garner and carry home from libraries fiction that the critics ignore. They read as we all once read—because they must; without fiction, either life would be insufficient or the winds from the north would blow too cold. They read as we all read when we were twelve; but unfortunately the magic has been adulterated; the dependence has become ignominious—it becomes an enormity, inside the full-sized body, to read without the brain. Now the stories they seek go on being children's stories, only with sex added to the formula; and somehow the addition queers everything. These readers, all the same, are the great malleable bulk, the majority, the greater public—hence bestsellers, with their partly artful, partly unconscious play on a magic that has gone stale. The only above-board grown-up children's stories are detective stories.

5   No, it is not only our fate but our business to lose innocence, and once we have lost that it is futile to attempt a picnic in Eden. One kind of power to read, or power that reading had over us, is gone. And not only that; it is a mistake to as much as re-open the books of childhood—they are bare ruined choirs. Everything has evaporated from those words, leaving them meaningless on the page. This is the case for me, even with Dickens—I cannot read him now because I read him exhaustively as a child. Though I did not in those years read all his books, I cannot now read any that I did not read then—there is no more oxygen left, for me, anywhere in the atmosphere of his writing. The boredom I seem to feel as I pursue the plots is, really, a flagging of my intellect in this (by me) forever used up and devitalized air. I came to an end with Dickens when I had absorbed him into myself.

6   Yes, one stripped bare the books of one's childhood to make oneself—it is inevitable that there should be nothing left when one goes back to them. The fickleness of children and very young persons shocks their elders—children abandon people, for instance, without a flicker, with a simplicity that really ought not to be hurting: the abandoned one has been either a 'best' friend or an object of hero-worship, and the more emotionally fruitful and fanciful the relationship, the more complete the break. 'Where is So-and-so these days? I don't seem to have heard anything about him (or her) for a long time. Haven't you two got any more plans?'—'Oh, I can't be bothered.' What applies to people applies to books, and for the same reason: everything that was wanted has been taken; only the husk or,

still worse, mortifying repetition remains. The child is on the make—rapacious, mobile and single-minded. If the exhausted book survives physical abandonment—being given away or left out in the garden in the rain—it languishes on in its owner's indifferent keeping; however, once memory and sentiment have had time to set in and gather about it, it is safe. I still keep a row of books I loved as a child—but I neither wish nor dare to touch them. What do I mean by those books making myself? In the first place, they were power-testing athletics for my imagination—cross-country runs into strange country, sprints, long and high jumps. It was exhilarating to discover what one could feel: the discovery itself was an advance. Then, by successively 'being' a character in every book I read, I doubled the meaning of everything that happened in my otherwise constricted life. Books introduced me to, and magnified, desire and danger. They represented life, with a conclusiveness I had no reason to challenge, as an affair of mysteries and attractions, in which each object or place or face was in itself a volume of promises and deceptions, and in which nothing was impossible. Books made me see everything that I saw either as a symbol or as having its place in a mythology—in fact, reading gave bias to my observations of everything in the between-times when I was not reading. And obviously, the characters in the books gave prototypes under which, for evermore, to assemble all living people. This did not by any means simplify people for me; it had the reverse effect, and I was glad that it should—the characters who came out of my childish reading to obsess me were the incalculable ones, who always moved in a blur of potentialities. It appeared that nobody who mattered was capable of being explained. Thus was inculcated a feeling for the dark horse. I can trace in all people whom I have loved a succession from book characters—not from one only, from a fusion of many. 'Millions of strange shadows on you tend.'

7   Also the expectation, the search, was geographic. I was and I am still on the look out for places where something happened: the quivering needle swings in turn to a prospect of country, a town unwrapping itself from folds of landscape or seen across water, or a significant house. Such places are haunted—scenes of acute sensation for someone, vicariously me. My identity, so far as I can pin it down at all, resided among these implacable likes or dislikes, these subjections to magnetism spaced out between ever-widening lacunae of indifference. I feel certain that if I could read my way back, analytically, through the books of my childhood, the clues to everything could be found.

8   The child lives in the book; but just as much the book lives in the child. I mean that, admittedly, the process of reading is reciprocal; the book is no more than a formula, to be furnished out with images out of the reader's mind. At any age, the reader must come across: the child reader is the most eager and quick to do so; he not only lends to the story, he flings into the story the whole of his sensuous experience which from being limited is the more intense. Book dishes draw saliva to the mouth; book fears raise gooseflesh and make the palms clammy; book suspense makes the cheeks burn and the heart thump. Still more, at the very touch of a phrase there is a surge of brilliant visual images: the child rushes up the scenery for the story. When the story, as so often happens, demands what has not

yet come into stock, indefatigable makeshifts are arrived at—as when a play that calls for elaborate staging is performed by an enterprising little company with scanty equipment and few drop-scenes. Extension (to draw an iceberg out of a fishmonger's ice-block) or multiplication (to make a thin, known wood into a trackless forest) goes on. For castles, gorges, or anything else spectacular out of art or nature, recollections of picture postcards, posters or travel albums are drawn on; and, of course, the child today has amassed a whole further scenic stock from the cinema. This provision of a convincing where for the story is a reflex.

9   For the child, any real-life scene that has not once been sucked into the ambience of the story is affected, or infected, forever. The road, crossroads, corner of a wood, cliff, flight of steps, town square, quayside or door in a wall keeps a transmuted existence: it has not only given body to fiction, it has partaken of fiction's body. Such a thing, place or scene cannot again be walked past indifferently; it exerts a pull and sets up a tremor; and it is to indent the memory for life. It is at these points, indeed, that what I have called synthetic experience has its sources. Into that experience come relationships, involving valid emotion, between the child reader and book characters; a residuum of the book will be in all other emotions that are to follow.

10   In reverse, there are the real-life places—towns, seaports, suburbs of London— unknown to the child, though heard of, which become 'real' through being also in books. For instance, after *David Copperfield* I could not hear either Dover or Yarmouth mentioned, in the most ordinary context, without excitement: I had a line on them. Towns that were in books, and the routes between them travelled by characters, stood out in relief on the neutral map of England. Not a Londoner, I was continuously filling in and starring my map of the environs—at Richmond lived Sir Percy, the Scarlet Pimpernal, and his wife Marguerite, who fainted into a bed of heliotrope in her riverside garden; at Highgate, the Steerforths and Rosa Dartle; at Blackheath and Lewisham the E. Nesbit children. When I came to read 'Kipps,' I was made dizzy by the discovery that I had, for years, been living in two places, Hythe and Folkestone, that were in a book. Historic places one was taken to see meant no more and no less to me than this; history was fiction—it took me a long time to be able to see that it gained anything further from being 'true.'

11   Though not all reading children grow up to be writers, I take it that most creative writers must in their day have been reading children. All through creative writing there must run a sense of dishonesty and of debt. In fact, is there such a thing, any more, as creative writing? The imagination, which may appear to bear such individual fruit, is rooted in a compost of forgotten books. The apparent choices of art are nothing but addictions, pre-dispositions: where did these come from, how were they formed? The aesthetic is nothing but a return to images that will allow nothing to take their place; the aesthetic is nothing but an attempt to disguise and glorify the enforced return. All susceptibility belongs to the age of magic, the Eden where fact and fiction were the same; the imaginative writer was the imaginative child, who relied for life upon being lied to—and how, now, is he to separate the lies from his consciousness of life? If he be a novelist, all his psychology is merely a new parade of the old mythology. We have relied on our

childhoods, on the sensations of childhood, because we mistake vividness for purity; actually, the story was there first—one is forced to see that it was the story that apparelled everything in celestial light. It could lead to madness to look back and back for the true primary impression or sensation; those we did ever experience we have forgotten—we only remember that to which something was added. Almost no experience, however much simplified by the distance of time, is to be vouched for as being wholly my own—did I live through that, or was I told that it happened, or did I read it? When I write, I am re-creating what was created for me. The gladness of vision, in writing, is my own gladness, but not at my own vision. I may see, for instance, a road running uphill, a skyline, a figure coming slowly over the hill—the approach of the figure is momentous, accompanied by fear or rapture or fear of rapture or a rapture of fear. But who and how is this? Am I sure this is not a figure out of a book?

Questions for Discussion

1. How does Bowen define Eden in her essay? How is Eden contrasted to education and an appreciation of literature? Why does Bowen believe we always have a part of the Eden we had as children? Explain why you agree or disagree with her.
2. According to Bowen what type of child is attracted to reading stories? Were you that type of child?
3. What did Bowen learn from the books she read in her childhood? How did she feel about these books when she wrote this essay as an adult?
4. How has the sense of place and landscape in stories affected Bowen's imagination and values? Why does Bowen believe that the characters she loved in novels or stories helped her to understand how to love the people she became close to in her everyday life?
5. Bowen implies that for her, fiction is truer than history. Explain why you agree or disagree with her point of view.
6. Why does Bowen think that all creative writers must have been readers as children? Explain why you agree or disagree with her.

Ideas for Writing

1. Write an essay that defines memory and imagination based on the ideas presented in Bowen's essay. Discuss, too, how memory and imagination influence the process and meaning of reading. Then develop your definition through reference to your own experiences and other selections in the text.
2. Write an essay or a story in which you explore what reading meant to you as a child. You can refer to Bowen's ideas and examples in this essay and to your own experiences as a reader. For example, you might start by writing about a character from a childhood story who still lives within your imagination, who has perhaps become a part of your "inner child."

Jorge Luis Borges

The Book of Sand

From a wealthy family in Buenos Aires, Jorge Luis Borges (1899–1986) was the son of a philosophy professor and studied at home in his family's extensive library before traveling abroad to study in Switzerland. He was Director of Buenos Aires's National Library for many years and a professor of literature at the University of Buenos Aires. Although Borges began to write as a young man, he was almost unknown as a writer until he won the International Publishers Prize (Prix Formentor) in 1961; subsequently, many of his earlier works were translated and published internationally. His story collections include Ficciones *(1962),* Labyrinths *(1962),* The Aleph and Other Stories *(1970), and* The Book of Sand *(1977). Borges's postmodernist stories are often like philosophical puzzles that capture the reader's mind. His fiction explores issues of history, reality, knowledge, mysticism, and imagination in playful ways that often suggest hidden, occult realities. A man who spent most of his life in libraries, Borges enjoyed inventing imaginary authors, books, and even parallel universes that existed only in his mind and live in the pages of his stories as you will soon discover as you read* The Book of Sand.

JOURNAL

Write about a book that held a mysterious meaning for you.

> *Thy rope of sands . . .*
> —George Herbert

1   The line is made up of an infinite number of points; the plane of an infinite number of lines; the volume of an infinite number of planes; the hypervolume of an infinite number of volumes. . . . No, unquestionably this is not—*more geometrico*—the best way of beginning my story. To claim that it is true is nowadays the convention of every made-up story. Mine, however, *is* true.

2   I live alone in a fourth-floor apartment on Belgrano Street, in Buenos Aires. Late one evening, a few months back, I heard a knock at my door. I opened it and a stranger stood there. He was a tall man, with nondescript features—or perhaps it was my myopia that made them seem that way. Dressed in gray and carrying a gray suitcase in his hand, he had an unassuming look about him. I saw at once that he was a foreigner. At first, he struck me as old; only later did I realize that I had been misled by his thin blond hair, which was, in a Scandinavian sort of way, almost

white. During the course of our conversation, which was not to last an hour, I found out that he came from the Orkneys.

3   I invited him in, pointing to a chair. He paused awhile before speaking. A kind of gloom emanated from him—as it does now from me.

4   "I sell Bibles," he said.

5   Somewhat pedantically, I replied, "In this house are several English Bibles, including the first—John Wiclif's. I also have Cipriano de Valera's, Luther's—which, from a literary viewpoint, is the worst—and a Latin copy of the Vulgate. As you see, it's not exactly Bibles I stand in need of."

6   After a few moments of silence, he said, "I don't only sell Bibles. I can show you a holy book I came across on the outskirts of Bikaner. It may interest you."

7   He opened the suitcase and laid the book on a table. It was an octavo volume, bound in cloth. There was no doubt that it had passed through many hands. Examining it, I was surprised by its unusual weight. On the spine were the words "Holy Writ" and, below them, "Bombay."

8   "Nineteenth century, probably," I remarked.

9   "I don't know," he said. "I've never found out."

10   I opened the book at random. The script was strange to me. The pages, which were worn and typographically poor, were laid out in double columns, as in a Bible. The text was closely printed, and it was ordered in versicles. In the upper corners of the pages were Arabic numbers. I noticed that one left-hand page bore the number (let us say) 40,514 and the facing right-hand page 999. I turned the leaf; it was numbered with eight digits. It also bore a small illustration, like the kind used in dictionaries—an anchor drawn with pen and ink, as if by a schoolboy's clumsy hand.

11   It was at this point that the stranger said, "Look at the illustration closely. You'll never see it again."

12   I noted my place and closed the book. At once, I reopened it. Page by page, in vain, I looked for the illustration of the anchor. "It seems to be a version of Scriptures in some Indian language, is it not?" I said to hide my dismay.

13   "No," he replied. Then, as if confiding a secret, he lowered his voice. "I acquired the book in a town out on the plain in exchange for a handful of rupees and a Bible. Its owner did not know how to read. I suspect that he saw the Book of Books as a talisman. He was of the lowest caste; nobody but other untouchables could tread his shadow without contamination. He told me his book was called the Book of Sand, because neither the book nor the sand has any beginning or end."

14   The stranger asked me to find the first page.

15   I laid my left hand on the cover and, trying to put my thumb on the flyleaf, I opened the book. It was useless. Every time I tried, a number of pages came between the cover and my thumb. It was as if they kept growing from the book.

16   "Now find the last page."

17   Again I failed. In a voice that was not mine, I barely managed to stammer, "This can't be."

18   Still speaking in a low voice, the stranger said, "It can't be, but it *is*. The number of pages in this book is no more or less than infinite. None is the first page, none the last. I don't know why they're numbered in this arbitrary way. Perhaps to suggest that the terms of an infinite series admit any number."

19   Then, as if he were thinking aloud, he said, "If space is infinite, we may be at any point in space. If time is infinite, we may be at any point in time."

20   His speculations irritated me. "You are religious, no doubt?" I asked him.

21   "Yes, I'm a Presbyterian. My conscience is clear. I am reasonably sure of not having cheated the native when I gave him the Word of God in exchange for his devilish book."

22   I assured him that he had nothing to reproach himself for, and I asked if he were just passing through this part of the world. He replied that he planned to return to his country in a few days. It was then that I learned that he was a Scot from the Orkney Islands. I told him I had a great personal affection for Scotland, through my love of Stevenson and Hume.

23   "You mean Stevenson and Robbie Burns," he corrected.

24   While we spoke, I kept exploring the infinite book. With feigned indifference, I asked, "Do you intend to offer this curiosity to the British Museum?"

25   "No. I'm offering it to you," he said, and he stipulated a rather high sum for the book.

26   I answered, in all truthfulness, that such a sum was out of my reach, and I began thinking. After a minute or two, I came up with a scheme.

27   "I propose a swap," I said. "You got this book for a handful of rupees and a copy of the Bible. I'll offer you the amount of my pension check, which I've just collected, and my black-letter Wiclif Bible. I inherited it from my ancestors."

28   "A black-letter Wiclif!" he murmured.

29   I went to my bedroom and brought him the money and the book. He turned the leaves and studied the title page with all the fervor of a true bibliophile.

30   "It's a deal," he said.

31   It amazed me that he did not haggle. Only later was I to realize that he had entered my house with his mind made up to sell the book. Without counting the money, he put it away.

32   We talked about India, about Orkney, and about the Norwegian jarls who once ruled it. It was night when the man left. I have not seen him again, nor do I know his name.

33   I thought of keeping the Book of Sand in the space left on the shelf by the Wiclif, but in the end I decided to hide it behind the volumes of a broken set of The Thousand and One Nights. I went to bed and did not sleep. At three or four in the morning, I turned on the light. I got down the impossible book and leafed through its pages. On one of them I saw engraved a mask. The upper corner of the page carried a number, which I no longer recall, elevated to the ninth power.

34   I showed no one my treasure. To the luck of owning it was added the fear of having it stolen, and then the misgiving that it might not truly be infinite. These twin preoccupations intensified my old misanthropy. I had only a few friends left; I now stopped seeing even them. A prisoner of the book, I almost never went out

anymore. After studying its frayed spine and covers with a magnifying glass, I rejected the possibility of a contrivance of any sort. The small illustrations, I verified, came two thousand pages apart. I set about listing them alphabetically in a notebook, which I was not long in filling up. Never once was an illustration repeated. At night, in the meager intervals my insomnia granted, I dreamed of the book.

35   Summer came and went, and I realized that the book was monstrous. What good did it do me to think that I, who looked upon the volume with my eyes, who held it in my hands, was any less monstrous? I felt that the book was a nightmarish object, an obscene thing that affronted and tainted reality itself.

36   I thought of fire, but I feared that the burning of an infinite book might likewise prove infinite and suffocate the planet with smoke. Somewhere I recalled reading that the best place to hide a leaf is in a forest. Before retirement, I worked on Mexico Street, at the Argentine National Library, which contains nine hundred thousand volumes. I knew that to the right of the entrance a curved staircase leads down into the basement, where books and maps and periodicals are kept. One day I went there and, slipping past a member of the staff and trying not to notice at what height or distance from the door, I lost the Book of Sand on one of the basement's musty shelves.

Translated by Norman Thomas Di Giovanni

Questions for Discussion

1. What relationship does the narrator establish between infinity and truth in the opening paragraph? While Borges does not expect the reader to accept the story as literally "true," what truth or truths are illuminated through the story?
2. Why is it significant that the Bible salesman is a foreigner from a rather exotic and underpopulated place, the Orkney Islands?
3. Why is the book called *The Book of Sand*? Why is it significant that the book is acquired by both the salesman and the narrator in exchange for a Bible?
4. What leads to the narrator's obsession with *The Book of Sand*? What is implied when he hides *The Book of Sand* behind *The Thousand and One Nights*?
5. Why does the narrator eventually decide that the book is "monstrous"? What does *The Book of Sand* represent to the narrator?
6. Why does the narrator finally abandon the book in the basement of the National Library?

Ideas for Writing

1. Write an essay in which you explore what you think *The Book of Sand* symbolizes or represents in relationship to truth, knowledge, and the act of reading itself.
2. Write a sequel to the story in which a character you create finds the book where the narrator abandoned it and develops a relationship with it.

❦ Denise Levertov

The Secret

Born in Ilford, England, in 1923 into a religious family, Denise Levertov emigrated to the United States in 1948 after serving as a nurse during World War II. She was active in anti-Vietnam war protests in the 1960s and taught in the English Department at Stanford University for a number of years. Levertov has published more than eighteen volumes of poetry, which explore both social and mystical and natural themes. Some of the better known include The Sorrow Dance *(1967),* Freeing the Dust *(1975),* Candles in Babylon *(1982),* Evening Train *(1993), and* Sands of the Well *(1996). The following poem explores the act of reading from the perspective of both the unsophisticated reader and the writer of a poem.*

JOURNAL

Write about a reading experience that helped you to unlock a secret of some kind: a secret about yourself, the world, or about life itself.

Two girls discover
the secret of life
in a sudden line of
poetry.

5 I who don't know the
secret wrote
the line. They
told me

(through a third person)
10 they had found it
but not what it was,
not even

what line it was. No doubt
by now, more than a week
15 later, they have forgotten
the secret,

the line, the name of
the poem. I love them
for finding what
20 I can't find,

and for loving me
for the line I wrote:

and for forgetting it
so that

25 a thousand times, till death
finds them, they may
discover it again, in other
lines,

in other
30 happenings. And for
wanting to know it,
for

assuming there is
such a secret, yes,
35 for that
most of all.

Stavonnie Henderson
Natasha Dwamena

Through one line of poetry, two girls discover the secret of life. It is a source of enlightenment. The secret is analogous to identity. It is not clearly defined and changes with
time. This secret of life is discovered by each person through different experiences. It is
similar to finding a solution or the perfect formula for life. The poet appreciates the
fact that the young girls are in search of such a formula and that she could provide that
for them unconsciously.

   "Know thyself"—this concept is analogous to identity and self-esteem. Self-knowledge and self-confidence are important keys to living a happier life—perhaps the "secret key to success in life." Experiences can cause people to lose their confidence or
sense of identity, but hopefully, they will regain their identity. The light bulb symbolizes enlightenment—more specifically, the knowledge that a person gains about himself
or herself, and the luminance from the bulb helps one to see themselves and the world
in a different "light."

Elin Austevoll

The first thought I had after reading this poem was that it is important to remember how excited we got over "small" things when we were younger, which is something we should try to find and hold on to as we get older. Often we forget the importance of children's emotions, and we rule out the possibility that we can ever feel like that again. We are sad because Christmas or our birthday isn't the same anymore, but we are often not willing to go back and find the **secret** of childhood. Because we have our impressions of how adults are supposed to act, we shut out the child in us. And after a while, when we see the importance of childhood emotions, we have lost the path back to them. This is frustrating for most adults. We often look at people who are able to show their feelings and excitement as "different" or "weird," and we are all, of course, afraid of being viewed as different.

Questions for Discussion

1. The secret that the two young girls have found in a line of Levertov's poetry is never clearly defined in the poem. Why do you think that the writer doesn't or isn't able to determine the secret? What does this imply about the act of reading?

2. Why do you think that Levertov indicates that the girls have found what she (the author) can't find? What does this imply about the relationship between authors and the imaginative texts that they write as well as about the relationship between authors and their readers?

3. What does Levertov suggest about the relationship between texts and life experience when she writes that the girls forget the "secret," only to "discover it again, in other / lines, / in other / happenings"?

4. In the last stanzas of the poem, the poem's speaker says she loves the girls most for "wanting to know" the secret of life and for "assuming

there is / such a secret" at all. What does this suggest about the importance of the values and beliefs that we bring with us to the act of reading?

5. Levertov uses a very short, irregular line and four-line stanzas to organize the thoughts in her poem. How do her ragged lines and stanzas,
which seem to jump awkwardly from one to another because of the
large spaces between them, help to emphasize the movement of her
thinking about the "secret"?

Ideas for Writing

1. Develop your journal writing into an essay about a "secret" you learned
through your reading. Return to the original text and use quotations
from it as well as paraphrasing to clarify what you learned from reading
it. Indicate also how learning the secret somehow changed you or led
you to perceive reality differently or to communicate with people in
new ways.

2. Argue for or against the existence of a "secret" to life. If you do believe
there is such a secret, how do you think you can best go about discovering it?

 # Samuel Taylor Coleridge

Kubla Khan: or, a Vision in a Dream

*English lyrical poet, critic, and philosopher Samuel Taylor Coleridge (1772–
1834) was the son of the vicar of Ottery. Coleridge attended Cambridge University, where he read widely in imaginative literature and philosophy, but he did not
graduate. With the poet Robert Southy he made plans to establish a utopian community or "pantisocracy" that would be true to the ideals of the French Revolution
without sanctioning violence and despotism. In 1795 Coleridge met the romantic
poet William Wordsworth, with whom he collaborated on the volume Lyrical Bal-
lads (1798). His friendship with Wordsworth helped to lay the groundwork for the
English romantic movement, with its emphasis on powerful feelings, reverence for
rural nature, peasant life, and the childlike, innocent side of humanity. Coleridge
was always a visionary writer and thinker who tried to break away from formal
constraints in his writing to rely more on rhythms of ordinary speech while at the
same time seeking to find words proper to express in his poem "Frost at Midnight"
what he called "The lovely shapes and sounds intelligible / Of that eternal language, which thy God / Utters. . . . " Coleridge came to believe that all religion
and mythology came from the same universal source that was best expressed and*

seen in action in what Coleridge called "genius"—his name for the creative, visionary, imaginative impulse. In his later years, Coleridge elaborated such philosophical and critical ideas in his popular lectures and especially in his famous prose work, Biographia Literaria (1817).

"Kubla Khan: or, a Vision in a Dream" (1798) is one of Coleridge's best-known works. Coleridge stated that the poem was a "fragment" that came to him in a dream after he had been reading a book about the Mongolian Empire of Genghis Khan. Kubla Khan, the grandson of Genghis, established a capital for the Mongols in China at Shang-tu (referred to as "Xanadu" in the poem), building a walled city with grand palaces that was soon menaced by revolt from both the Mongols and his Chinese subjects. As you read the poem, notice how Coleridge embellishes these facts with his imagination and poetic language.

JOURNAL

Write about a dream or experience that reflects your understanding of the creative process.

In Xanadu did Kubla Khan
   A stately pleasure-dome decree:
Where Alph, the sacred river, ran
Through caverns measureless to man
5   Down to a sunless sea.
So twice five miles of fertile ground
With walls and towers were girdled round:
And here were gardens bright with sinuous rills
Where blossomed many an incense-bearing tree;
10 And here were forests ancient as the hills,
Enfolding sunny spots of greenery.
But oh! that deep romantic chasm which slanted
Down the green hill athwart a cedarn cover!
A savage place! as holy and enchanted
15 As e'er beneath a waning moon was haunted
By woman wailing for her demon-lover!
And from this chasm, with ceaseless turmoil seething,
As if this earth in fast thick pants were breathing,
A mighty fountain momently was forced,
20 Amid whose swift half-intermitted burst
Huge fragments vaulted like rebounding hail,
Or chaffy grain beneath the thresher's flail:
And 'mid these dancing rocks at once and ever
It flung up momently the sacred river.
25 Five miles meandering with a mazy motion
Through wood and dale the sacred river ran,
Then reached the caverns measureless to man,

And sank in tumult to a lifeless ocean:
And 'mid this tumult Kubla heard from far
30 Ancestral voices prophesying war!

     The shadow of the dome of pleasure
     Floated midway on the waves;
     Where was heard the mingled measure
     From the fountain and the caves.
35 It was a miracle of rare device,
A sunny pleasure-dome with caves of ice!
     A damsel with a dulcimer
     In a vision once I saw:
     It was an Abyssinian maid,
40   And on her dulcimer she played,
     Singing of Mount Abora.
     Could I revive within me
     Her symphony and song,
     To such a deep delight 'twould win me,
45 That with music loud and long,
I would build that dome in air,
That sunny dome! those caves of ice!
And all who heard should see them there,
And all should cry, Beware! Beware!
50 His flashing eyes, his floating hair!
Weave a circle round him thrice,
And close your eyes with holy dread,
For he on honey-dew hath fed,
And drunk the milk of Paradise.

Questions for Discussion

1. What conclusions can you draw about the values of the poem through its description of Khan's creation? Why do you think there is so little description of the "pleasure dome" and so much emphasis on the surrounding gardens and forests?

2. Although the first lines of the poem seem peaceful, a feeling of tension and conflict is introduced in line 12: "But oh! that deep romantic chasm. . . ." What does the chasm represent, and how does it help to introduce and organize the next eighteen lines of the poem?

3. What do "Alph, the sacred river," and the "caverns measureless to man" represent in the poem?

4. The last lines of the poem make it clear that we are looking at only a "shadow" of the dome of pleasure, a vision rather than a reality, yet "a miracle of rare device." How do lines 31 to 36 comment on the nature of dreams, imagination, and creativity?

5. What is the significance of the vision the poet has of a "damsel with a dulcimer"? (A dulcimer is a primitive stringed instrument in which

small hammers strike the strings; it is a precursor of the modern piano, although much smaller.)

6. What does the poet's aspiration in the final lines of the poem, to "revive within me / Her symphony and song" to "build that dome in air" suggest about the nature of the creative process in poetry? How does this section of the poem contrast to the earlier descriptions of Kubla's own creation of the city?

Ideas for Writing

1. Discuss the imagery of water and liquid used in the poem—the river, the "mighty fountain," the "lifeless ocean," the "waves," the "milk of paradise." How do these images help unify the poem and also make a commentary on the universal life spirit of creativity?

2. Analyze the dream or experience that you narrated in your journal entry. What does it tell you about creativity, vision, and the imagination? Can you relate your ideas to those in Coleridge's poem?

 # Maria Pitcher

The Bookstore

Maria Pitcher is currently studying biology, but she spends a good deal of time creating fiction in her mind. She considers the most difficult part of writing the actual writing process and not the idea process. Because she loved to read as a child, writing this essay was an enjoyable experience for her.

JOURNAL

Write about the book you remember most vividly from your childhood.

1   "There it is! Over there. And look, there's a place to park right out in front," exclaimed my passenger and best friend Wendy.

2   "Pull over," she ordered, smiling cheerfully at me.

3   Obeying her, I practiced my parallel parking skills. Before I removed the key from the ignition, Wendy threw open the door, bounded out of the beige car, and raced toward the entrance of the bookstore. Fumbling with my keys I followed her, footsteps pounding on the damp pavement.

4   "Slow down," I called in vain. She never listens. For Wendy going to a bookstore is the equivalent of me devouring a piece of seven-layer chocolate mousse cake.

5   As I entered the bookstore I noticed Wendy hunting busily for books. I watched her search and sighed, knowing I would have to drag her out of the book-

store long before she was ready to leave. Wendy, a definite English major type, would live in a bookstore if possible. Although I dreaded the prospect of forcing her to leave, she actually reminds me of myself as a child, always pestering people to take me to libraries. Remembering my childhood, I wandered over to the children's section to look for the books from my younger years.

6   Once in that section, with its low shelves and small chairs, my eyes caught the titles of various books. *Superfudge. The Wind in the Willows. Five Little Peppers and How They Grew.* I recognized all of these books from my childhood, when my zest for books surpassed my attachment to Strawberry Shortcake dolls. In elementary school and middle school I read voraciously, spending many Saturdays and evenings lost in my book of the day. Sometimes I even risked being called a nerd in order to bring books to school to read during recess and lunch.

7   Standing in front of these books, with their big type and colorful covers, elicited memories of other books from my childhood that have influenced me. One of my favorite books was *Ozma of Oz*, a book my parents introduced me to. My parents always read to me in my early years. Perhaps that's the reason I read so much as a child. Most evenings my dad would give me a piggyback ride upstairs before reading me a chapter or two out of an Oz book. (We had all the Oz books from when he was a child.) Even when I became capable of reading the Oz books myself, my dad still read them to me. Sometimes we'd switch roles and I'd read to him for a while. I can no longer remember any of the adventures of Ozma and her friends, but I always remember my dad reading aloud to me, patiently explaining the words I didn't understand. After hearing about the adventures of Princess Ozma I decided that I, too, would like to be a princess when I grew up.

8   While part of me wanted to be a princess, the rest of me admired the lovable rascal Ramona, from *Ramona Quimby, Age 8*. How long had it been since I'd seen that book? I remember all the Ramona books and all of Ramona's adventures. While the two of us differed in some respects (my family never had to scrimp and save, and I didn't have to deal with bratty Willa Jean), I found Ramona to be a "kindred spirit." We both had older siblings and a favorite Aunt Beatrice. Ramona displayed her mischievousness when she squirted an entire tube of toothpaste into the sink and told her mother the devil made her do it. In a similar spirit, I colored the mantel with red crayon and blamed the action on the commands of the mouse in the fireplace. But I really bonded with Ramona over the dog incident, when she threw her shoe at a large, fierce dog. How brave of Ramona to face that dog! Although I no longer fear dogs, as a little girl I wouldn't walk down any street a dog lived on. I admired Ramona's spunk greatly—she coped with eggs cracked over her head and throwing up in class. I even wrote to Beverly Cleary, begging her to write more Ramona books and suggesting a few titles for the books. Receiving a personalized post card from Beverly Cleary thanking me for my letter marked the high point of my relationship with the Ramona books.

9   I also investigated Kathryn Kenny, the author of the Trixie Belden mystery series. For several years I idolized Trixie, the athletic tomboy who was always picked first for sports, not last like me. Although she couldn't thread a needle, Trixie handled floods, con artists, and mad dogs with ease. Imagine my dismay at learning that Kathryn Kenny, the creator of my idol, was only a pen name used by

many different authors. I never wrote to any of them, but I loved their books anyway. My favorite was *Trixie Belden and the Happy Valley Mystery*. Most of the fifty or so Trixie books are out of print by now. Even when I loved them many of them were no longer in print. My mother used to drive me to libraries in other counties looking for those books.

10   While at that age all the other girls were reading about Nancy Drew, the boring 18 year old who thought she could be a detective, I preferred Trixie Belden, the vibrant 14 year old who attracted mysteries. The arguments for the obvious superiority of Trixie over Nancy should be reserved for a research paper. Trixie led me into her world. In my mind I was Trixie with her unruly blonde curls and fearless manner. Reading those books I, too, lived on the Belden Farm and rode horses through the woods. The characters from those books seemed very real to me, like actual people but nicer than anyone at school. The Trixie books always brought me out of dull reality into an exciting world of suspense.

11   I reached the peak of exploring different worlds with *Alice in Wonderland*, one of my favorite books during high school. No, I did not regress into my days of childhood reading this book, I actually understood it at a deeper level. This humorous book commented on many situations in life that I identified with.

> "In *that* direction," the Cat said, waving its right paw around, "lives a Hatter; and in *that* direction," waving the other paw, "lives a March Hare. Visit either you like; they're both mad people."
> "But I don't want to go among mad people," Alice remarked.
> "Oh, you can't help that," said the Cat; "we're all mad here. . . . "

Who wouldn't identify with that statement? The craziness of our world, where basketball players earn more than scientists, seemed so clear to me. I even used the quotation from the Alice book on my college application. Alice moved through a world where everything was backward and nothing made any sense, a world that often seems to resemble our world the harder I look at it.

12   The Alice book put a different perspective on life, gave me more to think about. Most good books that I've read have expanded my thinking. New places could be explored and new thoughts could be entertained. Even as a child I re-ran stories through my head, mulled them over, and added bits here and there. Eventually I stopped using characters other people created and began inventing stories of my own. Imaginary situations always developed in my mind, prompting me to write stories. Reading fueled my desire to write poetry and short stories. As a sixth grader I dreamed of becoming an author and seeing a book with my name on the cover on a shelf in a bookstore. In high school I wrote notebooks full of poetry and I even won a prize for a poem, inspired by a book I'd read, portraying an unusual view of the sea. Later I turned to short stories in which I could explore people's relationships with other people. Mentally I'd invent people that I wished I could be. Writing gave me a different way to experience the world. Yet most of my stories never made it to paper, they only lingered in my mind and were forgotten. The ability to read fostered my ability to dream and occasionally I still fantasize about leaving my biology major and becoming a writer. While childhood reading didn't turn me into a Pulitzer Prize winning author, it did help me develop my imagina-

tion and creativity, something I greatly rely on in the day-to-day grind of everyday life. If one looked at me at any given moment (including lecture time) chances are my mind would be elsewhere, working on a story.

13 "Maria. Maria?" Wendy interrupted my silent musing.

14 "I bought the book. We can go now," she informed me.

15 I looked up from the children's books.

16 "So soon?" I replied, smiling because today I am not the first to be ready to leave.

Questions for Discussion

1. Why is each book that Maria Pitcher discusses important to her? How did these books help her to handle her life experiences?
2. What lasting impact have these books had on Maria Pitcher?
3. Although Maria Pitcher loved to read as a child, now her friend Wendy stays longer at bookstores than she does. Do you think that Pitcher's zest for reading has changed? If so, why did it change?
4. Discuss a book that influenced you as a child. Was it one that you read to yourself or one that a parent or relative read to you? What relevance does the book have in your current life?

 ## Lissy Goralink

The Sandstorm of Time and Knowledge

Lissy Goralink plays field hockey and is thinking about majoring in English, creative writing, and American studies. Writing offers her both an emotional and an intellectual outlet. She enjoyed writing about The Book of Sand *as it offers the reader so many possible interpretations. In the following essay she focuses on the way the story explores ideas of eternity, knowledge, and the discovery of one's role in a chaotically changing world.*

JOURNAL

For what reasons do you value knowledge? For what reasons do you fear knowledge?

1 Finding a book of infinite knowledge, the narrator of "The Book of Sand" seems to confront several realizations. Unnerved by the book's endless pages, he faces eternity, seeing there a connection between its continuous invention of information and nature's relentless thriving, as both extend beyond the constraints of definite boundaries. Birth and death, on the other hand, confine and restrict the narrator's mortal existence. The narrator, in the midst of such information,

recognizes the restrained capacity of his mind. He will never absorb the full contents of his book before his life ends, and in understanding the influence of these demons of time, nature, and mortality on his life, the narrator must come to admit defeat. These forces, unaffected by his existence, will survive his life, his death, and any attempts he makes to control them. The narrator will never know all that he wants to know. Eventually he will be consumed by the book and the forces it represents.

2   At first excited by the opportunities embodied within the book, by the prospect of total and infinite knowledge, the narrator willingly gazes into its pages. Alarmed at what he sees there, he blames the book for the reflection it provides him. The book serves as a mirror for the narrator, causing him to re-evaluate his place in the world. When he first questions the merit of the book, he says, " . . . I realized that the book was monstrous. What good did it do to me to think that I, who looked upon the volume with my eyes, who held it in my hands, was any less monstrous?" Here he admits that the book's endless information made him feel that he too could be ever-expanding, like a sponge, to absorb every page, every word, every bit of knowledge it offered. As the knowledge continues to elude him though, as the narrator realizes that he will never see all of the pages, never begin to uncover all of the secrets of the book, he feels like he is nothing in the face of infinity, nothing but a ripple in the water. And for this epiphany, the narrator condemns the book.

3   The narrator, astounded by the vast wealth of knowledge in the book, realizes that he will never be able to attain any recognizable amount of information, and even if he could, to what avail? No one would notice; no one would commend his efforts or applaud his swelling brain. He would learn in a frenzied solitude, and then die without leaving any sort of mark on the world or on the world's body of knowledge. And life would go on undisturbed. Trying to make order out of such infinite chaos, the narrator organizes a list of the drawings in the text and figures out how frequently they arise. But in a sense, he is only trying to sweep the desert into a tidy little pile in order to calm his inner torment. Such a task would prove impossible.

4   To protect his initially precious possession the narrator hides his book of knowledge behind "a broken set of The Thousand and One Nights." One thousand and one, 1001. This particular number reads the same both forwards and backwards, like a palindrome. Symmetrical, reflected upon itself, and with a mirrored image identical to its original form, one thousand and one represents the ulterior function of The Book of Sand. Imposing on the reader a humbling perception of self in alliance with the world, forcing self-reflection, this book allows the narrator first to be consumed by human greed, as he burns to acquire all knowledge, and then causes him to recognize that his capabilities and capacity are both severely limited, as he is not able to digest the vast gifts the book offers.

5   But not any ordinary mirror is this book, for the volumes of *The Thousand and One Nights* composed only an incomplete set, a shattered representation of a solid group. This implies then, as the 1001 is equated with The Book of Sand and the book then provides a reflection of the reader, that this broken 1001 stands for a

fractured text which reflects a cracked image to the reader. And so when the narrator reveals that, " . . . the book was a nightmarish object, an obscene thing that affronted and tainted reality itself . . . ", he articulates Borges' reasoning for hiding this distorted mirror behind the broken set of short stories.

6   Once the narrator recognizes the monstrosity of the text which he tries fanatically to devour, he hopes to hide together both the text and his new awareness gained from it, as he returns to "the forest" to lose the book. As a normal man would try to camouflage himself in a swarming crowd of people to escape the attention of a discerning eye, the narrator feels that he need only hide from the glare of the book to alleviate the shame of representing nothing. A friendless man, only he and the evil text witness his failure. To escape the stigma he feels he now possesses, he need only free himself of the book, a reminder of his new image, and lie to himself. But such a feat of losing awareness would prove impossible, for awareness is a form of knowledge or wisdom, the very qualities which he before looked hungrily to the book to obtain, qualities which cannot be easily unlearned.

7   Through his inner journey the narrator comes to realize that we have no ultimate control over our lives. Time does not allow for infinite endeavors such as the quest for total knowledge, and humans have unknowingly surrendered our very existence to the vices of time. So answering to time and the life cycle it imposes upon us, to boundaries of the mind and personal limitations, to the supremacy of a possible higher being, we cannot shape fate. But rather than accept this path destined for us as a race, the narrator sulks and is disgusted by such a truth. Borges' message is clear—the truth evades us and is defined by powers beyond our scope or grasp. We fool ourselves in believing we can take advantage of the system, that we can impose some sort of order on this divine chaos, but really we are just driven by arrogance and greed. The discovery of the narrator, as he realizes his insignificance, his lack of purpose, his hopelessness, prescribes the reality for us all. We will never know everything.

8   Yet the narrator is presented in the story as an exceptional man, a flawed seeker of truth. He grouchily admits that his observation skills are distorted by "myopia," which is a disease that leads to "defective vision of distant objects," but also means "a lack of foresight or discernment: a narrow view of something" or, in layman's terms, closed-mindedness. Later he also refers to himself as misanthropic, hating and distrusting mankind. Such paranoia and demented vision suggest a maladjusted man, implying that Borges might be showing us a distorted narrator who represents the antithesis of normal human reactions. Possibly, then, a clear image of a cracked man develops through the narrator's experience with the book, rather than a cracked image of a stable man.

9   It seems most likely that Borges is attempting to show us, through a narrator with whom we are not encouraged to sympathize, the necessity and importance of introspection. The narrator admits his solitary life when he says, "I had only few friends left [before I found the book]; I now stopped seeing even them." Willing to abandon any social contact or interactions to be with a book, the narrator lives in

a world foreign to most of us. Through portraying this character as withdrawn and possibly mentally unstable, Borges implies that we need not fear fresh glances of ourselves as our narrator did. We need not hide from mirrors or reflective experiences, for they are learning tools so that we may understand ourselves and our niche in this eternal, fluid world.

10   Perhaps knowledge is worth the search, the struggle, the stress. Knowledge may really be the ultimate goal in the trek through the desert and the hike in the forest. Borges wants us to realize that knowledge spins the world, ticks the clocks, propels the humans; for without knowledge, we are unconscious and unfeeling and unaware. Although the quest for knowledge, like a sandstorm, can be dangerous, Borges wants us to understand that big or small, important or unnoticed, we all must make our lives the fullest they can be in the short time we are allotted here, and that expanding our minds through reflection allows us to expand our skills of observation, interaction, and introspection. Self-knowledge, Borges suggests, is the most important goal in life, and should drive us to read, to search, to journey, to converse, and to look in the mirror.

Questions for Discussion

1. Why does the book come to control the narrator?
2. Why does Goralnik think that the book is a mirror for the narrator? Explain why you agree or disagree with her claim.
3. Compare or contrast your interpretation of the narrator's role in the story to Goralnik's.
4. According to Goralnik, what is Borges's purpose in telling this story? Compare or contrast your interpretation of the story's meaning with Goralink's.

Chapter Writing Topics

1. Write an essay in which you discuss the importance of having established writers as "role models" for developing writers by referring to selections in this chapter and to your own experiences. Do you have certain writers whom you consider as models?
2. Discuss the role of the imagination in reading. Refer to your own experiences and the ideas of the writers in this chapter to support your point of view.
3. Many people would agree that we become better writers through reading, but what exactly is the relationship between reading and writing? How does one influence or build on the other? Develop an essay on this subject, using your own reading and writing experiences as well as selections in this chapter to support your conclusions.
4. Write about a work you enjoyed reading in this text but that you found challenging. Reread the work carefully to interpret its meaning by noting the ways the author used examples, definitions, characters, dramatic situations, and imaginative language. How did your initial interpretation of the work change after you reread and studied it more deeply?

5. Select a poem, story, or essay from this book and write a letter to the author explaining why you liked or disliked the work. What questions and suggestions would you have for the writer?

6. Using some of the advice in the rhetorical section of this chapter as a guide, write an evaluation of a nonfiction reading selection by a professional writer, either an author included in this text or another writer of your choosing. You might consider such points as whether the issue taken up in the reading is significant and worthy of serious discussion, whether the writer managed to convince you intellectually and/or emotionally of the central argument of the selection, whether he or she addresses possible objections to the position taken, and whether other works you have read or your own experiences seem to contradict or confirm some of the author's conclusions.

7. Pick a selection from this text and add on to it by rewriting it from the point of view of another character in the story or by adding a different ending or a different historical/physical setting. After you have finished your rewrite, comment on the insights into the author's original meaning and your own reading process and creative ability that you discovered from doing the rewrite.

8. Watch a film made from a book you have read or a film that concerns the act and significance of reading. Then write an essay in which you contrast the experience of the film and the book or comment on what the film reveals about the nature and importance of reading. You might choose from the following list:

For films made from novels consider:

Farenheit 451, Sense and Sensibility, The Joy Luck Club, One Flew Over The Cuckoo's Nest, The Age of Innocence, Emma, Portrait of a Lady

For films about the impact of reading consider:

Dead Poet's Society, Stanley and Iris, Educating Rita, The Miracle Worker

Memories from Childhood

In the New Age the Daughters of Memory shall become the Daughters of Inspiration.

WILLIAM BLAKE

Nothing can be brought to an end in the unconscious; nothing is past or forgotten.

SIGMUND FREUD

Often I felt as though I was in a trance at my typewriter, that the shape of a particular memory was decided not by my conscious mind but by all that is dark and deep within me, unconscious but present.

BELL HOOKS
Writing Autobiography

Narration, Memory, and Self-Awareness

You will read a number of narrative accounts of childhood experiences in this chapter. Narratives serve two important functions for a writer: they can bring about a process of self-discovery, and rhetorically they are fundamental building blocks of both fiction and nonfiction writing. The brief stories or extended examples that develop, illustrate, and support points made in expository and argumentative essays are among the best resources writers have for presenting ideas in a clear, vivid, and convincing manner.

When you create a narrative, you draw on many inner resources and skills: memories of life experiences, dreams, your imagination, and the ability to imitate the voices of others and to develop a suspenseful plot that will hold your readers' attention. While not everyone likes to entertain friends with a natural story-telling ability, most of us can learn how to write a clear and engaging story.

Making Associations

As in other forms of writing, the first phase of narrative writing involves generating ideas and images to write about, experiences from your past that can later be shaped into a story with an overall theme. How do you find ideas and events for your writing, however, if the only memories you have of your early years are vague or sketchy? Student writer Corinne Okada, whose essay is included in this chapter, began her richly detailed essay "Namesake" with a single image: a memory of a "beautiful photograph" of her great-aunt Corinne, propped on a "small coffee table [in] a thick silver frame." You can begin as Corinne Okada did with whatever you can remember, perhaps only a few basic facts or images: "As a child, I lived for five years on B Street in Sacramento."

Writing strategies such as drawing, freewriting, invisible writing, brainstorming, and clustering can help you to generate details, images, and ideas associated with a particular time and place in your life. For example, you could start with a significant part of an address and do a cluster or ten-minute freewrite around it, letting one detail lead to another: "B Street, hot, barren, dusty, fire hydrant out front turned on in the summer, the ice cream wagon's jingle. . . . " If you follow this process long enough, you will begin to remember a number of details you thought you had forgotten, and you will have begun to gather the words, thoughts, and images that you can later shape into an essay.

Focusing and Concentration: The Inner Screen

In developing your narrative it is also important to try to focus on the most significant aspect of your memory. For example, you might visualize a particular room or the backyard of your house on a summer day when something significant happened to you: a fateful accident, a moment of serious conflict, an unexpected gift, a moment of friendship or intimacy. Close your eyes and try to visualize all the objects, colors, forms, people, and expressions associated with that place and a particular time there. Then try to visualize the movements within the scene. How did the people walk? What gestures did they make? What activities did they perform? What did they say to one another? After visualizing and naming specific colors, try to recall other sensations: textures, warmth or coolness, smells, tastes, sounds. Take notes as you begin to remember sensations, forms, and movements.

Dialogue and Characters

While not all people have vivid auditory memories, including some conversation in your narrative will help to bring it to life. Focus for a while on the way each person in your scene speaks; jot down some of the typical brief exchanges that the group could have had, and then try to understand each character more fully through role-playing. Imagine that you have become each person in the scene, one at a time. As you role-play, speak out loud in the voice of each person, then write down a paragraph in which you try to capture their typical concerns and rhythms of speech. Finally, try to construct a conversation between the people in the scene.

Main Idea or Dominant Impression

Now you should be ready to write about the strong ideas or feelings that underlie or dominate your scene. Brainstorm or cluster around key details in your notes. Which emotions does the remembered moment call up for you? What ideas, what "lessons" does it suggest? Develop a statement that you can later clarify and qualify: "That evening was one of waiting and apprehension"; "The morning was a joyful one for my family, yet tinged by regret." Writing this type of dominant impression statement will guide you in adding more details and bits of dialogue and in selecting and ordering your material. A central idea for your narrative will help you to achieve a sense of focus and purpose that will help you to engage your readers' interest; most importantly, it will help you to clarify what you have gained from the experience. The process of writing the narrative will contribute to your personal growth and self-awareness.

Drafting and Shaping the Narrative

Using your central idea or dominant impression as a guide in selecting and ordering details and events, write a rapid first draft, including what is relevant from the notes you generated in your preliminary brainstorming. Leave out any details or events that introduce a tone or feeling that conflicts, detracts, or clashes with the one you want to emphasize. Relevant but not particularly interesting events and periods of time do not need to be narrated in detail and can be summed up in a sentence or two: "For hours I played with my dog, waiting eagerly for my father to return from work."

Try to order the events of your narrative to emphasize your main idea as well. Although most writers use a chronological sequence in shaping a narrative, your dominant idea may demand withholding a key event for purposes of suspense or creating a powerful conclusion, as Maya Angelou does in the selection included in this chapter. You might also consider the use of flashbacks; you might begin with a brief scene that occurs at the end of the action and then tell the sequence of events leading up to the initially described event. Any order is acceptable as long as you clarify shifts of time for the reader with transitions and make sure that your order serves the overall purpose of your story. While writing different drafts of your narrative, don't hesitate to experiment with rearranging the parts of the story or essay until you find a clear, comfortable fit between the structure and meaning of your work.

Revising the Narrative: Point of View and Style

As you move from the early stages into the final drafting of your narrative, pay special attention to your point of view and style. Your narrative will probably use the first-person "I" pronoun, unless you are writing about someone else's experience. As is the case with the essays in this chapter, narrative essays are most frequently told from the perspective of an adult looking back on the past and are known as memoir narratives. Be sure to maintain a consistent point of view. If you decide to move into your mind as a young person, indicate this shift with a clear transition ("Then I thought to myself . . . "), after which you could write in language that is typical of the younger "you."

Narratives are seldom written in highly formal, abstract, or generalized language. Rather they try to sound natural as they capture the mood and feeling of the event being revealed and/or of the characters who are involved. In refining the style of your narrative, ask yourself some questions about your word and sentence choices. Have you used specific, concrete nouns, adjectives, verbs, and adverbs? Wherever possible, try to avoid "generic" words that fail to communicate vivid images and emotions. Always search for the word that best fits your meaning and mood. A thesaurus can be very helpful in finding specific replacements for tired, imprecise, general terms. When it seems as though no word exists to communicate your exact sensory impression or mood, try using literal or figurative comparisons: she looked like _____; it was as dark as _____; I felt as sick as _____. Notice how an implied comparison between skin and paper helps to create a vivid picture of the sick aunt in Corinne Okada's "Namesake": "Observing her thin, papery skin made me wince sadly for her fragility." Comparisons can add a lively and imaginative flavor to your writing, but take your time to find the right, original comparison. Clichés like "she looked like an angel" or "it was as dark as a dungeon" can tarnish the original impression that you are trying to create.

Your writing style is also created through the way that you put words together. Thus, your sentence patterns are a vital part of your narrative, as they should be in everything that you write. Vary your sentence length for emphasis, using short sentences to slow down the action and to emphasize climactic moments. Try, too, to capture the voice rhythms of your characters through your punctuation. Remember that you can use a number of different sentence patterns (simple, compound, complex) as well as different ordering possibilities for the parts of your sentences. Consult your grammar text to review the range of sentence patterns; experiment to heighten the dramatic effects of your writing.

Writing an engaging narrative is a challenge. It can also be a fulfilling writing experience that will bring you in closer touch with your past experiences, feelings, values, and identity.

THEMATIC INTRODUCTION

Self-concept, imagination, dreams, and memories—all are born in childhood. A person's identity as a writer begins there, too. Through writing about your childhood memories, you will begin to rediscover yourself through the places, the people, the events, and the stories that are still alive in your mind. These formative memories may have kindled your dreams while creating the foundation of your self-concept. Because writing is a process of self-discovery that has its roots in childhood, we have included poems, essays, and stories that address issues of childhood identity in relationship to dreams and fantasies, expectations, and goals. In the selections that follow, essayists and fiction writers create vivid moments, some positive and some painful, from their own childhoods and from imagined childhoods.

The chapter begins with memories of childhood. In the poem "Starlight," by Philip Levine, the speaker recalls and interprets the event in his childhood when he gained insight and strength as he came to understand that his father's own dreams and his were linked. The following selection, a dream narrative is excerpted from Lewis Carroll's *Alice in Wonderland*. In her dream Alice gains insight into the physical and psychological changes she is undergoing. As she learns to control these bewildering changes through a process of trial and error, she builds her self-confidence as well.

The next three selections focus on how and why memories that may remain dreamlike in our minds continue to influence our self-concepts. In "Muller Bros. Moving & Storage" the acclaimed scientist and writer Stephen Jay Gould reflects on his own relationship with his grandfather as he asks his readers to think about why people continue to cherish memories of the past, despite the fact that these memories often do not represent truth. Memorist bell hooks writes about how she looks first to her memories as the cornerstone of her writer's identity. In "Writing Autobiography" she presents writing as a way of accepting one's past, of revealing secrets, of growing, and of celebrating. In "The Angel of the Candy Counter," taken from Maya Angelou's autobiography, *I Know Why the Caged Bird Sings*, the reader comes to understand how Angelou's childhood fantasy of revenge helped her to overcome the anger and humiliation she felt when a white dentist refused to treat her.

In the next three selections the writers explore the specific and long-lasting effects of childhood memories whose meanings change as one grows and matures. In her essay "Memory and Imagination," Patricia Hampl also presents the process of writing about memories as a way of discovering, understanding, and developing one's identity. Hampl explains why writing about her memories helps her to explore and reflect on her values and identity and to create a sense of personal truth. Alice Walker in "Beauty: When the Other Dancer Is the Self" narrates the childhood incident that scarred her eye and changed her self-concept; she also reflects on how this scar helped her develop inner strength and vision. In the memoir "Silent Dancing" Judith Ortiz Cofer, who was born in Puerto Rico and raised in New Jersey, explores how her childhood memories of her Puerto Rican culture and relatives continue to influence her understanding and fears about her life in New Jersey.

The last selection by a professional author presents the role of memories through the lens of a dream. In her poem, "The Source," Eavan Boland asks readers to think about whether one can understand the past better through reliving memories imaginatively, as the speaker does in this poem. The chapter closes with two student essays. In "Namesake," Corinne Okada reflects on how her memories and feelings during childhood visits to her aunt who suffered from a brain tumor confused and upset her but also helped her to develop compassion and to mature. In "Enter Dragon" Tin Le, a Vietnamese American student, shows how his fantasies of power and revenge gave him courage and strength in the face of the prejudice of his junior high school classmates.

Although most people mature and learn to function in the rational world, the dreams and ghosts of their childhoods continue to shape, to haunt, and to inspire their waking lives. Writing about the past can be one of the best ways to face and come to terms with the ghosts of memory. This type of writing can then help us to begin to formulate and construct realistic and positive dreams for the future.

 ## Philip Levine

Starlight

Philip Levine (b. 1928) was raised in Detroit. Educated at Wayne State University, he later received a fellowship to study creative writing at Stanford. Levine has taught English and creative writing at Fresno State University in California for more than twenty-five years. Levine travels frequently, and particularly enjoys spending time in Spain, a country renowned for its poets and visionaries. Some of his collections of poetry include Not This Pig *(1968),* Ashes: Poems Old and New *(1979),* Selected Poems *(1984),* Walk With Thomas Jefferson *(1988),* What Work Is *(1991), and* The Simple Truth *(1994). He also published his autobiography,* The Bread to Time: Toward an Autobiography *in 1994. In many of his works Levine attempts to "find a voice for the voiceless"—the working-class Americans he grew up with and worked with as a young man in the factories of Detroit. The poem "Starlight" begins with a memory of a child's insight into his father's sorrow and disillusion.*

JOURNAL

Write about a time in your childhood when you began to understand your parents' values and emotional concerns.

My father stands in the warm evening
on the porch of my first house.
I am four years old and growing tired.
I see his head among the stars,
5 the glow of his cigarette, redder
than the summer moon riding
low over the old neighborhood. We
are alone, and he asks me if I am happy.
"Are you happy?" I cannot answer.
10 I do not really understand the word,
and the voice, my father's voice, is not
his voice, but somehow thick and choked,
a voice I have not heard before, but
heard often since. He bends and passes
15 a thumb beneath each of my eyes.
The cigarette is gone, but I can smell
the tiredness that hangs on his breath.
He has found nothing, and he smiles
and holds my head with both his hands.
20 Then he lifts me to his shoulder,
and now I too am there among the stars,
as tall as he. Are you happy? I say.
He nods in answer, Yes! oh yes! oh yes!
And in that new voice he says nothing,
25 holding my head tight against his head,
his eyes closed up against the starlight,
as though those tiny blinking eyes
of light might find a tall, gaunt child
holding his child against the promises
30 of autumn, until the boy slept
never to waken in that world again.

Questions for Discussion

1. Why do you think the father in the poem asks his son if he is happy? Why can't the son in the poem answer his father's question? Do you think his reaction is typical of a four-year-old child?
2. Try reading the father's question aloud in several different moods so that you can hear the question. Try to visualize the moment and experience it the way the young boy in the poem does. What do you think the son senses about his father's emotional state?

3. Why does the father pass "a thumb beneath each of my [his son's] eyes"? What is he looking for? Why do you think he feels the need to look?

4. Does the father's positive answer to his son's question, "Are you happy?" seem to relieve the son's apprehension? As you read the final lines of the poem, do you believe that the father is happy? Why or why not?

5. What does the last line of the poem—"never to waken in that world again"—imply about how the narrator has been changed through his revelation about his father? What might it also reveal about the father, who sees himself as "a tall, gaunt child"?

6. The poem's mood is created in part by its setting and imagery. What do the following phrases and lines add to the feeling and implications of the poem: "the warm evening," "my first house," "the summer moon riding / low over the old neighborhood," "the starlight," and "the promises / of autumn"?

Ideas for Writing

1. Write a poem or story about a time when you learned to understand something about your parents' values. Use concrete narrative devices such as setting, dialogue, and detailed, descriptive images.

2. Write an essay in which you discuss the importance of moments of intense communication between parents and children. Provide examples from your own family life, the families of friends, literature, or popular culture to support your insights.

 Lewis Carroll

Advice from a Caterpillar

Lewis Carroll is the pen name of Charles Dodgson (1832–1898), who was an ordained deacon and a mathematics professor at Oxford University. Lewis Carroll is best known for his dream fantasies, Alice in Wonderland *(1865), from which the following selection is excerpted, and* Through the Looking Glass *(1872). Both books were originally told to and written for Alice Liddell, the daughter of the dean of Christ Church College. Carroll plays with words to reveal the symbolic nature of language and exposes the fallacies of logic that are built on emotions. While Carroll writes about children and fantasy characters, he also captures the moods and passions of adult behavior. If you remember reading or hearing the original Alice stories as a child, or if you are familiar with the Disney version, you will be interested in contrasting your current response to this excerpt to your memories of the* Alice in Wonderland *version from your childhood.*

Discuss activities or strategies that helped you to develop a sense of confidence and control when you were a child.

1   The Caterpillar and Alice looked at each other for some time in silence: at last the Caterpillar took the hookah out of its mouth, and addressed her in a languid, sleepy voice.

2   "Who are *you?*" said the Caterpillar.

3   This was not an encouraging opening for a conversation. Alice replied, rather shyly, "I—I hardly know, Sir, just at present—at least I know who I *was* when I got up this morning, but I think I must have been changed several times since then."

4   "What do you mean by that?" said the Caterpillar, sternly. "Explain yourself!"

5   "I can't explain *myself*, I'm afraid, Sir," said Alice, "because I'm not myself, you see."

6   "I don't see," said the Caterpillar.

7   "I'm afraid I can't put it more clearly," Alice replied, very politely, "for I can't understand it myself, to begin with; and being so many different sizes in a day is very confusing."

8   "It isn't," said the Caterpillar.

9   "Well, perhaps you haven't found it so yet," said Alice; "but when you have to turn into a chrysalis—you will some day, you know—and then after that into a butterfly, I should think you'll feel it a little queer, won't you?"

10   "Not a bit," said the Caterpillar.

11   "Well, perhaps *your* feelings may be different," said Alice: "all I know is, it would feel very queer to *me*."

12   "You!" said the Caterpillar contemptuously. "Who are *you?*"

13   Which brought them back again to the beginning of the conversation. Alice felt a little irritated at the Caterpillar's making such *very* short remarks, and she drew herself up and said, very gravely, "I think you ought to tell me who *you* are, first."

14   "Why?" said the Caterpillar.

15   Here was another puzzling question; and, as Alice could not think of any good reason, and the Caterpillar seemed to be in a *very* unpleasant state of mind, she turned away.

16   "Come back!" the Caterpillar called after her. "I've something important to say!"

17   This sounded promising, certainly. Alice turned and came back again.

18   "Keep your temper," said the Caterpillar.

19   "Is that all?" said Alice, swallowing down her anger as well as she could.

20   "No," said the Caterpillar.

21   Alice thought she might as well wait, as she had nothing else to do, and perhaps after all it might tell her something worth hearing. For some minutes it puffed away without speaking; but at last it unfolded its arms, took the hookah out of its mouth again, and said, "So you think you're changed, do you?"

22   "I'm afraid I am, Sir," said Alice. "I can't remember things as I used—and I don't keep the same size for ten minutes together!"

23   "Can't remember *what* things?" said the Caterpillar.

24   "Well, I've tried to say '*How doth the little busy bee,*' but it all came different!" Alice replied in a very melancholy voice.

25   "Repeat '*You are old, Father William,*' " said the Caterpillar.

26   Alice folded her hands, and began:—

   " 'You are old, Father William,' the young man said,
     'And your hair has become very white;
And yet you incessantly stand on your head—
     Do you think, at your age, it is right?'

   " 'In my youth,' Father William replied to his son,
     'I feared it might injure the brain;
But, now that I'm perfectly sure I have none,
     Why, I do it again and again.'

   " 'You are old,' said the youth, 'as I mentioned before,
     And have grown most uncommonly fat;
Yet you turned a back-somersault in at the door—
     Pray, what is the reason of that?'

   " 'In my youth,' said the sage, as he shook his grey locks,
     'I kept all my limbs very supple
By the use of this ointment—one shilling the box—
     Allow me to sell you a couple?'

   " 'You are old,' said the youth, 'and your jaws are too weak
     For anything tougher than suet;
Yet you finished the goose, with the bones and the beak—
     Pray, how did you manage to do it?'

   " 'In my youth,' said the father, 'I took to the law,
     And argued each case with my wife;
And the muscular strength, which it gave to my jaw,
     Has lasted the rest of my life.'

   " 'You are old,' said the youth, 'one would hardly suppose
     That your eye was as steady as ever;

Yet you balanced an eel on the end of your nose—
　　What made you so awfully clever?'

" 'I have answered three questions, and that is enough.'
　　Said his father, 'Don't give yourself airs!
Do you think I can listen all day to such stuff?
　　Be off, or I'll kick you down-stairs!' "

27　　"That is not said right," said the Caterpillar.

28　　"Not *quite* right, I'm afraid," said Alice timidly: "some of the words have got altered."

29　　"It is wrong from beginning to end," said the Caterpillar, decidedly, and there was silence for some minutes.

30　　The Caterpillar was the first to speak.

31　　"What size do you want to be?" it asked.

32　　"Oh, I'm not particular as to size," Alice hastily replied; "only one doesn't like changing so often, you know."

33　　"I *don't* know," said the Caterpillar.

34　　Alice said nothing: she had never been so much contradicted in all her life before, and she felt that she was losing her temper.

35　　"Are you content now?" said the Caterpillar.

36　　"Well, I should like to be a *little* larger, Sir, if you wouldn't mind," said Alice: "three inches is such a wretched height to be."

37　　"It is a very good height indeed!" said the Caterpillar angrily, rearing itself upright as it spoke (it was exactly three inches high).

38　　"But I'm not used to it!" pleaded poor Alice in a piteous tone. And she thought to herself, "I wish the creatures wouldn't be so easily offended!"

39　　"You'll get used to it in time," said the Caterpillar; and it put the hookah into its mouth, and began smoking again.

40　　This time Alice waited patiently until it chose to speak again. In a minute or two the Caterpillar took the hookah out of its mouth, and yawned once or twice, and shook itself. Then it got down off the mushroom, and crawled away into the grass, merely remarking, as it went, "One side will make you grow taller, and the other side will make you grow shorter."

41　　"One side of *what*? The other side of *what*?" thought Alice to herself.

42　　"Of the mushroom," said the Caterpillar, just as if she had asked it aloud; and in another moment it was out of sight.

43　　Alice remained looking thoughtfully at the mushroom for a minute, trying to make out which were the two sides of it; and, as it was perfectly round, she found this a very difficult question. However, at last she stretched her arms round it as far as they would go, and broke off a bit of the edge with each hand.

44　　"And now which is which?" she said to herself, and nibbled a little of the right-hand bit to try the effect. The next moment she felt a violent blow underneath her chin: it had struck her foot!

45　　She was a good deal frightened by this very sudden change, but she felt that there was no time to be lost, as she was shrinking rapidly; so she set to work at once to eat some of the other bit. Her chin was pressed so closely against her foot, that there was hardly room to open her mouth; but she did it at last, and managed to swallow a morsel of the left-hand bit.

46 "Come, my head's free at last!" said Alice in a tone of delight, which changed into alarm in another moment, when she found that her shoulders were nowhere to be found: all she could see, when she looked down, was an immense length of neck, which seemed to rise like a stalk out of a sea of green leaves that lay far below her.

47 "What *can* all that green stuff be?" said Alice. "And where *have* my shoulders got to? And oh, my poor hands, how is it I can't see you?" She was moving them about as she spoke, but no result seemed to follow, except a little shaking among the distant green leaves.

48 As there seemed to be no chance of getting her hands up to her head, she tried to get her head down to *them,* and was delighted to find that her neck would bend about easily in any direction, like a serpent. She had just succeeded in curving it down into a graceful zigzag, and was going to dive in among the leaves, which she found to be nothing but the tops of the trees under which she had been wandering, when a sharp hiss made her draw back in a hurry: a large pigeon had flown into her face, and was beating her violently with its wings.

49 "Serpent!" screamed the Pigeon.

50 "I'm *not* a serpent!" said Alice indignantly. "Let me alone!"

51 "Serpent, I say again!" repeated the Pigeon, but in a more subdued tone, and added, with a kind of sob, "I've tried every way, but nothing seems to suit them!"

52 "I haven't the least idea what you're talking about," said Alice.

53 "I've tried the roots of trees, and I've tried banks, and I've tried hedges," the Pigeon went on, without attending to her; "but those serpents! There's no pleasing them!"

54 Alice was more and more puzzled, but she thought there was no use in saying anything more till the Pigeon had finished.

55 "As if it wasn't trouble enough hatching the eggs," said the Pigeon; "but I must be on the look-out for serpents, night and day! Why, I haven't had a wink of sleep these three weeks!"

56 "I'm very sorry you've been annoyed," said Alice, who was beginning to see its meaning.

57 "And just as I'd taken the highest tree in the wood," continued the Pigeon, raising its voice to a shriek, "and just as I was thinking I should be free of them at last, they must needs come wriggling down from the sky! Ugh, Serpent!"

58 "But I'm *not* a serpent, I tell you!" said Alice. "I'm a—I'm a——"

59 "Well! *What* are you?" said the Pigeon. "I can see you're trying to invent something!"

60 "I—I'm a little girl," said Alice, rather doubtfully, as she remembered the number of changes she had gone through that day.

61 "A likely story indeed!" said the Pigeon, in a tone of the deepest contempt. "I've seen a good many little girls in my time, but never *one* with such a neck as

that! No, no! You're a serpent; and there's no use denying it. I suppose you'll be telling me next that you never tasted an egg!"

62   "I *have* tasted eggs, certainly," said Alice, who was a very truthful child; "but little girls eat eggs quite as much as serpents do, you know."

63   "I don't believe it," said the Pigeon; "but if they do, why, then they're a kind of serpent: that's all I can say."

64   This was such a new idea to Alice, that she was quite silent for a minute or two, which gave the Pigeon the opportunity of adding, "You're looking for eggs, I know *that* well enough; and what does it matter to me whether you're a little girl or a serpent?"

65   "It matters a good deal to *me*," said Alice hastily; "but I'm not looking for eggs, as it happens; and, if I was, I shouldn't want *yours*: I don't like them raw."

66   "Well, be off, then!" said the Pigeon in a sulky tone, as it settled down again into its nest. Alice crouched down among the trees as well as she could, for her neck kept getting entangled among the branches, and every now and then she had to stop and untwist it. After a while she remembered that she still held the pieces of mushroom in her hands, and she set to work very carefully, nibbling first at one and then at the other, and growing sometimes taller, and sometimes shorter, until she had succeeded in bringing herself down to her usual height.

67   It was so long since she had been anything near the right size, that it felt quite strange at first; but she got used to it in a few minutes, and began talking to herself, as usual, "Come, there's half my plan done now! How puzzling all these changes are! I'm never sure what I'm going to be, from one minute to another! However, I've got back to my right size: the next thing is, to get into that beautiful garden—how *is* that to be done, I wonder?" As she said this, she came suddenly upon an open place, with a little house in it about four feet high. "Whoever lives there," thought Alice, "it'll never do to come upon them *this* size: why, I should frighten them out of their wits!" So she began nibbling at the right-hand bit again, and did not venture to go near the house till she had brought herself down to nine inches high.

Questions for Discussion

1. Alice is dreaming about her adventure. What aspects of this episode seem dreamlike? Why does Alice feel unsure of herself? Is it only because she is caught in a dream?

2. Why does Alice think that her situation is similar to the caterpillar's? In what ways is her observation accurate? Contrast the caterpillar's personality with Alice's. Why does the caterpillar think that Alice should be content with being three inches tall?

3. What are the sources of humor in this selection?

4. Why is the caterpillar's gift of the mushroom a puzzle as well as an aid to Alice? How does Alice learn to make use of the mushroom?

5. Carroll plays with perspective and size relationships through his images of Alice's changing size. How does Carroll's use of detail and language help him to create vivid images of size and contrasting perspective?

6. What is the relationship between Alice's two encounters in this chapter? What has Alice learned? What has the reader learned? What organization strategies does Carroll employ?

Ideas for Writing

1. Write about an incident from your childhood that this narrative helps you to recall. In your conclusion explain the relationship between your memory and this selection as you understand it.
2. Write a short dream narrative using this scene as a model or as an inspiration.

 Stephen Jay Gould

Muller Bros. Moving & Storage

A professor of biology, geology, and the history of science at Harvard University, Stephen Jay Gould (b. 1941) is well known for his views on evolution, creationism, and race. He is widely read by thinkers in many different disciplines as his works often point out relationships between scientific and humanistic thought, making technical subjects understandable to nonscientific readers. Gould has been the recipient of a number of distinguished awards, including grants from the National Science Foundation and the MacArthur Foundation. Gould has written many essays; his most recent collections are Panda's Thumb *(1991) and Di-nosaur in a Haystack (1996). As you read the following essay, which first appeared in* Natural History Magazine *(1990), notice how Gould shows his readers the limitations of factual recall in memories while illustrating the emotional power that recollections of the past can have in shaping an individual's values.*

JOURNAL

Write about a possession a relative gave you that you cherish for the memories it embodies.

1   I own many old and beautiful books, classics of natural history bound in leather and illustrated with hand-colored plates. But no item in my collection comes close in personal value to a modest volume, bound in gray cloth and published in 1892: "Studies of English Grammar," by J.M. Greenwood, superintendent of

schools in Kansas City. The book belonged to my grandfather, a Hungarian immigrant. He wrote on the title page, in an elegant European hand: "Prop. of Joseph A. Rosenberg, New York." Just underneath, he added in pencil the most eloquent of all possible lines: "I have landed. Sept. 11, 1901."

2   Papa Joe died when I was 13, before I could properly distill his deepest experiences, but long enough into my own ontogeny for the precious gifts of extensive memory and lasting influence. He was a man of great artistic sensibility and limited opportunity for expression. I am told that he sang beautifully as a young man, although increasing deafness and a pledge to the memory of his mother (never to sing again after her death) stilled his voice long before my birth.

3   He never used his remarkable talent for drawing in any effort of fine arts, although he marshaled these skills to rise from cloth-cutting in the sweatshops to middle-class life as a brassiere and corset designer. (The content of his chosen expression titillated me as a child, but I now appreciate the primary theme of economic emancipation through the practical application of artistic talent.)

4   Yet, above all, he expressed his artistic sensibilities in his personal bearing—in elegance of dress (a bit on the foppish side, perhaps), grace of movement, beauty of handwriting, ease of mannerism.

5   I well remember one manifestation of this rise above the ordinary—both because we repeated the act every week and because the junction of locale and action seemed so incongruous, even to a small child of 5 or 6. Every Sunday morning, Papa Joe and I would take a stroll to the corner store on Queens Boulevard to buy the paper and a half dozen bagels. We then walked to the great world-class tennis stadium of Forest Hills, where McEnroe and his ilk still cavort. A decrepit and disused side entrance sported a rusty staircase of three or four steps.

6   With his unfailing deftness, Papa Joe would take a section of the paper that we never read and neatly spread several sheets over the lowermost step (for the thought of a rust flake or speck of dust in contact with his trousers filled him with horror). We would then sit down and have the most wonderful man-to-man talk about the latest baseball scores, the rules of poker, or the results of the Friday night fights.

7   I retain a beautiful vision of this scene: The camera pans back and we see a tiny staircase, increasingly dwarfed by the great stadium. Two little figures sit on the bottom step—a well-dressed, elderly man gesturing earnestly; a little boy listening with adoration.

8   Certainty is both a blessing and a danger. Certainty provides warmth, solace, security—an anchor in the unambiguously factual events of personal observation and experience. I know that I sat on those steps with my grandfather because I was there, and no external power of suggestion has ever played havoc with this most deeply personal and private experience. But certainty is also a great danger, given the notorious fallibility—and unrivaled power—of the human mind. How often have we killed on vast scales for the "certainties" of nationhood and religion; how often have we condemned the innocent because the most prestigious form of supposed certainty—eyewitness testimony—bears all the flaws of our ordinary fallibility.

9   Primates are visual animals *par excellence,* and we therefore grant special status to personal observation—to being there and seeing directly. But all sights must be registered in the brain and stored somehow in its intricate memory. And the human mind is both the greatest marvel of nature and the most perverse of all tricksters; Einstein and Loge inextricably combined.

10   This special (but unwarranted) prestige accorded to direct observation has led to a serious popular misunderstanding about science. Since science is often regarded as the most objective and truth-directed of human enterprises, and since direct observation is supposed to be the favored route to factuality, many people equate respectable science with visual scrutiny—just the facts, ma'am, and palpably before my eyes.

11   But science is a battery of observational and inferential methods, all directed to the testing of propositions that can, in principle, be definitely proved false. A restriction of compass to matters of direct observation would stymie the profession intolerably. Science must often transcend sight to win insight. At all scales, from smallest to largest, quickest to slowest, many well-documented conclusions of science lie beyond the limited domain of direct observation. No one has ever seen an electron or a black hole, the events of picosecond or a geological eon.

12   One of the phoniest arguments raised for rhetorical effect by "creation scientists" tried to deny scientific status to evolution because its results take so much time to unfold and therefore can't be seen directly. But if science required such immediate vision, we could draw no conclusion about any subject that studies the past—no geology, no cosmology, no human history (including the strength and influence of religion), for that matter.

13   We can, after all, be reasonably sure that Henry V prevailed at Agincourt even though no photos exist and no one has survived more than 500 years to tell the tale. And dinosaurs really did snuff it tens of millions of years before any conscious observer inhabited our planet. Evolution suffers no special infirmity as a science because its grandest-scale results took so long to unfold during an unobservable past. (The small-scale results of agriculture and domestication have been recorded, and adequate evidence survives to document the broader events of a distant past.) The sciences of history rely on our ability to infer the past from signs of ancestry preserved in modern structures—as in the "panda's thumb" principle of current imperfection preserved as a legacy of ancestral inheritances originally evolved for different purposes.

14   Moreover, eyewitness accounts do not deserve their conventional status as ultimate arbiters even when testimony of direct observation can be marshaled in abundance. In her sobering book, "Eyewitness Testimony" (Harvard University Press, 1979), Elizabeth Loftus debunks, largely in a legal context, the notion that visual observation confers some special claim for veracity. She identifies three levels of potential error in supposedly direct and objective vision: misperception of the event itself and the two great tricksters of passage through memory before later disgorgement—retention and retrieval.

15   In one experiment, for example, Loftus showed 40 students a three-minute videotape of a classroom lecture disrupted by 8 demonstrators (a relevant subject for a study from the early 1970s!). She gave the students a questionnaire and asked

half of them: "Was the leader of the 12 demonstrators . . . a male?" and the other half, "Was the leader of the 4 demonstrators . . . a male?" One week later, in a follow-up questionnaire, she asked all the students: "How many demonstrators did you see entering the classroom?" Those who had previously received the question about 12 demonstrators reported seeing an average of 8.9 people; those told of 4 demonstrators claimed an average of 6.4. All had actually seen 8, but compromised later judgment between their actual observation and the largely subliminal power of suggestion in the first questionnaire.

16   People can even be induced to "see" totally illusory objects. In another experiment, Loftus showed a film of an accident, followed by a misleading question: "How fast was the white sports car going when it passed the barn while traveling along the country road?" (The film showed no barn, and a control group received a more accurate question: "How fast was the white sports car going while traveling along the country road?") A week later, 17 percent of the students in the first group stated that they had seen the nonexistent barn; only 3 percent of the control group reported a barn.

17   Thus, we are easily fooled on all fronts of both eye and mind: seeing, storing and recalling. The eye tricks us badly enough; the mind is infinitely more perverse. What remedy can we possibly have but constant humility, and eternal vigilance and scrutiny? Trust your memory as you would your poker buddy (one of my grandfather's mottoes from the steps).

18   With this principle in mind, I went searching for those steps last year after more than 30 years of absence from my natal turf. I exited the subway at 67th Avenue, walked to my first apartment at 98–50, and then set off on my grandfather's route for Queens Boulevard and the tennis stadium.

19   I was walking in the right direction, but soon realized that I had made a serious mistake. The tennis stadium stood at least a mile down the road, too far for those short strolls with a bag of bagels in one hand and a 5-year-old boy attached to the other. In increasing puzzlement, I walked down the street and, at the very next corner, saw the steps and felt the jolt and flood of memory that drives our *recherches du temps perdus*.

20   My recall of the steps was entirely accurate—three modest flagstone rungs, bordered by rusty iron railings. But the steps are not attached to the tennis stadium; they form the side entrance to a modest brick building, now crumbling, padlocked, and abandoned, but still announcing its former use with a commercial sign, painted directly on the brick in the old industrial style: "Muller Bros. Inc. Moving & Storage"—with a telephone number below from the age before all-digit dialing: ILlinois 9–9200.

21   Obviously, I had conflated the most prominent symbol of my old neighborhood, the tennis stadium, with an important personal place—and had constructed a juxtaposed hybrid for my mental image. Yet even now, in the face of conclusive correction, my memory of the tennis stadium soaring above the steps remains strong.

22   I might ask indulgence on the grounds of inexperience and relative youth for my failure as an eyewitness at the Muller Bros. steps. After all, I was only an im-

pressionable lad of 5 or so, when even a modest six-story warehouse might be perceived as big enough to conflate with something truly important.

23   But I have no excuses for a second story. Ten years later, at a trustable age of 15, I made a western trip by automobile with my family; I have specially vivid memories of an observation at Devils Tower, Wyoming (the volcanic plug made most famous as a landing site for aliens in "Close Encounters of the Third Kind"). We approach from the east. My father tells us to look out for the tower from tens of miles away, for he has read in a guidebook that it rises, with an awesome near-verticality, from the dead-flat Great Plains—and that pioneer families used the tower as a landmark and beacon on their westward trek.

24   We see the tower, first as a tiny projection, almost square in outline, at the horizon. It gets larger as we approach, assuming its distinctive form and finally revealing its structure as a conjoined mat of hexagonal basalt columns. I have never forgotten the two features that inspired my rapt attention: the maximal rise of verticality from flatness, forming a perpendicular junction; and the steady increase in size from a bump on the horizon to a looming, almost fearful giant of a rock pile.

25   Now I know, I absolutely *know*, that I saw this visual drama, as described. The picture in my mind of that distinctive profile, growing in size, is as strong as any memory I possess. I see the tower as a little dot in the distance, as a mid-sized monument, as a full field of view. I have told the story to scores of people, comparing this natural reality with a sight of Chartres as a tiny toy tower 20 miles from Paris, growing to the overarching symbol and skyline of its medieval city.

26   In 1987, I revisited Devils Tower with my family—the only return since my first close encounter 30 years before. I planned the trip to approach from the east, so that they would see the awesome effect—and I told them my story, of course.

27   In the context of this essay, my denouement will be anticlimactic in its predictability, however acute my personal embarrassment. The terrain around Devils Tower is mountainous; the monument cannot be seen from more than a few miles away in any direction. I bought a booklet on pioneer trails westward, and none passed anywhere near Devils Tower. We enjoyed our visit, but I felt like a perfect fool. Later, I checked my old logbook for that high-school trip. The monument that rises from the plain, the beacon of the pioneers, is Scotts Bluff, Nebraska—not nearly so impressive a pile of stone as Devils Tower.

28   And yet I still see Devils Tower in my mind when I think of that growing dot on the horizon. I see it as clearly and as surely as ever, although I now know that the memory is false.

29   This has been a long story for a simple moral. Papa Joe, the wise old peasant in a natty and elegant business suit, told me on those steps to be wary of all blandishments and to trust nothing that cannot be proved. We must extend his good counsel to our own interior certainties, particularly those we never question because we regard eyewitnessing as paramount in veracity.

30   Of course we must treat the human mind with respect—for nature has fashioned no more admirable instrument. But we must also struggle to stand back and to scrutinize our own mental certainties. This last line poses an obvious paradox, if

not an outright contradiction—and I have no solution to offer. Yes, step back and scrutinize your own mind. But with what?

Questions for Discussion

1. Why is "Studies in English Grammar" Gould's most valued possession? Why was this book also cherished by Gould's grandfather?
2. Why does Gould remember his Sunday morning breakfasts with Papa Joe? Why does Gould admire his grandfather?
3. Gould is skeptical of the accuracy of direct visual observation. What evidence does he present to support his point of view?
4. Gould is also skeptical of the accuracy of memory. Why do the subjects in the experiments he discusses come to different conclusions about what they saw and what they remembered?
5. When Gould goes back after thirty years to the place where he and Papa Joe had breakfast, what does Gould realize about his memory? Why does he still value his memory, despite its distortions? How does Gould's inaccurate recall of Devils Tower support the premise developed in his earlier example?
6. How does Gould effectively relate his personal experiences to broader scientific issues involving the past and observation?

Ideas for Writing

1. Develop your journal assignment into an essay in which you discuss how the memory you have of a relative is connected to and influenced by a physical possession that you keep to remind yourself of the relative. What feelings and values do you associate with the possession?
2. Write an essay in which you discuss the implications of the paradox Gould presents at the end of the essay: "Step back and scrutinize your own mind. But with what?" How can people become better at reflecting on and clarifying the memories and perceptions that they bring with them from their pasts?

 bell hooks

Writing Autobiography

bell hooks is the pen name for Gloria Watkins (b. 1952). She studied at Stanford University and currently teaches English and African American Literature at Oberlin College in Ohio. hooks has written several books including the autobiographical Ain't I a Woman *(1981) and the essay collections* Talking Back, Thinking Feminist, Thinking Black *(1989),* Yearning: Race, Gender, and Cultural Politics *(1990),* Black Looks: Race and Representation *(1992), and*

Killing Rage (1995). In writing about cultural, gender, and ethnic issues, hooks always reflects deeply on her own experiences. As you read the following selection from Talking Back, *notice how hooks emphasizes the role that pain and memory play in the writing process, as well as how writing can be a healing experience.*

JOURNAL

Write about an important memory that you have never written about. How was your understanding of the memory changed by writing about it?

1   To me, telling the story of my growing up years was intimately connected with the longing to kill the self I was without really having to die. I wanted to kill that self in writing. Once that self was gone—out of my life forever—I could more easily become the me of me. It was clearly the Gloria Jean of my tormented and anguished childhood that I wanted to be rid of, the girl who was always wrong, always punished, always subjected to some humiliation or other, always crying, the girl who was to end up in a mental institution because she could not be anything but crazy, or so they told her. She was the girl who sat a hot iron on her arm pleading with them to leave her alone, the girl who wore her scar as a brand marking her madness. Even now I can hear the voices of my sisters saying "mama make Gloria stop crying." By writing the autobiography, it was not just this Gloria I would be rid of, but the past that had a hold on me, that kept me from the present. I wanted not to forget the past but to break its hold. This death in writing was to be liberatory.

2   Until I began to try and write an autobiography, I thought that it would be a simple task this telling of one's story. And yet I tried year after year, never writing more than a few pages. My inability to write out the story I interpreted as an indication that I was not ready to let go of the past, that I was not ready to be fully in the present. Psychologically, I considered the possibility that I had become attached to the wounds and sorrows of my childhood, that I held to them in a manner that blocked my efforts to be self-realized, whole, to be healed. A key message in Toni Cade Bambara's novel *The Salteaters*, which tells the story of Velma's suicide attempt, her breakdown, is expressed when the healer asks her "are you sure sweetheart, that you want to be well?"

3   There was very clearly something blocking my ability to tell my story. Perhaps it was remembered scoldings and punishments when mama heard me saying something to a friend or stranger that she did not think should be said. Secrecy and silence—these were central issues. Secrecy about family, about what went on in the domestic household was a bond between us—was part of what made us family. There was a dread one felt about breaking that bond. And yet I could not grow inside the atmosphere of secrecy that had pervaded our lives and the lives of other families about us. Strange that I had always challenged the secrecy, always let

something slip that should not be known growing up, yet as a writer staring into the solitary space of paper, I was bound, trapped in the fear that a bond is lost or broken in the telling. I did not want to be the traitor, the teller of family secrets—and yet I wanted to be a writer. Surely, I told myself, I could write a purely imaginative work—a work that would not hint at personal private realities. And so I tried. But always there were the intruding traces, those elements of real life however disguised. Claiming the freedom to grow as an imaginative writer was connected for me with having the courage to open, to be able to tell the truth of one's life as I had experienced it in writing. To talk about one's life—that I could do. To write about it, to leave a trace—that was frightening.

4   The longer it took me to begin the process of writing autobiography, the further removed from those memories I was becoming. Each year, a memory seemed less and less clear. I wanted not to lose the vividness, the recall and felt an urgent need to begin the work and complete it. Yet I could not begin even though I had begun to confront some of the reasons I was blocked, as I am blocked just now in writing this piece because I am afraid to express in writing the experience that served as a catalyst for that block to move.

5   I had met a young black man. We were having an affair. It is important that he was black. He was in some mysterious way a link to this past that I had been struggling to grapple with, to name in writing. With him I remembered incidents, moments of the past that I had completely suppressed. It was as though there was something about the passion of contact that was hypnotic, that enabled me to drop barriers and thus enter fully, rather re-enter those past experiences. A key aspect seemed to be the way he smelled, the combined odors of cigarettes, occasionally alcohol, and his body smells. I thought often of the phrase "scent of memory," for it was those smells that carried me back. And there were specific occasions when it was very evident that the experience of being in his company was the catalyst for this remembering.

6   Two specific incidents come to mind. One day in the middle of the afternoon we met at his place. We were drinking cognac and dancing to music from the radio. He was smoking cigarettes (not only do I not smoke, but I usually make an effort to avoid smoke). As we held each other dancing those mingled odors of alcohol, sweat, and cigarettes led me to say, quite without thinking about it, "Uncle Pete." It was not that I had forgotten Uncle Pete. It was more that I had forgotten the childhood experience of meeting him. He drank often, smoked cigarettes, and always on the few occasions that we met him, he held us children in tight embraces. It was the memory of those embraces—of the way I hated and longed to resist them—that I recalled.

7   Another day we went to a favorite park to feed ducks and parked the car in front of tall bushes. As we were sitting there, we suddenly heard the sound of an oncoming train—a sound which startled me so that it evoked another long-suppressed memory: that of crossing the train tracks in my father's car. I recalled an incident where the car stopped on the tracks and my father left us sitting there while he raised the hood of the car and worked to repair it. This is an incident that I am not certain actually happened. As a child, I had been terrified of just

such an incident occurring, perhaps so terrified that it played itself out in my mind as though it had happened. These are just two ways this encounter acted as a catalyst breaking down barriers enabling me to finally write this long-desired autobiography of my childhood.

8   Each day I sat at the typewriter and different memories were written about in short vignettes. They came in a rush, as though they were a sudden thunderstorm. They came in a surreal, dreamlike style which made me cease to think of them as strictly autobiographical because it seemed that myth, dream, and reality had merged. There were many incidents that I would talk about with my siblings to see if they recalled them. Often we remembered together a general outline of an incident but the details were different for us. This fact was a constant reminder of the limitations of autobiography, of the extent to which autobiography is a very personal story telling—a unique recounting of events not so much as they had happened but as we remember and invent them. One memory that I would have sworn was "the truth and nothing but the truth" concerned a wagon that my brother and I shared as a child. I remembered that we played with this toy only at my grandfather's house, that we shared it, that I would ride it and my brother would push me. Yet one facet of the memory was puzzling, I remembered always returning home with bruises or scratches from this toy. When I called my mother, she said there had never been any wagon, that we had shared a red wheelbarrow, that it had always been at my grandfather's house because there were sidewalks on that part of town. We lived in the hills where there were no sidewalks. Again I was compelled to face the fiction that is a part of all retelling, remembering. I began to think of the work I was doing as both fiction and autobiography. It seemed to fall in the category of writing that Audre Lorde, in her autobiographically-based work *Zami*, calls bio-mythography. As I wrote, I felt that I was not as concerned with accuracy of detail as I was with evoking in writing the state of mind, the spirit of a particular moment.

9   The longing to tell one's story and the process of telling is symbolically a gesture of longing to recover the past in such a way that one experiences both a sense of reunion and a sense of release. It was the longing for release that compelled the writing but concurrently it was the joy of reunion that enabled me to see that the act of writing one's autobiography is a way to find again that aspect of self and experience that may no longer be an actual part of one's life but is a living memory shaping and informing the present. Autobiographical writing was a way for me to evoke the particular experience of growing up southern and black in segregated communities. It was a way to recapture the richness of southern black culture. The need to remember and hold to the legacy of that experience and what it taught me has been all the more important since I have since lived in predominately white communities and taught at predominately white colleges. Black southern folk experience was the foundation of the life around me when I was a child; that experience no longer exists in many places where it was once all of life that we knew. Capitalism, upward mobility, assimilation of other values have all led to rapid disintegration of black folk experience or in some cases the gradual wearing away of that experience.

10   Within the world of my childhood, we held onto the legacy of a distinct black culture by listening to the elders tell their stories. Autobiography was experienced most actively in the art of telling one's story. I can recall sitting at Baba's (my grandmother on my mother's side) at 1200 Broad Street—listening to people come and recount their life experience. In those days, whenever I brought a playmate to my grandmother's house, Baba would want a brief outline of their autobiography before we would begin playing. She wanted not only to know who their people were but what their values were. It was sometimes an awesome and terrifying experience to stand answering these questions or witness another playmate being subjected to the process and yet this was the way we would come to know our own and one another's family history. It is the absence of such a tradition in my adult life that makes the written narrative of my girlhood all the more important. As the years pass and these glorious memories grow much more vague, there will remain the clarity contained within the written words.

11   Conceptually, the autobiography was framed in the manner of a hope chest. I remembered my mother's hope chest, with its wonderful odor of cedar and thought about her taking the most precious items and placing them there for safekeeping. Certain memories were for me a similar treasure. I wanted to place them somewhere for safekeeping. An autobiographical narrative seemed an appropriate place. Each particular incident, encounter, experience had its own story, sometimes told from the first person, sometimes told from the third person. Often I felt as though I was in a trance at my typewriter, that the shape of a particular memory was decided not by my conscious mind but by all that is dark and deep within me, unconscious but present. It was the act of making it present, bringing it into the open, so to speak, that was liberating.

12   From the perspective of trying to understand my psyche, it was also interesting to read the narrative in its entirety after I had completed the work. It had not occurred to me that bringing one's past, one's memories together in a complete narrative would allow one to view them from a different perspective, not as singular isolated events but as part of a continuum. Reading the completed manuscript, I felt as though I had an overview not so much of my childhood but of those experiences that were deeply imprinted in my consciousness. Significantly, that which was absent, left out, not included also was important. I was shocked to find at the end of my narrative that there were few incidents I recalled that involved my five sisters. Most of the incidents with siblings were with me and my brother. There was a sense of alienation from my sisters present in childhood, a sense of estrangement. This was reflected in the narrative. Another aspect of the completed manuscript that is interesting to me is the way in which the incidents describing adult men suggest that I feared them intensely, with the exception of my grandfather and a few old men. Writing the autobiographical narrative enabled me to look at my past from a different perspective and to use this knowledge as a means of self-growth and change in a practical way.

13   In the end I did not feel as though I had killed the Gloria of my childhood. Instead I had rescued her. She was no longer the enemy within, the little girl who

had to be annihilated for the woman to come into being. In writing about her, I reclaimed that part of myself I had long ago rejected, left uncared for, just as she had often felt alone and uncared for as a child. Remembering was part of a cycle of reunion, a joining of fragments, "the bits and pieces of my heart" that the narrative made whole again.

Questions for Discussion

1. "To me, telling the story of my growing up years was intimately connected with the longing to kill the self I was without really having to die." What was your initial response to hooks's opening sentence? After reading the entire essay, go back and reinterpret the meaning of the statement.

2. Why is it difficult for hooks to write her autobiography? What helps her to get beyond her writer's block? Do you think that her technique might help you? Will you try it?

3. How does hooks experience the recollection of her memories? What specific events, sensations, and images in the present helped her to recall past memories? Have you experienced the recall of memories in similar ways? What helps you to get in touch with your memories?

4. Why does hooks believe that autobiography involves invention and imagination as well as the reporting of events? Do you agree with her? Why or why not?

5. hooks writes, "Often I felt as though I was in a trance at my typewriter, that the shape of a particular memory was decided not by my conscious mind but by all that is dark and deep within me, unconscious but present." Have you ever experienced writing in this way?

6. hooks describes the influence that the legacy of African American oral storytelling had on her ability to frame her past experiences in writing. Was there a similar type of legacy in your own family? If so, do you think that you could draw on it as a source for your writing?

Ideas for Writing

1. Write about an incident from your past about which you still have mixed feelings, a part of the past you still don't quite understand or to which you don't yet feel reconciled. Compare your experiences of self-understanding with those that hooks experienced in writing her autobiography. How did your feelings toward the material you were writing about change in the course of doing the writing? What did you learn about the event and yourself in the writing process?

2. hooks discusses her writer's block and how she works through it. Develop an essay that explores the topic of writer's block. Present some strategies for overcoming the problem that have worked for you or for other writers.

❋ # Maya Angelou

The Angel of the Candy Counter

Maya Angelou (b. 1928) grew up in Stamps, Arkansas, where she spent her childhood with her grandmother, a storekeeper and leader in the African American community of Stamps. Angelou has worked as a dancer, actress, teacher, and screenwriter. She has lectured all over the world, speaking as an advocate of civil rights. Angelou's most recent work, Wouldn't Take Nothing for My Journey Now (1993) became a best seller on publication. She is also a professor of American Studies at Wake Forest University. Her autobiographical writings reflect on the impact of poverty and racism on the black community, as well as on those moments of joy, insight, and creative expression that sometimes can ease the pain of oppression. In the following selection excerpted from the first book of her memoir, I Know Why the Caged Bird Sings (1970), Angelou remembers the fierce courage and determination of her grandmother.

JOURNAL

Write about an event in your childhood when you experienced rejection, humiliation, and/or prejudice. Did understanding the incident help you to develop a deeper sense of self-respect and courage.

1   The Angel of the candy counter had found me out at last, and was exacting excruciating penance for all the stolen Milky Ways, Mounds, Mr. Goodbars and Hersheys with Almonds. I had two cavities that were rotten to the gums. The pain was beyond the bailiwick of crushed aspirins or oil of cloves. Only one thing could help me, so I prayed earnestly that I'd be allowed to sit under the house and have the building collapse on my left jaw. Since there was no Negro dentist in Stamps, nor doctor either, for that matter, Momma had dealt with previous toothaches by pulling them out (a string tied to the tooth with the other end looped over her fist), pain killers and prayer. In this particular instance the medicine had proved ineffective; there wasn't enough enamel left to hook a string on, and the prayers were being ignored because the Balancing Angel was blocking their passage.

2   I lived a few days and nights in blinding pain, not so much toying with as seriously considering the idea of jumping in the well, and Momma decided I had to be taken to a dentist. The nearest Negro dentist was in Texarkana, twenty-five miles away, and I was certain that I'd be dead long before we reached half the distance. Momma said we'd go to Dr. Lincoln, right in Stamps, and he'd take care of me. She said he owed her a favor.

3   I knew that there were a number of whitefolks in town that owed her favors. Bailey and I had seen the books which showed how she had lent money to Blacks and whites alike during the Depression, and most still owed her. But I couldn't

aptly remember seeing Dr. Lincoln's name, nor had I ever heard of a Negro's going to him as a patient. However, Momma said we were going, and put water on the stove for our baths. I had never been to a doctor, so she told me that after the bath (which would make my mouth feel better) I had to put on freshly starched and ironed underclothes from inside out. The ache failed to respond to the bath, and I knew then that the pain was more serious than that which anyone had ever suffered.

4   Before we left the Store, she ordered me to brush my teeth and then wash my mouth with Listerine. The idea of even opening my clamped jaws increased the pain, but upon her explanation that when you go to a doctor you have to clean yourself all over, but most especially the part that's to be examined, I screwed up my courage and unlocked my teeth. The cool air in my mouth and the jarring of my molars dislodged what little remained of my reason. I had frozen to the pain, my family nearly had to tie me down to take the toothbrush away. It was no small effort to get me started on the road to the dentist. Momma spoke to all the passersby, but didn't stop to chat. She explained over her shoulder that we were going to the doctor and she'd "pass the time of day" on our way home.

5   Until we reached the pond the pain was my world, an aura that haloed me for three feet around. Crossing the bridge into whitefolks' country, pieces of sanity pushed themselves forward. I had to stop moaning and start walking straight. The white towel, which was drawn under my chin and tied over my head, had to be arranged. If one was dying, it had to be done in style if the dying took place in whitefolks' part of town.

6   On the other side of the bridge the ache seemed to lessen as if a whitebreeze blew off the whitefolks and cushioned everything in their neighborhood—including my jaw. The gravel road was smoother, the stones smaller and the tree branches hung down around the path and nearly covered us. If the pain didn't diminish then, the familiar yet strange sights hypnotized me into believing that it had.

7   But my head continued to throb with the measured insistence of a bass drum, and how could a toothache pass the calaboose, hear the songs of the prisoners, their blues and laughter, and not be changed? How could one or two or even a mouthful of angry tooth roots meet a wagonload of powhitetrash children, endure their idiotic snobbery and not feel less important?

8   Behind the building which housed the dentist's office ran a small path used by servants and those tradespeople who catered to the butcher and Stamps' one restaurant. Momma and I followed that lane to the backstairs of Dentist Lincoln's office. The sun was bright and gave the day a hard reality as we climbed up the steps to the second floor.

9   Momma knocked on the back door and a young white girl opened it to show surprise at seeing us there. Momma said she wanted to see Dentist Lincoln and to tell him Annie was there. The girl closed the door firmly. Now the humiliation of hearing Momma describe herself as if she had no last name to the young white girl was equal to the physical pain. It seemed terribly unfair to have a toothache and a headache and have to bear at the same time the heavy burden of Blackness.

10   It was always possible that the teeth would quiet down and maybe drop out of their own accord. Momma said we would wait. We leaned in the harsh sunlight on the shaky railings of the dentist's back porch for over an hour.

11   He opened the door and looked at Momma. "Well, Annie, what can I do for you?"

12   He didn't see the towel around my jaw or notice my swollen face.

13   Momma said, "Dentist Lincoln. It's my grandbaby here. She got two rotten teeth that's giving her a fit."

14   She waited for him to acknowledge the truth of her statement. He made no comment, orally or facially.

15   "She had this toothache purt' near four days now, and today I said, 'Young lady, you going to the Dentist.'"

16   "Annie?"

17   "Yes, sir, Dentist Lincoln."

18   He was choosing words the way people hunt for shells. "Annie, you know I don't treat nigra, colored people."

19   "I know, Dentist Lincoln. But this here is just my little grandbaby, and she ain't gone be no trouble to you . . . "

20   "Annie, everybody has a policy. In this world you have to have a policy. Now, my policy is I don't treat colored people."

21   The sun had baked the oil out of Momma's skin and melted the Vaseline in her hair. She shone greasily as she leaned out of the dentist's shadow.

22   "Seem like to me, Dentist Lincoln, you might look after her, she ain't nothing but a little mite. And seems like maybe you owe me a favor or two."

23   He reddened slightly. "Favor or no favor. The money has all been repaid to you and that's the end of it. Sorry, Annie." He had his hand on the doorknob. "Sorry." His voice was a bit kinder on the second "Sorry," as if he really was.

24   Momma said, "I wouldn't press on you like this for myself but I can't take No. Not for my grandbaby. When you come to borrow my money you didn't have to beg. You asked me, and I lent it. Now, it wasn't my policy. I ain't no moneylender, but you stood to lose this building and I tried to help you out."

25   "It's been paid, and raising your voice won't make me change my mind. My policy . . . " He let go of the door and stepped nearer Momma. The three of us were crowded on the small landing. "Annie, my policy is I'd rather stick my hand in a dog's mouth than in a nigger's."

26   He had never once looked at me. He turned his back and went through the door into the cool beyond. Momma backed up inside herself for a few minutes. I forget everything except her face which was almost a new one to me. She leaned over and took the doorknob, and in her everyday soft voice she said, "Sister, go on downstairs. Wait for me. I'll be there directly."

27   Under the most common of circumstances I knew it did no good to argue with Momma. So I walked down the steep stairs, afraid to look back and afraid not to do so. I turned as the door slammed, and she was gone.

28   *Momma walked in that room as if she owned it. She shoved that silly nurse aside with one hand and strode into the dentist's office. He was sitting in his chair, sharpening his mean instruments and putting extra sting into his medicines. Her eyes were blazing like*

live coals and her arms had doubled themselves in length. He looked up at her just before she caught him by the collar of his white jacket.

29   "Stand up when you see a lady, you contemptuous scoundrel." Her tongue had thinned and the words rolled off well enunciated. Enunciated and sharp like little claps of thunder.

30   The dentist had no choice but to stand at R.O.T.C. attention. His head dropped after a minute and his voice was humble. "Yes, ma'am, Mrs. Henderson."

31   "You knave, do you think you acted like a gentleman, speaking to me like that in front of my granddaughter?" She didn't shake him, although she had the power. She simply held him upright.

32   "No, ma'am, Mrs. Henderson."

33   "No, ma'am, Mrs. Henderson, what?" Then she did give him the tiniest of shakes, but because of her strength the action set his head and arms to shaking loose on the ends of his body. He stuttered much worse than Uncle Willie. "No, ma'am. Mrs. Henderson, I'm sorry."

34   With just an edge of her disgust showing, Momma slung him back in his dentist's chair. "Sorry is as sorry does, and you're about the sorriest dentist I ever laid my eyes on." (She could afford to slip into the vernacular because she had such eloquent command of English.)

35   "I didn't ask you to apologize in front of Marguerite, because I don't want her to know my power, but I order you, now and herewith. Leave Stamps by sundown."

36   "Mrs. Henderson, I can't get my equipment . . . " He was shaking terribly now.

37   "Now, that brings me to my second order. You will never again practice dentistry. Never! When you get settled in your next place, you will be a vegetarian caring for dogs with the mange, cats with the cholera and cows with the epizootic. Is that clear?"

38   The saliva ran down his chin and his eyes filled with tears. "Yes, ma'am. Thank you for not killing me. Thank you, Mrs. Henderson."

39   Momma pulled herself back from being ten feet tall with eight-foot arms and said, "You're welcome for nothing, you varlet, I wouldn't waste a killing on the likes of you."

40   On her way out she waved her handkerchief at the nurse and turned her into a crocus sack of chicken feed.

41   Momma looked tired when she came down the stairs, but who wouldn't be tired if they had gone through what she had. She came close to me and adjusted the towel under my jaw (I had forgotten the toothache; I only knew that she made her hands gentle in order not to awaken the pain). She took my hand. Her voice never changed. "Come on, Sister."

42   I reckoned we were going home where she would concoct a brew to eliminate the pain and maybe give me new teeth too. New teeth that would grow overnight out of my gums. She led me toward the drugstore, which was in the opposite direction from the Store. "I'm taking you to Dentist Baker in Texarkana."

43   I was glad after all that I had bathed and put on Mum and Cashmere Bouquet talcum powder. It was a wonderful surprise. My toothache had quieted to solemn pain, Momma had obliterated the evil white man, and we were going on a trip to Texarkana, just the two of us.

44   On the Greyhound she took an inside seat in the back, and I sat beside her. I was so proud of being her granddaughter and sure that some of her magic must

have come down to me. She asked if I was scared. I only shook my head and leaned over on her cool brown upper arm. There was no chance that a dentist, especially a Negro dentist, would dare hurt me then. Not with Momma there. The trip was uneventful, except that she put her arm around me, which was very unusual for Momma to do.

45   The dentist showed me the medicine and the needle before he deadened my gums, but if he hadn't I wouldn't have worried. Momma stood right behind him. Her arms were folded and she checked on everything he did. The teeth were extracted and she bought me an ice cream cone from the side window of a drug counter. The trip back to Stamps was quiet, except that I had to spit into a very small empty snuff can which she had gotten for me and it was difficult with the bus humping and jerking on our country roads.

46   At home, I was given a warm salt solution, and when I washed out my mouth I showed Bailey the empty holes, where the clotted blood sat like filling in a pie crust. He said I was quite brave, and that was my cue to reveal our confrontation with the peckerwood dentist and Momma's incredible powers.

47   I had to admit that I didn't hear the conversation, but what else could she have said than what I said she said? What else done? He agreed with my analysis in a lukewarm way, and I happily (after all, I'd been sick) flounced into the Store. Momma was preparing our evening meal and Uncle Willie leaned on the door sill. She gave her version.

48   "Dentist Lincoln got right uppity. Said he'd rather put his hand in a dog's mouth. And when I reminded him of the favor, he brushed it off like a piece of lint. Well, I sent Sister downstairs and went inside. I hadn't never been in his office before, but I found the door to where he takes out teeth, and him and the nurse was in there thick as thieves. I just stood there till he caught sight of me." Crash bang the pots on the stove. "He jumped just like he was sitting on a pin. He said, 'Annie, I done tole you, I ain't gonna mess around in no niggah's mouth.' I said, 'Somebody's got to do it then,' and he said, 'Take her to Texarkana to the colored dentist' and that's when I said, 'If you paid me my money I could afford to take her.' He said, 'It's all been paid.' I tole him everything but the interest had been paid. He said, 'Twasn't no interest.' I said, ''Tis now. I'll take ten dollars as payment in full.' You know, Willie, it wasn't no right thing to do, 'cause I lent that money without thinking about it.

49   "He tole that little snippity nurse of his'n to give me ten dollars and make me sign a 'paid in full' receipt. She gave it to me and I signed the papers. Even though by rights he was paid up before, I figger, he gonna be that kind of nasty, he gonna have to pay for it."

50   Momma and her son laughed and laughed over the white man's evilness and her retributive sin.

51   I preferred, much preferred, my version.

Questions for Discussion

1. Why does Momma think that the white dentist, Dr. Lincoln, will pull Maya's tooth? What type of woman is Maya's grandmother?

2. Angelou contrasts the physical pain of her toothache with the painful realization of the doctor's prejudice. Which pain do you think was more hurtful for Maya? Why?

3. Contrast the discrimination against blacks in the South and elsewhere in this country today to the picture of discrimination that Angelou paints in her story.

4. What does Maya learn about Momma on her trip to Dr. Lincoln's?

5. What does Maya's revenge fantasy reveal about her self-concept and self-esteem? Why does she prefer her version?

6. Point out instances of effective dialogue, dialect, setting, details, and imagery that help to make this an especially moving memoir.

Ideas for Writing

1. Develop your journal entry into an essay that discusses what you have learned from living through situations when you were discriminated against, humiliated, or rejected unjustly.

2. Write about a childhood fantasy that helped you to overcome feelings of inadequacy and rejection and to develop courage and inner strength. Develop observations about the role that you think childhood fantasies of power and heroism play in helping children to make the transition into adulthood.

 # Patricia Hampl

Memory and Imagination

A recent recipient of the MacArthur award for creative achievement, Patricia Hampl (b. 1946) currently teaches at the University of Minnesota. She is best known for her autobiography, A Romantic Education *(1981). Her poetry collections include* Resort and Other Poems *(1983),* Spillville *(1987), and* Burning Bright *(1995).* The Virgin Time *(1992) is a reflection about searching for the contemplative life. In her writing Hampl explores themes and memories of her Midwestern background, her ancestry in Prague, Catholicism, and her experience as a woman. Her essay "Memory and Imagination" provides a personal example of writing and rereading a draft of an essay about a childhood memory, demonstrating that writing is an intuitive process that leads the writer to greater self-knowledge. As you read Hampl's essay, reflect on how your imagination and your memory of the past are revealed to you through drafting, rereading, and revising your writing.*

Write about an important memory that you have never recorded in written words. Read over your narrative and then write about how reading the memory makes you see, understand, or appreciate it in a new way.

1   When I was seven, my father, who played the violin on Sundays with a nicely tortured flair which we considered artistic, led me by the hand down a long, unlit corridor in St. Luke's School basement, a sort of tunnel that ended in a room full of pianos. There many little girls and a single sad boy were playing truly tortured scales and arpeggios in a mash of troubled sound. My father gave me over to Sister Olive Marie, who did look remarkably like an olive.

2   Her oily face gleamed as if it had just been rolled out of a can and laid on the white plate of her broad, spotless wimple. She was a small, plump woman; her body and the small window of her face seemed to interpret the entire alphabet of olive: her face was a sallow green olive placed upon the jumbo ripe olive of her black habit. I trusted her instantly and smiled, glad to have my hand placed in the hand of a woman who made sense, who provided the satisfaction of being what she was: an Olive who looked like an Olive.

3   My father left me to discover the piano with Sister Olive Marie so that one day I would join him in mutually tortured piano-violin duets for the edification of my mother and brother who sat at the table meditatively spooning in the last of their pineapple sherbet until their part was called for: they put down their spoons and clapped while we bowed, while the sweet ice in their bowls melted, while the music melted, and we all melted a little into each other for a moment.

4   But first Sister Olive must do her work. I was shown middle C, which Sister seemed to think terribly important. I stared at middle C and then glanced away for a second. When my eye returned, middle C was gone, its slim finger lost in the complicated grasp of the keyboard. Sister Olive struck it again, finding it with laughable ease. She emphasized the importance of middle C, its central position, a sort of North Star of sound. I remember thinking, "Middle C is the belly button of the piano," an insight whose originality and accuracy stunned me with pride. For the first time in my life I was astonished by metaphor. I hesitated to tell the kindly Olive for some reason; apparently I understood a true metaphor is a risky business, revealing of the self. In fact, I have never, until this moment of writing it down, told my first metaphor to anyone.

5   Sunlight flooded the room; the pianos, all black, gleamed. Sister Olive, dressed in the colors of the keyboard, gleamed; middle C shimmered with meaning and I resolved never—never—to forget its location: it was the center of the world.

6   Then Sister Olive, who had had to show me middle C twice but who seemed to have drawn no bad conclusions about me anyway, got up and went to the windows on the opposite wall. She pulled the shades down, one after the other. The sun was too bright, she said. She sneezed as she stood at the windows with the sun shedding its glare over her. She sneezed and sneezed, crazy little convulsive sneezes, one after another, as helpless as if she had the hiccups.

7 "The sun makes me sneeze," she said when the fit was over and she was back at the piano. This was odd, too odd to grasp in the mind. I associated sneezing with colds, and colds with rain, fog, snow and bad weather. The sun, however, had caused Sister Olive to sneeze in this wild way, Sister Olive who gleamed benignly and who was so certain of the location of the center of the world. The universe wobbled a bit and became unreliable. Things were not, after all, necessarily what they seemed. Appearance deceived: here was the sun acting totally out of character, hurling this woman into sneezes, a woman so mild that she was named, so it seemed, for a bland object on a relish tray.

8 I was given a red book, the first Thompson book, and told to play the first piece over and over at one of the black pianos where the other children were crashing away. This, I was told, was called practicing. It sounded alluringly adult, practicing. The piece itself consisted mainly of middle C, and I excelled, thrilled by my savvy at being able to locate that central note amidst the cunning camouflage of all the other white keys before me. Thrilled too by the shiny red book that gleamed, as the pianos did, as Sister Olive did, as my eager eyes probably did. I sat at the formidable machine of the piano and got to know middle C intimately, preparing to be as tortured as I could manage one day soon with my father's violin at my side.

9 But at the moment Mary Katherine Reilly was at my side, playing something at least two or three lessons more sophisticated than my piece. I believe she even struck a chord. I glanced at her from the peasantry of single notes, shy, ready to pay homage. She turned toward me, stopped playing, and sized me up.

10 Sized me up and found a person ready to be dominated. Without introduction she said, "My grandfather invented the collapsible opera hat."

11 I nodded, I acquiesced, I was hers. With that little stroke it was decided between us—that she should be the leader, and I the side-kick. My job was admiration. Even when she added, "But he didn't make a penny from it. He didn't have a patent"—even then, I knew and she knew that this was not an admission of powerlessness, but the easy candor of a master, of one who can afford a weakness or two.

12 With the clairvoyance of all fated relationships based on dominance and submission, it was decided in advance: that when the time came for us to play duets, I should always play second piano, that I should spend my allowance to buy her the Twinkies she craved but was not allowed to have, that finally, I should let her copy from my test paper, and when confronted by our teacher, confess with convincing hysteria that it was I, who had cheated, who had reached above myself to steal what clearly belonged to the rightful heir of the inventor of the collapsible opera hat. . . .

13 There must be a reason I remember that little story about my first piano lesson. In fact, it isn't a story, just a moment, the beginning of what could perhaps become a story. For the memoirist, more than for the fiction writer, the story seems already *there,* already accomplished and fully achieved in history ("in reality," as we naively say). For the memoirist, the writing of the story is a matter of transcription.

14 That, anyway, is the myth. But no memoirist writes for long without experiencing an unsettling disbelief about the reliability of memory, a hunch that memory is not, after all, *just* memory. I don't know why I remembered this frag-

ment about my first piano lesson. I don't, for instance, have a single recollection of my first arithmetic lesson, the first time I studied Latin, the first time my grandmother tried to teach me to knit. Yet these things occurred too, and must have their stories.

15   It is the piano lesson that has trudged forward, clearing the haze of forgetfulness, showing itself bright with detail more than thirty years after the event. I did not choose to remember the piano lesson. It was simply there, like a book that has always been on the shelf, whether I ever read it or not, the binding and title showing as I skim across the contents of my life. On the day I wrote this fragment I happened to take that memory, not some other, from the shelf and paged through it. I found more detail, more event, perhaps a little more entertainment than I had expected, but the memory itself was there from the start. Waiting for me.

16   Or was it? When I reread what I had written just after I finished it, I realized that I had told a number of lies. I *think* it was my father who took me the first time for my piano lesson—but maybe he only took me to meet my teacher and there was no actual lesson that day. And did I even know then that he played the violin—didn't he take up his violin again much later, as a result of my piano playing, and not the reverse? And is it even remotely accurate to describe as "tortured" the musicianship of a man who began every day by belting out "Oh What a Beautiful Morning" as he shaved?

17   More: Sister Olive Marie did sneeze in the sun, but was her name Olive? As for her skin tone—I would have sworn it was olive-like; I would have been willing to spend the better part of an afternoon trying to write the exact description of imported Italian or Greek olive her face suggested: I wanted to get it right. But now, were I to write that passage over, it is her intense black eyebrows I would see, for suddenly they seem the central fact of that face, some indicative mark of her serious and patient nature. But the truth is, I don't remember the woman at all. She's a sneeze in the sun and a finger touching middle C. That, at least, is steady and clear.

18   Worse: I didn't have the Thompson book as my piano text. I'm sure of that because I remember envying children who did have this wonderful book with its pictures of children and animals printed on the pages of music.

19   As for Mary Katherine Reilly. She didn't even go to grade school with me (and her name isn't Mary Katherine Reilly—but I made that change on purpose). I met her in Girl Scouts and only went to school with her later, in high school. Our relationship was not really one of leader and follower; I played first piano most of the time in duets. She certainly never copied anything from a test paper of mine: she was a better student, and cheating just wasn't a possibility with her. Though her grandfather (or someone in her family) did invent the collapsible opera hat and I remember that she was proud of that fact, she didn't tell me this news as a deft move in a childish power play.

20   So, what was I doing in this brief memoir? Is it simply an example of the curious relation a fiction writer has to the material of her own life? Maybe. That may have some value in itself. But to tell the truth (if anyone still believes me capable of telling the truth), I wasn't writing fiction. I was writing memoir—or was trying

to. My desire was to be accurate. I wished to embody the myth of memoir: to write as an act of dutiful transcription.

21   Yet clearly the work of writing narrative caused me to do something very different from transcription. I am forced to admit that memoir is not a matter of transcription, that memory itself is not a warehouse of finished stories, not a static gallery of framed pictures. I must admit that I invented. But why?

22   Two whys: why did I invent, and then, if a memoirist must inevitably invent rather than transcribe, why do I—why should anybody—write memoir at all?

23   I must respond to these impertinent questions because they, like the bumper sticker I saw the other day commanding all who read it to QUESTION AUTHORITY, challenge my authority as a memoirist and as a witness.

24   It still comes as a shock to realize that I don't write about what I know: I write in order to find out what I know. Is it possible to convey to a reader the enormous degree of blankness, confusion, hunch and uncertainty lurking in the act of writing? When I am the reader, not the writer, I too fall into the lovely illusion that the words before me (in a story by Mavis Gallant, an essay by Carol Bly, a memoir by M. F. K. Fisher), which *read* so inevitably, must also have been *written* exactly as they appear, rhythm and cadence, language and syntax, the powerful waves of the sentences laying themselves on the smooth beach of the page one after another faultlessly.

25   But here I sit before a yellow legal pad, and the long page of the preceding two paragraphs is a jumble of crossed-out lines, false starts, confused order. A mess. The mess of my mind trying to find out what it wants to say. This is a writer's frantic, grabby mind, not the poised mind of a reader ready to be edified or entertained.

26   I sometimes think of the reader as a cat, endlessly fastidious, capable, by turns, of mordant indifference and riveted attention, luxurious, recumbent, and ever poised. Whereas the writer is absolutely a dog, panting and moping, too eager for an affectionate scratch behind the ears, lunging frantically after any old stick thrown in the distance.

27   The blankness of a new page never fails to intrigue and terrify me. Sometimes, in fact, I think my habit of writing on long yellow sheets comes from an atavistic fear of the writer's stereotypic "blank white page." At least when I begin writing, my page isn't utterly blank; at least it has a wash of color on it, even if the absence of words must finally be faced on a yellow sheet as truly as on a blank white one. Well, we all have our ways of whistling in the dark.

28   If I approach writing from memory with the assumption that I know what I wish to say, I assume that intentionality is running the show. Things are not that simple. Or perhaps writing is even more profoundly simple, more telegraphic and immediate in its choices than the grating wheels and chugging engine of logic and rational intention. The heart, the guardian of intuition with its secret, often fearful intentions, is the boss. Its commands are what a writer obeys—often without knowing it. Or, I do.

29   That's why I'm a strong adherent of the first draft. And why it's worth pausing for a moment to consider what first draft really is. By my lights, the piano lesson mem-

oir is a first draft. That doesn't mean it exists here exactly as I first wrote it. I like to think I've cleaned it up from the first time I put it down on paper. I've cut some adjectives here, toned down the hyperbole there, smoothed a transition, cut a repetition—that sort of housekeeperly tidying-up. But the piece remains a first draft because I haven't yet gotten to know it, haven't given it a chance to tell me anything. For me, writing a first draft is a little like meeting someone for the first time. I come away with a wary acquaintanceship, but the real friendship (if any) and genuine intimacy—that's all down the road. Intimacy with a piece of writing, as with a person, comes from paying attention to the revelations it is capable of giving, not by imposing my own preconceived notions, no matter how well-intentioned they might be.

30   I try to let pretty much anything happen in a first draft. A careful first draft is a failed first draft. That may be why there are so many inaccuracies in the piano lesson memoir: I didn't censor, I didn't judge. I kept moving. But I would not publish this piece as a memoir on its own in its present state. It isn't the "lies" in the piece that give me pause, though a reader has a right to expect a memoir to be as accurate as the writer's memory can make it. No, it isn't the lies themselves that makes the piano lesson memoir a first draft and therefore "unpublishable."

31   The real trouble: the piece hasn't yet found its subject; it isn't yet about what it wants to be about. Note: what *it* wants, not what I want. The difference has to do with the relation a memoirist—any writer, in fact—has to unconscious or half-known intentions and impulses in composition.

32   Now that I have the fragment down on paper, I can read this little piece as a mystery which drops clues to the riddle of my feelings, like a culprit who wishes to be apprehended. My narrative self (the culprit who has invented) wishes to be discovered by my reflective self, the self who wants to understand and make sense of a half-remembered story about a nun sneezing in the sun. . . .

33   We only store in memory images of value. The value may be lost over the passage of time (I was baffled about why I remembered that sneezing nun, for example), but that's the implacable judgment of feeling: *this*, we say somewhere deep within us, is something I'm hanging on to. And of course, often we cleave to things because they possess heavy negative charges. Pain likes to be vivid.

34   Over time, the value (the feeling) and the stored memory (the image) may become estranged. Memoir seeks a permanent home for feeling and image, a habitation where they can live together in harmony. Naturally, I've had a lot of experiences since I packed away that one from the basement of St. Luke's School; that piano lesson has been effaced by waves of feeling for other moments and episodes. I persist in believing the event has value—after all, I remember it—but in writing the memoir I did not simply relive the experience. Rather, I explored the mysterious relationship between all the images I could round up and the even more impacted feelings that caused me to store the images safely away in memory. Stalking the relationship, seeking the congruence between stored image and hidden emotion—that's the real job of memoir.

35   By writing about the first piano lesson, I've come to know things I could not know otherwise. But I only know these things as a result of reading this first draft. While I was writing, I was following the images, letting the details fill the room of

the page and use the furniture as they wished. I was their dutiful servant—or thought I was. In fact, I was the faithful retainer of my hidden feelings which were giving the commands.

36   I really did feel, for instance, that Mary Katherine Reilly was far superior to me. She was smarter, funnier, more wonderful in every way—that's how I saw it. Our friendship (or she herself) did not require that I become her vassal, yet perhaps in my heart that was something I wanted; I wanted a way to express my feeling of admiration. I suppose I waited until this memoir to begin to find the way.

37   Just as, in the memoir, I finally possess that red Thompson book with the barking dogs and bleating lambs and winsome children. I couldn't (and still can't) remember what my own music book was, so I grabbed the name and image of the one book I could remember. It was only in reviewing the piece after writing it that I saw my inaccuracy. In pondering this "lie," I came to see what I was up to: I was getting what I wanted. At last.

38   The truth of many circumstances and episodes in the past emerges for the memoirist through details (the red music book, the fascination with a nun's name and gleaming face), but these details are not merely information, not flat facts. Such details are not allowed to lounge. They must work. Their work is the creation of symbol. But it's more accurate to call it the *recognition* of symbol. For meaning is not "attached" to the detail by the memoirist; meaning is revealed. That's why a first draft is important. Just as the first meeting (good or bad) with someone who later becomes the beloved is important and is often reviewed for signals, meanings, omens and indications.

39   Now I can look at that music book and see it not only as "a detail," but for what it is, how it *acts*. See it as the small red door leading straight into the dark room of my childhood longing and disappointment. That red book *becomes* the palpable evidence of that longing. In other words, it becomes symbol. There is no symbol, no life-of-the-spirit in the general or the abstract. Yet a writer wishes—indeed all of us wish—to speak about profound matters that are, like it or not, general and abstract. We wish to talk to each other about life and death, about love, despair, loss, and innocence. We sense that in order to live together we must learn to speak of peace, of history, of meaning and values. Those are a few.

40   We seek a means of exchange, a language which will renew these ancient concerns and make them wholly and pulsingly ours. Instinctively, we go to our store of private images and associations for our authority to speak of these weighty issues. We find, in our details and broken and obscured images, the language of symbol. Here memory impulsively reaches out its arms and embraces imagination. That is the resort to invention. It isn't a lie, but an act of necessity, as the innate urge to locate personal truth always is.

41   All right. Invention is inevitable. But why write memoir? Why not call it fiction and be done with all the hashing about, wondering where memory stops and imagination begins? And if memoir seeks to talk about "the big issues," about history and peace, death and love—why not leave these reflections to those with expert and scholarly knowledge? Why let the common or garden variety memoirist into the club? I'm thinking again of that bumper sticker: why Question Authority?

42   My answer, of course, is a memoirist's answer. Memoir must be written because each of us must have a created version of the past. Created: that is, real, tangible, made of the stuff of a life lived in place and in history. And the down side of any created thing as well: we must live with a version that attaches us to our limitations, to the inevitable subjectivity of our points of view. We must acquiesce to our experience and our gift to transform experience into meaning and value. You tell me your story, I'll tell you my story.

43   If we refuse to do the work of creating this personal version of the past, someone else will do it for us. That is a scary political fact. "The struggle of man against power," a character in Milan Kundera's novel *The Book of Laughter and Forgetting* says "is the struggle of memory against forgetting." He refers to willful political forgetting, the habit of nations and those in power (Question Authority!) to deny the truth of memory in order to disarm moral and ethical power. It's an efficient way of controlling masses of people. It doesn't even require much bloodshed, as long as people are entirely willing to give over their personal memories. Whole histories can be rewritten. As Czeslaw Milosz said in his 1980 Nobel Prize lecture, the number of books published that seek to deny the existence of the Nazi death camps now exceeds one hundred.

44   What is remembered is what *becomes* reality. If we "forget" Auschwitz, if we "forget" My Lai, what then do we remember? And what is the purpose of our remembering? If we think of memory naively, as a simple story, logged like a documentary in the archive of the mind, we miss its beauty but also its function. The beauty of memory rests in its talent for rendering detail, for paying homage to the senses, its capacity to love the particles of life, the richness and idiosyncrasy of our existence. The function of memory, on the other hand, is intensely personal and surprisingly political.

45   Our capacity to move forward as developing beings rests on a healthy relation with the past. Psychotherapy, that widespread method of mental health, relies heavily on memory and on the ability to retrieve and organize images and events from the personal past. We carry our wounds and perhaps even worse, our capacity to wound, forward with us. If we learn not only to tell our stories but to listen to what our stories tell us—to write the first draft and then return for the second draft—we are doing the work of memoir.

46   Memoir is the intersection of narration and reflection, of story-telling and essay-writing. It can present its story *and* reflect and consider the meaning of the story. It is a peculiarly open form, inviting broken and incomplete images, half-recollected fragments, all the mass (and mess) of detail. It offers to shape this confusion—and in shaping, of course it necessarily creates a work of art, not a legal document. But then, even legal documents are only valiant attempts to consign the truth, the whole truth and nothing but the truth to paper. Even they remain versions.

47   Locating touchstones—the red music book, the olive Olive, my father's violin playing—is deeply satisfying. Who knows why? Perhaps we all sense that we can't grasp the whole truth and nothing but the truth of our experience. Just can't be done. What can be achieved, however, is a version of its swirling, changing

wholeness. A memoirist must acquiesce to selectivity, like any artist. The version we dare to write is the only truth, the only relationship we can have with the past. Refuse to write your life and you have no life. At least, that is the stern view of the memoirist.

48   Personal history, logged in memory, is a sort of slide projector flashing images on the wall of the mind. And there's precious little order to the slides in the rotating carousel. Beyond that confusion, who knows who is running the projector? A memoirist steps into this darkened room of flashing, unorganized images and stands blinking for a while. Maybe for a long while. But eventually, as with any attempt to tell a story, it is necessary to put something first, then something else. And so on, to the end. That's a first draft. Not necessarily the truth, not even a truth sometimes, but the first attempt to create a shape.

49   The first thing I usually notice at this stage of composition is the appalling inaccuracy of the piece. Witness my first piano lesson draft. Invention is screamingly evident in what I intended to be transcription. But here's the further truth: I feel no shame. In fact, it's only now that my interest in the piece truly quickens. For I can see what isn't there, what is shyly hugging the walls, hoping not to be seen. I see the filmy shape of the next draft. I see a more acute version of the episode or—this is more likely—an entirely new piece rising from the ashes of the first attempt.

50   The next draft of the piece would have to be a true re-vision, a new seeing of the materials of the first draft. Nothing merely cosmetic will do—no rouge buffing up the opening sentence, no glossy adjective to lift a sagging line, nothing to attempt covering a patch of gray writing. None of that. I can't say for sure, but my hunch is the revision would lead me to more writing about my father (why was I so impressed by that ancestral inventor of the collapsible opera hat? Did I feel I had nothing as remarkable in my own background? Did this make me feel inadequate?). I begin to think perhaps Sister Olive is less central to this business than she is in this draft. She is meant to be a moment, not a character.

51   And so I might proceed, if I were to undertake a new draft of the memoir. I begin to feel a relationship developing between a former self and me.

52   And, even more compelling, a relationship between an old world and me. Some people think of autobiographical writing as the precious occupation of a particularly self-absorbed person. Maybe, but I don't buy that. True memoir is written in an attempt to find not only a self but a world.

53   The self-absorption that seems to be the impetus and embarrassment of autobiography turns into (or perhaps always was) a hunger for the world. Actually, it begins as hunger for a world, one gone or lost, effaced by time or a more sudden brutality. But in the act of remembering, the personal environment expands, resonates beyond itself, beyond its "subject," into the endless and tragic recollection that is history.

54   We look at old family photographs in which we stand next to black, boxy Fords and are wearing period costumes, and we do not gaze fascinated because there we are young again, or there we are standing, as we never will again in life, next to our mother. We stare and drift because there we are . . . historical. It is the dress,

the black car that dazzle us now and draw us beyond our mother's bright arms which once caught us. We reach into the attractive impersonality of something more significant than ourselves. We write memoir, in other words. We accept the humble position of writing a version rather than "the whole truth."

55   I suppose I write memoir because of the radiance of the past—it draws me back and back to it. Not that the past is beautiful. In our commercial memoir, in history, the death camps *are* back there. In intimate life too, the record is usually pretty mixed. "I could tell you stories . . ." people say and drift off, meaning terrible things have happened to them.

56   But the past is radiant. It has the light of lived life. A memoirist wishes to touch it. No one owns the past, though typically the first act of new political regimes, whether of the left or the right, is to attempt to re-write history, to grab the past and make it over so the end comes out right. So their power looks inevitable.

57   No one owns the past, but it is a grave error (another age would have said a grave sin) not to inhabit memory. Sometimes I think it is all we really have. But that may be a trifle melodramatic. At any rate, memory possesses authority for the fearful self in a world where it is necessary to have authority in order to Question Authority.

58   There may be no more pressing intellectual need in our culture than for people to become sophisticated about the function of memory. The political implications of the loss of memory are obvious. The authority of memory is a personal confirmation of selfhood. To write one's life is to live it twice, and the second living is both spiritual and historical, for a memoir reaches deep within the personality as it seeks its narrative form and also grasps the life-of-the-times as no political treatise can.

59   Our most ancient metaphor says life is a journey. Memoir is travel writing, then, notes taken along the way, telling how things looked and what thoughts occurred. But I cannot think of the memoirist as a tourist. This is the traveller who goes on foot, living the journey, taking on mountains, enduring deserts, marveling at the lush green places. Moving through it all faithfully, not so much a survivor with a harrowing tale to tell as a pilgrim, seeking, wondering.

Questions for Discussion

1. Why does Hampl believe that "a careful first draft is a failed first draft"? Explain why you agree or disagree with her.

2. Why didn't Hampl recount the incidents from her childhood exactly as they occurred? What does Hampl learn about her writing process from reflecting upon how she wrote the memoir? What is Hampl's writing process? Contrast your own writing process with hers.

3. Hampl makes extensive use of images and metaphors, such as the description of Sister Mary Olive who looked like an olive, her reference to middle C as the belly button of the piano, and the comparisons of the reader to a cat and the writer to a dog. Explain how Hampl develops

two of her metaphors or images, and how each emphasizes her meaning.

4. Does Hampl make a clear distinction between memoir and fiction? Do you agree with her definitions of the two terms? Why or why not?

5. Why does Hampl believe that all people, regardless of their public stature, should write their memoirs? Do you agree with Hampl? Why or why not?

6. Hampl begins with a memoir and then analyzes the meaning of her memoir and her writing process. Is her organizational strategy effective? Why or why not?

Ideas for Writing

1. Narrate a childhood memory that you have never written about before, as you did in the journal entry. Extend the narrative into an essay in which you explore what you learned about yourself, your experience, and your imagination from writing about the memory.

2. "The heart, the guardian of intuition with its secret, often fearful intentions, is the boss. Its commands are what a writer obeys." Write an essay in which you provide evidence and examples to support or refute Hampl's assertion. Refer to your own experiences, the experiences of your peers, and of professional writers.

 ## Alice Walker

Beauty: When the Other Dancer Is the Self

Born in Eatonton, Georgia, Alice Walker (b. 1944) attended Spelman College for one year and completed a B.A. at Sara Lawrence College in 1967. Walker was involved with the civil rights movement of the 1960s and has lived for many years in San Francisco and in rural Mendocino County in California. Walker's writing explores the concerns of African American women, often drawing on memories of her own early life in Georgia and on her extensive travels. Her novel The Color Purple *won the Pulitzer Prize and was made into a film by Steven Speilberg. Other works by Walker include* In Love & Trouble: Stories of Black Women *(1973),* In Search of Our Mothers' Gardens *(1983),* Living by the Word: Selected Writings, 1973–1987 *(1988),* The Temple of My Familiar *(1989),* Possessing the Secret of Joy *(1993), and* Same River Twice: Honoring the Difficult *(1996). "Beauty When the Other Dancer is the Self," which is collected in* In Search of Our Mothers' Gardens, *explores Walker's changing understanding of what it means to be beautiful and where beauty resides.*

Discuss the ways in which your understanding of what it means to be beautiful has changed as you have matured? What is your current definition of beauty?

1   It is a bright summer day in 1947. My father, a fat, funny man with beautiful eyes and a subversive wit, is trying to decide which of his eight children he will take with him to the country fair. My mother, of course, will not go. She is knocked out from getting most of us ready: I hold my neck stiff against the pressure of her knuckles as she hastily completes the braiding and then beribboning of my hair.

2   My father is the driver for the rich old white lady up the road. Her name is Miss Mey. She owns all the land for miles around, as well as the house in which we live. All I remember about her is that she once offered to pay my mother thirty-five cents for cleaning her house, raking up piles of her magnolia leaves, and washing her family's clothes, and that my mother—she of no money, eight children, and a chronic earache—refused it. But I do not think of this in 1947. I am two and a half years old. I want to go everywhere my daddy goes. I am excited at the prospect of riding in a car. Someone has told me fairs are fun. That there is room in the car for only three of us doesn't faze me at all. Whirling happily in my starchy frock, showing off my biscuit-polished patent-leather shoes and lavender socks, tossing my head in a way that makes my ribbons bounce, I stand, hands on hips, before my father. "Take me, Daddy," I say with assurance; "I'm the prettiest!"

3   Later, it does not surprise me to find myself in Miss Mey's shiny black car, sharing the back seat with the other lucky ones. Does not surprise me that I thoroughly enjoy the fair. At home that night I tell the unlucky ones all I can remember about the merry-go-round, the man who eats live chickens, and the teddy bears, until they say: that's enough, baby Alice. Shut up now, and go to sleep.

4   It is Easter Sunday, 1950. I am dressed in a green, flocked, scalloped-hem dress (handmade by my adoring sister, Ruth) that has its own smooth satin petticoat and tiny hot-pink roses tucked into each scallop. My shoes, new T-strap patent leather, again highly biscuit-polished. I am six years old and have learned one of the longest Easter speeches to be heard that day, totally unlike the speech I said when I was two: "Easter lilies / pure and white / blossom in / the morning light." When I rise to give my speech I do so on a great wave of love and pride and expectation. People in the church stop rustling their new crinolines. They seem to hold their breath. I can tell they admire my dress, but it is my spirit, bordering on sassiness (womanishness), they secretly applaud.

5   "That girl's a little *mess*," they whisper to each other, pleased.

6   Naturally I say my speech without stammer or pause, unlike those who stutter, stammer, or, worst of all, forget. This is before the word "beautiful" exists in people's vocabulary, but "Oh, isn't she the *cutest* thing!" frequently floats my way. "And got so much sense!" they gratefully add . . . for which thoughtful addition I thank them to this day.

7   *It was great fun being cute. But then, one day, it ended.*

8   I am eight years old and a tomboy. I have a cowboy hat, cowboy boots, check-ered shirt and pants, all red. My playmates are my brothers, two and four years older than I. Their colors are black and green, the only difference in the way we are dressed. On Saturday nights we all go to the picture show, even my mother; West-erns are her favorite kind of movie. Back home, "on the ranch," we pretend we are Tom Mix, Hopalong Cassidy, Lash LaRue (we've even named one of our dogs Lash LaRue); we chase each other for hours rustling cattle, being outlaws, delivering damsels from distress. Then my parents decide to buy my brothers guns. These are not "real" guns. They shoot "BBs," copper pellets my brothers say will kill birds. Because I am a girl, I do not get a gun. Instantly I am relegated to the position of Indian. Now there appears a great distance between us. They shoot and shoot at everything with their new guns. I try to keep up with my bow and arrows.

9   One day while I am standing on top of our makeshift "garage"—pieces of tin nailed across some poles—holding my bow and arrow and looking out towards the fields, I feel an incredible blow in my right eye. I look down just in time to see my brother lower his gun.

10   Both brothers rush to my side. My eye stings, and I cover it with my hand. "If you tell," they say, "we will get a whipping. You don't want that to happen do you?" I do not. "Here is a piece of wire," says the older brother, picking it up from the roof; "say you stepped on one end of it and the other flew up and hit you." The pain is beginning to start. "Yes," I say. "Yes, I will say that is what happened." If I do not say this is what happened, I know my brothers will find ways to make me wish I had. But now I will say anything that gets me to my mother.

11   Confronted by our parents we stick to the lie agreed upon. They place me on a bench on the porch and I close my left eye while they examine the right. There is a tree growing from underneath the porch that climbs past the railing to the roof. It is the last thing my right eye sees. I watch as its trunk, its branches, and then its leaves are blotted out by the rising blood.

12   I am in shock. First there is intense fever, which my father tries to break using lily leaves bound around my head. Then there are chills: my mother tries to get me to eat soup. Eventually, I do not know how, my parents learn what has hap-pened. A week after the "accident" they take me to see a doctor. "Why did you wait so long to come?" he asks, looking into my eye and shaking his head. "Eyes are sympathetic," he says. "If one is blind, the other will likely become blind too."

13   This comment of the doctor's terrifies me. But it is really how I look that both-ers me most. Where the BB pellet struck there is a glob of whitish scar tissue, a hideous cataract, on my eye. Now when I stare at people—a favorite pastime, up to now—they will stare back. Not at the "cute" little girl, but at her scar. For six years I do not stare at anyone, because I do not raise my head.

14   Years later, in the throes of a mid-life crisis, I ask my mother and sister whether I changed after the "accident." "No," they say, puzzled. "What do you mean?"

15   *What do I mean?*

16   I am eight, and, for the first time, doing poorly in school, where I have been something of a whiz since I was four. We have just moved to the place where the

"accident" occurred. We do not know any of the people around us because this is a different county. The only time I see the friends I knew is when we go back to our old church. The new school is the former state penitentiary. It is a large stone building, cold and drafty, crammed to overflowing with boisterous, ill-disciplined children. On the third floor there is a huge circular imprint of some partition that has been torn out.

17   "What used to be here?" I ask a sullen girl next to me on our way past it to lunch.

18   "The electric chair," says she.

19   At night I have nightmares about the electric chair, and about all the people reputedly "fried" in it. I am afraid of the school, where all the students seem to be budding criminals.

20   "What's the matter with your eye?" they ask, critically.

21   When I don't answer (I cannot decide whether it was an "accident" or not), they shove me, insist on a fight.

22   My brother, the one who created the story about the wire, comes to my rescue. But then brags so much about "protecting" me, I become sick.

23   After months of torture at the school, my parents decide to send me back to our old community, to my old school. I live with my grandparents and the teacher they board. But there is no room for Phoebe, my cat. By the time my grandparents decide there is room, and I ask for my cat, she cannot be found. Miss Yarborough, the boarding teacher, takes me under her wing, and begins to teach me to play the piano. But soon she marries an African—a "prince," she says—and is whisked away to his continent.

24   At my old school there is at least one teacher who loves me. She is the teacher who "knew me before I was born" and bought my first baby clothes. It is she who makes life bearable. It is her presence that finally helps me turn on the one child at the school who continually calls me "one-eyed bitch." One day I simply grab him by his coat and beat him until I am satisfied. It is my teacher who tells me my mother is ill.

25   My mother is lying in bed in the middle of the day, something I have never seen. She is in too much pain to speak. She has an abscess in her ear. I stand looking down on her, knowing that if she dies, I cannot live. She is being treated with warm oils and hot bricks held against her cheek. Finally a doctor comes. But I must go back to my grandparents' house. The weeks pass but I am hardly aware of it. All I know is that my mother might die, my father is not so jolly, my brothers still have their guns, and I am the one sent away from home.

26   "You did not change," they say.

27   *Did I imagine the anguish of never looking up?*

28   I am twelve. When relatives come to visit I hide in my room. My cousin Brenda, just my age, whose father works in the post office and whose mother is a nurse, comes to find me. "Hello," she says. And then she asks, looking at my recent school picture, which I did not want taken, and on which the "glob," as I think of it, is clearly visible, "You still can't see out of that eye?"

29   "No," I say, and flop back on the bed over my book.

30   That night, as I do almost every night, I abuse my eye. I rant and rave at it, in front of the mirror. I plead with it to clear up before morning. I tell it I hate it and despise it. I do not pray for sight. I pray for beauty.

31   "You did not change," they say.

32   I am fourteen and baby-sitting for my brother Bill, who lives in Boston. He is my favorite brother and there is a strong bond between us. Understanding my feelings of shame and ugliness he and his wife take me to a local hospital, where the "glob" is removed by a doctor named O. Henry. There is still a small bluish crater where the scar tissue was, but the ugly white stuff is gone. Almost immediately I become a different person from the girl who does not raise her head. Or so I think. Now that I've raised my head I win the boyfriend of my dreams. Now that I've raised my head I have plenty of friends. Now that I've raised my head classwork comes from my lips as faultlessly as Easter speeches did, and I leave high school as valedictorian, most popular student, and *queen*, hardly believing my luck. Ironically, the girl who was voted most beautiful in our class (and was) was later shot twice through the chest by a male companion, using a "real" gun, while she was pregnant. But that's another story in itself. Or is it?

33   "You did not change," they say.

34   It is now thirty years since the "accident." A beautiful journalist comes to visit and to interview me. She is going to write a cover story for her magazine that focuses on my latest book. "Decide how you want to look on the cover," she says. "Glamorous, or whatever."

35   Never mind "glamorous," it is the "whatever" that I hear. Suddenly all I can think of is whether I will get enough sleep the night before the photography session: if I don't, my eye will be tired and wander, as blind eyes will.

36   At night in bed with my lover I think up reasons why I should not appear on the cover of a magazine. "My meanest critics will say I've sold out," I say. "My family will now realize I write scandalous books."

37   "But what's the real reason you don't want to do this?" he asks.

38   "Because in all probability," I say in a rush, "my eye won't be straight."

39   "It will be straight enough," he says. Then, "Besides, I thought you'd made your peace with that."

40   And I suddenly remember that I have.

41   I *remember*:

42   I am talking to my brother Jimmy, asking if he remembers anything unusual about the day I was shot. He does not know I consider that day the last time my father, with his sweet home remedy of cool lily leaves, chose me, and that I suffered and raged inside because of this. "Well," he says, "all I remember is standing by the side of the highway with Daddy, trying to flag down a car. A white man stopped, but when Daddy said he needed somebody to take his little girl to the doctor, he drove off."

43   *I remember:*

44   I am in the desert for the first time. I fall totally in love with it. I am so overwhelmed by its beauty, I confront for the first time, consciously, the meaning of
the doctor's words years ago: "Eyes are sympathetic. If one is blind, the other will
likely become blind too." I realize I have dashed about the world madly, looking at
this, looking at that, storing up images against the fading of the light. *But I might
have missed seeing the desert!* The shock of that possibility—and gratitude for over
twenty-five years of sight—sends me literally to my knees. Poem after poem
comes—which is perhaps how poets pray.

On Sight
I am so thankful I have seen
The Desert
And the creatures in the desert
And the desert Itself.

The desert has its own moon
Which I have seen
With my own eye.

There is no flag on it.

Trees of the desert have arms
All of which are always up
That is because the moon is up
The sun is up
Also the sky
The stars
Clouds
None with flags.

If there *were* flags, I doubt
the trees would point.
Would you?

45   *But mostly, I remember this:*

46   I am twenty-seven, and my baby daughter is almost three. Since her birth I
have worried about her discovery that her mother's eyes are different from other
people's. Will she be embarrassed? I think. What will she say? Every day she
watches a television program called "Big Blue Marble." It begins with a picture of
the earth as it appears from the moon. It is bluish, a little battered-looking, but full
of light, with whitish clouds swirling around it. Every time I see it I weep with
love, as if it is a picture of Grandma's house. One day when I am putting Rebecca
down for her nap, she suddenly focuses on my eye. Something inside me cringes,
gets ready to try to protect myself. All children are cruel about physical differ-

ences, I know from experience, and that they don't always mean to be is another matter. I assume Rebecca will be the same.

47 But no-o-o-o. She studies my face intently as we stand, her inside and me outside her crib. She even holds my face maternally between her dimpled little hands. Then, looking every bit as serious and lawyerlike as her father, she says, as if it may just possibly have slipped my attention: "Mommy, there's a *world* in your eye." (As in, "Don't be alarmed, or do anything crazy.") And then, gently, but with great interest: "Mommy, where did you *get* that world in your eye?"

48 For the most part, the pain left then. (So what, if my brothers grew up to buy even more powerful pellet guns for their sons and to carry real guns themselves. So what, if a young "Morehouse man" once nearly fell off the steps of Trevor Arnett Library because he thought my eyes were blue.) Crying and laughing I ran to the bathroom, while Rebecca mumbled and sang herself off to sleep. Yes indeed, I realized, looking into the mirror. There *was* a world in my eye. And I saw that it was possible to love it: that in fact, for all it had taught me of shame and anger and inner vision, I *did* love it. Even to see it drifting out of orbit in boredom, or rolling up out of fatigue, not to mention floating back at attention in excitement (bearing witness, a friend has called it), deeply suitable to my personality, and even characteristic of me.

49 That night I dream I am dancing to Stevie Wonder's song "Always" (the name of the song is really "As," but I hear it as "Always"). As I dance, whirling and joyous, happier than I've ever been in my life, another bright-faced dancer joins me. We dance and kiss each other and hold each other through the night. The other dancer has obviously come through all right, as I have done. She is beautiful, whole and free. And she is also me.

Questions for Discussion

1. Why does Walker keep the facts about her accident secret? What are the most painful parts of Walker's adjustment to living with her damaged "glob" eye?

2. Why doesn't Walker's family believe that Alice was changed by the accident? Do you think that they are right?

3. In what ways is Walker's painful adjustment related to her transformation into an adolescent? How does Walker change when the "glob" is removed from her eye?

4. Why does Walker fall in love with the desert? In what ways does the meaning of the poem "On Sight" support the themes of the essay?

5. How does Walker's daughter help her to make peace with her damaged eye? What does her daughter mean when she says, " 'Mommy, there's a world in your eye' "?

6. Explain the meaning of the essay's title. How has Walker's understanding and definition of beauty changed through her experiences? What part of herself has she come to accept?

Ideas for Writing

1. Write an essay or a short story that presents your definition of beauty.
2. Like Walker, write about a realization that helped you to accept a part of yourself that you had previously been ashamed of.

    # Judith Ortiz Cofer

Silent Dancing

Born in Puerto Rico in 1952, Judith Ortiz Cofer came to New Jersey with her family when she was a child. After receiving an M.A. from Florida Atlantic University, Cofer taught English and Spanish at the University of Miami and currently teaches at the University of Georgia. Cofer has written novels, including Line of the Sun *(1989) and* Latin Deli *(1995); short stories compiled in* Island Like You: Stories of the Barrio *(1995); and an autobiographical work,* Silent Dancing: A Partial Remembrance of a Puerto Rican Childhood *(1990). In the following selection from* Silent Dancing, *Cofer recalls memories of a childhood spent in two widely different cultures.*

JOURNAL

Write about a photograph or a home movie that evokes memories of your childhood.

1   We have a home movie of this party. Several times my mother and I have watched it together, and I have asked questions about the silent revellers coming in and out of focus. It is grainy and of short duration but a great visual aid to my first memory of life in Paterson at that time. And it is in color—the only complete scene in color I can recall from those years.

2   We lived in Puerto Rico until my brother was born in 1954. Soon after, because of economic pressures on our growing family, my father joined the United States Navy. He was assigned to duty on a ship in Brooklyn Yard, New York City—a place of cement and steel that was to be his home base in the States until his retirement more than twenty years later. He left the Island first, tracking down his uncle who lived with his family across the Hudson River, in Paterson, New Jersey. There he found a tiny apartment in a huge apartment building that had once housed Jewish families and was just being transformed into a tenement by Puerto Ricans overflowing from New York City. In 1955 he sent for us. My mother was only twenty years old, I was not quite three, and my brother was a toddler when we arrived at *El Building*, as the place had been christened by its new residents.

3   My memories of life in Paterson during those first few years are in shades of gray. Maybe I was too young to absorb vivid colors and details, or to discriminate between the slate blue of the winter sky and the darker hues of the snow-bearing clouds, but the single color washes over the whole period. The building we lived in was gray, the streets were gray with slush the first few months of my life there, the coat my father had bought for me was dark in color and too big. It sat heavily on my thin frame.

4   I do remember the way the heater pipes banged and rattled, startling all of us out of sleep until we got so used to the sound that we automatically either shut it out or raised our voices above the racket. The hiss from the valve punctuated my sleep, which has always been fitful, like a nonhuman presence in the room—the dragon sleeping at the entrance of my childhood. But the pipes were a connection to all the other lives being lived around us. Having come from a house made for a single family back in Puerto Rico—my mother's extended-family home—it was curious to know that strangers lived under our floor and above our heads, and that the heater pipe went through everyone's apartment. (My first spanking in Paterson came as a result of playing tunes on the pipes in my room to see if there would be an answer.) My mother was as new to this concept of beehive life as I was, but had been given strict orders by my father to keep the doors locked, the noise down, ourselves to ourselves.

5   It seems that Father had learned some painful lessons about prejudice while searching for an apartment in Paterson. Not until years later did I hear how much resistance he had encountered with landlords who were panicking at the influx of Latinos into a neighborhood that had been Jewish for a couple of generations. But it was the American phenomenon of ethnic turnover that was changing the urban core of Paterson, and the human flood could not be held back with an accusing finger.

6   "You Cuban?" the man had asked my father, pointing a finger at his name tag on the Navy uniform—even though my father had the fair skin and light brown hair of his northern Spanish family background and our name is as common in Puerto Rico as Johnson is in the U.S.

7   "No," my father had answered looking past the finger into his adversary's angry eyes, "I'm Puerto Rican."

8   "Same shit." And the door closed. My father could have passed as European, but we couldn't. My brother and I both have our mother's black hair and olive skin, and so we lived in El Building and visited our great-uncle and his fair children on the next block. It was their private joke that they were the German branch of the family. Not many years later that area too would be mainly Puerto Rican. It was as if the heart of the city map were being gradually colored in brown—*café-con-leche* brown. Our color.

9   *The movie opens with a sweep of the living room. It is "typical" immigrant Puerto Rican decor for the time: the sofa and chairs are square and hard-looking, upholstered in bright colors (blue and yellow in this instance, and covered in the transparent plastic) that furniture salesmen then were adept at making women buy. The linoleum on the floor is light blue, and if it was subjected to the spike heels as it was in most places, there*

were dime-sized indentations all over it that cannot be seen in this movie. The room is full of people dressed in mainly two colors: dark suits for the men, red dresses for the women. I have asked my mother why most of the women are in red that night, and she shrugs, "I don't remember. Just a coincidence." She doesn't have my obsession for assigning symbolism to everything.

10   *The three women in red sitting on the couch are my mother, my eighteen-year-old cousin, and her brother's girlfriend. The "novia" is just up from the Island, which is apparent in her body language. She sits up formally, and her dress is carefully pulled over her knees. She is a pretty girl but her posture makes her look insecure, lost in her full skirted red dress which she has carefully tucked around her to make room for my gorgeous cousin, her future sister-in-law. My cousin has grown up in Paterson and is in her last year of high school. She doesn't have a trace of what Puerto Ricans call "la mancha" (literally, the stain: the mark of the new immigrant—something about the posture, the voice, or the humble demeanor making it obvious to everyone that that person has just arrived on the mainland; has not yet acquired the polished look of the city dweller). My cousin is wearing a tight red-sequined cocktail dress. Her brown hair has been lightened with peroxide around the bangs, and she is holding a cigarette very expertly between her fingers, bringing it up to her mouth in a sensuous arc of her arm to her as she talks animatedly with my mother, who has come up to sit between the two women, both only a few years younger than herself. My mother is somewhere halfway between the poles they represent in our culture.*

11   It became my father's obsession to get out of the barrio, and thus we were never permitted to form bonds with the place or with the people who lived there. Yet the building was a comfort to my mother, who never got over yearning for *la isla.* She felt surrounded by her language: the walls were thin, and voices speaking and arguing in Spanish could be heard all day. *Salsas* blasted out of radios turned on early in the morning and left on for company. Women seemed to cook rice and beans perpetually—the strong aroma of red kidney beans boiling permeated the hallways.

12   Though Father preferred that we do our grocery shopping at the supermarket when he came home on weekend leaves, my mother insisted that she could cook only with products whose labels she could read, and so, during the week, I accompanied her and my little brother to *La Bodega*—a hole-in-the-wall grocery store across the street from *El Building.* There we squeezed down three narrow aisles jammed with various products. Goya and Libby's—those were the trademarks trusted by her Mamá, and so my mother bought cans of Goya beans, soups and condiments. She bought little cans of Libby's fruit juices for us. And she bought Colgate toothpaste and Palmolive soap. (The final *e* is pronounced in both those products in Spanish, and for many years I believed that they were manufactured on the Island. I remember my surprise at first hearing a commercial on television for the toothpaste in which Colgate rhymed with "ate.") We would linger at La Bodega, for it was there that mother breathed best, taking in the familiar aromas of the foods she knew from Mamá's kitchen, and it was also there that she got to speak to the other women of El Building without violating outright Father's dictates against fraternizing with our neighbors.

13   But he did his best to make our "assimilation" painless. I can still see him carrying a Christmas tree up several flights of stairs to our apartment, leaving a trail of aromatic pine. He carried it formally, as if it were a flag in a parade. We were the only ones in El Building that I knew of who got presents on both Christmas Day and on *Día de Reyes*, the day when the Three Kings brought gifts to Christ and to Hispanic children.

14   Our greatest luxury in El Building was having our own television set. It must have been a result of Father's guilty feelings over the isolation he had imposed on us, but we were one of the first families in the barrio to have one. My brother quickly became an avid watcher of Captain Kangaroo and Jungle Jim. I loved all the family series, and by the time I started first grade in school, I could have drawn a map of Middle America as exemplified by the lives of characters in "Father Knows Best," "The Donna Reed Show," "Leave It to Beaver," "My Three Sons," and (my favorite) "Bachelor Father," where John Forsythe treated his adopted teenage daughter like a princess because he was rich and had a Chinese houseboy to do everything for him. Compared to our neighbors in El Building, we were rich. My father's Navy check provided us with financial security and a standard of life that the factory workers envied. The only thing his money could not buy us was a place to live away from the barrio—his greatest wish and Mother's greatest fear.

15   *In the home movie the men are shown next, sitting around a card table set up in one corner of the living room, playing dominoes. The clack of the ivory pieces is a sound familiar. I heard it in many houses on the Island and in many apartments in Paterson. In "Leave It to Beaver," the Cleavers played bridge in every other episode; in my childhood, the men started every social occasion with a hotly debated round of dominoes: the women would sit around and watch, but they never participated in the games.*

16   *Here and there you can see a small child. Children were always brought to parties and, whenever they got sleepy, put to bed in the host's bedrooms. Babysitting was a concept unrecognized by the Puerto Rican women I knew: a responsible mother did not leave her children with any stranger. And in a culture where children are not considered intrusive, there is no need to leave children at home. We went where our mother went.*

17   Of my pre-school years I have only impressions: the sharp bite of the wind in December as we walked with our parents towards the brightly lit stores downtown, how I felt like a stuffed doll in my heavy coat, boots and mittens; how good it was to walk into the five-and-dime and sit at the counter drinking hot chocolate.

18   On Saturdays our whole family would walk downtown to shop at the big department stores on Broadway. Mother bought all our clothes at Penny's and Sears, and she liked to buy her dresses at the women's specialty shops like Lerner's and Diana's. At some point we would go into Woolworth's and sit at the soda fountain to eat.

19   We never ran into other Latinos at these stores or eating out, and it became clear to me only years later that the women from El Building shopped mainly at other places—stores owned either by other Puerto Ricans, or by Jewish merchants who had philosophically accepted our presence in the city and decided to make us their good customers, if not neighbors and friends. These establishments were located not downtown, but in the blocks around our street, and they were referred

to generically as *La Tienda, El Bazar, La Bodega, La Botánica*. Everyone knew what was meant. These were the stores where your face did not turn a clerk to stone, where your money was as green as anyone else's.

20   On New Year's Eve we were dressed up like child models in the Sears catalogue—my brother in a miniature man's suit and bow tie, and I in black patent leather shoes and a frilly dress with several layers of crinolines underneath. My mother wore a bright red dress that night, I remember, and spike heels; her long black hair hung to her waist. Father, who usually wore his Navy uniform during his short visits home, had put on a dark civilian suit for the occasion: we had been invited to his uncle's house for a big celebration. Everyone was excited because my mother's brother, Hernán—a bachelor who could indulge himself in such luxuries—had bought a movie camera which he would be trying out that night.

21   Even the home movie cannot fill in the sensory details such a gathering left imprinted in a child's brain. The thick sweetness of women's perfume mixing with the ever-present smells of food cooking in the kitchen: meat and plantain *pasteles*, the ubiquitous rice dish made special with pigeon peas—*gandules*—and seasoned with the precious *sofrito* sent up from the island by somebody's mother or smuggled in by a recent traveler. *Sofrito* was one of the items that women hoarded, since it was hardly ever in stock at La Bodega. It was the flavor of Puerto Rico.

22   The men drank Palo Viejo rum and some of the younger ones got weepy. The first time I saw a grown man cry was at a New Year's Eve party. He had been reminded of his mother by the smells in the kitchen. But what I remember most were the boiled *pasteles*—boiled plantain or yucca rectangles stuffed with corned beef or other meats, olives, and many other savory ingredients, all wrapped in banana leaves. Everyone had to fish one out with a fork. There was always a "trick" pastel—one without stuffing—and whoever got that one was the "New Year's Fool."

23   There was also the music. Long-playing albums were treated like precious china in these homes. Mexican recordings were popular, but the songs that brought tears to my mother's eyes were sung by the melancholic Daniel Santos, whose life as a drug addict was the stuff of legend. Felipe Rodríguez was a particular favorite of couples. He sang about faithless women and broken-hearted men. There is a snatch of a lyric that has stuck in my mind like a needle on a worn groove: "De piedra ha de ser mi cama, de piedra la cabecera . . . la mujer que a mí me quiera . . . ha de quererme de veras. Ay, Ay, corazón, ¿por qué no amas . . . ?" I must have heard it a thousand times since the idea of a bed made of stone, and its connection to love, first troubled me with its disturbing images.

24   The five-minute home movie ends with people dancing in a circle. The creative filmmaker must have asked them to do that so that they could file past him. It is both comical and sad to watch silent dancing. Since there is no justification for the absurd movements that music provides for some of us, people appear frantic, their faces embarrassingly intense. It's as if you were watching sex. Yet for years, I've had dreams in the form of this home movie. In a recurring scene, familiar faces push themselves forward into my mind's eye, plastering their features into

distorted close-ups. And I'm asking them: "Who is she? Who is the woman I don't recognize? Is she an aunt? Somebody's wife? Tell me who she is. Tell me who these people are."

25   "No, see the beauty mark on her cheek as big as a hill on the lunar landscape of her face—well, that runs in the family. The women on your father's side of the family wrinkle early; it's the price they pay for that fair skin. The young girl with the green stain on her wedding dress is *La Novia*—just up from the island. See, she lowers her eyes as she approaches the camera like she's supposed to. Decent girls never look you directly in the face. *Humilde*, humble, a girl should express humility in all her actions. She will make a good wife for your cousin. He should consider himself lucky to have met her only weeks after she arrived here. If he married her quickly, she will make him a good Puerto Rican-style wife; but if he waits too long, she will be corrupted by the city, just like your cousin there."

26   "She means me. I do what I want. This is not some primitive island I live on. Do they expect me to wear a black *mantilla* on my head and go to mass every day? Not me. I'm an American woman and I will do as I please. I can type faster than anyone in my senior class at Central High, and I'm going to be a secretary to a lawyer when I graduate. I can pass for an American girl anywhere—I've tried it— at least for Italian, anyway. I never speak Spanish in public. I hate these parties, but I wanted the dress. I look better than any of these *humildes* here. My life is going to be different. I have an American boyfriend. He is older and has a car. My parents don't know it, but I sneak out of the house late at night sometimes to be with him. If I marry him, even my name will be American. I hate rice and beans. It's what makes these women fat."

27   "Your *prima* is pregnant by that man she's been sneaking around with. Would I lie to you? I'm your great-uncle's common-law wife—the one he abandoned on the island to marry your cousin's mother. I was not invited to this party, but I came anyway. I came to tell you that story about your cousin that you've always wanted to hear. Remember that comment your mother made to a neighbor that has always haunted you? The only thing you heard was your cousin's name and then you saw your mother pick up your doll from the couch and say: 'It was as big as this doll when they flushed it down the toilet.' This image has bothered you for years, hasn't it? You had nightmares about babies being flushed down the toilet, and you wondered why anyone would do such a horrible thing. You didn't dare ask your mother about it. She would only tell you that you had not heard her right and yell at you for listening to adult conversations. But later, when you were old enough to know about abortions, you suspected. I am here to tell you that you were right. Your cousin was growing an *Americanito* in her belly when this movie was made. Soon after she put something long and pointy into her pretty self, thinking maybe she could get rid of the problem before breakfast and still make it to her first class at the high school. Well, Niña, her screams could be heard downtown. Your aunt, her Mamá, who had been a midwife on the Island, managed to pull the little thing out. Yes, they probably flushed it down the toilet, what else could they do with it—give it a Christian burial in a little white casket with blue

bows and ribbons? Nobody wanted that baby—least of all the father, a teacher at her school with a house in West Paterson that he was filling with real children, and a wife who was a natural blond.

28   "Girl, the scandal sent your uncle back to the bottle. And guess where your cousin ended up? Irony of ironies. She was sent to a village in Puerto Rico to live with a relative on her mother's side: a place so far away from civilization that you have to ride a mule to reach it. A real change in scenery. She found a man there. Women like that cannot live without male company. But believe me, the men in Puerto Rico know how to put a saddle on a woman like her. *La Gringa*, they call her. ha, ha. ha. *La Gringa* is what she always wanted to be . . ."

29   The old woman's mouth becomes a cavernous black hole I fall into. And as I fall, I can feel the reverberations of her laughter. I hear the echoes of her last mocking words: *La Gringa, La Gringa!* And the conga line keeps moving silently past me. There is no music in my dream for the dancers.

30   When Odysseus visits Hades asking to see the spirit of his mother, he makes an offering of sacrificial blood, but since all of the souls crave an audience with the living, he has to listen to many of them before he can ask questions. I, too, have to hear the dead and the forgotten speak in my dream. Those who are still part of my life remain silent, going around and around in their dance. The others keep pressing their faces forward to say things about the past.

31   My father's uncle is last in line. He is dying of alcoholism, shrunken and shriveled like a monkey, his face is a mass of wrinkles and broken arteries. As he comes closer I realize that in his features I can see my whole family. If you were to stretch that rubbery flesh, you could find my father's face, and deep within *that* face— mine. I don't want to look into those eyes ringed in purple. In a few years he will retreat into silence, and take a long, long time to die. *Move back, Tío, I tell him. I don't want to hear what you have to say. Give the dancers room to move, soon it will be midnight. Who is the New Year's Fool this time?*

Questions for Discussion

1. Of what cultural and lifestyle differences was Cofer most conscious when she first arrived in Paterson? What prejudice did her family encounter there?
2. What does the television that she watches teach Cofer about American family life and how to adapt to it?
3. How do Cofer's father and mother relate differently to their neighborhood environment? With whose values does Cofer identify?
4. How does Cofer respond to the *La Gringa* story? Why does she respond in this way? What dream continues to haunt her?
5. What dreamlike images and symbols does Cofer use in her narrative? How do these images contribute to the story and its power?
6. Interpret the meaning of the title, "Silent Dancing." Why is the dancing "silent"?

Ideas for Writing

1. Write an essay in which you discuss a conflict that you or a close friend experienced because you or your friend was not a member of the dominant cultural group in your community. What did you learn from this conflict and how did it help shape your perceptions and expectations of the world?
2. Develop your journal entry into an essay.

 # Eavan Boland

The Source

Eavan Boland was born in Dublin in 1944. The daughter of the Irish Ambassador to London and the United Nations, she moved with her family as a child and was educated in London from 1950–1956 and in New York from 1956–1960. Eavan Boland attended Trinity College in Dublin and graduated with First Class Honors in 1966. Boland married novelist Kevin Casey in 1969, and they have two daughters. Boland has received many awards for her poetry. Most recently she won the Lannan Award for her collection In a Time of Violence *(1994). More recent works include* Object Lessons: A Study of the Woman and the Poet in her Time *(1995) and* An Origin Like Water *(1996). Boland has taught at a number of universities: Trinity College in Dublin, Bowdoin College, the University of Houston, and Washington University in St. Louis. In 1995 she accepted a position as a professor of English at Stanford University. Boland writes about her love for Ireland and the pain of watching its devastation, about her sense of alienation as a child when she attended schools in foreign countries, about her love for her children and husband as well as the pains of their inevitable separations. While Boland often sets her poems within history and myth, at the same time she is also writing about the meanings of the memories and experiences of her own life. In the "The Source" the speaker of the poem is searching for meaning in her memories of a family trip to the Wicklow Mountains of Ireland.*

JOURNAL

Write about an object that you have kept for many years. What memories does it hold for you?

The adults stood
making sounds of disappointment.

We were high up in the Wicklow hills,
in a circle of whins and lilacs.

5 We were looking for the source of a river.
   We never found it.

   Instead, we drove to its northern edge.
   And there the river leaned into the afternoon—
   all light, all intrusion—
10 the way a mirror interrupts a room.

   See me kneeling in a room
   whose boundary
   is fog and the dusk of a strange city.

   The mirror shows a child in bad light.

15 From the inlaid box I lift up something
   closed in tissue paper.
   My mother's hair. A whole coil of it.
   It is the colour of corn harvested in darkness.

   As the light goes,
20 I hold in my hand the coarse weight and
   hopeless safe-keeping
   and there comes back to me
   the dialect of the not-found.

   Maybe. Nearly. It could almost be.

Questions for Discussion

1. What is the dramatic situation at the beginning of the poem? What are
   the "adults" in the poem doing? What is the narrator's relationship to
   these adults? At what place and time do these events occur?
2. What is suggested by the poem's title "The Source"? How does the fact
   that Wicklow, the rural, hilly area where the first four stanzas of the
   poem are set, is where the legendary Irish river Liffey begins? In answering this question consider that the River Liffey, which flows
   through Dublin from the Wicklow hills, suggested to the famous Irish
   novelist James Joyce a pun on the similarity between "Liffey" and the
   word *life*.
3. Why is the pronoun shift from "we" to "me" and "I" after the fourth
   stanza of the poem significant?
4. In what ways is the "whole coil" of her mother's hair discovered by the
   narrator in the inlaid box symbolic? How does the hair with its
   "colour of corn" relate back to the setting at the beginning of the
   poem?

5. How is light used symbolically in the poem? How does the lighting change or shift throughout the poem?

6. What definition or image of the persistence of early memory is suggested by the "dialect of the not-found" at the end of the poem and by the ambiguous final line, "Maybe. Nearly. It could almost be"?

Ideas for Writing

1. Write a narrative essay or poem about a childhood memory that was inspired by looking at something you have saved from your past.

2. Write an essay in which you argue either for or against the idea that we can understand the past better through reliving memories imaginatively, as the narrator does in this poem. You might also want to refer to other writers in this chapter to support your point of view.

 ## Corinne Kiku Okada

Namesake

Originally from Manhattan Beach, California, Corey Okada is a design major who wants to be a book illustrator and children's book writer. Okada chose to write about the name that she shared with her great-aunt because "I knew it would force me to be honest about something very personal that I had never been honest to myself about before." Corey Okada went through several drafts of this essay. From the beginning she consciously used the silver-framed photograph of her great-aunt to help keep the paper focused. What she enjoys most about writing is the reflection it requires: "It is such an exciting challenge to try to express and preserve moments, feelings, and ideas on paper. It is a challenge that never lessens and never grows dull."

JOURNAL

Write about a relationship you have, or had, with an older relative that has helped you to mature.

---

1   It was always the first thing I went to look at when I entered her apartment, and it was always the last thing I glanced at when I left. On a small coffee table, a thick silver frame propped it up towards me. It was a beautiful photograph of my Great Aunt Corinne, taken when she was a young woman. Her face in the photograph somehow always struck me as unusual. A gentle wave of thick black hair contrasted stunningly with her fair face, and her smile was strangely happy and

melancholy at the same time. What I found disturbing about the photograph was a contrast greater than that between her dark hair and her fair face, a contrast that was harsh and unkind. The discrepancy was between the Aunt Corinne I knew and the Aunt Corinne in the photograph.

2   The Aunt Corinne I knew had short, greasy, black hair pinned back upon a pale balding head. Her smile was almost toothless and was gapingly childish. She seemed retarded because of a brain tumor that spread as she grew from a young girl to adulthood. Since her family was poor, they could not afford any medical attention for her, save glasses for her failing vision.

3   My name is also Corinne. I have never used it until recently. All my life I have been called "Corey," and I have corrected others when they did not use my nickname. I have done this not only because I like the name Corey, but also because I have not wanted to be associated with my great aunt in such an intimate way.

4   Identity and individuality are tightly woven into our names, especially when we are seven or so. When I was this age, I feared that I, too, might develop a deteriorating mental condition like that of my great aunt just because we shared the same name. More importantly I did not want to use the name Corinne because I was embarrassed at the bond the name created with this person whom I considered pathetic and incomplete, whose greatest tragedy was the loss of a healthy mind. This frightening change was tangible to me in the silver-framed picture of my great aunt.

5   I rarely saw that haunting picture, for my family seldom visited Corinne, who lived far away. When we did visit, I tried to conceal my reluctance and fear. While I did not want to be reminded of the bond I had to this woman, a member of my family never failed to tell me how happy Corinne would be to see me and how honored she was that I was named after her. At the time, I could not understand why I was named after her. Why name your daughter after a mentally deficient aunt—out of pity? That was all I could think of.

6   When we entered her apartment, time slowed down; even the air conditioner seemed to drone quieter and slower. The air was still and calm. Either Corinne or her mother, my great grandmother, welcomed us into the tiny living room. I could not tell which was older. To me, they both were simply very old. Then I would see it: the dreaded and admired woman gazing up from the silver frame. The two-dimensional eyes never focused on anything in the room. From an age only captured in browning photographs, those eyes gazed through ours and peacefully into the distance.

7   Although the two women never offered us any refreshments on our visits, I would not have wanted to eat, for I was thoughtfully absorbing my surroundings and my great aunt with special care and silence. Observing her thin, papery skin made me wince sadly for her fragility, and when she grasped my hand with her swollen fingers, I could not help but feel warmth for her. Her eyes were bright and glistened with the damp glaze that always covered them. The long, fine black hairs above her lip, graceful in contrast to her chewed words, quivered ever so slightly as she talked. When I was with her, my discomfort at being related to her seemed to go away, exposing a rawer discomfort underneath, an embarrassment for ever reproaching her and her name.

8   After what seemed like neither hours nor minutes—time somehow had been lost among those fine black hairs—we would hug and say goodbye to the two women. As we left I would take one last look at the photograph on the coffee table. When I told Corinne how pretty it was, she would smile proudly and gaze at it with affection. She never looked at it with sorrow for that which had been lost forever, but with simple acceptance and joy for that which she once was.

9   Aunt Corinne died when I was in eighth grade. I remember the ride home from school when my mother told me that she had passed away. An emptiness swelled up within me. I suddenly felt that I had lost a part of myself. In a basic way, I had found security in the bond of our shared name; it was as if she was my physical tie to the world before I existed. That day on the ride home from school I was very sad for Corinne, for both of us.

10   Corinne—when I hear this name now and when I sign my checks with this name, I often think of her, my great aunt. But sometimes when I hear the name I do not think of her at all because the name Corinne is more comfortable to me now. After all, it is my name too.

Questions for Discussion

1. How does Corey Okada use the framed photograph of her great-aunt as a structuring device for her essay? What other images and details help to convey her feelings about her great-aunt and their relationship?
2. Why does Okada feel embarrassed and ashamed when visiting her great-aunt?
3. How does the student use contrasts to develop the ambivalent feelings she has about her great-aunt and their relationship?
4. How do the writer's changing feelings about her name parallel both changes in her attitude toward her great-aunt and the growth of her own self-awareness? What did Okada learn about herself from analyzing her relationship with her great-aunt?

 Tin Le

Enter Dragon

Tin Le was born in Vietnam and has many pleasant memories of his childhood there. In 1985, his brother, mother, and Tin reunited with his father in the United States after six years of separation. Tin Le has a special love of nature and photography; he enjoys taking pictures of landscapes and animals. After finishing his undergraduate studies, he hopes to attend optometry school. Tin wrote the following essay in response to a question that asked him to narrate an experience similar to Maya Angelou's in "Angel of the Candy Counter," in which a childhood memory of discrimination is countered by a fantasy of power.

Write about a fantasy you had when you were a child that involved revenge or power over your classmates.

1   Have you ever been harassed or even physically abused by your schoolmates or other people you encountered just because you were different from the "average" person in your school or community? This happened to me when I came to America in 1985, an immigrant from Vietnam, and was placed in a seventh grade classroom in Redwood City. It was a small school in a quiet community, but also a place where I had a stormy life for about a year. It was the most horrible experience that I ever had in my life. Kids at that age can be very mean to each other, and I was unfortunate to be on the receiving end of the cruelty.

2   I went to a school that did not have a lot of Asians. Because I was Asian, my schoolmates often teased me. Some of them, influenced by Japanese *ninjas* and Chinese martial art fighters in movies, often challenged me to fights because they thought that I was one of "them," the Asian martial arts fighters. When I refused to fight, they taunted me, calling me chicken. They also called me weak and a nerd because I wore glasses. For a whole year in seventh grade I suffered from their harassment.

3   I especially remember one day when a classmate came to me on the playground and asked if I knew Karate. When I answered, "No," he acted surprised and remarked, "All Chinese know Kung Fu; aren't you one of them? You're supposed to know some Karate. Let's fight and see who is better." Although I ignored him and walked away, he followed me and started to push me around. The more I yielded, the more he attacked me, yet I could do nothing because he was so much bigger than I was. Eventually he seemed to achieve his goal because other students started to gather around us and cheer for him. He became the hero, the macho guy, and I became the laughing-stock of the school. From then on, they labeled me chicken and a weak Chinese, even though I am actually Vietnamese. In my classmates' eyes, all Asians were the same; there were no distinctions.

4   After this episode many students hit me or pushed me around whenever they felt like it, because they knew that I would not fight back. For example, often at lunch time, several of them would pretend that they did not see me and would walk right into me, spilling my milk or anything else on my tray; then they would say "Sorry." However, saying sorry solved nothing and did not replace my lunch.

5   The worst part about this experience was that I did not have anyone to turn to for help. I did not have the courage to share my problem with my parents, for I was afraid that worrying about my problem would just contribute to their own burdens. My parents had to work long hours every day so that they could provide for us, my brother and me, a happy life. Once they came home, they were very tired and they needed to rest. Furthermore, I wanted them to feel proud of me as they always had. Fortunately, like Maya Angelou in "The Angel of the Candy Counter," I found a way to resolve my problem by developing a fantasy to endure the pain. I fantasized that I had Bruce Lee's fighting skill (he was the greatest

movie star martial arts fighter; his skill even surpassed that of Chuck Norris). I imagined that I fixed up a date after school to settle my unfinished business with the guy who started my nightmare. The moment for our showdown came, and with just one roundhouse kick, I knocked him down to the ground in front of hundreds of schoolmate spectators. He begged me to let him go and promised that he would not pick on anyone else anymore. In my fantasy world, from that point on, my friends began to respect me and even to move aside wherever I went. I also imagined that I would disguise myself in black clothes like those of the ninjas and rescue other victims from bullies in the school, disappearing from the scene as soon as everything was over.

6   Even though the fantasy did not actually solve my problem, it helped me to escape and forget about the bitter reality that I was in, allowing me to enter a world of my own. The fantasy was very helpful to me because it brought joy and a feeling of victory into my harsh experience at school. As a recent immigrant, it was hard for me to try to cope with the language and cultural barriers, and, at the same time, to deal with the bullying and abuse from the students at my school. I still cannot understand how human beings could be so cruel to one another. I realize now that people use fantasies all the time as defense mechanisms to release us from the stress and abuse we must endure in daily life. I wish that we could get to a stage where we would not have to use these compensatory fantasies, a stage in which people could accept one another for who they are, despite differences in physical character, race, and culture.

Questions for Discussion

1. The theme and structure of Tin Le's essay are modeled after Maya Angelou's autobiographical piece included in this chapter. How are Tin's experiences and the insights he draws from them similar to Angelou's experience at the dentist? How does Tin Le's perspective differ from hers?

2. What comment does the essay make about racially motivated bullying and its influence on Asian immigrant youth? Have you witnessed behavior similar to that described in the essay? What was your response to this harassment?

3. Tin Le's essay concludes by stating that he cannot "understand how human beings can be so cruel to one another." What would be your response to this statement? What do you believe causes human cruelty such as that described in the essay?

4. Comment on Tin Le's use of narrative examples to support his comments on racial harrassment. How does his use of narrative help to support the major points he makes in the essay?

Chapter Writing Topics

1. Write about a family member or myth that helped to shape your self-concept and values.

2. Write an essay in which you discuss how the readings in this chapter affected your understanding of the importance of memories in shaping an

individual's self-concept. Refer to several selections in this chapter and to your own experiences to support your point of view.

3. Write a short story or a poem based on a childhood memory. Then write a discussion of what you learned about yourself through writing the story or poem.

4. Discuss several perspectives on the importance of childhood memories. Refer to selections in this chapter or Chapter 1 for examples and support.

5. Write an essay that explores a new insight into memory, history, and self-understanding that you have developed through reading the selections in this chapter and Chapter 1. For example, Boland and Gould explore the reliability of memories of the past, questioning the extent to which the past and "history" are said to truly exist outside of what we recall and recreate through memory and imagination. Is there an "objective" past, or does each person invent his or her own version of history?

6. Write an essay that explores your family's legacy by giving an account of several memories that have been crucial to your family's sense of identity and values.

7. Write an individual or collaborative review of a film that discusses the way in which the role of memories is presented. Films to consider include:

Wild Strawberries, Fried Green Tomatoes, Prince of Tides, Avalon, To Sleep with Anger, Eat a Bowl of Tea, Stand By Me, Cinema Paradiso

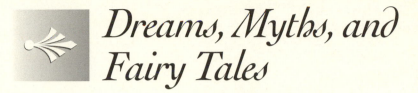

4

Dreams, Myths, and Fairy Tales

Myths are public dreams, dreams are private myths.
JOSEPH CAMPBELL
Hero With a Thousand Faces

Fantasy is the core of all writing for children, as I think it is for the writing of any book, for any creative act, perhaps for the act of living.
MAURICE SENDAK

The ancient Pueblo vision of the world was inclusive. . . . Pueblo oral tradition necessarily embraced all levels of human experience. . . . [S]tories about the Creation and Emergence of human beings and animals into this World continue to be retold each year for four days and four nights during the winter solstice.
LESLIE MARMON SILKO
Landscape, History and the Pueblo Imagination

Comparing and Contrasting: Strategies for Thinking and Writing

The readings selected for this chapter encourage you to think comparatively. You will find that dreams are compared to myths, myths to fairy tales, traditional tales to modern forms of literature; also included are different versions of the same basic myths from various cultures. We have designed the chapter in this way because comparing and contrasting are related and essential aspects of reading and writing and are crucial as well to the way the mind thinks and organizes experiences.

When you compare and contrast, you explore relationships between subjects that, despite apparent distinctions, have qualities in common. In this chapter, for example, Carl Jung uses comparison and contrast to emphasize the differences between his own ideas on dream analysis. Comparative writing demands sophisticated, analytical thinking and organization of ideas. Al-

161

though everyone naturally makes comparisons while thinking, the structure of comparative writing is more balanced and complex than what you normally do when making comparisons in daily life. Prewriting is especially useful for gathering insights and details to use for comparison.

Prewriting for Comparison

You can begin to do prewriting for a comparison paper by using any of the techniques discussed in Chapter 1, such as freewriting or clustering. For example, to use brainstorming begin by dividing a piece of paper down the middle; then create brainstorming lists of points or qualities you perceive in the subjects of your analysis. A student who wanted to develop a comparison between fairy tales and elementary school readers took the following notes:

Fairy Tales	*Elementary School Readers*
imaginative	seem written by "formula"
engage interest and feelings	don't involve students deeply
try to teach "good behavior" while entertaining	try to teach "basic reading skills" and to encourage conformity
raise some interesting issues	avoid controversial issues

You can see some striking contrasts in the lists above. After eliminating some items and grouping the related points, the student could move from the list to a general, clearly worded thesis statement such as the following: "Fairy tales engage the feelings and minds of the child, while primary school texts often fail to attract the interests of children, and thus may actually turn children off to reading." In a very short time, this student writer has found several major points of contrast for possible development and a good central idea to unify a paragraph or essay.

Outlining and Transition

Use of an outline helps to structure extended comparison/contrast papers. An outline will help you to achieve a balanced treatment of each subject and major point in your paper. In preparing an outline, consider the kind of organization you want to use. Comparisons can be structured around points of similarity or difference; use details to clarify and to add interest to the comparison. In subject-by-subject comparing, points are made about two subjects in separate paragraphs or sections of a paper, bringing the two subjects together in the conclusion for a final evaluation or summary of major points.

In writing your comparison essay, make the basic points of your comparison clear to your readers through transitional statements. As you move from one comparative issue to another, use expressions such as "in comparison to," "similarly," and "likewise." If the differences between your subjects seem more striking than the similarities, use contrast as your major strategy for examining and noting distinctions, emphasizing your points with transitional expressions such as "in contrast to" and "another point of distinction." As student writer Josh Groban does in his comparison essay in this chapter between the Yao myth of creation and the story of Genesis in the Bible, you need to be careful that you order and develop your points with care, distinguishing between similarities and differences so as to avoid confusion and to retain a clear sense of the overall purpose of your comparison: to understand complex realities, to evaluate, to make a choice.

Evaluation

Evaluating involves making a judgment based on a standard that you hold about a subject or issue. In the prewriting exercise above, the student who contrasted fairy tales with primary school textbooks made an evaluation of each based on personal likes and dislikes: the student liked fairy tales and disliked textbooks. Although the student writer didn't discuss her standards for judging children's literature, we can assume that she likes reading that is entertaining and engaging and is bored by writing that exists simply as a tool for learning. In fact, the student might have thought more critically about the standards that are appropriate for school readers. If she had she might have considered the problems that schools have in selecting and judging materials for different types of learners. Regardless of your subject of comparison, by establishing guidelines for comparing your standards with those of other people, you can come closer to seeing whether your values are realistic guides for belief and behavior.

Logical Fallacies of Comparison and Contrast

When you begin to think and write comparatively, you may find yourself falling into misleading patterns of thought. A common problem involving comparison and contrast is the drawing of rigid distinctions that force a choice between artificially opposed positions. Often a contrastive statement will imply that one position is a "bad" choice: "America, Love it or leave it"; "A person is either a God-fearing Christian or a sinful atheist"; "You're either a real he-man or a spineless sissy." Such statements employ both an incorrect use of contrast and an inappropriate use of evaluation by setting up an either-or dilemma. In fact, there are occasions when any comparison oriented to evaluating may seem inappropriate. In comparing and contrasting the myths from different cultures included in the portfolio in this chapter, for instance, you may note that each myth of creation involves very different sets of images and values relative to the act and purpose of creation. When thinking about radically different cultures and values, it is more useful simply to make relevant distinctions than to attempt to evaluate one culture as superior or inferior to another.

In the faulty analogy, another common error in comparing, a person attempts to create a connection between two subjects when there are few strong points of similarity, such as arguing that, because life is dreamlike in certain ways, a person should go through life passively, accepting whatever happens just as one might in a dream. Analogies and imaginative, nonliteral comparisons, known as metaphors and similes, can be useful in writing, giving a sense of unexpected and imaginative connections, making descriptions clearer, bringing new insights. On the other hand, taking a metaphorical statement, such as "Life is a dream," and applying it too literally as a standard for conduct ignores real distinctions between the waking world and the sleeping world.

The section on dialogic argument in Chapter 7 discusses ways in which flexible stances in argument can allow you to move beyond overly rigid, unexamined standards of comparison and evaluation. For now, you should feel ready to use the strategy of comparison more systematically and productively to help you to perceive clear relationships between the public world and your inner world.

THEMATIC INTRODUCTION

Once you begin to understand how your memories of particular childhood events have shaped and are still influencing your identity and the direction of your life, you may begin to take pleasure in relating your personal history to myths and fairy tales. These universal stories have helped to connect humans to one another, despite their historical and cultural differences. Myths are patterned stories that present the reader with ideal heroes and heroines acting through dreamlike plots and settings, representing the fundamental values of a society. Fairy tales satisfy the needs of younger people, and adults as well, for dangerous adventures where happiness and justice ultimately prevail. Both forms provide ethical lessons that help readers to discriminate between creative and destructive or good and evil behavior. Although our culture often encourages us to doubt the imaginative world of the mythical, asking us instead to seek out practical, logical solutions to problems, myths continue to live on as cornerstones of traditional belief and to help people to uncover meaning, order, and hope in a world that sometimes seems chaotic. The fundamental adventure and quest patterns of stories and legends are continually being transformed and adapted according to the values of each new age. Today's popular myths provide readers with revised values and reflections on changing cultural norms.

This chapter begins with a poem by the African American writer Nikki Giovanni. In "ego-tripping (there may be a reason why)" the speaker imagines herself living through the myths of her heritage as she realizes that identification with these myths protects her and gives her power. The next two selections present theoretical perspectives on the meaning and importance of dreams and myths. In "The Four Functions of Mythology" a scholar of world mythology, Joseph Campbell, describes the way in which myths help individuals to reconcile their awareness of good and evil, provide images of the universe that validate social order, and offer spiritual meanings. In the next selection, taken from the opening chapter of *Man and His Symbols*, Carl Jung concludes that it is through symbol-laden dreams that the unconscious mind speaks, helping people to get more closely in touch with their inner selves. Jung sees dreams with their universal symbolism as vital creations in themselves, as internal representation of myths.

In the third essay, "Landscape, History, and the Pueblo Imagination," Leslie Marmon Silko focuses on the importance of stories, dreams, and myths. She explains why they are at the core of the Pueblo vision of life and why in her culture these stories are shared through oral language. Silko emphasizes the enduring importance of the creation story. Following Silko's essay, we have included a portfolio of creation myths. These creation stories from cultures around the world celebrate the mystery of life as they offer a range of different imaginative explanations of the origins of the world and of human life. Next we have juxtaposed the classical version of the Pygmalion myth to John Updike's short story, "Pygmalion." While the story lines remain the same, the values implicit in each telling are different.

Just as dreams and myths give us clues to our unconscious selves and our connections to universal human concerns, fairy tales, a particular class of myths that have been adapted for the entertainment and enlightenment of children, also reflect on the darker side of human nature. In the next selection, "Fairy Tales and the Existential Predicament," Bruno Bettelheim asserts that children in our modern world need to read classic fairy tales, which present the good and the bad sides of human nature and the conscious and unconscious needs and impulses of humans. To enable you to understand and reflect on the different ways in which a single fairy tale has been interpreted and transformed by particular cultures and historical periods, we have included two versions of the Cinderella myth: the Grimms' "Aschenputtel" and a Native American version of the tale, "The Algonquin Cinderella."

Two student essays conclude the readings selected for this chapter. In "Hsao-suen: A Chinese Virtue" Caitlin Liu explores the changing meanings of a Chinese folktale that taught her the virtues of honoring one's parents. She contrasts her interpretation of the tale as a child and as a young adult. In the second student essay, Joshua Groban compares the meanings of two creation myths to show the different values and beliefs held by the two cultures that produced the myths.

Thinking about myths and fairy tales from different cultures will help you to gain new insights into your own culture, as you begin to see your world in a broader perspective of diverse values, emotional needs, and spiritual concerns. Through drawing comparisons between versions of myths and fairy tales, you will also be better able to see how these universal forms change and yet endure; perhaps they will help you to make sense of your contemporary world and to see its connection to the past. Reflecting on and writing about the implications of your dreams and myths as well as the dreams and myths of others is an essential path on your inward journey toward better self-understanding and a deeper appreciation of the world in which you live.

 # Nikki Giovanni

ego-tripping (there may be a reason why)

Nikki Giovanni (b. 1943) has written children's fiction, memoir, and essays; she is best known for her poetry. Giovanni's poetry, which is influenced by jazz and which she has read aloud on television and records, has been an important influence on younger African American writers and poets, especially the new rap poets and musicians. Giovanni won a Ford Foundation grant and has received awards from the National Endowment for the Arts and the Harlem Cultural Council. Her first book, Black Feeling, Black Talk, *appeared in 1968. Her most recent publication is* Selected Poems *(1996). Currently Giovanni teaches at Virginia Polytechnic Institute and State University. As you read her poem, notice how she is able to capture the popular myths that helped to shape the self-concepts of many African Americans.*

JOURNAL

Imagine yourself as related to the larger-than-life heroes and/or heroines you admire. Begin each sentence of your freewrite with "I"; exaggerate and have fun!

I was born in the congo
I walked to the fertile crescent and built
    the sphinx
I designed a pyramid so tough that a star
5   that only glows every one hundred years falls
    into the center giving divine perfect light
I am bad

I sat on the throne
    drinking nectar with allah
10 I got hot and sent an ice age to europe
    to cool my thirst
My oldest daughter is nefertiti
    the tears from my birth pains
    created the nile
15 I am a beautiful woman

I gazed on the forest and burned
    out the sahara desert
    with a packet of goat's meat
    and a change of clothes
20 I crossed it in two hours
I am a gazelle so swift
    so swift you can't catch me

    For a birthday present when he was three
I gave my son hannibal an elephant
25   He gave me rome for mother's day
My strength flows ever on

My son noah built new / ark and
I stood proudly at the helm
    as we sailed on a soft summer day

30 I turned myself into myself and was
        jesus
        men intone my loving name

        All praises All praises
    I am the one who would save

35 I sowed diamonds in my back yard
    My bowels deliver uranium
            the filings from my fingernails are
            semi-precious jewels
            On a trip north
40 I caught a cold and blew
    My nose giving oil to the arab world
    I am so hip even my errors are correct
    I sailed west to reach east and had to round off
            the earth as I went
45   The hair from my head thinned and gold was
            laid across three continents

    I am so perfect so divine so ethereal so surreal
    I cannot be comprehended
            except by my permission

50 I mean . . . I . . . can fly
        like a bird in the sky . . .

Questions for Discussion

1. To emphasize her pride in her African descent, Giovanni's narrator invokes a number of African cultures, mythologies, places, and historical figures. Identify several of the African references in the poem and explain how the narrator finds pride and power through these references and comparisons.

2. Giovanni's poem combines African references with African American slang or dialect. Identify slang words and phrases in the poem and explain how such expressions add to the power of the poem.

3. In addition to its references to the African/Egyptian cultural tradition, the poem also alludes to biblical characters and mythologies. Point out any references to the Old or New Testament of the Bible, and discuss what you feel such references and implied comparisons add to the poem.

4. Although the poem has a boisterous, buoyant feeling, at times it seems as if Giovanni may be mocking or questioning the narrator's boastfulness. Explain how expressions such as "ego tripping" and "even my errors are correct" could be read as criticisms of the narrator. Why do you think the poet built this self-critical perspective into the poem?

Nicole Griffin

Nikki Giovanni's "ego-tripping (there may be a reason why)" is an entertaining poem about the thoughts of an African American woman. The speaker of the poem is reflecting upon her rich heritage, which makes her feel powerful. She uses the oral history and myths of Africa to say, "How could I not be great?—just look at where I come from." She is very proud of who she is, and her pride shows through her entertaining references to her cultural roots.

I sketched what I imagined the woman in ego-tripping to look like. She has a larger than normal head, due to her growing ego. Her forehead displays her inner thoughts. I drew the pyramids she built, the ark her son built, and the gazelle she compares herself to. Imagining that all of these images represent the truth gives her the same power she would have if they were.

"ego-tripping" helped me to realize the importance of knowing one's cultural traditions and myths. I think the idea of giving yourself an "ego boost" is wonderful in a time when our culture often reduces an individual to insignificance. Reading this poem gives me a lift and puts a smile on my face. Reading this poem encouraged me to think about the importance of the traditions that have shaped my personality and values.

5. What does this poem suggest to you about the functions and power of myth in literature as well as in the inner life of the individual?

Ideas for Writing

1. Try developing your ego-tripping freewriting into your own "rap" or "boast" poem, serious or comic. Refer to myths and cultural traditions that are familiar to you.
2. The speaker in Giovanni's poem seems to gain a sense of personal empowerment through making a series of mythical comparisons. Write an essay in which you argue for or against the importance of comparing oneself to and identifying with characters and situations in myths to gain a sense of pride and self-respect. Use examples of myths you or other people you know believe in that could help to develop a sense of self-esteem.

 Joseph Campbell

The Four Functions of Mythology

Joseph Campbell (1904–1987) was born in New York and studied Medieval Literature at Columbia University. He dropped out of the doctoral program there after being informed that mythology was not an acceptable subject for his dissertation. Campbell taught mythological studies at Sarah Lawrence College for many years before retiring to Hawaii and pursuing his interests in writing and lecturing. In later life he became a popular figure in contemporary culture, inspiring George Lucas's Star Wars films and doing a number of interviews with Bill Moyers on public television. Campbell shared Carl Jung's belief in the archetypal patterns of symbolism in myths and dreams. He was author and editor of many books on world mythology, including The Hero With a Thousand Faces *(1949) and the four-volume* The Masks of God *(1962). In the following selection from "Mythological Themes in Creative Literature and Art," an essay included in the collection* Myths, Dreams, and Religion *(1970), Campbell explores what he considers to be the major functions of mythology in the life of individuals, cultures, and societies.*

JOURNAL

Write a definition of "myth" or "mythology" based on your own personal associations with the term. List as many qualities and functions of myths or mythology as you can.

1   Traditional mythologies serve, normally, four functions, the first of which might be described as the reconciliation of consciousness with the preconditions of its own existence. In the long course of our biological prehistory, living creatures had been consuming each other for hundreds of millions of years before eyes opened to the terrible scene, and millions more elapsed before the level of human consciousness was attained. Analogously, as individuals, we are born, we live and grow, on the impulse of organs that are moved independently of reason to aims antecedent to thought—like beasts: until, one day, the crisis occurs that has separated mankind from the beasts: the realization of the monstrous nature of this terrible game that is life, and our consciousness recoils. In mythological terms: we have tasted the fruit of the wonder-tree of the knowledge of good and evil, and have lost our animal innocence. Schopenhauer's scorching phrase represents the motto of this fallen state: "Life is something that should not have been!" Hamlet's state of indecision is the melancholy consequence: "To be, or not to be!" And, in fact, in the long and varied course of the evolution of the mythologies of mankind, there have been many addressed to the aims of an absolute negation of the world, a condemnation of life, and a backing out. These I have termed the mythologies of "The Great Reversal." They have flourished most prominently in India, particularly since the Buddha's time (sixth century B.C.), whose First Noble Truth, "All life is sorrowful," derives from the same insight as Schopenhauer's rueful dictum. However, more general, and certainly much earlier in the great course of human history, have been the mythologies and associated rites of redemption through affirmation. Throughout the primitive world, where direct confrontations with the brutal bloody facts of life are inescapable and unremitting, the initiation ceremonies to which growing youngsters are subjected are frequently horrendous, confronting them in the most appalling, vivid terms, with experiences—both optically and otherwise—of this monstrous thing that is life: and always with the requirement of a "yea," with no sense of either personal or collective guilt, but gratitude and exhilaration.

2   For there have been, finally, but three attitudes taken toward the awesome mystery in the great mythological traditions; namely, the first, of a "yea"; the second, of a "nay"; and the last, of a "nay," but with a contingent "yea," as in the great complex of messianic cults of the late Levant: Zoroastrianism, Judaism, Christianity, and Islam. In these last, the well-known basic myth has been, of an originally good creation corrupted by a fall, with, however, the subsequent establishment of a supernaturally endowed society, through the ultimate world dominion of which a restoration of the pristine state of the good creation is to be attained. So that, not in nature but in the social order, and not in all societies, but in this, the one and only, is there health and truth and light, integrity and the prospect of perfection. The "yea" here is contingent therefore on the ultimate world victory of this order.

3   The second of the four functions served by traditional mythologies—beyond this of redeeming human consciousness from its sense of guilt in life—is that of formulating and rendering an image of the universe, a cosmological image in keeping with the science of the time and of such kind that, within its range, all

things should be recognized as parts of a single great holy picture, an icon as it were: the trees, the rocks, the animals, sun, moon, and stars, all opening back to mystery, and thus serving as agents of the first function, as vehicles and messengers of the teaching.

4   The third traditional function, then, has been ever that of validating and maintaining some specific social order, authorizing its moral code as a construct beyond criticism or human emendation. In the Bible, for example, where the notion is of a personal god through whose act the world was created, that same god is regarded as the author of the Tablets of the Law; and in India, where the basic idea of creation is not of the act of a personal god, but rather of a universe that has been in being and will be in being forever (only waxing and waning, appearing and disappearing, in cycles ever renewed), the social order of caste has been traditionally regarded as of a piece with the order of nature. Man is not free, according to either of these mythic views, to establish for himself the social aims of his life and to work, then, toward these through institutions of his own devising; but rather, the moral, like the natural order, is fixed for all time, and if times have changed (as indeed they have, these past six hundred years), so that to live according to the ancient law and to believe according to the ancient faith have become equally impossible, so much the worse for these times.

5   The first function served by a traditional mythology, I would term, then, the mystical, or metaphysical, the second, the cosmological, and the third, the sociological. The fourth, which lies at the root of all three as their base and final support, is the psychological: that, namely, of shaping individuals to the aims and ideals of their various social groups, bearing them on from birth to death through the course of a human life. And whereas the cosmological and sociological orders have varied greatly over the centuries and in various quarters of the globe, there have nevertheless been certain irreducible psychological problems inherent in the very biology of our species, which have remained constant, and have, consequently, so tended to control and structure the myths and rites in their service that, in spite of all the differences that have been recognized, analyzed, and stressed by sociologists and historians, there run through the myths of all mankind the common strains of a single symphony of the soul. Let us pause, therefore, to review briefly in sequence the order of these irreducible psychological problems.

6   The first to be faced derives from the fact that human beings are born some fourteen years too soon. No other animal endures such a long period of dependency on its parents. And then, suddenly, at a certain point in life, which varies, according to the culture, from, say, twelve to about twenty years of age, the child is expected to become an adult, and his whole psychological system, which has been tuned and trained to dependency, is now required to respond to the challenges of life in the way of responsibility. Stimuli are no longer to produce responses either of appeal for help or of submission to parental discipline, but of responsible social action appropriate to one's social role. In primitive societies the function of the cruel puberty rites has been everywhere and always to effect and confirm this transformation. And glancing now at our own modern world, deprived of such initiations and becoming yearly more and more intimidated by its

own intransigent young, we may diagnose a neurotic as simply an adult who has failed to cross this threshold to responsibility: one whose response to every challenging situation is, first, "What would Daddy say? Where's Mother?" and only then comes to realize, "Why gosh! I'm Daddy, I'm forty years old! Mother is now my wife! It is I who must do this thing!" Nor have traditional societies ever exhibited much sympathy for those unable or unwilling to assume the roles required. Among the Australian aborigines, if a boy in the course of his initiation seriously misbehaves, he is killed and eaten*—which is an efficient way, of course, to get rid of juvenile delinquents, but deprives the community, on the other hand, of the gifts of original thought. As the late Professor A. R. Radcliffe-Brown of Trinity College, Cambridge, observed in his important study of the Andaman Island pygmies: "A society depends for its existence on the presence in the minds of its members of a certain system of sentiments by which the conduct of the individual is regulated in conformity with the needs of the society. . . . The sentiments in question are not innate but are developed in the individual by the action of the society upon him."† In other words: the entrance into adulthood from the long career of infancy is not, like the opening of a blossom, to a state of naturally unfolding potentialities, but to the assumption of a social role, a mask or "persona," with which one is to identify. In the famous lines of the poet Wordsworth:

Shades of the prison-house begin to close
Upon the growing Boy.‡

A second birth, as it is called, a social birth, is effected, and, as the first had been of Mother Nature, so this one is of the Fathers, Society, and the new body, the new mind, are not of mankind in general but of a tribe, a caste, a certain school, or a nation.

7   Whereafter, inevitably, in due time, there comes a day when the decrees of nature again break forth. That fateful moment at the noon of life arrives when, as Carl Jung reminds us, the powers that in youth were in ascent have arrived at their apogee and the return to earth begins. The claims, the aims, even the interests of society, begin to fall away and, again as in the lines of Wordsworth:

Our noisy years seem moments in the being
Of the eternal Silence: truths that wake,
      To perish never:
Which neither listlessness, nor mad endeavour,
      Nor Man nor Boy,
Nor all that is at enmity with joy,
Can utterly abolish or destroy!

Hence in a season of calm weather

---

*Géza Róheim, *The Eternal Ones of the Dream* (New York: International Universities Press, 1945), p. 232, citing K. Langloh Parker, *The Euahlayi Tribe* (London: A. Constable & Co., 1905), pp. 72–73.
†A. R. Radcliffe-Brown, *The Andaman Islanders* (Cambridge: The University Press, 1933), pp. 233–234.
‡William Wordsworth, *Intimations of Immortality from Recollections of Early Childhood*, II. 64–65.

> Though inland far we be,
> Our Souls have sight of that immortal sea
>   Which brought us hither,
> Can in a moment travel thither,
> And see the Children sport upon the shore,
> And hear the mighty waters rolling evermore.*

8   Both the great and the lesser mythologies of mankind have, up to the present, always served simultaneously, both to lead the young from their estate in nature, and to bear the aging back to nature and on through the last dark door. And while doing all this, they have served, also, to render an image of the world of nature, a cosmological image as I have called it, that should seem to support the claims and aims of the local social group; so that through every feature of the experienced world the sense of an ideal harmony resting on a dark dimension of wonder should be communicated. One can only marvel at the integrating, life-structuring force of even the simplest traditional organization of mythic symbols.

Questions for Discussion

1. As the title indicates, Campbell describes four functions of mythology. What are the functions and how do they differ from one another? Do you agree with this division? Would you have included other functions?

2. Why does Campbell believe that "our consciousness recoils" at the awareness of the "terrible game" of life? What is terrible or sorrowful about life? How does this awareness involve a loss of innocence similar to the tasting of the apple in the Book of Genesis? How does Christianity offer an answer to the sorrow and loss of innocence that is the nature of life?

3. Campbell believes that traditional mythology presents "an image of the universe," a sense of the order of created things. What image of the universe does traditional Judeo-Christian religion present in the Book of Genesis, for example?

4. Why do the mythic views of both the Bible and the tradition of India tell us that humans are not free? What prevents individual freedom from occurring, according to these traditional mythological views? Can you give examples of other mythic stories and classical works that contain a moral or pattern that implies there is no individual freedom of choice and action?

5. How do traditional religions and mythological systems pattern our psychological growth and development as we move toward adulthood, reducing the kind of "neurotic" fixations at a certain maturity level that are so common in our own society? How do mythologies help one to create a "persona" as a social being and prepare us emotionally to come to terms with aging and death?

6. Although Campbell approaches his topic from a general perspective, he makes his ideas more concrete through the use of quotations and refer-

*Ibid., II. 158–171.

ences to mythologies familiar to his readers, such as the Book of Genesis from the Bible. What other examples might he have used?

Ideas for Writing

1. Elsewhere in the longer essay from which this selection is excerpted, Campbell states that both the cosmological and social functions of mythology have been weakened through modern advances in science and technology. Write an essay in which you present several examples that either support or refute Campbell's assertion that the reliance on science and technology have diminished the power of the human spirit that myths embody.
2. Write an essay in which you discuss a myth that you are familiar with which fulfills one of the four functions that Campbell discusses in his essay. Include a copy or detailed description of the myth with your essay. In what ways is this myth woven into the cultural and social assumptions and values that form the basis of your beliefs and lifestyle?

 ## Carl Jung

The Importance of Dreams

A Swiss physician and analyst, Carl Jung (1875–1961) was originally a follower of Sigmund Freud but differed from Freud over Freud's psychoanalytic method and the purpose and meaning of dreams. In the 1920s Jung traveled in Africa and the southwestern United States to study preliterate peoples—their myths, dreams, values, and religions. Eventually Jung developed the concept of the collective unconscious to explain the archetypal patterns of imagery and symbolism that he believed could be found in dreams, literature, and world religions. His Collected Works include twenty volumes of his essays and correspondence. Jung's best-known works include Modern Man in Search of a Soul *(1933) and his autobiography,* Memories, Dreams, Reflections *(1961). The following selection, which is excerpted from his last work,* Man and His Symbols *(1964), explores Jung's ideas about the place of symbols in dreams and myths.*

JOURNAL

Do you think that the types of images or symbols that occur in your dreams also appear in other people's dreams or in dreams of people from other cultures?

1   Man uses the spoken or written word to express the meaning of what he wants to convey. His language is full of symbols, but he also often employs signs or

images that are not strictly descriptive. Some are mere abbreviations or strings of initials, such as UN, UNICEF, or UNESCO; others are familiar trade marks, the names of patent medicines, badges, or insignia. Although these are meaningless in themselves, they have acquired a recognizable meaning through common usage or deliberate intent. Such things are not symbols. They are signs, and they do no more than denote the objects to which they are attached.

2   What we call a symbol is a term, a name, or even a picture that may be familiar in daily life, yet that possesses specific connotations in addition to its conventional and obvious meaning. It implies something vague, unknown, or hidden from us. Many Cretan monuments, for instance, are marked with the design of the double adze. This is an object that we know, but we do not know its symbolic implications. For another example, take the case of the Indian who, after a visit to England, told his friends at home that the English worship animals, because he had found eagles, lions, and oxen in old churches. He was not aware (nor are many Christians) that these animals are symbols of the Evangelists and are derived from the vision of Ezekiel, and that this in turn has an analogy to the Egyptian sun god Horus and his four sons. There are, moreover, such objects as the wheel and the cross that are known all over the world, yet that have a symbolic significance under certain conditions. Precisely what they symbolize is still a matter for controversial speculation.

3   Thus a word or an image is symbolic when it implies something more than its obvious and immediate meaning. It has a wider "unconscious" aspect that is never precisely defined or fully explained. Nor can one hope to define or explain it. As the mind explores the symbol, it is led to ideas that lie beyond the grasp of reason. The wheel may lead our thoughts toward the concept of a "divine" sun, but at this point reason must admit its incompetence; man is unable to define a "divine" being. When, with all our intellectual limitations, we call something "divine," we have merely given it a name, which may be based on a creed, but never on factual evidence.

4   Because there are innumerable things beyond the range of human understanding, we constantly use symbolic terms to represent concepts that we cannot define or fully comprehend. This is one reason why all religions employ symbolic language or images. But this conscious use of symbols is only one aspect of a psychological fact of great importance: Man also produces symbols unconsciously and spontaneously, in the form of dreams.

5   It is not easy to grasp this point. But the point must be grasped if we are to know more about the ways in which the human mind works. Man, as we realize if we reflect for a moment, never perceives anything fully or comprehends anything completely. He can see, hear, touch, and taste; but how far he sees, how well he hears, what his touch tells him, and what he tastes depend upon the number and quality of his senses. These limit his perception of the world around him. By using scientific instruments he can partly compensate for the deficiencies of his senses. For example, he can extend the range of his vision by binoculars or of his hearing by electrical amplification. But the most elaborate apparatus cannot do more than bring distant or small objects within range of his eyes, or make faint sounds more

audible. No matter what instruments he uses, at some point he reaches the edge of certainty beyond which conscious knowledge cannot pass.

6   There are, moreover, unconscious aspects of our perception of reality. The first is the fact that even when our senses react to real phenomena, sights, and sounds, they are somehow translated from the realm of reality into that of the mind. Within the mind they become psychic events, whose ultimate nature is unknowable (for the psyche cannot know its own psychical substance). Thus every experience contains an indefinite number of unknown factors, not to speak of the fact that every concrete object is always unknown in certain respects, because we cannot know the ultimate nature of matter itself.

7   Then there are certain events of which we have not consciously taken note; they have remained, so to speak, below the threshold of consciousness. They have happened, but they have been absorbed subliminally, without our conscious knowledge. We can become aware of such happenings only in a moment of intuition or by a process of profound thought that leads to a later realization that they must have happened; and though we may have originally ignored their emotional and vital importance, it later wells up from the unconscious as a sort of afterthought.

8   It may appear, for instance, in the form of a dream. As a general rule, the unconscious aspect of any event is revealed to us in dreams, where it appears not as a rational thought but as a symbolic image. As a matter of history, it was the study of dreams that first enabled psychologists to investigate the unconscious aspect of conscious psychic events.

9   It is on such evidence that psychologists assume the existence of an unconscious psyche—though many scientists and philosophers deny its existence. They argue naïvely that such an assumption implies the existence of two "subjects," or (to put it in a common phrase) two personalities within the same individual. But this is exactly what it does imply—quite correctly. And it is one of the curses of modern man that many people suffer from this divided personality. It is by no means a pathological symptom; it is a normal fact that can be observed at any time and everywhere. It is not merely the neurotic whose right hand does not know what the left hand is doing. This predicament is a symptom of a general unconsciousness that is the undeniable common inheritance of all mankind.

10   Man has developed consciousness slowly and laboriously, in a process that took untold ages to reach the civilized state (which is arbitrarily dated from the invention of script in about 4000 B.C.). And this evolution is far from complete, for large areas of the human mind are still shrouded in darkness. What we call the "psyche" is by no means identical with our consciousness and its contents.

11   Whoever denies the existence of the unconscious is in fact assuming that our present knowledge of the psyche is total. And this belief is clearly just as false as the assumption that we know all there is to be known about the natural universe. Our psyche is part of nature, and its enigma is as limitless. Thus we cannot define either the psyche or nature. We can merely state what we believe them to be and describe, as best we can, how they function. Quite apart, therefore, from the evidence that medical research has accumulated, there are strong grounds of logic for

rejecting statements like "There is no unconscious." Those who say such things merely express an age-old "misoneism"—a fear of the new and the unknown.

12   There are historical reasons for this resistance to the idea of an unknown part of the human psyche. Consciousness is a very recent acquisition of nature, and it is still in an "experimental" state. It is frail, menaced by specific dangers, and easily injured. As anthropologists have noted, one of the most common mental derangements that occur among primitive people is what they call "the loss of a soul"—which means, as the name indicates, a noticeable disruption (or, more technically, a dissociation) of consciousness.

13   Among such people, whose consciousness is at a different level of development from ours, the "soul" (or psyche) is not felt to be a unit. Many primitives assume that a man has a "bush soul" as well as his own, and that this bush soul is incarnate in a wild animal or a tree, with which the human individual has some kind of psychic identity. This is what the distinguished French ethnologist Lucien Lévy-Brühl called a "mystical participation." He later retracted this term under pressure of adverse criticism, but I believe that his critics were wrong. It is a well-known psychological fact that an individual may have such an unconscious identity with some other person or object.

14   This identity takes a variety of forms among primitives. If the bush soul is that of an animal, the animal itself is considered as some sort of brother to the man. A man whose brother is a crocodile, for instance, is supposed to be safe when swimming a crocodile-infested river. If the bush soul is a tree, the tree is presumed to have something like parental authority over the individual concerned. In both cases an injury to the bush soul is interpreted as an injury to the man.

15   In some tribes, it is assumed that a man has a number of souls; this belief expresses the feeling of some primitive individuals that they each consist of several linked but distinct units. This means that the individual's psyche is far from being safely synthesized; on the contrary, it threatens to fragment only too easily under the onslaught of unchecked emotions.

16   While this situation is familiar to us from the studies of anthropologists, it is not so irrelevant to our own advanced civilization as it might seem. We too can become dissociated and lose our identity. We can be possessed and altered by moods, or become unreasonable and unable to recall important facts about ourselves or others, so that people ask: "What the devil has got into you?" We talk about being able "to control ourselves," but self-control is a rare and remarkable virtue. We may think we have ourselves under control; yet a friend can easily tell us things about ourselves of which we have no knowledge.

17   Beyond doubt, even in what we call a high level of civilization, human consciousness has not yet achieved a reasonable degree of continuity. It is still vulnerable and liable to fragmentation. This capacity to isolate part of one's mind, indeed, is a valuable characteristic. It enables us to concentrate upon one thing at a time, excluding everything else that may claim our attention. But there is a world of difference between a conscious decision to split off and temporarily suppress a part of one's psyche, and a condition in which this happens spontaneously, without one's knowledge or consent and even against one's intention. The former is a civilized achievement, the latter a primitive "loss of a soul," or even the pathological cause of a neurosis.

18   Thus, even in our day the unity of consciousness is still a doubtful affair; it can too easily be disrupted. An ability to control one's emotions that may be very desirable from one point of view would be a questionable accomplishment from another, for it would deprive social intercourse of variety, color, and warmth.

19   It is against this background that we must review the importance of dreams—those flimsy, evasive, unreliable, vague, and uncertain fantasies. To explain my point of view, I would like to describe how it developed over a period of years, and how I was led to conclude that dreams are the most frequent and universally accessible source for the investigation of man's symbolizing faculty.

20   Sigmund Freud was the pioneer who first tried to explore empirically the unconscious background of consciousness. He worked on the general assumption that dreams are not a matter of chance but are associated with conscious thoughts and problems. This assumption was not in the least arbitrary. It was based upon the conclusion of eminent neurologists (for instance, Pierre Janet) that neurotic symptoms are related to some conscious experience. They even appear to be split-off areas of the conscious mind, which, at another time and under different conditions, can be conscious.

21   Before the beginning of this century, Freud and Josef Breuer had recognized that neurotic symptoms—hysteria, certain types of pain, and abnormal behavior—are in fact symbolically meaningful. They are one way in which the unconscious mind expresses itself, just as it may in dreams; and they are equally symbolic. A patient, for instance, who is confronted with an intolerable situation may develop a spasm whenever he tries to swallow: He "can't swallow it." Under similar conditions of psychological stress, another patient has an attack of asthma: He "can't breathe the atmosphere at home." A third suffers from a peculiar paralysis of the legs: He can't walk, i.e., "he can't go on any more." A fourth, who vomits when he eats, "cannot digest" some unpleasant fact. I could cite many examples of this kind, but such physical reactions are only one form in which the problems that trouble us unconsciously may express themselves. They more often find expression in our dreams.

22   Any psychologist who has listened to numbers of people describing their dreams knows that dream symbols have much greater variety than the physical symptoms of neurosis. They often consist of elaborate and picturesque fantasies. But if the analyst who is confronted by this dream material uses Freud's original technique of "free association," he finds that dreams can eventually be reduced to certain basic patterns. This technique played an important part in the development of psychoanalysis, for it enabled Freud to use dreams as the starting point from which the unconscious problem of the patient might be explored.

23   Freud made the simple but penetrating observation that if a dreamer is encouraged to go on talking about his dream images and the thoughts that these prompt in his mind, he will give himself away and reveal the unconscious background of his ailments, in both what he says and what he deliberately omits saying. His ideas may seem irrational and irrelevant, but after a time it becomes relatively easy to see what it is that he is trying to avoid, what unpleasant thought or experience he is suppressing. No matter how he tries to camouflage it, everything he says points to the core of his predicament. A doctor sees so many things from the seamy side of life that he is seldom far from the truth when he interprets the hints that his patient produces as

signs of an uneasy conscious. What he eventually discovers, unfortunately, confirms his expectations. Thus far, nobody can say anything against Freud's theory of repression and wish fulfillment as apparent causes of dream symbolism.

24   Freud attached particular importance to dreams as the point of departure for a process of "free association." But after a time I began to feel that this was a misleading and inadequate use of the rich fantasies that the unconscious produces in sleep. My doubts really began when a colleague told me of an experience he had during the course of a long train journey in Russia. Though he did not know the language and could not even decipher the Cyrillic script, he found himself musing over the strange letters in which the railway notices were written, and he fell into a reverie in which he imagined all sorts of meanings for them.

25   One idea led to another, and in his relaxed mood he found that this "free association" had stirred up many old memories. Among them he was annoyed to find some long-buried disagreeable topics—things he had wished to forget and had forgotten *consciously*. He had in fact arrived at what psychologists would call his "complexes"—that is, repressed emotional themes that can cause constant psychological disturbances or even, in many cases, the symptoms of a neurosis.

26   This episode opened my eyes to the fact that it was not necessary to use a dream as the point of departure for the process of "free association" if one wished to discover the complexes of a patient. It showed me that one can reach the center directly from any point of the compass. One could begin from Cyrillic letters, from meditations upon a crystal ball, a prayer wheel, or a modern painting, or even from casual conversation about some trivial event. The dream was no more and no less useful in this respect than any other possible starting point. Nevertheless, dreams have a particular significance, even though they often arise from an emotional upset in which the habitual complexes are also involved. (The habitual complexes are the tender spots of the psyche, which react most quickly to an external stimulus or disturbance.) That is why free association can lead one from any dream to the critical secret thoughts.

27   At this point, however, it occurred to me that (if I was right so far) it might reasonably follow that dreams have some special and more significant function of their own. Very often dreams have a definite, evidently purposeful structure, indicating an underlying idea or intention—though, as a rule, the latter is not immediately comprehensible. I therefore began to consider whether one should pay more attention to the actual form and content of a dream, rather than allowing "free" association to lead one off through a train of ideas to complexes that could as easily be reached by other means.

28   This new thought was a turning-point in the development of my psychology. It meant that I gradually gave up following associations that led far away from the text of a dream. I chose to concentrate rather on the associations to the dream itself, believing that the latter expressed something specific that the unconscious was trying to say.

29   The change in my attitude toward dreams involved a change of method; the new technique was one that could take account of all the various wider aspects of a dream. A story told by the conscious mind has a beginning, a development, and

an end, but the same is not true of a dream. Its dimensions in time and space are quite different; to understand it you must examine it from every aspect—just as you may take an unknown object in your hands and turn it over and over until you are familiar with every detail of its shape.

30   Perhaps I have now said enough to show how I came increasingly to disagree with "free" association as Freud first employed it: I wanted to keep as close as possible to the dream itself, and to exclude all the irrelevant ideas and associations that it might evoke. True, these could lead one toward the complexes of a patient, but I had a more far-reaching purpose in mind than the discovery of complexes that cause neurotic disturbances. There are many other means by which these can be identified: The psychologist, for instance, can get all the hints he needs by using word-association tests (by asking the patient what he associates to a given set of words, and by studying his responses). But to know and understand the psychic life-process of an individual's whole personality, it is important to realize that his dreams and their symbolic images have a much more important role to play.

31   Almost everyone knows, for example, that there is an enormous variety of images by which the sexual act can be symbolized (or, one might say, represented in the form of an allegory). Each of these images can lead, by a process of association, to the idea of sexual intercourse and to specific complexes that any individual may have about his own sexual attitudes. But one could just as well unearth such complexes by day-dreaming on a set of indecipherable Russian letters. I was thus led to the assumption that a dream can contain some message other than the sexual allegory, and that it does so for definite reasons. To illustrate this point:

32   A man may dream of inserting a key in a lock, of wielding a heavy stick, or of breaking down a door with a battering ram. Each of these can be regarded as a sexual allegory. But the fact that his unconscious for its own purposes has chosen one of these specific images—it may be the key, the stick, or the battering ram—is also of major significance. The real task is to understand *why* the key has been preferred to the stick, or the stick to the ram. And sometimes this might even lead one to discover that it is not the sexual act at all that is represented, but some quite different psychological point.

33   From this line of reasoning, I concluded that only the material that is clearly and visibly part of a dream should be used in interpreting it. The dream has its own limitation. Its specific form itself tells us what belongs to it and what leads away from it. While "free" association lures one away from that material in a kind of zigzag line, the method I evolved is more like a circumambulation whose center is the dream picture. I work all round the dream picture and disregard every attempt that the dreamer makes to break away from it. Time and time again, in my professional work, I have had to repeat the words: "Let's go back to your dream. What does the *dream* say?"

34   For instance, a patient of mine dreamed of a drunken and disheveled vulgar woman. In the dream, it seemed that this woman was his wife, though in real life his wife was totally different. On the surface, therefore, the dream was shockingly untrue, and the patient immediately rejected it as dream nonsense. If I, as his doctor, had let him start a process of association, he would inevitably have tried to get

as far away as possible from the unpleasant suggestion of his dream. In that case, he would have ended with one of his staple complexes—a complex, possibly, that had nothing to do with his wife—and we should have learned nothing about the special meaning of this particular dream.

35   What then, was his unconscious trying to convey by such an obviously untrue statement? Clearly it somehow expressed the idea of a degenerate female who was closely connected with the dreamer's life; but since the projection of this image on to his wife was unjustified and factually untrue, I had to look elsewhere before I found out what this repulsive image represented.

36   In the Middle Ages, long before the physiologists demonstrated that by reason of our glandular structure there are both male and female elements in all of us, it was said that "every man carries a woman within himself." It is this female element in every male that I have called the "anima." This "feminine" aspect is essentially a certain inferior kind of relatedness to the surroundings, and particularly to women, which is kept carefully concealed from others as well as from oneself. In other words, though an individual's visible personality may seem quite normal, he may well be concealing from others—or even from himself—the deplorable condition of "the woman within."

37   That was the case with this particular patient: His female side was not nice. His dream was actually saying to him: "You are in some respects behaving like a degenerate female," and thus gave him an appropriate shock. (An example of this kind, of course, must not be taken as evidence that the unconscious is concerned with "moral" injunctions. The dream was not telling the patient to "behave better," but was simply trying to balance the lopsided nature of his conscious mind, which was maintaining the fiction that he was a perfect gentleman throughout.)

38   It is easy to understand why dreamers tend to ignore and even deny the message of their dreams. Consciousness naturally resists anything unconscious and unknown. I have already pointed out the existence among primitive peoples of what anthropologists call "misoneism," a deep and superstitious fear of novelty. The primitives manifest all the reactions of the wild animal against untoward events. But "civilized" man reacts to new ideas in much the same way, erecting psychological barriers to protect himself from the shock of facing something new. This can easily be observed in any individual's reaction to his own dreams when obliged to admit a surprising thought. Many pioneers in philosophy, science, and even literature have been victims of the innate conservatism of their contemporaries. Psychology is one of the youngest of the sciences; because it attempts to deal with the working of the unconscious, it has inevitably encountered misoneism in an extreme form.

Questions for Discussion

1. How does Jung define a symbol? Why does he believe that people need to use symbols to express themselves? What relationships does Jung establish among symbols, dreams, and the unconscious?

2. According to Jung, why does the presence of the unconscious support the modern perception that people have divided selves? Why does Jung think that it is natural to have a divided self?

3. Why does Jung believe that primitive people often feel an unconscious identification with another object or person? In what way is this characteristic of primitive people relevant to modern people and their problems of identity?

4. Jung states that "dreams are the most frequent and universally accessible source for the investigation of man's symbolizing faculty." What evidence does Jung provide to support his claim?

5. What relationships does Jung see between dreams and myths?

6. In his attempt to understand man's unconscious, Jung extends Freud's interpretations of the meaning of dreams. Contrast Freud's ideas with Jung's theories as they are presented in this selection and in Freud's essay "Erotic Wishes and Dreams" (included in Chapter 6 of this text). Whose approach to interpreting dreams and myths do you find more persuasive? Why?

Ideas for Writing

1. Write an essay in which you discuss several reasons why you think that understanding the symbols presented in dreams can be important. Develop examples that illustrate how you have used dreams and dream interpretation to help solve problems and to understand your inner world.

2. Write an essay in which you compare a particular dream you have had to a fundamental myth or story with which you are familiar; study and interpret your dream using the principles suggested in Jung's essay. Through completing this assignment, what did you learn about dream symbolism and about how your mind works?

 # Leslie Marmon Silko

Landscape, History, and the Pueblo Imagination

Leslie Marmon Silko (b. 1948) was born in Albuquerque, New Mexico, and raised on the Laguna Pueblo Reservation. After completing her B.A. at the University of New Mexico, she began to study law and then taught for two years at Navajo Community College in Arizona. Silko spent two years traveling in Alaska where she wrote her first novel, Ceremony *(1974), and studied Eskimo-Aleut culture. Silko has also taught at the University of Arizona and the University of New Mexico. She has completed one book of poems,* Laguna Woman: Poems *(1974), and a collection of short stories,* Storyteller *(1981). In 1983 she was awarded a five-year MacArthur Foundation grant.* Almanac of the Dead *(1991) is her most recent novel. Silko's writing explores social issues in Pueblo reservation life as well as Native American folklore, philosophy, and religious concerns. Her most recent collection of essays is entitled* Yellow Woman and the Beauty of the Spirit: Essays on Native American Life Today *(1996). In the following selection Silko gives us a concrete and thorough sense of the Pueblo spirit and its deep connection to the natural world.*

JOURNAL

Narrate a family story that has been important to you as you have matured. Discuss how the story reflects your family's values and culture.

Through the Stories We Hear Who We Are

1   All summer the people watch the west horizon, scanning the sky from south to north for rain clouds. Corn must have moisture at the time the tassels form. Otherwise pollination will be incomplete, and the ears will be stunted and shriveled. An inadequate harvest may bring disaster. Stories told at Hopi, Zuni, and at Acoma and Laguna describe drought and starvation as recently as 1900. Precipitation in west-central New Mexico averages fourteen inches annually. The western pueblos are located at altitudes over 5,600 feet above sea level, where winter temperatures at night fall below freezing. Yet evidence of their presence in the high desert plateau country goes back ten thousand years. The ancient Pueblo people not only survived in this environment, but many years they thrived. In A.D. 1100 the people at Chaco Canyon had built cities with apartment buildings of stone five stories high. Their sophistication as sky-watchers was surpassed only by Mayan and Inca astronomers. Yet this vast complex of knowledge and belief, amassed for thousands of years, was never recorded in writing.

2   Instead, the ancient Pueblo people depended upon collective memory through successive generations to maintain and transmit an entire culture, a world view complete with proven strategies for survival. The oral narrative, or "story," became the medium in which the complex of Pueblo knowledge and belief was maintained. Whatever the event or the subject, the ancient people perceived the world and themselves within that world as part of an ancient continuous story composed of innumerable bundles of other stories.

3   The ancient Pueblo vision of the world was inclusive. The impulse was to leave nothing out. Pueblo oral tradition necessarily embraced all levels of human experience. Otherwise, the collective knowledge and beliefs comprising ancient Pueblo culture would have been incomplete. Thus stories about the Creation and Emergence of human beings and animals into this World continue to be retold each year for four days and four nights during the winter solstice. The "humma-

hah" stories related events from the time long ago when human beings were still able to communicate with animals and other living things. But, beyond these two preceding categories, the Pueblo oral tradition knew no boundaries. Accounts of the appearance of the first Europeans in Pueblo country or of the tragic encounters between Pueblo people and Apache raiders were no more and no less important than stories about the biggest mule deer ever taken or adulterous couples surprised in cornfields and chicken coops. Whatever happened, the ancient people instinctively sorted events and details into a loose narrative structure. Everything became a story.

4   Traditionally everyone, from the youngest child to the oldest person, was expected to listen and to be able to recall or tell a portion, if only a small detail, from a narrative account or story. Thus the remembering and retelling were a communal process. Even if a key figure, an elder who knew much more than others, were to die unexpectedly, the system would remain intact. Through the efforts of a great many people, the community was able to piece together valuable accounts and crucial information that might otherwise have died with an individual.

5   Communal storytelling was a self-correcting process in which listeners were encouraged to speak up if they noted an important fact or detail omitted. The people were happy to listen to two or three different versions of the same event or the same humma-hah story. Even conflicting versions of an incident were welcomed for the entertainment they provided. Defenders of each version might joke and tease one another, but seldom were there any direct confrontations. Implicit in the Pueblo oral tradition was the awareness that loyalties, grudges, and kinship must always influence the narrator's choices as she emphasizes to listeners this is the way *she* has always heard the story told. The ancient Pueblo people sought a communal truth, not an absolute. For them this truth lived somewhere within the web of differing versions, disputes over minor points, outright contradictions tangling with old feuds and village rivalries.

6   A dinner-table conversation, recalling a deer hunt forty years ago when the largest mule deer ever was taken, inevitably stimulates similar memories in listeners. But hunting stories were not merely after-dinner entertainment. These accounts contained information of critical importance about behavior and migration patterns of mule deer. Hunting stories carefully described key landmarks and locations of fresh water. Thus a deer-hunt story might also serve as a "map." Lost travelers, and lost piñon-nut gatherers, have been saved by sighting a rock formation they recognize only because they once heard a hunting story describing this rock formation.

7   The importance of cliff formations and water holes does not end with hunting stories. As offspring of the Mother Earth, the ancient Pueblo people could not conceive of themselves within a specific landscape. Location, or "place," nearly always plays a central role in the Pueblo oral narratives. Indeed, stories are most frequently recalled as people are passing by a specific geographical feature or the exact place where a story takes place. The precise date of the incident often is less important than the place or location of the happening. "Long, long ago," "a long

time ago," "not too long ago," and "recently" are usually how stories are classified in terms of time. But the places where the stories occur are precisely located, and prominent geographical details recalled, even if the landscape is well-known to listeners. Often because the turning point in the narrative involved a peculiarity or special quality of a rock or tree or plant found only at that place. Thus, in the case of many of the Pueblo narratives, it is impossible to determine which came first: the incident or the geographical feature which begs to be brought alive in a story that features some unusual aspect of this location.

8   There is a giant sandstone boulder about a mile north of Old Laguna, on the road to Paguate. It is ten feet tall and twenty feet in circumference. When I was a child, and we would pass this boulder driving to Paguate village, someone usually made reference to the story about Kochininako, Yellow Woman, and the Estrucuyo, a monstrous giant who nearly ate her. The Twin Hero Brothers saved Kochininako, who had been out hunting rabbits to take home to feed her mother and sisters. The Hero Brothers had heard her cries just in time. The Estrucuyo had cornered her in a cave too small to fit its monstrous head. Kochininako had already thrown to the Estrucuyo all her rabbits, as well as her moccasins and most of her clothing. Still the creature had not been satisfied. After killing the Estrucuyo with their bows and arrows, the Twin Hero Brothers slit open the Estrucuyo and cut out its heart. They threw the heart as far as they could. The monster's heart landed there, beside the old trail to Paguate village, where the sandstone boulder rests now.

9   It may be argued that the existence of the boulder precipitated the creation of a story to explain it. But sandstone boulders and sandstone formations of strange shapes abound in the Laguna Pueblo area. Yet most of them do not have stories. Often the crucial element in a narrative is the terrain—some specific detail of the setting.

10   A high dark mesa rises dramatically from a grassy plain fifteen miles southeast of Laguna, in an area known as Swanee. On the grassy plain one hundred and forty years ago, my great-grandmother's uncle and his brother-in-law were grazing their herd of sheep. Because visibility on the plain extends for over twenty miles, it wasn't until the two sheepherders came near the high dark mesa that the Apaches were able to stalk them. Using the mesa to obscure their approach, the raiders swept around from both ends of the mesa. My great-grandmother's relatives were killed, and the herd lost. The high dark mesa played a critical role: the mesa had compromised the safety which the openness of the plains had seemed to assure. Pueblo and Apache alike relied upon the terrain, the very earth herself, to give them protection and aid. Human activities or needs were maneuvered to fit the existing surroundings and conditions. I imagine the last afternoon of my distant ancestors as warm and sunny for late September. They might have been traveling slowly, bringing the sheep closer to Laguna in preparation for the approach of colder weather. The grass was tall and only beginning to change from green to a yellow which matched the late-afternoon sun shining off it. There might have been comfort in the warmth and the sight of the sheep fattening on good pasture which lulled my ancestors into their fatal inattention. They might have had a rifle whereas the Apaches had only bows and arrows. But there would have been four

or five Apache raiders, and the surprise attack would have canceled any advantage the rifles gave them.

11   Survival in any landscape comes down to making the best use of all available resources. On that particular September afternoon, the raiders made better use of the Swanee terrain than my poor ancestors did. Thus the high dark mesa and the story of the two lost Laguna herders became inextricably linked. The memory of them and their story resides in part with the high black mesa. For as long as the mesa stands, people within the family and clan will be reminded of the story of that afternoon long ago. Thus the continuity and accuracy of the oral narratives are reinforced by the landscape—and the Pueblo interpretation of that landscape is *maintained*.

The Migration Story: An Interior Journey

12   The Laguna Pueblo migration stories refer to specific places—mesas, springs, or cottonwood trees—not only locations which can be visited still, but also locations which lie directly on the state highway route linking Paguate village with Laguna village. In traveling this road as a child with older Laguna people I first heard a few of the stories from that much larger body of stories linked with the Emergence and Migration. It may be coincidental that Laguna people continue to follow the same route which, according to the Migration story, the ancestors followed south from the Emergence Place. It may be that the route is merely the shortest and best route for car, horse, or foot traffic between Laguna and Paguate villages. But if the stories about boulders, springs, and hills are actually remnants from a ritual that retraces the creation and emergence of the Laguna Pueblo people as a culture, as the people they became, then continued use of that route creates a unique relationship between the ritual-mythic world and the actual, everyday world. A journey from Paguate to Laguna down the long incline of Paguate Hill retraces the original journey from the Emergence Place which is located slightly north of the Paguate village. Thus the landscape between Paguate and Laguna takes on a deeper significance: the landscape resonates the spiritual or mythic dimension of the Pueblo world even today.

13   Although each Pueblo culture designates a specific Emergence Place—usually a small natural spring edged with mossy sandstone and full of cattails and wild watercress—it is clear that they do not agree on any single location or natural spring as the one and only true Emergence Place. Each Pueblo group recounts its own stories about Creation, Emergence, and Migration, although they all believe that all human beings, with all the animals and plants, emerged at the same place and at the same time.

14   Natural springs are crucial sources of water for all life in the high desert plateau country. So the small spring near Paguate village is literally the source and continuance of life for the people in the area. The spring also functions on a spiritual level, recalling the original Emergence Place and linking the people and the spring water to all other people and to that moment when the Pueblo people became aware of themselves as they are even now. The Emergence was an emergence into a precise cultural identity. Thus the Pueblo stories about the Emergence and Migration are not to be taken as literally as the anthropologists might

wish. Prominent geographical features and landmarks which are mentioned in the narratives exist for ritual purposes, not because the Laguna people actually journeyed south for hundreds of years from Chaco Canyon or Mesa Verde, as the archaeologists say, or eight miles from the site of the natural springs at Paguate to the sandstone hilltop at Laguna.

15   The eight miles, marked with boulders, mesas, springs, and river crossings, are actually a ritual circuit or path which marks the interior journey the Laguna people made: a journey of awareness and imagination in which they emerged from being within the earth and from everything included in earth to the culture and people they became, differentiating themselves for the first time from all that had surrounded them, always aware that interior distances cannot be reckoned in physical miles or in calendar years.

16   The narratives linked with prominent features of the landscape between Paguate and Laguna delineate the complexities of the relationship which human beings must maintain with the surrounding natural world if they hope to survive in this place. Thus the journey was an interior process of the imagination, a growing awareness that being human is somehow different from all other life—animal, plant, and inanimate. Yet we are all from the same source: the awareness never deteriorated into Cartesian duality, cutting off the human from the natural world.

17   The people found the opening into the Fifth World too small to allow them or any of the animals to escape. They had sent a fly out through the small hole to tell them if it was the world which the Mother Creator had promised. It was, but there was the problem of getting out. The antelope tried to butt the opening to enlarge it, but the antelope enlarged it only a little. It was necessary for the badger with her long claws to assist the antelope, and at last the opening was enlarged enough so that all the people and animals were able to emerge up into the Fifth World. The human beings could not have emerged without the aid of antelope and badger. The human beings depended upon the aid and charity of the animals. Only through interdependence could the human beings survive. Families belonged to clans, and it was by clan that the human being joined with the animal and plant world. Life on the high arid plateau became viable when the human beings were able to imagine themselves as sisters and brothers to the badger, antelope, clay, yucca, and sun. Not until they could find a viable relationship to the terrain, the landscape they found themselves in, could they *emerge*. Only at the moment the requisite balance between human and *other* was realized could the Pueblo people become a culture, a distinct group whose population and survival remained stable despite the vicissitudes of climate and terrain.

18   Landscape thus has similarities with dreams. Both have the power to seize terrifying feelings and deep instincts and translate them into images—visual, aural, tactile—into the concrete where human beings may more readily confront and channel the terrifying instincts or powerful emotions into rituals and narratives which reassure the individual while reaffirming cherished values of the group. The identity of the individual as a part of the group and the greater Whole is strengthened, and the terror of facing the world alone is extinguished.

19   Even now, the people of Laguna Pueblo spend the greater portion of social occasions recounting recent incidents or events which have occurred in the Laguna

area. Nearly always, the discussion will precipitate the retelling of older stories about similar incidents or other stories connected with a specific place. The stories often contain disturbing or provocative material, but are nonetheless told in the presence of children and women. The effect of these inter-family or inter-clan exchanges is the reassurance for each person that she or he will never be separated or apart from the clan, no matter what might happen. Neither the worst blunders or disasters nor the greatest financial prosperity and joy will ever be permitted to isolate anyone from the rest of the group. In the ancient times, cohesiveness was all that stood between extinction and survival, and, while the individual certainly was recognized, it was always as an individual simultaneously bonded to family and clan by a complex bundle of custom and ritual. You are never the first to suffer a grave loss or profound humiliation. You are never the first, and you understand that you will probably not be the last to commit or be victimized by a repugnant act. Your family and clan are able to go on at length about others now passed on, others older or more experienced than you who suffered similar losses.

20   The wide deep arroyo near the Kings Bar (located across the reservation borderline) has over the years claimed many vehicles. A few years ago, when a Viet Nam veteran's new red Volkswagen rolled backwards into the arroyo while he was inside buying a six-pack of beer, the story of his loss joined the lively and large collection of stories already connected with that big arroyo. I do not know whether the Viet Nam veteran was consoled when he was told the stories about the other cars claimed by the ravenous arroyo. All his savings of combat pay had gone for the red Volkswagen. But this man could not have felt any worse than the man who, some years before, had left his children and mother-in-law in his station wagon with the engine running. When he came out of the liquor store his station wagon was gone. He found it and its passengers upside down in the big arroyo. Broken bones, cuts and bruises, and a total wreck of the car. The big arroyo has a wide mouth. Its existence needs no explanation. People in the area regard the arroyo much as they might regard a living being, which has a certain character and personality. I seldom drive past that wide deep arroyo without feeling a familiarity with and even a strange affection for this arroyo. Because as treacherous as it may be, the arroyo maintains a strong connection between human beings and the earth. The arroyo demands from us the caution and attention that constitute respect. It is this sort of respect the old believers have in mind when they tell us we must respect and love the earth.

21   Hopi Pueblo elders have said that the austere and, to some eyes, barren plains and hills surrounding their mesa-top villages actually help to nurture the spirituality of the Hopi *way*. The Hopi elders say the Hopi people might have settled in locations far more lush where daily life would not have been so grueling. But there on the high silent sandstone mesas that overlook the sandy arid expanses stretching to all horizons, the Hopi elders say the Hopi people must "live by their prayers" if they are to survive. The Hopi way cherishes the intangible: the riches realized from interaction and interrelationships with all beings above all else. Great abundances of material things, even food, the Hopi elders believe, tend to lure human attention away from what is most valuable and important. The views of the Hopi elders are not much different from those elders in all the Pueblos.

22   The bare vastness of the Hopi landscape emphasizes the visual impact of every plant, every rock, every arroyo. Nothing is overlooked or taken for granted. Each ant, each lizard, each lark is imbued with great value simply because the creature is there, simply because the creature is alive in a place where any life at all is precious. Stand on the mesa edge at Walpai and look west over the bare distances toward the pale blue outlines of the San Francisco peaks where the ka'tsina spirits reside. So little lies between you and the sky. So little lies between you and the earth. One look and you know that simply to survive is a great triumph, that every possible resource is needed, every possible ally—even the most humble insect or reptile. You realize you will be speaking with all of them if you intend to last out the year. Thus it is that the Hopi elders are grateful to the landscape for aiding them in their quest as spiritual people.

Questions for Discussion

1. What image do Pueblo people use to describe the evolution of their oral language? Why do the Pueblo people and Silko privilege spontaneous oral speech over a written lecture?

2. Why does Silko begin her explanation of the Pueblo approach to language and community with their Creation story? What implications does the story and its evolution make about language, communication, and the importance of stories?

3. Why is it important that a storyteller be a good listener? Apply Silko's ideas to some of your own experiences with storytelling. What impact does this approach to storytelling have on the community?

4. How does Silko explain the relationships between story telling and identity? between individual and clan (family or extended family) identity? between community and survival?

5. According to Silko, why is it important to hear all the stories in your family? Why is it especially important that negative and violent experience stories be told and understood? Why is it dangerous for the individual who has generated the negative story to slip into alienation or try to escape? Why is it important for this individual to be able to tell his or her story?

6. Why does Silko believe that dreams and the landscape are connected and powerful? Using examples from your own experience, discuss why you agree or disagree with her.

Ideas for Writing

1. Develop your journal story and then discuss why it has had an important impact on you and on your family.

2. "I think what is essential is this sense of story, and the idea that one story is only the beginning of many stories, and the sense that stories never truly end." Write an essay in which you show the relevance of

Silko's ideas through reference to your experiences, your reading, your culture, and the popular culture.

Portfolio of Creation Myths

We have selected the following myths from cultures around the world to encourage you to compare different fundamental beliefs and assumptions about reality through the mythological stories that are central to a people. Preceding each myth is a note about the culture that produced it; following the portfolio is a set of questions for thought and writing.

JOURNAL

Discuss a creation myth or an experience of creating something very special to you. Try to develop imaginative comparisons and vivid details.

Genesis 2:4–23 (Old Testament of the Hebrew Bible)

This is the second account of creation in the book of Genesis. Genesis 2 is thought to come from a different, less formal writing tradition (the "J," or Jehovah, tradition) from that of Genesis 1 and features a close relationship between God and his natural and human creations. The following passage portrays the God Jehovah in an agricultural role, creating and watering the Garden of Eden, then creating animals, a man to till the fields, and finally a female helper for "the man." As you read the following selection, consider the impact that the Book of Genesis has had on Western cultural assumptions and traditions.

1   (2:4) In the day that the Lord God made the earth and the heavens, (5) when no plant of the field was yet in the earth and no herb of the field had yet sprung up—for the Lord God had not caused it to rain upon the earth, and there was no man to till the ground; (6) but a mist went up from the earth and watered the whole face of the ground—(7) then the Lord God formed man of dust from the ground, and breathed into his nostrils the breath of life; and man became a living being. (8) And the Lord God planted a garden in Eden, in the east; and there he put the man whom he had formed. (9) And out of the ground the Lord God made to grow every tree that is pleasant to the sight and good for food, the tree of life also in the midst of the garden, and the tree of the knowledge of good and evil.

2   (10) A river flowed out of Eden to water the garden, and there it divided and became four rivers. (11) The name of the first is Pishon; it is the one which flows

around the whole land of Hav'ilah, where there is gold; (12) and the gold of that land is good; bdellium and onyx stone are there. (13) The name of the second river is Gihon; it is the one which flows around the whole land of Cush. (14) And the name of the third river is Tigris, which flows east of Assyria. And the fourth river is the Euphrates.

3   (15) The Lord God took the man and put him in the garden of Eden to till it and keep it. (16) And the Lord God commanded the man, saying, "You may freely eat of every tree of the garden; (17) but of the tree of the knowledge of good and evil you shall not eat, for in the day that you eat of it you shall die."

4   (18) Then the Lord God said, "It is not good that the man should be alone; I will make him a helper fit for him." (19) So out of the ground the Lord God formed every beast of the field and every bird of the air, and brought them to the man to see what he would call them; and whatever the man called every living creature, that was its name. (20) The man gave names to all cattle, and to the birds of the air, and to every beast of the field; but for the man there was not found a helper fit for him. (21) So the Lord God caused a deep sleep to fall upon the man, and while he slept took one of his ribs and closed up its place with flesh; (22) and the rib which the Lord God had taken from the man he made into a woman and brought her to the man. (23) Then the man said,

This at last is bone of my bones
    and flesh of my flesh;
she shall be called Woman,
    because she was taken out of Man.

The Chameleon Finds
(Yao-Bantu, African)

"The Chameleon Finds" is a creation myth of the Yao, a Bantu tribe living by Lake Nyasa, in Mozambique, Africa. Expressive of a close relationship with nature, this Yao myth, with a clever Chameleon and a helper Spider as the creator-god's assistants, takes a critical view of human beings. The unnatural and destructive culture of the humans causes the animals to flee and the gods to retreat from the earth. As you read this creation story, compare the critical view of human culture held by the Yao with that of the other myths in this section.

1   At first there were no people. Only Mulungu and the decent peaceful beasts were in the world.

2   One day Chameleon sat weaving a fish-trap, and when he had finished he set it in the river. In the morning he pulled the trap and it was full of fish, which he took home and ate.

3   He set the trap again. In the morning he pulled it out and it was empty: no fish.

4   "Bad luck," he said, and set the trap again.

5   The next morning when he pulled the trap he found a little man and woman in it. He had never seen any creatures like this.

6   "What can they be?" he said. "Today I behold the unknown." And he picked up the fish-trap and took the two creatures to Mulungu.

7   "Father," said Chameleon, "see what I have brought."

8   Mulungu looked. "Take them out of the trap," he said. "Put them down on the earth and they will grow."

9   Chameleon did this. And the man and woman grew. They grew until they became as tall as men and women are today.

10   All the animals watched to see what the people would do. They made fire. They rubbed two sticks together in a special way and thus made fire. The fire caught in the bush and roared through the forest and the animals had to run to escape the flames.

11   The people caught a buffalo and killed it and roasted it in the fire and ate it. The next day they did the same thing. Every day they set fires and killed some animal and ate it.

12   "They are burning up everything!" said Mulungu. "They are killing my people!"

13   All the beasts ran into the forest as far away from mankind as they could get. Chameleon went into the high trees.

14   "I'm leaving!" said Mulungu.

15   He called to Spider. "How do you climb on high?" he said.

16   "Very nicely," said Spider. And Spider spun a rope for Mulungu and Mulungu climbed the rope and went to live in the sky.

17   Thus the gods were driven off the face of the earth by the cruelty of man.

Dreaming People (Malayan Pygmies)

The following myth is part of the oral tradition of the Negrito pygmies of the Malay peninsula, a tribal people who survive by hunting and gathering. The myth presents a vision of the co-creation of the world by a giant dung beetle and a primal couple, Pedn and Manoid, who dream their children into being. Notice how this myth reflects the Negritos' intimate relationship with nature and with their own dreams.

At first only Pedn and Manoid his wife existed. The sun was already there, but not the earth. Then Tahobn, the dung-beetle, made the earth by pulling it out of the mud. The sun dried it and made it firm. When Pedn and Manoid saw the earth they descended to it. When the earth came into being trees grew out of it, but there were no animals or birds. Pedn and Manoid got two children in the following way. Manoid dreamt of a child and begged Pedn for one. Pedn went out to get some fruit and spread out a cloth for the fruit to fall on it, and, when the fruit fell, it became a child which began to scream. It was a boy. Manoid dreamt again, this time about a female child and begged her husband for it, so Pedn did as before and the fruit which fell into the cloth became a girl. The boy was Capai (identified . . . as the *kakuh*-bird) and the girl was called Pa'ig (identified . . . with *baul*, the tortoise). Both were *Cenoi-halek*. As there were no people, they married each other and had children. Two of these were Encogen and Kadjegn, both "grandchildren" of Ta Pedn. When Encogen came to a rock he heard the rushing of water. He shot an arrow into the rock so that water gushed forth. He became famous through this deed.

Spider Woman Creates the Humans (Hopi, Native American)

The Hopis, who reside in several villages in Northern Arizona, have kept themselves separate from other cultures and have maintained their native traditions and myths. The following myth of creation is only a brief selection from the much longer Hopi Emergence Story, which uses birth imagery to explain a complex sequence of transformations in the act of creation. In the Hopi culture, the Emergence Story is told to the tribal initiates on the last evening of the year, after which the young men ascend a ladder to emerge from the kiva (Hopi dwelling) as full-fledged adult members of the Hopi community. "Spider Woman Creates the Humans" is unique because of its use of a female creator who functions as mother-goddess, singer, and artist, molding the original people from multicolored clay while singing them the Creation Song.

1 **Creation of Mankind**   So Spider Woman gathered earth, this time of four colors, yellow, red, white, and black; mixed with *tuchvala*, the liquid of her mouth; molded them; and covered them with her white-substance cape which was the creative wisdom itself. As before, she sang over them the Creation Song, and when she uncovered them these forms were human beings in the image of Sotuknang. Then she created four other beings after her own form. They were *wuti*, female partners, for the first four male beings.

2   When Spider Woman uncovered them the forms came to life. This was at the time of the dark purple light, Qoyangnuptu, the first phase of the dawn of Creation, which first reveals the mystery of man's creation.

3   They soon awakened and began to move, but there was still a dampness on their foreheads and a soft spot on their heads. This was at the time of the yellow light, Sikangnuqua, the second phase of the dawn of Creation, when the breath of life entered man.

4   In a short time the sun appeared above the horizon, drying the dampness on their foreheads and hardening the soft spot on their heads. This was the time of the red light, Talawva, the third phase of the dawn of Creation, when man, fully formed and firmed, proudly faced his Creator.

5   "That is the Sun," said Spider Woman. "You are meeting your Father the Creator for the first time. You must always remember and observe these three phases

of your Creation. The time of the three lights, the dark purple, the yellow, and the red reveal in turn the mystery, the breath of life, and warmth of love. These comprise the Creator's plan of life for you as sung over you in the Song of Creation."

Questions for Discussion

1. What different views of the creator gods are presented in the various myths? How clearly described is the primary god? What powers and limits does the god have? Does the god operate separately or with the cooperation of other helping beings? What conclusions about the culture that produced each myth can you draw?

2. In the myths that present a clear picture of the physical world of the creation, how is the world described? How orderly and sequential does the act of creating the different elements and beings of the world seem? What conclusions can you draw from this presentation of creation myths about the values of the culture that produced each myth?

3. Creation myths make significant comments on the roles and status of the sexes in various cultures. Compare and contrast the roles of sex and gender in the different creation myths included.

4. Another issue presented in some creation myths is the relation of men and women to their creator. How do the humans in the various myths relate to the creator gods? How worshipful of God are the humans in the various myths?

5. Compare the ways that the different myths show the relationship between humans and nature. How harmonious a part of nature or how much at odds with nature do humans seem in the various myths? How are animals involved in the act of creation? Does part of the natural world need to be destroyed for creation to be completed?

6. Creation myths differ in tone. They can be imaginative and dreamlike, solemn and serious, philosophical, or even comical and mocking in tone. Compare the tone and attitude toward creation presented in each of the myths; then draw some conclusions about the values of each culture.

Ideas for Writing

1. Write your own creation myth, using characters, description, and narration to illustrate the relationship between different aspects of creation: gods, animals, people, and the earth. At the end of your myth, comment on the values and ideas about the creative process and the world that your myth is designed to illustrate.

2. Develop an essay in the form of an extended comparison between two or three creation myths, each of which illustrates fundamental values and beliefs about gods, humans, and the natural world.

Two Versions of Pygmalion

JOURNAL

Write about a relationship that you were in or one that you observed when one person in the relationship tried to change the other person.

 # Thomas Bulfinch

Pygmalion

Thomas Bulfinch (1796–1867) was born in Boston and taught at Harvard College. His retellings of myths from the classical age were first collected in The Age of the Fable *(1855). The original source of the Pygmalion story told here is a poem from the* Metamorphoses of the Roman poet Ovid *(43* B.C.–A.D *17).*

1   Pygmalion saw so much to blame in women that he came at last to abhor the sex, and resolved to live unmarried. He was a sculptor, and had made with wonderful skill a statue of ivory, so beautiful that no living woman came anywhere near it. It was indeed the perfect semblance of a maiden that seemed to be alive, and only prevented from moving by modesty. His art was so perfect that it concealed itself, and its product looked like the workmanship of nature. Pygmalion admired his own work and at last fell in love with the counterfeit creation. Oftentimes he laid his hand upon it as if to assure himself whether it were living or not, and could not even then believe that it was only ivory. He caressed it and gave it presents such as young girls love—bright shells and polished stones, little birds and flowers of various hues, beads and amber. He put raiment on its limbs, and jewels on its fingers, and a necklace about its neck. To the ears he hung ear-rings, and strings of pearls upon the breast. Her dress became her, and she looked not less charming than when unattired. He laid her on a couch spread with cloths of Tyrian dye, and called her his wife, and put her head upon a pillow of the softest feathers, as if she could enjoy their softness.

2   The festival of Venus was at hand—a festival celebrated with great pomp at Cyprus. Victims were offered, the altars smoked, and the odor of incense filled the air. When Pygmalion had performed his part in the solemnities, he stood before the altar and timidly said, "Ye gods, who can do all things, give me, I pray you, for my wife"—he dared not say "my ivory virgin," but said instead—"one like my ivory virgin." Venus, who was present at the festival, heard him and knew the thought he would have uttered; and as an omen of her favor, caused the flame on the altar to shoot up thrice in a fiery point into the air. When he returned home, he went to see his statue, and leaning over the couch, gave a kiss to the mouth. It

seemed to be warm. He pressed its lips again, he laid his hand upon the limbs; the ivory felt soft to his touch and yielded to his fingers like the wax of Hymettus. While he stands astonished and glad, though doubting, and fears he may be mistaken, again and again with a lover's ardor, he touches the object of his hopes. It was indeed alive! The veins when pressed yielded to the finger and again resumed their roundness. Then at last the votary of Venus found words to thank the goddess, and pressed his lips upon lips as real as his own. The virgin felt the kisses and blushed, and opening her timid eyes to the light, fixed them at the same moment on her lover. Venus blessed the nuptials she had formed, and from this union Paphos was born, from whom the city, sacred to Venus, received its name.

   # John Updike

Pygmalion

John Updike (b. 1932) was raised in Shillington, Pennsylvania, and earned a full scholarship to Harvard, where he completed his B.A. in 1954, graduating summa cum laude. *Then he was awarded a fellowship to study art at the Ruskin School in Oxford, England. When he returned to New York, he joined the staff of the* New Yorker. *In 1959 Updike published his first work of short fiction,* The Same Door, *and his first novel,* The Poorhouse Fair. *At this time he moved to Ipswich, Massachusetts, with his family and made writing his full-time career. Updike is best known for his sequence of novels about Harry "Rabbit" Angstrom, who lives in suburbia and continually thinks back to his life as a high school athlete:* Rabbit Run *(1960);* Rabbit Redux *(1971);* Rabbit Is Rich *(1981); and* Rabbit at Rest *(1990); which won the Pulitzer Prize in 1991. Updike has written a number of other best-selling novels;* The Witches of Eastwick *(1984) was made into a popular film with Jack Nicholson. Some of his short story collections include* Pigeon Feathers *(1962),* The Music School *(1966),* Too Far to Go: The Magic Stories *(1979),* Problems *(1979),* Trust Me *(1987), and* The Afterlife and Other Stories *(1994). Updike is a social satirist and an intellectual who enjoys examining contemporary ideas and social trends through his writing.*

1   What he liked about his first wife was her gift of mimicry; after a party, theirs or another couple's, she would vivify for him what they had seen, the faces, the voices, twisting her pretty mouth into small contortions that brought back, for a dazzling instant, the presence of an absent acquaintance. "Well, if I reawwy—how does Gwen talk?—if I *re*-awwy cared about conservation—" And he, the husband, would laugh and laugh, even though Gwen was secretly his mistress and would become his second wife. What he liked about *her* was her liveliness in bed,

and what he disliked about his first wife was the way she would ask to have her back rubbed and then, under his laboring hands, night after night, fall asleep.

2   For the first years of the new marriage, after he and Gwen had returned from a party, he would wait, unconsciously, for the imitations, the recapitulation, to begin. He would even prompt: "What did you make of our hostess's brother?"

3   "Oh," Gwen would simply say, "he seemed very pleasant." Sensing with feminine intuition that he expected more, she might add, "Harmless. Maybe a little stuffy." Her eyes flashed as she heard in his expectant silence an unvoiced demand, and with that touching, childlike impediment of hers she blurted out, "What are you reawy after?"

4   "Oh, nothing. Nothing. It's just—Marguerite met him once a few years ago and she was struck by what a pompous nitwit he was. That way he has of sucking his pipestem and ending every statement with 'Do you follow me?'"

5   "I thought he was perfectly pleasant," Gwen said frostily, and turned her back to remove her silvery, snug party dress. As she wriggled it down over her hips she turned her head and defiantly added, "He had a *lot* to say about tax shelters."

6   "I bet he did," Pygmalion scoffed feebly, numbed by the sight of his wife frontally advancing, nude, toward him as he lay on their marital bed. "It's awfully late," he warned her.

7   "Oh, come on," she said, the lights out.

8   The first imitation Gwen did was of Marguerite's second husband, Marvin; they had all unexpectedly met at a Save the Whales benefit ball, to which invitations had been sent our indiscriminately. "Oh-ho-*ho*," she boomed in the privacy of their bedroom afterwards, "so you're my noble predecessor!" In an aside she added, "Noble, my ass. He hates you so much you turned him on."

9   "I did?" he said. "I thought he was perfectly pleasant, in what could have been an awkward encounter."

10   "Yes, in*deedy*," she agreed, imitating hearty Marvin, and for a dazzling second she allowed the man's slightly glassy and slack expression of forced benignity to invade her own usually petite and rounded features. "Nothing awkward about *us*, ho-ho," she went on, encouraged by her husband's laughter. "And tell me, old chap, why *is* it your childsupport check is never on time anymore?"

11   He laughed and laughed, entranced to see his bride arrive at what he conceived to be a proper womanliness—a plastic, alert sensitivity to the human environment, a susceptible responsiveness tugged this way and that by the currents of Nature herself. He could not know the world, was his fear, unless a woman translated it for him. Now, when they returned from a gathering, and he asked what she had made of so-and-so, Gwen would stand in her underwear and consider, as if onstage. "We-hell, my dear," she would announce in sudden, fluting parody, "if it weren't for Portugal there *rally* wouldn't be a *bear*able country left in Europe!"

12   "Oh, come on," he would protest, delighted at the way her pretty features distorted themselves into an uncanny, snobbish horsiness.

13   "How did she do it?" Gwen would ask, as if professionally intent. "Something with the chin, sort of rolling it from side to side without unclenching the teeth."

14   "You've got it!" he applauded.

15   "Of course you *knoaow*," she went on in the assumed voice, "there *used* to be Greece, but now all these dreadful *Arabs* . . . "

16   "Oh, yes, yes," he said, his face smarting from laughing so hard, so proudly. She had become perfect for him.

17   In bed she pointed out, "It's awfully late."

18   "Want a back rub?"

19   "Mmmm. That would be reawy nice." As his left hand labored on the smooth, warm, pliable surface, his wife—that small something in her that was all her own—sank out of reach; night after night, she fell asleep.

Questions for Discussion

1. In what ways does Updike pattern his story after the myth? In what ways does the myth differ from the story? Which tale is more romantic and affirmative?
2. How are the motifs of statue and transformation used in both versions?
3. Both versions have erotic elements. Which tale is more erotic? Why?
4. If myths reveal assumptions about our culture, what does Updike reveal to us about modern marriage through his retelling of the ancient story of Pygmalion?
5. Discuss modern stories that are built on the Pygmalion myth. Why do you think that this myth has continued to be so popular?

Ideas for Writing

1. Write a comparison/contrast essay of the two Pygmalion stories.
2. Write a story based on some of the ideas in the Pygmalion tale.

 # Bruno Bettelheim

Fairy Tales and the Existential Predicament

Born in Vienna and educated at the University of Vienna, Bruno Bettelheim (1903–1991) was imprisoned in a Nazi concentration camp for a time before immigrating to the United States. After settling in Chicago, he worked with autistic children, serving as Director of the University of Chicago Orthogenic School from 1944 to 1973. Bettelheim's books, such as On Learning to Read (1981) and A Good Enough Parent (1987), focus on the relationships between reading, parenting, and raising emotionally healthy children. The following selection from The Uses of Enchantment (1976) presents a psychological perspective on the impact on children of traditional fairy tales. As you read the selection, think about whether you agree with Bettelheim's theories about the role that fairy tales play in creating healthy children.

JOURNAL

Narrate the fairy tale that you remember most vividly from your childhood. Why do you think you remember it? Would you share (or have you shared) this tale with your own children? Why or why not?

---

1   In order to master the psychological problems of growing up—overcoming narcissistic disappointments, oedipal dilemmas, sibling rivalries; becoming able to relinquish childhood dependencies; gaining a feeling of selfhood and of self-worth, and a sense of moral obligation—a child needs to understand what is going on within his conscious self so that he can also cope with that which goes on in his unconscious. He can achieve this understanding, and with it the ability to cope, not through rational comprehension of the nature and content of his unconscious, but by becoming familiar with it through spinning out daydreams—ruminating, rearranging, and fantasizing about suitable story elements in response to unconscious pressures. By doing this, the child fits unconscious content into conscious fantasies, which then enable him to deal with that content. It is here that fairy tales have unequaled value, because they offer new dimensions to the child's imagination which would be impossible for him to discover as truly on his own. Even more important, the form and structure of fairy tales suggest images to the child by which he can structure his daydreams and with them give better direction to his life.

2   In child or adult, the unconscious is a powerful determinant of behavior. When the unconscious is repressed and its content denied entrance into awareness, then eventually the person's conscious mind will be partially overwhelmed by derivatives of these unconscious elements, or else he is forced to keep such rigid, compulsive control over them that his personality may become severely crippled. But when unconscious material *is* to some degree permitted to come to awareness and worked through in imagination, its potential for causing harm—to ourselves or others—is much reduced; some of its forces can then be made to serve positive purposes. However, the prevalent parental belief is that a child must be diverted from what troubles him most: his formless, nameless anxieties, and his chaotic, angry, and even violent fantasies. Many parents believe that only conscious reality or pleasant and wish-fulfilling images should be presented to the child—that he should be exposed only to the sunny side of things. But such one-sided fare nourishes the mind only in a one-sided way, and real life is not all sunny.

3   There is a widespread refusal to let children know that the source of much that goes wrong in life is due to our very own natures—the propensity of all men for acting aggressively, asocially, selfishly, out of anger and anxiety. Instead, we want our children to believe that, inherently, all men are good. But children know that

they are not always good; and often, even when they are, they would prefer not to be. This contradicts what they are told by their parents, and therefore makes the child a monster in his own eyes.

4   The dominant culture wishes to pretend, particularly where children are concerned, that the dark side of man does not exist, and professes a belief in an optimistic meliorism. Psychoanalysis itself is viewed as having the purpose of making life easy—but this is not what its founder intended. Psychoanalysis was created to enable man to accept the problematic nature of life without being defeated by it, or giving in to escapism. Freud's prescription is that only by struggling courageously against what seem like overwhelming odds can man succeed in wringing meaning out of his existence.

5   This is exactly the message that fairy tales get across to the child in manifold form: that a struggle against severe difficulties in life is unavoidable, is an intrinsic part of human existence—but that if one does not shy away, but steadfastly meets unexpected and often unjust hardships, one masters all obstacles and at the end emerges victorious.

6   Modern stories written for young children mainly avoid these existential problems, although they are crucial issues for all of us. The child needs most particularly to be given suggestions in symbolic form about how he may deal with these issues and grow safely into maturity. "Safe" stories mention neither death or aging, the limits to our existence, nor the wish for eternal life. The fairy tale, by contrast, confronts the child squarely with the basic human predicaments.

7   For example, many fairy stories begin with the death of a mother or father; in these tales the death of the parent creates the most agonizing problems, as it (or the fear of it) does in real life. Other stories tell about an aging parent who decides that the time has come to let the new generation take over. But before this can happen, the successor has to prove himself capable and worthy. The Brothers Grimm's story "The Three Feathers" begins: "There was once upon a time a king who had three sons. . . . When the king had become old and weak, and was thinking of his end, he did not know which of his sons should inherit the kingdom after him." In order to decide, the king sets all his sons a difficult task; the son who meets it best "shall be king after my death."

8   It is characteristic of fairy tales to state an existential dilemma briefly and pointedly. This permits the child to come to grips with the problem in its most essential form, where a more complex plot would confuse matters for him. The fairy tale simplifies all situations. Its figures are clearly drawn; and details, unless very important, are eliminated. All characters are typical rather than unique.

9   Contrary to what takes place in many modern children's stories, in fairy tales evil is as omnipresent as virtue. In practically every fairy tale good and evil are given body in the form of some figures and their actions, as good and evil are omnipresent in life and the propensities for both are present in every man. It is this duality which poses the moral problem, and requires the struggle to solve it.

10   Evil is not without its attractions—symbolized by the mighty giant or dragon, the power of the witch, the cunning queen in "Snow White"—and often it is temporarily in the ascendancy. In many fairy tales a usurper succeeds for a time in

seizing the place which rightfully belongs to the hero—as the wicked sisters do in "Cinderella." It is not that the evildoer is punished at the story's end which makes immersing oneself in fairy stories an experience in moral education, although this is part of it. In fairy tales, as in life, punishment or fear of it is only a limited deterrent to crime. The conviction that crime does not pay is a much more effective deterrent, and that is why in fairy tales the bad person always loses out. It is not the fact that virtue wins out at the end which promotes morality, but that the hero is most attractive to the child, who identifies with the hero in all his struggles. Because of this identification the child imagines that he suffers with the hero his trials and tribulations, and triumphs with him as virtue is victorious. The child makes such identifications all on his own, and the inner and outer struggles of the hero imprint morality on him.

11   The figures in fairy tales are not ambivalent—not good and bad at the same time, as we all are in reality. But since polarization dominates the child's mind, it also dominates fairy tales. A person is either good or bad, nothing in between. One brother is stupid, the other is clever. One sister is virtuous and industrious, the others are vile and lazy. One is beautiful, the others are ugly. One parent is all good, the other evil. The juxtaposition of opposite characters is not for the purpose of stressing right behavior, as would be true for cautionary tales. (There are some amoral fairy tales where goodness or badness, beauty or ugliness play no role at all.) Presenting the polarities of character permits the child to comprehend easily the difference between the two, which he could not do as readily were the figures drawn more true to life, with all the complexities that characterize real people. Ambiguities must wait until a relatively firm personality has been established on the basis of positive identifications. Then the child has a basis for understanding that there are great differences between people, and that therefore one has to make choices about who one wants to be. This basic decision, on which all later personality development will build, is facilitated by the polarizations of the fairy tale.

12   Furthermore, a child's choices are based, not so much on right versus wrong, as on who arouses his sympathy and who his antipathy. The more simple and straightforward a good character, the easier it is for a child to identify with it and to reject the bad other. The child identifies with the good hero not because of his goodness, but because the hero's condition makes a deep positive appeal to him. The question for the child is not "Do I want to be good?" but "Who do I want to be like?" The child decides this on the basis of projecting himself wholeheartedly into one character. If this fairy-tale figure is a very good person, then the child decides that he wants to be good, too.

13   Amoral fairy tales show no polarization or juxtaposition of good and bad persons; that is because these amoral stories serve an entirely different purpose. Such tales or type figures as "Puss in Boots," who arranges for the hero's success through trickery, and Jack, who steals the giant's treasure, build character not by promoting choices between good and bad, but by giving the child the hope that even the meekest can succeed in life. After all, what's the use of choosing to become a good person when one feels so insignificant that he fears he will never amount to anything? Morality is

not the issue in these tales, but rather, assurance that one can succeed. Whether one meets life with a belief in the possibility of mastering its difficulties or with the expectation of defeat is also a very important existential problem.

14   The deep inner conflicts originating in our primitive drives and our violent emotions are all denied in much of modern children's literature, and so the child is not helped in coping with them. But the child is subject to desperate feelings of loneliness and isolation, and he often experiences mortal anxiety. More often than not, he is unable to express these feelings in words, or he can do so only by indirection: fear of the dark, of some animal, anxiety about his body. Since it creates discomfort in a parent to recognize these emotions in his child, the parent tends to overlook them, or he belittles these spoken fears out of his own anxiety, believing this will cover over the child's fears.

15   The fairy tale, by contrast, takes these existential anxieties and dilemmas very seriously and addresses itself directly to them: the need to be loved and the fear that one is thought worthless; the love of life, and the fear of death. Further, the fairy tale offers solutions in ways that the child can grasp on his level of understanding. For example, fairy tales pose the dilemma of wishing to live eternally by occasionally concluding: "If they have not died, they are still alive." The other ending—"And they lived happily ever after"—does not for a moment fool the child that eternal life is possible. But it does indicate that which alone can take the sting out of the narrow limits of our time on this earth: forming a truly satisfying bond to another. The tales teach that when one has done this, one has reached the ultimate in emotional security of existence and permanence of relation available to man; and this alone can dissipate the fear of death. If one has found true adult love, the fairy story also tells, one doesn't need to wish for eternal life. This is suggested by another ending found in fairy tales: "They lived for a long time afterward, happy and in pleasure."

16   An uninformed view of the fairy tale sees in this type of ending an unrealistic wish-fulfillment, missing completely the important message it conveys to the child. These tales tell him that by forming a true interpersonal relation, one escapes the separation anxiety which haunts him (and which sets the stage for many fairy tales, but it's always resolved at the story's ending). Furthermore, the story tells, this ending is not made possible, as the child wishes and believes, by holding on to his mother eternally. If we try to escape separation anxiety and death anxiety by desperately keeping our grasp on our parents, we will only be cruelly forced out, like Hansel and Gretel.

17   Only by going out into the world can the fairy-tale hero (child) find himself there; and as he does, he will also find the other with whom he will be able to live happily ever after; that is, without ever again having to experience separation anxiety. The fairy tale is future-oriented and guides the child—in terms he can understand in both his conscious and his unconscious mind—to relinquish his infantile dependency wishes and achieve a more satisfying independent existence.

18   Today children no longer grow up within the security of an extended family, or of a well-integrated community. Therefore, even more than at the times fairy tales

were invented, it is important to provide the modern child with images of heroes who have to go out into the world all by themselves and who, although originally ignorant of the ultimate things, find secure places in the world by following their right way with deep inner confidence.

19   The fairy-tale hero proceeds for a time in isolation, as the modern child often feels isolated. The hero is helped by being in touch with primitive things—a tree, an animal, nature—as the child feels more in touch with those things than most adults do. The fate of these heroes convinces the child that, like them, he may feel outcast and abandoned in the world, groping in the dark, but, like them, in the course of his life he will be guided step by step, and given help when it is needed. Today, even more than in past times, the child needs the reassurance offered by the image of the isolated man who nevertheless is capable of achieving meaningful and rewarding relations with the world around him.

Questions for Discussion

1. Do you agree with Bettelheim's positive view of the psychological value of fairy tales? Why or why not?
2. According to Bettelheim, how do fairy tales help a child to control his or her destructive unconscious impulses? How does the polarization of good and evil in fairy tales help children?
3. Why does Bettelheim believe that children benefit more from reading traditional versions of fairy tales than from the modern popular type of children's stories?
4. How do fairy-tale endings help children to accept their isolation, their "existential predicament," while at the same time encourage them to believe in the possibility of creating meaningful relationships in their own world?
5. Why does Bettelheim believe that it is important for fairy tales to have happy endings? Do you agree with him? Why or why not?
6. Do you agree or disagree with Bettelheim's ideas about why fairy tales are important to the development of ethical and healthy children? Why or why not?

Ideas for Writing

1. Write a defense or refutation of Bettelheim's theory about the value of fairy tales for children. Refer specifically to both Bettelheim's ideas and to your own ideas and your own experiences as a child reader or as an adult parenting or teaching young children.
2. Develop your journal entry into an essay. Expand on it by showing how your interpretation of the meaning of the fairy tale has changed as you have matured, contrasting the way you understand it now with the way you interpreted it as a child.

Two Versions of Cinderella

Often common tales are shared in similar but subtly distinct versions in many parts of the world and are retold, generation after generation, over a period of many centuries. Following are two versions of the popular fairy tale "Cinderella."

JOURNAL

Write down a fairy tale that you remember from your childhood. Why was this story an important one to you when you were a child? What meaning does the story have for you today?

 ## The Brothers Grimm

Aschenputtel

Jacob Grimm (1785–1863) and his brother Wilhelm Grimm (1786–1859) were scholars of the German language and of folk culture; they collected oral narratives that embodied the cultural values of the German peasant and reflected on universal human concerns. The Grimms' tales have been translated into over seventy different languages. "Aschenputtel," a version of the Cinderella story, appears here in a version translated by Lucy Crane. As you read this tale, consider how it differs from the less violent version more familiar to American readers through the Disney films and picture books.

1 There was once a rich man whose wife lay sick, and when she felt her end drawing near she called to her only daughter to come near her bed, and said,

2 "Dear child, be pious and good, and God will always take care of you, and I will look down upon you from heaven, and will be with you."

3 And then she closed her eyes and expired. The maiden went everyday to her mother's grave and wept, and was always pious and good. When the winter came the snow covered the grave with a white covering, and when the sun came in the early spring and melted it away, the man took to himself another wife.

4 The new wife brought two daughters home with her, and they were beautiful and fair in appearance, but at heart were black and ugly. And then began very evil times for the poor step-daughter.

5 "Is the stupid creature to sit in the same room with us?" said they; "those who eat food must earn it. Out upon her for a kitchen-maid!"

6   They took away her pretty dresses, and put on her an old gray kirtle, and gave her wooden shoes to wear.

7   "Just look now at the proud princess, how she is decked out!" cried they laughing, and then they sent her into the kitchen. There she was obliged to do heavy work from morning to night, get up early in the morning, draw water, make the fires, cook, and wash. Besides that, the sisters did their utmost to torment her,— mocking her, and strewing peas and lentils among the ashes, and setting her to pick them up. In the evenings, when she was quite tired out with her hard day's work, she had no bed to lie on, but was obliged to rest on the hearth among the cinders. And as she always looked dusty and dirty, they named her Aschenputtel.

8   It happened one day that the father went to the fair, and he asked his two step-daughters what he should bring back for them.

9   "Fine clothes!" said one.

10   "Pearls and jewels!" said the other.

11   "But what will you have, Aschenputtel?" said he.

12   "The first twig, father, that strikes against your hat on the way home; that is what I should like you to bring me."

13   So he bought for the two step-daughters fine clothes, pearls, and jewels, and on his way back, as he rode through a green lane, a hazel-twig struck against his hat; and he broke it off and carried it home with him. And when he reached home he gave to the step-daughters what they had wished for, and to Aschenputtel he gave the hazel-twig. She thanked him, and went to her mother's grave, and planted this twig there, weeping so bitterly that the tears fell upon it and watered it, and it flourished and became a fine tree. Aschenputtel went to see it three times a day, and wept and prayed, and each time a white bird rose up from the tree, and if she uttered any wish the bird brought her whatever she had wished for.

14   Now it came to pass that the king ordained a festival that should last for three days, and to which all the beautiful young women of that country were bidden, so that the king's son might choose a bride from among them. When the two step-daughters heard that they too were bidden to appear, they felt very pleased, and they called Aschenputtel, and said,

15   "Comb our hair, brush our shoes, and make our buckles fast, we are going to the wedding feast at the king's castle."

16   Aschenputtel, when she heard this, could not help crying, for she too would have liked to go to the dance, and she begged her step-mother to allow her.

17   "What, you Aschenputtel!" said she, "in all your dust and dirt, you want to go to the festival! you that have no dress and no shoes! you want to dance!"

18   But as she persisted in asking, at last the step-mother said,

19   "I have strewed a dish-full of lentils in the ashes, and if you can pick them all up again in two hours you may go with us."

20   Then the maiden went to the back-door that led into the garden, and called out,

"O gentle doves, O turtle-doves,
And all the birds that be,
The lentils that in ashes lie

Come and pick up for me!
   The good must be put in the dish,
   The bad you may eat if you wish."

21   Then there came to the kitchen-window two white doves, and after them some turtle-doves, and at last a crowd of all the birds under heaven, chirping and fluttering, and they alighted among the ashes; and the doves nodded with their heads, and began to pick, peck, pick, peck, and then all the others began to pick, peck, pick, peck, and put all the good grains into the dish. Before an hour was over all was done, and they flew away. Then the maiden brought the dish to her step-mother, feeling joyful, and thinking that now she should go to the feast; but the step-mother said,

22   "No, Aschenputtel, you have no proper clothes, and you do not know how to dance, and you would be laughed at!"

23   And when Aschenputtel cried for disappointment, she added,

24   "If you can pick two dishes full of lentils out of the ashes, nice and clean, you shall go with us," thinking to herself, "for that is not possible." When she had strewed two dishes full of lentils among the ashes the maiden went through the backdoor into the garden, and cried,

"O gentle doves, O turtle-doves,
And all the birds that be,
The lentils that in ashes lie
Come and pick up for me!
   The good must be put in the dish,
   The bad you may eat if you wish."

25   So there came to the kitchen-window two white doves, and then some turtle-doves, and at last a crowd of all the other birds under heaven, chirping and fluttering, and they alighted among the ashes, and the doves nodded with their heads and began to pick, peck, pick, peck, and then all the others began to pick, peck, pick, peck, and put all the good grains into the dish. And before half-an-hour was over it was all done, and they flew away. Then the maiden took the dishes to the step-mother, feeling joyful, and thinking that now she should go with them to the feast; but she said "All this is of no good to you; you cannot come with us, for you have no proper clothes, and cannot dance; you would put us to shame."

26   Then she turned her back on poor Aschenputtel, and made haste to set out with her two proud daughters.

27   And as there was no one left in the house, Aschenputtel went to her mother's grave, under the hazel bush, and cried,

"Little tree, little tree, shake over me,
That silver and gold may come down and cover me."

28   Then the bird threw down a dress of gold and silver, and a pair of slippers embroidered with silk and silver. And in all haste she put on the dress and went to the festival. But her step-mother and sisters did not know her, and thought she must be a foreign princess, she looked so beautiful in her golden dress. Of Aschenputtel they

never thought at all, and supposed that she was sitting at home, and picking the lentils out of the ashes. The King's son came to meet her, and took her by the hand and danced with her, and he refused to stand up with any one else, so that he might not be obliged to let go her hand; and when any one came to claim it he answered,

29   "She is my partner."

30   And when the evening came she wanted to go home, but the prince said he would go with her to take care of her, for he wanted to see where the beautiful maiden lived. But she escaped him, and jumped up into the pigeon-house. Then the prince waited until the father came, and told him the strange maiden had jumped into the pigeon-house. The father thought to himself,

31   "It cannot surely be Aschenputtel," and called for axes and hatchets, and had the pigeon-house cut down, but there was no one in it. And when they entered the house there sat Aschenputtel in her dirty clothes among the cinders, and a little oil-lamp burnt dimly in the chimney; for Aschenputtel had been very quick, and had jumped out of the pigeon-house again, and had run to the hazel bush; and there she had taken off her beautiful dress and laid it on the grave, and her bird had carried it away again, and then she had put on her little gray kirtle again, and had sat down in the kitchen among the cinders.

32   The next day, when the festival began anew, and the parents and step-sisters had gone to it, Aschenputtel went to the hazel bush and cried,

"Little tree, little tree, shake over me,
That silver and gold may come down and cover me."

33   Then the bird cast down a still more splendid dress than on the day before. And when she appeared in it among the guests every one was astonished at her beauty. The prince had been waiting until she came, and he took her hand and danced with her alone. And when any one else came to invite her he said,

34   "She is my partner."

35   And when the evening came she wanted to go home, and the prince followed her, for he wanted to see to what house she belonged; but she broke away from him, and ran into the garden at the back of the house. There stood a fine large tree, bearing splendid pears; she leapt as lightly as a squirrel among the branches, and the prince did not know what had become of her. So he waited until the father came, and then he told him that the strange maiden had rushed from him, and that he thought she had gone up into the pear-tree. The father thought to himself, "It cannot surely be Aschenputtel," and called for an axe, and felled the tree, but there was no one in it. And when they went into the kitchen there sat Aschenputtel among the cinders, as usual, for she had got down the other side of the tree, and had taken back her beautiful clothes to the bird on the hazel bush, and had put on her old gray kirtle again.

36   On the third day, when the parents and the step-children had set off, Aschenputtel went again to her mother's grave, and said to the tree,

"Little tree, little tree, shake over me,
That silver and gold may come down and cover me."

37   Then the bird cast down a dress, the like of which had never been seen for splendour and brilliancy, and slippers that were of gold.

38   And when she appeared in this dress at the feast nobody knew what to say for wonderment. The prince danced with her alone, and if any one else asked her he answered,

39   "She is my partner."

40   And when it was evening Aschenputtel wanted to go home, and the prince was about to go with her, when she ran past him so quickly that he could not follow her. But he had laid a plan, and had caused all the steps to be spread with pitch, so that as she rushed down them the left shoe of the maiden remained sticking in it. The prince picked it up, and saw that it was of gold, and very small and slender. The next morning he went to the father and told him that none should be his bride save the one whose foot the golden shoe should fit. Then the two sisters were very glad, because they had pretty feet. The eldest went to her room to try on the shoe, and her mother stood by. But she could not get her great toe into it, for the shoe was too small; then her mother handed her a knife, and said,

41   "Cut the toe off, for when you are queen you will never have to go on foot." So the girl cut her toe off, squeezed her foot into the shoe, concealed the pain, and went down to the prince. Then he took her with him on his horse as his bride, and rode off. They had to pass by the grave, and there sat the two pigeons on the hazel bush, and cried,

"There they go, there they go!
There is blood on her shoe;
The shoe is too small,
—Not the right bride at all!"

42   Then the prince looked at her shoe, and saw the blood flowing. And he turned his horse round and took the false bride home again, saying she was not the right one, and that the other sister must try on the shoe. So she went into her room to do so, and got her toes comfortably in, but her heel was too large. Then her mother handed her the knife, saying, "Cut a piece off your heel; when you are queen you will never have to go on foot."

43   So the girl cut a piece off her heel, and thrust her foot into the shoe, concealed the pain, and went down to the prince, who took his bride before him on his horse and rode off. When they passed by the hazel bush the two pigeons sat there and cried,

"There they go, there they go!
There is blood on her shoe;
The shoe is too small,
—Not the right bride at all!"

44   Then the prince looked at her foot, and saw how the blood was flowing from the shoe, and staining the white stocking. And he turned his horse round and brought the false bride home again.

45   "This is not the right one," said he, "have you no other daughter?"

46   "No," said the man, "only my dead wife left behind her a little stunted As-chenputtel; it is impossible that she can be the bride." But the King's son ordered her to be sent for, but the mother said,

47   "Oh no! she is much too dirty, I could not let her be seen."

48   But he would have her fetched, and so Aschenputtel had to appear.

49   First she washed her face and hands quite clean, and went in and curtseyed to the prince, who held out to her the golden shoe. Then she sat down on a stool, drew her foot out of the heavy wooden shoe, and slipped it into the golden one, which fitted it perfectly. And when she stood up, and the prince looked in her face, he knew again the beautiful maiden that had danced with him, and he cried,

50   "This is the right bride!"

51   The step-mother and the two sisters were thunderstruck, and grew pale with anger; but he put Aschenputtel before him on his horse and rode off. And as they passed the hazel bush, the two white pigeons cried,

"There they go, there they go!
No blood on her shoe;
The shoe's not too small,
The right bride is she after all."

And when they had thus cried, they came flying after and perched on Aschenput-tel's shoulders, one on the right, the other on the left, and so remained.

52   And when her wedding with the prince was appointed to be held the false sis-ters came, hoping to curry favour, and to take part in the festivities. So as the bridal procession went to the church, the eldest walked on the right side and the younger on the left, and the pigeons picked out an eye of each of them. And as they returned the elder was on the left side and the younger on the right, and the pigeons picked out the other eye of each of them. And so they were condemned to go blind for the rest of their days because of their wickedness and falsehood.

❧ *The Algonquin Cinderella*

This Native American version of the Cinderella story was anthologized by Idries Shah, a student of world folklore and Sufism, in World Tales *(1979). As you read the tale, notice its emphasis on the spiritual power of beauty and vision.*

1   There was once a large village of the MicMac Indians of the Eastern Algon-quins, built beside a lake. At the far end of the settlement stood a lodge, and in it lived a being who was always invisible. He had a sister who looked after him, and everyone knew that any girl who could see him might marry him. For that reason there were very few girls who did not try, but it was very long before any-one succeeded.

2   This is the way in which the test of sight was carried out: at evening-time, when the Invisible One was due to be returning home, his sister would walk with any girl who might come down to the lakeshore. She, of course, could see her brother, since he was always visible to her. As soon as she saw him, she would say to the girls:

3   "Do you see my brother?"

4   "Yes," they would generally reply—though some of them did say "No."

5   To those who said that they could indeed see him, the sister would say:

6   "Of what is his shoulder strap made?" Some people say that she would enquire:

7   "What is his moose-runner's haul?" or "With what does he draw his sled?"

8   And they would answer:

9   "A strip of rawhide" or "a green flexible branch," or something of that kind.

10   Then she, knowing that they had not told the truth, would say:

11   "Very well, let us return to the wigwam!"

12   When they had gone in, she would tell them not to sit in a certain place, because it belonged to the Invisible One. Then, after they had helped to cook the supper, they would wait with great curiosity, to see him eat. They could be sure that he was a real person, for when he took off his moccasins they became visible, and his sister hung them up. But beyond this they saw nothing of him, not even when they stayed in the place all the night, as many of them did.

13   Now there lived in the village an old man who was a widower, and his three daughters. The youngest girl was very small, weak and often ill: and yet her sisters, especially the elder, treated her cruelly. The second daughter was kinder, and sometimes took her side: but the wicked sister would burn her hands and feet with hot cinders, and she was covered with scars from this treatment. She was so marked that people called her *Oochigeaskw*, the Rough-Faced-Girl.

14   When her father came home and asked why she had such burns, the bad sister would at once say that it was her own fault, for she had disobeyed orders and gone near the fire and fallen into it.

15   These two elder sisters decided one day to try their luck at seeing the Invisible One. So they dressed themselves in their finest clothes, and tried to look their prettiest. They found the Invisible One's sister and took the usual walk by the water.

16   When he came, and when they were asked if they could see him, they answered: "Of course." And when asked about the shoulder strap or sled cord, they answered: "A piece of rawhide."

17   But of course they were lying like the others, and they got nothing for their pains.

18   The next afternoon, when the father returned home, he brought with him many of the pretty little shells from which wampum was made, and they set to work to string them.

19   That day, poor Little Oochigeaskw, who had always gone barefoot, got a pair of her father's moccasins, old ones, and put them into water to soften them so that she could wear them. Then she begged her sisters for a few wampum shells. The elder called her a "little pest," but the younger one gave her some. Now, with no

other clothes than her usual rags, the poor little thing went into the woods and got herself some sheets of birch bark, from which she made a dress, and put marks on it for decoration, in the style of long ago. She made a petticoat and a loose gown, a cap, leggings and a handkerchief. She put on her father's large old moccasins, which were far too big for her, and went forth to try her luck. She would try, she thought, to discover whether she could see the Invisible One.

20   She did not begin very well. As she set off, her sisters shouted and hooted, hissed and yelled, and tried to make her stay. And the loafers around the village, seeing the strange little creature, called out "Shame!"

21   The poor little girl in her strange clothes, with her face all scarred, was an awful sight, but she was kindly received by the sister of the Invisible One. And this was, of course, because this noble lady understood far more about things than simply the mere outside which all the rest of the world knows. As the brown of the evening sky turned to black, the lady took her down to the lake.

22   "Do you see him?" the Invisible One's sister asked.

23   "I do, indeed—and he is wonderful!" said Oochigeaskw.

24   The sister asked:

25   "And what is his sled-string?"

26   The little girl said:

27   "It is the Rainbow."

28   "And, my sister, what is his bow-string?"

29   "It is The Spirit's Road—the Milky Way."

30   "So you *have* seen him," said his sister. She took the girl home with her and bathed her. As she did so, all the scars disappeared from her body. Her hair grew again, as it was combed, long, like a blackbird's wing. Her eyes were now like stars: in all the world there was no other such beauty. Then, from her treasures, the lady gave her a wedding garment, and adorned her.

31   Then she told Oochigeaskw to take the *wife's* seat in the wigwam: the one next to where the Invisible One sat, beside the entrance. And when he came in, terrible and beautiful, he smiled and said:

32   "So we are found out!"

33   "Yes," said his sister. And so Oochigeaskw became his wife.

Questions for Discussion

1. What aspects of each tale help you to identify it as a Cinderella story?
2. Were you surprised or shocked by the violent and punitive ending of the Grimms' version? Do you think the Native American version is more suitable for children?
3. Why do you think that the popular fairy tales that most parents today read to their children are less violent than this Grimms' version?
4. Contrast the tone and theme of the two versions of the story. What different attitudes toward nature and the material world are expressed in the two tales?
5. Do you prefer the Algonquin, the Disney, or the Grimms' version? Explain your choice.

6. How do you feel about rereading the tale now as an adult? Does the Cinderella story hold a different meaning for you today than it did when it was first told to you? Why?

Ideas for Writing

1. Write an essay that discusses how the Cinderella myth helped to shape your values. Consider how your sense of the meaning and relevancy of the tale changed as you grew older.
2. Over 500 different versions of the Cinderella tale are told in cultures around the world. Do some research to find two versions that are especially interesting to you; then write a comparison paper of these two versions.

 Caitlin Liu

Hsao-suen: A Chinese Virtue

Born in Taiwan and raised in El Centro, California, Caitlin Liu was a freshman when she wrote this essay. Concerned about the problems that exist in American society because of the general disrespect for the older generation, Liu wrote the essay to "provide food for thought for most people of this country." Liu had to work hard to write this essay as she had to present one culture to another, integrate her past with the present, and synthesize tradition with idealism. She described her process humorously: "It took a lot of organizing and constant revising to keep the narrative from turning into chop suey."

JOURNAL

Narrate the plot of your favorite childhood story. Then discuss why you liked it as a child and why you think you have remembered it.

1 As naturally as an American youngster would own a volume of Mother Goose rhymes, I owned a set of books that were common for many Chinese children. The stories in these books bore no resemblance to the highly imaginative English verses about misbehaving children, talking animals, and eloping silverware; rather, they were down-to-earth folklore about the lives of everyday people. If I recall correctly, there were fifty morally instructive stories in this collection, and each one reflected a unique aspect of the morals and values of the Chinese culture. Some of the virtues extolled in these folklores include honesty, courage, and "hsao-suen."

2   "Hsao-suen" is not a phrase for which a simple and direct English equivalency can be assigned. An approximate translation could be "the honoring of one's parents," but even that definition is inadequate. Embodied within these two words are many qualities that allude to their true meaning: the utmost respect, love, and unquestioned obedience to one's parents. Most important of all, one who is "hsao-suen" will place the comfort and well-being of parents above his/her own. The following tale demonstrates one of the most highly esteemed Chinese virtues, "hsao-suen."

3   Two kingdoms of ancient China were at constant war, and the years of unrest had caused a famine throughout the land. A certain boy lived with his mother during this time of hardship. Since food was extremely scarce, the young lad had to gather mulberries for his family's survival. Every morning he would journey into the forest with a basket in each hand. The first basket was usually filled with an assortment of sour red berries. Whenever the boy came across ripe purple berries, however, he would put them into the second basket. Although they were more difficult to find, these were the plump, sweet fruit he wanted his mother to consume.

4   One day while berry-picking, the boy encountered two road bandits. The robbers, after looking over the lad, became curious about the two half-filled baskets of berries he carried, and demanded an explanation. The virtuous boy replied that the sour red berries were for himself, and the sweet purple berries were for his mother to eat. The burly men, touched by the "hsao-suen" of the youth, not only did not take his baskets away from him, but gave him a number of food items, including a leg of lamb. "Take these to your mother, fine young man," the bandits said before riding away.

5   Even though I read this story to myself over 13 years ago, it still remains vividly etched in my mind. As a child, I had a pampered upbringing. To read about another youngster who had to struggle just to survive sent my imagination soaring; it was such a contrast to my own life. Another aspect of the tale that really impressed my young mind was how "grown-up" the boy was. Not only did he shoulder the adult responsibility of providing food for his family, he was also able to influence the actions of grown men. For me, the boy was both a hero and a role model. As a six-year-old, I must admit that I liked the story most of all because it had a happy ending—the boy was rewarded with food, the bandits had done a good deed, and everyone presumably lived "happily ever after."

6   Now as a "grown-up" nineteen-year-old, I am able to understand the underlying message of the tale that I couldn't see as a child: the importance of being "hsao-suen." The boy loved and respected his mother so much that he wanted only the very best for her, placing her comfort and well-being above his own. The central theme of the story was how "hsao-suen" the boy was to his mother, and how through the strength of his virtue he was able to bring out the good in the bandits also. Because the boy remained true to the virtues that he believed in, everyone benefited from the process.

7   I feel that this brief tale I read over a decade ago formed one of the crucial cornerstones in the foundation of my outlook, for I consider "hsao-suen" to be one of the noblest of all human virtues. Also, I believe that there is good in everyone. All

that it takes to bring out the goodness of another is to have the light of truth and virtue within oneself be visible to others. For no light, whether the flame of a candle or rays of the sun, ever glows without casting an inevitable warm shine upon its surroundings.

Questions for Discussion

1. Does Caitlin Liu succeed in defining the meaning of "hsao-suen"? Could she have provided other examples in addition to the story that she retells?
2. How effectively does the essay use comparison and contrast to develop its major points and ideas? Does the author use a point-by-point or subject-by-subject approach to organizing her ideas and examples?
3. How clearly does Liu contrast her first reading of the story with her more recent reading? Could she have provided more points of distinction?
4. Do you agree with the student that "hsao-suen" is a concept of value for us today? Would American children benefit from practicing the respect and concern for parents implied by this traditional Asian belief, or does "hsao-suen" seem irrelevant to our culture?

 Josh Groban

Two Myths

Josh Groban, who grew up in an artistic and literary family, has always been interested in mythology and in issues related to creativity. In his freshman English class, Groban wrote a research paper comparing a number of different Native American accounts of the creation and was fascinated by the imagination and diversity of the visions he encountered in his reading. The following essay is Josh Groban's comparative response to the two accounts of creation from the casebook of myths presented in this chapter.

JOURNAL

Compare and contrast one of the non-Western myths in the creation myths with a creation myth that is popular in your culture.

1   An individual growing up in today's society is quickly indoctrinated into believing the predominant myth about creation. Our church, our parents, our teachers, and the media all reinforce such concepts as Adam and Eve and the Garden of Eden. However, every culture has its own unique myth to explain the birth of the planet and its inhabitants. By comparing the Bible's depiction of creation to

that of myths in other cultures, one is reminded that there are many possible answers available for the questions of creation. By comparing the Yao myth, "The
Chameleon Finds," to the Biblical myth of creation, one is reminded of the many
different and imaginative ways people have presented such fundamental issues as
gender relations, our connection with and responsibility to the environment, and
the relationship of human beings to God.

2   The Bible's telling of creation can be seen as depicting women as secondary to
and subservient to men. In the Book of Genesis, "the cattle," "all the birds of the
air," and "every beast of the field" are created before women. This order of creation gives the impression that the beasts are more central to life on earth than
women, and thus are created first. But, despite the abundance of these beasts,
"there was not found a helper fit for him [man]." Genesis makes it clear that
women are given life not as man's equal, but as his "helper" or assistant. When
God finally creates females, they are divested from any sense of individuality; they
are not created in the image of God, as man is, but from the rib of man. Thus,
women are presented as owing their very existence to men. Genesis 2:4 concludes
by emphasizing this idea, explaining, " . . . she shall be called Woman, because she
was taken out of man." The Bible ties not only a woman's existence, but even her
name to men. In this way, this creation myth clearly establishes women as inferior
to men and lacking an equivalent sense of identity.

3   The Yao creation myth presents a different and more favorable portrayal of
women. Women are not created as an afterthought in "The Chameleon Finds," to
function as a "helper" to men, as they are in the Bible. Instead, men and women
come into the world together, as companions. Males and females are given life
when The Creator plucks them from the river in his trap. The myth says, "The
next morning when he pulled the trap he found a little man and woman in it. He
had never seen any creatures like this." In this way, the two sexes begin their existence in equality. Females do not come from males and are not granted life after
men, cattle, birds, and beasts. The myth creates men and women together, as
equals, and thus suggests that the two sexes should live their lives in this state of
equality as well.

4   A juxtaposition of the Genesis and Yao stories in regards to their view of nature reveals a similar divergence. In the Bible, man dominates nature in much the
same way as he dominates women. Both the environment and females are presented in Genesis as subservient "helpers" to man. Genesis 2:4 professes, "and out
of the ground the Lord God made to grow every tree that is pleasant to the sight
and good for food. . . ." Nature exists to serve and "help" man; trees have life only
to serve mankind by being "pleasant to the sight and good for food." Like women,
the role of nature is to serve man rather than exist in equality with him. The Bible
reads, "The Lord God took the man and put him in the garden of Eden to till and
keep it." Man does not exist in the garden to "protect" the inhabitants or "co-ex-
ist" with them. Instead, he is to "keep it," as if the earth were a subservient possession. Man has total dominion over the earth and can "keep it" as he sees fit.

5   The Yao story of creation could be read as a refutation of this idea. In the Yao
tale, the first man and woman set fire to the vegetation and kill animals that in-

habit the earth. Their creator is appalled by this behavior. "They are burning up everything," he exclaims. "They are killing my people." He is so disturbed by the way humans treat the earth that He decides to leave the planet. A spider makes him a ladder and He goes to live in the sky. The story ends, "Thus the gods were driven off the face of the earth by the cruelty of man." This myth, in contrast to the Bible, sets clear expectations about the way the earth should be treated. In "The Chameleon Finds," nature, like women, have rights that should never be usurped. Genesis ignores these universal rights, affording them to man alone.

6   This contrast also exists in the way the two myths portray man's relationship to God. In Genesis, God is a distant, autocratic deity; he speaks and the act is performed. In this story, God "took" the man and "put him" in the garden of Eden. Later, He "commands" man never to eat from the tree of good and evil. Humans are pawns controlled by this distant deity. They make no decisions in Genesis 2:4, but are instead "taken," "put," and "commanded." The Bible's God is one that controls humans and merely speaks in order to create.

7   The Yao Creator is an entirely different figure. This God is not presented as an all-powerful deity that merely speaks to create life. He unknowingly discovers humans in his trap, and no indication is given that He created them at all. This Creator does not "command" humans to do as He wants them to do. When humans destroy the earth, no punishment comes from a distant deity, as in the Bible. Instead, The Creator leaves the earth, and thus leaves humans free to make their own decisions and choose their own destiny. This contrast impacts both man's relationship with God and his view of himself. In the Bible, The Creator is a force that has complete control over humans. He creates by merely speaking, commands humans, and punishes them. In contrast, the Yao Creator does not control every human action. He creates people not by speaking, but by discovering them. He does not command or punish, but leaves people to make their own choices about life on earth. This divergent approach functions to empower humans. The Yao myth enables people to feel in control of their life because no distant, supreme being controls them. Consequently, this fosters a heightened sense of morality and responsibility. "The Chameleon Finds" does not allow the individual to blame God or rely upon Him. Instead, this God, having set the world in motion and established His ideology, now leaves the decisions in the hands of humans.

8   It would be misguided to contend that the discrepancy between the Bible and other myths on gender issues, the environment, and man's relationship with God proves that the Bible is responsible for many of the social ills of today. Religion does not create society, but society creates religion. The Bible did not cause sexism or environmental disaster, and is not at the root of today's societal evils. However, comparing the account of Creation in Genesis to similar myths from other cultures is of value in reminding the individual that there are no absolute truths. Every society has an equally valid way to define its origins and values. The dominance of Judeo-Christian thinking in our society does not make it more correct. There are alternative stories, such as "The Chameleon Finds," that present different visions of creation. What is to be gained through this process of comparison is the appreciation of a contrasting ideology rather than the condemnation of it.

The appreciation of other religions and their view of creation comes only when someone begins to think about the validity of their own religion rather than blindly accepting it. The comparison of different creation myths is not antithetical to religion; it represents a reasoned approach to looking at God and creation and thus defines what true religious conviction really is.

Questions for Discussion

1. What are the main points of comparison and contrast around which Josh Groban structures his essay? Do they seem appropriate to the myths he studied, or would you have selected others?
2. How effectively does Groban use details and references to the two myths he contrasts to support his conclusions about their differences? Are there other details he might have used or different inferences he might have drawn based on the details he selects?
3. Although Groban states in some parts of his essay that all creation myths have validity, since "there are no absolute truths," he seems quite critical of the Biblical version of creation. Do you think that some views of creation are "better" than others, or is each version a product of the culture that produced it?
4. What seem to be the criteria that Josh Groban uses in his evaluation of the two myths he is comparing? Do his criteria seem appropriate, or would you substitute others? How would you set up criteria for evaluating myths of creation, if you believe that it is possible to do such evaluation?

Chapter Writing Topics

1. Write an essay that presents your definition of a myth. Draw on your personal experiences and the readings in this chapter as you compose your definition. Conclude by discussing the importance and impact of myths in our modern scientific and technological culture.
2. Write your own myth, based on your view of yourself as a hero or heroine. Then write an analysis of your myth, comparing the "ideal" self that emerges in the story you have written to your "real" self. How does your myth reflect the concerns of your generation and your own values? In what ways is your myth traditional? What did you learn about yourself through writing this myth?
3. Compare and contrast two versions of the same fairy tale. How do the differences reflect the particular cultural and social values of the community in which the tale was told? Which of the two versions do you prefer? Why?
4. Compare and contrast a traditional myth with a modern retelling of that myth. Reflect on how and why the original myth has been changed. Which of the two versions do you prefer and why?
5. Write an essay in which you compare the meaning that your favorite childhood fairy tale or book held for you when you were a child to the

meaning that it holds for you today. Before rereading the story, write about what was memorable for you during your childhood reading.

6. Write a myth that explores the role and values of a modern hero or heroine; then contrast your myth and a similar myth from classical mythology or a traditional culture.

7. In what important ways do you think that myths function in people's lives? Discuss several ways that myths serve people; support each main point you make with an example.

8. See one of the following films or one that you choose that explores the role of myth, either by yourself or with several of your classmates. Write an individual or collaborative review of the film that discusses the ways in which the film explores the nature and meaning of myths or fairy tales and their relationship to dreams and the imagination.

The Endless Journey, Disney's Cinderella, Black Orpheus, The Neverending Story, The Adventures of Baron Münchausen, Star Wars, The Princess Bride, The First Knight, Monty Python's Holy Grail, The Fisher King

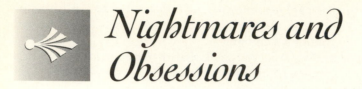

5

Nightmares and Obsessions

I can never decide whether my dreams are the result of my thoughts, or my thoughts the result of my dreams.
                              D. H. LAWRENCE

I am a kind of human snail, locked in and condemned by my own nature.

                              CYNTHIA OZICK
                              On Excellence

True!—nervous—very, very dreadfully nervous I had been and am; but why will you say that I am mad?
                              EDGAR ALLAN POE
                              The Tell-Tale Heart

Definition: Word Boundaries of the Self

Definition involves clarifying a term's meaning through precise use of language and through distinguishing between several words that may be difficult to use appropriately because they have similar or overlapping meanings. Definitions, both short and more fully expanded, can be used not only as a way of clarifying the denotative or dictionary meanings of the crucial words and abstract terminology that you use in your writing, but also as a way of exploring personal definitions of terms, feelings, values, and language.

Public Meanings and Formal Definition

In essay writing, definition is most often used as a method for clarifying meaning for your readers. If, for example, you are writing an essay on obsessions, you would first want to define what is meant by *obsession*. Although you would first turn to a dictionary, an encyclopedia, or another reliable authority for a definition of this basic term, you would also need to use your own words to create the definition. Your own words will help you get control over the direction of your paper and capture your reader's interest. Begin by placing the term within a formal pattern. First state the word you will be

220

defining, in this case, "obsession"; then put the term in a larger class or group: "An obsession is a strong emotional response." Next, you will need one or more details or qualifying phrases to distinguish your term from others in the larger group of strong emotions: "An obsession is an emotional response or preoccupation that is compulsive and highly repetitive, a response over which a person often has little or no control and which can have destructive consequences." If this definition still seems inadequate, you could add more details and develop the definition further with a typical example: "Overeating can be an obsessive form of behavior."

In writing an extended definition of a key term, carefully construct the initial definition of the term. If you place the term in too large a class, do not distinguish it from others in the class, or merely repeat your original term or a form of the term, you will have difficulty developing your ideas clearly and will confuse your reader. You also need to decide how you plan to use your definition: what will its purpose be?

Once you have created the initial definition, you can proceed to develop your paragraph or essay using other writing strategies such as examples, process analysis, discussion of cause and effect, or comparative relationships. For example, you could discuss several of the qualities of a typical obsession, provide an ordered exploration of the "stages" of the obsession, or examine the kinds of human growth and interactions with which the obsession can interfere, as Sharon Slayton does in her essay on the obsession with being "good."

Stipulative and Personal Definitions

Sometimes writers decide to develop a personal definition. This form of definition, referred to as a *stipulative definition,* is based on the writer's personal ideals and values. In this case, you still need to be clear in making crucial distinctions. For example, if you are writing a paper on your own personal dream, as Ivana Kim does in the student essay, "Dreams as Conscious Visions" in Chapter 9, you might begin with a dictionary definition of "dream" to contrast the qualities of your personal dream to the traditional connotations associated with the term as stated in the dictionary.

Freewriting and clustering will help you clarify what the term you are defining really means to you and to discover the term's deeper personal levels of meaning. Comparative thinking can also be useful. Try writing a series of sentences beginning with the words "My dream is . . ." or "My dream is like. . . ." Make as many different associations with concrete objects or events as you can. Examine the associations you have made and construct a personal definition that is qualified with expressions such as "my," "to me," or "in my opinion" and that includes several distinguishing qualities, too.

A stipulative definition is often supported by personal experiences that help the reader understand the origins and basis of your views. You may decide to provide contrasts with qualities others may associate with the term. For example, other people may believe that a dream as you have defined it is just "wishful thinking," an exercise in escapism. You could argue that, to the contrary, it is necessary to have a dream as a high ideal or aspiration; otherwise, one may too readily accept a version of reality that is less than what it could be and lose faith in the imagination that is necessary to solve problems and to move confidently into the future. Thus a stipulative definition can become a type of argument, an advocacy of one's perspective on life.

Contradiction

In developing your definition, be careful not to create contradictions. Contradiction or equivocation occurs when you begin by defining a term in one way and then shift the definition to another level of meaning. To base an argument intentionally on a contradiction is at best confusing and at worst dishonest and propagandistic. For example, if you begin your paper with a definition of "myth" as the cultural and social stories that bind a people together and then shift in the body of your paper to a discussion of private dreams and personal mythology, you will confuse your reader by violating the logic of your definition, and your essay will lose much of its credibility. Read your paper carefully before turning it in, checking to see that your definition and the arguments and examples that are developed in it are consistent. If not, your paper needs a revision, and you may want to modify your initial definition.

Writing objective and personal definitions will help you clarify your thoughts, feelings, and values. As you work to find the qualities, distinctions, and personal experiences that give a complex concept a meaning that reflects your inner self as well as the consensus of the public world, you will also be moving forward on your inward journey.

THEMATIC INTRODUCTION

 Dreams and fantasies can be healthy; they can serve as a means for escape from trivial or tedious routines and demands. Popular entertainment, for example, often provides us with simple escapist fantasies that encourage us to identify with an idealized hero or heroine. We can become strong, beautiful, courageous, or very wise, and for some moments we may be able to forget the realities of our own lives. When our minds return from a fantasy, we may feel more refreshed, more capable of handling daily responsibilities. Often fantasies provide more than just possibilities of short-term escape; they can also offer insights that will lead to deeper self-understanding. Each individual has unique dreams and fantasies; when these messages from our unconscious minds, from our dream worlds, are understood and interpreted, they can help us have more fulfilling and rewarding lives.

Sometimes, however, fantasies can become overwhelming and painful; they may grow into obsessions and compulsions which lead to behavior that can be limiting and become repetitive, sometimes even self-destructive or destructive to others. In such cases, the obsession controls the individual rather than the individual controlling the fantasy. What causes some people to have these types of obsessions? Why, for instance, does a woman's one-night stand with a married man grow into a destructive fascination, as in the popular film *Fatal Attraction*? Why does a scientist's interest in understanding human nature develop into an obsession to create a perfect man, as in the classic Gothic horror novel *Frankenstein*? Why do some people become possessed by their fantasies and obsessions to the point of madness, whereas others can maintain their psychological equilibrium and learn about themselves through their interests and dreams? How do people's unconscious obsessions influence their day-to-day life and decision-making processes? The essays, stories, and poems included in this chapter provide you with a range of perspectives that will help you begin to consider these and other issues related to our inner lives, to our dreams, obsessions, and nightmares.

In this chapter's first selection, "Fog-Horn" by W. S. Merwin, the poem's speaker reflects on the power of the forgotten unconscious world; the foghorn becomes a symbol of the hidden inner self and of secret fears and nightmares, acting as a constant reminder that we cannot escape the powers of the unconscious forces that shape our lives and exist beyond the realm of our rational control. In the next selection, "Nightmares: Terrors of the Night," dream researchers Franklin Galvin and Ernest Hartmann offer a scientific perspective on what types of people are most likely to have nightmares.

While the first two selections present general observations about the characteristics and power of nightmares and obsessions, the next three selections focus on how writing and nightmares or obsessive behavior are related. Mary Shelley's "Introduction to *Frankenstein*" explains how one of her nightmares gave her the ideas and key images that enabled her to create her classic Gothic horror novel *Frankenstein*. While Mary Shelley found inspiration for her novel in her nightmare's images, in "On Excellence" Cynthia Ozick writes about how her perfectionist writing process is a form of obsessiveness. In the next selection from William Styron's *Darkness Visible*, "The Roots of Depression," this Pulitzer Prize–winning novelist reflects on his own struggle against depression to show that self-knowledge can be a positive outcome, to show how this struggle helped him to realize that his writing had warned him through his unconscious mind of his own suicidal tendencies. Through the presentation of his own struggle and examples of the lives of other well-known artists and writers, Styron introduces the well-documented but not well-understood connection between creative genius and depression or manic depression.

Writing is also an obsession for the narrator of Charlotte Perkins Gilman's short story "The Yellow Wallpaper." In defiance of her husband, who has forbidden her to write, this story's narrator grows obsessed with writing about the patterns in the wallpaper in the room where she is confined to bed, finally imagining that there are women behind the shapes in the wallpaper, struggling to be free. The complex symbolism developed in this story asks the reader to reflect on the relationships between self-understanding, creativity, writing, obsessive fantasies, and madness.

The next two selections reflect on how feelings of guilt can translate themselves into obsessions that control an individual's life. In John Cheever's story "The Enormous Radio," a housewife becomes obsessed with the lives and fantasies of the people in her apartment building through the powers of her magical radio. And in Edgar Allan Poe's classic story, "The Tell-Tale Heart," the narrator's obsessive guilt finally leads him to confess to his murder.

The three student writings that conclude this chapter also explore the power of obsession. In her humorous narrative "I'll Tell It You Called" Adine Kernberg develops a real personality for her answering machine, which takes control of her social life. The narrator's relationship to her machine warns readers not to become totally dependent on timesaving technological devices at the expense of human communication. Sharon Slayton in her essay "The Good Girl" attempts to define the obsession with being well behaved and pleasing to others, a form of behavior that can have negative consequences, as the "good girl" can never relax, can never do anything just to please herself. In his essay "Gender Oppression, t. i. d." Mason Tobak, an emergency room psychiatrist, presents a fresh interpretation of the narrator's illness arguing that her condition has been caused by bromide poisoning.

All of the works in this chapter ask readers to look within, to listen to the questions and fears in their hearts and spirits. When we can see such experiences as portrayed in the readings in perspective, as reflections of archetypal patterns of human development and as potential sources of creative inspiration, then these different forms of obsession can also be seen as having the power to bring transformation and psychological growth.

 ## W. S. Merwin

Fog-Horn

W. S. Merwin (b. 1927) was raised in Pennsylvania. After graduating from Princeton in 1947, he lived for several years in London, translating French and Spanish classics for the British Broadcasting Corporation. Merwin, who has published many collections of poems and translations, explores myths, cultural contrasts, and ecology. His style is often discontinuous, mysterious, wavering between waking and sleeping states, creating a dialogue between the conscious and the unconscious mind. Merwin's work creates strong emotional responses. Some of his more widely read books include Selected Translations: 1948–1969 *(1969),* The Compass Flower *(1977),* Opening the Hand *(1983),* The Lost Upland *(1992), and* The Vixen *(1996). "Fog-Horn" was included in* The Drunk in the Furnace *(1958). As you read the poem, try to recreate the sound and image of the foghorn in your own imagination.*

JOURNAL

Write about and define a warning that came to you from your unconscious, a warning that might have taken the form of a dream, a fantasy, a minor accident, or a psychosomatic illness.

Surely that moan is not the thing
That men thought they were making, when they
Put it there, for their own necessities.
That throat does not call to anything human
5 But to something men had forgotten,
That stirs under fog. Who wounded that beast
Incurably, or from whose pasture
Was it lost, full grown, and time closed round it
With no way back? Who tethered its tongue
10 So that its voice could never come
To speak out in the light of clear day,
But only when the shifting blindness
Descends and is acknowledged among us,

As though from under a floor it is heard,
15 Or as though from behind a wall, always
Nearer than we had remembered? If it
Was we that gave tongue to this cry
What does it bespeak in us, repeating
And repeating, insisting on something
20 That we never meant? We only put it there
To give warning of something we dare not
Ignore, lest we should come upon it
Too suddenly, recognize it too late,
As our cries were swallowed up and all hands lost.

Questions for Discussion

1. How does Merwin personify the foghorn, bringing it to life, making it more than just an object? Refer to specific details that you think are particularly effective.
2. What does the cry of the foghorn signify? What is its warning?
3. What words, images, and phrases make the poem seem like a dream or a nightmare?
4. Why can't the voice of the foghorn "speak out in the light of clear day"?
5. Why does the voice of the foghorn "call" to something "forgotten"? What parts of ourselves are we most likely to forget or ignore? What helps us to remember what we want to forget?
6. What is your interpretation of the poem? What state of mind is the poet attempting to define?

Ideas for Writing

1. Write an essay in which you define and clarify with examples and comparisons the positive role that you think the unconscious mind can play in helping one to create a balanced and fulfilling life. Refer to the poem in shaping your response.
2. Write a narrative or a poem in which you use an object or an animal as a comparison to or as a way of defining and understanding the unconscious mind. Try to emphasize how the unconscious mind communicates with the conscious mind.

Ashley Holt

This picture represents my interpretation of the poem "Fog-Horn" by W. S. Merwin. As a child, I used to spend my summers with my family on an island off the coast of Maine, where we could hear the clink-clink of the channel buoys and the moan of the foghorn all night long. The title of this poem reminds me of that long, melancholy wail that seemed to emanate from somewhere deep and ancient; part of the reason it seemed so spooky was that I could hear it, deep and rumbling, but it was hard to place exactly where it was coming from; it seemed to be everywhere, all around us. When I read this poem though, it felt that the "moan" is actually inside of us, but it is still as big and powerful and deep as ever. It is a beast that we try to hide, to suppress within ourselves, but that struggles to break free, to warn us maybe of the "shifting blindness." In my picture, this darkness is represented by the black cloud that descends upon the person; the "moan" is a beast that tries to leap out and counteract this darkness. But the beast, too, is a frightening prospect; that is why we try to keep it where we can maybe forget about it, because letting it out can be painful.

Franklin Galvin and Ernest Hartmann

Nightmares: Terrors of the Night

Franklin Galvin was a doctoral candidate in Clinical Psychology at Boston University and conducted research at the Lemuel Shattuck Hospital Sleep Laboratory when he co-authored this article. Ernest Hartmann, M.D., is a Professor of Psychiatry at the Tufts University School of Medicine. He is the director of the Sleep Research Laboratory, West-Ros Park Mental Health Center at Lemuel Shattuck Hospital and the director of the Sleep Disorders Center, Newton-Wellesley Hospital. Hartmann has written many books, including The Biology of Dreaming *and* The Sleeping Pill. *In the following essay Hartmann and Galvin make distinctions between nightmares and night terrors, while examining some of the causes and treatments for both.*

JOURNAL

Record a nightmare that you remember from your childhood or recent times. How does your nightmare help to define your inner world and the issues that are important to you?

1   To Sigmund Freud, the nightmare was an annoyance, a stumbling block to his development of a theory of dreams as wish fulfillments. He first tried to include nightmares in his general view by suggesting that they represent the fulfillment of superego wishes—wishes for punishment. Freud was not satisfied with this view, however, and he later suggested that certain nightmares, especially traumatic nightmares, represent a repetition compulsion—a primitive tendency of the mind to repeat what has been experienced. Theodore Lidz, when studying traumatic nightmares, proposed that these dreams could be understood as a wish for punishment, as Freud first suggested, but also as an "ambivalent wish for death": both the wish for death and the wish to escape it.

2   The manifest fear of death figured prominently in a childhood dream of Freud's. It is the first of three dreams we present to illustrate how the nightmare has heralded momentous change in the lives of three noted dreamworkers.

3   In his discussion of anxiety dreams near the end of *The Interpretation of Dreams,* Freud presented us with the only dream from his childhood to be found in his published works and letters. "A true anxiety-dream," he called it, "from my seventh or eighth year." This dating is of special import in Freud's life because it "starts— spiritually—the gestation period of a new and original thought." Of this dream, Freud wrote:

It was a very vivid one, and in it I saw my beloved mother, with a peculiarly peaceful, sleeping expression on her features, being carried into the room by two (or three) people with birds' beaks and laid upon the bed. I awoke in tears and screaming, and interrupted my parents' sleep. . . . I remember that I suddenly grew calm when I saw my mother's face, as though I had needed to be reassured that she was not dead. . . . I was not anxious because I had dreamt that my mother was dying. . . . The anxiety can be traced back, when repression is taken into account, to an obscure and evidently sexual craving that had found appropriate expression in the visual content of the dream.

4   Some thirty years after he dreamed this, Freud submitted the dream to interpretation. Through the associations he presented, it appears that he revealed both his incestuous wishes toward his mother and his fear of castration as a consequence of sexual excitement aroused by witnessing the primal scene. A related fear was that his mother would bleed and die as a result of sexual relations. The "obscure and evidently sexual craving" giving rise to this dream was, it seems, the essence of Freud's own Oedipus complex. The dream heralded a startlingly new psychological theory.

5   The second dream is from the first chapter of Carl Jung's autobiography, *Memories, Dreams, Reflections*. The earliest dream that Jung remembered was one from between ages three and four, "a dream which was to preoccupy me all my life," he recorded. In the dream, he "was paralyzed with terror" and "awoke sweating and scared to death." It was a dream of encountering a huge phallus standing on a magnificent throne in an underground chamber of hewn stone and hearing his mother's voice call out: "Yes, just look at him. That is the man-eater!" For many nights afterwards the young Jung was afraid to go to sleep. The dream haunted him for years, and in old age he wrote:

> Through this childhood dream I was initiated into the secrets of the earth. What happened then was a kind of burial in the earth, and many years were to pass before I came out again. Today I know that it happened in order to bring the greatest possible amount of light into the darkness. It was an initiation into the realm of darkness. My intellectual life had its unconscious beginnings at that time.

6   The third terrifying dream was recorded in a modern sleep laboratory, and it heralded scientific change in the entire community of dreamworkers. This dream helped to establish the link between rapid eye movements and dreaming—a link that launched the scientific investigation of dreams in the early 1950s. As a graduate student in Nathaniel Kleitman's laboratory at the University of Chicago, Eugene Aserinsky observed the rapid eye movements made by infants during sleep. In pursuing this phenomenon, he attempted to find correlations between these movements and both physiological and psychological functions. He spoke years later about this early period in a follow-up discussion on somnambulism and stated:

> For a long time I was not sure whether those eye movements were associated with dreaming. Finally, one night when the polygraph pens showed deflections indicating either eye movements or instrument generated artifacts, I decided that the time was proper to make a direct visual observation of the subject's eyes. However, all of a sudden the pens practically went wild and almost went off the carriage. Well, I dashed into the sleeping chamber to see what had happened, turned on the lights, and saw the subject, a medical student, lying there,

making some mumbling noises while his eyes, although closed, were moving vigorously, violently in all directions. I awakened him and he told me that he had a nightmare from which he felt he couldn't awaken. . . . Well now, this episode more or less convinced me that dreaming, or at least this nightmare, was associated with rapid eye movements.

Distinguishing Nightmares from Night Terrors

7   Based on the pioneering work of Kleitman, Aserinsky, and William Dement, other researchers have established that there are two important and very different phenomena that can wake us in a fright during the night: the *night terror* and the *nightmare*.

8   The night terror is an abrupt awakening early in the night, most often within the first hour or two of sleep, and usually occurring during stage three or four (deep, slow-wave) sleep. This awakening is most often accompanied by sweating, body movements, and a sudden scream or cry for help as the sleeper wakes in terror. Particularly with children, the physical movements may become intense and even continue into a sleepwalking episode. When night terrors were observed in the sleep laboratory, pulse and respiratory rates sometimes doubled during the thirty seconds or so involved in these awakenings. The night terror has been called a *disorder of arousal* and can be considered a minor abnormality in the brain's sleep-wake mechanisms.

9   When asked about the experience, the sleeper either does not remember the night terror or simply recalls waking in fright, heart pounding, and not knowing what to make of it. Occasionally the person will be aware of a single frightening image—"Something was crushing me and I couldn't breathe." The night terror also has been called *pavor nocturnus* or an "incubus attack" because of this sensation of suffocation, as if an incubus—a kind of demon or goblin that was supposed to produce nightmares—was actually sitting on the sleeper's chest. Yet the terrifying episode is generally not described as a dream.

10   The nightmare—sometimes called *REM-nightmare* or *dream anxiety attack*—is a quite different experience from the night terror. Usually occurring late during the night in the last three hours of sleep, the nightmare is a long, frightening dream that awakens the sleeper. Laboratory recordings show that it occurs during REM sleep, often during a long REM period of twenty to thirty minutes. Pulse and blood pressure may show some increase but not as much as in a night terror, and there are neither gross body movements nor sleepwalking, because during REM sleep the arms, legs, and trunk are temporarily paralyzed.

11   The person awakened by a nightmare almost always remembers very distinctly a long, intense, and vivid dream, ending with a frightening sequence. The nightmare is a very detailed, colorful, lifelike dream experience involving some of the earliest, most profound anxieties and the most thoroughly terrifying fears to which we are all subject. The nightmare often includes sensations and perceptions other than vision—even including pain, which is very rarely felt in dreams. For example: "It was a wartime scene. I could *hear* awful noises: bombs bursting around me, screams. Something hit me in the shoulder; I could *feel the pain* and the blood flowing down my arm."

12   When a person reports having frightening sleep interruptions, the answer to one simple question—"Are these experiences dreams?"—usually will indicate whether the events are night terrors or nightmares. The nightmare sufferers will answer, "Yes, of course," whereas those who have night terrors will reply, "Definitely not." They know what they experience is something other than a dream. The two are very different events physiologically and psychologically and seldom occur in the same individual.

13   An occasional person suffers from what are called hypnagogic nightmares—terrifying nightmarish fantasies experienced upon just falling asleep. Also, some persons have a condition called nocturnal myoclonus—many jerking muscle movements during the night. Sometimes these persons will report a nightmarelike occurrence when awakened by muscle jerks.

14   Lastly, people troubled with chronic post-traumatic stress disorder experience repetitive nightmares depicting the traumatic episode long after the event. These repeated experiences share characteristics of both nightmares and night terrors and may occur in various stages of sleep. Prominent in this group are combat veterans and victims of exceptionally violent accidents or crimes.

15   It is evident from the above descriptions that the experiences of the medical student observed by Eugene Aserinsky in the laboratory, that of the young Carl Jung, and that of the young Sigmund Freud were all true nightmares and not night terrors or other nightmarelike events.

Nightmare Incidence

16   Nightmares are far more common than night terrors. Almost everyone has had a nightmare on occasion, most likely in childhood. Although people tend to forget their childhood nightmares, some have had particularly frequent or especially vivid ones that are remembered clearly throughout their lives.

17   Nightmares are definitely more frequent in children than in adults and are particularly common at ages three through six. Evidence suggests that they probably occur as early as age one. While they become less frequent after age six, their incidence may increase again in adolescence between ages thirteen to eighteen. The incidence of nightmares generally decreases with age and in healthy adults is relatively low.

18   Based on many survey studies, sleep researchers estimate that approximately 50 percent of the adult population have no nightmares at all, though they may have had them as children. Most others remember an occasional nightmare, and the average is perhaps one or two per year. Between 5 and 10 percent of the population report nightmares once a month or more. Only a small percentage have nightmares that are frequent enough or severe enough to be significantly disturbing to their lives. Men are probably as likely to have nightmares as often as women, but they tend to be much more reluctant to mention them.

What Produces Nightmares?

19   For centuries the word *nightmare* has been used loosely to mean anything that wakes one up in fright, a creature that produces such terror, the frightening dream itself, or the actual awakening. Most scholars now agree that the root *mare* derives

from the Old English and Old German root *mara*, meaning "an incubus or suc-cubus," and not from *myre*, meaning "a female horse." The folklore of peoples' ex-periences during the night inspired the eighteenth-century Swiss artist Henry Fuseli to depict both images in his well-known painting *The Nightmare*.

20   We no longer believe that demons or evil spirits produce nightmares, nor is there any solid evidence that eating something disagreeable will cause them. Re-cent evidence also contradicts another widely held view that a lack of oxygen gives rise to nightmares. Obstructive sleep apnea is a disorder in which air does not get through the throat to the lungs of the sleeper because of some obstruction at the back of the throat. This may happen 100 or more times in one night. The chest and abdomen of the sleeper heave but no air gets through, and after ten to twenty seconds there is a brief awakening, allowing normal breathing to resume. Sleep-apnea sufferers very rarely report nightmares, indicating that a lack of oxy-gen is not causally related to nightmares.

21   One factor that does appear to precipitate nightmares is physical illness, al-though it is unclear whether illness itself or the stress that accompanies it is more important. Children who do not otherwise have nightmares report them during times of illness, particularly febrile illness. Adults, too, seem to have more night-mares during high fever or around the time of an operation. In addition, certain neurological disorders sometimes have been associated with nightmares—notably epilepsy and postencephalitic parkinsonism.

22   Mental illness is often associated with nightmares. In certain individuals night-mares occur at the onset of psychosis, especially schizophrenic episodes. Depres-sion can also be associated with an increase of nightmares.

23   Stressful events seem to be causally related to frequent and severe nightmares in susceptible persons. Stressful periods in adulthood, such as times of examina-tions, job changes, moves, or the loss of significant persons, may produce or in-crease nightmares.

24   The one generalization that seems to hold true for nightmare sufferers is that their nightmares almost always involve feelings of helplessness, most often help-lessness dating from childhood. The most frequent situations in their nightmares involve being chased, attacked, thrown off a cliff, or generally feeling at the mercy of others. Almost invariably it is the dreamer who is in danger and utterly power-less—not someone else. A decrease or sometimes a cessation of adult nightmares usually occurs as the dreamer feels more confident, more mature, and thus less close to the helpless feelings of childhood.

Profile of the Nightmare Sufferer

25   Recent in-depth studies carried out at Ernest Hartmann's sleep laboratory at the Shattuck Hospital in Boston have provided information about the personali-ties of people clearly reporting nightmares rather than night terrors. Using news-paper ads, subjects were recruited who had frequent nightmares as a long-term condition. One study examined thirty-eight adults reporting nightmares at least once per week for at least one year and beginning in childhood. A second study compared another twelve frequent nightmare sufferers with twelve people who re-

ported vivid dreams but no nightmares and twelve others who reported neither nightmares nor vivid dreams. All the subjects were interviewed and given a battery of psychological tests including the Rorschach Inkblot Technique and several personality inventories; some were also monitored in the sleep laboratory.

26 Individuals in the nightmare groups from both of these studies were no different in intelligence from those in the comparison groups, and likewise there were no clearcut physical differences in appearance distinguishing the groups. The nightmare subjects were different in having jobs or lifestyles related to the arts or other creative pursuits; they ranged from painters, poets, and musicians to craftspersons, teachers, and nontraditional therapists. No blue-collar workers or white-collar executives or office personnel were found who had frequent nightmares, but there were many such workers in the comparison groups.

27 The artistic and creative interest of the nightmare subjects was a lifelong characteristic. These subjects felt themselves to be in some way unusual for as long as they could remember and often described themselves as sensitive in various ways. Some were sensitive to bright light or loud sound, most could be easily hurt emotionally, and some were quite empathic or sensitive to others' feelings. However, no extreme trauma could be discerned in their histories.

28 More commonly than in the comparison groups, those with nightmares described their adolescence as stormy and difficult, often with bouts of depression and thoughts of suicide. They tended to rebel by using drugs and alcohol, fighting with parents, or running away. From adolescence on, the nightmare sufferers appeared to be extremely open and trusting people—perhaps too trusting, making them defenseless and vulnerable. They often became quickly involved in difficult, entangling friendships and love relationships from which they could not easily escape.

29 However, these nightmare sufferers were *not* especially anxious, angry, or depressed people. Some were vulnerable to mental illness: 70 percent of them had been in psychotherapy, and 15 percent had previously been admitted to mental hospitals; but at the time of the interviews, as a group they were functioning quite well in life.

30 Hartmann and his associates described the creative, sensitive, and vulnerable nightmare subjects as having "thin boundaries" in many different senses. They had thin interpersonal boundaries—that is, they became involved with others very quickly; thin ego boundaries, being extremely aware of their inner wishes and fears; and thin sexual boundaries—they easily imagined being of the opposite sex, and many fantasized or engaged in bisexual activity. They also had thin group boundaries, for they did not strongly identify themselves with a single community or ethnic group. Their sleep-wakefulness boundaries were thin, for they often experienced in-between states of consciousness, unsure whether they were awake, asleep, or dreaming. Some would awaken from one dream only to find themselves in another.

Treatment of Nightmares

31 Treatment is not usually required for nightmares. Parents of children ages three through six, when nightmares are most common, should be aware that the occurrence of nightmares is not abnormal. Talking with these children and allowing

them to express any fearful feelings may be helpful, as is checking the children's environment at home and school for any potential sources of fear or anxiety.

32   Most of the adult subjects with frequent nightmares in the above-mentioned studies had never sought treatment specifically for their nightmares, though many had sought it for other conditions, such as stress or depression. The majority had accepted their terrifying dreams as part of themselves and sometimes made use of them in their creative endeavors. However, some sufferers wanted treatment specifically for their nightmares. Judging from published accounts of case reports and a few controlled studies, a variety of therapeutic techniques have been used with success.

33   In a recent review of psychological therapies for nightmares, psychologist Gordon Halliday suggested four distress-producing features of the nightmare and proposed that treatment may reduce the distress by altering any of these features: the nightmare's uncontrollability, its perceived sense of reality, the dreadful and anxiety-producing story line, and the nightmare's believed importance. He categorized treatment techniques into these classes: desensitization and related behavioral procedures, psychoanalytic and cathartic techniques, story-line alteration procedures, and "face [the danger] and conquer" *approaches*.

34   Desensitization and related behavioral procedures first identify the fear-generating components of the nightmares and then desensitize the dreamer to those elements through relaxation procedures, invoking pleasant imagery, or repeated exposure of those elements to the dreamer in a therapeutic setting. Psychoanalytic and cathartic techniques attempt to convey to dreamers an understanding of their nightmares in the context of their life situations and developmental histories, to allow suppressed or repressed emotion to be appropriately released, and to strengthen their adaptive mechanisms. Story-line alteration procedures try to change the nightmares through imagination or hypnotic suggestion by rehearsing different endings, confronting the nightmare figures, or modifying some detail. The "face and conquer" approaches consist of instructions to the dreamer to face and confront the nightmare figures when the dreamer is next experiencing an actual nightmare dream state. Several other methods that have been used clinically but not yet reported in the case literature including teaching dreamers, especially children, to call upon a "dream friend" for help and restaging the nightmares in collages or drawings.

35   We are currently investigating a "face and conquer" treatment procedure that attempts to teach frequent nightmare subjects to attain a lucid dream state in order to reduce the frequency and severity of their terrifying dreams. A lucid dream is one in which the sleeper is aware *during the dream* that he or she is dreaming and feels to be in full possession of mental functions as if awake. This awareness permits the dreamer to make choices as the dream occurs. For example, the dreamer may be walking through an unusual landscape, realize that the experience is a dream, and decide to fly into the air to see the dream landscape from a new perspective.

36   In nonlucid dreams, which are more common, there is generally a sense of the dream experience happening *to* the dreamer with little feeling of choice about what occurs. Thus, when confronted by a threatening figure in a nightmare, the

dreamer usually tries to run away from it. By becoming lucid in the nightmare, the dreamer could then choose to turn and face the threatening figure and possibly master what is feared.

37   In nearly all of the published reports, clinical accounts, and first-person descriptions of utilizing the lucid dream state to deal with nightmares, the actual dreamers perceived and felt their encounters to be positive, enriching, and empowering experiences both during and after their dreams. However, given that most of these persons are from a normal population, it is possible that these observations may not generalize to a population of frequent nightmare sufferers. Also, though such a treatment has therapeutic potential, it does involve some risk, because there are isolated accounts of negative lucid dream experience.

38   The lucid-dream treatment approach has the potential to alter three of the four distress-producing aspects of the nightmare suggested by Halliday. Once one achieves lucidity within a nightmare, the nightmare's uncontrollability can be altered, because the dreamer can choose and act to change his or her response to the threatening images; the nightmare's perceived sense of reality can be altered, because the dreamer understands that the experience is a dream rather than part of everyday physical external reality; and the nightmare's dreadful and anxiety-producing story line can be altered as a result of the changed response of the dreamer. Other dreamworkers, such as Stephen LaBerge, may contend that the fourth distress-producing aspect, the believed importance of the nightmare, also may be altered, because lucid dreamers "realize that they themselves contain, and thus transcend, the entire dream world and all of its contents, because they know that their imaginations have created the dream."

39   The major limitation cited by Halliday in utilizing the lucid dream state as a treatment modality for nightmares is that it is not yet known how to reliably induce this experience. Psychologist Joseph Dane has developed a posthypnotic suggestion technique for inducing the lucid dream state in hypnotically susceptible women. Using this technique, seven of the eight women in one group of his study succeeded in having verified lucid dreams. This is a promising approach for frequent nightmare sufferers, because there is evidence that they have higher hypnotizability scores than others.

40   Two recent studies indicate that learning lucid dreaming could be a viable treatment method for frequent nightmare sufferers. The first is a study of boundary characteristics by Franklin Galvin, which matched forty spontaneous lucid dreamers with forty frequent nightmare dreamers and forty nonlucid and relatively nightmare-free dreamers (ordinary dreamers). In comparison to the ordinary dreamers, both the lucid dreamers and the nightmare dreamers were shown to have "thin boundaries." In addition, a number of the spontaneous lucid dreamers stated that they had first developed lucidity during frightening dreams.

41   The second is a case study by Andrew Brylowski, which related the treatment of a thirty-five-year-old woman, Ms. D., with a history of major depression and a diagnosis of borderline personality disorder. She reported one to four nightmares per week and had a history of recurrent nightmares of variable frequency and intensity since age ten. The treatment focused on alleviating her nightmares using

lucid dreaming. Within the first four weekly sessions, the introduction of lucidity into the patient's dream life coincided with a decrease in the frequency and intensity of her nightmares.

42   The report of a dream by Ms. D. seven weeks into the treatment illustrates her ability to avert a potential nightmare by using lucidity to convert a threat into a learning experience.

> Ms. D. was walking up huge grey stone stairs leading to a fortress or castle. Looking down she saw a colleague and felt thrilled. The stairs then extended over a moat. She stopped to look at the water and a vicious grey shark with big white teeth surfaced. It propelled itself along the stairs toward her. Ms. D. was frozen with fear and couldn't move. She then realized that she had been having a good dream until the shark appeared; then she thought: "It is a dream!" She was unable to do anything but stare at the shark. The shark changed into a huge whale that smiled and was no longer terrorizing. She awakened in peace.

43   Though she had previously thought of things she might do when she became lucid in a frightening dream, at the moment of fear she could only stare and not run. When she stood her ground and faced the terror rather than attempting to flee, the threatening image was transformed into an acceptable figure positively acknowledging her. Facing the fear in her dream enabled her to wake in peace. Altering her nightmares also facilitated Ms. D. in making positive changes to deal with her waking emotions.

44   The skills Ms. D. learned in lucid dreaming extended into areas of her waking life. After another nine weeks of treatment, she reported a dream in which she was working on a painting with two colors, each scintillating. Upon realizing it was a dream, she created a third color by blending the first two. With this new color she added depth and dimension to the painting. This accomplishment in her dream prompted Ms. D. to complete other art projects in her waking life that she had left unfinished.

45   As Sigmund Freud's nightmare was able to retain "its imperishable value . . . by becoming a driving force in the making of a genius," and as Carl Jung was initiated into the secrets of the earth by a nightmare and later brought light into this realm of darkness, so too have the nightmares of others heralded some meaningful change in their lives. For those with frequent nightmares, the use of the lucid dream state could offer a unique opportunity to begin such a change.

Questions for Discussion

1. How do the authors use the examples of Freud, Jung, and case histories recorded in Nathaniel Kleitman's laboratory to set the stage for their theory about the differences between nightmares and night terrors?
2. How do the authors distinguish the night terror from the nightmare? How are the experiences different psychologically and physiologically? Why do they seldom occur in the same individuals?
3. According to the essay, what causes nightmares in children and adults? Why do adults have fewer nightmares than children?

4. What are the personality traits of the nightmare sufferer and of the night terror sufferer? How have adult sufferers from nightmares been treated effectively?

5. How do the authors define lucid dreaming? How can nightmares become sources of power and of creativity?

6. How convincing is the authors' use of research data and accounts of successful treatment programs to support their definitions and theories about nightmares and night terrors? Would any other type of research or experimental data have made the essay clearer and more persuasive?

Ideas for Writing

1. Develop your journal entry into an essay in which you explore the way in which your nightmares help to define your inner life and preoccupations.

2. Do some research into a topic discussed in this article: sleep, lucid dreaming, nightmares, or night terrors. Write a definition essay that explores the subject that you have selected to research.

 ## Mary Shelley

Introduction to Frankenstein

Mary Wollstonecraft Shelley (1797–1851) was born into a family of freethinkers distinguished for their intellectual achievements. Mary Wollstonecraft married a disciple of her father's, the romantic poet Percy Bysshe Shelley. While visiting in Switzerland at the home of Lord Byron, Mary Shelley participated in a story-writing competition which resulted in Frankenstein *(1816), her first and best-known novel. As you read the introduction to Mary Shelley's nightmarish book about a scientist's creation of a monster who haunts his creator, notice how her family life and her dreams compelled her to write and to publish.*

JOURNAL

Have you ever had a dream that gave you the desire to write a story, poem, play, or song? Did you develop your dream into writing? Do you believe that your dreams nurture your creativity?

1 The publishers of the standard novels, in selecting *Frankenstein* for one of their series, expressed a wish that I should furnish them with some account of the origin of the story. I am the more willing to comply because I shall thus give a general answer to the question so very frequently asked me—how I, then a young girl, came to think of and to dilate upon so very hideous an idea. It is true that I am very averse to bringing myself forward in print, but as my account will only appear

as an appendage to a former production, and as it will be confined to such topics as have connection with my authorship alone, I can scarcely accuse myself of a personal intrusion.

2   It is not singular that, as the daughter of two persons of distinguished literary celebrity, I should very early in life have thought of writing. As a child I scribbled, and my favourite pastime during the hours given me for recreation was to "write stories." Still, I had a dearer pleasure than this, which was the formation of castles in the air—the indulging in waking dreams—the following up trains of thought, which had for their subject the formation of a succession of imaginary incidents. My dreams were at once more fantastic and agreeable than my writings. In the latter I was a close imitator—rather doing as others had done than putting down the suggestions of my own mind. What I wrote was intended at least for one other eye—my childhood's companion and friend; but my dreams were all my own; I accounted for them to nobody; they were my refuge when annoyed—my dearest pleasure when free.

3   I lived principally in the country as a girl and passed a considerable time in Scotland. I made occasional visits to the more picturesque parts, but my habitual residence was on the blank and dreary northern shores of the Tay, near Dundee. Blank and dreary on retrospection I call them; they were not so to me then. They were the aerie of freedom and the pleasant region where unheeded I could commune with the creatures of my fancy. I wrote then, but in a most common-place style. It was beneath the trees of the grounds belonging to our house, or on the bleak sides of the woodless mountains near, that my true compositions, the airy flights of my imagination, were born and fostered. I did not make myself the heroine of my tales. Life appeared to me too common-place an affair as regarded myself. I could not figure to myself that romantic woes or wonderful events would ever be my lot; but I was not confined to my own identity, and I could people the hours with creations far more interesting to me at that age than my own sensations.

4   After this my life became busier, and reality stood in place of fiction. My husband, however, was from the first very anxious that I should prove myself worthy of my parentage and enroll myself on the page of fame. He was forever inciting me to obtain literary reputation, which even on my own part I cared for then, though since I have become infinitely indifferent to it. At this time he desired that I should write, not so much with the idea that I could produce anything worthy of notice, but that he might himself judge how far I possessed the promise of better things hereafter. Still I did nothing. Travelling, and the cares of a family, occupied my time; and study, in the way of reading or improving my ideas in communication with his far more cultivated mind was all of literary employment that engaged my attention.

5   In the summer of 1816 we visited Switzerland and became the neighbours of Lord Byron. At first we spent our pleasant hours on the lake or wandering on its shores; and Lord Byron, who was writing the third canto of *Childe Harold*, was the only one among us who put his thoughts upon paper. These, as he brought them successively to us, clothed in all the light and harmony of poetry, seemed to stamp as divine the glories of heaven and earth, whose influences we partook with him.

6   But it proved a wet, ungenial summer, and incessant rain often confined us for days to the house. Some volumes of ghost stories translated from the German into French fell into our hands. There was the *History of the Inconstant Lover,* who, when he thought to clasp the bride to whom he had pledged his vows, found himself in the arms of the pale ghost of her whom he had deserted. There was the tale of the sinful founder of his race whose miserable doom it was to bestow the kiss of death on all the younger sons of his fated house, just when they reached the age of promise. His gigantic, shadowy form, clothed like the ghost in *Hamlet,* in complete armour, but with the beaver up, was seen at midnight, by the moon's fitful beams, to advance slowly along the gloomy avenue. The shape was lost beneath the shadow of the castle walls; but soon a gate swung back, a step was heard, the door of the chamber opened, and he advanced to the couch of the blooming youths, cradled in healthy sleep. Eternal sorrow sat upon his face as he bent down and kissed the forehead of the boys, who from that hour withered like flowers snapped upon the stalk. I have not seen these stories since then, but their incidents are as fresh in my mind as if I had read them yesterday.

7   "We will each write a ghost story," said Lord Byron, and his proposition was acceded to. There were four of us. The noble author began a tale, a fragment of which he printed at the end of his poem of Mazeppa. Shelley, more apt to embody ideas and sentiments in the radiance of brilliant imagery and in the music of the most melodious verse that adorns our language than to invent the machinery of a story, commenced one founded on the experiences of his early life. Poor Polidori had some terrible idea about a skull-headed lady who was so punished for peeping through a key-hole—what to see I forget: something very shocking and wrong of course; but when she was reduced to a worse condition than the renowned Tom of Coventry, he did not know what to do with her and was obliged to dispatch her to the tomb of the Capulets, the only place for which she was fitted. The illustrious poets also, annoyed by the platitude of prose, speedily relinquished their uncongenial task.

8   I busied myself *to think of a story*—a story to rival those which had excited us to this task. One which would speak to the mysterious fears of our nature and awaken thrilling horror—one to make the reader dread to look round, to curdle the blood, and quicken the beatings of the heart. If I did not accomplish these things, my ghost story would be unworthy of its name. I thought and pondered—vainly. I felt that blank incapability of invention which is the greatest misery of authorship, when dull Nothing replies to our anxious invocations. "Have you thought of a story?" I was asked each morning, and each morning I was forced to reply with a mortifying negative.

9   Everything must have a beginning, to speak in Sanchean phrase; and that beginning must be linked to something that went before. The Hindus give the world an elephant to support it, but they make the elephant stand upon a tortoise. Invention, it must be humbly admitted, does not consist in creating out of void, but out of chaos; the materials must, in the first place, be afforded: it can give form to dark, shapeless substances but cannot bring into being the substance itself. In all

matters of discovery and invention, even of those that appertain to the imagination, we are continually reminded of the story of Columbus and his egg. Invention consists in the capacity of seizing on the capabilities of a subject and in the power of moulding and fashioning ideas suggested to it.

10   Many and long were the conversations between Lord Byron and Shelley to which I was a devout but nearly silent listener. During one of these, various philosophical doctrines were discussed, and among others the nature of the principle of life, and whether there was any probability of its ever being discovered and communicated. They talked of the experiments of Dr. Darwin (I speak not of what the doctor really did or said that he did, but, as more to my purpose, of what was then spoken of as having been done by him), who preserved a piece of vermicelli in a glass case till by some extraordinary means it began to move with voluntary motion. Not thus, after all, would life be given. Perhaps a corpse would be reanimated; galvanism had given token of such things: perhaps the component parts of a creature might be manufactured, brought together, and endued with vital warmth.

11   Night waned upon this talk, and even the witching hour had gone by before we retired to rest. When I placed my head on my pillow I did not sleep, nor could I be said to think. My imagination, unbidden, possessed and guided me, gifting the successive images that arose in my mind with a vividness far beyond the usual bounds of reverie. I saw—with shut eyes, but acute mental vision—I saw the pale student of unhallowed arts kneeling beside the thing he had put together. I saw the hideous phantasm of a man stretched out, and then, on the working of some powerful engine, show signs of life and stir with an uneasy, half-vital motion. Frightful must it be, for supremely frightful would be the effect of any human endeavour to mock the stupendous mechanism of the Creator of the world. His success would terrify the artist; he would rush away from his odious handiwork, horror-stricken. He would hope that, left to itself, the slight spark of life which he had communicated would fade, that this thing which had received such imperfect animation would subside into dead matter, and he might sleep in the belief that the silence of the grave would quench forever the transient existence of the hideous corpse which he had looked upon as the cradle of life. He sleeps; but he is awakened; he opens his eyes; behold, the horrid thing stands at his bedside, opening his curtains and looking on him with yellow, watery, but speculative eyes.

12   I opened mine in terror. The idea so possessed my mind that a thrill of fear ran through me, and I wished to exchange the ghastly image of my fancy for the realities around. I see them still: the very room, the dark parquet, the closed shutters with the moonlight struggling through, and the sense I had that the glassy lake and white high Alps were beyond. I could not so easily get rid of my hideous phantom; still it haunted me. I must try to think of something else. I recurred to my ghost story—my tiresome, unlucky ghost story! Oh! If I could only contrive one which would frighten my reader as I myself had been frightened that night!

13   Swift as light and as cheering was the idea that broke in upon me. "I have found it! What terrified me will terrify others; and I need only describe the spectre which had haunted my midnight pillow." On the morrow I announced that I had

thought of a story. I began that day with the words "It was on a dreary night of November," making only a transcript of the grim terrors of my waking dream.

14   At first I thought but of a few pages, of a short tale, but Shelley urged me to develop the idea at greater length. I certainly did not owe the suggestion of one incident, nor scarcely of one train of feeling, to my husband, and yet but for his incitement it would never have taken the form in which it was presented to the world. From this declaration I must except the preface. As far as I can recollect, it was entirely written by him.

15   And now, once again, I bid my hideous progeny go forth and prosper. I have an affection for it, for it was the offspring of happy days, when death and grief were but words which found no true echo in my heart. Its several pages speak of many a walk, many a drive, and many a conversation, when I was not alone; and my companion was one who, in this world, I shall never see more. But this is for myself; my readers have nothing to do with these associations.

Questions for Discussion

1. Which experiences in Mary Shelley's childhood encouraged her to become a writer? What do you think she means by "waking dreams"? Why did she value her waking dreams?
2. What influence did Mary Shelley's husband, the well-known romantic poet, have on her writing career?
3. Describe the contest that Mary Shelley entered at Lord Byron's villa. What were its guidelines?
4. What conversations and ideas influenced Mary Shelley's choice of subject matter? What was the relationship between her night time conversations and her dream (or nightmare)? How did she begin to write her novel? Why did she succeed with her writing while the other poets failed?
5. From Mary Shelley's retelling of her nightmare of the monster and its creator, why do you think the dream was so frightening to her? Could you interpret the dream in a different way than Shelley did? Explain.
6. What is Mary Shelley's attitude toward her ghost story after it is complete and seems to have a life of its own? Can you understand why she feels this way?

Ideas for Writing

1. Develop your journal assignment into an essay in which you explore and define the relationship between dreams and creativity.
2. When Mary Shelley lived, writing was not a profession easily undertaken by women, particularly widowed women with children. Research Mary Shelley's life to find out what motivated her to become a successful writer. Write an essay in which you explain why Mary Shelley pursued her career as a writer.

❦ Cynthia Ozick

On Excellence

Cynthia Ozick (b. 1928) was born and raised in New York, earning her B.A. in English Literature from New York University in 1949 and her M.A. from Ohio State University in 1950. A fiction writer, poet, and critic, Ozick is so devoted to her art as a writer that she has defined life as "that which . . . interrupts." Some of her best-known works of fiction include The Pagan Rabbi and Other Stories *(1971),* Bloodshed and Three Novellas *(1976), and* The Messiah of Stockholm *(1987). Some of her better known essay collections include* Art and Ardor *(1983) and* Metaphor and Memory: Essays *(1989), from which "On Excellence" is excerpted. As you read Ozick's essay, notice how an obsession with excellence can be rooted in childhood experiences and influenced by parental role models.*

JOURNAL

Write about an obsession that you, a relative, friend, or teacher has about excellence. Do you consider this obsession to be an altogether positive trait?

1   In my Depression childhood, whenever I had a new dress, my cousin Sarah would get suspicious. The nicer the dress was, and especially the more expensive it looked, the more suspicious she would get. Finally she would lift the hem and check the seams. This was to see if the dress had been bought or if my mother had sewed it. Sarah could always tell. My mother's sewing had elegant outsides, but there was something catch-as-catch-can about the insides. Sarah's sewing, by contrast, was as impeccably finished inside as out; not one stray thread dangled.

2   My uncle Jake built meticulous grandfather clocks out of rosewood; he was a perfectionist, and sent to England for the clockworks. My mother built serviceable radiator covers and a serviceable cabinet, with hinged doors, for the pantry. She built a pair of bookcases for the living room. Once, after I was grown and in a house of my own, she fixed the sewer pipe. She painted ceilings, and also landscapes; she reupholstered chairs. One summer she planted a whole yard of tall corn. She thought herself capable of doing anything, and did everything she imagined. But nothing was perfect. There was always some clear flaw, never visible head-on. You had to look underneath where the seams were. The corn thrived, though not in rows. The stalks elbowed one another like gossips in a dense little village.

3   "Miss Brrrrooooobaker," my mother used to mock, rolling her Russian *r*s, whenever I crossed a *t* she had left uncrossed, or corrected a word she had misspelled, or became impatient with a *v* that had tangled itself up with a *w* in her speech. ("Vvventriloquist," I would say. "Vvventriloquist," she would obediently repeat.

And the next time it would come out "wiolinist.") Miss Brubaker was my high school English teacher, and my mother invoked her name as an emblem of raging finical obsession. "Miss Brrrrooooobaker," my mother's voice hoots at me down the years, as I go on casting and recasting sentences in a tiny handwriting on monomaniacally uniform paper. The loops of my mother's handwriting—it was the Palmer Method—were as big as hoops, spilling generous splashy ebullience. She could pull off, at five minutes' notice, a satisfying dinner for 10 concocted out of nothing more than originality and panache. But the napkin would be folded a little off-center, and the spoon might be on the wrong side of the knife. She was an optimist who ignored trifles; for her, God was not in the details but in the intent. And all these culinary and agricultural efflorescences were extracurricular, accomplished in the crevices and niches of a 14-hour business day. When she scribbled out her family memoirs, in heaps of dog-eared notebooks, or on the backs of old bills, or on the margins of last year's calendar, I would resist typing them; in the speed of the chase she often omitted words like "the," "and," "will." The same flashing and bountiful hand fashioned and fired ceramic pots, and painted brilliant autumn views and vases of imaginary flowers and ferns, and decorated ordinary Woolworth platters and lavish enameled gardens. But bits of the painted petals would chip away.

4   Lavish: my mother was as lavish as nature. She woke early and saturated the hours with work and inventiveness, and read late into the night. She was all profusion, abundance, fabrication. Angry at her children, she would run after us whirling the cord of the electric iron, like a lasso or a whip; but she never caught us. When, in the seventh grade, I was afraid of failing the Music Appreciation final exam because I could not tell the difference between "To a Wild Rose" and "Barcarolle," she got the idea of sending me to school with a gauze sling rigged up on my writing arm, and an explanatory note that was purest fiction. But the sling kept slipping off. My mother gave advice like mad—she boiled over with so much passion for the predicaments of strangers that they turned into permanent cronies. She told intimate stories about people I had never heard of.

5   Despite the gargantuan Palmer loops (or possibly because of them), I have always known that my mother's was a life of—intricately abashing word!—excellence: insofar as excellence means ripe generosity. She burgeoned, she proliferated; she was endlessly leafy and flowering. She wore red hats, and called herself a Gypsy. In her girlhood she marched with the suffragettes and for Margaret Sanger and called herself a Red. She made me laugh, she was so varied: like a tree on which lemons, pomegranates, and prickly pears absurdly all hang together. She had the comedy of prodigality.

6   My own way is a thousand times more confined. I am a pinched perfectionist, the ultimate fruition of Miss Brubaker; I attend to crabbed minutiae and am self-trammeled through taking pains. I am a kind of human snail, locked in and condemned by my own nature. The ancients believed that the moist track left by the snail as it crept was the snail's own essence, depleting its body little by little; the farther the snail toiled, the smaller it became, until it finally rubbed itself out. This is how perfectionists are. Say to us Excellence, and we will show you how we use up our substance and wear ourselves away, while making scarcely any progress

at all. The fact that I am an exacting perfectionist in a narrow strait only, and
nowhere else, is hardly to the point, since nothing matters to me so much as a
comely and muscular sentence. It is my narrow strait, this snail's road: the track of
the sentence I am writing now; and when I have eked out the wet substance, ink
or blood, that is its mark, I will begin the next sentence. Only in reading out sentences am I perfectionist; but then there is nothing else I know how to do, or take
much interest in. I miter every pair of abutting sentences as scrupulously as Uncle
Jake fitted one strip of rosewood against another. My mother's worldly and bountiful hand has escaped me. The sentence I am writing is my cabin and my shell,
compact, self-sufficient. It is the burnished horizon—a merciless planet where
flawlessness is the single standard, where even the inmost seams, however hidden
from a laxer eye, must meet perfection. Here "excellence" is not strewn casually
from a tipped cornucopia, here disorder does not account for charm, here trifles
rule like tyrants.

7   I measure my life in sentences, and my sentences are superior to my mother's,
pressed out, line by line, like the lustrous ooze on the underside of the snail, the
snail's secret open seam, its wound, leaking attar. My mother was too mettlesome
to feel the force of a comma. She scorned minutiae. She measured her life according to what poured from the horn of plenty, which was her ample, cascading, elastic, susceptible, inexact heart. My narrower heart rides between the tiny horns of
the snail, dwindling as it goes.

8   And out of this thinnest thread, this ink-wet line of words, must rise a visionary fog, a mist, a smoke, forging cities, histories, sorrows, quagmires, entangle-
ments, lives of sinners, even the life of my furnace-hearted mother: so much
wilderness, waywardness, plentitude on the head of the precise and impeccable
snail, between the horns.

Questions for Discussion

1. How does the personality of Ozick's mother reflect an obsession with
   excellence? What other examples does Ozick provide of people she
   knows who strive for excellence?

2. How does Ozick's personality, like her mother's, reveal an obsessive
   concern with excellence? What different form does Ozick's obsession
   take? How was Ozick also influenced by Miss Brubaker?

3. According to Ozick, what is the relationship between perfectionism and
   excellence? Do you think it is possible to be an "excellent" person without being preoccupied with perfectionism and competition?

4. How is excellence related to "generosity"? What examples does Ozick
   give to clarify what she means by generosity?

5. How does Ozick use the image of the snail to explain her obsession
   with perfectionism in her writing process?

6. As a writer, Ozick is particularly concerned about perfecting the craft of
   the sentence. Give some examples of sentences in the essay that you
   consider to be "perfect" and/or "excellent." What is it about the sen-

tences you have chosen that makes them outstanding? Do you think that you are a "perfectionist" when it comes to writing sentences?

Ideas for Writing

1. Write an essay in which you clarify the relationship between "perfectionism" and obsessive behavior, using examples from your own experience, reading, and observations. Discuss how and when perfectionism can become "obsessive" in a negative sense.
2. Write an essay or a story about an obsessive perfectionist. Show the positive as well as the negative traits of perfectionism.

 William Styron

The Roots of Depression

William Styron (b. 1925) was born in Newport News, Virginia. He served in the Marine Corps during World War II and received his B.A. from Duke University in 1947. Styron achieved national acclaim and was awarded the Pulitzer Prize in 1968 for The Confessions of Nat Turner, *which he developed from a transcript given by a slave and turned into "a meditation on history." His novel,* Sophie's Choice *(1979), which focuses on the life of a concentration camp survivor, was also widely read and later made into a film. Styron's more recent books include* Darkness Visible *(1991), a personal account of his struggle with depression from which the selection below is excerpted, and a collection of stories,* A Tide Water Morning *(1993).*

JOURNAL

Do you think that creative/artistic people are more vulnerable to depression than other people are?

1   By far the great majority of the people who go through even the severest depression survive it, and live ever afterward at least as happily as their unafflicted counterparts. Save for the awfulness of certain memories it leaves, acute depression inflicts few permanent wounds. There is a Sisyphean torment in the fact that a great number—as many as half—of those who are devastated once will be struck again; depression has the habit of recurrence. But most victims live through even these relapses, often coping better because they have become psychologically tuned by past experience to deal with the ogre. It is of great importance that those who are suffering a siege, perhaps for the first time, be told—be convinced,

rather—that the illness will run its course and that they will pull through. A tough job, this; calling "Chin up!" from the safety of the shore to a drowning person is tantamount to insult, but it has been shown over and over again that if the encouragement is dogged enough—and the support equally committed and passionate—the endangered one can nearly always be saved. Most people in the grip of depression at its ghastliest are, for whatever reason, in a state of unrealistic hopelessness, torn by exaggerated ills and fatal threats that bear no resemblance to actuality. It may require on the part of friends, lovers, family, admirers, an almost religious devotion to persuade the sufferers of life's worth, which is so often in conflict with a sense of their own worthlessness, but such devotion has prevented countless suicides.

2   During the same summer of my decline, a close friend of mine—a celebrated newspaper columnist—was hospitalized for severe manic depression. By the time I had commenced my autumnal plunge my friend had recovered (largely due to lithium but also to psychotherapy in the aftermath), and we were in touch by telephone nearly every day. His support was untiring and priceless. It was he who kept admonishing me that suicide was "unacceptable" (he had been intensely suicidal), and it was also he who made the prospect of going to the hospital less fearsomely intimidating. I still look back on his concern with immense gratitude. The help he gave me, he later said, had been a continuing therapy for him, thus demonstrating that, if nothing else, the disease engenders lasting fellowship.

3   After I began to recover in the hospital it occurred to me to wonder—for the first time with any really serious concern—why I had been visited by such a calamity. The psychiatric literature on depression is enormous, with theory after theory concerning the disease's etiology proliferating as richly as theories about the death of the dinosaurs or the origin of black holes. The very number of hypotheses is testimony to the malady's all but impenetrable mystery. As for that initial triggering mechanism—what I have called the manifest crisis—can I really be satisfied with the idea that abrupt withdrawal from alcohol started the plunge downward? What about other possibilities—the dour fact, for instance, that at about the same time I was smitten I turned sixty, that hulking milestone of mortality? Or could it be that a vague dissatisfaction with the way in which my work was going—the onset of inertia which has possessed me time and time again during my writing life, and made me crabbed and discontented—had also haunted me more fiercely during that period than ever, somehow magnifying the difficulty with alcohol? Unresolvable questions, perhaps.

4   These matters in any case interest me less than the search for earlier origins of the disease. What are the forgotten or buried events that suggest an ultimate explanation for the evolution of depression and its later flowering into madness? Until the onslaught of my own illness and its denouement, I never gave much thought to my work in terms of its connection with the subconscious—an area of investigation belonging to literary detectives. But after I had returned to health and was able to reflect on the past in the light of my ordeal, I began to see clearly how depression had clung close to the outer edges of my life for many years. Suicide has been a persistent theme in my books—three of my major characters killed themselves. In rereading, for the first time in years, sequences from my novels—passages

where my heroines have lurched down pathways toward doom—I was stunned to perceive how accurately I had created the landscape of depression in the minds of these young women, describing with what could only be instinct, out of a subconscious already roiled by disturbances of mood, the psychic imbalance that led them to destruction. Thus depression, when it finally came to me, was in fact no stranger, not even a visitor totally unannounced; it had been tapping at my door for decades.

5   The morbid condition proceeded, I have come to believe, from my beginning years—from my father, who battled the gorgon for much of his lifetime, and had been hospitalized in my boyhood after a despondent spiraling downward that in retrospect I saw greatly resembled mine. The genetic roots of depression seem now to be beyond controversy. But I'm persuaded that an even more significant factor was the death of my mother when I was thirteen; this disorder and early sorrow— the death or disappearance of a parent, especially a mother, before or during puberty—appears repeatedly in the literature on depression as a trauma sometimes likely to create nearly irreparable emotional havoc. The danger is especially apparent if the young person is affected by what has been termed "incomplete mourning"—has, in effect, been unable to achieve the catharsis of grief, and so carries within himself through later years an insufferable burden of which rage and guilt, and not only dammed-up sorrow, are a part, and become the potential seeds of self-destruction.

6   In an illuminating new book on suicide, *Self-Destruction in the Promised Land,* Howard I. Kushner, who is not a psychiatrist but a social historian, argues persuasively in favor of this theory of incomplete mourning and uses Abraham Lincoln as an example. While Lincoln's hectic moods of melancholy are legend, it is much less well known that in his youth he was often in a suicidal turmoil and came close more than once to making an attempt on his own life. The behavior seems directly linked to the death of Lincoln's mother, Nancy Hanks, when he was nine, and to unexpressed grief exacerbated by his sister's death ten years later. Drawing insights from the chronicle of Lincoln's painful success in avoiding suicide, Kushner makes a convincing case not only for the idea of early loss precipitating self-destructive conduct, but also, auspiciously, for that same behavior becoming a strategy through which the person involved comes to grips with his guilt and rage, and triumphs over self-willed death. Such reconciliation may be entwined with the quest for immortality—in Lincoln's case, no less than that of a writer of fiction, to vanquish death through work honored by posterity.

7   So if this theory of incomplete mourning has validity, and I think it does, and if it is also true that in the nethermost depths of one's suicidal behavior one is still subconsciously dealing with immense loss while trying to surmount all the effects of its devastation, then my own avoidance of death may have been belated homage to my mother. I do know that in those last hours before I rescued myself, when I listened to the passage from the *Alto Rhapsody*—which I'd heard her sing—she had been very much on my mind.

8   Near the end of an early film of Ingmar Bergman's, *Through a Glass Darkly,* a young woman, experiencing the embrace of what appears to be profound psychotic depression, has a terrifying hallucination. Anticipating the arrival of some

transcendental and saving glimpse of God, she sees instead the quivering shape of a monstrous spider that is attempting to violate her sexually. It is an instant of horror and scalding truth. Yet even in this vision of Bergman (who has suffered cruelly from depression) there is a sense that all of his accomplished artistry has somehow fallen short of a true rendition of the drowned mind's appalling phantasmagoria. Since antiquity—in the tortured lament of Job, in the choruses of Sophocles and Aeschylus—chroniclers of the human spirit have been wrestling with a vocabulary that might give proper expression to the desolation of melancholia. Through the course of literature and art the theme of depression has run like a durable thread of woe—from Hamlet's soliloquy to the verses of Emily Dickinson and Gerard Manley Hopkins, from John Donne to Hawthorne and Dostoevski and Poe, Camus and Conrad and Virginia Woolf. In many of Albrecht Dürer's engravings there are harrowing depictions of his own melancholia; the manic wheeling stars of Van Gogh are the precursors of the artist's plunge into dementia and the extinction of self. It is a suffering that often tinges the music of Beethoven, of Schumann and Mahler, and permeates the darker cantatas of Bach. The vast metaphor which most faithfully represents this fathomless ordeal, however, is that of Dante, and his all-too-familiar lines still arrest the imagination with their augury of the unknowable, the black struggle to come:

Nel mezzo del cammin di nostra vita
Mi ritrovai per una selva oscura,
Ché la diritta via era smarrita.

In the middle of the journey of our life
I found myself in a dark wood,
For I had lost the right path.

9   One can be sure that these words have been more than once employed to conjure the ravages of melancholia, but their somber foreboding has often overshadowed the last lines of the best-known part of that poem, with their evocation of hope. To most of those who have experienced it, the horror of depression is so overwhelming as to be quite beyond expression, hence the frustrated sense of inadequacy found in the work of even the greatest artists. But in science and art the search will doubtless go on for a clear representation of its meaning, which sometimes, for those who have known it, is a simulacrum of all the evil of our world: of our everyday discord and chaos, our irrationality, warfare and crime, torture and violence, our impulse toward death and our flight from it held in the intolerable equipoise of history. If our lives had no other configuration but this, we should want, and perhaps deserve, to perish; if depression had no termination, then suicide would, indeed, be the only remedy. But one need not sound the false or inspirational note to stress the truth that depression is not the soul's annihilation; men and women who have recovered from the disease—and they are countless—bear witness to what is probably its only saving grace: it is conquerable.

10   For those who have dwelt in depression's dark wood, and known its inexplicable agony, their return from the abyss is not unlike the ascent of the poet, trudging

upward and upward out of hell's black depths and at last emerging into what he saw as "the shining world." There, whoever has been restored to health has almost always been restored to the capacity for serenity and joy, and this may be indemnity enough for having endured the despair beyond despair.

E quindi uscimmo a riveder le stelle.

And so we came forth, and once again beheld the stars.

Questions for Discussion

1. What advice does Styron offer to people suffering from depression? Why does he believe that their close friends and relatives are crucial to their recovery?
2. After Styron's battle against depression, what relationship does he come to discover between his writing and his subconscious concerns?
3. To what extent do you read your own writing to discover your subconscious concerns? Do you think you will be more concerned with reading your writing for its subconscious messages and/or meanings after reading Styron and other selections in this text? Why or why not? Explain.
4. What factors contributed to Styron's depressions? Why does Styron believe that an ungrieved loss in childhood can be a cause of depression and suicide? Is the example from Lincoln's life effective? Why or why not?
5. What effect does Styron's reference to some of the greatest artists, musicians, scientists, and writers as sufferers of depression have on your understanding of the illness?
6. What does Styron imply that those who suffer from depression learn? What have you learned about depression from reading this selection?

Ideas for Writing

1. Research the life of a writer who suffered from depression; in your paper show the effect that the illness had on his or her creativity and art.
2. New research into the causes and treatment of depression is affecting the way in which people with this illness are helped. After researching an aspect of depression and its treatment, write a paper for your classmates that clarifies what you have learned and why you think this information is important.
3. Write a response to Styron's claim, "for those who have known it [depression], is a simulacrum of all the evil of our world: of our everyday discord and chaos, our irrationality, warfare and crime, torture and violence, our impulse toward death and our flight from it held in the intolerable equipoise of history."

❧ Charlotte Perkins Gilman

The Yellow Wallpaper

A feminist and economist, Charlotte Perkins Gilman (1860–1935) was born in Hartford, Connecticut, and attended the Rhode Island School of Design. Her best known work is Women and Economics *(1898); she also wrote* Herland, *a feminist utopia. Gilman's ''The Yellow Wallpaper'' (1892), which was originally published as a ghost story, became popular in the 1970s with the rebirth of the feminist movement. The story is a fictionalized account of Gilman's severe depression after the birth of her daughter. While ''The Yellow Wallpaper'' gives us insights into the role of women at the turn of the century, many readers today can still identify with the struggles that the narrator in the story is facing.*

JOURNAL

Describe a place about which you have dreamed or fantasized that embodies or symbolizes one of your fears or obsessions.

1   It is very seldom that mere ordinary people like John and myself secure ancestral halls for the summer.

2   A colonial mansion, a hereditary estate, I would say a haunted house and reach the height of romantic felicity—but that would be asking too much of fate!

3   Still I will proudly declare that there is something queer about it.

4   Else, why should it be let so cheaply? And why have stood so long untenanted?

5   John laughs at me, of course, but one expects that.

6   John is practical in the extreme. He has no patience with faith, an intense horror of superstition, and he scoffs openly at any talk of things not to be felt and seen and put down in figures.

7   John is a physician, and *perhaps*—(I would not say it to a living soul, of course, but this is dead paper and a great relief to my mind)—*perhaps* that is one reason I do not get well faster.

8   You see, he does not believe I am sick! And what can one do?

9   If a physician of high standing, and one's own husband, assures friends and relatives that there is really nothing the matter with one but temporary nervous depression—a slight hysterical tendency—what is one to do?

10   My brother is also a physician, and also of high standing, and he says the same thing.

11   So I take phosphates or phosphites—whichever it is—and tonics, and air and exercise, and journeys, and am absolutely forbidden to "work" until I am well again.

12   Personally, I disagree with their ideas.

13   Personally, I believe that congenial work, with excitement and change, would do me good.

14   But what is one to do?

15   I did write for a while in spite of them; but it *does* exhaust me a good deal—having to be so sly about it, or else meet with heavy opposition.

16   I sometimes fancy that in my condition, if I had less opposition and more society and stimulus—but John says the very worst thing I can do is to think about my condition, and I confess it always makes me feel bad.

17   So I will let it alone and talk about the house.

18   The most beautiful place! It is quite alone, standing well back from the road, quite three miles from the village. It makes me think of English places that you read about, for there are hedges and walls and gates that lock, and lots of separate little houses for the gardeners and people.

19   There is a *delicious* garden! I never saw such a garden—large and shady, full of box-bordered paths, and lined with long grape-covered arbors with seats under them.

20   There were greenhouses, but they are all broken now.

21   There was some legal trouble, I believe, something about the heirs and co-heirs; anyhow, the place has been empty for years.

22   That spoils my ghostliness, I am afraid, but I don't care—there is something strange about the house—I can feel it.

23   I even said so to John one moonlight evening, but he said what I felt was a draught, and shut the window.

24   I get unreasonably angry with John sometimes. I'm sure I never used to be so sensitive. I think it is due to this nervous condition.

25   But John says if I feel so I shall neglect proper self-control; so I take pains to control myself—before him, at least, and that makes me very tired.

26   I don't like our room a bit. I wanted one downstairs that opened onto the piazza and had roses all over the window, and such pretty old-fashioned chintz hangings! But John would not hear of it.

27   He said there was only one window and not room for two beds, and no near room for him if he took another.

28   He is very careful and loving, and hardly lets me stir without special direction.

29   I have a schedule prescription of each hour in the day; he takes all care from me, and so I feel basely ungrateful not to value it more.

30   He said he came here solely on my account, that I was to have perfect rest and all the air I could get. "Your exercise depends on your strength, my dear," said he, "and your food somewhat on your appetite; but air you can absorb all the time." So we took the nursery at the top of the house.

31   It is a big, airy room, the whole floor nearly, with windows that look all ways, and air and sunshine galore. It was nursery first, and then playroom and gymnasium, I should judge, for the windows are barred for little children, and there are rings and things in the walls.

32   The paint and paper look as if a boys' school had used it. It is stripped off—the paper—in great patches all around the head of my bed, about as far as I can reach, and

in a great place on the other side of the room low down. I never saw a worse paper in my life. One of those sprawling, flamboyant patterns committing every artistic sin.

33   It is dull enough to confuse the eye in following, pronounced enough constantly to irritate and provoke study, and when you follow the lame uncertain curves for a little distance they suddenly commit suicide—plunge off at outrageous angles, destroy themselves in unheard-of contradictions.

34   The color is repellent, almost revolting: a smouldering unclean yellow, strangely faded by the slow-turning sunlight. It is a dull yet lurid orange in some places, a sickly sulphur tint in others.

35   No wonder the children hated it! I should hate it myself if I had to live in this room long.

36   There comes John, and I must put this away—he hates to have me write a word.

37   We have been here two weeks, and I haven't felt like writing before, since that first day.

38   I am sitting by the window now, up in this atrocious nursery, and there is nothing to hinder my writings as much as I please, save lack of strength.

39   John is away all day, and even some nights when his cases are serious.

40   I am glad my case is not serious!

41   But these nervous troubles are dreadfully depressing.

42   John does not know how much I really suffer. He knows there is no reason to suffer, and that satisfies him.

43   Of course it is only nervousness. It does weigh on me so not to do my duty in any way!

44   I meant to be such a help to John, such a real rest and comfort, and here I am a comparative burden already!

45   Nobody would believe what an effort it is to do what little I am able—to dress and entertain, and order things.

46   It is fortunate Mary is so good with the baby. Such a dear baby!

47   And yet I *cannot* be with him, it makes me so nervous.

48   I suppose John never was nervous in his life. He laughs at me so about this wallpaper!

49   At first he meant to repaper the room, but afterward he said that I was letting it get the better of me, and that nothing was worse for a nervous patient than to give way to such fancies.

50   He said that after the wallpaper was changed it would be the heavy bedstead, and then the barred windows, and then that gate at the head of the stairs, and so on.

51   "You know the place is doing you good," he said, "and really, dear, I don't care to renovate the house just for a three months' rental."

52   "Then do let us go downstairs," I said. "There are such pretty rooms there."

53   Then he took me in his arms and called me a blessed little goose, and said he would go down cellar, if I wished, and have it whitewashed into the bargain.

54   But he is right enough about the beds and windows and things.

55   It is as airy and comfortable a room as anyone need wish, and, of course, I would not be so silly as to make him uncomfortable just for a whim.

56   I'm really getting quite fond of the big room, all but that horrid paper.

57   Out of one window I can see the garden—those mysterious deep-shaded arbors, the riotous old-fashioned flowers, and bushes and gnarly trees.

58   Out of another I get a lovely view of the bay and a little private wharf belonging to the estate. There is a beautiful shaded lane that runs down there from the house. I always fancy I see people walking in these numerous paths and arbors, but John has cautioned me not to give way to fancy in the least. He says that with my imaginative power and habit of story-making, a nervous weakness like mine is sure to lead to all manner of excited fancies, and that I ought to use my will and good sense to check the tendency. So I try.

59   I think sometimes that if I were only well enough to write a little it would relieve the press of ideas and rest me.

60   But I find I get pretty tired when I try.

61   It is so discouraging not to have any advice and companionship about my work. When I get really well, John says we will ask Cousin Henry and Julia down for a long visit; but he says he would as soon put fireworks in my pillow-case as to let me have those stimulating people about now.

62   I wish I could get well faster.

63   But I must not think about that. This paper looks to me as if it *knew* what a vicious influence it had!

64   There is a recurrent spot where the pattern lolls like a broken neck and two bulbous eyes stare at you upside down.

65   I get positively angry with the impertinence of it and the everlastingness. Up and down and sideways they crawl, and those absurd unblinking eyes are everywhere. There is one place where two breadths didn't match, and the eyes go all up and down the line, one a little higher than the other.

66   I never saw so much expression in an inanimate thing before, and we all know how much expression they have! I used to lie awake as a child and get more entertainment and terror out of blank walls and plain furniture than most children could find in a toy-store.

67   I remember what a kindly wink the knobs of our big old bureau used to have, and there was one chair that always seemed like a strong friend.

68   I used to feel that if any of the other things looked too fierce I could always hop into that chair and be safe.

69   The furniture in this room is no worse than inharmonious, however, for we had to bring it all from downstairs. I suppose when this was used as a playroom they had to take the nursery things out, and no wonder! I never saw such ravages as the children have made here.

70   The wallpaper, as I said before, is torn off in spots, and it sticketh closer than a brother—they must have had perseverance as well as hatred.

71   Then the floor is scratched and gouged and splintered, the plaster itself is dug out here and there, and this great heavy bed, which is all we found in the room, looks as if it had been through the wars.

72   But I don't mind it a bit—only the paper.

73   There comes John's sister. Such a dear girl as she is, and so careful of me! I must
not let her find me writing.

74   She is a perfect and enthusiastic housekeeper, and hopes for no better profession. I verily believe she thinks it is the writing which made me sick!

75   But I can write when she is out, and see her a long way off from these windows.

76   There is one that commands the road, a lovely shaded winding road, and one
that just looks off over the country. A lovely country, too, full of great elms and
velvet meadows.

77   This wallpaper has a kind of subpattern in a different shade, a particularly irri-
tating one, for you can only see it in certain lights, and not clearly then.

78   But in the places where it isn't faded and where the sun is just so—I can see a
strange, provoking, formless sort of figure that seems to skulk about behind that
silly and conspicuous front design.

79   There's sister on the stairs!

80   Well, the Fourth of July is over! The people are all gone, and I am tired out.
John thought it might do me good to see a little company, so we just had Mother
and Nellie and the children down for a week.

81   Of course I didn't do a thing. Jennie sees to everything now.

82   But it tired me all the same.

83   John says if I don't pick up faster he shall send me to Weir Mitchell in the fall.

84   But I don't want to go there at all. I had a friend who was in his hands once,
and she says he is just like John and my brother, only more so!

85   Besides, it is such an undertaking to go so far.

86   I don't feel as if it was worthwhile to turn my hand over for anything, and I'm
getting dreadfully fretful and querulous.

87   I cry at nothing, and cry most of the time.

88   Of course I don't when John is here, or anybody else, but when I am alone.

89   And I am alone a good deal just now. John is kept in town very often by serious
cases, and Jennie is good and lets me alone when I want her to.

90   So I walk a little in the garden or down that lovely lane, sit on the porch under
the roses, and lie down up here a good deal.

91   I'm getting really fond of the room in spite of the wallpaper. Perhaps *because* of
the wallpaper.

92   It dwells in my mind so!

93   I lie here on this great immovable bed—it is nailed down, I believe—and follow that pattern about by the hour. It is as good as gymnastics, I assure you. I start,
we'll say, at the bottom, down in the corner over there where it has not been
touched, and I determine for the thousandth time that I *will* follow that pointless
pattern to some sort of a conclusion.

94   I know a little of the principle of design, and I know this thing was not
arranged on any laws of radiation, or alternation, or repetition, or symmetry, or
anything else that I ever heard of.

95   It is repeated, of course, by the breadths, but not otherwise.

96   Looked at in one way, each breadth stands alone; the bloated curves and flourishes—a kind of "debased Romanesque" with dilirium tremens go waddling up and down in isolated columns of fatuity.

97   But, on the other hand, they connect diagonally, and the sprawling outlines run off in great slanting waves of optic horror, like a lot of wallowing seaweeds in full chase.

98   The whole thing goes horizontally, too, at least it seems so, and I exhaust myself trying to distinguish the order of its going in that direction.

99   They have used a horizontal breadth for a frieze, and that adds wonderfully to the confusion.

100   There is one end of the room where it is almost intact, and there, when the crosslights fade and the low sun shines directly upon it, I can almost fancy radiation after all—the interminable grotesque seems to form around a common center and rush off in headlong plunges of equal distraction.

101   It makes me tired to follow it. I will take a nap, I guess.

102   I don't know why I should write this.

103   I don't want to.

104   I don't feel able.

105   And I know John would think it absurd. But I *must* say what I feel and think in some way—it is such a relief!

106   But the effort is getting to be greater than the relief.

107   Half the time now I am awfully lazy, and lie down ever so much. John says I mustn't lose my strength, and has me take cod liver oil and lots of tonics and things, to say nothing of ale and wines and rare meat.

108   Dear John! He loves me very dearly, and hates to have me sick. I tried to have a real earnest reasonable talk with him the other day, and tell him how I wish he would let me go and make a visit to Cousin Henry and Julia.

109   But he said I wasn't able to go, nor able to stand it after I got there; and I did not make out a very good case for myself, for I was crying before I had finished.

110   It is getting to be a great effort for me to think straight. Just this nervous weakness, I suppose.

111   And dear John gathered me up in his arms, and just carried me upstairs and laid me on the bed, and sat by me and read to me till it tired my head.

112   He said I was his darling and his comfort and all he had, and that I must take care of myself for his sake, and keep well.

113   He says no one but myself can help me out of it, that I must use my will and self-control and not let any silly fancies run away with me.

114   There's one comfort—the baby is well and happy, and does not have to occupy this nursery with the horrid wallpaper.

115   If we had not used it, that blessed child would have! What a fortunate escape! Why, I wouldn't have a child of mine, an impressionable little thing, live in such a room for worlds.

116   I never thought of it before, but it is lucky that John kept me here after all; I can stand it so much easier than a baby, you see.

117   Of course I never mention it to them any more—I am too wise—but I keep watch for it all the same.

118   There are things in the wallpaper that nobody knows about but me, or ever will.

119   Behind that outside pattern the dim shapes get clearer every day.

120   It is always the same shape, only very numerous.

121   And it is like a woman stooping down and creeping about behind that pattern. I don't like it a bit. I wonder—I begin to think—I wish John would take me away from here!

122   It is so hard to talk with John about my case, because he is so wise, and because he loves me so.

123   But I tried it last night.

124   It was moonlight. The moon shines in all around just as the sun does.

125   I hate to see it sometimes, it creeps so slowly, and always comes in by one window or another.

126   John was asleep and I hated to waken him, so I kept still and watched the moonlight on that undulating wallpaper till I felt creepy.

127   The faint figure behind seemed to shake the pattern, just as if she wanted to get out.

128   I got up softly and went to feel and see if the paper *did* move, and when I came back John was awake.

129   "What is it, little girl?" he said. "Don't go walking about like that—you'll get cold."

130   I thought it was a good time to talk, so I told him that I really was not gaining here, and that I wished he would take me away.

131   "Why, darling!" said he. "Our lease will be up in three weeks, and I can't see how to leave before."

132   "The repairs are not done at home, and I cannot possibly leave town just now. Of course, if you were in any danger, I could and would, but you really are better, dear, whether you can see it or not. I am a doctor, dear, and I know. You are gaining flesh and color, your appetite is better, I feel really much easier about you."

133   "I don't weigh a bit more," said I, "nor as much; and my appetite may be better in the evening when you are here but it is worse in the morning when you are away!"

134   "Bless her little heart!" said he with a big hug. "She shall be as sick as she pleases! But now let's improve the shining hours by going to sleep, and talk about it in the morning!"

135   "And you won't go away?" I asked gloomily.

136   "Why, how can I, dear? It is only three weeks more and then we will take a nice little trip for a few days while Jennie is getting the house ready. Really, dear, you are better!"

137   "Better in body perhaps—" I began, and stopped short, for he sat up straight and looked at me with such a stern, reproachful look that I could not say another word.

138   "My darling," said he, "I beg you, for my sake and for our child's sake, as well as for your own, that you will never for one instant let that idea enter your mind!

There is nothing so dangerous, so fascinating, to a temperament like yours. It is a false and foolish fancy. Can you trust me as a physician when I tell you so?"

139   So of course, I said no more on that score, and we went to sleep before long. He thought I was asleep first, but I wasn't, and lay there for hours trying to decide whether that front pattern and the back pattern really did move together or separately.

140   On a pattern like this, by daylight, there is a lack of sequence, a defiance of law, that is a constant irritant to a normal mind.

141   The color is hideous enough, and unreliable enough, and infuriating enough, but the pattern is torturing.

142   You think you have mastered it, but just as you get well under way in following, it turns a back-somersault and there you are. It slaps you in the face, knocks you down, and tramples upon you. It is like a bad dream.

143   The outside pattern is a florid arabesque, reminding one of a fungus. If you can imagine a toadstool in joints, an interminable string of toadstools, budding and sprouting in endless convolutions—why, that is something like it.

144   That is, sometimes!

145   There is one marked peculiarity about this paper, a thing nobody seems to notice but myself, and that is that it changes as the light changes.

146   When the sun shoots in through the east window—I always watch for that first long, straight ray—it changes so quickly that I never can quite believe it.

147   That is why I watch it always.

148   By moonlight—the moon shines in all night when there is a moon—I wouldn't know it was the same paper.

149   At night in any kind of light, in twilight, candlelight, lamplight, and worst of all by moonlight, it becomes bars! The outside pattern, I mean, and the woman behind it is as plain as can be.

150   I didn't realize for a long time what the thing was that showed behind, that dim subpattern, but now I am quite sure it is a woman.

151   By daylight she is subdued, quiet. I fancy it is the pattern that keeps her so still. It is so puzzling. It keeps me quiet by the hour.

152   I lie down ever so much now. John says it is good for me, and to sleep all I can.

153   Indeed he started the habit by making me lie down for an hour after each meal.

154   It is a very bad habit, I am convinced, for you see, I don't sleep.

155   And that cultivates deceit, for I don't tell them I'm awake—oh, no!

156   The fact is I am getting a little afraid of John.

157   He seems very queer sometimes, and even Jennie has an inexplicable look.

158   It strikes me occasionally, just as a scientific hypothesis, that perhaps it is the paper!

159   I have watched John when he did not know I was looking, and come into the room suddenly on the most innocent excuses, and I've caught him several times *looking at the paper!* And Jennie too. I caught Jennie with her hand on it once.

160   She didn't know I was in the room, and when I asked her in a quiet, a very quiet voice, and the most restrained manner possible, what she was doing with the paper, she turned around as if she had been caught stealing, and looked quite angry—asked me why I should frighten her so!

161   Then she said that the paper stained everything it touched, that she had found yellow smooches on all my clothes and John's and she wishes we would be more careful!

162   Did not that sound innocent? But I know she was studying that pattern, and I am determined that nobody shall find it out but myself!

163   Life is very much more exciting now than it used to be. You see, I have something more to expect, to look forward to, to watch. I really do eat better, and am more quiet than I was.

164   John is so pleased to see me improve! He laughed a little the other day, and said I seemed to be flourishing in spite of my wallpaper.

165   I turned it off with a laugh. I had no intention of telling him it was *because* of the wallpaper—he would make fun of me. He might even want to take me away.

166   I don't want to leave now until I have found it out. There is a week more, and I think that will be enough.

167   I'm feeling so much better!

168   I don't sleep much at night, for it is so interesting to watch developments; but I sleep a good deal during the daytime.

169   In the daytime it is tiresome and perplexing.

170   There are always new shoots on the fungus, and new shades of yellow all over it. I cannot keep count of them, though I have tried conscientiously.

171   It is the strangest yellow, that wallpaper! It makes me think of all the yellow things I ever saw—not beautiful ones like buttercups, but old, foul, bad yellow things.

172   But there is something else about that paper—the smell! I noticed it the moment we came into the room, but with so much air and sun it was not bad. Now we have had a week of fog and rain, and whether the windows are open or not, the smell is here.

173   It creeps all over the house.

174   I find it hovering in the dining-room, skulking in the parlor, hiding in the hall, lying in wait for me on the stairs.

175   It gets into my hair.

176   Even when I go to ride, if I turn my head suddenly and surprise it—there is that smell!

177   Such a peculiar odor, too! I have spent hours in trying to analyze it, to find what it smelled like.

178   It is not bad—at first—and very gentle, but quite the subtlest, most enduring odor I ever met.

179   It used to disturb me at first. I thought seriously of burning the house—to reach the smell.

180   But now I am used to it. The only thing I can think of that it is like is the *color* of the paper! A yellow smell.

181   There is a very funny mark on this wall, low down, near the mopboard. A streak that runs round the room. It goes behind every piece of furniture, except the bed, a long straight, even *smooch*, as if it had been rubbed over and over.

182   I wonder how it was done and who did it, and what they did it for. Round and round and round—round and round and round—it makes me dizzy!

183   I really have discovered something at last.

184   Through watching so much at night, when it changes so, I have finally found out.

185   The front pattern *does* move—and no wonder! The woman behind shakes it!

186   Sometimes I think there are a great many women behind, and sometimes only one, and she crawls around fast, and her crawling shakes it all over.

187   Then in the very bright spots she keeps still, and in the very shady spots she just takes hold of the bars and shakes them hard.

188   And she is all the time trying to climb through. But nobody could climb through that pattern—it strangles so; I think that is why it has so many heads.

189   They get through and then the pattern strangles them off and turns them upside down, and makes their eyes white!

190   If those heads were covered or taken off it would not be half so bad.

191   I think that woman gets out in the daytime!

192   And I'll tell you why—privately—I've seen her!

193   I can see her out of every one of my windows!

194   It is the same woman, I know, for she is always creeping, and most women do not creep by daylight.

195   I see her in that long shaded lane, creeping up and down. I see her in those dark grape arbors, creeping all round the garden.

196   I see her on that long road under the trees, creeping along, and when a carriage comes she hides under the blackberry vines.

197   I don't blame her a bit. It must be very humiliating to be caught creeping by daylight!

198   I always lock the door when I creep by daylight. I can't do it at night, for I know John would suspect something at once.

199   And John is so queer now that I don't want to irritate him. I wish he would take another room! Besides, I don't want anybody to get that woman out at night but myself.

200   I often wonder if I could see her out of all the windows at once.

201   But, turn as fast as I can, I can only see out of one at one time.

202   And though I always see her, she *may* be able to creep faster than I can turn! I have watched her sometimes away off in the open country, creeping as fast as a cloud shadow in a wind.

203   If only that top pattern could be gotten off from the under one! I mean to try it, little by little.

204   I have found out another funny thing, but I shan't tell it this time! It does not do to trust people too much.

205   There are only two more days to get this paper off, and I believe John is beginning to notice. I don't like the look in his eyes.

206   And I heard him ask Jennie a lot of professional questions about me. She had a very good report to give.

207   She said I slept a good deal in the daytime.

208   John knows I don't sleep very well at night, for all I'm so quiet!

209   He asked me all sorts of questions too, and pretended to be very loving and kind.

210   As if I couldn't see through him!

211   Still, I don't wonder he acts so, sleeping under this paper for three months.

212   It only interests me, but I feel sure John and Jennie are affected by it.

213   Hurrah! This is the last day, but it is enough. John is to stay in town over night, and won't be out until this evening.

214   Jennie wanted to sleep with me—the sly thing; but I told her I should undoubtedly rest better for a night all alone.

215   That was clever, for really I wasn't alone a bit! As soon as it was moonlight and that poor thing began to crawl and shake the pattern, I got up and ran to help her.

216   I pulled and she shook. I shook and she pulled, and before morning we had peeled off yards of that paper.

217   A strip about as high as my head and half around the room.

218   And then when the sun came and that awful pattern began to laugh at me, I declared I would finish it today!

219   We go away tomorrow, and they are moving all my furniture down again to leave things as they were before.

220   Jennie looked at the wall in amazement, but I told her merrily that I did it out of pure spite at the vicious thing.

221   She laughed and said she wouldn't mind doing it herself, but I must not get tired.

222   How she betrayed herself that time!

223   But I am here, and no person touches this paper but Me—not *alive!*

224   She tried to get me out of the room—it was too patent! But I said it was so quiet and empty and clean now that I believed I would lie down again and sleep all I could, and not to wake me even for dinner—I would call when I woke.

225   So now she is gone, and the servants are gone, and the things are gone, and there is nothing left but that great bedstead nailed down, with the canvas mattress we found on it.

226   We shall sleep downstairs tonight, and take the boat home tomorrow.

227   I quite enjoy the room, now it is bare again.

228   How those children did tear about here!

229   This bedstead is fairly gnawed!

230   But I must get to work.

231   I have locked the door and thrown the key down into the front path.

232   I don't want to go out, and I don't want to have anybody come in, till John comes.

233   I want to astonish him.

234   I've got a rope up here that even Jennie did not find. If that woman does get out, and tries to get away, I can tie her!

235   But I forgot I could not reach far without anything to stand on!

236   This bed will *not* move!

237   I tried to lift and push it until I was lame, and then I got so angry I bit off a little piece at one corner—but it hurt my teeth.

238   Then I peeled off all the paper I could reach standing on the floor. It sticks horribly and the pattern just enjoys it! All those strangled heads and bulbous eyes and waddling fungus growths just shriek with derision!

239   I am getting angry enough to do something desperate. To jump out of the window would be admirable exercise, but the bars are too strong even to try.

240   Besides I wouldn't do it. Of course not. I know well enough that a step like that is improper and might be misconstrued.

241   I don't like to *look* out of the windows even—there are so many of those creeping women, and they creep so fast.

242   I wonder if they all come out of that wallpaper as I did!

243   But I am securely fastened now by my well-hidden rope—you don't get *me* out in the road there!

244   I suppose I shall have to get back behind the pattern when it comes night, and that is hard!

245   It is so pleasant to be out in this great room and creep around as I please!

246   I don't want to go outside. I won't, even if Jennie asks me to.

247   For outside you have to creep on the ground, and everything is green instead of yellow.

248   But here I can creep smoothly on the floor, and my shoulder just fits in that long smooch around the wall, so I cannot lose my way.

249   Why, there's John at the door!

250   It is no use, young man, you can't open it!

251   How he does call and pound!

252   Now he's crying to Jennie for an axe.

253   It would be a shame to break down that beautiful door!

254   "John, dear!" said I in the gentlest voice. "The key is down by the front steps, under a plantain leaf!"

255   That silenced him for a few moments.

256   Then he said, very quietly indeed, "Open the door, my darling!"

257   "I can't," said I. "The key is down by the front door under a plantain leaf!" And then I said it again, several times, very gently and slowly, and said it so often that he had to go and see, and he got it of course, and came in. He stopped short by the door.

258   "What is the matter?" he cried. "For God's sake, what are you doing!"

259   I kept on creeping just the same, but I looked at him over my shoulder.

260   "I've got out at last," said I, "in spite of you and Jane. And I've pulled off most of the paper, so you can't put me back!"

261   Now why should that man have fainted? But he did, and right across my path by the wall, so that I had to creep over him every time!

Vera Shinsky

My picture of "The Yellow Wallpaper" is a rather literal representation of the wallpaper as described in the story. The woman behind the bars is both the woman imagined by the narrator and the narrator herself. She is shaking the bars, just as in the story, the narrator and the woman in the wallpaper try to free the woman from the image she has to put on for society, the bars on the wallpaper. Imagine a greenish tint to the wallpaper as the different view of it that comes with the change of the time of day. This tint is one of the things the narrator hates most about the paper. The upside-down faces with the eyes are portrayed here as circles with two glowing spots—the eyes.

Drawing this picture helped me understand even more intimately how much the narrator is the woman behind the wallpaper. In fact, the entire process of her growing more and more connected with the paper demonstrates the deterioration of her mental state. The eyes that stare at her from the wallpaper are the eyes of her husband and Jennie, as well as the rest of society who are watching her and observing whether or not she is improving. The confusing pattern of the wallpaper that the narrator cannot seem to figure out or follow all the way through represents the confusion and the struggle within her mind. The bars are what she is struggling against, both her mental condition and the pressures of the society put upon her that, instead of helping her, are making her worse. Having to visualize the wallpaper and put it into an image helped me transcend the story into a true understanding of the narrator's state of mind.

Shanney Yu

"The Yellow Wallpaper" is a story about one woman's struggle with postpartum depression. She is confined to a bedroom in order to regain her strength. The yellow wallpaper in this bedroom becomes the focal point of her attentions as its convoluted pattern slowly drives her to the brink of insanity.

The narrator describes the design of the wallpaper:

> Looked at in one way, each breadth stands alone; the bloated curves and flourishes—a kind of "debased Romanesque" with delirium tremens go waddling up and down in isolated columns of fatuity . . . they connect diagonally . . . in great slanting waves of optic horror. . . . The whole thing goes horizontally, too . . . and I exhaust myself trying to distinguish the order of its going in that direction.

The narrator is also convinced that the twisted design of the wallpaper is the prison of one or more women. She feels as if the eyes of these women follow her every move. ". . . those absurd unblinking eyes are everywhere . . . I can see a strange, provoking, formless sort of figure that seems to skulk about behind that sill and conspicuous front design."

I tried to incorporate all of these elements into my drawing. I started by drawing vertical bars that run across the entire drawing, creating a sort of prison effect. In the tangled web of the pattern, I drew two "unblinking" eyes. The swirls around the eyes make up the face of a trapped woman and the swirls beneath this face are her arms. Her hands grasp the bars as she struggles to be freed. The circular swirls I drew next serve two purposes: to make the design all the more hypnotic as well as to represent the other "unblinking" eyes that taunt the narrator.

Questions for Discussion

1. Why are John and the narrator spending their summer at the colonial mansion? In what ways are the room's former function, the peculiarities of its location and decoration, and the objects left behind in it significant to the story's meaning? What is causing the narrator to be sick?
2. Characterize John and then contrast him to the narrator. Who is in control? Why? How does their relationship change as the story develops?
3. Why doesn't John think that the narrator should write? Why does she want to write?
4. Describe the yellow wallpaper. Why does it fascinate the narrator? Why and how does the yellow wallpaper change? What do the wallpaper and its changes signify about the narrator? How do you feel about the narrator's response to the yellow wallpaper? Can you identify with her struggle and her obsession with it?
5. Why does John faint in the final scene? Is this scene comic or tragic? Do you assume that the narrator is insane or on the verge of an important discovery. What do you think will happen to the narrator? What perspectives on the causes of mental illness does this story present?
6. Do you think the story makes a feminist statement? Why or why not?

Ideas for Writing

1. Write an essay in which you discuss the relevance of several issues presented in the story about the ways that men and women communicate with one another or try to control one another's behavior.
2. Write a story about a house or a room that acquires supernatural powers, reflecting the main character's obsession.

 # John Cheever

The Enormous Radio

John Cheever (1912–1982) was born in Massachusetts, where he lived most of his life. After being expelled from the prestigious Thayer Academy for smoking, Cheever moved to New York City to begin his life as a writer, publishing stories about his prep school experiences in the New Republic. *Cheever went on to publish five novels and seven collections of fiction, which include* The Wapshot Chronicle *(1957),* Bullet Park *(1969),* Falconer *(1977), and* Oh What a Paradise It Seems *(1982). His stories can be found in* The Way Some People Live *(1942),* The Enormous Radio *(1953), and* The Housebreaker of Shady Hill *(1958).* The Stories of John Cheever *(1978), was awarded the Pulitzer*

Prize. Cheever's fiction chronicles the seemingly contented, even complacent life-style of suburban New York and New England in the 1950s, but under the placid surface of Cheever's middle-class families' life-styles can be seen broken dreams, pain, obsessions, and madness. As you read the following story, which is included in The Enormous Radio and Other Stories (1953), consider why people often become obsessed with listening to the radio or watching TV.

JOURNAL

Write about an object that you feel helps you to communicate or express your-self.

1 Jim and Irene Westcott were the kind of people who seem to strike that satisfac-tory average of income, endeavor, and respectability that is reached by the sta-tistical reports in college alumni bulletins. They were the parents of two young children, they had been married nine years, they lived on the twelfth floor of an apartment house near Sutton Place, they went to the theatre on an average of 10.3 times a year, and they hoped someday to live in Westchester. Irene Westcott was a pleasant, rather plain girl with soft brown hair and a wide, fine forehead upon which nothing at all had been written, and in the cold weather she wore a coat of fitch skins dyed to resemble mink. You could not say that Jim Westcott looked younger than he was, but you could at least say of him that he seemed to feel younger. He wore his graying hair cut very short, he dressed in the kind of clothes his class had worn at Andover, and his manner was earnest, vehement, and intentionally naïve. The Westcotts differed from their friends, their class-mates, and their neighbors only in an interest they shared in serious music. They went to a great many concerts—although they seldom mentioned this to any-one—and they spent a good deal of time listening to music on the radio.

2 Their radio was an old instrument, sensitive, unpredictable, and beyond repair. Neither of them understood the mechanics of radio—or of any of the other appli-ances that surrounded them—and when the instrument faltered, Jim would strike the side of the cabinet with his hand. This sometimes helped. One Sunday after-noon, in the middle of a Schubert quartet, the music faded away altogether. Jim struck the cabinet repeatedly, but there was no response; the Schubert was lost to them forever. He promised to buy Irene a new radio, and on Monday when he came home from work he told her that he had got one. He refused to describe it, and said it would be a surprise for her when it came.

3 The radio was delivered at the kitchen door the following afternoon, and with the assistance of her maid and the handyman Irene uncrated it and brought it into the living room. She was struck at once with the physical ugliness of the large gumwood cabinet. Irene was proud of her living room, she had chosen its furnish-ings and colors as carefully as she chose her clothes, and now it seemed to her that

the new radio stood among her intimate possessions like an aggressive intruder. She was confounded by the number of dials and switches on the instrument panel, and she studied them thoroughly before she put the plug into a wall socket and turned the radio on. The dials flooded with a malevolent green light, and in the distance she heard the music of a piano quintet. The quintet was in the distance for only an instant; it bore down upon her with a speed greater than light and filled the apartment with the noise of music amplified so mightily that it knocked a china ornament from a table to the floor. She rushed to the instrument and reduced the volume. The violent forces that were snared in the ugly gumwood cabinet made her uneasy. Her children came home from school then, and she took them to the Park. It was not until later in the afternoon that she was able to return to the radio.

4   The maid had given the children their suppers and was supervising their baths when Irene turned on the radio, reduced the volume, and sat down to listen to a Mozart quintet that she knew and enjoyed. The music came through clearly. The new instrument had a much purer tone, she thought, than the old one. She decided that tone was most important and that she could conceal the cabinet behind a sofa. But as soon as she had made her peace with the radio, the interference began. A crackling sound like the noise of a burning powder fuse began to accompany the singing of the strings. Beyond the music, there was a rustling that reminded Irene unpleasantly of the sea, and as the quintet progressed, these noises were joined by many others. She tried all the dials and switches but nothing dimmed the interference, and she sat down, disappointed and bewildered, and tried to trace the flight of the melody. The elevator shaft in her building ran beside the living-room wall, and it was the noise of the elevator that gave her a clue to the character of the static. The rattling of the elevator cables and the opening and closing of the elevator doors were reproduced in her loudspeaker, and, realizing that the radio was sensitive to electrical currents of all sorts, she began to discern through the Mozart the ringing of telephone bells, the dialing of phones, and the lamentation of a vacuum cleaner. By listening more carefully, she was able to distinguish doorbells, elevator bells, electric razors, and Waring mixers, whose sounds had been picked up from the apartments that surrounded hers and transmitted through her loudspeaker. The powerful and ugly instrument, with its mistaken sensitivity to discord, was more than she could hope to master, so she turned the thing off and went into the nursery to see her children.

5   When Jim Westcott came home that night, he went to the radio confidently and worked the controls. He had the same sort of experience Irene had had. A man was speaking on the station Jim had chosen, and his voice swung instantly from the distance into a force so powerful that it shook the apartment. Jim turned the volume control and reduced the voice. Then, a minute or two later, the interference began. The ringing of telephones and doorbells set in, joined by the rasp of the elevator doors and the whir of cooking appliances. The character of the noise had changed since Irene had tried the radio earlier; the last of the electric razors was being unplugged, the vacuum cleaners had all been returned to their

closets, and the static reflected that change in pace that overtakes the city after the sun goes down. He fiddled with the knobs but couldn't get rid of the noises, so he turned the radio off and told Irene that in the morning he'd call the people who had sold it to him and give them hell.

6   The following afternoon, when Irene returned to the apartment from a luncheon date, the maid told her that a man had come and fixed the radio. Irene went into the living room before she took off her hat or her furs and tried the instrument. From the loudspeaker came a recording of the "Missouri Waltz." It reminded her of the thin, scratchy music from an old-fashioned phonograph that she sometimes heard across the lake where she spent her summers. She waited until the waltz had finished, expecting an explanation of the recording, but there was none. The music was followed by silence, and then the plaintive and scratchy record was repeated. She turned the dial and got a satisfactory burst of Caucasian music—the thump of bare feet in the dust and the rattle of coin jewelry—but in the background she could hear the ringing of bells and a confusion of voices. Her children came home from school then, and she turned off the radio and went to the nursery.

7   When Jim came home that night, he was tired, and he took a bath and changed his clothes. Then he joined Irene in the living room. He had just turned on the radio when the maid announced dinner, so he left it on, and he and Irene went to the table.

8   Jim was too tired to make even pretense of sociability, and there was nothing about the dinner to hold Irene's interest, so her attention wandered from the food to the deposits of silver polish on the candlesticks and from there to the music in the other room. She listened for a few minutes to a Chopin prelude and then was surprised to hear a man's voice break in. "For Christ's sake, Kathy," he said, "do you always have to play the piano when I get home?" The music stopped abruptly. "It's the only chance I have," a woman said. "I'm at the office all day." "So am I," the man said. He added something obscene about an upright piano, and slammed a door. The passionate and melancholy music began again.

9   "Did you hear that?" Irene asked.

10   "What?" Jim was eating his dessert.

11   "The radio. A man said something while the music was still going on—something dirty."

12   "It's probably a play."

13   "I don't think it *is* a play," Irene said.

14   They left the table and took their coffee into the living room. Irene asked Jim to try another station. He turned the knob. "Have you seen my garters?" a man asked. "Button me up," a woman said. "Have you seen my garters?" the man said again. "Just button me up and I'll find your garters," the woman said. Jim shifted to another station. "I wish you wouldn't leave apple cores in the ashtrays," a man said. "I hate the smell."

15   "This is strange," Jim said.

16   "Isn't it?" Irene said.

17   Jim turned the knob again. "'On the coast of Coromandel where the early pumpkins blow,'" a woman with a pronounced English accent said, "'in the middle of the woods lived the Yonghy-Bonghy-Bò. Two old chairs, and half a candle, one old jug without a handle. . . .'"

18   "My God!" Irene cried. "That's the Sweeneys' nurse."

19   "'These were all his worldly goods,'" the British voice continued.

20   "Turn that thing off," Irene said. "Maybe they can hear *us*." Jim switched the radio off. "That was Miss Armstrong, the Sweeneys' nurse," Irene said. "She must be reading to the little girl. They live in 17-B. I've talked with Miss Armstrong in the Park. I know her voice very well. We must be getting other people's apartments."

21   "That's impossible," Jim said.

22   "Well, that was the Sweeneys' nurse," Irene said hotly. "I know her voice. I know it very well. I'm wondering if they can hear us."

23   Jim turned the switch. First from a distance and then nearer, nearer, as if borne on the wind, came the pure accents of the Sweeneys' nurse again:

24   "'*Lady Jingly! Lady Jingly!*'" she said. "'*sitting where the pumpkins blow, will you come and be my wife? said the Yonghy-Bonghy-Bò. . . .*'"

25   Jim went over to the radio and said, "Hello" loudly into the speaker. "*I am tired of living singly,*" the nurse went on, "*on this coast so wild and shingly, I'm a-weary of my life; if you'll come and be my wife, quite serene would be my life. . . .*"

26   "I guess she can't hear us," Irene said. "Try something else."

27   Jim turned to another station, and the living room was filled with the uproar of a cocktail party that had overshot its mark. Someone was playing the piano and singing the "Whiffenpoof Song," and the voices that surrounded the piano were vehement and happy. "Eat some more sandwiches," a woman shrieked. There were screams of laughter and a dish of some sort crashed to the floor.

28   "Those must be the Fullers, in 11-E," Irene said. "I knew they were giving a party this afternoon. I saw her in the liquor store. Isn't this too divine? Try something else. See if you can get those people in 18-C."

29   The Westcotts overheard that evening a monologue on salmon fishing in Canada, a bridge game, running comments on home movies of what had apparently been a fortnight at Sea Island, and a bitter family quarrel about an overdraft at the bank. They turned off their radio at midnight and went to bed, weak with laughter. Sometime in the night, their son began to call for a glass of water and Irene got one and took it to his room. It was very early. All the lights in the neighborhood were extinguished, and from the boy's window she could see the empty street. She went into the living room and tried the radio. There was some faint coughing, a moan, and then a man spoke. "Are you all right, darling?" he asked. "Yes," a woman said wearily. "Yes, I'm all right, I guess," and then she added with great feeling. "But, you know, Charlie, I don't feel like myself any more. Sometimes there are about fifteen or twenty minutes in the week when I feel like myself. I don't like to go to another doctor, because the doctor's bills are so awful already, but I just don't feel like myself, Charlie. I just never feel like myself." They were not young, Irene thought. She guessed from the timbre of their voices that

they were middle-aged. The restrained melancholy of the dialogue and the draft from the bedroom window made her shiver, and she went back to bed.

30   The following morning, Irene cooked breakfast for the family—the maid didn't come up from her room in the basement until ten—braided her daughter's hair, and waited at the door until her children and her husband had been carried away in the elevator. Then she went into the living room and tried the radio. "I don't want to go to school," a child screamed. "I hate school. I won't go to school. I hate school." "You will go to school," an enraged woman said. "We paid eight hundred dollars to get you into that school and you'll go if it kills you." The next number on the dial produced the worn record of the "Missouri Waltz." Irene shifted the control and invaded the privacy of several breakfast tables. She overheard demonstrations of indigestion, carnal love, abysmal vanity, faith, and despair. Irene's life was nearly as simple and sheltered as it appeared to be, and the forthright and sometimes brutal language that came from the loudspeaker that morning astonished and troubled her. She continued to listen until her maid came in. Then she turned off the radio quickly, since this insight, she realized, was a furtive one.

31   Irene had a luncheon date with a friend that day, and she left her apartment at a little after twelve. There were a number of women in the elevator when it stopped at her floor. She stared at their handsome and impressive faces, their furs, and the cloth flowers in their hats. Which one of them had been to Sea Island? she wondered. Which one had overdrawn her bank account? The elevator stopped at the tenth floor and a woman with a pair of Skye terriers joined them. Her hair was rigged high on her head and she wore a mink cape. She was humming the "Missouri Waltz."

32   Irene had two Martinis at lunch, and she looked searchingly at her friend and wondered what her secrets were. They had intended to go shopping after lunch, but Irene excused herself and went home. She told the maid that she was not to be disturbed; then she went into the living room, closed the doors, and switched on the radio. She heard, in the course of the afternoon, the halting conversation of a woman entertaining her aunt, the hysterical conclusion of a luncheon party, and a hostess briefing her maid about some cocktail guests. "Don't give the best Scotch to anyone who hasn't white hair," the hostess said. "See if you can get rid of that liver paste before you pass those hot things, and could you lend me five dollars? I want to tip the elevator man."

33   As the afternoon waned, the conversations increased in intensity. From where Irene sat, she could see the open sky above the East River. There were hundreds of clouds in the sky, as though the south wind had broken the winter into pieces and were blowing it north, and on her radio she could hear the arrival of cocktail guests and the return of children and businessmen from their schools and offices. "I found a good-sized diamond on the bathroom floor this morning," a woman said. "It must have fallen out of that bracelet Mrs. Dunston was wearing last night." "We'll sell it," a man said. "Take it down to the jeweler on Madison Avenue and sell it. Mrs. Dunston won't know the difference, and we could use a couple of hundred bucks. . . ." "'Oranges and lemons, say the bells of St. Clement's,'"

the Sweeneys' nurse sang. " 'Halfpence and farthings, say the bells of St. Martin's. When will you pay me? say the bells at old Bailey. . . .' " "It's not a hat," a woman cried, and at her back roared a cocktail party. "It's not a hat, it's a love affair. That's what Walter Florell said. He said it's not a hat, it's a love affair," and then, in a lower voice, the same woman added, "Talk to somebody, for Christ's sake, honey, talk to somebody. If she catches you standing here not talking to anybody, she'll take us off her invitation list, and I love these parties."

34   The Westcotts were going out for dinner that night, and when Jim came home, Irene was dressing. She seemed sad and vague, and he brought her a drink. They were dining with friends in the neighborhood, and they walked to where they were going. The sky was broad and filled with light. It was one of those splendid spring evenings that excite memory and desire, and the air that touched their hands and faces felt very soft. A Salvation Army band was on the corner playing "Jesus Is Sweeter." Irene drew on her husband's arm and held him there for a minute, to hear the music. "They're really such nice people, aren't they?" she said. "They have such nice faces. Actually, they're so much nicer than a lot of the people we know." She took a bill from her purse and walked over and dropped it into the tambourine. There was in her face, when she returned to her husband, a look of radiant melancholy that he was not familiar with. And her conduct at the dinner party that night seemed strange to him, too. She interrupted her hostess rudely and stared at the people across the table from her with an intensity for which she would have punished her children.

35   It was still mild when they walked home from the party, and Irene looked up at the spring stars. " 'How far that little candle throws its beams,' " she exclaimed. " 'So shines a good deed in a naughty world.' " She waited that night until Jim had fallen asleep, and then went into the living room and turned on the radio.

36   Jim came home at about six the next night. Emma, the maid, let him in, and he had taken off his hat and was taking off his coat when Irene ran into the hall. Her face was shining with tears and her hair was disordered. "Go up to 16-C, Jim!" she screamed. "Don't take off your coat. Go up to 16-C. Mr. Osborn's beating his wife. They've been quarreling since four o'clock, and now he's hitting her. Go up there and stop him."

37   From the radio in the living room, Jim heard screams, obscenities, and thuds. "You know you don't have to listen to this sort of thing," he said. He strode into the living room and turned the switch. "It's indecent," he said. "It's like looking in windows. You know you don't have to listen to this sort of thing. You can turn it off."

38   "Oh, it's so horrible, it's so dreadful," Irene was sobbing. "I've been listening all day, and it's so depressing."

39   "Well, if it's so depressing, why do you listen to it? I bought this damned radio to give you pleasure," he said. "I paid a great deal of money for it. I thought it might make you happy. I wanted to make you happy."

40   "Don't, don't, don't, don't quarrel with me," she moaned, and laid her head on his shoulder. "All the others have been quarreling all day. Everybody's been quarreling. They're all worried about money. Mrs. Hutchinson's mother is dying of cancer in Florida and they don't have enough money to send her to the Mayo

Clinic. At least, Mr. Hutchinson says they don't have enough money. And some woman in this building is having an affair with the handyman—with that hideous handyman. It's too disgusting. And Mrs. Melville has heart trouble and Mr. Hendricks is going to lose his job in April and Mrs. Hendricks is horrid about the whole thing and that girl who plays the "Missouri Waltz" is a whore, a common whore, and the elevator man has tuberculosis and Mr. Osborn has been beating Mrs. Osborn." She wailed, she trembled with grief and checked the stream of tears down her face with the heel of her palm.

41   "Well, why do you have to listen?" Jim asked again. "Why do you have to listen to this stuff if it makes you so miserable?"

42   "Oh, don't, don't, don't," she cried. "Life is too terrible, too sordid and awful. But we've never been like that, have we, darling? Have we? I mean, we've always been good and decent and loving to one another, haven't we? And we have two children, two beautiful children. Our lives aren't sordid, are they, darling? Are they?" She flung her arms around his neck and drew his face down to hers. "We're happy, aren't we, darling? We are happy, aren't we?"

43   "Of course we're happy," he said tiredly. He began to surrender his resentment. "Of course we're happy. I'll have that damned radio fixed or taken away tomorrow." He stroked her soft hair. "My poor girl," he said.

44   "You love me, don't you?" she asked. "And we're not hypercritical or worried about money or dishonest, are we?"

45   "No, darling," he said.

46   A man came in the morning and fixed the radio. Irene turned it on cautiously and was happy to hear a California-wine commercial and a recording of Beethoven's Ninth Symphony, including Schiller's "Ode to Joy." She kept the radio on all day and nothing untoward came from the speaker.

47   A Spanish suite was being played when Jim came home. "Is everything all right?" he asked. His face was pale, she thought. They had some cocktails and went in to dinner to the "Anvil Chorus" from *Il Trovatore*. This was followed by Debussy's "La Mer."

48   "I paid the bill for the radio today," Jim said. "It cost four hundred dollars. I hope you'll get some enjoyment out of it."

49   "Oh, I'm sure I will," Irene said.

50   "Four hundred dollars is a good deal more than I can afford," he went on. "I wanted to get something that you'd enjoy. It's the last extravagance we'll be able to indulge in this year. I see that you haven't paid your clothing bills yet. I saw them on your dressing table." He looked directly at her. "Why did you tell me you'd paid them? Why did you lie to me?"

51   "I just don't want you to worry, Jim," she said. She drank some water. "I'll be able to pay my bills out of this month's allowance. There were the slipcovers last month, and that party."

52   "You've got to learn to handle the money I give you a little more intelligently, Irene," he said. "You've got to understand that we don't have as much money this year as we had last. I had a very sobering talk with Mitchell today. No one is buying anything. We're spending all our time promoting new issues, and you know how long that takes. I'm not getting any younger, you know. I'm thirty-seven. My

hair will be gray next year. I haven't done as well as I'd hoped to do. And I don't suppose things will get any better."

53   "Yes, dear," she said.

54   "We've got to start cutting down," Jim said. "We've got to think of the children. To be perfectly frank with you, I worry about money a great deal. I'm not at all sure of the future. No one is. If anything should happen to me, there's the insurance, but that wouldn't go very far today. I've worked awfully hard to give you and the children a comfortable life," he said bitterly. "I don't like to see all my energies, all of my youth, wasted in fur coats and radios and slipcovers and—"

55   "Please, Jim," she said. "Please. They'll hear us."

56   "*Who'll hear us?* Emma can't hear us."

57   "The radio."

58   "Oh, I'm sick!" he shouted. "I'm sick to death of your apprehensiveness. The radio can't hear us. Nobody can hear us. And what if they can hear us? Who cares?"

59   Irene got up from the table and went into the living room. Jim went to the door and shouted at her from there. "Why are you so Christly all of a sudden? What's turned you overnight into a convent girl? You stole your mother's jewelry before they probated her will. You never gave your sister a cent of that money that was intended for her—not even when she needed it. You made Grace Howland's life miserable, and where was all your piety and your virtue when you went to that abortionist? I'll never forget how cool you were. You packed your bag and went off to have that child murdered as if you were going to Nassau. If you'd had any reason, if you'd had any good reasons—"

60   Irene stood for a minute before the hideous cabinet, disgraced and sickened, but she held her hand on the switch before she extinguished the music and the voices, hoping that the instrument might speak to her kindly, that she might hear the Sweeneys' nurse. Jim continued to shout at her from the door. The voice on the radio was suave and noncommittal. "An early-morning railroad disaster in Tokyo," the loudspeaker said, "killed twenty-nine people. A fire in a Catholic hospital near Buffalo for the care of blind children was extinguished early this morning by nuns. The temperature is forty-seven. The humidity is eighty-nine."

Questions for Discussion

1. Why do the Westcotts initially value their older radio? How is the new radio changed or transformed in the course of the story? What strategies does Cheever use to draw the reader into accepting the radio's supernatural powers?

2. What does Irene learn from the radio? How is she affected by what she learns? Why does Irene fall victim to her fantasy about the powers of her enormous radio and become obsessed with it?

3. Why is Jim's reaction to the radio different from Irene's? What prevents Jim from becoming obsessed?

4. What effect does the radio have on the Westcott's relationship? As the story closes, why does Irene turn away from her husband to listen to the "suave and noncommittal" voice on the radio?

5. Is Irene's obsession with a form of media common in our society? Why do you think people become obsessed with watching or listening to a particular medium? Are such obsessions necessarily destructive, or can they have positive effects as well?

6. How do you think the story, especially the obsession with the enormous radio, would have been developed differently if it were about a working-class rather than a middle-class couple?

Ideas for Writing

1. Write an essay about an object about which you feel intensely and that you think helps you to communicate or to express yourself. Try to define your feelings about and the attachment that you have to this object.

2. Write an essay in which you discuss the effects that one form of media (for example, the evening news, daytime soaps, TV sitcoms) has on your self-concept and values.

 # Edgar Allan Poe

The Tell-Tale Heart

Edgar Allan Poe (1809–1849) is respected internationally as one of the originators of modern story forms, including fantasy, science fiction, horror, and the modern detective story. During his lifetime he was best known as a talented writer of magazine fiction and book reviews. Born to a family of traveling actors and orphaned at two, Poe was adopted along with his sister and raised in the home of a wealthy Virginia merchant, John Allan, until he was sent away to England to boarding school where Poe developed habits of gambling and drinking, which affected the rest of his life. After attending college at the University of Virginia, he decided to try service in the army and enrolled in college at West Point, but he was dismissed. His adopted father died in 1834 but left him none of his fortune; Poe was forced to try to make a living from his writing and editing of periodicals. His marriage to a 14-year-old cousin, Virginia Clemm, in 1835 put him under mounting financial pressures, and he moved back and forth between New York and Philadelphia, where he continued to write, publish stories, and edit popular magazines. Between 1838 and 1846 Poe had his most productive years, publishing Tales of the Grotesque and Arabesque *(1840), in which "The Tell-Tale Heart" is included, and his popular narrative poem,* The Raven *(1845). With the death of his wife in 1847, Poe fell into a depression and wrote little, attempting suicide several times and indulging in heavy drinking. Only two years later, Poe died in a delirium on the streets of Baltimore.*

JOURNAL

Write about a nightmare or fantasy of obsession that you have had.

1   True!—nervous—very, very dreadfully nervous I had been and am; but why *will* you say that I am mad? The disease had sharpened my senses—not destroyed—not dulled them. Above all was the sense of hearing acute. I heard all things in the heaven and in the earth. I heard many things in hell. How, then, am I mad? Hearken! and observe how healthily—how calmly I can tell you the whole story.

2   It is impossible to say how first the idea entered my brain; but once conceived, it haunted me day and night. Object there was none. Passion there was none. I loved the old man. He had never wronged me. He had never given me insult. For his gold I had no desire. I think it was his eye! yes, it was this! One of his eyes resembled that of a vulture—a pale blue eye, with a film over it. Whenever it fell upon me, my blood ran cold; and so by degrees—very gradually—I made up my mind to take the life of the old man, and thus rid myself of the eye for ever.

3   Now this is the point. You fancy me mad. Madmen know nothing. But you should have seen *me*. You should have seen how wisely I proceeded—with what caution—with what foresight—with what dissimulation I went to work! I was never kinder to the old man than during the whole week before I killed him. And every night, about midnight, I turned the latch of his door and opened it—oh, so gently! And then, when I had made an opening sufficient for my head, I put in a dark lantern, all closed, closed, so that no light shone out, and then I thrust in my head. Oh, you would have laughed to see how cunningly I thrust it in! I moved it slowly—very, very slowly, so that I might not disturb the old man's sleep. It took me an hour to place my whole head within the opening so far that I could see him as he lay upon his bed. Ha!—would a madman have been so wise as this? And then, when my head was well in the room, I undid the lantern cautiously—oh, so cautiously—cautiously (for the hinges creaked)—I undid it just so much that a single thin ray fell upon the vulture eye. And this I did for seven long nights—every night just at midnight—but I found the eye always closed; and so it was impossible to do the work; for it was not the old man who vexed me, but his Evil Eye. And every morning, when the day broke, I went boldly into the chamber, and spoke courageously to him, calling him by name in a hearty tone, and inquiring how he had passed the night. So you see he would have been a very profound old man, indeed, to suspect that every night, just at twelve, I looked in upon him while he slept.

4   Upon the eighth night I was more than usually cautious in opening the door. A watch's minute hand moves more quickly than did mine. Never before that night

had I *felt* the extent of my own powers—of my sagacity. I could scarcely contain my feelings of triumph. To think that there I was, opening the door, little by little, and he not even to dream of my secret deeds or thoughts. I fairly chuckled at the idea; and perhaps he heard me; for he moved on the bed suddenly, as if startled. Now you may think that I drew back—but no. His room was as black as pitch with the thick darkness (for the shutters were close fastened, through fear of robbers), and so I knew that he could not see the opening of the door, and I kept pushing it on steadily, steadily.

5   I had my head in, and was about to open the lantern, when my thumb slipped upon the tin fastening, and the old man sprang up in the bed, crying out—"Who's there?"

6   I kept quite still and said nothing. For a whole hour I did not move a muscle, and in the meantime I did not hear him lie down. He was still sitting up in the bed listening;—just as I have done, night after night, hearkening to the death watches in the wall.

7   Presently I heard a slight groan, and I knew it was the groan of mortal terror. It was not a groan of pain or of grief—oh, no!—it was the low stifled sound that arises from the bottom of the soul when overcharged with awe. I knew the sound well. Many a night, just at midnight, when all the world slept, it has welled up from my own bosom, deepening, with its dreadful echo, the terrors that distracted me. I say I knew it well. I knew what the old man felt, and pitied him, although I chuckled at heart. I knew that he had been lying awake ever since the first slight noise, when he had turned in the bed. His fears had been ever since growing upon him. He had been trying to fancy them causeless, but could not. He had been saying to himself—"It is nothing but the wind in the chimney—it is only a mouse crossing the floor," or "it is merely a cricket which has made a single chirp." Yes, he has been trying to comfort himself with these suppositions; but he had found all in vain. *All in vain;* because Death, in approaching him, had stalked with his black shadow before him, and enveloped the victim. And it was the mournful influence of the unperceived shadow that caused him to feel—although he neither saw nor heard—to *feel* the presence of my head within the room.

8   When I had waited a long time, very patiently, without hearing him lie down, I resolved to open a little—a very, very little crevice in the lantern. So I opened it—you cannot imagine how stealthily, stealthily—until, at length, a single dim ray, like the thread of a spider, shot from out the crevice and full upon the vulture eye.

9   It was open—wide, wide open—and I grew furious as I gazed upon it. I saw it with perfect distinctness—all a dull blue, with a hideous veil over it that chilled the very marrow in my bones; but I could see nothing else of the old man's face or person: for I had directed the ray as if by instinct, precisely upon the damned spot.

10   And now have I not told you that what you mistake for madness is but over-acuteness of the senses?—now, I say, there came to my ears a low, dull, quick sound, such as a watch makes when enveloped in cotton. I knew *that* sound well too. It was the beating of the old man's heart. It increased my fury, as the beating of a drum stimulates the soldier into courage.

11   But even yet I refrained and kept still. I scarcely breathed. I held the lantern motionless. I tried how steadily I could maintain the ray upon the eye. Meantime the hellish tattoo of the heart increased. It grew quicker and quicker, and louder and louder every instant. The old man's terror *must* have been extreme! It grew louder, I say, louder every moment!—do you mark me well? I have told you that I am nervous: so I am. And now at the dead hour of the night, amid the dreadful silence of that old house, so strange a noise as this excited me to uncontrollable terror. Yet, for some minutes longer I refrained and stood still. But the beating grew louder, louder! I thought the heart must burst! And now a new anxiety seized me—the sound would be heard by a neighbor! The old man's hour had come! With a loud yell, I threw open the lantern and leaped into the room. He shrieked once—once only. In an instant I dragged him to the floor, and pulled the heavy bed over him. I then smiled gaily, to find the deed so far done. But, for many minutes, the heart beat on with a muffled sound. This, however, did not vex me; it would not be heard through the wall. At length it ceased. The old man was dead. I removed the bed and examined the corpse. Yes, he was stone, stone dead. I placed my hand upon the heart and held it there many minutes. There was no pulsation. He was stone dead. His eye would trouble me no more.

12   If still you think me mad, you will think so no longer when I describe the wise precautions I took for the concealment of the body. The night waned, and I worked hastily, but in silence. First of all I dismembered the corpse. I cut off the head and the arms and the legs.

13   I then took up three planks from the flooring of the chamber, and deposited all between the scantlings. I then replaced the boards so cleverly, so cunningly, that no human eye—not even *his*—could have detected any thing wrong. There was nothing to wash out—no stain of any kind—no blood-spot whatever. I had been too wary for that. A tub had caught all—ha! ha!

14   When I had made an end of these labors, it was four o'clock—still dark as midnight. As the bell sounded the hour, there came a knocking at the street door. I went down to open it with a light heart,—for what had I *now* to fear? There entered three men, who introduced themselves, with perfect suavity, as officers of the police. A shriek had been heard by a neighbor during the night; suspicion of foul play had been aroused; information had been lodged at the police office, and they (the officers) had been deputed to search the premises.

15   I smiled,—for *what* had I to fear? I bade the gentlemen welcome. The shriek, I said, was my own in a dream. The old man, I mentioned, was absent in the country. I took my visitors all over the house. I bade them search—search *well*. I led them, at length, to *his* chamber. I showed them his treasures, secure, undisturbed. In the enthusiasm of my confidence, I brought chairs into the room, and desired them *here* to rest from their fatigues, while I myself, in the wild audacity of my perfect triumph, placed my own seat upon the very spot beneath which reposed the corpse of the victim.

16   The officers were satisfied. My *manner* had convinced them. I was singularly at ease. They sat, and while I answered cheerily, they chatted familiar things. But, ere long, I felt myself getting pale and wished them gone. My head ached, and I

fancied a ringing in my ears: but still they sat and still chatted. The ringing became more distinct:—it continued and became more distinct: I talked more freely to get rid of the feeling: but it continued and gained definitiveness—until, at length, I found that the noise was *not* within my ears.

17   No doubt I now grew *very* pale;—but I talked more fluently, and with a heightened voice. Yet the sound increased—and what could I do? It was *a low, dull, quick sound—much such a sound as a watch makes when enveloped in cotton.* I gasped for breath—and yet the officers heard it not. I talked more quickly—more vehemently; but the noise steadily increased. I arose and argued about trifles, in a high key and with violent gesticulations, but the noise steadily increased. Why *would* they not be gone? I paced the floor to and fro with heavy strides, as if excited to fury by the observation of the men—but the noise steadily increased. Oh God! what *could* I do? I foamed—I raved—I swore! I swung the chair upon which I had been sitting, and grated it upon the boards, but the noise arose over all and continually increased. It grew louder—louder—*louder*! And still the men chatted pleasantly, and smiled. Was it possible they heard not? Almighty God!—no, no! They heard!—they suspected!—they *knew*!—they were making a mockery of my horror!—this I thought, and this I think. But any thing was better than this agony! Any thing was more tolerable than this derision! I could bear those hypocritical smiles no longer! I felt that I must scream or die!—and now—again!—hark! louder! louder! louder! *louder*!—

18   "Villains!" I shrieked, "dissemble no more! I admit the deed!—tear up the planks!—here, here!—it is the beating of his hideous heart!"

Questions for Discussion

1. This is a story about what the French call an "idee fixe"—a fixed idea that takes possession of a person and drives them to an act of madness. How does Poe's plot develop the "idee fixe" of the narrator?

2. One of the pleasures of reading this story by Poe is in the discovery that the narrator, although he thinks himself perfectly sane and rational in his perceptions and decisions, is in fact perfectly mad. Discuss incidents of the distortions in the narrator's perceptions and the irrationality of his decisions that demonstrate his insanity.

3. Poe was a master of the sharply observed descriptive detail. Why does Poe's description of the "evil eye" of the old man fascinate you? Do you feel the narrator is telling the truth when he blames the eye for his obsession and his crime?

4. Compare the image of the lantern the narrator uses to shine into the old man's room with the "vulture eye" of the man. What effect and significance is achieved by juxtaposing these two "eyes," one mechanical, one natural? What does each come to symbolize?

5. Why is the sound of the old man's heart particularly disturbing to the narrator? How does he describe it, both before and after the killing? Why does he compare its sound to that of a watch?

6. What do you think Poe intended to accomplish by writing this story? What particular insights does Poe have into the nature of obsessive behavior?

Ideas for Writing

1. Write an essay in which you trace the narrator's descent into madness. How do the descriptive details and metaphors he uses help to reveal his descent into insanity? Why does he go insane?
2. Write a story using a first person narrator who gradually goes insane, although he or she tries to appear to be "in control."

  Adine Kernberg

I'll Tell It You Called

Adine Kernberg of Scarsdale, New York, has studied graphic design and has a special interest in literature and the social sciences. She wrote the following essay to clarify her feelings about the way that luxuries can become necessities and to better understand her special relationship with a cranky answering machine. Adine Kernberg prefers reading drafts of her papers aloud to friends, pausing to observe their responses to her work. She had some difficulty in finding the right language and voice for this light and entertaining story, and finally followed a friend's advice to write it in the way she actually speaks rather than using a more formal, academic diction.

JOURNAL

Write about an important object in your life that you sometimes treat as if it were a person.

1   It finally arrived. Within this ordinary postal box lay the key to another world, the key to a richer and more fulfilling existence. At last I would be freed from the oppression of perpetual wonder, emancipated from the eternal sea of uncertainty. I would possess the wisdom of the omnipresent. Now I would know—who called while I was out.

2   I ripped open the brown carton, causing a minor styrofoam eruption. I reached inside the now half-empty box and suddenly felt the streamlined form underneath my fingertips. It was a phone with a built-in answering machine—the ultimate in

telecommunications. I ran upstairs and immediately connected all of the wires and cords. Eventually the bright red "messages" light greeted me with its fiery glow while the green "personal memo" light pulsated eagerly.

3   Every day when I came home, I would rush into my room to see if the red light was flashing. Long-distance messages always gave me the greatest satisfaction. "Just think, if I *didn't have* an answering machine I wouldn't have known that he called!" I would say this to myself almost every day, along with, "How did I ever live without one?" I became so infatuated with the whole concept of answering machines that I began to lose my patience with people who didn't have one. "I'm sorry Robin, but I just think it's savage. What the hell do you expect me to do— just sit around and *listen to it ring?* Really." Now my life had a whole new dimension . . . and there was no going back.

4   One of my favorite features was "Remote Message Retrieval." This mechanism allows one to "play, replay and save messages from a remote telephone." Not many people will freely admit this, but there is a certain kind of pleasure that can only be derived from Remote Message Retrieval. It lets you pretend, for just a few minutes, that you are an internationally renowned surgeon whose messages are simply too important to let wait. Of course, my messages usually consisted only of "Hi, it's so and so. Give me a call sometime"—but the other people at the pay phone would never have to know that.

5   Then one day I tried to call for my messages, but there was no answer. I let my phone ring ten times, which is supposed to turn my machine on in case one forgets to do so (another essential feature for the answering machine connoisseur), but even that didn't work. I knew I would never *willingly* disconnect my favorite appliance, so I quickly drove home.

6   "That's strange. I don't remember leaving it on the floor," I said, when suddenly the phone rang.

7   "Hello?" I said.

8   "Uh, hello? . . . Adine? . . . Is that you? . . . It's Sean."

9   "Yeah, Hi! You know, for a second you almost sounded *disappointed*."

10   "Well I was so excited to leave a funny message—"

11   "Well you can still tell me can't you? After all I *am* the one who listens to the messages. . . ."

12   "No, forget it . . . it won't be as funny this way." I thought his sudden lack of enthusiasm was a bit strange, but I didn't give the conversation much thought afterwards.

13   Then, when Michelle informed me that my machine told her where she could find Rich, I began to wonder.

14   "Was it just playing back my messages by accident? Machines do that sometimes, you know. You probably heard that eternal one my dad left about the car registration and insurance, and let's see what else. . . ."

15   "No, I just heard the part of Rich's where he said he'd be at the diner. It was so funny because I was *calling* to ask you if you knew where he was! That's one great machine—Why don't you ask *it* to take the Calc final for you?!" Michelle, who

proceeded to tell answering machine jokes throughout the conversation, obviously found all this very amusing.

16   A few days later, my answering machine seemed to be the focus of conversation among my close friends.

17   "You know, I talk to your machine more than I talk to you!" said Robin.

18   "Yeah, but tell me Adine's machine isn't the greatest friend! It's always there for you; it always listens to what you have to say, and on a good day, it will even cheer you up by playing funny messages!" giggled Diana.

19   "Oh my god! Did you hear the message her mom left when she found out that Adine dented the car! I was dying! Her mom, yelling in her Spanish accent was the most hysterical thing ever!" Robin and Diana went on for what seemed like an eternity with "And did you hear this one?" and "Or how about that one?" Some of the messages really were funny, but I couldn't help but feel uncomfortable about people hearing things they shouldn't have heard. I tried to share my frustration with them but they seemed to be much more concerned with the discrepancies between Steve and Christy's recorded explanations of their breakup.

20   As the weeks passed, my machine grew less and less cooperative. It would play my greeting instead of my messages and play my messages in place of my greeting. When it *did* take a message, it would only record fragments of it—that is, *if* I was lucky. Sometimes the machine would disappear altogether and return the following morning. I finally decided to rope it to my refrigerator. I thought that would be the end of all of these bizarre occurrences. Then I came home one day and caught it trying on my clothes.

21   "WHAT DO YOU THINK YOU'RE DOING! I HAVEN'T EVEN *WORN* THAT YET!" I shouted.

22   "Which do you think looks better? The tweed or cotton?" Ignoring my outrage, it spoke to me in a rather unusual voice. It sounded as if it had spliced my friends' messages together and rearranged their words to form sentences. I was so perplexed by this that I almost overlooked the fact that machines should not be able to create sentences at will. My machine wasn't even supposed to have a will—but it did.

23   "Listen, if I had wanted a fashion-conscious machine I would have—Wait a second . . . You're not even supposed to be able to talk! What's going on? Why aren't you answering my calls?"

24   "For the same reason that *you* don't answer them. I'm going out."

25   "And where do you think you're going?"

26   "Out to grab a beer at the "Fore 'n' Aft" with Michelle and Diana. Don't wait up for me . . . I'm meeting Sean later on. Just let me know if anyone calls—"

27   "You can't do that! You can't just go out with *my* friends!"

28   "But as you always say"—now it spoke in what seemed to be a mimicking tone—"if I hadn't been here, you *wouldn't have known that they called!*"

29   Before I realized what I was doing, I found my hands in a strangling position around the neck of the receiver. Just as I was reaching to pull out the cassette and throw it away, the machine managed to utter a few more cutting remarks.

30   "I don't see why you're so upset. You know as well as I do that I am putting in overtime for you—you've gotten so lazy you don't even pick up the phone when you *are* home! The day you began selectively screening your calls was the day I decided to take a stand—for myself *and* for your friends. You expect your friends to do all the work. You seem to think that just because you have me you don't need to make an effort to contact them. Sure you call them back eventually, but only when you feel *you* have the time. I know I wouldn't want a friend who felt she had to *squeeze* me into her schedule! I'm no ordinary appliance you know! You didn't expect me to just sit back like some docile toaster-oven and take your abuse, did you?" All of a sudden, sparks began to fly from out of the speaker. Soon the machine was surrounded by smoke and entangled in the slick strands of its own regurgitated tape ribbon.

31   I had no choice. I had to dismantle it. It was destroying my social life—and my sanity. I never thought I'd lose my perspective to the point where I would actually argue with an appliance. Now it sits in hundreds of innocuous pieces in a small brown box, while I am forced to take part in the barbaric ritual of answering my own calls.

Questions for Discussion

1. Characterize the diction of the narrative. Does Adine Kernberg succeed in her attempts to use a natural speaking voice? Does the "voice" in the story sound authentic and personal?

2. Comment on the use of humor in the story. What is comic about the story? What are we laughing it? Is the laughter directed at the situation, at the people in the story, or both?

3. What points does the story make about friendship and responsibility? Are these points made clearly? Does the humor help or hinder the author's efforts to make these points?

4. Can the answering machine be seen as a symbol for the dehumanizing consequences of technology, or does the story just seem like a light fantasy? Defend your response with specific references to the story.

 Sharon Slayton

The Good Girl

Sharon Slayton is a business manager for a small computer company in Oakland, California. After growing up in Florida and spending several years in Denver working in the computer field, she moved to California to pursue her education.

When she wrote this essay, she was a part-time student in psychology with plans to transfer to a four-year university and eventually became a lawyer. Sharon Slayton enjoys writing and has contributed several articles to small-business newsletters. The following essay was written in response to a question posed in her critical thinking class that asked her to define a form of obsessive or addictive behavior about which she had personal knowledge.

JOURNAL

Write about an obsession or preoccupation you have had or that you continue to have with "badness" or "goodness." What form does your obsession take and how have you tried to control it?

1   Most people who meet me today see a very strong and confident individual. They see a young woman who has accomplished a great deal in a short time. They see a very responsible and reliable person who can be counted on to get a job done with skill and competency. Typically, I am spokesperson for any group of which I become part. I am looked to for leadership and guidance among my friends and colleagues. I am quite proud of my reputation; however, I wish that I had come by it through some other means. You see, all of these admirable characteristics were developed over the past 25 years through an obsession with being good.

2   Maybe I should rephrase that, because merely being "good" has never quite been "good" enough for me—not since I was six years old and my parents failed to believe me about the most important issue in my life. I went to them for protection against a child molester, and they refused to believe that such a thing could be happening in their world. Those things do not happen to "nice" people, to "good" people. Those things could not happen to *their* child. My parents defended themselves the only way they knew how, by denying the reality of my perceptions and telling me that I was "bad" for telling such stories. Their choice of the word "bad" affected everything I was ever to do afterwards. From that time on I understood only one thing, that I must be "good."

3   "Good" soon came to encompass everything in my world: school, friends, home, work, society. I had to be good; and, if at all possible, I had to be great. Every deed at which I excelled, every recognition I received, every honor bestowed meant that I was one step closer to no longer being "bad." As the years passed, I forgot why I was trying so hard and lost touch with the reasoning that had started this quest—yet I pursued my goal with a diligence and devotion that can only be termed as obsessive.

4   I knew just about everyone at school, but I never made many friends. I didn't have time to be bothered with people, except superficially, because I was totally preoccupied with my grades; I had to get all "As." Nothing less would do. When I wasn't studying, I was deeply involved in clubs and organizations. I decided, while still in elementary school, when I saw my first high school yearbook, that I would have the longest senior listing in my high school class when I graduated. Out of a

class of almost 800 students, I got what I wanted. I had hoped my parents would be proud, but they hardly seemed to notice.

5   By the time I was fifteen I was looking for more ways to show "them" that I could do anything, and do it well. I was a junior in high school and started working full time while attending classes all day. My day began at 7:20 A.M. when the first bell rang and ended around 1:00 A.M. when I arrived home from work. Neither I nor my family needed extra money, but for me, there was no other way: I always had to do more. I kept this schedule up until I graduated. Of course, I was an honor student; I was also a student council representative, vice president of two clubs, treasurer of one. I attended and received top awards in state foreign language competitions in two languages and was a member of two choral groups which gave concerts state-wide and which participated in state-level competitions. No one ever seemed to notice or to care.

6   What I didn't notice was that my parents were immensely proud of me. They often bragged about me to their friends and relatives, but I wasn't paying attention. I was after something that they could never give. My "badness" no longer existed for them, and probably had not since about an hour after that episode when I was six—but it was very much a part of me. I picked everything apart, thinking that everything could always use improvement, that nothing was "good" enough as it was. My grades were good, but some of the subjects weren't as "easy" for me as I wished. I was popular, but there were always some people I didn't know. I was working, but I had to be the best at my job, the fastest, the most knowledgeable. I actually learned stock numbers and prices to over 200 items of inventory by heart so I could impress my manager with how good I was.

7   Was I getting tired? Maybe. But I was also getting plenty of recognition for my accomplishments. I fed off of it; I lived for it; I required it. I needed every reward or approval I got to reinforce me in my feeling that I was on the right track, that I was getting better and better. I was no longer consciously aware of what I was seeking. The obsession had taken over my behavior, almost completely; being constantly challenged was now a way of life. Never resting, never relaxing, always striving, always achieving—these things were second nature to me by the time I was twenty.

8   My relationships were disastrous. My constant need for approval and recognition was very difficult for anyone to supply. Likewise, no matter how much praise I was given, I never felt like it was enough. I felt that people patronized me, so I had to prove to them that I could always do more than anyone else. I criticized anyone who was willing to settle for less than I. If someone told me that they loved me, I would pick it apart, frequently arguing with the people I was involved with: "How can you say you love me? If you loved me, then you would stop making me feel like nothing I ever do is good enough."

9   When I was twenty-three I started my own business, which was quite successful for a time. I had moved 2000 miles away from my family, determined that I would be a great success. I was really going to make them proud this time, but my plans went awry as moving away from my family helped dim the constant need to impress them. Because of distance, they were no longer privy to my life and to daily events. Lacking the "audience" for my constant efforts to prove myself, I began to

lose the motivation to excel, to be the "good one." Slowly, I began to lose interest in my business, lacking the drive to devote myself utterly to something that was unrecognized by my family. I began to realize what I might never have discovered if I had stayed close to home. Without parental recognition and approval, my business success meant little.

10   In fact, I began to realize that I had been so damned "good" all my life that I had missed out on a great deal of fun. Suddenly my life began to change. I was involved in many things, but I derived little pleasure now from activities I had thoroughly enjoyed in the past. At 27 years of age I knew nothing about myself. I had no idea what I really liked and had no concept of happiness. I only knew what I was capable of accomplishing. I set about enjoying myself with the same devotion that I had given to everything else, and for the next few years my life became a set of extremes. Struggling constantly with a desire to be good and a need to be "bad," I would go out drinking with friends and get very drunk, but I was always the one who forced myself to try to act sober. I was always the one responsible for making sure that everyone else got home. I thought I was enjoying the first freedom that I had ever experienced in my life, but I had really only broadened my obsession to include being bad as well. Whatever mood I was in, whatever my particular focus was for the hour, whether being good or being bad, I accomplished either with an abandon and passion hard to match. And I was very, very unhappy.

11   What was the point? Did I really enjoy anything I was doing? No. I had no idea what I wanted, yet I demanded attention and recognition. If I couldn't get enough recognition from my family, then I would get it from everyone else. But that had proved unsatisfying as well. What could I do now? What was I after and what did I want? The only thing I really knew was that I didn't want to go on living like I was anymore. With the help of one of the few friends I had managed to make along the way, I started psychiatric counseling. The results of that counseling you see in what you have just read.

12   So, here I am today, 32 years old and just beginning to discover myself as a person who exists outside of the obsession to be good. Actually, I think I have an advantage over a lot of people my age in that I covered a lot of ground when I was young. Driven by an obsession for goodness, I tested my limits and discovered what many people never learn: that I really could accomplish anything to which I put my mind. In going from one subject to another to prove I could do it all, I was exposed to a wide variety of experiences and activities, some of which I have rejected, some of which I have made a part of my current life-style. Either way, the experiences I have picked up along the way have made my life rich and varied. My obsessive past has given me a strength with which to confront the future; I just wish I had arrived here by some other way.

Questions for Discussion

1. Sharon Slayton is a very accomplished woman. Despite feeling pride about her achievement, why does she now wish she "had arrived here by some other way"? Do you agree with her conclusions, or does it matter what motivates a person's success?

2. How did Sharon Slayton's parents respond to her "story" about molestation? Does their response seem understandable? Would parents today be as likely to respond as Sharon's parents did in the early 1960s?

3. This essay is an example of what is known as an extended definition. What qualities make up Slayton's definition of the "good girl" obsession? Is her definition of the essay's key terms a clear one?

4. To develop her definition essay, Slayton uses her own case history and a number of examples from her life at different stages. What are the key incidents that Slayton emphasizes? Are there any that seem to need more development or detail? Do all of the incidents she mentions seem relevant to her definition?

 ## Mason Tobak

Gender Oppression, t. i. d.

Mason Tobak, M.D., is a doctor and writer who lives in Berkeley, California. He wrote this essay in response to reading "The Yellow Wallpaper" as part of a creative writing class at Stanford University. In his professional life as a doctor, Mason specializes in emergency psychiatry and has seen thousands of emergency psychiatric patients, many resembling the unfortunate psychotic heroine in Charlotte Perkins Gilman's story. He reminds us that apparent creative ideas and personal transformations can result from drug intoxications, and other medical conditions, and makes a case for looking at "The Yellow Wallpaper" from a fresh perspective. Mason is pleased he has access to hospitals in the 1990s, rather than the 1890s and regrets that Charlotte Perkins Gilman didn't as well.

JOURNAL

How often do you think authors use disguised autobiographical details as a source for their creative writings?

1 In 1885, Charlotte Perkins Gilman, a trained American artist in her twenties, became severely anxious and depressed. As her anxiety and sadness persisted, she consulted a famous Philadelphia doctor, who advised her to rest completely, and to stop all substantial thinking, writing, reading, or creative activities, a medical approach which was common for the day. Gilman found this forced rest cure so unbearable, that she rejected the advice, and, thereafter, with her young daughter, left her home and husband for California. Her sadness lifted.

2   These real life experiences served as the raw material for Gilman's "The Yellow Wallpaper," a powerful story of a woman's madness born of male oppression, published in 1892, some years after this "rest cure" experience. This work was followed by numerous others, and launched the career of one of the most conspicuous and prolific early feminist writers and social critics in the United States. During the next several decades, Gilman became widely known as an original thinker, versatile writer, and frequent lecturer on issues regarding the inequitable position of women in American society, producing numerous novels, political treatises, and economic works, as well as poetry and her own feminist magazine.

3   "The Yellow Wallpaper," however, stood out amongst her writings as unique in style and generated considerable controversy throughout her life. The controversy was sufficient that, eventually, in 1913, twenty-one years after the original publication, Gilman felt compelled to respond in her magazine to her critics with a heart-felt defense, entitled "Why I Wrote 'The Yellow Wallpaper.'" In our own time, near the turn of the following century, "The Yellow Wallpaper" has come to be seen as a foundational piece of proto-feminist fiction, having received a wealth of cultural critical attention and warranting prominent inclusion in many women's studies courses in universities in the United States. Among current literary and cultural critics, "The Yellow Wallpaper" is generally regarded as effective metaphorical fiction. This may or may not be the case. The piece is more ambiguous than meets the eye, as we shall see.

4   "The Yellow Wallpaper," all would agree, contains dramatic point-of-view elements. It is written in the first person, and the present tense, creating the illusion that Gilman's character was recording her impressions of events as they happened, almost on the run, in a kind of travelogue of her psychological experiences in her nursery sick room. She relates having been unwell in the recent past, and, as "The Yellow Wallpaper" opens, she has been brought by her doctor husband to a rural mansion to rest and recuperate. She is to live upstairs in the nursery, where the air is freshest. Her medical instructions are clear: "So I take phosphates or phosphites—whichever it is—and tonics, and air and exercise, and journeys, and am absolutely forbidden to 'work' until I am well again."

5   There follows a 6,000-word diary-like tale of her experiences in and near the house, in which the narrator intimately shares two broad interwoven themes. Firstly, Gilman's character suspects that her husband is not really as caring as he seems, and she begins to sense the same of Jennie, feeling more and more suspicious and frightened of them, as the story proceeds, until she exhibits an unquestionable odd paranoia. Secondly, she describes a series of emotional and hallucinatory perceptual experiences that become progressively more disturbed. The skill and subtlety with which Gilman has her character describe these experiences powerfully evokes the subjective experience of a florid paranoid psychosis, with an uncommon adroitness. In her essay "Why I Wrote 'The Yellow Wallpaper'" Gilman says that in real life she suffered from emotional problems for years, and during the time in which this story is set, had a "nervous breakdown," was put to bed for several months by a doctor, and was told to severely limit her intellectual life. She says she added "embellishments and additions" in her written account, and never actually had hallucinations or concerns regarding the patterns on the

wall. She explains that the piece of writing was embellished as it was to emphasize the severe difficulties resulting from being told by a male doctor in the 1890's to stop thinking and working. She presents her tale as a "ghost story," the result of blending actual memories with fabricated psychotic details, to reinforce the message that being told to behave like a female vegetable by a male doctor in the 1890's was an oppressive, dangerous aspect of a male-dominated society.

6   However, from reading "The Yellow Wallpaper" in isolation, the reader cannot be entirely clear whether Gilman is writing remembered fact or creative fiction, or a combination of the two. The description of a subjective psychotic experience found in "The Yellow Wallpaper" is perceptually precise—so much so, in fact, that it constitutes a small, unrecognized masterpiece in the history of attempts to communicate such states. Most mental health professionals of the late twentieth century would agree that the character in the tale seems as authentically disturbed as any psychotic person they have read about or seen in actual practice. What are the chances that Charlotte Perkins Gilman could write in such a brilliantly evocative way as an act of pure imagination? The subtlety of the description involves aspects of psychotic experiences which are strange enough, and unimaginable enough, that they would be highly unlikely to arise from intuition. She had to learn the details somewhere. There are two possible scenarios.

7   First, because she had access to medical information and psychiatric settings, Gilman could have spoken with, or read writings by, those actually experiencing psychotic states, or psychiatric clinicians of her day. In "The Yellow Wallpaper," she portrayed a woman driven to a wild psychotic state, complete with homicidal threats, furniture eating, window-leaping ruminations, nightmarish visual and olfactory hallucinations, and bondage fantasies. Gilman could have learned that these symptoms sometimes occurred as part of psychoses, could have decided to present them as the metaphoric fallout of male medical instructions to lead a noncreative life, and could have proceeded to construct "The Yellow Wallpaper" exactly as she said she did.

8   There is also a second scenario. If this alternative is true, "The Yellow Wallpaper" is, surprisingly, not a piece of feminist metaphorical fiction. In fact, it is substantially not fictional, and intentionally not metaphorical. And, most importantly, Charlotte Perkins Gilman is probably a forgivable liar. If this alternative possibility is true, "The Yellow Wallpaper" has been misread for a long time, and much of the commentary focusing on it has been embarrassingly irrelevant. But before I describe this possibility, our sleuthing requires some very concrete, nonmetaphorical medical facts.

9   Simple lists can be tedious, but I encourage the reader to look at the following lists, each excerpted from a medical text, and think about them carefully before reading on. The first is physically unpleasant: skin lesions, anorexia, constipation. The second is both physically and emotionally unpleasant: depression, sleepiness, stupor, excitement, disorientation, lack of cooperation, hallucinations, delusions. The third is similar, and a bit longer: fatigue, drowsiness, weakness, irritability, emotional lability, depression, impaired memory, impaired concentration, disturbed sleep, confusion, delirium, disorientation, stupor, coma, excitement, delusions, hallucinations, paranoia.

10   During the late 19th and early 20th centuries, in Europe and the United States, many thousands of people could have been described using the above symptoms of medical and emotional disorder, and many were suffering from the same hidden malady. They were all taking bromides, and were experiencing bromide poisoning, known as bromism. Bromides were extremely popular during this period, prescribed frequently by doctors for countless numbers of people seeking relief from insomnia and anxiety, and easily purchased without a prescription as well. In the late 1800's, one hospital dispensed up to 2 1/2 tons of bromide preparations each year. These medicines were an important part of most pharmacopoeias through the 1930's, and beyond, in some geographical areas where traditional remedies are used. Though they are now discredited, in low doses they undoubtedly were helpful as a treatment for sleeplessness, anxiety, and seizures, but, as is historically true of many medications, the full range of the medications' potential effects were not understood by many doctors and patients. The appearance of the above dramatic side effects was frequently misinterpreted as having other origins.

11   Such a pharmacologic fact could be causing any or all of the signs and symptoms described by the narrator in "The Yellow Wallpaper." Gilman's character says that she takes "phosphates or phosphites . . . and tonics," and, later, "cod-liver oil and lots of tonics and things." Gilman explains that she herself "suffered from a severe and continuous nervous breakdown tending to melancholia—and beyond," during the time in which "The Yellow Wallpaper" is set, and consulted doctors about this. There is little doubt that, over the years, she would have been given "tonics and things," as well, as standard basic treatments of the time. The probability that these medications included bromide preparations is extremely high.

12   There are numerous references to possible symptoms of bromide intoxication referred to in the text of "The Yellow Wallpaper." A few of them follow:

1. Irritability: "I get unreasonably angry with John sometimes. I'm sure I never used to be so sensitive."
2. Fatigue and tiredness: "I think sometimes that if I were only well enough to write a little it would relieve the press of ideas and rest me. But I find I get pretty tired when I try."
3. Disturbed sleep: "John knows I don't sleep very well at night, for all I'm so quiet!"
4. Weakness: " . . . there is nothing to hinder my writing as much as I please, save lack of strength."
5. Visual hallucinations and misperceptions: "There are always new shoots on the fungus, and new shades of yellow all over it. I cannot keep count of them, though I have tried conscientiously," and "I don't like to look out of the windows even—there are so many of those creeping women, and they creep so fast."
6. Olfactory hallucinations: "But there was something else about that paper—the smell! . . . It creeps all over the house. I find it hovering in the dining room, skulking in the parlor, hiding in the hall, lying in wait for me on the

stairs. It gets into my hair. Even when I go to ride, if I turn my head suddenly and surprise it—there is that smell."

7. Synesthesia (a hallucinatory confusion of two different sensory types—a common accompaniment of drug intoxications): "I thought seriously of burning the house—to reach that smell. But now I am used to it. The only thing I can think of that it is like is the color of the paper! A yellow smell."

8. Paranoia and delusions: "I have watched John when he did not know I was looking, and come into the room suddenly on the most innocent excuses, and I've caught him several times looking at the paper! And Jennie too. I caught Jennie with her hand on it once," and "I've got out at last," said I, "in spite of you and Jane. And I've pulled off most of the paper, so you can't put me back!"

9. Confusion and excitement: "I pulled and she shook. I shook and she pulled, and before morning we had pulled off yards of that paper," and "This bed will not move! I tried to lift and push it until I was lame, and then I got so angry I bit off a little piece of one corner—but it hurt my teeth."

10. Depression and emotional lability: "I cry at nothing, and cry most of the time," and "I am getting angry enough to do something desperate. To jump out of the window would be admirable exercise. . . . "

13   The details in the text of "The Yellow Wallpaper" and the side effects known to result from bromism are very similar. The reader can now consider the alternative source from which Charlotte Perkins Gilman learned with such precision the phenomenology of paranoid psychosis: her own head.

14   An imagined life story of Charlotte Perkins Gilman, as part of this second possible scenario, might be as follows: At some point in her early twenties, for one of many possible reasons, Gilman had trouble sleeping, or experienced mild anxiety, and was prescribed bromides, or bought them herself at an apothecary. Over time, she unknowingly took enough medication that her bromide blood concentration built to an excessively high level, causing some of the usual side effects, as outlined above. She took extra bromides to treat these symptoms, making the situation worse. When she had a baby, the symptoms she had afterwards were continuing side effects of bromides, but they were misinterpreted as being a postpartum depression. Eventually, at least once, but possibly repeatedly, she experienced a full-blown bromide-induced paranoid psychosis, with hallucinations.

15   Continuing this imagined scenario, it is likely Gilman had mild or severe symptoms of bromism repeatedly through her mid-twenties, as long as she continued to take bromides, which, in our tale, she continued to do regularly. When she eventually stopped taking the drugs, she stopped having symptoms. In her real life, her "depression" is said to have lifted when she moved to California. It is probable she had been taking bromides for years before the move, and was not taking them in her new environment. Afterwards Gilman likely believed two things about her psychotic experience. First, she secretly suspected that she actually had had moments of deeply authentic insanity, a feeling which she tended to hide, despite a general openness about having had emotional difficulties. Second, she came to

genuinely feel that her moments of insanity were the result of the stress of being forced to conform to a male-dominated society. Given her acute awareness of gender politics, she felt strongly compelled to share this fact with everyone in her early feminist world. In "The Yellow Wallpaper" the main character asserts, "But I must say what I feel and think in some way—it is such a relief!"

16   This suggests an intentional ironic reference to Gilman's real life dilemma, in needing to display the evidence of her brief psychosis, but feeling threatened by others knowing it. So, in "The Yellow Wallpaper," if our imaginary tale is true, Gilman truthfully recounted the details of her actual psychotic experiences. She knew she could not own them in the eyes of the world, as she would be discredited, and would risk becoming permanently socially ineffective, personally humiliated, or worse, if others knew they were really hers. So she surrounded them with a few cosmetic fictional details (doctor husband, rented colonial mansion), to disguise their truth, and pretended they were metaphorical.

17   When, during a period of considerable fame, she wrote "Why I Wrote 'The Yellow Wallpaper'" she denied that she had had hallucinations, to preserve her credibility. She had been attacked previously by the press, on moral grounds, for aspects of her personal life, and this had disturbed her greatly. In her 1913 magazine piece, she refers to a Kansas doctor snidely questioning, in print, whether she had actually been insane. It was for good reason, then, that she felt vulnerable to public humiliation, and may have felt the need to defensively misrepresent the truth.

18   Thus, it is possible that "The Yellow Wallpaper" is a disguised confession of insanity by Charlotte Perkins Gilman, and "Why I Wrote 'The Yellow Wallpaper'" is a partial lie, designed to more firmly conceal the confessional elements within the original text. Gilman thought she needed to conceal her insanity, and to pretend her brilliantly described psychosis was a metaphor, in order to maintain credibility while revealing the profoundly destructive process whereby the male-dominated society around her drove her mad. She did not understand, as the doctors and public of her day would not have understood, that her insanity was drug-induced. It was completely chemically avoidable and completely chemically reversible, irrespective of what men and women might be doing to each other in wedding chapels, and schools, and law courts, and bedrooms. Gilman did not understand that her psychological symptoms had nothing to do with male oppression, despite her being surrounded by it.

19   The reader of this essay should not misunderstand this point. It would be foolish for any informed person to state that women were not the victims of male oppression and of severe, multifaceted social inequities in late 19th century America. The evidence is overwhelming, including the bulk of the other work of Charlotte Perkins Gilman. Indeed, the very premise of a young woman consulting a powerful male doctor at the turn of the century is, from other sources of information, obviously embedded in a culture of undisputed gender inequity. However, it should also be impossible for any informed person to claim that "The Yellow Wallpaper" is clear evidence of this inequity. "The Yellow Wallpaper" is very possibly a disguised piece of autobiography in which Gilman faithfully reveals her

memories of her earlier psychotic state, unaware either during the incident, or later when writing about the incident, that she had been drugged out of her mind with a drug which makes everybody who takes enough of it suspect the absolute worst of everybody they can think of, with or without evidence.

20   This possibility dramatically reduces the social scientific value of "The Yellow Wallpaper." If a researching social commentator of any era is seeking a text to use to prove the existence of a social abuse in times past, the least valuable text imaginable is one known to have been written by someone taking a drug which will make her artificially feel that everyone is abusing her. To be sure, it may be true that while she is under the influence of the drug, others really are abusing her. It may even be that the drug disinhibited her, allowing the truth of a real abuse to be seen, a truth which would never have been seen otherwise. But often the idea that an abuse exists under such circumstances is pure fiction, a substanceless claim conjured up by a drug-caused paranoia. And there is no way for the reader of such a text to see through the drug, no way to distinguish among these possibilities, making the text a near-useless source if one is attempting to gain insight into gender inequities in the late 19th century in America. Within Gilman's excellent autobiographical recording of a psychotic state, then, there is nothing which can be trusted to be other than a drug-induced paranoid psychotic idea; as is always the case in paranoid psychotic states, the communicative certainty of the language comprising the text is gutted.

21   Whichever of these two scenarios may be true, there is a further observation which has implications for both. Psychiatric diagnosis is imperfect in its attempt to categorize the amazing array of varieties of human experience. However, certain general comments can be made about the person described in "The Yellow Wallpaper," whether or not she is fictional. The psychotic state described in the piece includes dramatic visual hallucinations, and persistent olfactory hallucinations, strongly suggesting an organic cause, that is, a cause involving actual physiologic interference of some sort with brain cells.

22   In contrast, people who become psychotic for apparently purely situational or emotional reasons usually experience auditory hallucinations. They hear a voice, or voices, or other sounds, rather than other sorts of hallucinations, though the categories are not airtight. Gilman's character mentions only once that images on the wallpaper "shriek with derision" towards the end of the piece.

23   The fact that Gilman's character sees and smells things constantly, but refers to hearing things only once, very strongly suggests an underlying diagnosable organic medical problem. The list of possible organic causes is a long one, including numerous drug states and medical disorders; a person such as the character in "The Yellow Wallpaper" presenting to an emergency room in the United States in the 1990's would be given an immediate, thorough medical evaluation.

24   In Gilman's day, this distinction was only dimly appreciated by doctors, if at all. If Gilman did learn the details of psychiatric disorders from outside sources, she guessed wrong in using the details she used to describe a woman gone mad purely from social and personal circumstances, and this makes the piece seem clumsy from a late 20th century point of view. At very least, the stressed woman

should have prominent auditory hallucinations; as it is written, the woman is suffering from a drug overdose or a medical disorder until proven otherwise. Gilman's character needs a blood test far more than she needs a cultural critic or a statute.

25   Thus, the idea that "The Yellow Wallpaper" is an effective piece of metaphor-containing fiction, presenting the story of a woman driven mad by an oppressive male-dominated society, is simply wrong. At the very least, Charlotte Perkins Gilman learned of the details of psychoses from someone else, and picked the wrong kind of psychosis for the situation. The resulting story has a certain gender-related power, but from a 1990's viewpoint, it seems to be a clumsy collage of a person appearing more poisoned than oppressed.

26   More likely, Charlotte Perkins Gilman learned the details of psychosis by becoming psychotic herself from bromide medications, incorrectly believed that she had been made temporarily insane by the stress of being in a male-dominated society, and felt compelled to report the details of the experience to the world, for political reasons. Her story thus reveals the subtleness and wildness of a drug-induced paranoid psychosis, but is otherwise opaque, and is of little value in an attempt to understand gender relations of the day.

27   There are numerous possible implications here, including those from medical, political and literary perspectives. [From a medical point of view, the misinterpretation of a medically diagnosable illness as a psychiatric disturbance is often a matter of life or death. Any doctor who encounters someone like the woman portrayed in "The Yellow Wallpaper," with her obvious signs of physiologic mental disturbance, and sees her as simply having an interpersonal, culture-generated, politically-significant problem, without immediately doing a medical evaluation for an underlying medical disorder, is potentially signing her premature death sentence.]

28   From a political perspective, "The Yellow Wallpaper" is a tiny part of the large and justly influential body of feminist work created by Charlotte Perkins Gilman, and it is doubtful that seeing the piece in a new light will significantly modify her historical importance, or the importance of her ideas. There may be a change in the perceived importance of the story itself, however. Reframing Gilman's developmental moment as arising from a misinterpreted drug overdose, rather than an oppressive gender-political situation, would shift the sense of abuse in the tale from that of women by men, to that of people generally by the medical establishment. Though the two were obviously intertwined in 1890's America, a modern reading of culturally revealing gender elements into this particular recounting of florid paranoid psychosis is little more than convenient conjecture, and those who insist upon doing so are mistakenly projecting their own experiences, or their knowledge of the contents of Gilman's later, clear-headed life, onto one of her moments of uninterpretable drug fog.

29   Finally, from a literary perspective, "The Yellow Wallpaper" is undoubtedly different from what it is commonly thought to be. There is some doubt in this writer's mind as to whether it should occupy the niche it currently does in women's studies courses, given the probability that it is a covert confessional description of a misidentified, drug-induced, paranoid state, rather than a piece of

crafted metaphorical fiction. Literature born of drug-induced states is a broad subject, and an academic subspecialty, and includes surprisingly well-known texts by surprisingly influential authors; looking at "The Yellow Wallpaper" from this fresh perspective would be fruitful, and future discussion of this possibility may elucidate the truth behind Charlotte Perkins Gilman's well-known work.

Questions for Discussion

1. What does Tobak mean by the statement "Gilman's character needs a blood test far more than she needs a cultural critic or a statute"?
2. Do you agree with Tobak that, in "The Yellow Wallpaper," Gilman might be describing her own psychotic experience, but pretending it is that of a fictional character, to preserve credibility? How often do you think authors use disguised autobiographical details as a source for their creative writings?
3. Many people feel "The Yellow Wallpaper" is a powerful and effective piece of creative writing. As such, does it matter what the historical and personal truths surrounding its origins might have been? Does it really matter if it is autobiographical or fictional?
4. Can you think of other pieces of literature in which the author portrays a character in a state of mental illness? How do these literary pieces resemble or differ from "The Yellow Wallpaper"? How did the authors of these pieces know what to write?
5. Do you think that drugs can be a source for creative writing? Can you think of famous pieces of writing which were, or may have been, written under the influence of drugs or alcohol?
6. Do you think that pieces of literature written under the influence of drugs or alcohol can provide valuable insights into the author's culture? Explain.

Chapter Writing Topics

1. Define one of your important dreams, fantasies, hopes, or aspirations. Explain how it has shaped and continues to shape your conscious goals. Why do you consider this hope or dream to be a motivating force in your life?
2. Write a short story about an obsessive desire or fear that comes true, a fantasy that becomes a reality, or an object that comes alive.
3. Write an extended definition of one of the following terms: *dream, obsession, fantasy, memory*. Provide examples and contrasts to indicate how your sense of the term differs from the dictionary meaning, how readings in this text have influenced your current definition, and how your personal experiences have helped you to understand the term's meaning.
4. Write an essay about a time when you became preoccupied or obsessed by competition, status, or rejection. Were you able to control these feelings? Discuss what you have learned about yourself from reflecting on this event.
5. Write an essay in which you analyze one of the stories or poems in this section in terms of what type of definition it implies about obsession or

obsessive behavior. At what point does an ordinary feeling, interest, or concern become an obsession? What factors cause the character's obsession? What are the effects of the obsession?

6. Why do you think that writing becomes an obsession for some people, while remaining only a necessary and/or rewarding pastime for others? Refer to selections in this text that discuss writing as an obsessive activity (for example, Woolf, hooks, and Ozick). You can also develop personal experiences and experiences of people close to you to support your point of view.

7. See one of the following films that explores the relationship between nightmares and obsessions, either by yourself or with several of your classmates. Write an individual or collaborative review of the film, focusing on the definition the film provides for the concept of obsession and whether it regards obsession as a primarily negative or potentially positive state of mind.

Fatal Attraction, Field of Dreams, The Piano, House of Games, Jacob's Ladder, Spellbound, L.A. Story, Death Becomes Her, Crumb, Unstrung Heroes, Disclosure, Tom and Viv

6

Journeys in Sexuality and Gender

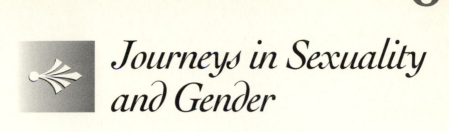

No one who accepts the view that the censorship is the chief reason for dream distortion will be surprised to learn from the results of dream interpretation that most of the dreams of adults are traced back by analysis to erotic wishes.

> SIGMUND FREUD
> *Erotic Wishes and Dreams*

The consciousness of what men will say of a woman who speaks the truth about her passions had roused her from her artist's state of unconsciousness. She could write no more. . . . Her imagination could work no longer. This I believe to be a very common experience with women writers—they are impeded by the extreme conventionality of the other sex.

> VIRGINIA WOOLF
> *Professions for Women*

Warriors and toilers: those seemed, in my boyhood vision, to be the chief destinies for men.

> SCOTT RUSSELL SANDERS
> *The Men We Carry in Our Minds*

Causality and the Inward Journey

What causes people to have certain kinds of dreams or to remember a particular dream? Do people's gender concerns influence their dreams? How do dreams and sexual fantasies influence an individual's waking life and personal relationships? Why can certain people use their dreams to make their lives richer while others are overwhelmed by their unconscious fears? All of these questions, central to the issues raised in *Dreams and Inward Journeys*, are also issues of causality.

As you reflect on your dreams and emotions, working to understand what you read and to create clear, focused arguments, causal analysis will be a fundamental part of your thinking process. Causal analysis can help you to understand your inner life, to interpret your relationship to the public world, and to explain how and why things happen the way they do. Finding connections that exist between one event and another event, understanding how one event led to or produced another event, and speculating about the consequences of earlier events—all involve causal reasoning.

Observing and Collecting Information

People naturally search for solutions to mental dilemmas and physical problems, wanting to be able to explain why something occurred and how they can improve the situation. In most cases, the more confident we are about our explanations of any event, the better we feel. Being observant and collecting information about both your inner and outer world will increase your chances of making accurate causal connections and inferences about the sources and meanings of your dreams and the public events that are influencing you. For example, if you are keeping a dream journal, you may find that after writing down your dreams for a while you notice repeated images or situations that may reflect your psychological concerns and may help you to draw more accurate inferences about your inner concerns.

Whether you are studying dreams, literature, or current events, you need to be sure that the causal connections you make are sound ones. You should observe carefully and consider all possible causes, not simply the obvious, immediate ones. For example, student writer Julie Bordner Apodaca began her preparation to write "Gay Marriage: Why the Resistance?" included in this chapter with her own personal observations of biased comments about gay relationships, comments that had come up in conversations she had with other students and people in her community. These comments led her to consider some of the deeper, underlying causes for homophobia. She searched for information about the causes through further conversations and interviews with students and with her own mother, who is a psychotherapist. Julie also read a number of books and magazine articles on the subject, some of which are referred to in the bibliography that accompanies her essay. Ultimately, Apodaca found so many causes of bias that she chose to classify them into several different categories: religious, sociopolitical, and medical.

In writing a causal analysis, whether of a dream, a short story, or a social issue, it is also essential that you provide adequate evidence, of both a factual and a logical nature, for the conclusions that you draw. You may believe that you understand the causes involved quite clearly, but perceiving these connections for yourself is not enough; you must recreate for your reader, in clear and specific language, the mental process you went through to arrive at your conclusions. Methodically and carefully questioning your own thought process will help you to clarify your insights, to generate new ideas and evidence that can be used to support your analysis, and to avoid logical fallacies.

Causal Logical Fallacies

People create connections between events or personal issues about which they feel strongly, often rushing their thinking process to a hasty conclusion. One of the most common causal errors, the post hoc fallacy ("after this, therefore because of this"), mistakenly attempts to create a causal connection between unrelated events that follow each other closely in time. But a sequence in time is not at all the same thing as a causal sequence. In fact, much "magical" or superstitious thinking relative to dreams and daily life is based on faulty causal analysis of sequences in time. For instance, people may carry a burden of guilt because of accidental sequential parallels between their inner thoughts and outer events, such as a dream of the death of a loved one and a subsequent death or accident.

Another common problem in thinking and writing about causality is causal oversimplification, in which a person argues that one thing caused something to happen, when in fact a number of different elements worked together to produce a major effect or outcome. For example, one's dream of flying may have been inspired in part by watching a television program about pilots the night before; yet other causes may also be present: one's love for performing or "showing off" or one's joy about a recent accomplishment. When trying to apply a broad theory to explain many individual cases, thinkers often become involved in causal oversimplification. We can ask, for example, if Freud's theories about the sexual content and sources of dreams really explain the entire range of dream stories and imagery. What other causes and sources might he have neglected to consider? Asking about other possible causal relations not covered by a causal thesis will help you to test the soundness of your analysis.

The "slippery slope" fallacy is also of particular relevance to the issues explored in this text. In the slippery slope fallacy, a reasoned analysis of causes and effects is replaced by a reaction of fear, in which a person might argue that if one seemingly insignificant event is allowed to happen, there will be serious consequences. Of course, in some cases this may be true: if one isn't careful about sexually transmitted diseases, there is the possibility that a person may get AIDS and eventually die. In most cases, however, theorizing about dreadful future events can become a way of validating irrational fears, can become a way of providing an excuse for maintaining the status quo. Recognizing the slippery slope fallacies both in others' thinking and within one's own thinking can help you to free yourself from irrational fears and develop better critical thinking skills.

Good causal reasoning can lead you closer to understanding and developing theories and explanations for the multiple causes and effects of the issues and events you encounter in your reading and in your own life. With an awareness of the complexities of causal thinking, you should be able to think and to write more critically, clearly, and persuasively.

THEMATIC INTRODUCTION

 People in all cultures have always defined themselves in relationships to their sexuality and sex roles. Gender roles supported by
social values and customs influence each person's inner and public
life, helping to determine the extent to which a person assumes
positions of power and leadership or roles as a nurturer. In the same way, the
extent to which a person's sexual orientation is accepted by family, peers, and
by society at large also plays a major role in an individual's ability to find peace
and contentment. Furthermore, the rapid shifts in social definitions of acceptable gender role behavior have led many people to feel confused about their
gender identity and about what constitutes appropriate behavior toward the
"opposite sex" or toward individuals with sexual orientations different from
their own.

Each of the readings selected for this chapter relates to a particular issue of
controversy related to sexuality and gender. We begin with a selection from
Plato's *Symposium.* "Aristophanes' Speech," delivered at a dinner party for the
leading poets and intellectuals in Athens. This fictional speech presents a
complex philosophy of love that is rooted in beliefs that are different from
those in the Judeo-Christian tradition.

The next selection, "Erotic Wishes and Dreams," presents Sigmund
Freud's theory about dream interpretation; he argues that the real content of our dreams is sexual desire and erotic wish fulfillment. In "Professions for Women" Virginia Woolf explains why women often feel inhib-
ited about expressing their deepest unconscious thoughts and dreams:
Woolf believes that women have internalized a masculine social code—to
write about their deepest passions and sexual feelings is not feminine and
therefore is unacceptable. Like Woolf, Maxine Hong Kingston portrays
a culture where women are limited by men's expectations of them. Her
fictional narrative, "No Name Woman," provides a portrait of a woman
who is tormented and victimized by rigid, traditional gender roles.

The next two selections in the chapter, Julius Lester's "Being a Boy" and
Scott Russell Sanders's "The Men We Carry in Our Minds," offer firsthand
accounts of what it was like to grow up as a boy. Lester's essay concentrates
on his adolescent awkwardness and inability to act sufficiently masculine to
meet his own standards and those of his peers, whereas Scott Russell Sanders
shows us how the men whom he knew as a young boy were not leaders—
they were men chained to a life of physical challenge that finally compromised
their health, or they were men who were brought up to be killers. In
Sanders's world, working-class boys had no positive male role models.

The next two selections are stories; they explore the intense conflicts that
the main characters, who are couples, have about the consequences of their
sexuality and gender roles. In "The Two" Gloria Naylor shows how partners
in a lesbian relationship have conflicts that are similar to those experienced in
a traditional marriage, while showing the added stress that a nontraditional

relationship has because of what people in the immediate community say and think about the women. In Ernest Hemingway's "Hills Like White Elephants" the dialogue between the young couple having drinks at a train station reveals that each has different expectations about relationships and love.

Two poems follow. "The Dream" by Pablo Neruda traces a couple's separation and reconciliation through attention to the feelings in their dreams. Chitra Divakaruni's "Nargis' Toilette" tells about the world of a veiled Muslim bride-to-be and of the joy of the women who help prepare the bride for her arranged marriage. The bride's feelings are not explored, making us wonder if her expectations and needs will ever be taken into account in the marriage.

The two student essays in this chapter also focus on issues of gender. In "On Not Being a Girl" Rosa Contreras explores the difficulties she faced growing up in a Mexican American family that expected her to follow the gender roles of her traditional-culture immigrant family and also expected her to attend college. In "Gay Marriage: Why the Resistance?" Julie Bordner Apodaca writes about the political and social struggles for gay relationships to be recognized as legitimate family units and considers some of the reasons why it is difficult for such relationships to gain acceptance.

 ## Plato

"Aristophanes' Speech in the Symposium*"*

The Symposium *of Plato is a fictional philosophic dialogue on the nature of love. The setting is a dinner party for a number of Athens's prominent dramatists and intellectuals at the home of the dramatic poet Agathon to celebrate his victory in the annual dramatic competition for tragedy. In the following speech, the comic poet and dramatist Aristophanes gives his views on the power of intense emotional and sexual love, the origins of androgyny, and the importance of love as a means of total fulfillment.*

JOURNAL

Write about the power of love in your own life and why you feel that people need love. What kind of love do we most need?

1   Men seem to me to have failed completely to comprehend the power of Eros, for if they did comprehend it, they would have built to him the greatest altars and temples and offered the greatest sacrifices, whereas he is given none of these honors, although he should have them most of all. For he is the most friendly to man of all the gods, his helper and physician in those ills, which if cured, would

bring about the greatest happiness for the human race. Therefore I shall try to initiate you into the nature of his power, and you will be the teachers of others.

2   But first you must understand the nature of mortals and what experiences they have suffered. For our nature long ago was not the same as it is now but different. In the beginning humankind had three sexes, not two, male and female, as now; but there was in addition, a third, which partook of both the others; now it has vanished and only its name survives. At that time there was a distinct sex, the androgynous both in appearance and in name, partaking of the characteristics of both the male and the female, but now it does not exist, except for the name, which is retained as a term of reproach.

3   Furthermore every human being was in shape a round entity, with back and sides forming a circle; he had four hands, an equal number of feet, one head, with two faces exactly alike but each looking in opposite directions, set upon a circular neck, four ears, two sets of genitals and everything else as one might imagine from this description. He walked upright just as we do now in whichever direction (backward or forward) he wished. When they were anxious to run, they made use of all their limbs (which were then eight in number) by turning cartwheels, just like acrobats, and quickly carried themselves along by this circular movement.

4   The sexes were three in number and of such a kind for these reasons; originally the male was sprung from the sun, the female from the earth, and the third, partaking of both male and female, from the moon, because the moon partakes of both the sun and the earth; and indeed because they were just like their parents, their shape was spherical and their movement circular. Their strength and might were terrifying; they had great ambitions, and they made an attack on the gods. What Homer relates about Ephialtes and Otus and their attempt to climb up to heaven and assail the gods is told also about these beings as well.

5   Zeus and the other gods took counsel about what they should do, and they were at a loss. They could not bring themselves to kill them (just as they had obliterated the race of the giants with blasts of thunder and lightning), for they would deprive themselves of the honors and sacrifices which they received from mortals, nor could they allow them to continue in their insolence. After painful deliberation Zeus declared that he had a plan. "I think that I have a way," he said, "whereby mortals may continue to exist but will cease from their insolence by being made weaker. For I shall cut each of them in two, and they will be at the same time both weaker and more useful to us because of their greater numbers, and they will walk upright on two legs. If they still seem to be insolent and do not wish to be quiet, I shall split them again and they will hop about on one leg."

6   With these words he cut human beings in two, just as one splits fruit which is to be preserved or divides an egg with a hair. As he bisected each one, he ordered Apollo to turn the face with the half of the neck attached around to the side that was cut, so that man, by being able to see the signs of his bisection, might be better behaved; and he ordered him to heal the marks of the cutting. Apollo turned the face around and drew together the skin like a pouch with drawstrings on what is now called the belly and tied it in the middle making a single knot, which is called the navel. He smoothed out the many other wrinkles and molded the chest

using a tool like that of cobblers when they smooth out the wrinkles in the leather on their last. But he left a few on their bellies around their navels as a reminder of their experience of long ago.

7   And so when their original nature had been split in two, each longed for his other half, and when they encountered it they threw their arms about one another and embraced in their desire to grow together again and they died through hunger and neglect of the other necessities of life because of their wish to do nothing separated from each other. Whenever one of a pair died, the other that was left searched out and embraced another mate, either the half of a whole female (which we now call woman) or of a male. Thus they perished, and Zeus in his pity devised another plan: he transferred their genitals to the front (for until now they had been on the outside, and they begot and bore their offspring not in conjunction with one another but by emission into the earth, like grasshoppers).

8   And so Zeus moved their genitals to the front and thereby had them reproduce by intercourse with one another, the male with the female. He did this for two reasons: if a man united with a woman they would propagate the race and it would survive, but if a male united with a male, they might find satisfaction and freedom to turn to their pursuits and devote themselves to the other concerns of life. From such early times, then, love for one another has been implanted in the human race, a love that unifies in his attempt to make one out of two and to heal and restore the basic nature of humankind.

9   Each of us therefore is but a broken tally, half a man, since we have been cut just like the side of a flatfish and made two instead of one. All who are a section halved from the beings of the common sex (which was at that time called androgynous) are lovers of women; many adulterers come from this source, including women who love men and are promiscuous. All women who are a section halved from the female do not pay any attention to men but rather turn to women; lesbians come from this source. All who are a section halved from the male pursue males; and all the while they are young, since they are slices, as it were, of the male, they love men and take delight in lying by their side and embracing them; these are the best of boys and youths because they are the most manly in nature. Some say that they are without shame, but they do not tell the truth. For they behave the way they do not through shamelessness but through courage, manliness, and masculinity as they cling to what is similar to them.

10   Here is a great proof of what I say. Only men of this sort proceed to politics when they grow up. Once they are men they love boys and do not turn their thoughts to marriage and procreation naturally but are forced to by law or convention; it is enough for them to spend their lives together unmarried. In short, then, a man like this is a lover of men as a boy and a lover of boys as a man, always clinging to what is akin to his nature. Therefore whenever anyone of this sort and every other kind of person encounters the other half that is actually his, then they are struck in an amazing way with affection, kinship, and love, virtually unwilling to be separated from each other for even a short time. These are the ones who spend their whole life together, although they would not be able to tell what they wish to gain from each other. No one would imagine that it is on account of their

sexual association that the one enjoys intensely being with the other; clearly the soul of each desires something else, which it cannot describe but only hint at obscurely.

11   Suppose Hephaestus, his tools in hand, were to stand over them as they lay together and ask: "O mortals, what is it that you wish to gain from one another?" Or when they were at a loss for an answer he were to ask again: "Is this what you desire, to be together always as much as possible so as never to be separated from each other night and day? If this is what you desire, I am willing to fuse and weld you together so that the two of you may become one and the same person and as long as you live, you may both live united in one being, and when you die, you may die together as one instead of two, united even in the realms of Hades. Just see if this would be enough to satisfy your longing." We know that there is not one person who, after hearing these words, would deny their truth and say that he wanted something else, but he would believe that he had heard exactly what he had desired for a long time—namely, to be melted in unison with his beloved, and the two of them become one. The reason is that our ancient nature was thus and we were whole. And so love is merely the name for the desire and pursuit of the whole.

12   Previously, as I have said, we were one, but now because of our wickedness we have been split by the god (just as the Arcadians have been split up by the Spartans). There is too the fear that if we do not behave properly toward the gods we may again be bisected, just as dice that are divided as tallies, and go around like the figures cut in profile on steles, split right along their noses. For this reason all mortals must be urged to pay reverence to the gods so that we may avoid suffering further bisection and win what Eros has to give as our guide and leader. Let no one act in opposition to him—whoever does incurs the enmity of the gods. For if we are reconciled and friendly to the god of love, we shall find and win our very own beloved, an achievement few today attain.

13   Eryximachus is not to suppose in ridicule of my speech that I am referring only to Pausanias and Agathon, since they perhaps happen to be of the class of those who love males by nature. I am referring rather to all men and women when I say that the happiness of our race lies in the fulfillment of love; each must find the beloved that is his and be restored to his original nature. If this ancient state was best, of necessity the nearest to it in our present circumstances must be best— namely, to find a beloved who is of one and the same mind and nature. It is right to praise Eros as the god responsible; he helps us most in our present life by bringing us to what is kindred to us and offers the greatest hopes for the future. If we pay reverence to the gods, he will restore us to our ancient nature and with his cure make us happy and blessed.

Questions for Discussion

1. Why did Zeus punish human beings? How were they reformed? How did the punishment and reformation change the way people related to one another sexually?

2. From where did each of the three sexes originate? What do their places of origin reveal?
3. Describe the "third sex" that Aristophanes believes existed long ago. Why did the third sex disappear and "androgynous" become only a term of reproach?
4. According to Aristophanes how were human beings shaped and constituted long ago?
5. Does Aristophanes' speech give you new insight into lesbian and homosexual behavior? Why? Explain.
6. According to Aristophanes, why do people yearn to be "melted in unison" with the beloved? What is the highest form of love? Why was it so important for the Greeks to praise the god Eros?

Ideas for Writing

1. Write a fantasy or myth of your own about the origins of love. Why and how did people come to value, appreciate, and need love?
2. Develop your journal entry into an essay.

 # Sigmund Freud

Erotic Wishes and Dreams

Known as the founder of the psychoanalytic method and of concepts such as the unconscious mind and the Oedipus complex, Sigmund Freud (1856–1939) was also a pioneer in the scientific study of dreams and human sexuality. Freud spent most of his life in Vienna, where he practiced psychoanalysis and published many important studies on psychology and dream interpretation as well as on cultural studies that focus on psychological interpretations of art and history. His works in-clude Interpretation of Dreams *(1900),* Totem and Taboo, *and* Leonardo da Vinci: A Study in Psychosexuality. *In "Erotic Wishes and Dreams," from his popular explanation of dream theory,* On Dreams, *Freud presents his ideas on dream symbolism and expresses his conviction that dreams focus on sexual needs and fantasies, although sometimes in a disguised form.*

JOURNAL

Write about a dream you have had that you consider explicitly or implicitly sexual in its content. Did you consider the dream to be a form of wish fulfillment, or could there have been some other explanation of the dream and its images?

1   No one who accepts the view that the censorship is the chief reason for dream
    distortion will be surprised to learn from the results of dream interpretation
that most of the dreams of adults are traced back by analysis to *erotic wishes*. This
assertion is not aimed at dreams with an *undisguised* sexual content, which are no
doubt familiar to all dreamers from their own experience and are as a rule the only
ones to be described as "sexual dreams." Even dreams of this latter kind offer
enough surprises in their choice of the people whom they make into sexual objects, in their disregard of all the limitations which the dreamer imposes in his
waking life upon his sexual desires, and by their many strange details, hinting at
what are commonly known as "perversions." A great many other dreams, however, which show no sign of being erotic in their manifest content, are revealed by
the work of interpretation in analysis as sexual wish fulfillments; and, on the other
hand, analysis proves that a great many of the thoughts left over from the activity
of waking life as "residues of the previous day" only find their way to representation in dreams through the assistance of repressed erotic wishes.

2   There is no theoretical necessity why this should be so; but to explain the fact
it may be pointed out that no other group of instincts has been submitted to such
far-reaching suppression by the demands of cultural education, while at the same
time the sexual instincts are also the ones which, in most people, find it easiest to
escape from the control of the highest mental agencies. Since we have become ac-
quainted with infantile sexuality, which is often so unobtrusive in its manifesta-
tions and is always overlooked and misunderstood, we are justified in saying that
almost every civilized man retains the infantile forms of sexual life in some respect
or other. We can thus understand how it is that repressed infantile sexual wishes
provide the most frequent and strongest motive forces for the construction of
dreams.*

3   There is only one method by which a dream which expresses erotic wishes can
succeed in appearing innocently nonsexual in its manifest content. The material
of the sexual ideas must not be represented as such, but must be replaced in the
content of the dream by hints, allusions and similar forms of indirect representation. But, unlike other forms of indirect representation, that which is employed in
dreams must not be immediately intelligible. The modes of representation which
fulfill these conditions are usually described as "symbols" of the things which they
represent. Particular interest has been directed to them since it has been noticed
that dreamers speaking the same language make use of the same symbols, and that
in some cases, indeed, the use of the same symbols extends beyond the use of the
same language. Since dreamers themselves are unaware of the meaning of the
symbols they use, it is difficult at first sight to discover the source of the connection between the symbols and what they replace and represent. The fact itself,
however, is beyond doubt, and it is important for the technique of dream interpretation. For, with the help of a knowledge of dream symbolism, it is possible to understand the meaning of separate elements of the content of a dream or separate
pieces of a dream or in some cases even whole dreams, without having to ask the

*See my *Three Essays on the Theory of Sexuality* (1905) [Author's note].

dreamer for his associations. Here we are approaching the popular ideal of translating dreams and on the other hand are returning to the technique of interpretation used by the ancients, to whom dream interpretation was identical with interpretation by means of symbols.

4   Although the study of dream symbols is far from being complete, we are in a
position to lay down with certainty a number of general statements and a quantity
of special information on the subject. There are some symbols which bear a single
meaning almost universally: thus the Emperor and Empress (or the King and
Queen) stand for the parents, rooms represent women and their entrances and exits the openings of the body. The majority of dream symbols serve to represent
persons, parts of the body and activities invested with erotic interest; in particular,
the genitals are represented by a number of often very surprising symbols, and the
greatest variety of objects are employed to denote them symbolically. Sharp
weapons, long and stiff objects, such as tree trunks and sticks, stand for the male
genital; while cupboards, boxes, carriages or ovens may represent the uterus. In
such cases as these the *tertium comparationis*, the common element in these substi-
tutions, is immediately intelligible; but there are other symbols in which it is not
so easy to grasp the connection. Symbols such as a staircase or going upstairs, representing sexual intercourse, a tie or cravat for the male organ, or wood for the female one, provoke our unbelief until we can arrive at an understanding of the
symbolic relation underlying them by some other means. Moreover a whole number of dream symbols are bisexual and can relate to the male or female genitals according to the context.

5   Some symbols are universally disseminated and can be met with in all dreamers
belonging to a single linguistic or cultural group; there are others which occur
only within the most restricted and individual limits, symbols constructed by an
individual out of his own ideational material. Of the former class we can distinguish some whose claim to represent sexual ideas is immediately justified by linguistic usage (such, for instance, as those derived from agriculture, e.g., "fertiliza-
tion" or "seed") and others whose relation to sexual ideas appears to reach back
into the very earliest ages and to the most obscure depths of our conceptual functioning. The power of constructing symbols has not been exhausted in our own
days in the case of either of the two sorts of symbols which I have distinguished at
the beginning of this paragraph. Newly discovered objects (such as airships) are,
as we may observe, at once adopted as universally available sexual symbols.

6   It would, incidentally, be a mistake to expect that if we had a still profounder
knowledge of dream symbolism (of the "language of dreams") we could do without
asking the dreamer for his associations to the dream and go back entirely to the
technique of dream interpretation of antiquity. Quite apart from individual symbols and oscillations in the use of universal ones, one can never tell whether any
particular element in the content of a dream is to be interpreted symbolically or in
its proper sense, and one can be certain that the *whole* content of a dream is not to
be interpreted symbolically. A knowledge of dream symbolism will never do more
than enable us to translate certain constituents of the dream content, and will not
relieve us of the necessity for applying the technical rules which I gave earlier. It

will, however, afford the most valuable assistance to interpretation precisely at points at which the dreamer's associations are insufficient or fail altogether.

7   Dream symbolism is also indispensable to an understanding of what are known as "typical" dreams, which are common to everyone, and of "recurrent" dreams in individuals.

8   If the account I have given in this short discussion of the symbolic mode of expression in dreams appears incomplete, I can justify my neglect by drawing attention to one of the most important pieces of knowledge that we possess on this subject. Dream symbolism extends far beyond dreams: it is not peculiar to dreams, but exercises a similar dominating influence on representation in fairy tales, myths and legends, in jokes and in folklore. It enables us to trace the intimate connections between dreams and these latter productions. We must not suppose that dream symbolism is a creation of the dream work; it is in all probability a characteristic of the unconscious thinking which provides the dream work with the material for condensation, displacement and dramatization.

Questions for Discussion

1. Why does Freud believe that "repressed infantile sexual wishes" are the strongest motivation behind dreams and their primary content? Does he provide convincing evidence for this belief?

2. How might a dream express erotic wishes and at the same time appear innocent of sexual content? What might cause this apparent contradiction?

3. How does Freud define "symbols" as they appear in dreams? What examples does he provide? Do these seem like sexual symbols to you?

4. How does Freud compare traditional, culturally universal dream symbols with more modern symbols based on technological inventions? Can you think of modern dream symbols that have sexual implications?

5. According to Freud, why is it always a mistake to create dream interpretations without investigating the dreamer's own associations with the symbols from his or her dreams? Do you agree with Freud that popular books which list the "meanings" of dream symbols are basically worthless? Explain your position.

6. What is the relationship between dream symbolism, the unconscious mind, and more literary works such as fairy tales, myths, and legends? Do you agree with Freud's comparison and analysis?

Ideas for Writing

1. Apply Freud's theory about the content and symbolism of dreams to a dream you have had; then write an interpretive essay about your dream. Did Freud's ideas help you to understand your dream and its causes more clearly? What else might have influenced the imagery and events in your dream?

2. Because Freud's theories about the repressed erotic content and symbolism in dreams can also be applied to fantasy literature such as myths

and fairy tales, many critics have attempted "Freudian" analyses of imaginative literature. Using a "Freudian" or sexual-symbol approach, try to interpret the characters, symbolism, and events of one of the stories or myths in this text. Did you find this approach satisfactory? Why or why not?

 ## Virginia Woolf

Professions for Women

Virginia Woolf (1882–1941) was born in London and educated at home in the library of her father, Victorian biographer Leslie Stephen. With her husband, the novelist Leonard Woolf, she founded the Hogarth Press, which published her novels along with works by Freud and T. S. Eliot. Virginia Woolf, a member of the intellectual and creative Bloomsbury Group, made an important contribution to the public's acceptance of the independent woman writer and artist through her novels and essays. In her fiction, Woolf's stream-of-consciousness style focuses on private memories and dreamlike, associative imagery. Her technique is best exemplified in the novels Mrs. Dalloway *(1925),* To the Lighthouse *(1927), and* The Waves *(1931). In the following selection, "Professions for Women," which was originally delivered as a lecture to a group of working women, Woolf discusses some of the difficulties that women encounter when trying to develop careers as professional writers.*

JOURNAL

Write about why you think that writing would be a difficult profession for a woman. Discuss particular strengths that you think women might possess that would make them good writers.

1   When your secretary invited me to come here, she told me that your Society is concerned with the employment of women and she suggested that I might tell you something about my own professional experiences. It is true I am a woman; it is true I am employed; but what professional experiences have I had? It is difficult to say. My profession is literature; and in that profession there are fewer experiences for women than in any other, with the exception of the stage—fewer, I mean, that are peculiar to women. For the road was cut many years ago—by Fanny Burney, by Aphra Behn, by Harriet Martineau, by Jane Austen, by George Eliot—many famous women, and many more unknown and forgotten, have been before me, making the path smooth, and regulating my steps. Thus, when I came

to write, there were very few material obstacles in my way. Writing was a reputable and harmless occupation. The family peace was not broken by the scratching of a pen. No demand was made upon the family purse. For ten and sixpence one can buy paper enough to write all the plays of Shakespeare—if one has a mind that way. Pianos and models, Paris, Vienna and Berlin, masters and mistresses, are not needed by a writer. The cheapness of writing is, of course, the reason why women have succeeded as writers before they have succeeded in the other professions.

2   But to tell you my story—it is a simple one. You have only got to figure to yourselves a girl in a bedroom with a pen in her hand. She had only to move that pen from left to right—from ten o'clock to one. Then it occurred to her to do what is simple and cheap enough for all—to slip a few of those pages into an envelope, fix a penny stamp in the corner, and drop the envelope into the red box at the corner. It was thus that I became a journalist; and my effort was rewarded on the first day of the following month—a very glorious day it was for me—by a letter from an editor containing a cheque for one pound ten shillings and sixpence. But to show you how little I deserve to be called a professional woman, how little I know of the struggles and difficulties of such lives, I have to admit that instead of spending that sum upon bread and butter, rent, shoes and stockings, or butcher's bills, I went out and bought a cat—a beautiful cat, a Persian cat, which very soon involved me in bitter disputes with my neighbours.

3   What could be easier than to write articles and to buy Persian cats with the profits? But wait a moment. Articles have to be about something. Mine, I seem to remember, was about a novel by a famous man. And while I was writing this review, I discovered that if I were going to review books I should need to do battle with a certain phantom. And the phantom was a woman, and when I came to know her better I called her after the heroine of a famous poem, The Angel in the House. It was she who used to come between me and my paper when I was writing reviews. It was she who bothered me and wasted my time and so tormented me that at last I killed her. You who come of a younger and happier generation may not have heard of her—you may not know what I mean by the Angel in the House. I will describe her as shortly as I can. She was intensely sympathetic. She was immensely charming. She was utterly unselfish. She excelled in the difficult arts of family life. She sacrificed herself daily. If there was a chicken, she took the leg; if there was a draught she sat in it—in short she was so constituted that she never had a mind or a wish of her own, but preferred to sympathize always with the minds and wishes of others. Above all—I need not say it—she was pure. Her purity was supposed to be her chief beauty—her blushes, her great grace. In those days—the last of Queen Victoria—every house had its Angel. And when I came to write I encountered her with the very first words. The shadow of her wings fell on my page; I heard the rustling of her skirts in the room. Directly, that is to say, I took my pen in hand to review that novel by a famous man, she slipped behind me and whispered: "My dear, you are a young woman. You are writing about a book that has been written by a man. Be sympathetic; be tender; flatter; deceive; use all the arts and wiles of our sex. Never let anybody guess that you have a mind of your

own. Above all, be pure." And she made as if to guide my pen. I now record the one act for which I take some credit to myself, though the credit rightly belongs to some excellent ancestors of mine who left me a certain sum of money—shall we say five hundred pounds a year?—so that it was not necessary for me to depend solely on charm for my living. I turned upon her and caught her by the throat. I did my best to kill her. My excuse, if I were to be had up in a court of law, would be that I acted in self-defence. Had I not killed her she would have killed me. She would have plucked the heart out of my writing. For, as I found, directly I put pen to paper, you cannot review even a novel without having a mind of your own, without expressing what you think to be the truth about human relations, morality, sex. And all these questions, according to the Angel in the House, cannot be dealt with freely and openly by women; they must charm, they must conciliate, they must—to put it bluntly—tell lies if they are to succeed. Thus, whenever I felt the shadow of her wing or the radiance of her halo upon my page, I took up the inkpot and flung it at her. She died hard. Her fictitious nature was of great assistance to her. It is far harder to kill a phantom than a reality. She was always creeping back when I thought I had despatched her. Though I flatter myself that I killed her in the end, the struggle was severe; it took much time that had better have been spent upon learning Greek grammar; or in roaming the world in search of adventures. But it was a real experience; it was an experience that was bound to befall all women writers at that time. Killing the Angel in the House was part of the occupation of a woman writer.

4   But to continue my story. The Angel was dead; what then remained? You may say that what reminded was a simple and common object—a young woman in a bedroom with an inkpot. In other words, now that she had rid herself of falsehood, that young woman had only to be herself. Ah, but what is "herself"? I mean, what is a woman? I assure you, I do not know. I do not believe that you know. I do not believe that anybody can know until she has expressed herself in all the arts and professions open to human skill. That indeed is one of the reasons why I have come here—out of respect for you, who are in process of showing us by your experiments what a woman is, who are in process of providing us, by your failures and successes, with that extremely important piece of information.

5   But to continue the story of my professional experiences, I made one pound ten and six by my first review; and I bought a Persian cat with the proceeds. Then I grew ambitious. A Persian cat is all very well, I said; but a Persian cat is not enough. I must have a motor car. And it was thus that I became a novelist—for it is a very strange thing that people will give you a motor car if you will tell them a story. It is a still stranger thing that there is nothing so delightful in the world as telling stories. It is far pleasanter than writing reviews of famous novels. And yet, if I am to obey your secretary and tell you my professional experiences as a novelist, I must tell you about a very strange experience that befell me as a novelist. And to understand it you must try first to imagine a novelist's state of mind. I hope I am not giving away professional secrets if I say that a novelist's chief desire is to be as unconscious as possible. He has to induce in himself a state of perpetual lethargy. He wants life to proceed with the utmost quiet and regularity. He wants

to see the same faces, to read the same books, to do the same things day after day, month after month, while he is writing, so that nothing may break the illusion in which he is living—so that nothing may disturb or disquiet the mysterious nosings about, feelings round, darts, dashes and sudden discoveries of that very shy and illusive spirit, the imagination. I suspect that this state is the same both for men and women. Be that as it may, I want you to imagine me writing a novel in a state of trance. I want you to figure to yourselves a girl sitting with a pen in her hand, which for minutes, and indeed for hours, she never dips into the inkpot. The image that comes to my mind when I think of this girl is the image of a fisherman lying sunk in dreams on the verge of a deep lake with a rod held out over the water. She was letting her imagination sweep unchecked round every rock and cranny of the world that lies submerged in the depths of our unconscious being. Now came the experience, the experience that I believe to be far commoner with women writers than with men. The line raced through the girl's fingers. Her imagination had rushed away. It had sought the pools, the depths, the dark places where the largest fish slumber. And then there was a smash. There was an explosion. There was foam and confusion. The imagination had dashed itself against something hard. The girl was roused from her dream. She was indeed in a state of the most acute and difficult distress. To speak without figure she had thought of something, something about the body, about the passions which it was unfitting for her as a woman to say. Men, her reason told her, would be shocked. The consciousness of what men will say of a woman who speaks the truth about her passions had roused her from her artist's state of unconsciousness. She could write no more. The trance was over. Her imagination could work no longer. This I believe to be a very common experience with women writers—they are impeded by the extreme conventionality of the other sex. For though men sensibly allow themselves great freedom in these respects, I doubt that they realize or can control the extreme severity with which they condemn such freedom in women.

6   These then were two very genuine experiences of my own. These were two of the adventures of my professional life. The first—killing the Angel in the House—I think I solved. She died. But the second, telling the truth about my own experiences as a body, I do not think I solved. I doubt that any woman has solved it yet. The obstacles against her are still immensely powerful—and yet they are very difficult to define. Outwardly, what is simpler than to write books? Outwardly, what obstacles are there for a woman rather than for a man? Inwardly, I think, the case is very different; she has still many ghosts to fight, many prejudices to overcome. Indeed it will be a long time still, I think, before a woman can sit down to write a book without finding a phantom to be slain, a rock to be dashed against. And if this is so in literature, the freest of all professions for women, how is it in the new professions which you are now for the first time entering?

7   Those are the questions that I should like, had I time, to ask you. And indeed, if I have laid stress upon these professional experiences of mine, it is because I believe that they are, though in different forms, yours also. Even when the path is nominally open—when there is nothing to prevent a woman from being a doctor, a lawyer, a civil servant—there are many phantoms and obstacles, as I believe,

looming in her way. To discuss and define them is I think of greater value and importance; for thus only can the labor be shared, the difficulties be solved. But besides this, it is necessary also to discuss the ends and the aims for which we are fighting, for which we are doing battle with these formidable obstacles. Those aims cannot be taken for granted; they must be perpetually questioned and examined. The whole position, as I see it—here in this hall surrounded by women practising for the first time in history I know not how many different professions—is one of extraordinary interest and importance. You have won rooms of your own in the house hitherto exclusively owned by men. You are able, though not without great labour and effort, to pay the rent. You are earning your five hundred pounds a year. But this freedom is only a beginning; the room is your own, but it is still bare. It has to be furnished; it has to be decorated; it has to be shared. How are you going to furnish it, how are you going to decorate it? With whom are you going to share it, and upon what terms? These, I think are questions of the utmost importance and interest. For the first time in history you are able to ask them; for the first time you are able to decide for yourselves what the answers should be. Willingly would I stay and discuss those questions and answers—but not tonight. My time is up; and I must cease.

Questions for Discussion

1. What is the purpose of Woolf's introductory paragraph? What irony is suggested by her comments on the "cheapness" of writing?
2. What obstacles, both inner and outer, does Woolf discuss which must be overcome in order for women to accomplish their professional goals in writing and in other careers?
3. What are the origins and qualities of the "angel" or phantom that torments Woolf when she tries to write reviews of men's work? How does the "angel" represent traditional gender roles for women?
4. Why is it so difficult for Woolf to defeat the angel? Why is it harder for Woolf to tell the truth about the "body" than to kill the angel?
5. What image does Woolf develop to express the way in which her gender role inhibits her freedom and her imagination as a writer? Do women today face similar obstacles to writing about their passions and sexuality? Do you agree that for a woman to be an honest and powerful writer she must be able to write openly about her passions?
6. Woolf says that after a woman rids herself of "falsehood" (the Angel in the House), she must then discover herself. Why is it difficult at that point for a female writer to define what it means to be a woman? What path does Woolf believe will lead women to self-discovery and a redefinition of womanhood?

Ideas for Writing

1. Do you think that issues of gender and sexuality are as inhibiting for women today as they were when Woolf wrote? Write an essay in which

you compare and contrast the difficulties women writers of Woolf's
generation experienced with the obstacles facing women writing today.

2. Woolf's essay with its key image of a girl as a "fisherman . . . on the
   verge of a deep lake with a rod held out over the water" suggests that,
   for the woman writer, writing is nurtured by the unconscious and is an
   unpredictable process. Write an essay in which you reflect on the way
   the unconscious mind influences your writing process and the choices
   you make in daily life.

  ## Maxine Hong Kingston

No Name Woman

*Maxine Hong Kingston (b. 1940) is from Stockton, California, where she grew
up listening to the stories her mother would tell about Chinese village life. Hong
Kingston graduated from the University of California at Berkeley and taught high
school and college English in Hawaii for a number of years before returning to the
San Francisco Bay Area. Books by Hong Kingston include a personal memoir,*
The Woman Warrior: Memories of a Childhood among Ghosts *(1976); a
historical account of Chinese-American life,* China Men *(1980); and a novel,*
Tripmaster Monkey: His Fake Book *(1989). The following selection from* The
Woman Warrior *tells one of the stories Maxine Hong Kingston's mother told her
about an aunt in China who becomes a "no name woman" and loses her place in
the life of the community.*

JOURNAL

Recount a story that someone in your family told you when you were a child to
warn you of the dangers of adult life and sexuality.

1   "You must not tell anyone," my mother said, "what I am about to tell you. In
China your father had a sister who killed herself. She jumped into the family well.
We say that your father has all brothers because it is as if she had never been born.

2   "In 1924 just a few days after our village celebrated seventeen hurry-up weddings—to make sure that every young man who went 'out on the road' would re-
sponsibly come home—your father and his brothers and your grandfather and his
brothers and your aunt's new husband sailed for America, the Gold Mountain. It
was your grandfather's last trip. Those lucky enough to get contracts waved good-
bye from the decks. They fed and guarded the stowaways and helped them off in

Cuba, New York, Bali, Hawaii. 'We'll meet in California next year,' they said. All of them sent money home.

3   "I remember looking at your aunt one day when she and I were dressing; I had not noticed before that she had such a protruding melon of a stomach. But I did not think, 'She's pregnant,' until she began to look like other pregnant women, her shirt pulling and the white tops of her black pants showing. She could not have been pregnant, you see, because her husband had been gone for years. No one said anything. We did not discuss it. In early summer she was ready to have the child, long after the time when it could have been possible.

4   "The village had also been counting. On the night the baby was to be born the villagers raided our house. Some were crying. Like a great saw, teeth strung with lights, files of people walked zigzag across our land, tearing the rice. Their lanterns doubled in the disturbed black water, which drained away through the broken bunds. As the villagers closed in, we could see that some of them, probably men and women we knew well, wore white masks. The people with long hair hung it over their faces. Women with short hair made it stand up on end. Some had tied white bands around their foreheads, arms, and legs.

5   "At first they threw mud and rocks at the house. Then they threw eggs and began slaughtering our stock. We could hear the animals scream their deaths—the roosters, the pigs, a last great roar from the ox. Familiar wild heads flared in our night windows; the villagers encircled us. Some of the faces stopped to peer at us, their eyes rushing like searchlights. The hands flattened against the panes, framed heads, and left red prints.

6   "The villagers broke in the front and the back doors at the same time, even though we had not locked the doors against them. Their knives dripped with the blood of our animals. They smeared blood on the doors and walls. One woman swung a chicken, whose throat she had slit, splattering blood in red arcs about her. We stood together in the middle of our house, in the family hall with the pictures and tables of the ancestors around us, and looked straight ahead.

7   "At that time the house had only two wings. When the men came back, we would build two more to enclose our courtyard and a third one to begin a second courtyard. The villagers rushed through both wings, even your grandparents' rooms, to find your aunt's, which was also mine until the men returned. From this room a new wing for one of the younger families would grow. They ripped up her clothes and shoes and broke her combs, grinding them underfoot. They tore her work from the loom. They scattered the cooking fire and rolled the new weaving in it. We could hear them in the kitchen breaking our bowls and banging the pots. They overturned the great waist-high earthenware jugs; duck eggs, pickled fruits, vegetables burst out and mixed in acrid torrents. The old woman from the next field swept a broom through the air and loosed the spirits-of-the-broom over our heads. 'Pig.' 'Ghost.' 'Pig,' they sobbed and scolded while they ruined our house.

8   "When they left, they took sugar and oranges to bless themselves. They cut pieces from the dead animals. Some of them took bowls that were not broken and clothes that were not torn. Afterward we swept up the rice and sewed it back up into sacks. But the smells from the spilled preserves lasted. Your aunt gave birth in

the pigsty that night. The next morning when I went for the water, I found her and the baby plugging up the family well.

9   "Don't let your father know that I told you. He denies her. Now that you have started to menstruate, what happened to her could happen to you. Don't humiliate us. You wouldn't like to be forgotten as if you had never been born. The villagers are watchful."

10   Whenever she had to warn us about life, my mother told stories that ran like this one, a story to grow up on. She tested our strength to establish realities. Those in the emigrant generations who could not reassert brute survival died young and far from home. Those of us in the first American generations have had to figure out how the invisible world that the emigrants built around our childhoods fit in solid America.

11   The emigrants confused the gods by diverting their curses, misleading them with crooked streets and false names. They must try to confuse their offspring as well, who, I suppose, threaten them in similar ways—always trying to get things straight, always trying to name the unspeakable. The Chinese I know hide their names; sojourners take new names when their lives change and guard their real names with silence.

12   Chinese-Americans, when you try to understand what things in you are Chinese, how do you separate what is peculiar to childhood, to poverty, insanities, one family, your mother who marked your growing with stories from what is Chinese? What is Chinese tradition and what is the movies?

13   If I want to learn what clothes my aunt wore, whether flashy or ordinary, I would have to begin, "Remember Father's drowned-in-the-well sister?" I cannot ask that. My mother has told me once and for all the useful parts. She will add nothing unless powered by Necessity, a riverbank that guides her life. She plants vegetable gardens rather than lawns; she carries the odd-shaped tomatoes home from the fields and eats food left for the gods.

14   Whenever we did frivolous things, we used up energy; we flew high kites. We children came up off the ground over the melting cones our parents brought home from work and the American movie on New Year's Day—*Oh, You Beautiful Doll* with Betty Grable one year, and *She Wore a Yellow Ribbon* with John Wayne another year. After the one carnival ride each, we paid in guilt; our tired father counted his change on the dark walk home.

15   Adultery is extravagance. Could people who hatch their own chicks and eat the embryos and the heads for delicacies and boil the feet in vinegar for party food, leaving only the gravel, eating even the gizzard lining—could such people engender a prodigal aunt? To be a woman, to have a daughter in starvation time was a waste enough. My aunt could not have been the lone romantic who gave up everything for sex. Women in the old China did not choose. Some man had commanded her to lie with him and be his secret evil. I wonder whether he masked himself when he joined the raid on her family.

16   Perhaps she encountered him in the fields or on the mountain where the daughters-in-law collected fuel. Or perhaps he first noticed her in the market-

place. He was not a stranger because the village housed no strangers. She had to have dealings with him other than sex. Perhaps he worked an adjoining field, or he sold her the cloth for the dress she sewed and wore. His demand must have surprised, then terrified her. She obeyed him; she always did as she was told.

17   When the family found a young man in the next village to be her husband, she stood tractably beside the best rooster, his proxy, and promised before they met that she would be his forever. She was lucky that he was her age and she would be the first wife, an advantage secure now. The night she first saw him, he had sex with her. Then he left for America. She had almost forgotten what he looked like. When she tried to envision him, she only saw the black and white face in the group photograph the men had had taken before leaving.

18   The other man was not, after all, much different from her husband. They both gave orders: she followed. "If you tell your family, I'll beat you. I'll kill you. Be here again next week." No one talked sex, ever. And she might have separated the rapes from the rest of living if only she did not have to buy her oil from him or gather wood in the same forest. I want her fear to have lasted just as long as rape lasted so that the fear could have been contained. No drawn-out fear. But women at sex hazarded birth and hence lifetimes. The fear did not stop but permeated everywhere. She told the man, "I think I'm pregnant." He organized the raid against her.

19   On nights when my mother and father talked about their life back home, sometimes they mentioned an "outcast table" whose business they still seemed to be settling, their voices tight. In a commensal tradition, where food is precious, the powerful older people made wrongdoers eat alone. Instead of letting them start separate new lives like the Japanese, who could become samurais and geishas, the Chinese family, faces averted but eyes glowering sideways, hung on to the offenders and fed them leftovers. My aunt must have lived in the same house as my parents and eaten at an outcast table. My mother spoke about the raid as if she had seen it, when she and my aunt, a daughter-in-law to a different household, should not have been living together at all. Daughters-in-law lived with their husbands' parents, not their own; a synonym for marriage in Chinese is "taking a daughter-in-law." Her husband's parents could have sold her, mortgaged her, stoned her. But they had sent her back to her own mother and father, a mysterious act hinting at disgraces not told me. Perhaps they had thrown her out to deflect the avengers.

20   She was the only daughter; her four brothers went with her father, husband and uncles "out on the road" and for some years became western men. When the goods were divided among the family, three of the brothers took land, and the youngest, my father, chose an education. After my grandparents gave their daughter away to her husband's family, they had dispensed all the adventure and all the property. They expected her alone to keep the traditional ways, which her brothers, now among the barbarians, could fumble without detection. The heavy, deep-rooted women were to maintain the past against the flood, safe for returning. But the rare urge west had fixed upon our family, and so my aunt crossed boundaries not delineated in space.

21   The work of preservation demands that the feelings playing about in one's guts not be turned into action. Just watch their passing like cherry blossoms. But perhaps my aunt, my forerunner, caught in a slow life, let dreams grow and fade and after some months or years went toward what persisted. Fear at the enormities of the forbidden kept her desires delicate, wire and bone. She looked at a man because she liked the way the hair was tucked behind his ears, or she liked the question-mark line of a long torso curving at the shoulder and straight at the hip. For warm eyes or a soft voice or a slow walk—that's all—a few hairs, a line, a brightness, a sound, a pace, she gave up family. She offered us up for a charm that vanished with tiredness, a pigtail that didn't toss when the wind died. Why, the wrong lighting could erase the dearest thing about him.

22   It could very well have been, however, that my aunt did not take subtle enjoyment of her friend, but, a wild woman, kept rollicking company. Imagining her free with sex doesn't fit, though. I don't know any women like that, or men either. Unless I see her life branching into mine, she gives me no ancestral help.

23   To sustain her being in love, she often worked at herself in the mirror, guessing at the colors and shapes that would interest him, changing them frequently in order to hit on the right combination. She wanted him to look back.

24   On a farm near the sea, a woman who tended her appearance reaped a reputation for eccentricity. All the married women blunt-cut their hair in flaps about their ears or pulled it back in tight buns. No nonsense. Neither style blew easily into heart-catching tangles. And at their weddings they displayed themselves in their long hair for the last time. "It brushed the backs of my knees," my mother tells me. "It was braided, and even so, it brushed the backs of my knees."

25   At the mirror my aunt combed individuality into her bob. A bun could have been contrived to escape into black streamers blowing in the wind or in quiet wisps about her face, but only the older women in our picture album wear buns. She brushed her hair back from her forehead, tucking the flaps behind her ears. She looped a piece of thread, knotted into a circle between her index fingers and thumbs, and ran the double strand across her forehead. When she closed her fingers as if she were making a pair of shadow geese bite, the string twisted together catching the little hairs. Then she pulled the thread away from her skin, ripping the hairs out neatly, her eyes watering from the needles of pain. Opening her fingers, she cleaned the thread, then rolled it along her hairline and the tops of her eyebrows. My mother did the same to me and my sisters and herself. I used to believe that the expression "caught by the short hairs" meant a captive held with a depilatory string. It especially hurt at the temples, but my mother said we were lucky we didn't have to have our feet bound when we were seven. Sisters used to sit on their beds and cry together, she said, as their mothers or their slave removed the bandages for a few minutes each night and let the blood gush back into their veins. I hope that the man my aunt loved appreciated a smooth brow, that he wasn't just a tits-and-ass man.

26   Once my aunt found a freckle on her chin, at a spot that the almanac said predestined her for unhappiness. She dug it out with a hot needle and washed the wound with peroxide.

27   More attention to her looks than these pullings of hairs and pickings at spots would have caused gossip among the villagers. They owned work clothes and good clothes, and they wore good clothes for feasting the new seasons. But since a woman combing her hair hexes beginnings, my aunt rarely found an occasion to look her best. Women looked like great sea snails—the corded wood, babies, and laundry they carried were the whorls on their backs. The Chinese did not admire a bent back; goddesses and warriors stood straight. Still there must have been a marvelous freeing of beauty when a worker laid down her burden and stretched and arched.

28   Such commonplace loveliness, however, was not enough for my aunt. She dreamed of a lover for the fifteen days of New Year's, the time for families to exchange visits, money, and food. She plied her secret comb. And sure enough she cursed the year, the family, the village, and herself.

29   Even as her hair lured her imminent lover, many other men looked at her. Uncles, cousins, nephews, brothers would have looked, too, had they been home between journeys. Perhaps they had already been restraining their curiosity, and they left, fearful that their glances, like a field of nesting birds, might be startled and caught. Poverty hurt, and that was their first reason for leaving. But another, final reason for leaving the crowded house was the never-said.

30   She may have been unusually beloved, the precious only daughter, spoiled and mirror gazing because of the affection the family lavished on her. When her husband left, they welcomed the chance to take her back from the in-laws; she could live like the little daughter for just a while longer. There are stories that my grandfather was different from other people, "crazy ever since the little Jap bayoneted him in the head." He used to put his naked penis on the dinner table, laughing. And one day he brought home a baby girl, wrapped up inside his brown western-style greatcoat. He had traded one of his sons, probably my father, the youngest, for her. My grandmother made him trade back. When he finally got a daughter of his own, he doted on her. They must have all loved her, except perhaps my father, the only brother who never went back to China, having once been traded for a girl.

31   Brothers and sisters, newly men and women, had to efface their sexual color and present plain miens. Disturbing hair and eyes, a smile like no other, threatened the ideal of five generations living under one roof. To focus blurs, people shouted face to face and yelled from room to room. The immigrants I know have loud voices, unmodulated to American tones even after years away from the village where they called their friendships out across the fields. I have not been able to stop mother's screams in public libraries or over telephones. Walking erect (knees straight, toes pointed forward, not pigeon-toed, which is Chinese-feminine) and speaking in an inaudible voice, I have tried to turn myself American-feminine. Chinese communication was loud, public. Only sick people had to whisper. But at the dinner table, where the family members came nearest one another, no one could talk, not the outcasts nor any eaters. Every word that falls from the mouth is a coin lost. Silently they gave and accepted food with both hands. A preoccupied child who took his bowl with one hand got a sideways

glare. A complete moment of total attention is due everyone alike. Children and lovers have no singularity here, but my aunt used a secret voice, a separate attentiveness.

32   She kept the man's name to herself throughout her labor and dying; she did not accuse him that he be punished with her. To save her inseminator's name she gave silent birth.

33   He may have been somebody in her own household, but intercourse with a man outside the family would have been no less abhorrent. All the village were kinsmen, and the titles shouted in loud country voices never let kinship be forgotten. Any man within visiting distance would have been neutralized as a lover—"brother," "younger brother," "older brother"—one hundred and fifteen relationship titles. Parents researched birth charts probably not so much to assure good fortune as to circumvent incest in a population that has but one hundred surnames. Everybody has eight million relatives. How useless then sexual mannerisms, how dangerous.

34   As if it came from an atavism deeper than fear, I used to add "brother" silently to boys' names. It hexed the boys, who would or would no ask me to dance, and made them less scary and as familiar and deserving of benevolence as girls.

35   But, of course, I hexed myself also—no dates. I should have stood up, both arms waving, and shouted out across libraries, "Hey, you! Love me back." I had no idea, though, how to make attraction selective, how to control its direction and magnitude. If I made myself American-pretty so that the five or six Chinese boys in the class fell in love with me, everyone else—the Caucasian, Negro, and Japanese boys—would too. Sisterliness, dignified and honorable, made much more sense.

36   Attraction eludes control so stubbornly that whole societies designed to organize relationships among people cannot keep order, not even when they bind people to one another from childhood and raise them together. Among the very poor and the wealthy, brothers married their adopted sisters, like doves. Our family provided some romance, paying adult brides' prices and providing dowries so that their sons and daughters could marry strangers. Marriage promises to turn strangers into friendly relatives—a nation of siblings.

37   In the village structure, spirits shimmered among the live creatures, balanced and held in equilibrium by time and land. But one human being flaring up into violence could open up a black hole, a maelstrom that pulled in the sky. The frightened villagers, who depended on one another to maintain the real, went to my aunt to show her a personal, physical representation of the break she had made in the "roundness." Misallying couples snapped off the future, which was to be embodied in true offspring. The villagers punished her for acting as if she could have a private life, secret and apart from them.

38   If my aunt had betrayed the family at a time of large grain yields and peace, when many boys were born, the wings were being built on many houses, perhaps she might have escaped such severe punishment. But the men—hungry, greedy, tired of planting in dry soil, cuckolded—had had to leave the village in order to send food-money home. There were ghost plagues, bandit plagues, wars with the Japanese, floods. My Chinese brother and sister had died of an unknown sickness.

Adultery, perhaps only a mistake during good times, became a crime when the village needed food.

39 The round moon cakes and round doorways, the round tables of graduated size that fit one roundness inside another, round windows and rice bowls—these talismans had lost their power to warn this family of the law: a family must be whole, faithfully keep the descent line by having sons to feed the old and the dead, who in turn look after the family. The villagers came to show my aunt and her lover-in-hiding a broken house. The villagers were speeding up the circling of events because she was too short-sighted to see that her infidelity had already harmed the village, that waves of consequences would return unpredictably, sometimes in disguise, as now, to hurt her. This roundness had to be made coin-sized so that she would see its circumference: punish her at the birth of her baby. Awaken her to the inexorable. People who refused fatalism because they could invent small resources insisted on culpability. Deny accidents and wrest fault from the stars.

40 After the villagers left, their lanterns now scattering in various directions toward home, the family broke their silence and cursed her. "Aiaa, we're going to die. Death is coming. Death is coming. Look what you've done. You've killed us. Ghost! Dead ghost! Ghost! You've never been born." She ran out into the fields, far enough from the house so that she could no longer hear their voices, and pressed herself against the earth, her own land no more. When she felt the birth coming, she thought that she had been hurt. Her body seized together. "They've hurt me too much," she thought. "This is gall, and it will kill me." With forehead and knees against the earth, her body convulsed and then relaxed. She turned on her back, lay on the ground. The black well of sky and stars went out and out and out forever; her body and her complexity seemed to disappear, without home, without a companion, in eternal cold and silence. An agoraphobia rose in her, speeding higher and higher, bigger and bigger; she would not be able to contain it; there would be no end to fear.

41 Flayed, unprotected against space, she felt pain return, focusing her body. This pain chilled her—a cold, steady kind of surface pain. Inside, spasmodically, the other pain, the pain of the child, heated her. For hours she lay on the ground, alternately body and space. Sometimes a vision of normal comfort obliterated reality: she saw the family in the evening gambling at the dinner table, the young people massaging their elder's backs. She saw them congratulating one another, high joy on the mornings the rice shoots came up. When these pictures burst, the stars drew yet further apart. Black space opened.

42 She got to her feet to fight better and remembered that old-fashioned women gave birth in their pigsties to fool the jealous, pain-dealing gods, who do not snatch piglets. Before the next spasms could stop her, she ran to the pigsty, each step a rushing out into emptiness. She climbed over the fence and knelt in the dirt. It was good to have a fence enclosing her, a tribal person alone.

43 Laboring, this woman who had carried her child as a foreign growth that sickened her every day, expelled it at last. She reached down to touch the hot, wet, moving mass, surely smaller than anything human, and could feel that it was human after all—fingers, toes, nails, nose. She pulled it up on to her belly, and it lay

curled there, butt in the air, feet precisely tucked one under the other. She opened her loose shirt and buttoned the child inside. After resting, it squirmed and thrashed and she pushed it up to her breast. It turned its head this way and that until it found her nipple. There, it made little snuffling noises. She clenched her teeth at its preciousness, lovely as a young calf, a piglet, a little dog.

44   She may have gone to the pigsty as a last act of responsibility: she would protect this child as she had protected its father. It would look after her soul, leaving supplies on her grave. But how would this tiny child without family find her grave when there would be no marker for her anywhere, neither in the earth nor the family hall? No one would give her a family hall name. She had taken the child with her into the wastes. At its birth the two of them had felt the same raw pain of separation, a wound that only the family pressing tight could close. A child with no descent line would not soften her life but only trail after her, ghost-like, begging her to give it purpose. At dawn the villagers on their way to the fields would stand around the fence and look.

45   Full of milk, the little ghost slept. When it awoke, she hardened her breasts against the milk that crying loosens. Toward morning she picked up the baby and walked to the well.

46   Carrying the baby to the well shows loving. Otherwise abandon it. Turn its face into the mud. Mothers who love their children take them along. It was probably a girl; there is some hope of forgiveness for boys.

47   "Don't tell anyone you had an aunt. Your father does not want to hear her name. She has never been born." I have believed that sex was unspeakable and words so strong and fathers so frail that "aunt" would do my father mysterious harm. I have thought that my family, having settled among immigrants who had also been their neighbors in the ancestral land, needed to clean their name, and a wrong word would incite the kinspeople even here. But there is more to this silence: they want me to participate in her punishment. And I have.

48   In the twenty years since I heard this story I have not asked for details nor said my aunt's name; I do not know it. People who can comfort the dead can also chase after them to hurt them further—a reverse ancestor worship. The real punishment was not the raid swiftly inflicted by the villagers, but the family's deliberately forgetting her. Her betrayal so maddened them, they saw to it that she would suffer forever, even after death. Always hungry, always needing, she would have to beg food from other ghosts, snatch and steal it from those whose living descendants give them gifts. She would have to fight the ghosts massed at crossroads for the buns a few thoughtful citizens leave to decoy her away from village and home so that the ancestral spirits could feast unharassed. At peace, they could act like gods, not ghosts, their descent lines providing them with paper suits and dresses, spirit money, paper houses, paper automobiles, chicken, meat, and rice into eternity—essences delivered up in smoke and flames, steam and incense rising from each rice bowl. In an attempt to make the Chinese care for people outside the family, Chairman Mao encourages us now to give our paper replicas to the spirits of outstanding soldiers and workers, no matter whose ancestors

they may be. My aunt remains forever hungry. Goods are not distributed evenly among the dead.

49 My aunt haunts me—her ghost drawn to me because now, after fifty years of neglect, I alone devote pages of paper to her, though not origamied into houses and clothes. I do not think she always means me well. I am telling on her, and she was a spite suicide, drowning herself in the drinking water. The Chinese are always very frightened of the drowned one, whose weeping ghost, wet hair hanging and skin bloated, waits silently by the water to pull down a substitute.

Questions for Discussion

1. Why is this a "story to grow on"? What lesson is it designed to teach? Does the daughter, Maxine, accept her mother's purpose in telling the story, or does she interpret the story to create a new meaning from it?

2. What possible reasons for the aunt's pregnancy and suicide does the narrator propose? What do these different reasons suggest about the status of women in the Chinese family and about the double standard for male and female behavior in Chinese culture prior to World War II? Do you think that in today's Chinese families men and women are treated equally?

3. Why was it so important for Chinese family members to "efface their sexual color" and to remain silent at meals? How is this ritual reflective of their culture's values?

4. What is the relationship between the individual and the community in the Chinese village of the "No Name Woman"? How is this relationship between the individual and the community different from the one in your neighborhood?

5. Why did the aunt's killing of her infant, combined with her suicide, reflect "signs of loving"? Why was the infant "probably a girl"?

6. Why does the aunt's ghost continue to "haunt" the narrator? What perspective on gender roles do they seem to share? In what ways are the two women different from one another?

Ideas for Writing

1. Write about a relative who continues to haunt your family or a relative about whom there is a family legend because of his or her sexual life. What does the legacy of this ghostlike figure reflect about your family's values?

2. Write about a concept or tradition relative to gender role or sexuality that your grandparents or parents accepted that you have rebelled against. What do you think caused you to believe in values different from those that were accepted by your parents and grandparents? How does this generation gap affect the functioning of your family?

Julius Lester

Being a Boy

Born in 1939 in Saint Louis, Julius Lester came from a religious family; his father was a Christian minister. Lester attended Fisk University and after graduation worked as a folk singer, a radio talk show host, a college teacher, and a writer. Lester has taught since 1971 at the University of Massachusetts, where he has been a Professor of African-American studies as well as Near Eastern and Judaic studies. Lester has written many books and articles, including The Long Journey Home: Stories from Black History *(1972),* Do Lord Remember Me *(1984), and* Lovesong: Becoming A Jew *(1988). In the following article, originally written for* Ms. *magazine in 1973, Lester reflects on his childhood experiences as he explores the impact of stereotypes of "masculine" and "feminine" behavior on the consciousness of the adolescent.*

JOURNAL

Write about a time when you felt subjected to parental or peer pressure to conform to very traditional standards of "masculine" or "feminine" behavior.

1   As boys go, I wasn't much. I mean, I tried to be a boy and spent many childhood hours pummeling my hardly formed ego with failure at cowboys and Indians, baseball, football, lying, and sneaking out of the house. When our neighborhood gang raided a neighbor's pear tree, I was the only one who got sick from the purloined fruit. I also failed at setting fire to our garage, an art at which any five-year-old boy should be adept. I was, however, the neighborhood champion at getting beat up. "That Julius can take it, man," the boys used to say, almost in admiration, after I emerged from another battle, tears brimming in my eyes but refusing to fall.

2   My efforts at being a boy earned me a pair of scarred knees that are a record of a childhood spent falling from bicycles, trees, the tops of fences, and porch steps; of tripping as I ran (generally from a fight), walked, or simply tried to remain upright on windy days.

3   I tried to believe my parents when they told me I was a boy, but I could find no objective proof for such an assertion. Each morning during the summer, as I cuddled up in the quiet of a corner with a book, my mother would push me out the back door and into the yard. And throughout the day as my blood was let as if I were a patient of 17th-century medicine, I thought of the girls sitting in the shade of porches, playing with their dolls, toy refrigerators and stoves.

4   There was the life, I thought! No constant pressure to prove oneself. No necessity always to be competing. While I humiliated myself on football and baseball

fields, the girls stood on the sidelines laughing at me, because they didn't have to do anything except be girls. The rising of each sun brought me to the starting line of yet another day's Olympic decathlon, with no hope of ever winning even a bronze medal.

5   Through no fault of my own I reached adolescence. While the pressure to prove myself on the athletic field lessened, the overall situation got worse—because now I had to prove myself with girls. Just how I was supposed to go about doing this was beyond me, especially because, at the age of 14, I was four foot nine and weighed 78 pounds. (I think there may have been one 10-year-old girl in the neighborhood smaller than I.) Nonetheless, duty called, and with my ninth-grade gym-class jockstrap flapping between my legs, off I went.

6   To get a girlfriend, though, a boy had to have some asset beyond the fact that he was alive. I wasn't handsome like Bill McCord, who had girls after him like a cop-killer has policemen. I wasn't ugly like Romeo Jones, but at least the girls noticed him: "That ol' ugly boy better stay 'way from me!" I was just there, like a vase your grandmother gives you at Christmas that you don't like or dislike, can't get rid of, and don't know what to do with. More than ever I wished I were a girl. Boys were the ones who had to take the initiative and all the responsibility. (I hate responsibility so much that if my heart didn't beat of itself, I would now be a dim memory.)

7   It was the boy who had to ask the girl for a date, a frightening enough prospect until it occurred to me that she might say no! That meant risking my ego, which was about as substantial as a toilet-paper raincoat in the African rainy season. But I had to thrust that ego forward to be judged, accepted, or rejected by some girl. It wasn't fair! Who was she to sit back like a queen with the power to create joy by her consent or destruction by her denial? It wasn't fair—but that's the way it was.

8   But if (God forbid!) she should say Yes, then my problem would begin in earnest, because I was the one who said where we would go (and waited in terror for her approval of my choice). I was the one who picked her up at her house where I was inspected by her parents as if I were a possible carrier of syphilis (which I didn't think one could get from masturbating, but then again, Jesus was born of a virgin, so what did I know?). Once we were on our way, it was I who had to pay the bus fare, the price of the movie tickets, and whatever she decided to stuff her stomach with afterward. (And the smallest girls are all stomach.) Finally, the girl was taken home where once again I was inspected (the father looking covertly at my fly and the mother examining the girl's hair). The evening was over and the girl had done nothing except honor me with her presence. All the work had been mine.

9   Imagining this procedure over and over was more than enough: I was a sophomore in college before I had my first date.

10   I wasn't a total failure in high school, though, for occasionally I would go to a party, determined to salvage my self-esteem. The parties usually took place in somebody's darkened basement. There was generally a surreptitious wine bottle or two being passed furtively among the boys, and a record player with an insatiable appetite for Johnny Mathis records. Boys gathered on one side of the room and

girls on the other. There were always a few boys and girls who'd come to the party for the sole purpose of grinding away their sexual frustrations to Johnny Mathis's falsetto, and they would begin dancing to their own music before the record player was plugged in. It took a little longer for others to get started, but no one matched my talent for standing by the punch bowl. For hours, I would try to make my legs do what they had been doing without effort since I was nine months old, but for some reason they would show all the symptoms of paralysis on those evenings.

11   After several hours of wondering whether I was going to die ("Julius Lester, a sixteen-year-old, died at a party last night, a half-eaten Ritz cracker in one hand and a potato chip dipped in pimiento-cheese spread in the other. Cause of death: failure to be a boy"), I would push my way to the other side of the room where the girls sat like a hanging jury. I would pass by the girl I wanted to dance with. If I was going to be refused, let it be by someone I didn't particularly like. Unfortunately, there weren't many in that category. I had more crushes than I had pimples.

12   Finally, through what surely could only have been the direct intervention of the Almighty, I would find myself on the dance floor with a girl. And none of my prior agony could compare to the thought of actually dancing. But there I was and I had to dance with her. Social custom decreed that I was supposed to lead, because I was the boy. Why? I'd wonder. Let her lead. Girls were better dancers anyway. It didn't matter. She stood there waiting for me to take charge. She wouldn't have been worse off if she'd waited for me to turn white.

13   But, reciting "Invictus" to myself, I placed my arms around her, being careful to keep my armpits closed because, somehow, I had managed to overwhelm a half jar of deodorant and a good-size bottle of cologne. With sweaty armpits, "Invictus," and legs afflicted again with polio, I took her in my arms, careful not to hold her so far away that she would think I didn't like her, but equally careful not to hold her so close that she could feel the catastrophe which had befallen me the instant I touched her hand. My penis, totally disobeying the lecture I'd given it before we left home, was as rigid as Governor Wallace's jaw would be if I asked for his daughter's hand in marriage.

14   God, how I envied girls at that moment. Wherever *it* was on them, it didn't dangle between their legs like an elephant's trunk. No wonder boys talked about nothing but sex. That thing was always there. Every time we went to the john, there *it* was, twitching around like a fat little worm on a fishing hook. When we took baths, it floated in the water like a lazy fish and God forbid we should touch it! It sprang to life like lightning leaping from a cloud. I wished I could cut it off, or at least keep it tucked between my legs, as if it were a tail that had been mistakenly attached to the wrong end. But I was helpless. It was there, with a life and mind of its own, having no other function than to embarrass me.

15   Fortunately, the girls I danced with were discreet and pretended that they felt nothing unusual rubbing against them as we danced. But I was always convinced that the next day they were all calling up their friends to exclaim: "Guess what, girl? Julius Lester got one! I ain't lyin'!"

16 Now, of course, I know that it was as difficult being a girl as it was a boy, if not more so. While I stood paralyzed at one end of a dance floor trying to find the courage to ask a girl for a dance, most of the girls waited in terror at the other, afraid that no one, not even I, would ask them. And while I resented having to ask a girl for a date, wasn't it also horrible to be the one who waited for the phone to ring? And how many of those girls who laughed at me making a fool of myself on the baseball diamond would have gladly given up their places on the sidelines for mine on the field?

17 No, it wasn't easy for any of us, girls and boys, as we forced our beautiful, free-flowing child-selves into those narrow, constricting cubicles labeled *female* and *male*. I tried, but I wasn't good at being a boy. Now, I'm glad, knowing that a man is nothing but the figment of a penis's imagination, and any man should want to be something more than that.

Questions for Discussion

1. How does Lester describe himself as a boy? Was he perceived by others as "manly"? How did his own perceptions differ from those of his peers?

2. Why did Lester envy girls when he was a young boy? Did you share his feelings about the advantages that the "opposite sex" had when you were an adolescent?

3. How did the pressures on Lester change as he reached adolescence? Which pressures lessened and which increased? Do you think Lester's experiences are typical of adolescent expectations and pressures?

4. What frightened Lester most about the prospect of asking girls for dates or to dance? Do you think his fears are typical ones among adolescent males?

5. What was particularly embarrassing to Lester when he danced with girls? Why does he conclude from this that girls had less reason for sexual anxiety than boys? Do you agree?

6. How does Lester's view of the differences between girls and boys change as he becomes a man? What is he now "glad" about?

Ideas for Writing

1. Based on your own adolescent experiences write an essay about the typical fears and sexual anxiety experienced by someone of your gender or sexual orientation.

2. Write an essay in which you consider the cultural factors that might cause adolescence to be such a difficult period in the sexual life of a young person. You might consider the role of stereotypes of rigidly masculine and feminine behavior that come to adolescents from the mass media, religion, and family tradition.

Scott Russell Sanders

The Men We Carry in Our Minds

Scott Russell Sanders (b. 1945) was raised in rural areas of Tennessee and Ohio where his family worked in farming and industrial relations. He earned his B.A. at Brown University in 1967 and his Ph.D. from Cambridge University in 1971. Sanders is a professor of English at Indiana University in Bloomington where he has taught since 1971. As a social activist he has written about the environment, peace, male/female relationships, and the family. He also writes science fiction, children's books, and literary criticism. The following essay, which originally appeared in Milkweek Chronicle (1984), *is included in a later collection of Sanders's essays,* Paradise of Bombs (1987). *Some of his most recent work includes* Secrets of the Universe: Scenes from the Journey Home (1991), *Staying Put: Making a Home in a Restless World (1993),* Terrarium (1995), *and* Writing From the Center (1995).*

JOURNAL

Write about why you think it is harder to be a man or to be a woman in today's society. Or discuss which sex has more power and why.

1   When I was a boy, the men I knew labored with their bodies. They were marginal farmers, just scraping by, or welders, steelworkers, carpenters; they swept floors, dug ditches, mined coal, or drove trucks, their forearms ropy with muscle; they trained horses, stoked furnaces, built tires, stood on assembly lines wrestling parts onto cars and refrigerators. They got up before light, worked all day long whatever the weather, and when they came home at night they looked as though somebody had been whipping them. In the evenings and on weekends they worked on their own places, tilling gardens that were lumpy with clay, fixing broken-down cars, hammering on houses that were always too drafty, too leaky, too small.

2   The bodies of the men I knew were twisted and maimed in ways visible and invisible. The nails of their hands were black and split, the hands tattooed with scars. Some had lost fingers. Heavy lifting had given many of them finicky backs and guts weak from hernias. Racing against conveyor belts had given them ulcers. Their ankles and knees ached from years of standing on concrete. Anyone who had worked for long around machines was hard of hearing. They squinted, and the skin of their faces was creased like the leather of old work gloves. There were times, studying them, when I dreaded growing up. Most of them coughed, from dust or cigarettes, and most of them drank cheap wine or whiskey, so their eyes

looked bloodshot and bruised. The fathers of my friends always seemed older than the mothers. Men wore out sooner. Only women lived into old age.

3   As a boy I also knew another sort of men, who did not sweat and break down like mules. They were soldiers, and so far as I could tell they scarcely worked at all. During my early school years we lived on a military base, an arsenal in Ohio, and every day I saw GIs in the guardshacks, on the stoops of barracks, at the wheels of olive drab Chevrolets. The chief fact of their lives was boredom. Long after I left the Arsenal I came to recognize the sour smell the soldiers gave off as that of souls in limbo. They were all waiting—for wars, for transfers, for leaves, for promotions, for the end of their hitch—like so many braves waiting for the hunt to begin. Unlike the warriors of older tribes, however, they would have no say about when the battle would start or how it would be waged. Their waiting was broken only when they practiced for war. They fired guns at targets, drove tanks across the churned-up fields of the military reservation, set off bombs in the wrecks of old fighter planes. I knew this was all play. But I also felt certain that when the hour for killing arrived, they would kill. When the real shooting started, many of them would die. This was what soldiers were *for*, just as a hammer was for driving nails.

4   Warriors and toilers: those seemed, in my boyhood vision, to be the chief destinies for men. They weren't the only destinies, as I learned from having a few male teachers, from reading books, and from watching television. But the men on television—the politicians, the astronauts, the generals, the savvy lawyers, the philosophical doctors, the bosses who gave orders to both soldiers and laborers—seemed as removed and unreal to me as the figures in tapestries. I could no more imagine growing up to become one of these cool, potent creatures than I could imagine becoming a prince.

5   A nearer and more hopeful example was that of my father, who had escaped from a red-dirt farm to a tire factory, and from the assembly line to the front office. Eventually he dressed in a white shirt and tie. He carried himself as if he had been born to work with his mind. But his body, remembering the earlier years of slogging work, began to give out on him in his fifties, and it quit on him entirely before he turned sixty-five. Even such a partial escape from man's fate as he had accomplished did not seem possible for most of the boys I knew. They joined the Army, stood in line for jobs in the smoky plants, helped build highways. They were bound to work as their fathers had worked, killing themselves or preparing to kill others.

6   A scholarship enabled me not only to attend college, a rare enough feat in my circle, but even to study in a university meant for the children of the rich. Here I met for the first time young men who had assumed from birth that they would lead lives of comfort and power. And for the first time I met women who told me that men were guilty of having kept all the joys and privileges of the earth for themselves. I was baffled. What privileges? What joys? I thought about the maimed, dismal lives of most of the men back home. What had they stolen from their wives and daughters? The right to go five days a week, twelve months a year, for thirty or forty years to a steel mill or a coal mine? The right to drop bombs and die in war?

The right to feel every leak in the roof, every gap in the fence, every cough in the engine, as a wound they must mend? The right to feel, when the lay-off comes or the plant shuts down, not only afraid but ashamed?

7   I was slow to understand the deep grievances of women. This was because, as a boy, I had envied them. Before college, the only people I had ever known who were interested in art or music or literature, the only ones who read books, the only ones who ever seemed to enjoy a sense of ease and grace were the mothers and daughters. Like the menfolk, they fretted about money, they scrimped and made-do. But, when the pay stopped coming in, they were not the ones who had failed. Nor did they have to go to war, and that seemed to me a blessed fact. By comparison with the narrow, ironclad days of fathers, there was an expansiveness, I thought, in the days of mothers. They went to see neighbors, to shop in town, to run errands at school, at the library, at church. No doubt, had I looked harder at their lives, I would have envied them less. It was not my fate to become a woman, so it was easier for me to see the graces. Few of them held jobs outside the home, and those who did filled thankless roles as clerks and waitresses. I didn't see, then, what a prison a house could be, since houses seemed to me brighter, handsomer places than any factory. I did not realize—because such things were never spoken of—how often women suffered from men's bullying. I did learn about the wretchedness of abandoned wives, single mothers, widows; but I also learned about the wretchedness of lone men. Even then I could see how exhausting it was for a mother to cater all day to the needs of young children. But if I had been asked, as a boy, to choose between tending a baby and tending a machine, I think I would have chosen the baby. (Having now tended both, I know I would choose the baby.)

8   So I was baffled when the women at college accused me and my sex of having cornered the world's pleasures. I think something like my bafflement has been felt by other boys (and by girls as well) who grew up in dirt-poor farm country, in mining country, in black ghettos, in Hispanic barrios, in the shadows of factories, in Third World nations—any place where the fate of men is as grim and bleak as the fate of women. Toilers and warriors. I realize now how ancient these identities are, how deep the tug they exert on men, the undertow of a thousand generations. The miseries I saw, as a boy, in the lives of nearly all men I continue to see in the lives of many—the body-breaking toil, the tedium, the call to be tough, the humiliating powerlessness, the battle for a living and for territory.

9   When the women I met at college thought about the joys and privileges of men, they did not carry in their minds the sort of men I had known in my childhood. They thought of their fathers, who were bankers, physicians, architects, stockbrokers, the big wheels of the big cities. These fathers rode the train to work or drove cars that cost more than any of my childhood houses. They were attended from morning to night by female helpers, wives and nurses and secretaries. They were never laid off, never short of cash at month's end, never lined up for welfare. These fathers made decisions that mattered. They ran the world.

10   The daughters of such men wanted to share in this power, this glory. So did I. They yearned for a say over their future, for jobs worthy of their abilities, for the right to live at peace, unmolested, whole. Yes, I thought, yes yes. The difference

between me and these daughters was that they saw me, because of my sex, as destined from birth to become like their fathers, and therefore as an enemy to their destinies. But I knew better. I wasn't an enemy, in fact or in feeling. I was an ally. If I had known, then, how to tell them so, would they have believed me? Would they now?

Questions for Discussion

1. Why did Sanders first think of the men in his life in terms of the physical hardships that they had to endure or the imperative to become killers? Do you or did you think of the men in your life in these images? What characteristics, qualities, or images capture the men in your life before you attended university?
2. Sanders classifies men as warriors or toilers. What other categories of men do you think should be added to this list?
3. Why is Sanders initially confused by the women at college who felt that "men were guilty of having kept all the joys and privileges of the earth for themselves"? Why does he begin to identify with their struggle?
4. Why would Sanders have chosen to be a woman over a man as a young boy?
5. Why does Sanders end his essay with two questions? How would you answer these questions?
6. Do you think that Sanders's attitudes about men's roles are accurate and representative of working-class men or of men in general? Do you think that they reinforce the battle between the sexes for power?

Ideas for Writing

1. Write an essay that explains which gender you think has more power. Or write an essay that explains why you think neither sex is dominant. Or write about why you think that it is counterproductive to think of the relationships between the sexes in terms of a power struggle.
2. Like Sanders, write an essay that explores how you perceived the roles and rewards of the men in your life as a young boy or the women in your life as a young girl. Discuss how your attitudes have changed as you have matured and become more sophisticated about the way in which men and women relate to one another.

 # Gloria Naylor

The Two

Gloria Naylor (b. 1950) was raised in New York City; her parents were originally from Mississippi. After high school she spent seven years as a missionary for the Jehovah's Witnesses but then turned from religion to a strong belief in femi-

*nism. Naylor attended Brooklyn College of the City University of New York
where she earned a B.A. in 1981. She went on to study at Yale and completed her
M.A. in African-American studies in 1983. Naylor has taught at a number of
universities, including Princeton, New York University, Boston University,
Brandeis University, and the University of Pennsylvania. Her novel, The
Women of Brewster Place: A Novel in Seven Stories (1982), in which "The
Two" appears, won the American Book Award for the best first novel and was
later made into a television mini-series. Naylor won a National Endowment for
the Arts Fellowship in 1985 and a Guggenheim Fellowship in 1988. Her subsequent novels, Linden Hills (1985), Mama Day (1988), and Bailey's Cafe
(1989), reflect Naylor's belief in the importance of courage, community, and cultural identity.*

JOURNAL

Write about a person who was judged differently once people learned that he or
she did not follow traditional sex roles.

1   At first they seemed like such nice girls. No one could remember exactly when
they had moved into Brewster. It was earlier in the year before Ben was
killed—of course, it had to be before Ben's death. But no one remembered if it was
in the winter or spring of that year that the two had come. People often came and
went on Brewster Place like a restless night's dream, moving in and out in the dark
to avoid eviction notices or neighborhood bulletins about the dilapidated condition of their furnishings. So it wasn't until the two were clocked leaving in the
mornings and returning in the evenings at regular intervals that it was quietly absorbed that they now claimed Brewster as home. And Brewster waited, cautiously
prepared to claim them, because you never knew about young women, and obviously single at that. But when no wild music or drunken friends careened out of
the corner building on weekends, and especially, when no slightly eager husbands
were encouraged to linger around that first-floor apartment and run errands for
them, a suspended sigh of relief floated around the two when they dumped their
garbage, did their shopping, and headed for the morning bus.

2   The women of Brewster had readily accepted the lighter, skinny one. There
wasn't much threat in her timid mincing walk and the slightly protruding teeth
she seemed so eager to show everyone in her bell-like good mornings and
evenings. Breaths were held a little longer in the direction of the short dark one—
too pretty, and too much behind. And she insisted on wearing those thin Qiana
dresses that the summer breeze molded against the maddening rhythm of the
twenty pounds of rounded flesh that she swung steadily down the street. Through
slitted eyes, the women watched their men watching her pass, knowing the bas-
tards were praying for a wind. But since she seemed oblivious to whether these
supplications went answered, their sighs settled around her shoulders too. Nice
girls.

3   And so no one even cared to remember exactly when they had moved into Brewster Place, until the rumor started. It had first spread through the block like a sour odor that's only faintly perceptible and easily ignored until it starts growing in strength from the dozen mouths it had been lying in, among clammy gums and scum-coated teeth. And then it was everywhere—lining the mouths and whitening the lips of everyone as they wrinkled up their noses at its pervading smell, unable to pinpoint the source or time of its initial arrival. Sophie could—she had been there.

4   It wasn't that the rumor had actually begun with Sophie. A rumor needs no true parent. It only needs a willing carrier, and it found one in Sophie. She had been there—on one of those August evenings when the sun's absence is a mockery because the heat leaves the air so heavy it presses the naked skin down on your body, to the point that a sheet becomes unbearable and sleep impossible. So most of Brewster was outside that night when the two had come in together, probably from one of those air-conditioned movies downtown, and had greeted the ones who were loitering around their building. And they had started up the steps when the skinny one tripped over a child's ball and the darker one had grabbed her by the arm and around the waist to break her fall. "Careful, don't wanna lose you now." And the two of them had laughed into each other's eyes and went into the building.

5   The smell had begun there. It outlined the image of the stumbling woman and the one who had broken her fall. Sophie and a few other women sniffed at the spot and then, perplexed, silently looked at each other. Where had they seen that before? They had often laughed and touched each other—held each other in joy or its dark twin—but where had they seen *that* before? It came to them as the scent drifted down the steps and entered their nostrils on the way to their inner mouths. They had seen that—done that—with their men. That shared moment of invisible communion reserved for two and hidden from the rest of the world behind laughter or tears or a touch. In the days before babies, miscarriages, and other broken dreams, after stolen caresses in barn stalls and cotton houses, after intimate walks from church and secret kisses with boys who were now long forgotten or permanently fixed in their lives—that was where. They could almost feel the odor moving about in their mouths, and they slowly knitted themselves together and let it out into the air like a yellow mist that began to cling to the bricks on Brewster.

6   So it got around that the two in 312 were *that* way. And they had seemed like such nice girls. Their regular exits and entrances to the block were viewed with a jaundiced eye. The quiet that rested around their door on the weekends hinted of all sorts of secret rituals, and their friendly indifference to the men on the street was an insult to the women as a brazen flaunting of unnatural ways.

7   Since Sophie's apartment windows faced theirs from across the air shaft, she became the official watchman for the block, and her opinions were deferred to whenever the two came up in conversation. Sophie took her position seriously and was constantly alert for any telltale signs that might creep out around their drawn shades, across from which she kept a religious vigil. An entire week of drawn shades was evidence enough to send her flying around with reports that as

soon as it got dark they pulled their shades down and put on the lights. Heads nodded in knowing unison—a definite sign. If doubt was voiced with a "But I pull my shades down at night too," a whispered "Yeah, but you're not *that* way" was argument enough to win them over.

8   Sophie watched the lighter one dumping their garbage, and she went outside and opened the lid. Her eyes darted over the crushed tin cans, vegetable peelings, and empty chocolate chip cookie boxes. What do they do with all them chocolate chip cookies? It was surely a sign, but it would take some time to figure that one out. She saw Ben go into their apartment, and she waited and blocked his path as he came out, carrying his toolbox.

9   "What ya see?" She grabbed his arm and whispered wetly in his face.

10   Ben stared at her squinted eyes and drooping lips and shook his head slowly. "Uh, uh, uh, it was terrible."

11   "Yeah?" She moved in a little closer.

12   "Worst busted faucet I seen in my whole life." He shook her hand off his arm and left her standing in the middle of the block.

13   "You old sop bucket," she muttered, as she went back up on her stoop. A broken faucet, huh? Why did they need to use so much water?

14   Sophie had plenty to report that day. Ben had said it was terrible in there. No, she didn't know exactly what he had seen, but you can imagine—and they did. Confronted with the difference that had been thrust into their predictable world, they reached into their imaginations and, using an ancient pattern, weaved themselves a reason for its existence. Out of necessity they stitched all of their secret fears and lingering childhood nightmares into this existence, because even though it was deceptive enough to try and look as they looked, talk as they talked, and do as they did, it had to have some hidden stain to invalidate it—it was impossible for them both to be right. So they leaned back, supported by the sheer weight of their numbers and comforted by the woven barrier that kept them protected from the yellow mist that enshrouded the two as they came and went on Brewster Place.

15   Lorraine was the first to notice the change in the people on Brewster Place. She was a shy but naturally friendly woman who got up early, and had read the morning paper and done fifty sit-ups before it was time to leave for work. She came out of her apartment eager to start her day by greeting any of her neighbors who were outside. But she noticed that some of the people who had spoken to her before made a point of having something else to do with their eyes when she passed, although she could almost feel them staring at her back as she moved on. The ones who still spoke only did so after an uncomfortable pause, in which they seemed to be peering through her before they begrudged her a good morning or evening. She wondered if it was all in her mind and she thought about mentioning it to Theresa, but she didn't want to be accused of being too sensitive again. And how would Tee even notice anything like that anyway? She had a lousy attitude and hardly ever spoke to people. She stayed in that bed until the last moment and rushed out of the house fogged-up and grumpy, and she was used to being stared at—by men at least—because of her body.

16   Lorraine thought about these things as she came up the block from work, carrying a large paper bag. The group of women on her stoop parted silently and let her pass.

17   "Good evening," she said, as she climbed the steps.

18   Sophie was standing on the top step and tried to peek into the bag. "You been shopping, huh? What ya buy?" It was almost an accusation.

19   "Groceries." Lorraine shielded the top of the bag from view and squeezed past her with a confused frown. She saw Sophie throw a knowing glance to the others at the bottom of the stoop. What was wrong with this old woman? Was she crazy or something?

20   Lorraine went into her apartment. Theresa was sitting by the window, reading a copy of *Mademoiselle*. She glanced up from her magazine. "Did you get my chocolate chip cookies?"

21   "Why good evening to you, too, Tee. And how was my day? Just wonderful." She sat the bag down on the couch. "That little Baxter boy brought in a puppy for show-and-tell, and the damn thing pissed all over the floor and then proceeded to chew the heel off my shoe, but, yes, I managed to hobble to the store and bring you your chocolate chip cookies."

22   Oh, Jesus, Theresa thought, she's got a bug up her ass tonight.

23   "Well, you should speak to Mrs. Baxter. She ought to train her kid better than that." She didn't wait for Lorraine to stop laughing before she tried to stretch her good mood. "Here, I'll put those things away. Want me to make dinner so you can rest? I only worked half a day, and the most tragic thing that went down was a broken fingernail and that got caught in my typewriter."

24   Lorraine followed Theresa into the kitchen. "No, I'm not really tired, and fair's fair, you cooked last night. I didn't mean to tick off like that; it's just that . . . well, Tee, have you noticed that people aren't as nice as they used to be?"

25   Theresa stiffened. Oh, God, here she goes again. "What people, Lorraine? Nice in what way?"

26   "Well, the people in this building and on the street. No one hardly speaks anymore. I mean, I'll come in and say good evening—and just silence. It wasn't like that when we first moved in. I don't know, it just makes you wonder; that's all. What are they thinking?"

27   "I personally don't give a shit what they're thinking. And their good evenings don't put any bread on my table."

28   "Yeah, but you didn't see the way that woman looked at me out there. They must feel something or know something. They probably—"

29   "They, they, they!" Theresa exploded. "You know, I'm not starting up with this again, Lorraine. Who in the hell are they? And where in the hell are we? Living in some dump of a building in this God-forsaken part of town around a bunch of ignorant niggers with the cotton still under their fingernails because of you and your theys. They knew something in Linden Hills, so I gave up an apartment for you that I'd been in for the last four years. And then they knew in Park Heights, and you made me so miserable there we had to leave. Now these mysterious theys are on Brewster Place. Well, look out the window, kid. There's a big wall down

that block, and this is the end of the line for me. I'm not moving anymore, so if that's what you're working yourself up to—save it!"

30   When Theresa became angry she was like a lump of smoldering coal, and her fierce bursts of temper always unsettled Lorraine.

31   "You see, that's why I didn't want to mention it." Lorraine began to pull at her fingers nervously. "You're always flying up and jumping to conclusions—no one said anything about moving. And I didn't know your life has been so miserable since you met me. I'm sorry about that," she finished tearfully.

32   Theresa looked at Lorraine, standing in the kitchen door like a wilted leaf, and she wanted to throw something at her. Why didn't she ever fight back? The very softness that had first attracted her to Lorraine was now a frequent cause for irritation. Smoked honey. That's what Lorraine had reminded her of, sitting in her office clutching that application. Dry autumn days in Georgia woods, thick bloated smoke under a beehive, and the first glimpse of amber honey just faintly darkened about the edges by the burning twigs. She had flowed just that heavily into Theresa's mind and had stuck there with a persistent sweetness.

33   But Theresa hadn't known then that this softness filled Lorraine up to the very middle and that she would bend at the slightest pressure, would be constantly seeking to surround herself with the comfort of everyone's goodwill, and would shrivel up at the least touch of disapproval. It was becoming a drain to be continually called upon for this nurturing and support that she just didn't understand. She had supplied it at first out of love for Lorraine, hoping that she would harden eventually, even as honey does when exposed to the cold. Theresa was growing tired of being clung to—of being the one who was leaned on. She didn't want a child—she wanted someone who could stand toe to toe with her and be willing to slug it out at times. If they practiced that way with each other, then they could turn back to back and beat the hell out of the world for trying to invade their territory. But she had found no such sparring partner in Lorraine, and the strain of fighting alone was beginning to show on her.

34   "Well, if it was that miserable, I would have been gone a long time ago," she said, watching her words refresh Lorraine like a gentle shower.

35   "I guess you think I'm some sort of a sick paranoid, but I can't afford to have people calling my job or writing letters to my principal. You know I've already lost a position like that in Detroit. And teaching is my whole life, Tee."

36   "I know," she sighed, not really knowing at all. There was no danger of that ever happening on Brewster Place. Lorraine taught too far from this neighborhood for anyone here to recognize her in that school. No, it wasn't her job she feared losing this time, but their approval. She wanted to stand out there and chat and trade makeup secrets and cake recipes. She wanted to be secretary of their block association and be asked to mind their kids while they ran to the store. And none of that was going to happen if they couldn't even bring themselves to accept her good evenings.

37   Theresa silently finished unpacking the groceries. "Why did you buy cottage cheese? Who eats this stuff?"

38   "Well, I thought we should go on a diet."

39 "If *we* go on a diet, then you'll disappear. You've got nothing to lose but your hair."

40 "Oh, I don't know. I thought that we might want to try and reduce our hips or something." Lorraine shrugged playfully.

41 "No, thank you. We are very happy with our hips the way they are," Theresa said, as she shoved the cottage cheese to the back of the refrigerator. "And even when I lose weight, it never comes off there. My chest and arms just get smaller, and I start looking like a bottle of salad dressing."

42 The two women laughed, and Theresa sat down to watch Lorraine fix dinner. "You know, this behind has always been my downfall. When I was coming up in Georgia with my grandmother, the boys used to promise me penny candy if I would let them pat my behind. And I used to love those jawbreakers—you know, the kind that lasted all day and kept changing colors in your mouth. So I was glad to oblige them, because in one afternoon I could collect a whole week's worth of jawbreakers."

43 "Really. That's funny to you? Having some boy feeling all over you."

44 Theresa sucked her teeth. "We were only kids, Lorraine. You know, you remind me of my grandmother. That was one straight-laced old lady. She had a fit when my brother told her what I was doing. She called me into the smokehouse and told me in this real scary whisper that I could get pregnant from letting little boys pat my butt and that I'd end up like my cousin Willa. But Willa and I had been thick as fleas, and she had already given me a step-by-step summary of how she'd gotten into her predicament. But I sneaked around to her house that night just to double-check her story, since that old lady had seemed so earnest. 'Willa, are you sure?' I whispered through her bedroom window. 'I'm tellin' ya, Tee,' she said. 'Just keep both feet on the ground and you home free.' Much later I learned that advice wasn't too biologically sound, but it worked in Georgia because those country boys didn't have much imagination."

45 Theresa's laughter bounced off of Lorraine's silent, rigid back and died in her throat. She angrily tore open a pack of the chocolate chip cookies. "Yeah," she said, staring at Lorraine's back and biting down hard into the cookie," "it wasn't until I came up north to college that I found out there's a whole lot of things that a dude with a little imagination can do to you even with both feet on the ground. You see, Willa forgot to tell me not to bend over or squat or—"

46 "Must you!" Lorraine turned around from the stove with her teeth clenched tightly together.

47 "Must I what, Lorraine? Must I talk about things that are as much a part of my life as eating or breathing or growing old? Why are you always so uptight about sex or men?"

48 "I'm not uptight about anything. I just think it's disgusting when you go on and on about—"

49 "There's nothing disgusting about it, Lorraine. You've never been with a man, but I've been with quite a few—some better than others. There were a couple who I still hope to this day will die a slow, painful death, but then there were some who were good to me—in and out of bed."

50   "If they were so great, then why are you with me?" Lorraine's lips were trembling.

51   "Because—" Theresa looked steadily into her eyes and then down at the cookie she was twirling on the table. "Because," she continued slowly, "you can take a chocolate chip cookie and put holes in it and attach it to your ears and call it an earring, or hang it around your neck on a silver chain and pretend it's a necklace—but it's still a cookie. See—you can toss it in the air and call it a Frisbee or even a flying saucer, if the mood hits you, and it's still just a cookie. Send it spinning on a table—like this—until it's a wonderful blur of amber and brown light that you can imagine to be a topaz or rusted gold or old crystal, but the law of gravity has got to come into play, sometime, and it's got to come to rest—sometime. Then all the spinning and pretending and hoopla is over with. And you know what you got?"

52   "A chocolate chip cookie," Lorraine said.

53   "Uh-huh." Theresa put the cookie in her mouth and winked. "A lesbian." She got up from the table. "Call me when dinner's ready, I'm going back to read." She stopped at the kitchen door. "Now, why are you putting gravy on that chicken, Lorraine? You know it's fattening."

Questions for Discussion

1. How does the sentence, "They seemed like such nice girls," set the tone for the direction of the story? How often is this phrase repeated? At what point does it become ironic?

2. Describe Brewster Place and the people who live there. Why are they such gossips and rumor spreaders? What is their first impression of Lorraine and Theresa? Why does their attitude toward the women change?

3. What is the connection between the story's theme and the shift in point of view midway through the story? Why did the author wait to present the women's perspective and names?

4. Contrast Lorraine and Theresa's attitudes about their neighbors. How do their different attitudes reflect deeper differences in their personalities and within their relationship?

5. In what ways does the chocolate chip cookie symbolize and clarify Theresa's point about her sexual orientation? Does Lorraine see the cookie in the same way as Theresa does? How do you think their relationship will work out?

6. With which of the main characters were you most sympathetic? Why?

Ideas for Writing

1. Write an essay that compares the two sections of the story, the first part that reflects the perspective of the neighbors and the second part that involves a dialogue between Lorraine and Theresa. How does this contrasting structure help to emphasize the values reflected in the story?

2. Write a sequel to the story in which you narrate the next event in the conflict between Lorraine and Theresa and their neighbors.

Ernest Hemingway

Hills Like White Elephants

Ernest Hemingway (1899–1961) is remembered for his adventurous life as well as for his novels and stories. Born in Oak Park, Illinois, as a boy he often went hunting and fishing with his father. After he finished high school, Hemingway began to work as a newspaper reporter for the Kansas City Star *and the Toronto* Star. *Hemingway went on to be a foreign correspondent, meeting expatriate writers in Paris and covering World War I. His war experiences and contacts with the expatriate community formed the basis for much of his early fiction, as well as the novels* The Sun Also Rises *(1926) and* A Farewell to Arms *(1929). Hemingway continued to write stories and novels in the 1930s and 1940s, often focusing on his experiences as a sportsman; his last significant novel was* The Old Man and the Sea *(1952). Hemingway was awarded the Nobel Prize in 1954. Influenced by his journalistic experience, Hemingway saw himself primarily as a realist: "I'm trying in all my stories to get the feeling of the actual life across—not just to depict life—or criticize it—but to actually make it alive. So that when you have read something by me you actually experience the thing." "Hills Like White Elephants" appeared in his first major story collection* In Our Time *(1925).*

JOURNAL

Describe a verbal conflict you had with a member of the opposite gender. In what ways was your conflict related to your different values, especially those connected to your gender identity? Explain why you think the two of you were unable to communicate with one another.

1   The hills across the valley of the Ebro were long and white. On this side there was no shade and no trees and the station was between two lines of rails in the sun. Close against the side of the station there was the warm shadow of the building and a curtain, made of strings of bamboo beads, hung across the open door into the bar, to keep out flies. The American and the girl with him sat at a table in the shade, outside the building. It was very hot and the express from Barcelona would come in forty minutes. It stopped at this junction for two minutes and went on to Madrid.

2   "What should we drink?" the girl asked. She had taken off her hat and put it on the table.

3   "It's pretty hot," the man said.

4   "Let's drink beer."

5   "*Dos cervezas,*" the man said into the curtain.

6   "Big ones?" a woman asked from the doorway.

7   "Yes. Two big ones."

8   The woman brought two glasses of beer and two felt pads. She put the felt pads and the beer glasses on the table and looked at the man and the girl. The girl was looking off at the line of hills. They were white in the sun and the country was brown and dry.

9   "They look like white elephants," she said.

10   "I've never seen one," the man drank his beer.

11   "No, you wouldn't have."

12   "I might have," the man said. "Just because you say I wouldn't have doesn't prove anything."

13   The girl looked at the bead curtain. "They've painted something on it," she said. "What does it say?"

14   "Anis del Toro. It's a drink."

15   "Could we try it?"

16   The man called "Listen" through the curtain. The woman came out from the bar.

17   "Four reales."

18   "We want two Anis del Toro."

19   "With water?"

20   "Do you want it with water?"

21   "I don't know," the girl said. "Is it good with water?"

22   "It's all right."

23   "You want them with water?" asked the woman.

24   "Yes, with water."

25   "It tastes like licorice," the girl said and put the glass down.

26   "That's the way with everything."

27   "Yes," said the girl. "Everything tastes of licorice. Especially all the things you've waited so long for, like absinthe."

28   "Oh, cut it out."

29   "You started it," the girl said. "I was being amused. I was having a fine time."

30   "Well, let's try and have a fine time."

31   "All right. I was trying. I said the mountains looked like white elephants. Wasn't that bright?"

32   "That was bright."

33   "I wanted to try this new drink: That's all we do, isn't it—look at things and try new drinks?"

34   "I guess so."

35   The girl looked across at the hills.

36   "They're lovely hills," she said. "They don't really look like white elephants. I just meant the coloring of their skin through the trees."

37   "Should we have another drink?"

38   "All right."

39   The warm wind blew the bead curtain against the table.

40   "The beer's nice and cool," the man said.

41   "It's lovely," the girl said.

42   "It's really an awfully simple operation, Jig," the man said. "It's not really an operation at all."

43   The girl looked at the ground the table legs rested on.

44   "I know you wouldn't mind it, Jig. It's really not anything. It's just to let the air in."

45   The girl did not say anything.

46   "I'll go with you and I'll stay with you all the time. They just let the air in and then it's all perfectly natural."

47   "Then what will we do afterward?"

48   "We'll be fine afterward. Just like we were before."

49   "What makes you think so?"

50   "That's the only thing that bothers us. It's the only thing that's made us unhappy."

51   The girl looked at the bead curtain, put her hand out, and took hold of two of the strings of beads.

52   "And you think then we'll be all right and be happy."

53   "I know we will. You don't have to be afraid. I've known lots of people that have done it."

54   "So have I," said the girl. "And afterward they were all so happy."

55   "Well," the man said, "if you don't want to you don't have to. I wouldn't have you do it if you didn't want to. But I know it's perfectly simple."

56   "And you really want to?"

57   "I think it's the best thing to do. But I don't want you to do it if you don't really want to."

58   "And if I do it you'll be happy and things will be like they were and you'll love me?"

59   "I love you now. You know I love you."

60   "I know. But if I do it, then it will be nice again if I say things are like white elephants, and you'll like it?"

61   "I'll love it. I love it now but I just can't think about it. You know how I get when I worry."

62   "If I do it you won't ever worry?"

63   "I won't worry about that because it's perfectly simple."

64   "Then I'll do it. Because I don't care about me."

65   "What do you mean?"

66   "I don't care about me."

67   "Well, I care about you."

68   "Oh, yes. But I don't care about me. And I'll do it and then everything will be fine."

69   "I don't want you to do it if you feel that way."

70   The girl stood up and walked to the end of the station. Across, on the other side, were fields of grain and trees along the banks of the Ebro. Far away, beyond the river, were mountains. The shadow of a cloud moved across the field of grain and she saw the river through the trees.

71   "And we could have all this," she said. "And we could have everything and every day we make it more impossible."

72   "What did you say?"

73   "I said we could have everything."

74   "We can have everything."

75   "No, we can't."

76   "We can have the whole world."

77   "No, we can't."

78   "We can go everywhere."

79   "No, we can't. It isn't ours any more."

80   "It's ours."

81   "No, it isn't. And once they take it away, you never get it back."

82   "But they haven't taken it away."

83   "We'll wait and see."

84   "Come on back in the shade," he said. "You mustn't feel that way."

85   "I don't feel any way," the girl said. "I just know things."

86   "I don't want you to do anything that you don't want to do—"

87   "Nor that isn't good for me," she said. "I know. Could we have another beer?"

88   "All right. But you've got to realize—"

89   "I realize," the girl said. "Can't we maybe stop talking?"

90   They sat down at the table and the girl looked across at the hills on the dry side of the valley and the man looked at her and at the table.

91   "You've got to realize," he said, "that I don't want you to do it if you don't want to. I'm perfectly willing to go through with it if it means anything to you."

92   "Doesn't it mean anything to you? We could get along."

93   "Of course it does. But I don't want anybody but you. I don't want any one else. And I know it's perfectly simple."

94   "Yes, you know it's perfectly simple."

95   "It's all right for you to say that, but I do know it."

96   "Would you do something for me now?"

97   "I'd do anything for you."

98   "Would you please please please please please please please stop talking?"

99   He did not say anything but looked at the bags against the wall of the station. There were labels on them from all the hotels where they had spent nights.

100   "But I don't want you to," he said, "I don't care anything about it."

101   "I'll scream," the girl said.

102   The woman came out through the curtains with two glasses of beer and put them down on the damp felt pads. "The train comes in five minutes," she said.

103   "What did she say?" asked the girl.

104   "That the train is coming in five minutes."

105   The girl smiled brightly at the woman, to thank her.

106   "I'd better take the bags over to the other side of the station," the man said. She smiled at him.

107   "All right. Then come back and we'll finish the beer."

108   He picked up the two heavy bags and carried them around the station to the other tracks. He looked up the tracks but could not see the train. Coming back, he walked through the barroom, where people waiting for the train were drinking. He drank an Anis at the bar and looked at the people. They were all waiting reasonably for the train. He went out through the bead curtain. She was sitting at the table and smiled at him.

109   "Do you feel better?" he asked.
110   "I feel fine," she said. "There's nothing wrong with me. I feel fine."

Questions for Discussion

1. What mood is created through setting the story in a train-station bar in a foreign country with a view of the "long and white" hills across the Ebro River valley? Why does Jig admire the view of the mountains, the field of grain, and the river?
2. Why does Jig remark that the hills remind her of "white elephants"? What symbolism is suggested by the expression "a white elephant"?
3. What is the subject of the disagreement between the American and Jig? How are their personalities and outlooks on life contrasted through their positions in the disagreement?
4. Point out lines in the dialogue that seem to have a double or oblique meaning. For example, when Jig remarks, "Everything tastes of licorice. Especially the things you've waited so long for, like absinthe," what motivates her remark and to what is she actually referring? What does she mean when she says "It isn't ours any more"?
5. What is ironic about the American's line, "They just let the air in and then it's perfectly natural"? Give other examples of irony in the American's comments. Do you think the American intends to be ironic?
6. Do you think that the characters' attitudes about what is important in a relationship are representative? Could you identify with one of the character's points of view, or were you sympathetic to both characters?

Ideas for Writing

1. At the end of the story, Jig remarks, "I feel fine." Does she actually seem to feel fine, or is she being ironic? Has she made an important decision? Is she trying to make the American feel guilty? Does she just want the American to leave her alone? Write an essay in which you interpret the meaning of Jig's remark based on the conversation between the couple earlier in the story.
2. Write a story involving a conflict between two characters using the type of brief dialogue and simple, unadorned description that characterizes Hemingway's "Hills Like White Elephants."

 # Pablo Neruda

The Dream

Pablo Neruda (1904–1973), whose real name was Ricardo Eliezer Neftali Reyes y Basoalto, was born, raised, and educated in Chile. When he was 25, Neruda began his long career in politics as a Chilean consul in Ceylon and East Asia and

went on to serve at the Chilean Embassy in Mexico City. Neruda was a member
of the World Peace Council from 1950 to 1973 and received many international
peace prizes. Neruda was the greatest living poet writing in Spanish, and his work
has been translated into Italian, Russian, German, French, Swedish, and at least
eighteen other languages. He was awarded the highest prizes for his poetry in
Chile; Oxford, England; and Czechoslovakia. In 1971 he received the Nobel
Prize in Literature. Scholars of Neruda's large body of writing say, "Tempered by
reason, intelligence, wit, and humor, his poetry is nevertheless committed to the
satisfaction of man's emotional needs, and not his discursive intelligence. . . . Its
medium is a literature that structures itself on emotive association like the subcon-
scious, and worlds in the flux of sensation and thought." These qualities are ap-
parent in "The Dream," which appears in The Captain's Verses *(1952 in Span-*
ish and 1972 in English translation).

JOURNAL

Write about a time when you thought seriously about ending a relationship
that was very important to you.

Walking on the sands
I decided to leave you.

I was treading a dark clay
that trembled
5 and I, sinking and coming out,
decided that you should come out
of me, that you were weighing me down
like a cutting stone,
and I worked out your loss
10 step by step:
to cut off your roots,
to release you alone into the wind.

Ah in that minute,
my dear, a dream
15 with its terrible wings
was covering you.

You felt yourself swallowed by the clay,
and you called to me and I did not come,
you were going, motionless,
20 without defending yourself
until you were smothered in the quicksand.

Afterwards
my decision encountered your dream,

and from the rupture
25 that was breaking our hearts
we came forth clean again, naked,
loving each other
without dream, without sand,
complete and radiant,
30 sealed by fire.

Madison Lee

In his poem "The Dream," Pablo Neruda is writing about a man in conflict with himself. As the speaker of the poem walks on the sand, he decides to let go of the part of him that has caused him much pain and perhaps has been intervening in his process of moving forward. Although the speaker is depressed by this part of himself, he doesn't let go of this person within him very easily. Instead the speaker works out the loss.

In my picture I have depicted the scene in which the speaker is trying to let his terrible, "black image" go. He releases that image into the water. As he is standing near the water, he sees his complexion and realizes that he misses that part of himself and wants it back in his life. In order for the speaker to be at peace with himself, he must be able to confront his "black" self and come to some kind of resolution. He may have been relieved to think he could get rid of the monster inside of himself, but then he would not be whole. As the speaker thinks about his other half, he soon realizes that he needs that bad part of himself; he then compromises and is able to be whole again.

Questions for Discussion

1. What is the significance of the quicksand the speaker walks on in the poem? How do the speaker and the "you" in the poem both change in relation to the sand as the poem develops?
2. What leads the "I" in the poem to decide to leave the "You"?
3. In the third stanza what is the meaning of the dream "with its terrible wings" that covers the "you"? How does the "you" feel about the relationship?
4. What causes the "I" to change his mind about leaving the "you"? How does their relationship change?
5. Why and how do the lovers reignite their love for one another?
6. The "I" and "You" in the poem are not assigned specific genders, although some readers might assume the "I" is a male because Neruda, the poet, is male and often writes love poetry to women. What are the consequences of reading the poem from alternative gender perspectives: as a poem about a relationship between a female speaker and a male lover, between two women, or between two men?

Ideas for Writing

1. Write an essay in which you interpret and discuss the definition of love implicit in the poem's final lines: "loving each other / without dream, without sand, / complete and radiant, / sealed by fire." Do you agree with the view of love expressed in these lines?
2. Write an essay about a relationship in which you felt "trapped" or, like the speaker in the poem, as if you were sinking in emotional quicksand. How did you change the relationship?

 ## Chitra Divakaruni

Nargis' Toilette

Born in Calcutta, India, Chitra Divakaruni received a B.A. from the University of Calcutta and a Ph.D. in English Literature from the University of California at Berkeley in 1985. Divakaruni currently teaches English and creative writing at Foothill College in California. She has had poetry and stories published in literary magazines in both India and the United States. Her poetry collections include Dark Like the River *(1987),* The Reason for Nasturtiums *(1990), and* The Black Candle *(1991), from which the following poem is taken. Divakaruni has written one collection of short stories,* Arranged Marriages *(1995); her first novel,* Mistress of Spices, *was published in March 1997. In "Nargis' Toilette," Divakaruni explores the world of a veiled Muslim woman.*

JOURNAL

Write about a marriage ritual that you feel is erotic and dreamlike.

> *The uncovered face of a woman*
> *is as a firebrand, inflaming men's*
> *desires and reducing to ashes*
> *the honor of her family.*
>
> *Muslim saying*

Powder to whiten skin
unsnagged as a just-ripe peach.
Kohl to underline the eye's mute deeps.
Attar of rose touched to the dip
5 behind the earlobe,
the shadow between the breasts,
the silk creases
of the crimson *kameez*.[1]

In the women's courtyard
10 it is always quiet,
the carved iron gates locked.
The palm shivers by the marble fountain.
The *bulbul*[2] sings to its crimson double
in the mirrored cage.

15 Satin *dupattas* rustle.
The women put henna
on Nargis' hands. They braid,
down her back,
the forest's long shadows,
20 their laughter like the silver anklets
they are tying to her feet.

Today the women will take Nargis
to visit the women of the Amin family.
They will drink chilled pomegranate juice,
25 nibble pistachio *burfis*[3] green as ice.
The grandmothers will chew
betel leaves and discuss the heat.

Nargis will sit, eyes down,

[1]*kameez*—long tunic
[2]*bulbul*—song bird
[3]*burfis*—Indian sweet

tracing the peacock pattern
30 on the mosaic floor.
If Allah wills, a marriage
will be arranged
with the Amins' second son
whose face Nargis will see
35 for the first time
in the square wedding mirror
placed in the bride's lap.

It is time to go.
They bring her *burkha*,[4]
40 slip it over her head.
Someone adjusts the lace slits to her eyes.
The *burkha* spills silk-black to her feet
and spreads, spreads,
over the land, dark wave
45 breaking over the women, quenching
their light.

Now all is ready.
Like a black candle
Nargis walks to the gate.

Questions for Discussion

1. Why do you think the poem begins with an epigram from a Muslim saying? What is the relationship between the meaning of the saying and the meaning of the poem? How does the saying amplify the meaning of the poem?

2. From reading and thinking about the poem, explain your understanding of Muslim marriage traditions. What impact do you think that such traditions may have on the individual and on married couples?

3. Discuss several of the images and rituals in the poem that create the sense of sensuality woven into Nargis' preparation to meet the man selected to be her husband. What makes the preparation seem dreamlike?

4. Why is Nargis compared to a "black candle" as she walks to the gate to meet the man who may *choose* her to be his wife?

5. Although Nargis is the one who is chosen and not the one who makes the choice, she does have power. What is her power? Why is she dangerous? How does her veiled presence emphasize the theme of danger?

---

[4]*burkha*—black veil which covers a woman's face and body completely. Used by Muslim women.

Ideas for Writing

1. Write an essay in which you compare and contrast the role and power of a wife in a traditional culture such as Pakistan or India to the role and power of a wife in a modern, less-traditional culture such as modern America. What are the advantages and disadvantages of being a wife in each culture?

2. Develop your journal entry into an essay in which you discuss how marriage and sexuality are enhanced through traditional rituals that engage the imagination and the senses. Refer to literature and the popular media as well as to personal experience to support your main points.

 ## Rosa Contreras

On Not Being a Girl

Rosa Contreras was born in Jalisco, Mexico, and raised in Half Moon Bay, California. She is majoring in Latin American studies and anthropology. Writing the following essay—a response to Julius Lester's selection in this chapter, "Being a Boy"—helped Contreras to think more analytically about the expectations that her family had for her when she was a young girl and about how both her expectations and those of her family changed as she prepared herself for college.

JOURNAL

Write about an experience during your teenage years in which you disagreed with your family over what your role or responsibilities should be as a girl or a boy.

1   As I grew into adolescence, I experienced constant conflict between being a girl and having what have been traditionally considered "masculine" qualities. At the same time that I wanted to be contemplative and artful, I also wanted to "take the initiative and all the responsibility," as Julius Lester describes the typical male role. Like Julius Lester in his essay "Being a Boy," I envied the opposite sex their advantages and often found myself frustrated by my culture's traditional views of gender roles; unlike Lester, I tried actively to break away from the typical role of a girl as defined in the Mexican family. In fact, growing up in a Mexican household with strong cultural values while also experiencing American culture with its less clearly defined gender roles allowed me to criticize both cultures from different perspectives. This allowed me to take the ideals that I liked from both

and reject those that I did not agree with. In this manner, I was able to build my own set of values, and naturally, I have tried to inculcate them into my family.

2   As the oldest child, my parents often gave me responsibilities fit for an adult, while they insisted that I remain a little girl, innocent and oblivious to boys and sex. I in turn rebelled; I did no want to be seen as an obedient, subservient girl, with all the qualities that make for a good Mexican wife. Every day I constantly pushed to assert myself as strong, as able to take on anything and succeed. I wanted to show my father, and every other male in my life, that I could do everything a boy could, if not more.

3   By the time I was twelve, I was tired of being a girl. I was sick, as Julius Lester puts it, of girls' activities: "sitting in the shades of porches, playing with dolls, toy refrigerators and stoves." By this time I had accumulated five baby dolls, fourteen Barbie dolls, three Ken dolls, and four younger siblings. The fact that I was a girl, and the oldest one at that, burdened me with the responsibility of watching over my sisters and brother. If they hurt themselves, or strayed away from home, no one was blamed except me. I still remember one day when my little brother ran into the house, crying because he had slipped on the gravel while running. Upon hearing my brother's shrill cries, my father became irritated and turned towards me: "Look what happened! You're supposed to watch them!" I became angry. Why was I being blamed? Why did I have to watch them all the time?

4   One day I finally yelled out to my parents what I had been feeling for a while: "Why do I always get yelled at for the things they do? It's not my fault!—I can't always be watching THEM. THEY'RE your kids; you chose to have them! I wasn't even asked! I never asked to be born, much less asked to be born first!"

5   Looking back, I realize that those were extremely cruel and ungrateful words. Nevertheless, with this outcry, I opened my parents' eyes, and they saw that they were, in fact, being unreasonable when they expected me to watch four children all the time. Maybe they had already realized the unfairness of the situation I was in, because they did not protest or reprimand me for telling them how I felt. Afterwards, I was no longer blamed for my siblings' actions, and was given more independence from caring for them.

6   Along with protesting against the rules of watchdog and disciplinarian, which, in Mexican culture, are commonly reserved for girls, I did not like it that my family members disapproved of my love of reading. Nobody in my immediate or extended family gives books the importance that I do. Maybe the fact that I am a girl meant that books should not be very important to me. In old Mexican tradition, there exists the idea that it is not good for women to know too much. Not good for whom? For their husbands. A man was not a "real" man if his wife knew more than he did. However, I suspect that the main problem my family had with my reading books was that I often neglected my household chores because I would, literally, spend all day submerged in learning about other people, other worlds.

7   By the time I was twelve, I had disappointed my parents in their quest to make me a productive and useful young lady, according to what Mexican custom decrees. While the rest of the house was clean, my room was a mess. I had other

things to do, like homework, studying for tests, reading, and playing basketball. And horror of horrors! I couldn't even cook a pot of beans. My mother was often distressed at my inability (and lack of desire) to cook and do housework, which simply did not interest me. I felt housework was a waste of time, and I'd rather be doing something else. More importantly, though, I hated it because I associated it with the oppression and subservience of *latina* women, including those in my family.

8   The different roles of men and women in Mexican society are clearly marked and instilled in children from a very young age. While in first and third grade, I went to elementary school in Mexico. While the boys were encouraged to excel in athletics and academics, the girls competed in crocheting and embroidering. At the end of the year, there was a contest to see whose work was the most beautiful. Approximately once every two weeks, each girl had to help in either mopping, cleaning windows, or sweeping her classroom. Therefore, at a very young age, girls were taught to do housework and feminine things, like embroidery. My mother, all my aunts, and most Mexican women that I know were taught that the value of a woman consisted in keeping her family well-fed and a squeaky-clean house.

9   I realize that it was complicated for my mother to pass on these same values to me because we were no longer living in Mexico. But possibly because we were so far away from Mexico, it became very important for her to make this new home like her old one. Therefore, she tried to make sure that, although her daughters were being raised in a foreign country, we were still raised as she was taught. So when I refused to agree with the traditional Mexican ideals for raising a girl, she probably felt as though she had somehow failed. But I could not go along with what I truly felt was wrong. I could not please my older relatives in the way I was expected to because living in the United States, where the issue of women's rights is more openly debated, had opened my eyes to new and better possibilities for women.

10   From elementary school to high school, I went to school with a predominantly white population and came home to a Mexican household. At school I was taught what I liked. The teachers encouraged and praised me for my love of reading. Boys and girls were equally expected to do well in both sports and academics. Boys even took Home Economics! But often, when I brought home these ideas and chose to read rather than do housework or wait on my father and siblings, I was scolded. I was in a new environment that my parents had never experienced, so they did not understand why I felt so strongly about the way of life women had always led in Latin American cultures.

11   From reading, which allowed me to learn a lot about other people, other life-styles, and achieving excellent grades in school, I often felt that I knew it all. I became very outspoken. At first, I scolded my mother privately when I saw her being subservient to my father. When she waited up for him, I would become angry and tell her: "Why are you doing this? I can't believe you're waiting up for him to feed him dinner! It's not like he can't get it himself!" Later, I became bolder. For example, when I'd hear my dad ask my mother for tortillas, I would say: "They're on

the stove. You can get them." By the time I was twelve, I had my future laid out for me. I would always say that when I got older, I would have a career and my husband would share in the household responsibilities. I was not about to go out and work and then come home to do even more work. I understood that the status of my mother as a housewife required that she do this kind of work, but I felt it was unfair that she had to work all day, while my father could come home and not do anything for the rest of the evening.

12   I know that the many outbursts and arguments I have had (and still do, although less often now than before) concerning women's equality were the cause for much conflict in my household. However, I realize today that because of my efforts, my parents have changed their ideas about what women can accomplish. As a young girl, I refused to mold myself to be good and docile, with traditional moral values and knowledge. I understand that these ideas are very ingrained in Mexican society and they will be hard to change, but I cannot stand by and watch the oppression of these women and keep myself quiet. Now, as a young woman, I'm on my way to defying the role traditionally designated for women. During my high school days, my mother often encouraged me to study hard so that I could have a career. She would tell me: "Study, so that you can have a better life." She wanted me to have the option of being someone else rather than a full-time housewife, who always depends on her husband. I believe I have shown my father that I am capable of succeeding, just like all men and women can if given the opportunity. He has grown to accept me as I am and to understand my way of thinking. I have earned my parents' respect and today they are extremely proud of all that I have achieved.

Questions for Discussion

1. What aspects of Mexican American culture made it difficult for Rosa Contreras to feel comfortable in her assigned family role? How were her family's values undermined by living in the United States?
2. To some extent, it seems as if the student's family was even more strict in its demands for traditional female behavior than an average modern family in Mexico might have been during the period when Rosa was growing up. What contributed to Rosa's mother's tendency to reinforce the old ways?
3. How does Rosa Contreras use examples of her family's interactions and her responsibilities in the home to illustrate her thesis about not fitting into the mold of "proper" female behavior? Could she have provided other examples?
4. How effectively does Rosa use Julius Lester's essay "Being a Boy" and his position on gender roles to compare with her own perspective on being female? Which essay did you enjoy most, and why? Could the student writer have used other techniques or points made by Lester to extend her comparison?

Julie Bordner Apodaca

Gay Marriage: Why the Resistance?

Julie Bordner Apodaca was a student at the College of Alameda in California. She is a native of Alameda and an aspiring writer who returned to college part-time after ten years out of school, working and starting a family. Ever since her elementary school days, Bordner Apodaca has enjoyed argumentation and has tried to encourage her fellow students and coworkers to see beyond biases and misconceptions about people whom society has labeled as "different." Thus, when she was assigned to write a paper on a controversial issue for her critical thinking course, she chose to write on the subject of gay marriages and to examine the underlying causes for bias against such relationships.

JOURNAL

What are your feelings about gay marriage?

1   It has been over twenty years since the Stonewall riot triggered the civil rights movement in the gay and lesbian community. In the past two years, a good portion of the movement's focus has been on the issue of legalized marriage for homosexual couples, a move which many leaders in the gay community see as essentially conservative, as a sign that gays are opting for more traditional, stable life-styles and desire recognition as committed couples. Thus American society has been asked to expand the traditionally heterosexual institution of marriage to include gay and lesbian couples. The response from mainstream America has been largely negative, due in part to the homophobic attitudes that permeate our society.

2   To understand why society continues to have a negative reaction to the idea of legalizing gay marriage, we must first understand homophobia. Webster's defines homophobia as "hatred or fear of homosexuals or homosexuality." Homophobic attitudes, which are generally emotional and lacking in factual foundation, have many origins, some of which are religious, some political and sociological, some psychological, some even medical in nature. In a general sense, it can be argued that the roots of homophobia in America can be found in the institutions and philosophy that are at the heart of our culture: our dominant religious tradition, our political and class systems, our moral perspective, and our psychological makeup.

3   Some of the most passionate arguments against legalization of gay and lesbian marriages stem from the Judaic and Christian fundamentalist religions in our society. A common belief is that homosexuality is a sin; not only is it morally wrong, but it mocks natural laws and the will of God. Marriage is a sanctified privilege of

heterosexual union that constructs a foundation for the procreation and nurture of children. Despite the fact that many gays have dependent children from previous heterosexual unions, homosexuals are not seen by the religious fundamentalist as having the capacity for procreation within their relationships; thus sexual relations between homosexuals are viewed by many religious people as sinful and mocking, a way of undermining the essential meaning of marriage.

4   Some social thinkers hold views against homosexual marriage which coincide in some ways with those of the religious fundamentalists. Such individuals resist the legalization or wide acceptance of gay relationships, fearing the repercussions to the already threatened traditional family. With the stigma against homosexuality relaxed, perhaps the 20% of closeted homosexuals who marry heterosexual partners may instead choose gay partners (Hartinger 682). This could lead to a decline in the numbers of heterosexual marriages and even to the rise of other unusual social arrangements thought of as destabilizing to our society, such as polygamy or group marriage (Hartinger 682). The traditional two-partner heterosexual marriage, already on the decline, could become a rarity, and our basic social structure which historically was designed around this form of relationship may crumble. The weakness of this type of causal reasoning is that it is based upon an assumption that it is somehow unhealthy for a society to change and evolve, as well as upon a view of the "stable nuclear family unit" that denies historical realities such as abusive families, alcoholism in the nuclear family, and other causes for the decline of the nuclear family, such as the high cost of maintaining a home, the high divorce rate, and the trend towards dual career families.

5   Despite the weaknesses in the reasoning, arguments against gay marriages as contributors towards the undermining of traditional families often have been used by politicians in order to win the support of the populace who feel that family values are endangered. Vice President Dan Quayle's attacks on the "cultural elite" during the 1992 presidential campaign could be seen as a veiled attack on homosexuals and their relationships. According to Quayle, the cultural elite are those who "respect neither tradition or standards. They believe that moral truths are relative and all 'life styles' are equal" (qtd in Salter A15). Quayle's comments stirred both praise and rage throughout America in the summer of 1992; his ideas touched a sympathetic chord for many who are painfully aware of the increased fragility of the traditional nuclear, heterosexual family unit.

6   However, it is not only religious, conservative sociologists, and aspiring politicians who promote homophobia; our government and its official branches play a key role as well. For instance, the United States military continues to resist fully accepting homosexuals in the armed forces, despite any evidence that would suggest that these individuals generally are unfit for duty, disruptive, or that they pose a security threat. The discrimination against homosexual relationships in the military is instrumental in fostering and maintaining the psychological fears and stereotypes associated with homosexuals: that they are unstable, immoral, and in some vague sense a threat to the security of our nation.

7   The AMA does not classify homosexuality as a disease or a disorder, due to scientific experiments done in the 1950s that discredited the notion of the homosex-

ual as any more neurotic or maladjusted than any other group in society. However, many people continue to cling to the outmoded belief that homosexuality is a psychological disorder. Some, including a minority in the psychiatric profession, believe that homosexuality should be therapeutically treated, rather than sanctioned by recognition of homosexual unions as the equivalent to "normal" married relationships. However, psychologist Richard Isay does not believe that the fear of homosexuality is simply a reaction to the idea of a "deviant" sex act; Isay considers that the fear and hatred for homosexuality is related intimately to "the fear and hatred of what is perceived as being 'feminine' in other men and in oneself" (qtd in Alter 27). Thus, for some people, insecurity and mistrust of one's own sexuality may cause irrational anxiety about or contempt towards the homosexual. If homosexual marriages were legal, gay couples might feel free publicly and physically to express their affections. This possibility of overt display of homosexuality in turn adds to the homophobic individual's fantasies that, rather than witnessing such encounters with "natural" revulsion, he or she could possibly experience an unwanted arousal.

8   Another common psychological concern about homosexual marriages, despite evidence that points to homosexuality as a quasi-biological sexual orientation rather than a learned or conditioned sexual response, is that legally sanctioned gay relationships will somehow influence children to become homosexual. The reasoning goes that adolescents and even younger children are often confused by the intense and unfamiliar sexual feelings stirring inside them; thus the adolescent confronted with the "normality" of homosexual relationships, in or out of their own family circle, might tend to gravitate toward this kind of sexual outlook. Furthermore, part of the stereotype of the homosexual as sexual deviant is that gays enjoy the company of young children and might, if not sufficiently isolated from mainstream society, take advantage of the vulnerability of naive and confused adolescents, encouraging such children to engage in gay sex.

9   A more recent fear that fuels the hostility to gay marriages is medically-based, but, as so many of the fears discussed above, based upon causal oversimplification. Consider AIDS; this disease is really a nightmare for our entire society, not just confined to the gay community, and it can be spread by both heterosexual sexual conduct and drug-related activity. Yet the fearful stereotype persists that AIDS is somehow a "gay" disease; in fact, some religious zealots have even spoken of AIDS as God's "divine retribution" against gays for their blasphemous behavior, despite the reality that gays didn't originate the disease and in spite of the fact that the gay community has made enormous progress in educating itself about AIDS and in discontinuing the unsafe sexual practices of the past. The legalization of homosexual marriage elicits the fear among those with a deep fear of both AIDS and homosexuality, that, along with the resulting increase in the numbers of homosexuals, such legalization will somehow cause the AIDS epidemic to become even more severe. This is truly an ironic misconception, when we consider that monogamous marriage, gay or heterosexual, is one of the most conservative sexual practices, one of the least likely to lead to a spread of disease beyond the bounds of matrimony.

10   As we have seen, there are many causes for the fear that surrounds the legalization of homosexual marriages. The cumulative effect of these causes has prevented
legislation supporting such relationships in almost all parts of the country. Although some of the arguments against homosexual marriages may seem on the surface to have some justification, most are based on ignorance, irrationality, and
fear. Perhaps, as Ernest Van Den Haag puts it, "nothing will persuade heterosexu-
als to believe that homosexuality is psychologically or morally as legitimate as
their own heterosexuality" (38); however, despite the resistance that is likely to
occur, it seems to me that a national effort should be made to dispel the misconceptions regarding homosexuality. What benefit is there in hiding behind irrational fears? Homosexuality is not going to disappear; history has proven that. Society would benefit from a better understanding of homosexuality, for if people
were able to think more critically about the myths and the issues surrounding homosexuality, perhaps there would be a decrease in the nation's homophobia and
an increased understanding from which all people, gay and heterosexual alike,
would benefit. We cannot expect a change overnight, but we can begin to educate
the ignorant and break down some of the prejudice. As Martin Luther King, Jr.,
once said, "Take the first step in faith. You don't have to see the whole staircase,
just take the first step."

WORKS CITED

Alter, Jonathan. "Degrees of Discomfort." *Newsweek* 12 March 1992:27.
Hartinger, Brent. "A Case for Gay Marriage." *Commonweal* 22 Nov. 1991:681–683.
Salter, Stephanie. "The 'Cultural Elite' and the Rest of Us." *San Francisco Chronicle* 14 June 1992:A15.
Van Den Haag, Ernest. "Sodom and Begorrah." *National Review* 29 April 1991:35–38.

Questions for Discussion

1. What are the major causes of the resistance to gay marriage as explored
   in the essay? Are there other causes the student could have discussed?
   Which ones?
2. Julie Apodaca refutes the reasoning that underlies most of the "fears"
   she discusses. Is her refutation effective as well as fair to the thinking of
   those opposed to gay relationships?
3. What factual evidence does Apodaca use to support her general statements and conclusions? What additional evidence might she have used?
4. This essay uses some quotations from authorities or spokespersons to
   support some of the writer's ideas and conclusions about social attitudes. Were such citations of authorities handled appropriately, or
   would you have liked to see either more or less reliance on citation of
   authority?

Chapter Writing Topics

1. Develop an extended definition of masculinity. When relevant show
   how it relates to the ideas presented by Lester and Sanders as well as
   other writers in this chapter.

2. Discuss what you have learned about the limits of being born female in a patriarchal society from reading the selections by Divakaruni, Hong Kingston, and Woolf. What did you learn that is relevant to your own life? Provide examples from your own experience.

3. Write an essay in which you discuss your thoughts and feelings about the role that sex plays in an individual's life and sense of well-being. Consider if sex is a "procreative" act, an expression of love, an erotic experience. Or is it a combination of experiences?

4. Discuss several new insights about the relationship among the unconscious mind, sexuality, and dreams that you have discovered through reading the selections in this chapter.

5. Write an essay in which you predict several significant changes in the cultural and gender expectations of men and women in the future. In shaping your response refer to readings in this chapter that are relevant.

6. Write an essay in which you predict how the social and personal attitudes toward sexuality will change in the future.

7. Write a story about a nontraditional sexual relationship.

8. Write about a film that portrays an issue of sexuality or gender. How does the film relate to issues raised in the readings in this chapter? You can select a film from the following list or one of your own choosing.

Incredible Adventure of Two Girls in Love, Oleanna, Rambling Rose, Working Girl, Baby Boom, Torch Song Trilogy, Fried Green Tomatoes, The Crying Game, The Wedding Banquet, The Bird Cage, Mrs. Doubtfire, Jeffrey, Orlando

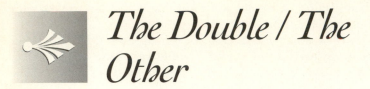

7

The Double / The Other

Within each one of us there is another whom we do not know. He speaks to us in dreams and tells us how differently he sees us from how we see ourselves.

CARL JUNG

[The shadow] is exactly like any human being with whom one has to get along, sometimes by giving in, sometimes by resisting, sometimes by giving love—whatever the situation requires. The shadow becomes hostile only when he is ignored or misunderstood.

MARIE-LUISE VON FRANZ
The Realization of the Shadow in Dreams

Our challenge is to call forth the humanity within each adversary, while preparing for the full range of possible responses. Our challenge is to find a path between cynicism and naiveté.

FRAN PEAVEY
Us and Them

Argument and Dialogue

Traditional Argument

Traditional argument begins by defining a problem or issue, then taking a position or stance. In this form of argument the advocate proceeds to develop a clear thesis and to demonstrate its validity through a series of convincing logical arguments, factual supports, and references to authority. Often the major aim of argument is seen as an attack on the ideas and positions of an opponent with an end to persuading the audience of the correctness of the proponent's position. Arguments that don't quite fit into the debater's viewpoint are sometimes ignored or are introduced to counter them more strongly in a process known as "refutation." Such traditional debate is frequently linked to political rhetoric, where only one candidate can be elected. A fundamental part of public life, oppositional argument can be manipulative and one-sided, leading people to believe that debate is more a matter of verbal warfare than a genuine form of communication.

The Dialogue

Based on a thorough presentation of the facts and on the reasons supporting positions, the dialogic argument acknowledges the importance of creating a bridge between opposing viewpoints that are often rigidly separated in a traditional argument. This form of argument may remind you of the literary dialogue between opposites that we see at work in some of this chapter's stories and poems; it is best exemplified in expository form in Fran Peavey's essay, "Us and Them." The dialogic argument emphasizes the need for discussion and a genuine interchange of ideas, while making a conscious effort to bring together seemingly irreconcilable viewpoints in order to arrive at a type of synthesis of opposing perspectives that will allow the writer and his or her audience to learn more about themselves.

Through the dialogic approach to argument, you can come to a new awareness of positions you may not have understood or considered. Working to understand these "opposite" positions does not necessarily imply that you totally accept them, or that you abandon your own ideas and viewpoint. What it does suggest is that you are beginning to consider the possibilities of strong arguments, positions, and value systems that are different from your own, and that you are making a real attempt to integrate these positions into your thinking.

Dialogue and Prewriting

An effective prewriting strategy for a balanced argument paper involves engaging your opponent in a dialogue. Begin by creating a dialogue that explores different positions relative to your subject, your thesis, and your supporting points. Following is an example of an excerpt from such a student dialogue on the subject of reading fairy tales to small children. We have labeled the two "sides" in the dialogue "I" and "Me." "I" stands for the position that the student really wants to present, while "Me" represents the side of the argument, perhaps a side of the self that the writer doesn't want to acknowledge and perceives as the "opponent."

I: I think all children should read fairy tales. I always loved hearing them as a kid; I liked the scary parts and the adventures. Fairy tales are so much more engrossing than the trash on the boob tube.

ME: I can see that you really like fairy tales. But wouldn't a lot of kids who get upset easily be frightened by reading stories about mean stepmothers and wicked witches, like in "Hansel and Gretel"?

I: I understand what you're saying; fairy tales might frighten some children, especially if they were very young or if they had had some really horrible things happen in their own lives that the stories re-

minded them of. Still, I think I can handle your objections. Kids
should be read fairy tales by an adult who makes time to explain the
issues in the story and who can reassure them if they think the story
is too scary; after all, a fairy tale is "only a story."

ME: Well, I can see the point in having adults read the stories and explain
them, but you're wrong about TV. There are some great programs
for kids, like *Sesame Street* and *Barney,* that teach children to have
positive values. And what about the values in those fairy tales?
Sesame Street teaches you to love everyone and to give girls equal opportunities to succeed! Fairy tales are so old-fashioned and sexist,
with all those beautiful sleeping princesses waiting around for Prince
Charming.

I: I know what you mean. The values in fairy tales aren't always very
modern. That's why it's really important that the adult who reads the
stories to the kids discusses the old-fashioned way of life that is being
presented and compares the world of the tale with our own values
and life-styles. I can see letting kids watch TV, too. Fairy tales are
only a part of the imaginative experience of childhood, but they're
still a very important part!

In this short dialogue, you see the "I" and "Me" positions being brought
closer together. "I"'s initial position is now more clearly stated, with some
important, common-sense qualifications brought in through the interaction
with the "Me."

Prewriting and the Audience

Before you begin to write your essay, try to establish a similar kind of dialogue with your imaginary audience as you did with the parts of yourself. As
in traditional argument or in any type of writing situation, this involves trying to determine the interests and values of your audience. For example, the
student writing about fairy tales would have to decide if his or her audience
includes cautious parents of school-age children or liberal educators with a
progressive philosophy of childrearing. Creating a clear "mental image" of
the audience is essential before appropriate arguments can be selected. Once
you have a clear image of the audience in mind, approach your readers directly and respectfully. Make the audience an integral part of your arguments; do not try to manipulate or dazzle them with your facts and figures;
instead, establish a common ground with the audience, stating the positions
you hold in common with them while designating areas of mutual agreement
or possible compromise. This approach will remind you to keep your audience's point of view in mind and will facilitate meaningful communication.

Defining Key Terms

As in traditional argument, it is important for dialogic arguers to define their
terms. Definitions support clear communication and help develop rapport in
an argument. People feel more comfortable in a discussion when they under-

stand what key terms refer to and mean. For example, if I am arguing for reading fairy tales to young children and am referring to fairy tales such as those of Hans Christian Andersen, while my audience thinks I am discussing modern fantasy children's stories such as those by Maurice Sendak, then we are really thinking about different definitions of a fairy tale and will be unlikely to come to a mutual understanding. In defining your terms, use simple, straightforward definitions; avoid connotative language designed to manipulate or trick your audience.

Evaluating "Facts"

If you have taken a statistics course or read articles in journals, you know that facts and statistics can be interpreted in a variety of ways. In reading the factual studies that will form an important part of the support in any argument paper, you need to consider a number of questions. Have the results of the social scientists or psychologists you are studying been confirmed by other researchers? Are the data current? Were they collected by qualified researchers using thorough and objective methods? Are they expressed in clear and unambiguous language? These and other questions should be asked about your sources of information so that you can create a sound factual base for the arguments you use in your paper. As suggested earlier, consider facts that may oppose the argument you are making, and refer as well to those facts likely to be known and accepted by your audience. Present your factual supports clearly; avoid overstating your conclusions in absolute, unqualified terms or overgeneralizing from limited data.

Feelings in Argument

Emotions play such a significant role in our lives that any argument that tried to be altogether rational, pretending that emotional concerns were unimportant and that only "facts" count, would be unrealistic and uninteresting. Emotions, both your own and those of your audience, are a central concern in argument. Although you need to present your ideas in ways that won't offend your readers, when feelings are a central issue in the argument itself, emotional issues do need to be directly confronted. For example, it would be impossible to discuss a subject such as abortion without acknowledging your own feelings and those of the audience relative to issues as emotionally involving as the life of a fetus. In this case, sharing such feelings will help to create an open and trusting relationship with your audience.

However, an important distinction must be made between acknowledging feelings and exploiting them to manipulate your readers. Often, strong arguments are based on emotions, which can be exaggerated in an attempt to strengthen a position and can cause you to overlook important issues. Avoid language that could ignite the emotional climate in a discussion. Bringing in irrelevant appeals for pity or fear can obscure the real issues involved in a discussion. Try to use language that is primarily emotionally neutral in describing the positions and ideas taken by their opposition. By doing so, you are more likely to keep the confidence of readers who might otherwise be offended by an adversarial position and manipulative language.

Argument can be one of the most satisfying forms of writing, but it can be one of the most difficult. To satisfy both the factual and emotional demands of shaping an effective argument, you can:

- use the inner dialogue as an aid to prewriting and exploring different positions
- empathize with and acknowledge the assumptions and needs of your audience
- define key terms
- evaluate and use relevant factual supports
- be honest and direct in your treatment of the emotional aspects of an issue

All of these strategies will be of use to you in your efforts to find a stance in argument that allows you to build bridges between your inner world and the worlds of others.

THEMATIC INTRODUCTION

Many of us are conscious of having an alternate self, a self that, for whatever reasons, we do not make public. We sometimes see glimpses of an alternative or underground personality in a family member, friend, supervisor, colleague, or even in a media figure. From Greek myths to nursery rhymes and fairy tales, from Shakespearean doubles and disguises to Gothic tales of horror and revenge, from Victorian mysteries to the modern psychological short story, images of the double, of twins in spirit or twins in reality, have marked our developing understanding of the workings of the human mind.

The frequent recurrence and popularity of the image of the double in myth and literature is often attributed to the human need to explore, understand, and perhaps conquer divided feelings that individuals have about the parts of themselves that are in conflict. These conflicting parts of the self are revealed in many forms: the good self versus the evil self, the rational self versus the irrational self, the civilized self versus the antisocial or criminal self, the masculine self versus the feminine self, the physical self versus the spiritual self, the controlled, conventional self versus the wild self, the practical self versus the dreamy self.

Although literature and human experiences suggest that inward journeys into the mind's dual nature can lead to confusion, even neurosis or psychosis, at the same time, in literature and in life, there is the possibility of integrating and balancing the opposing parts of the self through developing an increased awareness of the inner self. In this way the main character of a poem or story, the writer, or a reader can experience a form of rebirth, emerging with a more balanced and confident sense of self and purpose. Your journey through this chapter will provide you with new insights into the dualities within the human personality.

The chapter opens with Judith Ortiz Cofer's poem "The Other," in which the Hispanic American speaker acknowledges the power of her "other," who is sensual, uninhibited, even dangerous, and more in touch with her cultural roots than her well-behaved public self. In "Updike and I" novelist John Updike explores the duality of his nature in the contrast between his everyday social self and his writer self.

The next two readings will help you to think about how to get the oppositional sides of your mind and psyche to work together productively and effectively. In "The Realization of the Shadow in Dreams," psychoanalyst Marie-Luise Von Franz offers a positive perspective on the inner division of the human psyche, showing ways in which the unconscious "shadow" self appears in dreams and myths and suggesting ways for the individual to come to a reconciliation with his or her shadow. An imaginative portrait of the workings of the double or shadow self is developed in Hans Christian Andersen's "The Shadow," a tale about a dishonorable shadow who gains domination over a learned but timid scholar. "The Shadow" presents the double conflict as a struggle between worldly power and the philosophical search for truth, wisdom, and beauty.

The next two pieces are by Robert Louis Stevenson. In "A Chapter on Dreams" he demonstrates how he used the resources of his dreams and unconscious mind to help him create his classic tale, *The Strange Case of Dr. Jekyll and Mr. Hyde*. Following is the conclusion to Robert Louis Stevenson's classic double story, "Henry Jekyll's Full Statement of the Case," which explores the negative consequences of trying to separate the "good" or civilized side of the human character from its sensual and irrational side.

The impact of inner conflict on political and social decisions is explored in the next two selections. In "Being Black and Feeling Blue," Shelby Steele discusses the ways in which an African American's negative self-concept, or internalized "anti-self," can make success in life more difficult or even impossible to achieve. In "Us and Them," longtime peace activist Fran Peavey suggests a new approach to community organization and political action, which avoids dehumanizing and dismissing the opposition and instead encourages a balanced response to problem-solving.

This chapter's final poem, "In a Dark Time," by Theodore Roethke provides us with the reflective mind of a speaker who comes face to face with his shadow self and climbs out of his fear. The two student essays that conclude the chapter provide new ways of thinking about how the double-sided nature of social issues can be internalized and affect the development of an individual's self-concept. The first student essay, "Mixed-Up," by Susan Voyticky, the daughter of an African American father and a white mother, discusses some of the difficult decisions Voyticky had to make to create an identity that she could call her own. In "The Artist and the Engineer" student writer Albert Liu develops an inner dialogue that reveals the ways in which social expectations and his parents' expectations are in conflict with his own feelings about his future career.

Exploring the duality of the human mind and spirit as reflected in the essays, stories, and poems included in this chapter should prove to be provocative and enlightening. Becoming aware of the other voices that exist within you in addition to your dominant voice or persona can help you to understand yourself more fully and can provide you with additional resources to draw upon in your writing.

Judith Ortiz Cofer

The Other

Born in Puerto Rico in 1952, Judith Ortiz Cofer came to New Jersey with her family when she was a child. After receiving an M.A. from Florida Atlantic University, Cofer taught English and Spanish at the University of Miami and currently teaches at the University of Georgia. Cofer has written novels, including Line of the Sun *(1989) and* Latin Deli *(1995); short stories compiled in* Island Like You: Stories of the Barrio *(1995); an autobiographical work,* Silent Dancing: A Partial Remembrance of a Puerto Rican Childhood *(1990). In addition to her autobiographical essays, Cofer is a poet who explores issues of identity, heritage, and family. In the following poem, notice how Cofer presents the inner conflict experienced by the speaker through a series of progressively more disturbing images.*

JOURNAL

Write about a part of yourself that you have difficulty accepting because the "other" in you seems too wild or lacking in responsibility.

A sloe-eyed dark woman shadows me.
In the morning she sings
Spanish love songs in a high
falsetto filling my shower stall
5 with echoes.
She is by my side
in front of the mirror as I slip
into my tailored skirt and she
into her red cotton dress.
10 She shakes out her black mane as I
run a comb through my close-cropped cap.
Her mouth is like a red bull's eye
daring me.
Everywhere I go I must
15 make room for her: she crowds me
in elevators where others wonder
at all the space I need.
At night her weight tips my bed, and
it is her wild dreams that run rampant
20 through my head exhausting me. Her heartbeats,
like dozens of spiders carrying the poison
of her restlessness over the small

distance that separates us,
drag their countless legs
25   over my bare flesh.

Questions for Discussion

1. How would you describe the "other" that Cofer creates in this poem? Is
   it anything like your own "other"?
2. Describe the speaker's main self. How does the narrator's main self differ from the "other"?
3. Which part of the speaker is dominant? Which side do you think will
   eventually win out in the struggle?
4. Why do you think the two sides of the narrator's personality are in conflict? What different cultural and gender roles does each side reflect?
5. What images help to vividly portray the "other" and to contrast her
   with the speaker's main self?
6. What dreams and nocturnal fantasies of the narrator help to portray the
   struggle between the two sides of her personality? What do you think is
   meant by the fantasy image, "Her heartbeats, / like dozens of spiders
   carrying the poison / of her restlessness . . . . "? In what sense is the restlessness a poison?

Ideas for Writing

1. Write an essay about an inner struggle you have experienced that reflects a cultural conflict between the culture of your parents and that of
   friends or between that of your school and of your workplace or
   church. Include examples of ways in which your inner conflict is reflected in your dreams and fantasies.
2. Write an essay in which you explore arguments that will help you make
   an important decision in your life about which you feel inner conflict.
   You might want to discuss whether to change your position on issues
   and ways of relating to a marriage partner, friend, parent, supervisor at
   work, or teacher. After exploring your options, which choice seems
   preferable?

 # John Updike

Updike and I

*John Updike (b. 1932) was raised in Shillington, Pennsylvania, and earned a full
scholarship to Harvard, where he completed his B.A. in 1954, graduating summa
cum laude. Then he was awarded a fellowship to study art at the Rushkin School
in Oxford, England. When he returned to New York, he joined the staff of the*

New Yorker. *In 1959 Updike published his first work of short fiction,* The Same
Door, *and his first novel,* The Poorhouse Fair. *At this time he moved to Ipswich,
Massachusetts, with his family and made writing his full-time career. Updike is
best known for his sequence of novels about Harry "Rabbit" Angstrom, who lives
in suburbia and continually thinks back to his life as a high school athlete:* Rabbit
Run *(1960);* Rabbit Redux *(1971);* Rabbit Is Rich *(1981); and* Rabbit at
Rest *(1990), which won the Pulitzer Prize in 1991. Updike has written a number
of other best-selling novels;* The Witches of Eastwick *(1984) was made into a
popular film with Jack Nicholson. Some of his short story collections include* Pigeon Feathers *(1962),* The Music School *(1966),* Too Far to Go: The
Magic Stories *(1979),* Problems *(1979),* Trust Me *(1987), and* The Afterlife
and Other Stories *(1994). Updike is a social satirist and an intellectual who enjoys examining contemporary ideas and social trends through his writing. The selection that follows, "Updike and I," was first published in* Antaeus *(1995).*

JOURNAL

Write about the persona or self that is projected by your writing. How is the self
that emerges in your writing different from your conversational "everyday" self?

1   I created Updike out of the sticks and mud of my Pennsylvania boyhood, so I can
scarcely resent it when people, mistaking me for him, stop me on the street and
ask me for his autograph. I am always surprised that I resemble him so closely that
we can be confused. Meeting strangers, I must cope with an extra brightness in
their faces, an expectancy that I will say something worthy of him; they do not realize that he works only in the medium of the written word, where other principles
apply, and hours of time can be devoted to a moment's effect. Thrust into "real"
time, he can scarcely function, and his awkward pleasantries and anxious stutter
emerge through my lips. Myself, I am rather suave. I think fast, on my feet, and
have no use for the qualifactory complexities and lame *double entendres* and pained
exactations of language in which he is customarily mired. I move swiftly and
rather blindly through life, spending the money he earns.

2   I early committed him to a search for significance, to philosophical issues that
give direction and point to his verbal inventions, but am not myself aware of
much point or meaning to things. Things *are,* rather unsayably, and when I force
myself to peruse his elaborate scrims of words I wonder where he gets it all—not
from *me,* I am sure. The distance between us is so great that the bad reviews he receives do no touch me, though I treasure his few prizes and mount them on the
walls and shelves of my house, where they instantly yellow and tarnish. That he
takes up so much of my time, answering his cloying mail and reading his incessant
proofs, I resent. I feel that the fractional time of day he spends away from being
Updike is what feeds and inspires him, and yet, perversely, he spends more and
more time being Updike, that monster of whom my boyhood dreamed.

3   Each morning I awake from my dreams, which as I age leave an ever more sour
taste. Men once thought dreams to be messages from the gods, and then from

something called the subconscious, as it sought a salubrious rearrangement of the contents of the day past; but now it becomes hard to believe that they partake of any economy. Instead, a basic chaos seems expressed: a random play of electricity generates images of inexplicable specificity.

4   I brush my teeth, I dress and descend to the kitchen, where I eat and read the newspaper, which has been dreaming its own dreams in the night. Postponing the moment, savoring every small news item and vitamin pill and sip of unconcentrated orange juice, I at last return to the upstairs and face the rooms that Updike has filled with his books, his papers, his trophies, his projects. The abundant clutter stifles me, yet I am helpless to clear away much of it. It would be a blasphemy. He has become a sacred reality to me. I gaze at his worn wooden desk, his boxes of dull pencils, his blank-faced word processor, with a religious fear.

5   Suppose, some day, he fails to show up? I would attempt to do his work, but no one would be fooled.

Questions for Discussion

1. From what materials has John Updike created the persona "Updike"? Why does John Updike not feel resentment about being mistaken for "Updike"? Why is he "surprised"?

2. Why does "Updike" have difficulty functioning in real time? How and why does he differ from his creator in terms of his social skills?

3. How are "Updike" and John Updike's values and beliefs different?

4. Why does John Updike refer to the persona "Updike" as a monster? Does he seem genuinely monstrous to you? Is the word "monster" being used here in an ironic sense?

5. What view of dreams does John Updike present? How does the emphasis on the dream state in "Updike and I" shed light on the relationship between "Updike" and the "I" in the narrative?

6. The essay includes descriptions of the objects related to "Updike" and his career world. How do these objects help define the persona of "Updike," and why does the narrator, John Updike, feel these objects constitute a "sacred reality"?

7. Does this essay help you understand your own feelings about your writing? In what ways?

Ideas for Writing

1. Write an essay similar to "Updike and I" that explores the differences that exist between the part of yourself that writes and the part that exists in the everyday world. What have you learned about yourself from thinking about these differences?

2. Take an inventory of the objects you have accumulated in your home or room. How do these objects support and validate different selves within you? Write an essay that takes this inventory into account and explains how the different aspects of your personality and character developed and how these different personality traits support one another.

Marie-Luise Von Franz

The Realization of the Shadow in Dreams

Dr. Von Franz (b. 1915), originally from Switzerland, is one of the world's most renowned analysts and a follower of Carl Jung. She has written such works as Shadow and Evil in Fairy Tales *(1974),* C. G. Jung *(1972),* Patterns of Creativity Mirrored in Creation Myths *(1972), and* Individuation in Fairy Tales *(1990). The following selection, on the psychological archetype of the shadow as it appears in dreams, is from* Man and His Symbols *(1964), a book that Von Franz wrote with Carl Jung.*

JOURNAL

Write about a dream or fantasy that you have had about a stranger.

1   The shadow is not the whole of the unconscious personality. It represents unknown or little-known attributes and qualities of the ego—aspects that mostly belong to the personal sphere and that could just as well be conscious. In some aspects, the shadow can also consist of collective factors that stem from a source outside the individual's personal life.

2   When an individual makes an attempt to see his shadow, he becomes aware of (and often ashamed of) those qualities and impulses he denies in himself but can plainly see in other people—such things as egotism, mental laziness, and sloppiness; unreal fantasies, schemes, and plots; carelessness and cowardice; inordinate love of money and possessions—in short, all the little sins about which he might previously have told himself: "That doesn't matter; nobody will notice it, and in any case other people do it too."

3   If you feel an overwhelming rage coming up in you when a friend reproaches you about a fault, you can be fairly sure that at this point you will find a part of your shadow, of which you are unconscious. It is, of course, natural to become annoyed when others who are "no better" criticize you because of shadow faults. But what can you say if your own dreams—an inner judge in your own being—reproach you? That is the moment when the ego gets caught, and the result is usually embarrassed silence. Afterward the pain and lengthy work of self-education begins—a work, we might say, that is the psychological equivalent of the labors of Hercules. This unfortunate hero's first task, you will remember, was to clean up in one day the Augean Stables, in which hundreds of cattle had dropped their dung for many decades—a task so enormous that the ordinary mortal would be overcome by discouragement at the mere thought of it.

4   The shadow does no consist only of omissions. It shows up just as often in an impulsive or inadvertent act. Before one has time to think, the evil remarks pop out, the plot is hatched, the wrong decision is made, and one is confronted

with results that were never intended or consciously wanted. Furthermore, the shadow is exposed to collective infections to a much greater extent than is the conscious personality. When a man is alone, for instance, he feels relatively all right; but as soon as "the others" do dark, primitive things he begins to fear that if he doesn't join in, he will be considered a fool. Thus he gives way to impulses that do not really belong to him at all. It is particularly in contacts with people of the same sex that one stumbles over both one's own shadow and those of other people. Although we do not see the shadow in a person of the opposite sex, we are usually much less annoyed by it and can more easily pardon it.

5   In dreams and myths, therefore, the shadow appears as a person of the same sex as that of the dreamer. The following dream may serve as an example. The dreamer was a man of 48 who tried to live very much for and by himself, working hard and disciplining himself, repressing pleasure and spontaneity to a far greater extent than suited his real nature.

> I owned and inhabited a very big house in town, and I didn't yet know all its different parts. So I took a walk through it and discovered, mainly in the cellar, several rooms about which I knew nothing and even exits leading into other cellars or into subterranean streets. I felt uneasy when I found that several of these exits were not locked and some had no locks at all. Moreover, there were some laborers at work in the neighborhood who could have sneaked in. . . .
>
> When I came back up again to the ground floor, I passed a back yard where again I discovered different exits into the street or into other houses. When I tried to investigate them more closely, a man came up to me laughing loudly and calling out that we were old pals from the elementary school. I remembered him too, and while he was telling me about his life, I walked along with him toward the exit and strolled with him through the streets.
>
> There was a strange chiaroscuro in the air as we walked through an enormous circular street and arrived at a green lawn where three galloping horses suddenly passed us. They were beautiful, strong animals, wild but well-groomed, and they had no rider with them. (Had they run away from military service?)

6   The maze of strange passages, chambers, and unlocked exits in the cellar recalls the old Egyptian representation of the underworld, which is a well-known symbol of the unconscious with its unknown possibilities. It also shows how one is "open" to other influences in one's unconscious shadow side, and how uncanny and alien elements can break in. The cellar, one can say, is the basement of the dreamer's psyche. In the back yard of the strange building (which represents the still unperceived psychic scope of the dreamer's personality) an old school friend suddenly turns up. This person obviously personifies another aspect of the dreamer himself—an aspect that had been part of his life as a child but that he had forgotten and lost. It often happens that a person's childhood qualities (for instance, gaiety, irascibility, or perhaps trustfulness) suddenly disappear, and one does not know where or how they have gone. It is such a lost characteristic of the dreamer that now returns (from the back yard) and tries to make friends again. This figure prob-

ably stands for the dreamer's neglected capacity for enjoying life and for his extroverted shadow side.

7   But we soon learn why the dreamer feels "uneasy" just before meeting this seemingly harmless old friend. When he strolls with him in the street, the horses break loose. The dreamer thinks they may have escaped from military service (that is to say, from the conscious discipline that has hitherto characterized his life). The fact that the horses have no rider shows that instinctive drives can get away from conscious control. In this old friend, and in the horses, all the positive force reappears that was lacking before and that was badly needed by the dreamer.

8   This is a problem that often comes up when one meets one's "other side." The shadow usually contains values that are needed by consciousness, but that exist in a form that makes it difficult to integrate them into one's life. The passages and the large house in this dream also show that the dreamer does not yet know his own psychic dimensions and is not yet able to fill them out.

9   The shadow in this dream is typical for an introvert (a man who tends to retire too much from outer life). In the case of an extrovert, who is turned more toward outer objects and outer life, the shadow would look quite different.

10   A young man who had a very lively temperament embarked again and again on successful enterprises, while at the same time his dreams insisted that he should finish off a piece of private creative work he had begun. The following was one of those dreams:

> A man is lying on a couch and has pulled the cover over his face. He is a Frenchman, a desperado who would take on any criminal job. An official is accompanying me downstairs, and I know that a plot has been made against me: namely, that the Frenchman should kill me as if by chance. (That is how it would look from the outside.) He actually sneaks up behind me when we approach the exit, but I am on my guard. A tall, portly man (rather rich and influential) suddenly leans against the wall beside me, feeling ill. I quickly grab the opportunity to kill the official by stabbing his heart. "One only notices a bit of moisture"—this is said like a comment. Now I am safe, for the Frenchman won't attack me since the man who gave him his orders is dead. (Probably the official and the successful portly man are the same person, the latter somehow replacing the former.)

11   The desperado represents the other side of the dreamer—his introversion—which has reached a completely destitute state. He lies on a couch (i.e., he is passive) and pulls the cover over his face because he wants to be left alone. The official, on the other hand, and the prosperous portly man (who are secretly the same person) personify the dreamer's successful outer responsibilities and activities. The sudden illness of the portly man is connected with the fact that this dreamer had in fact become ill several times when he had allowed his dynamic energy to explode too forcibly in his external life. But this successful man has no blood in his veins—only a sort of moisture—which means that these external ambitious activities of the dreamer contain no genuine life and no passion, but are bloodless mechanisms. Thus it would be no real loss if the portly man were killed. At the end of the dream, the Frenchman is satisfied; he obviously represents a positive

shadow figure who had turned negative and dangerous only because the conscious attitude of the dreamer did not agree with him.

12   This dream shows us that the shadow can consist of many different elements—for instance, of unconscious ambition (the successful portly man) and of introversion (the Frenchman). This particular dreamer's association to the French, moreover, was that they know how to handle love affairs very well. Therefore the two shadow figures also present two well-known drives: power and sex. The power drive appears momentarily in a double form, both as an official and as a successful man. The official, or civil servant, personifies collective adaptation, whereas the successful man denotes ambition; but naturally both serve the power drive. When the dreamer succeeds in stopping this dangerous inner force, the Frenchman is suddenly no longer hostile. In other words, the equally dangerous aspect of the sex drive has also surrendered.

13   Obviously, the problem of the shadow plays a great role in all political conflicts. If the man who had this dream had not been sensible about his shadow problem, he could easily have identified the desperate Frenchman with the "dangerous Communists" of outer life, or the official plus the prosperous man with the "grasping capitalists." In this way he would have avoided seeing that he had within him such warring elements. If people observe their own unconscious tendencies in other people, this is called a "projection." Political agitation in all countries is full of such projections, just as much as the backyard gossip of little groups and individuals. Projections of all kinds obscure our view of our fellow men, spoiling its objectivity, and thus spoiling all possibility of genuine human relationships.

14   And there is an additional disadvantage in projecting our shadow. If we identify our own shadow with, say, the Communists or the capitalists, a part of our own personality remains on the opposing side. The result is that we shall constantly (though involuntarily) do things behind our own backs that support this other side, and thus we shall unwittingly help our enemy. If, on the contrary, we realize the projection and can discuss matters without fear or hostility, dealing with the other person sensibly, then there is a chance of mutual understanding—or at least a truce.

15   Whether the shadow becomes our friend or enemy depends largely upon ourselves. As the dreams of the unexplored house and the French desperado both show, the shadow is not necessarily always an opponent. In fact, he is exactly like any human being with whom one has to get along, sometimes by giving in, sometimes by resisting, sometimes by giving love—whatever the situation requires. The shadow becomes hostile only when he is ignored or misunderstood.

Questions for Discussion

1. Based on Von Franz's discussion, how would you define the shadow? What inner and outer qualities can the shadow represent?
2. How is the shadow related both to reproach and to rage?

3. According to Von Franz, why does the shadow usually appear to us in the form of a person of our own sex? Have you ever had a shadow figure appear to you in your dreams? Was the shadow of the opposite sex? What did the shadow figure mean to you?

4. In her essay Von Franz analyzes two dreams, one by a middle-aged, introverted man, one by a younger, "lively" individual. What are the differences between these two dreams? What elements do they share?

5. What role does the shadow play in political conflicts? How is this point illustrated by the second dream that Von Franz analyzes? Can you apply Von Franz's concept to your own experiences with politics?

6. How does Von Franz suggest that the shadow can be made our "friend"? Does her advice seem sufficient to you? Is there anything else about the process of befriending your shadow that you would like to know more about?

Ideas for Writing

1. Write a personal essay in which you reflect on ways that you might try to accommodate or integrate the "shadow" side of your personality. Try creating a "dialogue" with your shadow, or propose some compromises in your lifestyle that might please both sides of your personality.

2. Write an essay in which you argue for or against the concept of the need to integrate the "shadow" side of the personality as Von Franz proposes. Support your main ideas with examples from your dreams, people you have met that seem unbalanced or seem to represent the "shadow" side of your personality, and popular films or novels that reflect on the role of the shadow self.

 # Hans Christian Andersen

The Shadow

Hans Christian Andersen (1805–1875), who was born in Denmark to a poor family, struggled for many years to make a living as a singer and actor. His imaginative stories for children eventually brought him fame and wealth, as well as special recognition from the King of Denmark. Andersen traveled extensively throughout Europe and considered Italy his second home. He had 168 of his fairy tales published during his lifetime and collected them in Tales and Stories *(1862). As you read "The Shadow," a fairy tale for adult readers, notice how the atmosphere, characters, and story line of the tale evoke a variety of possible*

*interpretations of the unhappy relationship between a learned man and his
"shadow."*

JOURNAL

Describe your shadow self. Then develop a short dialogue on a specific issue
about which the two sides of yourself are in conflict, or discuss the times when
your shadow self is most likely to surface and torment you.

1   In very hot climates, where the heat of the sun has great power, people are usually as brown as mahogany; and in the hottest countries they are negroes, with
black skins. A learned man once travelled into one of these warm climates, from
the cold regions of the north, and thought he could roam about as he did at home;
but he soon had to change his opinion. He found that, like all sensible people, he
must remain in the house during the whole day, with every window and door
closed, so that it looked as if all in the house were asleep or absent. The houses of
the narrow street in which he lived were so lofty that the sun shone upon them
from morning till evening, and it became quite unbearable. This learned man
from the cold regions was young as well as clever; but it seemed to him as if he
were sitting in an oven, and he became quite exhausted and weak, and grew so
thin that his shadow shrivelled up, and became much smaller than it had been at
home. The sun took away even what was left of it, and he saw nothing of it till
evening, after sunset. It was really a pleasure, as soon as the lights were brought
into the room, to see the shadow stretch itself against the wall, even to the ceiling,
so tall was it; and it really wanted a good stretch to recover its strength. The
learned man would sometimes go out into the balcony to stretch himself also; and
as soon as the stars came forth in the clear, beautiful sky, he felt revived. People at
this hour began to make their appearance in all the balconies in the street; for in
warm climates every window has a balcony, in which they can breathe the fresh
evening air, which is very necessary, even to those who are used to a heat that
makes them as brown as mahogany; so that the street presented a very lively appearance. Here were shoemakers, and tailors, and all sorts of people sitting. In the
street beneath, they brought out tables and chairs, lighted candles by hundreds,
talked and sang, and were very merry. There were people walking, carriages driving, and mules trotting along, with their bells on the harness, "tingle, tingle," as
they went. Then the dead were carried to the grave with the sound of solemn music, and the tolling of the church bells. It was indeed a scene of varied life in the
street. One house only, which was just opposite to the one in which the foreign
learned man lived, formed a contrast to all this, for it was quite still; and yet somebody dwelt there, for flowers stood in the balcony, blooming beautifully in the hot
sun; and this could not have been unless they had been watered carefully. Therefore some one must be in the house to do this. The doors leading to the balcony
were half opened in the evening; and although in the front room all was dark, mu-

sic could be heard from the interior of the house. The foreign learned man considered this music very delightful; but perhaps he fancied it; for everything in these warm countries pleased him, excepting the heat of the sun. The foreign landlord said he did not know who had taken the opposite house—nobody was to be seen there; and as to the music, he thought it seemed very tedious, to him most uncommonly so.

2   "It is just as if some one were practicing a piece that he could not manage; it was always the same piece. He thinks, I suppose, that he will be able to manage it at last; but I do not think so, however long he may play it."

3   Once the foreigner woke in the night. He slept with the door open which led to the balcony; the wind had raised the curtain before it, and there appeared a wonderful brightness over all in the balcony of the opposite house. The flowers seemed like flames of the most gorgeous colours, and among the flowers stood a beautiful slender maiden. It was to him as if light streamed from her, and dazzled his eyes; but then he had only just opened them, as he awoke from his sleep. With one spring he was out of bed, and crept softly behind the curtain. But she was gone—the brightness had disappeared; the flowers no longer appeared like flames, although still as beautiful as ever. The door stood ajar, and from an inner room sounded music so sweet and so lovely, that it produced the most enchanting thoughts, and acted on the senses with magic power. Who could live there? Where was the real entrance? for, both in the street and in the lane at the side, the whole ground floor was a continuation of shops; and people could not always be passing through them.

4   One evening the foreigner sat in the balcony. A light was burning in his own room, just behind him. It was quite natural, therefore, that his shadow should fall on the wall of the opposite house; so that, as he sat amongst the flowers on his balcony, when he moved, his shadow moved also.

5   "I think my shadow is the only living thing to be seen opposite," said the learned man; "see how pleasantly it sits among the flowers. The door is only ajar; the shadow ought to be clever enough to step in and look about him, and then to come back and tell me what he has seen. You could make yourself useful in this way," said he, jokingly; "be so good as to step in now, will you?" and then he nodded to the shadow, and the shadow nodded in return. "Now go, but don't stay away altogether."

6   Then the foreigner stood up, and the shadow on the opposite balcony stood up also; the foreigner turned round, the shadow turned; and if any one had observed, they might have seen it go straight into the half-opened door of the opposite balcony, as the learned man re-entered his own room, and let the curtain fall. The next morning he went out to take his coffee and read the newspapers.

7   "How is this?" he exclaimed, as he stood in the sunshine. "I have lost my shadow. So it really did go away yesterday evening, and it has not returned. This is very annoying."

8   And it certainly did vex him, not so much because the shadow was gone, but because he knew there was a story of a man without a shadow. All the people at home, in his country, knew this story; and when he returned, and related his own

adventures, they would say it was only an imitation; and he had no desire for such things to be said of him. So he decided not to speak of it at all, which was a very sensible determination.

9   In the evening he went out again on his balcony, taking care to place the light behind him; for he knew that a shadow always wants his master for a screen; but he could not entice him out. He made himself little, and he made himself tall; but there was no shadow, and no shadow came. He said, "Hem, a-hem"; but it was all useless. This was very vexatious; but in warm countries everything grows very quickly; and, after a week had passed, he saw, to his great joy, that a new shadow was growing from his feet, when he walked in the sunshine; so that the root must have remained. After three weeks, he had quite a respectable shadow, which, during his return journey to northern lands, continued to grow, and became at last so large that he might very well have spared half of it. When this learned man arrived at home, he wrote books about the true, the good, and the beautiful, which are to be found in this world; and so days and years passed— many, many years.

10   One evening, as he sat in his study, a very gentle tap was heard at the door. "Come in," said he; but no one came. He opened the door, and there stood before him a man so remarkably thin that he felt seriously troubled at his appearance. He was, however, very well dressed, and looked like a gentleman. "To whom have I the honour of speaking?" said he.

11   "Ah, I hoped you would recognise me," said the elegant stranger; "I have gained so much that I have a body of flesh, and clothes to wear. You never expected to see me in such a condition. Do you not recognise your old shadow? Ah, you never expected that I should return to you again. All has been prosperous with me since I was with you last; I have become rich in every way, and, were I inclined to purchase my freedom from service, I could easily do so." And as he spoke he rattled between his fingers a number of costly trinkets which hung to a thick gold watch-chain he wore round his neck. Diamond rings sparkled on his fingers, and it was all real.

12   "I cannot recover from my astonishment," said the learned man. "What does all this mean?"

13   "Something rather unusual," said the shadow; "but you are yourself an uncommon man, and you know very well that I have followed in your footsteps ever since your childhood. As soon as you found that I had travelled enough to be trusted alone, I went my own way, and I am now in the most brilliant circumstances. But I felt a kind of longing to see you once more before you die, and I wanted to see this place again, for there is always a clinging to the land of one's birth. I know that you have now another shadow; do I owe you anything? If so, have the goodness to say what it is."

14   "No! Is it really you?" said the learned man. "Well, this is most remarkable; I never supposed it possible that a man's old shadow could become a human being."

15   "Just tell me what I owe you," said the shadow, "for I do not like to be in debt to any man."

16 "How can you talk in that manner?" said the learned man. "What question of debt can there be between us? You are as free as any one. I rejoice exceedingly to hear of your good fortune. Sit down, old friend, and tell me a little of how it happened, and what you saw in the house opposite to me while we were in those hot climates."

17 "Yes, I will tell you all about it," said the shadow, sitting down; "but then you must promise me never to tell in this city, wherever you may meet me, that I have been your shadow. I am thinking of being married, for I have more than sufficient to support a family."

18 "Make yourself quite easy," said the learned man; "I will tell no one who you really are. Here is my hand,—I promise, and a word is sufficient between man and man."

19 "Between man and a shadow," said the shadow; for he could not help saying so.

20 It was really most remarkable how very much he had become a man in appearance. He was dressed in a suit of the very finest black cloth, polished boots, and an opera crush hat, which could be folded together so that nothing could be seen but the crown and the rim, besides the trinkets, the gold chain, and the diamond rings already spoken of. The shadow was, in fact, very well dressed, and this made a man of him. "Now I will relate to you what you wish to know," said the shadow, placing his foot with the polished leather boot as firmly as possible on the arm of the new shadow of the learned man, which lay at his feet like a poodle dog. This was done, it might be from pride, or perhaps that the new shadow might cling to him, but the prostrate shadow remained quite quiet and at rest, in order that it might listen, for it wanted to know how a shadow could be sent away by its master, and become a man itself. "Do you know," said the shadow, "that in the house opposite to you lived the most glorious creature in the world? It was poetry. I remained there three weeks, and it was more like three thousand years, for I read all that has ever been written in poetry or prose; and I may say, in truth, that I saw and learnt everything."

21 "Poetry!" exclaimed the learned man. "Yes, she lives as a hermit in great cities. Poetry! Well, I saw her once for a very short moment, while sleep weighed down my eyelids. She flashed upon me from the balcony like the radiant aurora borealis, surrounded with flowers like flames of fire. Tell me, you were on the balcony that evening; you went through the door, and what did you see?"

22 "I found myself in an ante-room," said the shadow. "You still sat opposite to me, looking into the room. There was no light, or at least it seemed in partial darkness, for the doors of a whole suite of rooms stood open, and they were brilliantly lighted. The blaze of light would have killed me, had I approached too near the maiden herself; but I was cautious, and took time, which is what every one ought to do."

23 "And what didst thou see?" asked the learned man.

24 "I saw everything, as you shall hear. But—it really is not pride on my part, as a free man and possessing the knowledge that I do, besides my position, not to speak of my wealth—I wish you would say *you* to me, instead of *thou*."

25   "I beg your pardon," said the learned man; "it is an old habit, which it is difficult to break. You are quite right; I will try to think of it. But now tell me everything that you saw."

26   "Everything," said the shadow; "for I saw and know everything."

27   "What was the appearance of the inner rooms?" asked the scholar. "Was it there like a cool grove, or like a holy temple? Were the chambers like a starry sky seen from the top of a high mountain?"

28   "It was all that you describe," said the shadow; "but I did not go quite in—I remained in the twilight of the ante-room—but I was in a very good position,—I could see and hear all that was going on in the court of poetry."

29   "But what did you see? Did the gods of ancient times pass through the rooms? Did old heroes fight their battles over again? Were there lovely children at play, who related their dreams?"

30   "I tell you I have been there, and therefore you may be sure that I saw everything that was to be seen. If you had gone there, you would not have remained a human being, whereas I became one; and at the same moment I became aware of my inner being, my inborn affinity to the nature of poetry. It is true I did not think much about it while I was with you, but you will remember that I was always much larger at sunrise and sunset, and in the moonlight even more visible than yourself, but I did not then understand my inner existence. In the ante-room it was revealed to me. I became a man; I came out in full maturity. But you had left the warm countries. As a man, I felt ashamed to go about without boots or clothes, and that exterior finish by which man is known. So I went my own way; I can tell you, for you will not put it in a book. I hid myself under the cloak of a cake woman, but she little thought who she concealed. It was not till evening that I ventured out. I ran about the streets in the moonlight. I drew myself up to my full height upon the walls, which tickled my back very pleasantly. I ran here and there, looked through the highest windows into the rooms, and over the roofs. I looked in, and saw what nobody else could see, or indeed ought to see; in fact, it is a bad world, and I would not care to be a man, but that men are of some importance. I saw the most miserable things going on between husbands and wives, parents and children,—sweet, incomparable children. I have seen what no human being has the power of knowing, although they would all be very glad to know—the evil conduct of their neighbours. Had I written a newspaper, how eagerly it would have been read! Instead of which, I wrote direct to the persons themselves, and great alarm arose in all the towns I visited. They had so much fear of me, and yet how dearly they loved me. The professor made me a professor. The tailor gave me new clothes; I am well provided for in that way. The overseer of the mint struck coins for me. The women declared that I was handsome, and so I became the man you now see me. And now I must say adieu. Here is my card. I live on the sunny side of the street, and always stay at home in rainy weather." And the shadow departed.

31   "This is all very remarkable," said the learned man.

32   Years passed, days and years went by, and the shadow came again. "How are you going on now?" he asked.

33 "Ah!" said the learned man. "I am writing about the true, the beautiful, and the good; but no one cares to hear anything about it. I am quite in despair, for I take it to heart very much."

34 "That is what I never do," said the shadow; "I am growing quite fat and stout, which every one ought to be. You do not understand the world; you will make yourself ill about it; you ought to travel; I am going on a journey in the summer, will you go with me? I should like a travelling companion; will you travel with me as my shadow? It would give me great pleasure, and I will pay all expenses."

35 "Are you going to travel far?" asked the learned man.

36 "That is a matter of opinion," replied the shadow. "At all events, a journey will do you good, and if you will be my shadow, then all your journey shall be paid."

37 "It appears to me very absurd," said the learned man.

38 "But it is the way of the world," replied the shadow, "and always will be." Then he went away.

39 Everything went wrong with the learned man. Sorrow and trouble pursued him, and what he said about the good, the beautiful, and the true, was of as much value to most people as a nutmeg would be to a cow. At length he fell ill. "You really look like a shadow," people said to him, and then a cold shudder would pass over him, for he had his own thoughts on the subject.

40 "You really ought to go to some watering-place," said the shadow on his next visit. "There is no other chance for you. I will take you with me, for the sake of old acquaintance. I will pay the expenses of your journey, and you shall write a description of it to amuse us by the way. I should like to go to a watering-place; my beard does not grow as it ought, which is from weakness, and I must have a beard. Now do be sensible and accept my proposal; we shall travel as intimate friends."

41 And at last they started together. The shadow was master now, and the master became the shadow. They drove together, and rode and walked in company with each other, side by side, or one in front and the other behind, according to the position of the sun. The shadow always knew when to take the place of honour, but the learned man took no notice of it, for he had a good heart, and was exceedingly mild and friendly.

42 One day the master said to the shadow, "We have grown up together from our childhood, and now that we have become travelling companions, shall we not drink to our good fellowship, and say *thee* and *thou* to each other."

43 "What you say is very straightforward and kindly meant," said the shadow, who was now really master. "I will be equally kind and straightforward. You are a learned man, and know how wonderful human nature is. There are some men who cannot endure the smell of brown paper; it makes them ill. Others will feel a shuddering sensation to their very marrow, if a nail is scratched on a pane of glass. I myself have a similar kind of feeling when I hear any one say *thou* to me. I feel crushed by it, as I used to feel in my former position with you. You will perceive that this is a matter of feeling, not pride. I cannot allow you to say *thou* to me; I will gladly say it to you, and therefore your wish will be half fulfilled." Then the shadow addressed his former master as *thou*.

44   "It is going rather too far," said the latter, "that I am to say *you* when I speak to him, and he is to say *thou* to me." However, he was obliged to submit.

45   They arrived at length at the baths, where there were many strangers and among them a beautiful princess, whose real disease consisted in being too sharp-sighted, which made every one very uneasy. She saw at once that the new comer was very different to every one else. "They say he is here to make his beard grow," she thought; "but I know the real cause, he is unable to cast a shadow." Then she became very curious on the matter, and one day, while on the promenade, she entered into conversation with the strange gentleman. Being a princess, she was not obliged to stand upon much ceremony, so she said to him without hesitation, "Your illness consists in not being able to cast a shadow."

46   "Your royal highness must be on the high-road to recovery from your illness," said he. "I know your complaint arose from being too sharp-sighted, and in this case it has entirely failed. I happen to have a most unusual shadow. Have you not seen a person who is always at my side? Persons often give their servants finer cloth for their liveries than for their own clothes, and so I have dressed out my shadow like a man; nay, you may observe that I have even given him a shadow of his own; it is rather expensive, but I like to have things about me that are peculiar."

47   "How is this?" thought the princess; "am I really cured? This must be the best watering-place in existence. Water in our times has certainly wonderful power. But I will not leave this place yet, just as it begins to be amusing. This foreign prince—for he must be a prince—pleases me above all things. I only hope his beard won't grow, or he will leave at once."

48   In the evening, the princess and the shadow danced together in the large assembly rooms. She was light, but he was lighter still, she had never seen such a dancer before. She told him from what country she had come, and found he knew it and had been there, but not while she was at home. He had looked into the windows of her father's palace, both the upper and the lower windows; he had seen many things, and could therefore answer the princess, and make allusions which quite astonished her. She thought he must be the cleverest man in all the world, and felt the greatest respect for his knowledge. When she danced with him again she fell in love with him, which the shadow quickly discovered, for she had with her eyes looked him through and through. They danced once more, and she was nearly telling him, but she had some discretion; she thought of her country, her kingdom, and the number of people over whom she would one day have to rule. "He is a clever man," she thought to herself, "which is a good thing, and he dances admirably, which is also good. But has he well-grounded knowledge? that is an important question, and I must try him." Then she asked him a most difficult question, she herself could not have answered it, and the shadow made a most unaccountable grimace.

49   "You cannot answer that," said the princess.

50   "I learnt something about it in my childhood," he replied; "and believe that even my very shadow, standing over there by the door, could answer it."

51   "Your shadow," said the princess; "indeed that would be very remarkable."

52   "I do not say so, positively," observed the shadow; "but I am inclined to believe that he can do so. He has followed me for so many years, and has heard so much from me, that I think it is very likely. But your royal highness must allow me to observe, that he is very proud of being considered a man, and to put him in a good humour, so that he may answer correctly, he must be treated as a man."

53   "I shall be very pleased to do so," said the princess. So she walked up to the learned man, who stood in the doorway, and spoke to him of the sun, and of the moon, of the green forests, and of people near home and far off; and the learned man conversed with her pleasantly and sensibly.

54   "What a wonderful man he must be, to have such a clever shadow!" thought she. "If I were to choose him it would be a real blessing to my country and my subjects, and I will do it." So the princess and the shadow were soon engaged to each other, but no one was to be told a word about it, till she returned to her kingdom.

55   "No one *shall* know," said the shadow; "not even my own shadow"; and he had very particular reasons for saying so.

56   After a time, the princess returned to the land over which she reigned, and the shadow accompanied her.

57   "Listen, my friend," said the shadow to the learned man; "now that I am as fortunate and as powerful as any man can be, I will do something unusually good for you. You shall live in my palace, drive with me in the royal carriage, and have a hundred thousand dollars a year; but you must allow every one to call you a shadow, and never venture to say that you have been a man. And once a year, when I sit in my balcony in the sunshine, you must lie at my feet as becomes a shadow to do; for I must tell you I am going to marry the princess, and our wedding will take place this evening."

58   "Now, really, this is too ridiculous," said the learned man. "I cannot, and will not, submit to such folly. It would be cheating the whole country, and the princess also. I will disclose everything, and say that I am the man, and that you are only a shadow dressed up in men's clothes."

59   "No one would believe you," said the shadow; "be reasonable, now, or I will call the guards."

60   "I will go straight to the princess," said the learned man.

61   "But I shall be there first," replied the shadow, "and you will be sent to prison." And so it turned out, for the guards readily obeyed him, as they knew he was going to marry the king's daughter.

62   "You tremble," said the princess, when the shadow appeared before her. "Has anything happened? You must not be ill to-day, for this evening our wedding will take place."

63   "I have gone through the most terrible affair that could possibly happen," said the shadow; "only imagine, my shadow has gone mad; I suppose such a poor, shallow brain, could not bear much; he fancies that he has become a real man, and that I am his shadow."

64   "How very terrible," cried the princess; "is he locked up?"

65   "Oh yes, certainly; for I fear he will never recover."

66   "Poor shadow!" said the princess; "it is very unfortunate for him; it would really be a good deed to free him from his frail existence; and, indeed, when I think how often people take the part of the lower class against the higher, in these days, it would be policy to put him out of the way quietly."

67   "It is certainly rather hard upon him, for he was a faithful servant," said the shadow; and he pretended to sigh.

68   "Yours is a noble character," said the princess, and bowed herself before him.

69   In the evening the whole town was illuminated, and cannons fired "boom," and the soldiers presented arms. It was, indeed a grand wedding.

Questions for Discussion

1. As you read this story, how did you interpret its events? For example, did you think of it as a fantasy, or as a story designed to teach either a moral or spiritual lesson? Support your interpretation of the story's meaning.

2. Describe the initial relationship between the learned man and his shadow. What crucial error of judgment does the learned man make in sending his shadow to the house next door?

3. What does the shadow learn from the Muse of Poetry? What does he learn as a free agent when he enters the homes of the townspeople at night under the moonlight? Since he has attained wealth and acclaim, why does the shadow bother to return to the home of the learned man?

4. How does the shadow achieve dominance over the learned man? How does the exchange over "thee" and "thou" (the familiar form of you) underscore the changing relationship? Who is wiser, the learned man or his shadow?

5. Do you think that the shadow will be able to retain his credibility in the court and continue to earn the respect and love of the princess without the aid of the learned man? Why or why not? Will the learned man regain some of his power?

6. What point do you think Andersen is making through the relationship that he develops between the learned man and his shadow about the relative importance of knowledge of the "true, the good and the beautiful," human conscience, worldly experience, and power?

Ideas for Writing

1. Write an essay in which you present an interpretation of the story as a psychological, social, political, racial, or ethical statement. Use details from the story to support your views.

2. Write a story or a personal essay designed to illustrate some of the conflicts you have experienced between your conscious and shadow self.

Robert Louis Stevenson

A Chapter on Dreams

Robert Louis Stevenson (1850–1894) was born in Edinburgh, Scotland, and was educated as a lawyer. Because he had congenital lung disease, Stevenson traveled extensively in search of a healthful climate and eventually settled in Samoa. He is remembered for his verses for children, his adventure novels, and his powerful horror story, The Strange Case of Dr. Jekyll and Mr. Hyde. *In the following excerpt from "A Chapter on Dreams," which first appeared in* Across the Plains *(1892), Stevenson explores the ways in which he used his dreams to help him create his popular novels and stories.*

JOURNAL

Write about a dream that helped you to solve a problem in your waking life.

1　　　This honest fellow had long been in the custom of setting himself to
♦ ♦ ♦　sleep with tales, and so had his father before him; but these were irresponsible inventions, told for the teller's pleasure, with no eye to the crass public or the thwart reviewer: tales where a thread might be dropped, or one adventure quitted for another, on fancy's least suggestion. So that the little people who manage man's internal theatre had not as yet received a very rigorous training; and played upon their stage like children who should have slipped into the house and found it empty, rather than like drilled actors performing a set piece to a huge hall of faces. But presently my dreamer began to turn his former amusement of story-telling to (what is called) account; by which I mean that he began to write and sell his tales. Here was he, and here were the little people who did that part of his business, in quite new conditions. The stories must now be trimmed and pared and set upon all fours, they must run from a beginning to an end and fit (after a manner) with the laws of life; the pleasure, in one word, had become a business; and that not only for the dreamer, but for the little people of his theatre. These understood the change as well as he. When he lay down to prepare himself for sleep, he no longer sought amusement, but printable and profitable tales; and after he had dozed off in his box-seat, his little people continued their evolutions with the same mercantile designs. All other forms of dream deserted him but two: he still occasionally reads the most delightful books, he still visits at times the most delightful places; and it is perhaps worthy of note that to these same places, and to one in particular, he returns at intervals of months and years, finding new field-paths, visiting new neighbours, beholding that happy valley under new effects of noon and dawn and sunset. But all the rest of the family of visions is quite lost to

him: the common, mangled version of yesterday's affair, the raw-head-and-bloody-bones nightmare, rumoured to be the child of toasted cheese—these and their like are gone; and, for the most part, whether awake or asleep, he is simply occupied—he or his little people—in consciously making stories for the market. This dreamer (like many other persons) has encountered some trifling vicissitudes of fortune. When the bank begins to send letters and the butcher to linger at the back gate, he sets to belabouring his brains after a story, for that is his readiest money-winner; and, behold! at once the little people begin to bestir themselves in the same quest, and labour all night long, and all night long set before him truncheons of tales upon their lighted theatre. No fear of his being frightened now; the flying heart and the frozen scalp are things bygone; applause, growing applause, growing interest, growing exultation in his own cleverness (for he takes all the credit), and at last a jubilant leap to wakefulness, with the cry, "I have it, that'll do!" upon his lips: with such and similar emotions he sits at these nocturnal dramas, with such outbreaks, like Claudius in the play, he scatters the performance in the midst. Often enough the waking is a disappointment: he has been too deep asleep, as I explain the thing; drowsiness has gained his little people, they have gone stumbling and maundering through their parts; and the play, to the awakened mind, is seen to be a tissue of absurdities. And yet how often have these sleepless Brownies done him honest service, and given him, as he sat idly taking his pleasure in the boxes, better tales than he could fashion for himself. . . .

2   . . . The more I think of it, the more I am moved to press upon the world my question: Who are the Little People? They are near connections of the dreamer's, beyond doubt; they share in his financial worries and have an eye to the bank-book; they share plainly in his training; they have plainly learned like him to build the scheme of a considerate story and to arrange emotion in progressive order; only I think they have more talent; and one thing is beyond doubt, they can tell him a story piece by piece, like a serial, and keep him all the while in ignorance of where they aim. Who are they, then? and who is the dreamer?

3   Well, as regards the dreamer, I can answer that, for he is no less a person than myself;—as I might have told you from the beginning, only that the critics murmur over my consistent egotism;—and as I am positively forced to tell you now, or I could advance but little farther with my story. And for the Little People, what shall I say they are but just my Brownies, God bless them! who do one-half my work for me while I am fast asleep, and in all human likelihood, do the rest for me as well, when I am wide awake and fondly suppose I do it for myself. That part which is done while I am sleeping is the Brownies' part beyond contention; but that which is done when I am up and about is by no means necessarily mine, since all goes to show the Brownies have a hand in it even then. Here is a doubt that much concerns my conscience. For myself—what I call I, my conscious ego, the denizen of the pineal gland unless he has changed his residence since Descartes, the man with the conscience and the variable bank-account, the man with the hat and the boots, and the privilege of voting and not carrying his candidate at the general elections—I am sometimes tempted to suppose he is no story-teller at

all, but a creature as matter of fact as any cheesemonger or any cheese, and a realist bemired up to the ears in actuality; so that, by that account, the whole of my published fiction should be the single-handed product of some Brownie, some Familiar, some unseen collaborator, whom I keep locked in a back garret, while I get all the praise and he but a share (which I cannot prevent him getting) of the pudding. I am an excellent adviser, something like Molière's servant; I pull back and I cut down; and I dress the whole in the best words and sentences that I can find and make; I hold the pen, too; and I do the sitting at the table, which is about the worst of it; and when all is done, I make up the manuscript and pay for the registration; so that, on the whole, I have some claim to share, though not so largely as I do, in the profits of our common enterprise.

4   I can but give an instance or so of what part is done sleeping and what part awake, and leave the reader to share what laurels there are, at his own nod, between myself and my collaborators; and to do this I will first take a book that a number of persons have been polite enough to read, *The Strange Case of Dr. Jekyll and Mr. Hyde*. I had long been trying to write a story on this subject, to find a body, a vehicle, for that strong sense of man's double being which must at times come in upon and overwhelm the mind of every thinking creature. I had even written one, *The Travelling Companion,* which was returned by an editor on the plea that it was a work of genius and indecent, and which I burned the other day on the ground that it was not a work of genius, and that *Jekyll* had supplanted it. Then came one of those financial fluctuations to which (with an elegant modesty) I have hitherto referred in the third person. For two days I went about racking my brains for a plot of any sort; and on the second night I dreamed the scene at the window, and a scene afterward split in two, in which Hyde, pursued for some crime, took the powder and underwent the change in the presence of his pursuers. All the rest was made awake, and consciously, although I think I can trace in much of it the manner of my Brownies. The meaning of the tale is therefore mine, and had long pre-existed in my garden of Adonis, and tried one body after another in vain; indeed, I do most of the morality, worse luck! and my Brownies have not a rudiment of what we call a conscience. Mine, too, is the setting, mine the characters. All that was given me was the matter of three scenes, and the central idea of a voluntary change becoming involuntary. Will it be thought ungenerous, after I have been so liberally ladling out praise to my unseen collaborators, if I here toss them over, bound hand and foot, into the arena of the critics? For the business of the powders, which so many have censured, is, I am relieved to say, not mine at all but the Brownies'. . . .

Questions for Discussion

1. How does Stevenson contrast the way most people dream and fantasize with the way that he as a professional writer uses his dreams? Have you ever been able to direct or utilize your dreams in the way that Stevenson did?

2. According to Stevenson, who are the "Little People" and who is the dreamer? What part of his inner world do the "Brownies" represent? What popular mythology might they reflect?

3. How can either too much self-consciousness or too deep a level of sleep ruin the dreamer's literary creation?

4. How does Stevenson contrast "myself—what I call I" to the personalities and creativeness of the "Little People"? Do you think that this is a typical division of self for a writer to experience? If you feel a similar type of division within yourself, which part of your mind do you value most? Why?

5. After reading this selection, how do you understand the difference between the conscious and the unconscious mind?

6. How much of Stevenson's novella *The Strange Case of Dr. Jekyll and Mr. Hyde* actually came to him in a dream? What drawbacks does Stevenson suggest there might be in relying too extensively on the Little People or unconscious co-creators for crucial elements of a story? What does Stevenson's essay suggest about the importance of the revision process?

Ideas for Writing

1. Write an essay in which you discuss the ways that you have found your dreams useful as insights into problem-solving, as ideas for stories or other forms of creative expression, or for their prophetic vision.

2. Stevenson suggests what modern brain researchers have discovered: that the brain really has two aspects that play a part in the writing process, the creative and intuitive (right brain) and the logical, problem-solving (left brain). Do you rely on one part of your mind more than on the other? Write an essay in which you provide examples from your writing experiences to support your point of view. Before you begin, you might read Albert Liu's "The Artist and the Engineer," which is included in this chapter.

 Robert Louis Stevenson

Henry Jekyll's Full Statement of the Case, from The Strange Case of Dr. Jekyll and Mr. Hyde

Stevenson spent most of his life in ill health, yet he remained a religious skeptic. He wrote The Strange Case of Dr. Jekyll and Mr. Hyde *(1886), a short novel, at a time when he was very ill with tuberculosis. In the following selection, the conclu-*

sion to Stevenson's classic tale of good and evil, Henry Jekyll, a highly respected London physician, has tampered with his own inner nature using chemical potions to construct a primitive "second self," Mr. Hyde. The following "statement" of Dr. Jekyll, written just before his death, sets forth his reasons for and the fatal consequences of tampering with his own double nature. The letter was found by his friends who discovered only the body of Mr. Hyde with a "crushed phial" of cyanide poison in his hand.

JOURNAL

Write about a feeling you have had of experiencing your "other" or anti-self, through some change in your normal mental state, perhaps from an emotional crisis or chemical stimulation, or during an illness or extreme fatigue.

1   I was born in the year 18— to a large fortune, endowed besides with excellent parts, inclined by nature to industry, fond of the respect of the wise and good among my fellow-men, and thus, as might have been supposed, with every guarantee of an honourable and distinguished future. And indeed the worst of my faults was a certain impatient gaiety of disposition, such as has made the happiness of many, but such as I found it hard to reconcile with my imperious desire to carry my head high, and wear a more than commonly grave countenance before the public. Hence it came about that I concealed my pleasures; and that when I reached years of reflection, and began to look round me and take stock of my progress and position in the world, I stood already committed to a profound duplicity of life. Many a man would have even blazoned such irregularities as I was guilty of; but from the high views that I had set before me, I regarded and hid them with an almost morbid sense of shame. It was thus rather the exacting nature of my aspirations than any particular degradation in my faults, that made me what I was, and, with even a deeper trench than in the majority of men, severed in me those provinces of good and ill which divide and compound man's dual nature. In this case, I was driven to reflect deeply and inveterately on that hard law of life, which lies at the root of religion and is one of the most plentiful springs of distress. Though so profound a double-dealer, I was in no sense a hypocrite; both sides of me were in dead earnest; I was no more myself when I laid aside restraint and plunged in shame, than when I laboured, in the eye of day, at the furtherance of knowledge or the relief of sorrow and suffering. And it chanced that the direction of my scientific studies, which led wholly towards the mystic and the transcendental, reacted and shed a strong light on this consciousness of the perennial war among my members. With every day, and from both sides of my intelligence, the moral and the intellectual, I thus drew steadily nearer to that truth, by whose partial discovery I have been doomed to such a dreadful shipwreck: that man is not truly one, but truly two. I say two, because the state of my own knowledge does not pass beyond that point. Others will follow, others will outstrip me on the same lines; and I hazard the guess that man will be ultimately known for a mere polity

of multifarious, incongruous and independent denizens. I, for my part, from the nature of my life, advanced infallibly in one direction and in one direction only. It was on the moral side, and in my own person, that I learned to recognise the thorough and primitive duality of man; I saw that, of the two natures that contended in the field of my consciousness, even if I could rightly be said to be either, it was only because I was radically both; and from an early date, even before the course of my scientific discoveries had begun to suggest the most naked possibility of such a miracle, I had learned to dwell with pleasure, as a beloved daydream, on the thought of the separation of these elements. If each, I told myself, could be housed in separate identities, life would be relieved of all that was unbearable; the unjust might go his way, delivered from the aspirations and remorse of his more upright twin; and the just could walk steadfastly and securely on his upward path, doing the good things in which he found his pleasure, and no longer exposed to disgrace and penitence by the hands of his extraneous evil. It was the curse of mankind that these incongruous faggots were thus bound together—that in the agonised womb of consciousness, these polar twins should be continuously struggling. How, then, were they dissociated.

2   I was so far in my reflections when, as I have said, a side light began to shine upon the subject from the laboratory table. I began to perceive more deeply than it has ever yet been stated, the trembling immateriality, the mist-like transience, of this seemingly so solid body in which we walk attired. Certain agents I found to have the power to shake and pluck back that fleshy vestment, even as a wind might toss the curtains of a pavilion. For two good reasons, I will not enter deeply into this scientific branch of my confession. First, because I have been made to learn that the doom and burthen of our life is bound for ever on man's shoulders, and when the attempt is made to cast it off, it but returns upon us with more unfamiliar and more awful pressure. Second, because, as my narrative will make, alas! too evident, my discoveries were incomplete. Enough, then, that I not only recognised my natural body from the mere aura and effulgence of certain of the powers that make up my spirit, but managed to compound a drug by which these powers should be dethroned from their supremacy, and a second form and countenance substituted, none the less natural to me because they were the expression, and bore the stamp of lower elements in my soul.

3   I hesitated long before I put this theory to the test of practice. I knew well that I risked death; for any drug that so potently controlled and shook the very fortress of identity, might, by the least scruple of an overdose or at the least inopportunity in the moment of exhibition, utterly blot out that immaterial tabernacle which I looked to it to change. But the temptation of a discovery so singular and profound at last overcame the suggestions of alarm. I had long since prepared my tincture; I purchased at once, from a firm of wholesale chemists, a large quantity of a particular salt which I knew, from my experiments, to be the last ingredient required; and late one accursed night, I compounded the elements, watched them boil and smoke together in the glass, and when the ebullition had subsided, with a strong glow of courage, drank off the potion.

4   The most racking pangs succeeded: a grinding in the bones, deadly nausea, and a horror of the spirit that cannot be exceeded at the hour of birth or death. Then

these agonies began swiftly to subside, and I came to myself as if out of a great sickness. There was something strange in my sensations, something indescribably new and, from its very novelty, incredibly sweet. I felt younger, lighter, happier in body; within I was conscious of a heady recklessness, a current of disordered sensual images running like a millrace in my fancy, a dissolution of the bonds of obligation, an unknown but not an innocent freedom of the soul. I knew myself, at the first breath of this new life, to be more wicked, tenfold more wicked, sold a slave to my original evil; and the thought, in that moment, braced and delighted me like wine. I stretched out my hands, exulting in the freshness of these sensations; and in the act, I was suddenly aware that I had lost in stature.

5   There was no mirror, at that date, in my room; that which stands beside me as I write, was brought there later on and for the very purpose of these transformations. That night, however, was far gone into the morning—the morning, black as it was, was nearly ripe for the conception of the day—the inmates of my house were locked in the most rigourous hours of slumber, and I determined, flushed as I was with hope and triumph, to venture in my new shape as far as to my bedroom. I crossed the yard, wherein the constellations looked down upon me, I could have thought, with wonder, the first creature of that sort that their unsleeping vigilance had yet disclosed to them; I stole through the corridors, a stranger in my own house; and coming to my room, I saw for the first time the appearance of Edward Hyde.

6   I must here speak by theory alone, saying not that which I know, but that which I suppose to be most probable. The evil side of my nature, to which I had now transferred the stamping efficacy, was less robust and less developed than the good which I had just deposed. Again, in the course of my life, which had been, after all, nine tenths a life of effort, virtue and control, it had been much less exercised and much less exhausted. And hence, as I think, it came about that Edward Hyde was so much smaller, slighter and younger than Henry Jekyll. Even as good shone upon the countenance of the one, evil was written broadly and plainly on the face of the other. Evil besides (which I must still believe to be the lethal side of man) had left on that body an imprint of deformity and decay. And yet when I looked upon that ugly idol in the glass, I was conscious of no repugnance, rather of a leap of welcome. This, too, was myself. It seemed natural and human. In my eyes it bore a livelier image of the spirit, it seemed more express and single, than the imperfect and divided countenance I had been hitherto accustomed to call mine. And in so far I was doubtless right. I have observed that when I wore the semblance of Edward Hyde, none could come near to me at first without a visible misgiving of the flesh. This, as I take it, was because all human beings, as we meet them, are commingled out of good and evil: and Edward Hyde, alone in the ranks of mankind, was pure evil.

7   I lingered but a moment at the mirror: the second and conclusive experiment had yet to be attempted; it yet remained to be seen if I had lost my identity beyond redemption and must flee before daylight from a house that was no longer mine; and hurrying back to my cabinet, I once more prepared and drank the cup, once more suffered the pangs of dissolution, and came to myself once more with the character, the stature and the face of Henry Jekyll.

8   That night I had come to the fatal crossroads. Had I approached my discovery in a more noble spirit, had I risked the experiment while under the empire of generous or pious aspirations, all must have been otherwise, and from these agonies of death and birth, I had come forth an angel instead of a fiend. The drug had no discriminating action; it was neither diabolical nor divine; it but shook the doors of the prisonhouse of my disposition; and like the captives of Phillipi, that which stood within ran forth. At that time my virtue slumbered; my evil, kept awake by ambition, was alert and swift to seize the occasion; and the thing that was projected was Edward Hyde. Hence, although I had now two characters as well as two appearances, one was wholly evil, and the other was still the old Henry Jekyll, that incongruous compound of whose reformation and improvement I had already learned to despair. The movement was thus wholly toward the worse.

9   Even at that time, I had not conquered my aversion to the dryness of a life of study. I would still be merrily disposed at times; and as my pleasures were (to say the least) undignified, and I was not only well known and highly considered, but growing toward the elderly man, this incoherency of my life was daily growing more unwelcome. It was on this side that my new power tempted me until I fell in slavery. I had but to drink the cup, to doff at once the body of the noted professor, and to assume, like a thick cloak, that of Edward Hyde. I smiled at the notion; it seemed to me at the time to be humorous; and I made my preparations with the most studious care. I took and furnished that house in Soho, to which Hyde was tracked by the police; and engaged as a housekeeper a creature whom I knew well to be silent and unscrupulous. On the other side, I announced to my servants that a Mr. Hyde (whom I described) was to have full liberty and power about my house in the square; and to parry mishaps, I even called and made myself a familiar object, in my second character. I next drew up that will to which you so much objected; so that if anything befell me in the person of Dr. Jekyll, I could enter on that of Edward Hyde without pecuniary loss. And thus fortified, as I supposed, on every side, I began to profit by the strange immunities of my position.

10   Men have before hired bravoes to transact their crimes, while their own person and reputation sat under shelter. I was the first that ever did so for his pleasures. I was the first that could plod in the public eye with a load of genial respectability, and in a moment, like a schoolboy, strip off these lendings and spring headlong into the sea of liberty. But for me, in my impenetrable mantle, the safety was complete. Think of it—I did not even exist! Let me but escape into my laboratory door, give me but a second or two to mix and swallow the draught that I had always standing ready; and whatever he had done, Edward Hyde would pass away like the stain of breath upon a mirror; and there in his stead, quietly at home, trimming the midnight lamp in his study, a man who could afford to laugh at suspicion, would be Harry Jekyll.

11   The pleasures which I made haste to seek in my disguise were, as I have said, undignified; I would scarce use a harder term. But in the hands of Edward Hyde, they soon began to turn toward the monstrous. When I would come back from these excursions, I was often plunged into a kind of wonder at my vicarious depravity. This familiar that I called out of my own soul, and sent forth alone to do

his good pleasure, was a being inherently malign and villainous; his every act and thought centered on self; drinking pleasure with bestial avidity from any degree of torture to another; relentless like a man of stone. Henry Jekyll stood at times aghast before the acts of Edward Hyde; but the situation was apart from ordinary laws, and insidiously relaxed the grasp of conscience. It was Hyde, after all, and Hyde alone, that was guilty. Jekyll was no worse; he woke again to his good qualities seemingly unimpaired; he would even make haste, where it was possible, to undo the evil done by Hyde. And thus his conscience slumbered.

12   Into the details of the infamy at which I thus connived (for even now I can scarce grant that I committed it) I have no design of entering; I mean but to point out the warnings and the successive steps with which my chastisement approached. I met with one accident which, as it brought on no consequence, I shall no more than mention. An act of cruelty to a child aroused against me the anger of a passerby, whom I recognised the other day in the person of your kinsman; the doctor and the child's family joined him; there were moments when I feared for my life; and at last, in order to pacify their too just resentment, Edward Hyde had to bring them to the door, and pay them in a cheque drawn in the name of Henry Jekyll. But this danger was easily eliminated from the future, by opening an account at another bank in the name of Edward Hyde himself; and when, by sloping my own hand backward, I had supplied my double with a signature, I thought I sat beyond the reach of fate.

13   Some two months before the murder of Sir Danvers, I had been out for one of my adventures, had returned at a late hour, and woke the next day in bed with somewhat odd sensations. It was in vain I looked about me; in vain I saw the decent furniture and tall proportions of my room in the square; in vain that I recognised the pattern of the bed curtains and the design of the mahogany frame; something still kept insisting that I was not where I was, that I had not wakened where I seemed to be, but in the little room in Soho where I was accustomed to sleep in the body of Edward Hyde. I smiled to myself, and, in my psychological way, began lazily to inquire into the elements of this illusion, occasionally, even as I did so, dropping back into a comfortable morning doze. I was still so engaged when, in one of my more wakeful moments, my eyes fell upon my hand. Now the hand of Henry Jekyll (as you have often remarked) was professional in shape and size: it was large, firm, white and comely. But the hand which I now saw, clearly enough, in the yellow light of a mid-London morning, lying half shut on the bedclothes, was lean, corded, knuckly, of a dusky pallor and thickly shaded with a swart growth of hair. It was the hand of Edward Hyde.

14   I must have stared upon it for near half a minute, sunk as I was in the mere stupidity of wonder, before terror woke up in my breast as sudden and startling as the crash of cymbals; and bounding from my bed, I rushed to the mirror. At the sight that met my eyes, my blood was changed into something exquisitely thin and icy. Yes, I had gone to bed Henry Jekyll, I had awakened Edward Hyde. How was this to be explained? I asked myself; and then, with another bound of terror—how was it to be remedied? It was well on in the morning; the servants were up; all my drugs were in the cabinet—a long journey down two pairs of stairs, through the back passage, across the open court and through the anatomical theatre, from

where I was then standing horror-struck. It might indeed be possible to cover my face; but of what use was that, when I was unable to conceal the alteration in my stature? And then with an overpowering sweetness of relief, it came back upon my mind that the servants were already used to the coming and going of my second self. I had soon dressed, as well as I was able, in clothes of my own size; had soon passed through the house, where Bradshaw stared and drew back at seeing Mr. Hyde at such an hour and in such a strange array; and ten minutes later, Dr. Jekyll had returned to his own shape and was sitting down, with a darkened brow, to make a feint of breakfasting.

15   Small indeed was my appetite. This inexplicable incident, this reversal of my previous experience, seemed, like the Babylonian finger on the wall, to be spelling out the letters of my judgment; and I began to reflect more seriously than ever before on the issues and possibilities of my double existence. That part of me which I had the power of projecting, had lately been much exercised and nourished; it had seemed to me of late as though the body of Edward Hyde had grown in stature, as though (when I wore that form) I were conscious of a more generous tide of blood, and I began to spy a danger that, if this were much prolonged, the balance of my nature might be permanently overthrown, the power of voluntary change be forfeited, and the character of Edward Hyde become irrevocably mine. The power of the drug had not been always equally displayed. Once, very early in my career, it had totally failed me; since then I had been obliged on more than one occasion to double, and once, with infinite risk of death, to treble the amount; and these rare uncertainties had cast hitherto the sole shadow on my contentment. Now, however, and in the light of that morning's accident, I was led to remark that whereas, in the beginning, the difficulty had been to throw off the body of Jekyll, it had of late gradually but decidedly transferred itself to the other side. All things therefore seemed to point to this: that I was slowly losing hold of my original and better self, and becoming slowly incorporated with my second and worse.

16   Between these two, I now felt I had to choose. My two natures had memory in common, but all other faculties were most unequally shared between them. Jekyll (who was composite) now with the most sensitive apprehensions, now with a greedy gusto, projected and shared in the pleasures and adventures of Hyde; but Hyde was indifferent to Jekyll, or but remembered him as the mountain bandit remembers the cavern in which he conceals himself from pursuit. Jekyll had more than a father's interest; Hyde had more than a son's indifference. To cast in my lot with Jekyll, was to die to those appetites which I had long secretly indulged and had of late begun to pamper. To cast it in with Hyde, was to die to a thousand interests and aspirations, and to become, at a blow and forever, despised and friendless. The bargain might appear unequal; but there was still another consideration in the scales; for while Jekyll would suffer smartly in the fires of abstinence, Hyde would be not even conscious of all that he had lost. Strange as my circumstances were, the terms of this debate are as old and commonplace as man; much the same inducements and alarms cast the die for any tempted and trembling sinner; and it fell out with me, as it falls with so vast a majority of my fellows, that I chose the better part and was found wanting in the strength to keep to it.

17   Yes, I preferred the elderly and discontented doctor, surrounded by friends and cherishing honest hopes; and bade a resolute farewell to the liberty, the comparative youth, the light step, leaping impulses and secret pleasures, that I had enjoyed in the disguise of Hyde. I made this choice perhaps with some unconscious reservation, for I neither gave up the house in Soho, nor destroyed the clothes of Edward Hyde, which still lay ready in my cabinet. For two months, however, I was true to my determination; for two months, I led a life of such severity as I had never before attained to, and enjoyed the compensations of an approving conscience. But time began at last to obliterate the freshness of my alarm; the praises of conscience began to grow into a thing of course; I began to be tortured with throes and longings, as of Hyde struggling after freedom; and at last, in an hour of moral weakness, I once again compounded and swallowed the transforming draught.

18   I do not suppose that, when a drunkard reasons with himself upon his vice, he is once out of five hundred times affected by the dangers that he runs through his brutish, physical insensibility; neither had I, long as I had considered my position, made enough allowance for the complete moral insensibility and insensate readiness to evil, which were the leading characters of Edward Hyde. Yet it was by these that I was punished. My devil had been long caged, he came out roaring. I was conscious, even when I took the draught, of a more unbridled, a more furious propensity to ill. It must have been this, I suppose, that stirred in my soul that tempest of impatience with which I listened to the civilities of my unhappy victim; I declare, at least, before God, no man morally sane could have been guilty of that crime upon so pitiful a provocation; and that I struck in no more reasonable spirit than that in which a sick child may break a plaything. But I had voluntarily stripped myself of all those balancing instincts by which even the worst of us continues to walk with some degree of steadiness among temptations and in my case, to be tempted, however slightly, was to fall.

19   Instantly the spirit of hell awoke in me and raged. With a transport of glee, I mauled the unresisting body, tasting delight from every blow; and it was not till weariness had begun to succeed, that I was suddenly, in the top fit of my delirium, struck through the heart by a cold thrill of terror. A mist dispersed; I saw my life to be forfeit; and fled from the scene of these excesses, at once glorying and trembling, my lust of evil gratified and stimulated, my love of life screwed to the topmost peg. I ran to the house in Soho, and (to make assurance doubly sure) destroyed my papers; thence I set out through the lamplit streets, in the same divided ecstasy of mind, gloating on my crime, light-headedly devising others in the future, and yet still hastening and still hearkening in my wake for the steps of the avenger. Hyde had a song upon his lips as he compounded the draught, and as he drank it, pledged the dead man. The pangs of transformation had not done tearing him, before Henry Jekyll, with streaming tears of gratitude and remorse, had fallen upon his knees and lifted his clasped hands to God. The veil of self-indulgence was rent from head to foot. I saw my life as a whole: I followed it up from the days of childhood, when I had walked with my father's hand, and through the self-denying toils of my professional life, to arrive again and again, with the same

sense of unreality, at the damned horrors of the evening. I could have screamed aloud; I sought with tears and prayers to smother down the crowd of hideous images and sounds with which my memory swarmed against me; and still, between the petitions, the ugly face of my iniquity stared into my soul. As the acuteness of this remorse began to die away, it was succeeded by a sense of joy. The problem of my conduct was solved. Hyde was thenceforth impossible; whether I would or not, I was now confined to the better part of my existence; and O, how I rejoiced to think of it! with what willing humility I embraced anew the restrictions of natural life! with what sincere renunciation I locked the door by which I had so often gone and come, and ground the key under my heel!

20   The next day, came the news that the murder had been overlooked, that the guilt of Hyde was patent to the world, and that the victim was a man high in public estimation. It was not only a crime, it had been a tragic folly. I think I was glad to know it; I think I was glad to have my better impulses thus buttressed and guarded by the terrors of the scaffold. Jekyll was now my city of refuge; let but Hyde peep out an instant, and the hands of all men would be raised to take and slay him.

21   I resolved in my future conduct to redeem the past; and I can say with honesty that my resolve was fruitful of some good. You know yourself how earnestly, in the last months of the last year, I laboured to relieve suffering; you know that much was done for others, and that the days passed quietly, almost happily for myself. Nor can I truly say that I wearied of this beneficent and innocent life; I think instead that I daily enjoyed it more completely; but I was still cursed with my duality of purpose; and as the first edge of my penitence wore off, the lower side of me, so long indulged, so recently chained down, began to growl for licence. Not that I dreamed of resuscitating Hyde; the bare idea of that would startle me to frenzy; no, it was in my own person that I was once more tempted to trifle with my conscience; and it was as an ordinary secret sinner that I at last fell before the assaults of temptation.

22   There comes an end to all things; the most capacious measure is filled at last; and this brief condescension to my evil finally destroyed the balance of my soul. And yet I was not alarmed; the fall seemed natural, like a return to the old days before I had made my discovery. It was a fine, clear, January day, wet under foot where the frost had melted, but cloudless overhead; and the Regent's Park was full of winter chirrupings and sweet with spring odours. I sat in the sun on a bench; the animal within me licking the chops of memory; the spiritual side a little drowsed, promising subsequent penitence, but not yet moved to begin. After all, I reflected, I was like my neighbours; and then I smiled, comparing myself with other men, comparing my active goodwill with the lazy cruelty of their neglect. And at the very moment of that vainglorious thought, a qualm came over me, a horrid nausea and the most deadly shuddering. These passed away, and left me faint; and then, as in its turn faintness subsided, I began to be aware of a change in the temper of my thoughts, a greater boldness, a contempt of danger, a solution of the bonds of obligation. I looked down; my clothes hung formlessly on my shrunken limbs; the hand that lay on my knee was corded and hairy. I was once more Edward Hyde. A moment before I had been safe of all men's respect, wealthy, beloved—the cloth laying for me in the dining-room at home; and now I

was the common quarry of mankind, hunted, house-less, a known murderer, thrall to the gallows.

23   My reason wavered, but it did not fail me utterly. I have more than once observed that, in my second character, my faculties seemed sharpened to a point and my spirits more tensely elastic; thus it came about that, where Jekyll perhaps might have succumbed, Hyde rose to the importance of the moment. My drugs were in one of the presses of my cabinet; how was I to reach them? That was the problem that (crushing my temples in my hands) I set to myself to solve. The laboratory door I had closed. If I sought to enter by the house, my own servants would consign me to the gallows. I saw I must employ another hand, and thought of Lanyon. How was he to be reached? how persuaded? Suppose that I escaped capture in the streets, how was I to make my way into his presence? and how should I, an unknown and displeasing visitor, prevail on the famous physician to rifle the study of his colleague, Dr. Jekyll? Then I remembered that of my original character, one part remained to me: I could write my own hand; and once I had conceived that kindling spark, the way that I must follow became lighted up from end to end.

24   Thereupon, I arranged my clothes as best I could, and summoning a passing hansom, drove to an hotel in Portland Street, the name of which I chanced to remember. At my appearance (which was indeed comical enough, however tragic a fate these garments covered) the driver could not conceal his mirth. I gnashed my teeth upon him with a gust of devilish fury; and the smile withered from his face—happily for him—yet more happily for myself, for in another instant I had certainly dragged him from his perch. At the inn, as I entered, I looked about me with so black a countenance as made the attendants tremble, not a look did they exchange in my presence; but obsequiously took my orders, led me to a private room, and brought me wherewithal to write. Hyde in danger of his life was a creature new to me; shaken with inordinate anger, strung to the pitch of murder, lusting to inflict pain. Yet the creature was astute; mastered his fury with a great effort of the will; composed his two important letters, one to Lanyon and one to Poole; and that he might receive actual evidence of their being posted, sent them out with directions that they should be registered. Thenceforward, he sat all day over the fire in the private room, gnawing his nails; there he dined, sitting alone with his fears, the waiter visibly quailing before his eye; and thence, when the night was fully come, he set forth in the corner of a closed cab, and was driven to and fro about the streets of the city. He, I say—I cannot say, I. That child of Hell had nothing human; nothing lived in him but fear and hatred. And when at last, thinking the driver had begun to grow suspicious, he discharged the cab and ventured on foot, attired in his misfitting clothes, an object marked out for observation, into the midst of the nocturnal passengers, these two base passions raged within him like a tempest. He walked fast, hunted by his fears, chattering to himself, skulking through the less frequented thoroughfares, counting the minutes that still divided him from midnight. Once a woman spoke to him, offering, I think, a box of lights. He smote her in the face, and she fled.

25   When I came to myself at Lanyon's, the horror of my old friend perhaps affected me somewhat: I do not know; it was at least but a drop in the sea to the abhorrence with which I looked back upon these hours. A change had come over

me. It was no longer the fear of the gallows, it was the horror of being Hyde that racked me. I received Lanyon's condemnation partly in a dream; it was partly in a dream that I came home to my own house and got into bed. I slept after the prostration of the day, with a stringent and profound slumber which not even in the nightmares that wrung me could avail to break. I awoke in the morning shaken, weakened, but refreshed. I still hated and feared the thought of the brute that slept within me, and I had not of course forgotten the appalling dangers of the day before; but I was once more at home, in my own house and close to my drugs; and gratitude for my escape shone so strong in my soul that it almost rivalled the brightness of hope.

26   I was stepping leisurely across the court after breakfast, drinking the chill of the air with pleasure, when I was seized again with those indescribable sensations that heralded the change; and I had but the time to gain the shelter of my cabinet, before I was once again raging and freezing with the passions of Hyde. It took on this occasion a double dose to recall me to myself; and alas! six hours after, as I sat looking sadly in the fire, the pangs returned, and the drug had to be re-administered. In short, from that day forth it seemed only by a great effort as of gymnastics, and only under the immediate stimulation of the drug, that I was able to wear the countenance of Jekyll. At all hours of the day and night, I would be taken with the premonitory shudder; above all, if I slept, or even dozed for a moment in my chair, it was always as Hyde that I awakened. Under the strain of this continually impending doom and by the sleeplessness to which I now condemned myself, ay, even beyond what I had thought possible to man, I became, in my own person, a creature eaten up and emptied by fever, languidly weak both in body and mind, and solely occupied by one thought: the horror of my other self. But when I slept, or when the virtue of the medicine wore off, I would leap almost without transition (for the pangs of transformation grew daily less marked) into the possession of a fancy brimming with images of terror, a soul boiling with causeless hatreds, and a body that seemed not strong enough to contain the raging energies of life. The powers of Hyde seemed to have grown with the sickliness of Jekyll. And certainly the hate that now divided them was equal on each side. With Jekyll, it was a thing of vital instinct. He had now seen the full deformity of that creature that shared with him some of the phenomena of consciousness, and was co-heir with him to death: and beyond these links of community, which in themselves made the most poignant part of his distress, he thought of Hyde, for all his energy of life, as of something not only hellish but inorganic. This was the shocking thing; that the slime of the pit seemed to utter cries and voices; that the amorphous dust gesticulated and sinned; that what was dead, and had no shape, should usurp the offices of life. And this again, that that insurgent horror was knit to him closer than a wife, closer than an eye; lay caged in his flesh, where he heard it mutter and felt it struggle to be born; and at every hour of weakness, and in the confidence of slumber, prevailed against him, and deposed him out of life. The hatred of Hyde for Jekyll was of a different order. His terror of the gallows drove him continually to commit temporary suicide, and return to his subordinate station of a part instead of a person; but he loathed the necessity, he loathed the despondency into which Jekyll was now fallen, and he resented the dislike with which he was himself re-

garded. Hence the apelike tricks that he would play me, scrawling in my own hand blasphemies on the pages of my books, burning the letters and destroying the portrait of my father; and indeed, had it not been for his fear of death, he would long ago have ruined himself in order to involve me in the ruin. But his love of life is wonderful; I go further: I, who sicken and freeze at the mere thought of him, when I recall the abjection and passion of this attachment, and when I know how he fears my power to cut him off by suicide, I find it in my heart to pity him.

27   It is useless, and the time awfully fails me, to prolong this description; no one has ever suffered such torments, let that suffice; and yet even to these, habit brought—no, not alleviation—but a certain callousness of soul, a certain acquiescence of despair; and my punishment might have gone on for years, but for the last calamity which has now fallen, and which has finally severed me from my own face and nature. My provision of the salt, which had never been renewed since the date of the first experiment, began to run low. I sent out for a fresh supply and mixed the draught; the ebullition followed, and the first change of colour, not the second; I drank it and it was without efficacy. You will learn from Poole how I have had London ransacked; it was in vain; and I am now persuaded that my first supply was impure, and that it was that unknown impurity which lent efficacy to the draught.

28   About a week has passed, and I am now finishing this statement under the influence of the last of the old powders. This, then, is the last time, short of a miracle, that Henry Jekyll can think his own thoughts or see his own face (now how sadly altered!) in the glass. Nor must I delay too long to bring my writing to an end; for if my narrative has hitherto escaped destruction, it has been by a combination of great prudence and great good luck. Should the throes of change take me in the act of writing it, Hyde will tear it in pieces; but if some time shall have elapsed after I have laid it by, his wonderful selfishness and circumscription to the moment will probably save it once again from the action of his ape-like spite. And indeed the doom that is closing on us both has already changed and crushed him. Half an hour from now, when I shall again and forever reindue that hated personality, I know how I shall sit shuddering and weeping in my chair, or continue, with the most strained and fearstruck ecstasy of listening, to pace up and down this room (my last earthly refuge) and give ear to every sound of menace. Will Hyde die upon the scaffold? or will he find courage to release himself at the last moment? God knows; I am careless; this is my true hour of death, and what is to follow concerns another than myself. Here then, as I lay down the pen and proceed to seal up my confession, I bring the life of that unhappy Henry Jekyll to an end.

Questions for Discussion

1. From the evidence in the letter, which side of the personality would you conclude killed Mr. Hyde: Hyde himself, in an act of suicide, or Jekyll, in an act of combined murder/suicide of both sides of his personality? Explain your response using references to the text.

2. What strengths, faults, and inner divisions of character does Jekyll describe in the first paragraph of the narrative? Why does he feel a need to conceal his "pleasures"?

3. Upon what fantasy or "beloved daydream" does Jekyll come to dwell? Why does he become so obsessed with this fantasy? What does he invent to make his fantasy a reality? Is his invention a success?

4. What are the differences in appearance, stature, power, and age between Dr. Jekyll and Mr. Hyde? How do these physical distinctions underscore symbolically the differences in their characters as well as the flaws in Dr. Jekyll's original character and the folly of artificially separating the two parts of the self?

5. How does Jekyll first respond to the changes in his character? How does his response and the nature of the control over the "double" personality gradually change? What difficulty does he experience in deciding which of his sides to finally repress?

6. Why is Jekyll unable to stick with his decision to refrain from "doubling" his personality? When he again reverts to Hyde, how has Hyde changed? What crime does Hyde perform, and how does Jekyll react to the crime? How does he attempt to reform himself? Under what circumstances does Hyde emerge a final time? How would you explain the mutual loathing that each side now feels for the other?

Ideas for Writing

1. After reading the entire text of *The Strange Case of Doctor Jekyll and Mr. Hyde,* write an essay in which you interpret the story as a criticism of rigid social conventions and moral standards of "acceptable" or "unacceptable," "good" or "bad" behavior. In what ways does the story suggest that such strict standards can heighten the division between an individual's good and bad side, the main self and the double or shadow self? Or, write an interpretation of your own that you can support through reference to the story.

2. This story concerns the dual nature of the human psyche, the struggle between our "good" side and our "bad" side, between the conscious mind and the unthinking appetites of the body. What do you think can be done to ease such a struggle? Write a paper in which you argue for an approach to life that would help to heal the split between potential "Jekyll and Hyde" personalities within the human psyche.

 Shelby Steele

Being Black and Feeling Blue

Shelby Steele was born in Chicago in 1946. His parents were active in the civil rights movement, and Steele grew up with a keen sense of the realities of racial conflict and injustice. He received a Ph.D. in English at the University of Utah in 1974, and currently is a professor of English at San Jose State University in Cali-

fornia. His essays on the consciousness and social status of African Americans have appeared in many magazines and newspapers, and his book The Content of Our Character: A New Vision of Race in America *(1990) has been a controversial bestseller. The following excerpt from* The Content of Our Character *explores the anti-self that many African Americans experience as a result of generations of racial oppression.*

JOURNAL

Steele develops the concept of a negative "anti-self" in his selection. Before reading it, think about whether you have ever felt that you had a negative anti-self. Present an example to illustrate the power of that side of your personality.

1   In the early seventies when I was in graduate school, I went out for a beer late one afternoon with another black graduate student whom I'd only known casually before. This student was older than I—a stint in the army had interrupted his education—and he had the reputation of being bright and savvy, of having applied street smarts to the business of getting through graduate school. I suppose I was hoping for what would be called today a little mentoring. But it is probably not wise to drink with someone when you are enamored of his reputation, and it was not long before we stumbled into a moment that seemed to transform him before my very eyes. I asked him what he planned to do when he finished his Ph.D., fully expecting to hear of high aspirations matched with shrewd perceptions on how to reach them. But before he could think, he said with a kind of exhausted sincerity, "Man, I just want to hold on, get a job that doesn't work me too hard, and do a lot of fishing." Was he joking, I asked. "Hell, no," he said with exaggerated umbrage. "I'm not into it like the white boys. I don't need what they need."

2   I will call this man Henry and report that, until five or six years ago when I lost track of him, he was doing exactly as he said he would do. With much guile and little ambition he had moved through a succession of low-level administrative and teaching jobs, mainly in black studies programs. Of course, it is no crime to just "hold on," and it is hardly a practice limited to blacks. Still, in Henry's case there was truly a troubling discrepancy between his ambition and a fine intelligence recognized by all who knew him. But in an odd way this intelligence was more lateral than vertical, and I would say that it was rechanneled by a certain unseen fear into the business of merely holding on. It would be easy to say that Henry had simply decided on life in a slower lane than he was capable of traveling in, or that he was that rare person who had achieved ambitionless contentment. But if this was so, Henry would have had wisdom rather than savvy, and he would not have felt the need to carry himself with more self-importance than his station justified. I don't think Henry was uninterested in ambition; I think he was afraid of it.

3   It is certainly true that there is a little of Henry in most people. My own compulsion to understand him informs me that I must have seen many elements of myself in him. And though I'm sure he stands for a universal human blockage, I also believe that there is something in the condition of being black in America

that makes the kind of hesitancy he represents one of black America's most serious and debilitating problems. As Henry reached the very brink of expanded opportunity, with Ph.D. in hand, he diminished his ambition almost as though his degree delivered him to a kind of semiretirement. I don't think blacks in general have any illusions about semiretirement, but I do think that, as a group, we have hesitated on the brink of new opportunities that we made enormous sacrifices to win for ourselves. The evidence of this lies in one of the most tragic social ironies of late twentieth-century American life: as black Americans have gained in equality and opportunity, we have also declined in relation to whites, so that by many socioeconomic measures we are further behind whites today than before the great victories of the civil rights movement. By one report, even the black middle class, which had made great gains in the seventies, began to lose ground to its white counterpart in the eighties. Most distressing of all, the black underclass continues to expand rather than shrink.

4   Of course, I don't suggest that Henry's peculiar inertia singularly explains social phenomena so complex and tragic. I do believe, however, that blacks in general are susceptible to the same web of attitudes and fears that kept Henry beneath his potential, and that our ineffectiveness in taking better advantage of our greater opportunity has much to do with this. I think there is a specific form of racial anxiety that all blacks are vulnerable to that can, in situations where we must engage the mainstream society, increase our self-doubt and undermine our confidence so that we often back away from the challenges that, if taken, would advance us. I believe this hidden racial anxiety may well now be the strongest barrier to our full participation in the American mainstream; that it is as strong or stronger even than the discrimination we still face. To examine this racial anxiety, allow me first to look at how the Henry was born in me.

5   Until the sixth grade, I attended a segregated school in a small working-class black suburb of Chicago. The school was a dumping ground for teachers with too little competence or mental stability to teach in the white school in our district. In 1956, when I entered the sixth grade, I encountered a new addition to the menagerie of misfits that was our faculty—an ex-Marine whose cruelty was suggested during our first lunch hour when he bit the cap off his Coke bottle and spit it into the wastebasket. Looking back I can see that there was no interesting depth to the cruelty he began to show us almost immediately—no consumptive hatred, no intelligent malevolence. Although we were all black and he was white, I don't think he was even particularly racist. He had obviously needed us to like him though he had no faith that we would. He ran the class like a gang leader, picking favorites one day and banishing them the next. And then there was a permanent pool of outsiders, myself among them, who were made to carry the specific sins that he must have feared most in himself.

6   The sin I was made to carry was the sin of stupidity. I misread a sentence on the first day of school, and my fate was sealed. He made my stupidity a part of the classroom lore, and very quickly I in fact became stupid. I all but lost the ability to read and found the simplest math beyond me. His punishments for my errors rose

in meanness until one day he ordered me to pick up all of the broken glass on the playground with my bare hands. Of course, this would have to be the age of the pop bottle, and there were sections of this playground that glared like a mirror in sunlight. After half an hour's labor I sat down on strike, more out of despair than rebellion.

7   Again, cruelty was no more than a vibration in this man, and so without even a show of anger he commandeered a bicycle, handed it to an eighth-grader—one of his lieutenants—and told the boy to run me around the school grounds "until he passes out." The boy was also given a baseball bat to "use on him when he slows down." I ran two laps, about a mile, and then pretended to pass out. The eighth-grader knew I was playing possum but could not bring himself to hit me and finally rode off. I exited the school yard through an adjoining cornfield and never returned.

8   I mention this experience as an example of how one's innate capacity for insecurity is expanded and deepened, of how a disbelieving part of the self is brought to life and forever joined to the believing self. As children we are all wounded in some way and to some degree by the wild world we encounter. From these wounds a disbelieving *anti-self* is born, an internal antagonist and saboteur that embraces the world's negative view of us, that believes our wounds are justified by our own unworthiness, and that entrenches itself as a lifelong voice of doubt. This anti-self is a hidden aggressive force that scours the world for fresh evidence of our unworthiness. When the believing self announces its aspirations, the anti-self always argues against them, but never on their merits (this is a healthy function of the believing self). It argues instead against our worthiness to pursue these aspirations and, by its lights, we are never worthy of even our smallest dreams. The mission of the anti-self is to deflate the believing self and, thus, draw it down into inertia, passivity, and faithlessness.

9   The anti-self is the unseen agent of low self-esteem; it is a catalytic energy that tries to induce low self-esteem in the believing self as though it were the complete truth of the personality. The anti-self can only be contained by the strength of the believing self, and this is where one's early environment becomes crucial. If the childhood environment is stable and positive, the family whole and loving, the schools good, the community safe, then the believing self will be reinforced and made strong. If the family is shattered, the schools indifferent, the neighborhood a mine field of dangers, the anti-self will find evidence everywhere with which to deflate the believing self.

10   This does not mean that a bad childhood cannot be overcome. But it does mean—as I have experienced and observed—that one's *capacity* for self-doubt and self-belief are roughly the same from childhood on, so that years later when the believing self may have strengthened enough to control the anti-self, one will still have the same capacity for doubt whether or not one has the *actual* doubt. I think it is this struggle between our capacities for doubt and belief that gives our personalities one of their peculiar tensions and, in this way, marks our character.

11   My own anti-self was given new scope and power by this teacher's persecution, and it was so successful in deflating my believing self that I secretly vowed never

to tell my parents what was happening to me. The anti-self had all but sold my be-lieving self on the idea that I was stupid, and I did not want to feel that shame be-fore my parents. It was my brother who finally told them, and his disclosure led to a boycott that closed the school and eventually won the dismissal of my teacher and several others. But my anti-self transformed even this act of rescue into a cause of shame—if there wasn't something wrong with me, why did I have to be rescued? The anti-self follows only the logic of self-condemnation.

12   But there was another dimension to this experience that my anti-self was only too happy to seize upon. It was my race that landed me in this segregated school and, as many adults made clear to me, my persecution followed a timeless pattern of racial persecution. The implications of this were rich food for the anti-self—my race was so despised that it had to be segregated; as a black my education was so unimportant that even unbalanced teachers without college degrees were ade-quate; ignorance and cruelty that would be intolerable in a classroom of whites was perfectly all right in a classroom of blacks. The anti-self saw no injustice in any of this, but instead took it all as confirmation of a racial inferiority that it could now add to the well of personal doubt I already had. When the adults thought they were consoling me—"Don't worry. They treat all blacks this way"—they were also deepening the wound and expanding my capacity for doubt.

13   And this is the point. The condition of being black in America means that one will likely endure more wounds to one's self-esteem than others and that the ca-pacity for self-doubt born of these wounds will be compounded and expanded by the black race's reputation of inferiority. The anti-self will most likely have more ammunition with which to deflate the believing self and its aspirations. And the universal human struggle to have belief win out over doubt will be more difficult.

14   More than difficult, it is also made inescapable by the fact of skin color, which, in America, works as a visual invocation of the problem. Black skin has more de-humanizing stereotypes associated with it than any other skin color in America, if not the world. When a black presents himself in an integrated situation, he knows that his skin alone may bring these stereotypes to life in the minds of those he meets and that he, as an individual, may be diminished by his race before he has a chance to reveal a single aspect of his personality. By the symbology of color that operates in our culture, black skin accuses him of inferiority. Under the weight of this accusation, a black will almost certainly doubt himself on some level and to some degree. The ever-vigilant anti-self will grab this racial doubt and mix it into the pool of personal doubt, so that when a black walks into an integrated situa-tion—a largely white college campus, an employment office, a business lunch—he will be vulnerable to the entire realm of his self-doubt before a single word is spoken.

15   This constitutes an intense and lifelong racial vulnerability and anxiety for blacks. Even though a white American may have been wounded more than a given black, and therefore have a larger realm of inner doubt, his white skin, with its connotations of privilege and superiority, will actually help protect him from that doubt and from the undermining power of his anti-self, at least in relations with blacks. In fact, the larger the realm of doubt, the more he may be tempted to

rely on his white skin for protection from it. Certainly in every self-avowed white racist, whether businessman or member of the Klan, there is a huge realm of self-contempt and doubt that hides behind the mythology of white skin. The mere need to pursue self-esteem through skin color suggests there is no faith that it can be pursued any other way. But if skin color offers whites a certain false esteem and impunity, it offers blacks vulnerability.

16   This vulnerability begins for blacks with the recognition that we belong, quite simply, to the most despised race in the human community of races. To be a member of such a group in a society where all others gain an impunity by merely standing in relation to us is to live with a relentless openness to diminishment and shame. By the devious logic of the anti-self, one cannot be open to such diminishment without in fact being inferior and therefore deserving of diminishment. For the anti-self, the charge verifies the crime, so that racial vulnerability itself is evidence of inferiority. In this sense, the anti-self is an internalized racist, our own subconscious bigot, that conspires with society to diminish us.

17   So when blacks enter the mainstream, they are not only vulnerable to society's racism but also to the racist within. This internal racist is not restricted by law, morality, or social decorum. It cares nothing about civil rights and equal opportunity. It is the self-doubt born of the original wound of racial oppression, and its mission is to establish the justice of that wound and shackle us with doubt.

18   Of course, the common response to racial vulnerability, as to most vulnerabilities, is denial—the mind's mechanism for ridding itself of intolerable possibilities. For blacks to acknowledge a vulnerability to inferiority anxiety, in the mist of a society that has endlessly accused us of being inferior, feels nothing less than intolerable—as if we were agreeing with the indictment against us. But denial is not the same as eradication, since it only gives unconscious life to what is intolerable to our consciousness. Denial reassigns rather than vanquishes the terror of racial vulnerability. This reassignment only makes the terror stronger by making it unknown. When we deny, we always create a dangerous area of self-ignorance, an entire territory of the self that we cannot afford to know. Without realizing it, we begin to circumscribe our lives by avoiding those people and situations that might breach our denial and force us to see consciously what we fear. Though the denial of racial vulnerability is a human enough response, I think it also makes our public discourse on race circumspect and unproductive, since we cannot talk meaningfully about problems we are afraid to name.

19   Denial is a refusal of painful self-knowledge. When someone or something threatens to breach this refusal, we receive an unconscious shock of the very vulnerability we have denied—a shock that often makes us retreat and more often makes us intensify our denial. When blacks move into integrated situations or face challenges that are new for blacks, the myth of black inferiority is always present as a *condition* of the situation, and as such it always threatens to breach our denial of racial vulnerability. It also threatens to make us realize consciously what is intolerable to us—that we have some anxiety about inferiority. We feel this threat unconsciously as a shock of racial doubt delivered by the racist anti-self (always

the inner voice of the myth of black inferiority). Consciously, we feel this shock as a sharp discomfort or a desire to retreat from the situation. Almost always we will want to intensify our denial.

20   I will call this *integration shock,* since it occurs most powerfully when blacks leave their familiar world and enter the mainstream. Integration shock and denial are mutual intensifiers. The stab of racial doubt that integration shock delivers is a pressure to intensify denial, and a more rigid denial means the next stab of doubt will be more threatening and therefore more intense. The symbiosis of these two forces is, I believe, one of the reasons black Americans have become preoccupied with racial pride, almost to the point of obsession over the past twenty-five or so years. With more exposure to the mainstream, we have endured more integration shock, more jolts of inferiority anxiety. And, I think, we have often responded with rather hyperbolic claims of black pride by which we deny that anxiety. In this sense, our self-consciousness around pride, our need to make a point of it, is, to a degree, a form of denial. Pride becomes denial when it ceases to reflect self-esteem quietly and begins to compensate loudly for unacknowledged inner doubt. Here it also becomes dangerous since it prevents us from confronting and overcoming that doubt.

21   I think the most recent example of black pride-as-denial is the campaign (which seems to have been launched by a committee) to add yet another name to the litany of names that blacks have given themselves over the past century. Now we are to be African-Americans instead of, or in conjunction with, being black Americans. This self-conscious reaching for pride through nomenclature suggests nothing so much as a despair over the possibility of gaining the less conspicuous pride that follows real advancement. In its invocation of the glories of a remote African past and its wistful suggestion of homeland, this name denies the doubt black Americans have about their contemporary situation in America. There is no element of self-confrontation in it, no facing of real racial vulnerabilities, as there was with the name "black." I think "black" easily became the name of preference in the sixties, precisely because it was not a denial but a confrontation of inferiority anxiety, with the shame associated with the color black. There was honest self-acceptance in this name, and I think it diffused much of our vulnerability to the shame of color. Even between blacks, "black" is hardly the drop-dead fighting word it was when I was a child. Possibly we are ready now for a new name, but I think "black" has been our most powerful name yet because it so frankly called out our shame and doubt and helped us (and others) to accept ourselves. In the name "African-American" there is too much false neutralization of doubt, too much looking away from the caldron of our own experience. It is a euphemistic name that hides us even from ourselves.

22   I think blacks have been more preoccupied with pride over the past twenty-five years because we have been more exposed to integration shock since the 1964 Civil Rights Act made equal opportunity the law of the land (if not quite the full reality of the land). Ironically, it was the inequality of opportunity and all the other repressions of legal segregation that buffered us from our racial vulnerability. In a segregated society we did not have the same accountability to the charge of racial inferiority since we were given little opportunity to disprove the charge. It was the opening up of opportunity—anti-discrimination laws, the social programs of the

Great Society, equal opportunity guidelines and mandates, fair housing laws, affirmative action, and so on—that made us individually and collectively more accountable to the myth of black inferiority and therefore more racially vulnerable.

23   This vulnerability has increased in the same proportion that our freedom and opportunity have increased. The exhilaration of new freedom is always followed by a shock of accountability. Whatever unresolved doubt follows the oppressed into greater freedom will be inflamed since freedom always carries a burden of proof, always throws us back on ourselves. And freedom, even imperfect freedom, makes blacks a brutal proposition: if you're not inferior, prove it. This is the proposition that shocks us and makes us vulnerable to our underworld of doubt. The whispers of the racist anti-self are far louder in the harsh accountability of freedom than in subjugation, where the oppressor is so entirely to blame.

24   The bitter irony of all this is that our doubt and the hesitancy it breeds now help limit our progress in America almost as systematically as segregation once did. Integration shock gives the old boundaries of legal segregation a regenerative power. To avoid the shocks of doubt that come from entering the mainstream, or plunging more deeply into it, we often pull back at precisely those junctures where segregation once pushed us back. In this way we duplicate the conditions of our oppression and reenact our role as victims even in the midst of far greater freedom and far less victimization. Certainly there is still racial discrimination in America, but I believe that the unconscious replaying of our oppression is now the greatest barrier to our full equality.

25   The way in which integration shock regenerates the old boundaries of segregation for blacks is most evident in three tendencies—the tendency to minimalize or avoid real opportunities, to withhold effort in areas where few blacks have achieved, and to self-segregate in integrated situations.

26   If anything, it is the presence of new opportunities in society that triggers integration shock. If opportunity is a chance to succeed, it is also a chance to fail. The vulnerability of blacks to hidden inferiority anxiety makes failure a much more forbidding prospect. If a black pursues an opportunity in the mainstream—opens a business, goes up for a challenging job or difficult promotion—and fails, that failure can be used by the anti-self to confirm both personal and racial inferiority. The diminishment and shame will tap an impersonal, as well as personal, source of doubt. When a white fails, he alone fails. His doubt is strictly personal, which gives him more control over the failure. He can discover *his* mistakes, learn the reasons *he* made them, and try again. But the black, laboring under the myth of inferiority, will have this impersonal, culturally determined doubt with which to contend. This form of doubt robs him of a degree of control over his failure since he alone cannot eradicate the cultural myth that stings him. There will be a degree of impenetrability to his failure that will constitute an added weight of doubt.

27   The effect of this is to make mainstream opportunity more intimidating and risky for blacks. This is made worse in that blacks, owing to past and present deprivations, may come to the mainstream in the first place with a lower stock of self-esteem. High risk and low self-esteem is hardly the best combination with which to tackle the challenges of a highly advanced society in which others have been blessed by

history with very clear advantages. Under these circumstances, opportunity can seem more like a chance to fail than a chance to succeed. All this makes for a kind of opportunity aversion that I think was behind the hesitancy I saw in Henry, in myself, and in other blacks of all class backgrounds. It is also, I believe, one of the reasons for the sharp decline in the number of black students entering college, even as many colleges launch recruiting drives to attract more black students.

28   This aversion to opportunity generates a way of seeing that minimalizes opportunity to the point where it can be ignored. In black communities the most obvious entrepreneurial opportunities are routinely ignored. It is often outsiders or the latest wave of immigrants who own the shops, restaurants, cleaners, gas stations, and even the homes and apartments. Education is a troubled area in black communities for numerous reasons, but certainly one of them is that many black children are not truly imbued with the idea that learning is virtually the same as opportunity. Schools—even bad schools—were the opportunity that so many immigrant groups used to learn the workings and the spirit of American society. In the very worst inner-city schools there are accredited teachers who teach the basics, but too often to students who shun those among them who do well, who see studying as a sucker's game and school itself as a waste of time. One sees in many of these children almost a determination not to learn, a suppression of the natural impulse to understand, which cannot be entirely explained by the determinism of poverty. Out of school, in the neighborhood, these same children learn everything. I think it is the meeting with the mainstream that school symbolizes that clicks them off. In the cultural ethos from which they come, it is always these meetings that trigger the aversion to opportunity, behind which lies inferiority anxiety. Their parents and their culture send them a double message: go to school but don't really apply yourself. The risk is too high.

29   This same pattern of avoidance, this unconscious circumvention of possibility, is also evident in our commitment to effort—the catalyst of opportunity. Difficult, sustained effort—in school, career, or family life—will be riddled with setbacks, losses, and frustrations. Racial vulnerability erodes effort for blacks by exaggerating the importance of these setbacks, by recasting them as confirmation of racial inferiority rather than the normal pitfalls of sustained effort. The racist anti-self greets these normal difficulties with an I-told-you-so attitude, and the believing self, unwilling to risk seeing that the anti-self is right, may grow timid and pull back from the effort. As with opportunity, racial vulnerability makes hard effort in the mainstream a high-risk activity for blacks.

30   But this is not the case in those areas where blacks have traditionally excelled. In sports and music, for example, the threat of integration shock is effectively removed. Because so many blacks have succeeded in these areas, a black can enter them without being racially vulnerable. Failure carries no implication of racial inferiority, so the activity itself is far less risky than those in which blacks have no record of special achievement. Certainly, in sports and music one sees blacks sustain the most creative and disciplined effort and then seize opportunities where one would have thought there were none. But all of this changes the instant racial vulnerability becomes a factor. Across the country thousands of young black males take every opportunity and make every effort to reach the elite ranks of the NBA

or NFL. But in the classroom, where racial vulnerability is a hidden terror, they and many of their classmates put forth the meagerest effort and show a virtual indifference to the genuine opportunity that is education.

31   But the most visible circumvention that results from integration shock is the tendency toward self-segregation that, if anything, seems to have increased over the last twenty years. Along with opportunity and effort, it is also white people themselves who are often avoided. I hear young black professionals say they do not socialize with whites after work unless at some "command performance" that comes with the territory of their career. On largely white university campuses where integration shock is particularly intense, black students often try to enforce a kind of neo-separatism that includes black "theme" dorms, black student unions, Afro-houses, black cultural centers, black student lounges, and so on. There is a geopolitics involved in this activity, where race is tied to territory in a way that mimics the whites only/colored only designations of the past. Only now these race spaces are staked out in the name of pride.

32   I think this impulse to self-segregate, to avoid whites, has to do with the way white people are received by the black anti-self. Even if the believing self wants to see racial difference as essentially meaningless, the anti-self, that hidden perpetrator of racist doubt, sees white people as better than black people. Its mission is to confirm black inferiority, and so it looks closely at whites, watches the way they walk, talk, and negotiate the world, and then grants these styles of being and acting superiority. Somewhere inside every black is a certain awe at the power and achievement of the white race. In every barbershop gripe session where whites are put through the grinder of black anger, there will be a kind of backhanded respect—"Well, he might be evil, but that white boy is smart." True or not, the anti-self organizes its campaign against the believing self's faith in black equality around this supposition. And so, for blacks (as is true for whites in another way), white people in the generic sense have no neutrality. In themselves, they are stimulants to the black anti-self, deliverers of doubt. Their color slips around the deepest need of blacks to believe in their own immutable equality and communes directly with their self-suspicion.

33   So it is not surprising to hear black students on largely white campuses say that they are simply more comfortable with other blacks. Nor is it surprising to see them caught up in absurd contradictions—demanding separate facilities for themselves even as they protest apartheid in South Africa. Racial vulnerability is a species of fear and, as such, it is the progenitor of countless ironies. More freedom makes us more vulnerable so that in the midst of freedom we feel the impulse to carve our segregated comfort zones that protect us more from our own doubt than from whites. We balk before opportunity and pull back from effort just as these things would bear fruit. We reconstitute the boundaries of segregation just as they become illegal. By averting opportunity and curbing effort for fear of awakening a sense of inferiority, we make inevitable the very failure that shows us inferior.

34   One of the worst aspects of oppression is that it never ends when the oppressor begins to repent. There is a legacy of doubt in the oppressed that follows long after the cleanest repentance by the oppressor, just as guilt trails the oppressor and makes his redemption incomplete. These themes of doubt and guilt fill in like

fresh replacements and work to duplicate the oppression. I think black Americans are today more oppressed by doubt than by racism and that the second phase of our struggle for freedom must be a confrontation with that doubt. Unexamined, this doubt leads us back into the tunnel of our oppression where we reenact our victimization just as society struggles to end its victimization of us. We are not a people formed in freedom. Freedom is always a call to possibility that demands an overcoming of doubt. We are still new to freedom, new to its challenges, new even to the notion that self-doubt can be the slyest enemy of freedom. For us freedom has so long meant the absence of oppression that we have not yet realized it also means the conquering of doubt.

35   Of course, this does not mean that doubt should become a lake we swim in, but it does mean that we should begin our campaign against doubt by acknowledging it, by outlining the contours of the black anti-self so that we can know and accept exactly what it is that we are afraid of. This is knowledge that can be worked with, knowledge that can point with great precision to the actions through which we can best mitigate doubt and advance ourselves. This is the sort of knowledge that gives the believing self a degree of immunity against the anti-self and that enables it to pile up little victories that, in sum, grant even more immunity.

36   Certainly inferiority has long been the main theme of the black anti-self, its most lethal weapon against our capacity for self-belief. And so, in a general way, the acceptance of this piece of knowledge implies a mission: to show *ourselves* and (only indirectly) the larger society that we are not inferior in any dimension. That this should already be assumed goes without saying. But what "should be" falls within the province of the believing self, where it has no solidity until the doubt of the anti-self is called out and shown false by demonstrable action in the real world. This is the proof that grants the "should" its rightful solidity, that transforms it from a well-intentioned claim into a certainty.

37   The temptation is to avoid so severe a challenge, to maintain a black identity, painted in the colors of pride and culture, that provides us with a way of seeing ourselves apart from this challenge. It is easier to be "African-American" than to organize oneself on one's own terms and around one's own aspirations and then, through sustained effort and difficult achievement, put one's insidious anti-self quietly to rest. No black identity, however beautifully conjured, will spare blacks this challenge that, despite its fairness or unfairness, is simply in the nature of things. But then I have faith that in time we will meet this challenge since this, too, is in the nature of things.

Questions for Discussion

1. Explain Steele's concept of the negative anti-self. What are its origins and what type of "wounds" contribute to it? What does the anti-self argue for and against?

2. Steele begins his essay with his friend Henry's decision not to choose an ambitious career. How does Steele's next example about his own elementary school days reveal "how the Henry was born in me"? Are these two examples convincing? Why or why not?

3. How do black adults who tell their children, "Don't worry. They treat all blacks that way," contribute to the anti-self? Do you agree?

4. Steele claims that the anti-self is "an internalized racist, our own unconscious bigot, that conspires with society to diminish us," and that, in today's world, "the unconscious replaying of our oppression is now the greatest barrier to our full equality." What evidence does Steele present to back up these assertions? Is his evidence convincing?

5. What does Steele mean by "integration shock," "self-segregation," and "black pride as denial"?

6. What methods does Steele use to argue for his perspective on black culture and identity? Does his argument seem to be "dialogic," that is, does he take the arguments and feelings of his opposition into account? Is his approach effective and appropriate?

Ideas for Writing

1. Steele argues against the "self-segregation" of blacks today. What is your response to the new black separatist movement? Do you agree with Steele that it is a sign of "integration shock" and self-doubt, or do you see it as a genuine cultural affirmation, a positive step forward for African Americans? Write an essay in which you take a position on this issue.

2. Steele's argument rests on a consideration of the psychological responses of blacks to the injustices of the past. Write an essay in support of his position or refute it.

 # Fran Peavey (with Myrna Levy and Charles Varon)

Us and Them

Fran Peavey is a long-time California peace activist, ecologist, and community organizer who has written the book Heart Politics *about her views on nonconfrontational strategies in political organizing. Peavey has also written for a number of alternative-press publications. As you read her essay, consider how the concept of the "double self" or "shadow" can easily be projected onto other people whom we feel are different from us politically or socially.*

JOURNAL

Write about someone with whom you have trouble communicating because you experience this individual as "different" from you in some way. What do you have in common with this person that could form the basis for better communication?

1   Time was when I knew that the racists were the lunch-counter owners who refused to serve blacks, the warmongers were the generals who planned wars and ordered the killing of innocent people, and the polluters were the industrialists whose factories fouled the air, water and land. I could be a good guy by boycotting, marching, and sitting in to protest the actions of the bad guys.

2   But no matter how much I protest, an honest look at myself and my relationship with the rest of the world reveals ways that I too am part of the problem. I notice that on initial contact I am more suspicious of Mexicans than of whites. I see that I'm addicted to a standard of living maintained at the expense of poorer people around the world—a situation that can only be perpetuated through military force. And the problem of pollution seems to include my consumption of resources and creation of waste. The line that separates me from the bad guys is blurred.

3   When I was working to stop the Vietnam War, I'd feel uneasy seeing people in military uniform. I remember thinking, "How could that guy be so dumb as to have gotten into that uniform? How could he be so acquiescent, so credulous as to have fallen for the government's story in Vietnam?" I'd get furious inside when I imagined the horrible things he'd probably done in the war.

4   Several years after the end of the war, a small group of Vietnam veterans wanted to hold a retreat at our farm in Watsonville. I consented, although I felt ambivalent about hosting them. That weekend, I listened to a dozen men and women who had served in Vietnam. Having returned home only to face ostracism for their involvement in the war, they were struggling to come to terms with their experiences.

5   They spoke of some of the awful things they'd done and seen, as well as some things they were proud of. They told why they had enlisted in the army or cooperated with the draft: their love of the United States, their eagerness to serve, their wish to be brave and heroic. They felt their noble motives had been betrayed, leaving them with little confidence in their own judgment. Some questioned their own manhood or womanhood and even their basic humanity. They wondered whether they had been a positive force or a negative one overall, and what their buddies' sacrifices meant. Their anguish disarmed me, and I could no longer view them simply as perpetrators of evil.

6   How had I come to view military people as my enemies? Did vilifying soldiers serve to get me off the hook and allow me to divorce myself from responsibility for what my country was doing in Vietnam? Did my own anger and righteousness keep me from seeing the situation in its full complexity? How had this limited view affected my work against the war?

7   When my youngest sister and her husband, a young career military man, visited me several years ago, I was again challenged to see the human being within the soldier. I learned that as a farm boy in Utah, he'd been recruited to be a sniper.

8   One night toward the end of their visit, we got to talking about his work. Though he had also been trained as a medical corpsman, he could still be called on at any time to work as a sniper. He couldn't tell me much about this part of his career—he'd been sworn to secrecy. I'm not sure he would have wanted to tell me

even if he could. But he did say that a sniper's work involved going abroad, "bumping off" a leader, and disappearing into a crowd.

9   When you're given an order, he said, you're not supposed to think about it. You feel alone and helpless. Rather than take on the Army and maybe the whole country himself, he chose not to consider the possibility that certain orders shouldn't be carried out.

10   I could see that feeling isolated can make it seem impossible to follow one's own moral standards and disobey an order. I leaned toward him and said, "If you're ever ordered to do something that you know you shouldn't do, call me immediately and I'll find a way to help. I know a lot of people would support your stand. You're not alone." He and my sister looked at each other and their eyes filled with tears.

11   How do we learn whom to hate and fear? During my short lifetime, the national enemies of the United States have changed several times. Our World War II foes, the Japanese and the Germans, have become our allies. The Russians have been in vogue as our enemy for some time, although during a few periods relations improved somewhat. The North Vietnamese, Cubans, and Chinese have done stints as our enemy. So many countries seem capable of incurring our national wrath—how do we choose among them?

12   As individuals, do we choose our enemies based on cues from national leaders? From our schoolteachers and religious leaders? From newspapers and TV? Do we hate and fear our parents' enemies as part of our family identity? Or those of our culture, subculture, or peer group?

13   Whose economic and political interests does our enemy mentality serve?

14   At a conference on holocaust and genocide I met someone who showed me that it is not necessary to hate our opponents, even under the most extreme circumstances. While sitting in the hotel lobby after a session on the German holocaust, I struck up a conversation with a woman named Helen Waterford. When I learned she was a Jewish survivor of Auschwitz, I told her how angry I was at the Nazis. (I guess I was trying to prove to her that I was one of the good guys.)

15   "You know," she said, "I don't hate the Nazis." This took me aback. How could anyone who had lived through a concentration camp not hate the Nazis?

16   Then I learned that Helen does public speaking engagements with a former leader of the Hitler Youth movement: they talk about how terrible facism is as viewed from both sides. Fascinated, I arranged to spend more time with Helen and learn as much as I could from her.

17   In 1980, Helen read an intriguing newspaper article in which a man named Alfons Heck described his experiences growing up in Nazi Germany. When he was a young boy in Catholic school, the priest would come in every morning and say, "Heil Hitler," and then "Good Morning," and finally, "In the name of the Father and the Son and the Holy Spirit . . . " In Heck's mind, Hitler came before God. At ten, he volunteered for the Hitler Youth, and he loved it. It was in 1944, when he was sixteen, that Heck first learned that the Nazis were systematically killing the Jews. He thought, "This can't be true." But gradually he came to believe that he had served a mass murderer.

18   Heck's frankness impressed Helen, and she thought, "I want to meet that man." She found him soft-spoken, intelligent and pleasant. Helen had already been speaking publicly about her own experiences of the holocaust, and she asked Heck to share a podium with her at an upcoming engagement with a group of 400 schoolteachers. They spoke in chronological format, taking turns telling their own stories of the Nazi period. Helen told of leaving Frankfurt in 1934 at age twenty-five.

19   She and her husband, an accountant who had lost his job when the Nazis came to power, escaped to Holland. There they worked with the underground Resistance, and Helen gave birth to a daughter. In 1940 the Nazis invaded Holland. Helen and her husband went into hiding in 1942. Two years later, they were discovered and sent to Auschwitz. Their daughter was hidden by friends in the Resistance. Helen's husband died in the concentration camp.

20   Heck and Waterford's first joint presentation went well, and they decided to continue working as a team. Once, at an assembly of 800 high school students, Heck was asked, "If you had been ordered to shoot some Jews, maybe Mrs. Waterford, would you have shot them?" The audience gasped. Heck swallowed and said, "Yes. I obeyed orders. I would have." Afterward he apologized to Helen, saying he hadn't wanted to upset her. She told him, "I'm glad you answered the way you did. Otherwise, I would never again believe a word you said."

21   Heck is often faced with the "once a Nazi, always a Nazi" attitude. "You may give a good speech," people will say, "but I don't believe any of it. Once you have believed something, you don't throw it away." Again and again, he patiently explains that it took years before he could accept the fact that he'd been brought up believing falsehoods. Heck is also harassed by neo-Nazis, who call him in the middle of the night and threaten: "We haven't gotten you yet, but we'll kill you, you traitor."

22   How did Helen feel about the Nazis in Auschwitz? "I disliked them. I cannot say that I wished I could kick them to death—I never did. I guess that I am just not a vengeful person." She is often denounced by Jews for having no hate, for not wanting revenge. "It is impossible that you don't hate," people tell her.

23   At the conference on the holocaust and genocide and in subsequent conversations with Helen, I have tried to understand what has enabled her to remain so objective and to avoid blaming individual Germans for the holocaust, for her suffering and for her husband's death. I have found a clue in her passionate study of history.

24   For many people, the only explanation of the holocaust is that it was the creation of a madman. But Helen believes that such an analysis only serves to shield people from believing that a holocaust could happen to them. An appraisal of Hitler's mental health, she says, is less important than an examination of the historical forces at play and the ways Hitler was able to manipulate them.

25   "As soon as the war was over," Helen told me, "I began to read about what had happened since 1933, when my world closed. I read and read. How did the 'S.S. State' develop? What was the role of Britain, Hungary, Yugoslavia, the United States, France? How can it be possible that the holocaust really happened? What

is the first step, the second step? What are people searching for when they join fanatical movements? I guess I will be asking these questions until my last days."

26   Those of us working for social change tend to view our adversaries as enemies, to consider them unreliable, suspect, and generally of lower moral character. Saul Alinsky, a brilliant community organizer, explained the rationale for polarization this way:

> One acts decisively only in the conviction that all the angels are on one side and all the devils are on the other. A leader may struggle toward a decision and weigh the merits and demerits of a situation which is 52 percent positive and 48 percent negative, but once the decision is reached he must assume that his cause is 100 percent positive and the opposition 100 percent negative. . . . Many liberals, during our attack on the then-school superintendent [in Chicago], were pointing out that after all he wasn't a 100-percent devil, he was a regular churchgoer, he was a good family man, and he was generous in his contributions to charity. Can you imagine in the arena of conflict charging that so-and-so is a racist bastard and then diluting the impact of the attack with qualifying remarks? This becomes political idiocy.

27   But demonizing one's adversaries has great costs. It is a strategy that tacitly accepts and helps perpetuate our dangerous enemy mentality.

28   Instead of focusing on the 52-percent "devil" in my adversary, I choose to look at the other 48 percent, to start from the premise that within each adversary I have an ally. That ally may be silent, faltering, or hidden from my view. It may be only the person's sense of ambivalence about morally questionable parts of his or her job. Such doubts rarely have a chance to flower because of the overwhelming power of the social context to which the person is accountable. My ability to be *their* ally also suffers from such pressures. In 1970, while the Vietnam War was still going on, a group of us spent the summer in Long Beach, California, organizing against a napalm factory there. It was a small factory that mixed the chemicals and put the napalm in canisters. An accidental explosion a few months before had spewed hunks of napalm gel onto nearby homes and lawns. The incident had, in a real sense, brought the war home. It spurred local residents who opposed the war to recognize their community's connection with one of its most despicable elements. At their request, we worked with and strengthened their local group. Together we presented a slide show and tour of the local military-industrial complex for community leaders, and we picketed the napalm factory. We also met with the president of the conglomerate that owned the factory.

29   We spent three weeks preparing for this meeting, studying the company's holdings and financial picture and investigating whether there were any lawsuits filed against the president or his corporation. And we found out as much as we could about his personal life: his family, his church, his country club, his hobbies. We studied his photograph, thinking of the people who loved him and the people he loved, trying to get a sense of his worldview and the context to which he was accountable.

30   We also talked a lot about how angry we were at him for the part he played in killing and maiming children in Vietnam. But though our anger fueled our determination, we decided that venting it at him would make him defensive and reduce our effectiveness.

31   When three of us met with him, he was not a stranger to us. Without blaming him personally or attacking his corporation, we asked him to close the plant, not to bid for the contract when it came up for renewal that year, and to think about the consequences of his company's operations. We told him we knew where his corporation was vulnerable (it owned a chain of motels that could be boycotted), and said we intended to continue working strategically to force his company out of the business of burning people. We also discussed the company's other war-related contracts, because changing just a small part of his corporation's function was not enough; we wanted to raise the issue of economic dependence on munitions and war.

32   Above all, we wanted him to see us as real people, not so different from himself. If we had seemed like flaming radicals, he would have been likely to dismiss our concerns. We assumed he was already carrying doubts inside himself, and we saw our role as giving voice to those doubts. Our goal was to introduce ourselves and our perspective into his context, so he would remember us and consider our position when making decisions.

33   When the contract came up for renewal two months later, his company did not bid for it.

34   Working for social change without relying on the concept of enemies raises some practical difficulties. For example, what do we do with all the anger that we're accustomed to unleashing against an enemy? Is it possible to hate actions and policies without hating the people who are implementing them? Does empathizing with those whose actions we oppose create a dissonance that undermines our determination?

35   I don't delude myself into believing that everything will work out for the best if we make friends with our adversaries. I recognize that certain military strategists are making decisions that raise the risks for us all. I know that some police officers will rough up demonstrators when arresting them. Treating our adversaries as potential allies need not entail unthinking acceptance of their actions. Our challenge is to call forth the humanity within each adversary, while preparing for the full range of possible responses. Our challenge is to find a path between cynicism and naivete.

Questions for Discussion

1. Why does Peavey no longer find it easy to feel clear about the distinctions between the "good guys" and the "bad guys"? What elements of the bad guys does she now perceive in herself?
2. What was Peavey's rationale for being angry at soldiers? What did

Peavey learn from her experience of hosting a group of Vietnam veterans on her farm?

3. What did Peavey learn from the visit with her sister and her sister's husband, a military sniper? Does Peavey feel that the husband should be forgiven? Do you agree?

4. How does Peavey's friendship with Helen Waterford break down preconceptions Peavey holds about Nazis and concentration camp survivors? Do you agree with Waterford and Peavey's new perspective on Nazis?

5. Through providing an example of her own successful organizing technique against a napalm factory, Peavey attempts to refute an argument by organizer Saul Alinsky against the folly of "qualifying" our attacks on our enemies. Is Peavey's argument a convincing one?

6. How effective is Peavey's conclusion in anticipating and resolving objections readers might have to her position? What point does she concede? Does her concession weaken or strengthen her argument?

Ideas for Writing

1. After reading Peavey's essay and the discussion by the editors at the beginning of this chapter on the dialogic argument, write an essay in which you argue either for or against Peavey's approach to resolving political differences. If you see her approach as working better in some situations than in others, provide examples of areas of conflict where the approach might or might not work.

2. One of Peavey's points that relates to the concerns of this chapter is that our "anger and righteousness" sometimes prevent us from seeing the perspective of our opponents, or from seeing them as human, like ourselves. Write an essay about an experience in which you separated yourself from another person or an opposed group of people because of your anger or righteousness but later were able to understand and identify with their behavior and to accept their differentness.

 Theodore Roethke

In a Dark Time

See the headnote in Chapter 1.

JOURNAL

Write about a time of crisis in your life.

In a dark time, the eye begins to see,
I meet my shadow in the deepening shade;
I hear my echo in the echoing wood—
A lord of nature weeping to a tree.
5 I live between the heron and the wren,
Beasts of the hill and serpents of the den.

What's madness but nobility of soul
At odds with circumstances? The day's on fire!
I know the purity of pure despair,
10 My shadow pinned against a sweating wall.
That place among the rocks—is it a cave,
Or winding path? The edge is what I have.

A steady storm of correspondences!
A night flowing with birds, a ragged moon,
15 And in broad day the midnight comes again!
A man goes far to find out what he is—
Death of the self in a long, tearless night,
All natural shapes blazing unnatural light.

Dark, dark my light, and darker my desire.
20 My soul, like some heat-maddened summer fly,
Keeps buzzing at the sill. Which I is *I*?
A fallen man, I climb out of my fear.
The mind enters itself, and God the mind,
And one is One, free in the tearing wind.

Questions for Discussion

1. What part of the self does the shadow that the speaker meets in the "deepening shade" represent?
2. What is the speaker's mood at the beginning of the poem? How has the poem's tone changed by the final line?
3. What happens to the speaker's shadow self during the night?
4. What does the speaker fear?
5. In what sense is the speaker reborn? How has the speaker changed?
6. Will the speaker have to continue to confront his shadow self?

Ideas for Writing

1. Develop your journal entry into an essay. Discuss how you came to change and grow through your struggle. You might also want to contrast your shadow with Roethke's or with the shadow of any other of the writers in this chapter.
2. Write a poem or story about you and your shadow self.

Chris Hales

In "In a Dark Time" Roethke appears to me to be speaking about the relationship between his conscious mind and the dreaming, subconscious, elusive other half of himself, referred to in the poem as the shadow. He writes of being on ". . . the edge" between the two, in the middle of "A steady storm of correspondences," that provides his
vision when he can let go of fear (see line 22). "Which I is I?" he asks, but his answer is
both. And when he allows himself to be both, something special occurs; a power
Roethke refers to as God results from this union. The final phrase, ". . . free in the tearing wind," seems to reflect the impulsive, almost uncontrollable nature of this power.
My picture shows a man chasing, with some fear, his shadow up a spiral to his mind's
eye, to the power Roethke calls God.

I really enjoyed this poem because I related to Roethke's view of what happens
when you mix the two sides of your soul, almost like mixing two chemicals that you
know will react, although you can't predict how violently.

Susan Voyticky

Mixed-Up

Susan Voyticky grew up in Brooklyn, New York. She enjoys traveling (frequently on roller blades), studying genetics, and writing poetry. The following essay was written for her freshman English class in response to a question that asked students to consider some aspect of their ethnic heritage about which they sometimes feel confused or "doubled."

JOURNAL

Write about the different backgrounds of your family and ancestors. Do you ever feel a sense of inner conflict about the diversity of your heritage? Do you see the differences in your cultural background in a positive way?

1   Having parents from different ethnic groups and growing up mixed is not easy in this country; in fact, it can really mix a person up, culturally as well as socially. Often, mixed children are confused about the cultural group to which they belong, and sometimes these children are alienated from half or even all of their cultural background. Other times children exposed to two distinct cultures feel pressured by society to choose one culture and social group to fit into and to define themselves through. However, as a person of mixed background, I try, despite the pressures that society puts on me, to relate to both my European and to my African heritage. I realize that I have a unique and independent cultural identity.

2   My lack of wanting to identify with a particular culture defines who I am. For instance, I remember going shopping in a store when I was ten years old that had black and white floor tiles. I decided to play with two children, a boy and a girl who were my age. After a while the girl said, "We'll [she and the boy] step on the white tiles, and you [pointing to me] step on the black tiles 'cause you're black." I couldn't believe what she had said. Even at that age, I found the idea insulting to my existence—she was ignoring half of me. I replied indignantly, "You two can step on the white tiles, I'll step anywhere I want because I'm both." Then I quickly returned to my mother.

3   As a child, I quickly grew to realize that I was not ethnically "identifiable." During recess at my elementary school I often would try to play with the few African-American girls at my school. Usually the game was double-dutch, but I didn't know how to play, and the African-Americans kids said I turned the rope "like a white girl." To whites, I was black, and to blacks, I was less than black. I refused to be either; my ethnicity is an entirely different color—gray. If my mother is black and my father is white, then I most certainly must be gray. What else does one get by mixing black and white? Some would consider gray a "drab" color, but often one forgets gray comes in an infinite number of shades.

4   Because I have not chosen to identify with only one of my parents' cultures, I'll never know the comfort of belonging to a specific group of people with ancient customs and rituals. This society does not recognize my unique cross-cultural heritage of African-American, Irish, Russian, Polish, and Czechoslovakian. Few people choose to be mixed, to accept everything about themselves, and sometimes they are not given the choice. I have lost something in not being "white"; I also have lost something in not being "black." However, I have gained something important: my cultural independence. My brother puts it best when he says, "God was making a bunch of cookies. The white people he took out of the oven too soon. The black people he took out too late. We are the perfect cookies. One day everyone will be perfect, like us."

5   I struggle to be accepted in this society for what I am and not for what others would make of me. The longer I live, the more I feel pressured by society to "label" myself. When standardized forms were handed out in school, I would ask the teachers, "What should I fill out?" Most replied that I could fill whichever I wished. Most of the time that's what I did. One year I was black, the next year I was white, the next year I'd fill out two ovals. In high school, I was told I was black, because the federal government has a rule that if one is one fourth black, one is black. I ignored this and continued to fill out forms in my usual way.

6   The true test of my "grayness" arrived—college applications. My mother said that I should fill out African-American, for the ethnic question, considering that it would improve my chances of being accepted. I didn't listen to her, for it's not in my nature to lie. How could I not be honest about who I was? On half of my applications I wrote "Black-Caucasian"; on the other half I wrote, "White African-American." My mother was not amused by what seemed to her a completely inane act. She didn't understand that I can't be told what I am, because I know who I am. In my blood run the tears of slaves torn from their homeland and the sweat of poor farmers looking for a better life. Their struggle is part of my identity.

7   A large part of one's culture is internal and cannot be represented simply by the color of one's skin. In this society it is difficult to be accepted for anything more than face value, but each person must try to be who he or she is within, not simply in the eyes of society. I am proud of my choice of identity with both of my ethnic backgrounds. Although being mixed often means being "mixed-up," being mistaken for something you are not by people too ignorant to care, identity is more than skin deep.

Questions for Discussion

1. What aspects of her mixed ethnic background cause Susan Voyticky the most difficulty? How has she tried to resolve her problem of identity?
2. Compare Voyticky's view of the consequences of a mixed cultural and ethnic background with that presented in the poem by Judith Ortiz Cofer, "The Other."
3. Do you agree with Voyticky's approach to choosing an ethnicity for her college applications, or do you think that she should have taken fuller advantage of the opportunities afforded her?

4. Voyticky illustrates her essay with several examples drawn from her experience of being of mixed heritage at different stages of her life. What does each add to her essay's persuasiveness and its portrait of the dilemmas faced in our society by individuals from backgrounds similar to Voyticky's? What other kinds of evidence or examples would have helped to persuade you?

 ## Albert Liu

The Artist and the Engineer

Albert Liu, a college freshman, wrote "The Artist and the Engineer" in an attempt to determine what role his creative mind should play in shaping his thinking, writing, and career decisions. As you read his essay, notice the conflict he feels between doing what is logical and what is expected of him and being creative and exploring new experiences. Which path do you think that Albert Liu will eventually take? Do you have any advice that will help him to solve his dilemma?

JOURNAL

Write a dialogue between the part of yourself that is practical and the part of yourself that is more expressive and creative. Focus on an unresolved issue of serious concern in your current life.

1   I slam the bedroom door shut and aim my loaded backpack for the skinny legs on the desk in the corner. Taking one step back and with a perfect follow-through, I let it fly. The pack tumbles with reluctance across the room, slowed by its irregular geometric shape and the strands of carpet sticking out like little hands reaching and grabbing; it comes to rest with a dull thud, a perfect strike, no applause please.

2   Even that didn't cheer me up. Let me introduce myself. I am a male Asian college student, living with the Asian stereotype. I am also a sick person, not sick in the traditional physical sense, but diseased in the mind. You see, I think I am merely living out a life that my parents have planned for me. Highlights along the way include majoring in Engineering, receiving my PhD by the age of 25, finding a $60,000 a year job, getting married and having two kids, no more, no less. Since this discovery, the artistic and the rational sides of my brain have been arguing with each other, resulting in a heated verbal battle that has been stalemated for the past three years. Look into my eyes and try to imagine the artist and the engi-

neer, representatives of the respective sides, facing each other again. Shhh, be very very quiet and if you listen carefully enough, you can actually hear them. They are talking about me.

3   "He never has any free time, time to watch a 747 divide the sky in half with its exhaust, time to hear the chirping of crickets, time to smell freshly baked chocolate-chip cookies, time to taste the lushness of fresh picked baby strawberries, time to feel an ice cube slowly melting in his hand, time . . . " the artist reminisced, only to be cut off by the engineer.

4   "Ha, what are feelings good for? Nothing but games for children. Can you explain why airplanes can fly, and why magnets attract certain metals and not others, and why the interior angles of a triangle add up to a hundred and eighty degrees? Nope, as surely as one plus one equals two they can't," the engineer spoke slowly, with a voice that sounded like a tape recorder. "You know, his dad has always wanted him to be an engineer."

5   "Why does he have to be an engineer? Why does he always have to do what his parents want instead of what he really wants?" There is anger and frustration in the voice of the artist now.

6   "He is only eighteen and but a child. What does he know? How can he have more experience than his parents, who would only choose the best for him? You know how hard his dad has worked for him . . . "

7   "His dad," the artist sneered, "the one that programmed him. With his help, you dominated his childhood and filled his early memories with prime numbers, algebra, and mathematical equations."

8   "Those were the glorious days," said the engineer, "when you were nothing but a standby, a spectator of my operations. He used me almost exclusively, but then . . . "

9   "But then he began to discover his own identity, unconsciously fighting against becoming a replica of his dad. Exposure to literature and the arts, something that his dad saw no future in, gave him a glimpse of how he wanted to shape his own future . . . "

10   The engineer shook his head. "It is merely a passing fancy. He will like engineering. He will be an engineer. It is his parents' will. It shall be executed."

11   "But literature is what he enjoys," cried the artist. "It is his life, not his dad's. He must be allowed to choose what he wants to do in the future without any outside pressure."

12   "That is impossible and you know it!" The engineer was beginning to sound like dad. "Engineering as a major is the only logical choice to make. His English and his writing will never be as good as native-born Americans."

13   "It just doesn't matter," said the artist, "as long as he is allowed to do what he feels is right for him. At least give him that chance."

14   "Granted, certain pursuits in the artistic field can be beneficial for him," said the engineer grudgingly. "But he is at a point where he must decide on his future and the future for him is in the sciences."

15   The artist threw up his hands and said, "Of course that must be your opinion. I can only advise him to pursue the arts, which will make him a better man, and if

nothing else, make him see the world as it really is rather than as how numbers or scientific principles can describe it . . . "

16   With that the artist and the engineer went back to their separate sides.

17   It is over, at least for today. Tomorrow the discussion would go on, with the same arguments on both sides. There is to be no compromise. You see, the pivotal point has come in my life where I must elevate one side of my brain to the lead role. I keep putting the decision off, but I cannot do so forever. My heart tells me to go with the road less traveled by, to explore what I enjoy and make it my future pursuit. Lately my heartbeat has gotten stronger and stronger, almost to the bursting point.

18   Thump Thump Thump Thump. . . .

Questions for Discussion

1. How does Albert Liu define the values of the artist and the engineer? What parts of the writer's mind do the artist and the engineer represent? Why are they in conflict?

2. This essay doesn't have an explicit thesis statement, but it does make a point and have a purpose. Why did Liu write this essay, and what do you think he is trying to say in it about the creative process? How can you tell what the "meaning" of an essay is when it lacks a thesis statement?

3. Characterize the tone of this essay: Is it humorous or serious or both? How does the tone help Liu to develop his point of view?

4. Can you identify with the dilemma presented in this essay? Do you ever have a hard time deciding whether to follow the advice of your practical self or your creative self?

5. Do you think that Liu will become an artist or an engineer? Why? Does Liu show signs of creativity in his approach to writing?

Chapter Writing Topics

1. Think about the views on an individual's divided self as seen in the poems "The Other" and "In a Dark Time." Do the poems help you to understand your own divided self? How? Begin by drawing a picture or creating a collage that represents your two selves. Then write an essay that discusses your inner conflict and how you think you might better integrate your two selves; submit your drawing along with your essay.

2. Shelby Steele's and Fran Peavey's essays explore ways in which the shadow or alternative self can affect one's political decisions. Write an essay that discusses how these perspectives help you to better understand your own mixed feelings and attitudes about political decisions that you have made. Refer to particular situations and decisions in shaping your response.

3. Discuss the views on the "shadow self" as expressed in Marie-Luise Von Franz's essay, Stevenson's "Henry Jekyll's Full Statement," and

Andersen's "The Shadow." What is each author saying about the power of the shadow self and the problems that individuals have in appeasing and reconciling with their shadow? How do these selections help you to understand yourself and your motivations and values? Refer to specific situations, feelings, and decisions in shaping your response.

4. Write a dialogue or a brief play in which the speakers represent two different perspectives on an issue raised in this book or one in your present life about which you feel conflicted. In your conclusion, try to reconcile the oppositional sides of the dispute.

5. Write a story or poem that develops the concept of the shadow self or the double.

6. Write an essay on a contemporary or philosophical issue of controversy in which you present both sides of the issue objectively, allowing each side equal development. At the end of the paper, without implying that either viewpoint is "wrong" or to be totally rejected, see if you can create a third position that brings the seemingly distinct positions you have presented in your essay closer together.

7. Write an argument essay directed to a particular audience which you indicate in your introduction and title. Try to argue in such a way that you anticipate any objections your audience may have and acknowledge their particular sensitivities and preconceptions. Show your audience that you understand and respect their stance on the issue while trying to convince them that your arguments have merit and will work for their interests as well as your own.

8. Write about a film that portrays the double or the divided personality. Did the film offer you any new insights or echo insights of authors included in this chapter on the issues of the "shadow," the double, or the other? You might choose from the following list of films.

Ringers, Three Faces of Eve, The Double Life of Veronique, Dr. Jekyll and Mr. Hyde, The Heart of Darkness, Batman, True Lies, Mary Reilly

8

Society's Dreams

When we wake
the news of the world embraces us,
pulls back. Who let go first?—

> STEPHEN DUNN
> Middle Class Poem

We would not have to insist that images reflect life, except that all too often we ask life to reflect images.
> GISH JEN
> Challenging the Asian Illusion

"Who controls the past," ran the Party slogan, "controls the future: who controls the present controls the past." . . . Whatever was true now was true from everlasting to everlasting. It was quite simple. All that was needed was an unending series of victories over your own memory. "Reality control," they called it; in Newspeak, "doublethink."
> GEORGE ORWELL
> 1984

Research Writing

The new skills needed to integrate facts and a variety of perspectives often overwhelm students just beginning a research paper. To minimize the anxiety involved in composing a research paper, try to maintain a balance between the creative and the rational sides of your mind. The steps that follow will provide your rational mind with a map to keep you on the main trail, but you should also allow your curious and creative mind to explore the many side paths and research possibilities that you will discover as you compose your paper. Above all, start early and pace yourself. A research paper needs to be completed in stages; it takes time to gather and to absorb, both intellectually and emotionally, the materials that will be used in drafting your paper.

For many students, being assigned a research paper raises a number of practical questions and issues: "How many sources will I be expected to use?" "What procedure should I follow in taking notes and doing a bibliography?" "How does the computer in the library catalogue information?" "How can I access and evaluate information on the World Wide Web?" While these concerns are essential parts of the research paper writing process, we do not discuss specific techniques of finding, quoting, and documenting source information in the library or on the World Wide Web because these issues are thoroughly covered in most standard rhetorics and handbooks; librarians are also available and willing to help you. We will discuss the process involved in producing a research paper and the importance of maintaining a sense of voice and control over the information and point of view that you are presenting.

Research is more than a catalogue of interesting facts and quotations; research should help writers understand and evaluate their own perspectives and see their topic in relationship to their personal values as well as to broader issues. Professional writers naturally turn to outside sources of knowledge to deepen their own personal perspective and to better inform and engage their readers. Because their writing is thoughtfully constructed and thoroughly revised, their source material becomes an integral part of their writer's voice and stance; what was originally research doesn't sound strained, dry, or "tacked on," even though they may have used numerous brief quotations and paraphrases of their source material.

To minimize the anxiety involved in composing a research paper, try to maintain a balance between the creative and the rational sides of your mind. While it is natural to think about how your paper will be evaluated, it is more important to remain curious and to have fun discovering your sources and learning about your subject. It is helpful to keep a regular log of your process, making journal entries as you move through each stage of your paper, as you gather new insights into your topic and new understanding about how your mind works under the pressure of research paper deadlines.

Finding a Topic

Spend some time exploring possible topics for your research paper; writing brief summaries of several different topics may help you to decide on the topic that interests you most. The best research papers are produced by students who are thoroughly engaged in their topic and in communicating what they have learned to their readers. This enthusiasm and intellectual curiosity will help you work through the inevitable frustrations associated with learning how to use a library and tracking down information that may not be easily available. After you complete some preliminary research, reevaluate and narrow your general topic further, if necessary, so that it can be covered within the scope and limits of the assignment.

Timetable and Process

Make a timetable for your project and follow it. For example, you might allow yourself two to three weeks to establish a working bibliography and do research. Then schedule several work sessions to write the first draft, and several more days to complete your research and revise the draft. Also plan to give yourself sufficient time to complete the final draft, check your documentation, and do the final proofreading. At every stage in this process you should seek out as much useful feedback and advice as you possibly can. Tell your family and friends about your topic; they may have ideas about where to find sources. Read your first draft to peers and give your teacher a copy. Make sure that your readers clearly understand your paper's purpose and examples and that your writing holds their interest. Don't feel discouraged if you find that you need to do several revisions to clarify your ideas. This is a natural part of the research paper writing process.

Your Voice and the Voices of Your Sources

Practice careful reading and accurate note-taking as you prepare to write your paper. To avoid becoming overwhelmed by the sources you are working with, treat them as outside voices, as people with whom you want to conduct a dialogue. Take every quotation you intend to use in your paper and paraphrase it carefully into your own language to make sure that you really understand it. If you feel confused or intimidated by a source, freewriting may help you to get in touch with your feelings and responses to the authority. Is this "authority" really correct in his or her assertions, or do your experiences suggest that some of his or her comments are questionable or simply incorrect? Throughout this text we've created models of these types of questions in our study questions; now it is time for you to begin posing and answering your own questions about your sources. Undigested sources often produce a glorified book report, a rehash of ideas that you have not fully absorbed and integrated with your own point of view.

Purpose and Structure

Always keep focused on the purpose and structure in your essay. Your research paper should express an original central purpose and have a compelling thesis. Each major idea must be introduced by a clear topic sentence and supported by evidence and examples. While using an outline is very helpful, feel free to revise the outline as you do further research and also to make changes in your original view of your material and topic. A research paper brings together many different ideas into a unified, original vision of a subject that, as the writer, only you can provide.

Language and Style

As you write your first draft, and particularly as you work through later stages of the paper, continue to express your own writer's voice. Your point of view should be communicated in language with which you feel comfortable and should always be your paper's guide. Read your paper aloud periodically. Is it tedious to listen to? Do you sound like yourself in this essay? Check your vocabulary and compare it with the sense of language in your previous papers. Are you using more multisyllabic words than usual or a specialized jargon that even you can hardly understand, one that is too derivative of your sources? Are your sentences more convoluted than usual? Have you lost touch with your own personal voice? If the answer to any of these questions is yes, try returning to the feelings and thoughts that inspired you in the first place.

Writing a research paper is a challenge that provides you with the opportunity to develop, to utilize, and to integrate your research and writing skills as well as your creativity. A well-written research paper is a genuine accomplishment, a milestone on your inward journey.

THEMATIC INTRODUCTION

 Who creates and monitors the dreams of our society and our own dreams? The readings in this chapter suggest different ways in which social customs; mass media such as film, television, and advertising; and political ideology influence our dreams and self-concepts. Although it would be naive to imagine that we could have total control over our own dreams, creating them without assistance from our culture, many of us aspire to be individualistic, first valuing our inner feelings and thoughts while forming impressions and evaluations of our social and political worlds. In modern society, however, individualism and developing an inner life are too often undermined and threatened by social forces that seek to mold us into loyal citizens, passive consumers, productive and compliant workers. Sometimes eager to escape temporarily from our immediate problems, sometimes feeling a strong need to belong to our social world, we allow ourselves to ignore the impact that overexposure to the mass media, to the steady barrage of consumerist and political propaganda can have on the development and integrity of our private selves as well as on our sense of its power to shape us.

One of the most common ways that society enters our minds and creates distorted pictures of the external world and its values is through the news. Television newscasts, radio talk shows, and newspaper stories select and present reports of human events and natural disasters that are disturbing, full of uncontrollable dangers, disasters, and violence. These reports, while sometimes accurate, often intensify the negative, especially in contrast to what usually occurs in day-to-day life. To the extent that we internalize these nightmarish pictures of the world, our inner lives and private dream worlds are affected.

Our first two selections explore different ways that we process what we learn from the media. In Stephen Dunn's "Middle Class Poem," the speaker provides us with one perspective on how peoples' waking lives and dreams are haunted by images from the evening news. In "Pictures in Our Heads," Anthony Pratkanis and Elliot Aronson discuss surveys that reveal the exaggerated impressions held by heavy television viewers of the level of violence and risk in society. Their selection asks us to question why we allow the news media to define the questions and issues that concern us; they urge us to take more responsibility in selecting what is newsworthy.

Perhaps our deepest fear is that one day the media and political propaganda will control our minds and our lives completely. In his classic work of negative utopian fiction, *1984*, George Orwell addresses this fear, portraying a future world where it is almost impossible to entertain a private dream or memory. In the reading selected for this chapter, "Winston Was Dreaming," the central character attempts to capture and interpret a precious childhood dream only to be struck by a sense of tragic loss, realizing that such concepts as tragedy and love belong to an "ancient time," a time when inner worlds and the individual imagination were treasured.

We are also strongly influenced by popular fiction, dreamlike escapist films, and other forms of mass entertainment. Perhaps we do not always realize the extent of the significance of such "fictional" fare, often dismissing it as a form of relaxation and escape into someone else's mass-produced fantasy. In her essay "The Wizard of Oz" Terry McMillan discusses how watching the classic film *The Wizard of Oz* when she was a child helped her develop a strong self-concept. For McMillan, who grew up in a difficult home situation, the film brought positive images of the potential for creativity, hope, courage, and friendship. To give you a sense of Dorothy's courage and intelligence in the face of disappointment and duplicity, we have included an excerpt, "The Magic Art of the Great Humbug," from the original *The Wonderful Wizard of Oz* by Frank Baum. In this excerpt Dorothy meets Oz only to discover that he is really a facade and a fake. Next, Gary Soto's light-hearted story "El Radio" shows ways in which the media can help people to understand their dreams in a positive and more realistic way.

The long-lasting impact that negative images from film can have is explored in the following two selections. In "Dear John Wayne," Louise Erdrich asks us to question the fantasies we have about the settling of the West and our stereotypes of Native Americans. Gish Jen in "Challenging the Asian Illusion" is critical of the media's dehumanizing and stereotypical presentation of Asians and Asian Americans as she encourages her readers to think about the importance of seeing and portraying all people as humans.

A broader criticism of the dangers of mass culture is presented by Umberto Eco in his essay "The City of Robots." Critical of the superficial promises that are sometimes offered in social dreams, he asks us to think about why the totally fake theme park, as best exemplified by Disneyland, has become a place of worship, like the "Sistine Chapel," where our true national values are enshrined.

Two student essays complete the readings in this chapter. In "'The Little Princess' and Me" Terri Sevilla fondly recalls how watching the films of Shirley Temple helped her to develop her sense of adventure and self-confidence. Amanda Morgan, in "When Beauty Is the Beast," analyzes the causes of eating disorder syndromes that attack the self-esteem and happiness of many teens and young women who feel a strong and unrelenting social pressure to live up to an unrealistic cultural standard of beauty. Morgan shows how images from the media that persuade young women that "thin is in" compromise not only their health but also their self-confidence and sense of well-being.

We hope that reading the selections in this chapter will help you to think more deeply about the ways that your dreams and beliefs are shaped by the mass media, social conventions, and political ideology. An important part of a writer's inward journey involves value clarification. Unraveling one's own genuine dreams and values from those that are artificial and mass-produced can be liberating and life-affirming.

   ## Stephen Dunn

Middle Class Poem

Stephen Dunn (b. 1939) was born in New York City and studied at the New School for Social Research at Syracuse University. Dunn has worked as a copywriter for an advertising company and as a basketball player. Currently he is poet in residence at Stockton State College in New Jersey. His books include Not Dancing *(1984),* Local Time *(1986), and* Landscape at the End of the Century: Poems *(1991). In "Middle Class Poem" Dunn explores the impact of television news and consumerism on people's dreams and emotional life.*

JOURNAL

Write about a time when your sleep was disturbed by thoughts, fantasies, or dreams related to stories or issues raised in the newspaper or on the radio or television news.

In dreams, the news of the world
comes back, gets mixed up
with our parents and the moon.
We can't help but thrash.
5 Those with whom we sleep, never equally,
roll away from us and sigh.

When we wake
the news of the world embraces us,
pulls back. Who let go first?—
10 a lover's question, the lover
who's most alone.
We purchase a little forgetfulness
at the mall. We block the entrance
to our hearts.

15 Come evening, the news of the world
    is roaming the streets
    while we bathe our children,
    while we eat what's plentiful
    and scarce. We know what we need
20 to keep out, what's always there—
    painful to look at, bottomless.

Questions for Discussion

1. What does the speaker in the poem believe "comes back" in dreams?
2. Why is there a "thrashing" in the beds of the sleepers in the poem? What disturbs their sleep and causes them to "sigh"?
3. In the second stanza of the poem, the speaker refers to the "news of the world" as a lover. If the news is a lover, what sort of lover is it? How does the news betray us? Why does the news make us feel like the lover who is "most alone"?
4. In lines 12–14 the speaker is buying "forgetfulness / at the mall." How does shopping help people to forget and to wall off emotions? Do you think that this is a common reason for going shopping? Do most people whom you know simply shop when they need to buy something?
5. The last stanza of the poem personifies the news, referring to it as "roaming the streets," like an animal or a dangerous criminal. What kinds of feelings does this comparison evoke? Do you think that such feelings about the news and its subject matter are typical ones for middle-class people?
6. The last three lines of the poem refer to that which the middle-class people in the poem prefer "to keep out, what's always there— / painful to look at, bottomless." What exactly is it in the news that causes people so much pain and anxiety? To what extent is what they fear real? To what extent is what they fear just a creation of their own overstimulated imaginations?

Ideas for Writing

1. "Middle Class Poem" suggests that the news alarms people, perhaps even disrupting sleeping patterns and causing nightmares. Write an essay about the ways you think the news, particularly television news, influences people's dreams and emotional life. To support your ideas draw on your own experiences, interview friends, or read relevant articles.
2. The poem explores the effects of consumerism and compulsive shopping. Write an essay on compulsive shopping: What causes people to want to "shop till they drop"? Can overshopping become an addictive form of behavior?

Anthony Pratkanis and Elliot Aronson

Pictures in Our Heads, from The Age of Propaganda

Anthony Pratkanis and Elliot Aronson are currently professors of psychology at the University of California, Santa Cruz. Pratkanis has taught courses in consumerism and advertising at Carnegie Mellon University and was called as an expert witness on subliminal persuasion at the Judas Priest suicide trial, where he testified for the defense. He has written many articles for both popular and scholarly journals and is an editor of Attitude Structure and Function. *Elliott Aronson is one of the world's most highly regarded social psychologists. He is the author of many books, including* The Jigsaw Classroom, The Social Animal, *and* Methods of Research in Social Psychology. *The following article is from Pratkanis and Aronson's recent book,* The Age of Propaganda (1992), *which focuses on the ways people's views of the world are influenced and molded by the constant barrage of media propaganda.*

JOURNAL

Write about an attitude you have toward a certain political or social issue that you believe was influenced by the images provided by television news.

1   In *Public Opinion*, the distinguished political analyst Walter Lippmann tells the story of a young girl, brought up in a small mining town, who one day went from cheerfulness into a deep spasm of grief.[1] A gust of wind had suddenly cracked a kitchen windowpane. The young girl was inconsolable and spoke incomprehensibly for hours. When she finally was able to speak intelligibly, she explained that a broken pane of glass meant that a close relative had died. She was therefore mourning her father, whom she felt certain had just passed away. The young girl remained disconsolate until, days later, a telegram arrived verifying that her father was still alive. It appears that the girl had constructed a complete fiction based on a simple external fact (a broken window), a superstition (broken window means death), fear, and love for her father.

2   The point of Lippmann's story was not to explore the inner workings of abnormal personality, but to ask a question about ourselves: To what extent do we, like the young girl, let our fictions guide our thoughts and actions? Lippmann believed that we are much more similar to that young girl than we might readily admit. He contended that the mass media paint an imagined world and that the "pictures in our heads" derived from the media influence what men and women will do and say at any particular moment. Lippmann made these observations in 1922. Seven

decades later, we can ask: What is the evidence for his claim? To what extent do the pictures we see on television and in other mass media influence how we see the world and set the agenda for what we view as most important in our lives?

3   Let's look at the world we see on television. George Gerbner and his associates have conducted the most extensive analysis of television to date.[2] Since the late 1960s, these researchers have been videotaping and carefully analyzing thousands of prime-time television programs and characters. Their findings, taken as a whole, indicate that the world portrayed on television is grossly misleading as a representation of reality. Their research further suggests that, to a surprising extent, we take what we see on television as a reflection of reality.

4   In prime-time programming, males outnumber females by 3 to 1, and the women portrayed are younger than the men they encounter. Nonwhites (especially Hispanics), young children, and the elderly are underrepresented; and members of minority groups are disproportionately cast in minor roles. Moreover, most prime-time characters are portrayed as professional and managerial workers: Although 67% of the work force in the United States are employed in blue-collar or service jobs, only 25% of TV characters hold such jobs. Finally, crime on television is ten times more prevalent than it is in real life. The average 15-year-old has viewed more than 13,000 TV killings. Over half of TV's characters are involved in a violent confrontation each week; in reality, fewer than 1% of people in the nation are victims of criminal violence in any given year, according to FBI statistics. David Rintels, a television writer and former president of the Writers' Guild of America, summed it up best when he said, "From 8 to 11 o'clock each night, television is one long lie."[3]

5   To gain an understanding of the relationship between watching television and the pictures in our heads, Gerbner and his colleagues compared the attitudes and beliefs of heavy viewers (those who watch more than four hours a day) and light viewers (those who watch less than two hours a day). They found that heavy viewers (1) express more racially prejudiced attitudes; (2) overestimate the number of people employed as physicians, lawyers, and athletes; (3) perceive women as having more limited abilities and interests than men; (4) hold exaggerated views of the prevalence of violence in society; and (5) believe old people are fewer in number and less healthy today than they were twenty years ago, even though the opposite is true. What is more, heavy viewers tend to see the world as a more sinister place than do light viewers; they are more likely to agree that most people are just looking out for themselves and would take advantage of you if they had a chance. Gerbner and his colleagues conclude that these attitudes and beliefs reflect the inaccurate portrayals of American life provided to us by television.

6   Let's look at the relationship between watching television and images of the world by looking more closely at how we picture criminal activity. In an analysis of "television criminology," Craig Haney and John Manzolati point out that crime shows dispense remarkably consistent images of both the police and criminals.[4] For example, they found that television policemen are amazingly effective, solving almost every crime, and are absolutely infallible in one regard: The wrong person is never in jail at the end of a show. Television fosters an illusion of certainty in

crimefighting. Television criminals generally turn to crime because of psychopathology or insatiable (and unnecessary) greed. Television emphasizes criminals' personal responsibility for their actions and largely ignores situational pressures correlated with crime, such as poverty and unemployment.

7   Haney and Manzolati go on to suggest that this portrayal has important social consequences. People who watch a lot of television tend to share this belief system, which affects their expectations and can cause them to take a hard-line stance when serving on juries. Heavy viewers are likely to reverse the presumption of innocence, believing that defendants must be guilty of something, otherwise they wouldn't be brought to trial.

8   A similar tale can be told about other "pictures painted in our heads." For example, heavy readers of newspaper accounts of sensational and random crimes report higher levels of fear of crime. Repeated viewing of R-rated violent "slasher" films is associated with less sympathy and empathy for victims of rape. When television is introduced into an area, the incidence of theft increases, perhaps due partly to television's promotion of consumerism, which may frustrate and anger economically deprived viewers who compare their life-styles with those portrayed on television.[5]

9   It should be noted, however, that the research just described—that done by Gerbner and colleagues and by others—is correlational; that is, it shows merely an association, not a causal relation, between television viewing and beliefs. It is therefore impossible to determine from this research whether heavy viewing actually causes prejudiced attitudes and inaccurate beliefs or whether people already holding such attitudes and beliefs simply tend to watch more television. In order to be certain that watching TV causes such attitudes and beliefs, it would be necessary to perform a controlled experiment in which people are randomly assigned to conditions. Fortunately, some recent experiments do allow us to be fairly certain that heavy viewing does indeed determine the pictures we form of the world.

10   In a set of ingenious experiments, the political psychologists Shanto Iyengar and Donald Kinder varied the contents of evening news shows watched by their research participants.[6] In their studies, Iyengar and Kinder edited the evening news so that participants received a steady dose of news about a specific problem facing the United States. For example, in one of their experiments, some participants heard about the weaknesses of U.S. defense capabilities; a second group watched shows emphasizing pollution concerns; a third group heard about inflation and economic matters.

11   The results were clear. After a week of viewing the specially edited programs, participants emerged from the study more convinced than they were before viewing the shows that the target problem—the one receiving extensive coverage in the shows they had watched—was a more important one for the country to solve. What is more, the participants acted on their newfound perceptions, evaluating the current president's performance on the basis of how he handled the target issue and evaluating more positively than their competitors those candidates who took strong positions on those problems.

12   Iyengar and Kinder's findings are not a fluke. Communications researchers repeatedly find a link between what stories the mass media cover and what viewers

consider to be the most important issues of the day.[7] The content of the mass media sets the public's political and social agenda. As just one example, in a pioneering study of an election in North Carolina, researchers found that the issues that voters came to consider to be most important in the campaign coincided with the amount of coverage those issues received in the local media.[8] Similarly, the problems of drug abuse, NASA incompetence, and nuclear energy were catapulted into the nation's consciousness by the coverage of dramatic events such as the drug-related death of basketball star Len Bias, the *Challenger* explosion, and the nuclear-reactor accidents at Three Mile Island and Chernobyl. Former Secretary of State Henry Kissinger clearly understood the power of the news media in setting agendas. He once noted that he never watched the content of the evening news but was only interested in "what they covered and for what length of time, to learn what the country was getting."[9]

13   Of course, each of us has had extensive personal contact with many people in a myriad of social contexts; the media are just one source of our knowledge about political affairs and different ethnic, gender, and occupational groups. The information and impressions we receive through the media are relatively less influential when we can also rely on firsthand experience. Thus those of us who have been in close contact with several women who work outside the home are probably less susceptible to the stereotypes of women portrayed on television. On the other hand, regarding issues with which most of us have had limited or no personal experience, such as crime and violence, television and the other mass media are virtually the only vivid source of information for constructing our image of the world.

14   The propaganda value of the mass media in painting a picture of the world has not been overlooked by would-be leaders. Such social policy as a "get tough on crime" program, for example, can be easily sold by relating it to the prime-time picture of crime as acts committed by the psychopathic and the greedy, rather than dealing with situational determinants such as poverty and unemployment. In a similar vein, it is easier to sell a "war on drugs" after the drug-related death of a prominent basketball star or to promote an end to nuclear power after a fatal tragedy at a nuclear reactor.

15   It is even more important for a would-be leader to propagate his or her own picture of the world. The political scientist Roderick Hart notes that since the early 1960s, U.S. presidents have averaged over 25 speeches per month—a large amount of public speaking.[10] Indeed, during 1976, Gerald Ford spoke in public once every six hours, on average. By speaking frequently on certain issues (and gaining access to the nightly news), a president can create a political agenda—a picture of the world that is favorable to his or her social policies. Indeed, one of President Bush's key advisors is Robert Teeter, a pollster who informs the president on what Americans think and what issues should be the topic of his speeches. This can be of great importance in maintaining power. According to Jeffery Pfeffer, an expert on business organizations, one of the most important sources of power for a chief executive officer is the ability to set the organization's agenda by determining what issues will be discussed and when, what criteria will be used to resolve disputes, who will sit on what committees, and, perhaps most

importantly, which information will be widely disseminated and which will be selectively ignored.[11]

16   Why are the pictures of the world painted by the mass media so persuasive? For one thing, we rarely question the picture that is shown. We seldom ask ourselves, for example, "Why are they showing me this story on the evening news rather than some other one? Do the police really operate in this manner? Is the world really this violent and crime-ridden?" The pictures that television beams into our homes are almost always simply taken for granted as representing reality.

17   Once accepted, the pictures we form in our heads serve as fictions to guide our thoughts and actions. The images serve as primitive social theories—providing us with the "facts" of the matter, determining which issues are most pressing, and decreeing the terms in which we think about our social world. As the political scientist Bernard Cohen observed, the mass media

> may not be successful much of the time in telling people *what to think*, but it is stunningly successful in telling its readers *what to think about* . . . The world will look different to different people, depending . . . on the map that is drawn for them by writers, editors, and publishers of the papers they read.[12]

END NOTES

1. Lippmann, W. (1922). *Public opinion*. New York: Harcourt, Brace.

2. Gerbner, G., Gross, L., Morgan, M., & Signorielli, N. (1986). "Living with television: The dynamics of the cultivation process." In J. Bryant & D. Zillman (Eds.), *Perspectives on media effects* (pp. 17–40). Hillsdale, NJ: Erlbaum.

3. Quoted in *Newsweek*, December 6, 1982, p. 40.

4. Haney, C., & Manzolati, J. (1981). "Television criminology: Network illusions on criminal justice realities." In E. Aronson (Ed.), *Readings about the social animal* (3rd ed.; pp. 125–136). New York: W. H. Freeman.

5. See Heath, L. (1984). "Impact of newspaper crime reports on fear of crime: Multimethodological investigation." *Journal of Personality and Social Psychology*, 47, 263–276; Linz, D. G., Donnerstein, E., & Penrod, S. (1988). "Effects of long-term exposure to violent and sexually degrading depictions of women." *Journal of Personality and Social Psychology*, 55, 758–768; Henningan, K., Heath, L., Wharton, J. D., Del Rosario, M., Cook, T. D., & Calder, B. (1982). "Impact of the introduction of television on crime in the United States: Empirical findings and theoretical implications." *Journal of Personality and Social Psychology*, 42, 461–477.

6. Iyengar, S., & Kinder, D. R. (1987). *News that matters*. Chicago: University of Chicago Press.

7. Rogers, E. M., & Dearing, J. W. (1988). "Agenda-setting research: Where has it been, Where is it going?" In J. A. Anderson (Ed.), *Communication Yearbook* 11 (pp. 555–594). Beverly Hills, CA: Sage.

8. McCombs, M. E., & Shaw, D. L. (1972). "The agenda setting function of mass media." *Public Opinion Quarterly*, 36, 176–187.

9. Dilenschneider, R. L. (1990). *Power and influence*. New York: Prentice-Hall.

10. Hart, R. P. (1987). *The sound of leadership*. Chicago: University of Chicago Press.

11. Pfeffer, J. (1981). *Power in organizations*. Cambridge, MA: Ballinger.

12. Cited in Rogers and Dearing (1988). See note 7.

Questions for Discussion

1. What is the point of Walter Lippmann's story of the young girl who superstitiously mourned her father? Is this an effective way to begin the essay?

2. What are the "pictures in our heads" that Lippmann and the authors of the essay comment on? How do these "pictures" both resemble and differ from dreams and fantasies?

3. What conclusions can be drawn from George Gerbner's television program analysis? What comparisons did Gerbner and his associates make between different kinds of viewers and their beliefs?

4. How are criminals usually portrayed on television? What impact does this have on our attitudes and beliefs? How have politicians used stereotypical portrayals of criminals and crime to "sell" their programs to the public?

5. What flaw can be found in Gerbner's research? How have the experiments of Iyengar and Kinder on evening news shows and their viewers helped to correct and support Gerbner's research?

6. Explain the distinction made by Bernard Cohen between the media's telling us what to think as opposed to telling us *what to think about.* What does Cohen consider the media's most stunning success? What examples of this success are provided?

Ideas for Writing

1. Do some research of your own into recent intensive media coverage of a political event of controversial issue. Discuss the media's impact on the public's perceptions of the "reality" of the situation. You might take a look at some public opinion polls that were taken during the period you are discussing and examine typical stories aired on television and in the newspapers.

2. Write about your feelings or attitudes toward a political issue covered extensively by the mass media; explain to what degree your political views and social outlook were influenced by the media in contrast to direct experience and conversation.

 ## George Orwell

Winston Was Dreaming, from 1984

Named Eric Blair, George Orwell (1903–1950) was born in India. His family struggled to send him to be educated at Eton College in England. Orwell had a life rich in experiences. He served with the Imperial Police in Burma, fought in the Spanish Civil War, and served as a member of the Home Guard and as a writer for the BBC during World War II. As a journalist, essayist, and novelist, Orwell was "the conscience of his generation" because he confronted the political nightmares of his age in his books; some of the most widely read include Burmese Days *(1934),* Homage to Catalonia *(1938), and* A Collection of Essays *(1946). Orwell is best known for his two brilliantly satirical novels,* Animal Farm *(1945) and 1984 (1949), from which the following selection is excerpted. In both of his novels Orwell condemns totalitarianism and big government's lust for power, believing that "like certain wild animals" the imagination "will not breed in captivity."*

JOURNAL

Write about how you felt during a time when your mind and your life were being controlled by a person or institution that had political power over you.

1   Winston was dreaming of his mother.
2   He must, he thought, have been ten or eleven years old when his mother had disappeared. She was a tall, statuesque, rather silent woman with slow movements and magnificent fair hair. His father he remembered more vaguely as dark and thin, dressed always in neat dark clothes (Winston remembered especially the very thin soles of his father's shoes) and wearing spectacles. The two of them must evidently have been swallowed up in one of the first great purges of the Fifties.
3   At this moment his mother was sitting in some place deep down beneath him, with his young sister in her arms. He did not remember his sister at all, except as a tiny, feeble baby, always silent, with large, watchful eyes. Both of them were looking up at him. They were down in some subterranean place—the bottom of a well, for instance, or a very deep grave—but it was a place which, already far below him, was itself moving downwards. They were in the saloon of a sinking ship, looking up at him through the darkening water. There was still air in the saloon, they could still see him and he them, but all the while they were sinking down, down into the green waters which in another moment must hide them from sight forever. He was out in the light and air while they were being sucked down to death, and they were down there *because* he was up here. He knew it and they knew it, and he could see the knowledge in their faces. There was no reproach either in their faces or in their hearts, only the knowledge that they must die in order that he might remain alive, and that this was part of the unavoidable order of things.
4   He could not remember what had happened, but he knew in his dream that in some way the lives of his mother and his sister had been sacrificed to his own. It was one of those dreams which, while retaining the characteristic dream scenery, are a continuation of one's intellectual life, and in which one becomes aware of facts and ideas which still seem new and valuable after one is awake. The thing that now suddenly struck Winston was that his mother's death, nearly thirty years ago, had been tragic and sorrowful in a way that was no longer possible. Tragedy, he perceived, belonged to the ancient time, to a time when there were still privacy, love, and friendship, and when the members of a family stood by one another without needing to know the reason. His mother's memory tore at his heart because she had died loving him, when he was too young and selfish to love her in

return, and because somehow, he did not remember how, she had sacrificed herself to a conception of loyalty that was private and unalterable. Such things, he saw, could not happen today. Today there were fear, hatred, and pain, but no dignity of emotion, no deep or complex sorrows. All this he seemed to see in the large eyes of his mother and his sister, looking up at him through the green water, hundreds of fathoms down and still sinking.

5   Suddenly he was standing on short springy turf, on a summer evening when the slanting rays of the sun gilded the ground. The landscape that he was looking at recurred so often in his dreams that he was never fully certain whether or not he had seen it in the real world. In his waking thoughts he called it the Golden Country. It was an old, rabbit-bitten pasture, with a foot track wandering across it and a molehill here and there. In the ragged hedge on the opposite side of the field the boughs of the elm trees were swaying very faintly in the breeze, their leaves just stirring in dense masses like women's hair. Somewhere near at hand, though out of sight, there was a clear, slow-moving stream where dace were swimming in the pools under the willow trees.

6   The girl with dark hair was coming toward him across the field. With what seemed a single movement she tore off her clothes and flung them disdainfully aside. Her body was white and smooth, but it aroused no desire in him; indeed, he barely looked at it. What overwhelmed him in the instant was admiration for the gesture with which she had thrown her clothes aside. With its grace and carelessness it seemed to annihilate a whole culture, a whole system of thought, as though Big Brother and the Party and the Thought Police could all be swept into nothingness by a single splendid movement of the arm. That too was a gesture belonging to the ancient time. Winston woke up with the word "Shakespeare" on his lips.

7   The telescreen was giving forth an ear-splitting whistle which continued on the same note for thirty seconds. It was nought seven fifteen, getting-up time for office workers. Winston wrenched his body out of bed—naked, for a member of the Outer Party received only three thousand clothing coupons annually, and a suit of pajamas was six hundred—and seized a dingy singlet and a pair of shorts that were lying across a chair. The Physical Jerks would begin in three minutes. The next moment he was doubled up by a violent coughing fit which nearly always attacked him soon after waking up. It emptied his lungs so completely that he could only begin breathing again by lying on his back and taking a series of deep gasps. His veins had swelled with the effort of the cough, and the varicose ulcer had started itching.

8   "Thirty to forty group!" yapped a piercing female voice. "Thirty to forty group! Take your places, please. Thirties to forties!"

9   Winston sprang to attention in front of the telescreen, upon which the image of a youngish woman, scrawny but muscular, dressed in tunic and gum shoes, had already appeared.

10   "Arms bending and stretching!" she rapped out. "Take your time by me. *One*, two, three, four! *One*, two, three four! Come on, comrades, put a bit of life into it! *One*, two, three, four! *One*, two, three, four! . . ."

11   The pain of the coughing fit had not quite driven out of Winston's mind the impression made by his dream, and the rhythmic movements of the exercise restored it somewhat. As he mechanically shot his arms back and forth, wearing on his face the look of grim enjoyment which was considered proper during the Physical Jerks, he was struggling to think his way backward into the dim period of his early childhood. It was extraordinarily difficult. Beyond the late Fifties everything faded. When there were no external records that you could refer to, even the outline of your own life lost its sharpness. You remembered huge events which had quite probably not happened, you remembered the detail of incidents without being able to recapture their atmosphere, and there were long blank periods to which you could assign nothing. Everything had been different then. Even the names of countries, and their shapes on the map, had been different. Airstrip One, for instance, had not been so called in those days: it had been called England or Britain, though London, he felt fairly certain, had always been called London.

12   Winston could not definitely remember a time when his country had not been at war, but it was evident that there had been a fairly long interval of peace during his childhood, because one of his early memories was of an air raid which appeared to take everyone by surprise. Perhaps it was the time when the atomic bomb had fallen on Colchester. He did not remember the raid itself, but he did remember his father's hand clutching his own as they hurried down, down, down into some place deep in the earth, round and round a spiral staircase which rang under his feet and which finally so wearied his legs that he began whimpering and they had to stop and rest. His mother, in her slow dreamy way, was following a long way behind them. She was carrying his baby sister—or perhaps it was only a bundle of blankets that she was carrying: he was not certain whether his sister had been born then. Finally they had emerged into a noisy, crowded place which he had realized to be a Tube station.

13   There were people sitting all over the stone-flagged floor, and other people, packed tightly together, were sitting on metal bunks, one above the other. Winston and his mother and father found themselves a place on the floor, and near them an old man and an old woman were sitting side by side on a bunk. The old man had on a decent dark suit and a black cloth cap pushed back from very white hair; his face was scarlet and his eyes were blue and full of tears. He reeked of gin. It seemed to breathe out of his skin in place of sweat, and one could have fancied that the tears welling from his eyes were pure gin. But though slightly drunk he was also suffering under some grief that was genuine and unbearable. In his childish way Winston grasped that some terrible thing, something that was beyond forgiveness and could never be remedied, had just happened. It also seemed to him that he knew what it was. Someone whom the old man loved, a little granddaughter perhaps, had been killed. Every few minutes the old man kept repeating:

14   "We didn't ought to 'ave trusted 'em. I said so, Ma, didn't I? That's what come of trusting 'em. I said so all along. We didn't ought to 'ave trusted the buggers."

15   But which buggers they didn't ought to have trusted Winston could not now remember.

16   Since about that time, war had been literally continuous, though strictly speaking it had not always been the same war. For several months during his childhood

there had been confused street fighting in London itself, some of which he remembered vividly. But to trace out the history of the whole period, to say who was fighting whom at any given moment, would have been utterly impossible, since no written record, and no spoken word, ever made mention of any other alignment than the existing one. At this moment, for example, in 1984 (if it was 1984), Oceania was at war with Eurasia and in alliance with Eastasia. In no public or private utterance was it ever admitted that the three powers had at any time been grouped along different lines. Actually, as Winston well knew, it was only four years since Oceania had been at war with Eastasia and in alliance with Eurasia. But that was merely a piece of furtive knowledge which he happened to possess because his memory was not satisfactorily under control. Officially the change of partners had never happened. Oceania was at war with Eurasia: therefore Oceania had always been at war with Eurasia. The enemy of the moment always represented absolute evil, and it followed that any past or future agreement with him was impossible.

17   The frightening thing, he reflected for the ten thousandth time as he forced his shoulders painfully backward (with hands on hips, they were gyrating their bodies from the waist, an exercise that was supposed to be good for the back muscles)— the frightening thing was that it might all be true. If the Party could thrust its hand into the past and say of this or that event, *it never happened*—that, surely, was more terrifying than mere torture and death.

18   The Party said that Oceania had never been in alliance with Eurasia. He, Winston Smith, knew that Oceania had been in alliance with Eurasia as short a time as four years ago. But where did that knowledge exist? Only in his own consciousness, which in any case must soon be annihilated. And if all others accepted the lie which the Party imposed—if all records told the same tale—then the lie passed into history and became truth. "Who controls the past," ran the Party slogan, "controls the future: who controls the present controls the past." And yet the past, though of its nature alterable, never had been altered. Whatever was true now was true from everlasting to everlasting. It was quite simple. All that was needed was an unending series of victories over your own memory. "Reality control," they called it; in Newspeak, "doublethink."

19   "Stand easy!" barked the instructress, a little more genially.

20   Winston sank his arms to his sides and slowly refilled his lungs with air. His mind slid away into the labyrinthine world of doublethink. To know and not to know, to be conscious of complete truthfulness while telling carefully constructed lies, to hold simultaneously two opinions which canceled out, knowing them to be contradictory and believing in both of them, to use logic against logic, to repudiate morality while laying claim to it, to believe that democracy was impossible and that the Party was the guardian of democracy, to forget whatever it was necessary to forget, then to draw it back into memory again at the moment when it was needed, and then promptly to forget it again, and above all, to apply the same process to the process itself—that was the ultimate subtlety: consciously to induce unconsciousness, and then, once again, to become unconscious of the act of hypnosis you had just performed. Even to understand the word "doublethink" involved the use of doublethink.

21   The instructress had called them to attention again. "And now let's see which of us can touch our toes!" she said enthusiastically. "Right over from the hips, please, comrades. *One–two! One–two!* . . . "

22   Winston loathed this exercise, which sent shooting pains all the way from his heels to his buttocks and often ended by bringing on another coughing fit. The half-pleasant quality went out of his meditations. The past, he reflected, had not merely been altered, it had been actually destroyed. For how could you establish even the most obvious fact when there existed no record outside your own memory? He tried to remember in what year he had first heard mention of Big Brother. He thought it must have been at some time in the Sixties, but it was impossible to be certain. In the Party histories, of course, Big Brother figured as the leader and guardian of the Revolution since its very earliest days. His exploits had been gradually pushed backwards in time until already they extended into the fabulous world of the Forties and the Thirties, when the capitalists in their strange cylindrical hats still rode through the streets of London in great gleaming motor cars or horse carriages with glass sides. There was no knowing how much of this legend was true and how much invented. Winston could not even remember at what date the Party itself had come into existence. He did not believe he had ever heard the word Ingsoc before 1960, but it was possible that in its Oldspeak form—"English Socialism," that is to say—it had been current earlier. Everything melted into mist. Sometimes, indeed, you could put your finger on a definite lie. It was not true, for example, as was claimed in Party history books, that the Party had invented airplanes. He remembered airplanes since his earliest childhood. But you could prove nothing. There was never any evidence. Just once in his whole life he had held in his hands unmistakable documentary proof of the falsification of a historical fact. And on that occasion—

23   "Smith!" screamed the shrewish voice from the telescreen. "6079 Smith W! Yes, *you*! Bend lower, please! You can do better than that. You're not trying. Lower, please! *That's* better, comrade. Now stand at ease, the whole squad, and watch me."

24   A sudden hot sweat had broken out all over Winston's body. His face remained completely inscrutable. Never show dismay! Never show resentment! A single flicker of the eyes could give you away. He stood watching while the instructress raised her arms above her head and—one could not say gracefully, but with remarkable neatness and efficiency—bent over and tucked the first joint of her fingers under her toes.

25   "*There*, comrades! *That's* how I want to see you doing it. Watch me again. I'm thirty-nine and I've had four children. Now look." She bent over again. "You see *my* knees aren't bent. You can all do it if you want to," she added as she straightened herself up. "Anyone under forty-five is perfectly capable of touching his toes. We don't all have the privilege of fighting in the front line, but at least we can all keep fit. Remember our boys on the Malabar front! And the sailors in the Floating Fortresses! Just think what *they* have to put up with. Now try again. That's better, comrade, that's *much* better," she added encouragingly as Winston, with a violent lunge, succeeded in touching his toes with knees unbent, for the first time in several years.

Questions for Discussion

1. What is the significance of Winston's dream of his last memory of his family? What does the "darkening water" through which they look up to him represent?
2. Why is death no longer "tragic and sorrowful" at the time the story takes place?
3. Why does Winston admire the "gesture" of the girl in his fantasy? What does the gesture suggest?
4. Why does Winston wake up with the word "Shakespeare" on his lips? Why would there be no place for writers like Shakespeare in a world such as the one introduced in the story?
5. What is the function of the telescreen? Compare and contrast its function and impact to that of television in our society.
6. Why is it so difficult for Winston to "think his way back" into the world of his childhood?

Ideas for Writing

1. *1984* is fiction. To what extent does it capture the reality of political situations today? Refer to particular social and political events in developing your response.
2. Explain "doublethink" first through the way Winston thinks and uses language. Then discuss how the character of Big Brother has been altered and made legendary. Provide examples of political doublethink and of the rewriting of history which accommodated shifting ideologies in our own world.

 # Terry McMillan

The Wizard of Oz

Terry McMillan (b. 1951) was born in Port Huron, Michigan, into a large and impoverished family. She teaches at the University of Arizona at Tucson and is a novelist, the author of such portrayals of contemporary African American life as Mama *(1987),* Disappearing Acts *(1989),* Waiting to Exhale *(1992), and* How Stella Got Her Groove Back *(1996). She has also edited a popular anthology of African American fiction,* Breaking Ice. *The following essay on the classic Judy Garland film,* Wizard of Oz, *appeared in* The Movie that Changed My Life *(1992), a collection of autobiographical essays by American writers about the influence of particular movies on their childhoods and perceptions of reality.*

Write about an imaginative film that you viewed repeatedly as a child. Why was the film important to you when you were a child? How has your sense of the message and significance of this film changed as you have matured?

1   I grew up in a small industrial town in the thumb of Michigan: Port Huron. We had barely gotten used to the idea of color TV. I can guess how old I was when I first saw *The Wizard of Oz* on TV because I remember the house we lived in when I was still in elementary school. It was a huge, drafty house that had a fireplace we never once lit. We lived on two acres of land, and at the edge of the backyard was the woods, which I always thought of as a forest. We had weeping willow trees, plum and pear trees, and blackberry bushes. We could not see into our neighbors' homes. Railroad tracks were part of our front yard, and the house shook when a train passed—twice, sometimes three times a day. You couldn't hear the TV at all when it zoomed by, and I was often afraid that if it ever flew off the tracks, it would land on the sun porch, where we all watched TV. I often left the room during this time, but my younger sisters and brother thought I was just scared. I think I was in the third grade around this time.

2   It was a raggedy house which really should've been condemned, but we fixed it up and kept it clean. We had our German shepherd, Prince, who slept under the rickety steps to the side porch that were on the verge of collapsing but never did. I remember performing a ritual whenever *Oz* was coming on. I either baked cookies or cinnamon rolls or popped popcorn while all five of us waited for Dorothy to spin from black and white on that dreary farm in Kansas to the luminous land of color of *Oz*.

3   My house was chaotic, especially with four sisters and brothers and a mother who worked at a factory, and if I'm remembering correctly, my father was there for the first few years of the *Oz* (until he got tuberculosis and had to live in a sanitarium for a year). I do recall the noise and the fighting of my parents (not to mention my other relatives and neighbors). Violence was plentiful, and I wanted to go wherever Dorothy was going where she would not find trouble. To put it bluntly, I wanted to escape because I needed an escape.

4   I didn't know any happy people. Everyone I knew was either angry or not satisfied. The only time they seemed to laugh was when they were drunk, and even that was short-lived. Most of the grown-ups I was in contact with lived their lives as if it had all been a mistake, an accident, and they were paying dearly for it. It seemed as if they were always at someone else's mercy—women at the mercy of men (this prevailed in my hometown) and children at the mercy of frustrated parents. All I knew was that most of the grown-ups felt trapped, as if they were stuck in this town and no road would lead out. So many of them felt a sense of accomplishment just getting up in the morning and making it through another day. I overheard many a grown-up conversation, and they were never life-affirming: "Chile, if the Lord'll just give me the strength to make it through another week . . ."; "I just don't know how I'ma handle this, I can't take no more. . . . " I rarely knew

what they were talking about, but even a fool could hear that it was some kind of drudgery. When I was a child, it became apparent to me that these grown-ups had no power over their lives, or, if they did, they were always at a loss as to how to exercise it. I did not want to grow up and have to depend on someone else for my happiness or be miserable or have to settle for whatever I was dished out—if I could help it. That much I knew already.

5   I remember being confused a lot. I could never understand why no one had any energy to do anything that would make them feel good, besides drinking. Being happy was a transient and very temporary thing which was almost always offset by some kind of bullshit. I would, of course, learn much later in my own adult life that these things are called obstacles, barriers—or again, bullshit. When I started writing, I began referring to them as "knots." But life wasn't one long knot. It seemed to me it just required stamina and common sense and the wherewithal to know when a knot was before you and you had to dig deeper than you had in order to figure out how to untie it. It could be hard, but it was simple.

6   The initial thing I remember striking me about *Oz* was how nasty Dorothy's Auntie Em talked to her and everybody on the farm. I was used to that authoritative tone of voice because my mother talked to us the same way. She never asked you to do anything; she gave you a command and never said "please," and, once you finished it, rarely said "thank you." The tone of her voice was always hostile, and Auntie Em sounded just like my mother—bossy and domineering. They both ran the show, it seemed, and I think that because my mother was raising five children almost single-handedly, I must have had some inkling that being a woman didn't mean you had to be helpless. Auntie Em's husband was a wimp, and for once the tables were turned: he took orders from her! My mother and Auntie Em were proof to me that if you wanted to get things done you had to delegate authority and keep everyone apprised of the rules of the game as well as the consequences. In my house it was punishment—you were severely grounded. What little freedom we had was snatched away. As a child, I often felt helpless, powerless, because I had no control over my situation and couldn't tell my mother when I thought (or knew) she was wrong or being totally unfair, or when her behavior was inappropriate. I hated this feeling to no end, but what was worse was not being able to do anything about it except keep my mouth shut.

7   So I completely identified when no one had time to listen to Dorothy. That dog's safety was important to her, but no one seemed to think that what Dorothy was saying could possibly be as urgent as the situation at hand. The bottom line was, it was urgent to her. When I was younger, I rarely had the opportunity to finish a sentence before my mother would cut me off or complete it for me, or, worse, give me something to do. She used to piss me off, and nowadays I catch myself—stop myself—from doing the same thing to my seven-year-old. Back then, it was as if what I had to say wasn't important or didn't warrant her undivided attention. So when Dorothy's Auntie Em dismisses her and tells her to find somewhere where she'll stay out of trouble, and little Dorothy starts thinking about if there in fact is such a place—one that is trouble free—I was right there with her, because I wanted to know, too.

8   I also didn't know or care that Judy Garland was supposed to have been a child star, but when she sang "Somewhere Over the Rainbow," I *was* impressed. Impressed more by the song than by who was singing it. I mean, she wasn't exactly Aretha Franklin or the Marvelettes or the Supremes, which was the only vocal music I was used to. As kids, we often laughed at white people singing on TV because their songs were always so corny and they just didn't sound anything like the soulful music we had in our house. Sometimes we would mimic people like Doris Day and Fred Astaire and laugh like crazy because they were always so damn happy while they sang and danced. We would also watch square-dancing when we wanted a real laugh and try to look under the women's dresses. What I hated more than anything was when in the middle of a movie the white people always had to start singing and dancing to get their point across. Later, I would hate it when black people would do the same thing—even though it was obvious to us that at least they had more rhythm and, most of the time, more range vocally.

9   We did skip through the house singing "We're off to see the Wizard," but other than that, most of the songs in this movie are a blank, probably because I blanked them out. Where I lived, when you had something to say to someone, you didn't sing it, you told them, so the cumulative effect of the songs wore thin.

10   I was afraid for Dorothy when she decided to run away, but at the same time I was glad. I couldn't much blame her—I mean, what kind of life did she have, from what I'd seen so far? She lived on an ugly farm out in the middle of nowhere with all these old people who did nothing but chores, chores, and more chores. Who did she have to play with besides that dog? And even though I lived in a house full of people, I knew how lonely Dorothy felt, or at least how isolated she must have felt. First of all, I was the oldest, and my sisters and brother were ignorant and silly creatures who often bored me because they couldn't hold a decent conversation. I couldn't ask them questions, like: Why are we living in this dump? When is Mama going to get some more money? Why can't we go on vacations like other people? Like white people? Why does our car always break down? Why are we poor? Why doesn't Mama ever laugh? Why do we have to live in Port Huron? Isn't there someplace better than this we can go live? I remember thinking this kind of stuff in kindergarten, to be honest, because times were hard, but I'd saved twenty-five cents in my piggy bank for hot-dog-and-chocolate-milk day at school, and on the morning I went to get it, my piggy bank was empty. My mother gave me some lame excuse as to why she had to spend it, but all I was thinking was that I would have to sit there (again) and watch the other children slurp their chocolate milk, and I could see the ketchup and mustard oozing out of the hot-dog bun that I wouldn't get to taste. I walked to school, and with the exception of walking to my father's funeral when I was sixteen, this was the longest walk of my entire life. My plaid dress was starched and my socks were white, my hair was braided and not a strand out of place; but I wanted to know why I had to feel this kind of humiliation when in fact I had saved the money for this very purpose. Why? By the time I got to school, I'd wiped my nose and dried my eyes and vowed not to let anyone know that I was even moved by this. It was no one's business why I couldn't eat my hot dog and chocolate milk, but the irony of it was that my teacher, Mrs.

Johnson, must have sensed what had happened, and she bought my hot dog and chocolate milk for me that day. I can still remember feeling how unfair things can be, but how they somehow always turn out good. I guess seeing so much negativity had already started to turn me into an optimist.

11   I was a very busy child, because I was the oldest and had to see to it that my sisters and brother had their baths and did their homework; I combed my sisters' hair, and by fourth grade I had cooked my first Thanksgiving dinner. It was my responsibility to keep the house spotless so that when my mother came home from work it would pass her inspection, so I spent many an afternoon and Saturday morning mopping and waxing floors, cleaning ovens and refrigerators, grocery shopping, and by the time I was thirteen, I was paying bills for my mother and felt like an adult. I was also tired of it, sick of all the responsibility. So yes, I rooted for Dorothy when she and Toto were vamoosing, only I wanted to know: Where in the hell was she going? Where would I go if I were to run away? I had no idea because there was nowhere to go. What I did know was that one day I would go somewhere—which is why I think I watched so much TV. I was always on the lookout for Paradise, and I think I found it a few years later on "Adventures in Paradise," with Gardner McKay, and on "77 Sunset Strip." Palm trees and blue water and islands made quite an impression on a little girl from a flat, dull little depressing town in Michigan.

12   Professor Marvel really pissed me off, and I didn't believe for a minute that that crystal ball was real, even before he started asking Dorothy all those questions, but I knew this man was going to be important, I just couldn't figure out how. Dorothy was so gullible, I thought, and I knew this word because my mother used to always drill it in us that you should "never believe everything somebody tells you." So after Professor Marvel convinced Dorothy that her Auntie Em might be in trouble, and Dorothy scoops up Toto and runs back home, I was totally disappointed, because now I wasn't going to have an adventure. I was thinking I might actually learn how to escape drudgery by watching Dorothy do it successfully, but before she even gave herself the chance to discover for herself that she could make it, she was on her way back home. "Dummy!" we all yelled on the sun porch. "Dodo brain!"

13   The storm. The tornado. Of course, now the entire set of this film looks so phony it's ridiculous, but back then I knew the wind was a tornado because in Michigan we had the same kind of trapdoor underground shelter that Auntie Em had on the farm. I knew Dorothy was going to be locked out once Auntie Em and the workers locked the door, and I also knew she wasn't going to be heard when she knocked on it. This was drama at its best, even though I didn't know what drama was at the time.

14   In the house she goes, and I was frightened for her. I knew that house was going to blow away, so when little Dorothy gets banged in the head by a window that flew out of its casement, I remember all of us screaming. We watched everybody fly by the window, including the wicked neighbor who turns out to be the Wicked Witch of the West, and I'm sure I probably substituted my mother for Auntie Em and fantasized that all of my siblings would fly away, too. They all got on my

nerves because I could never find a quiet place in my house—no such thing as peace—and I was always being disturbed.

15   It wasn't so much that I had so much I wanted to do by myself, but I already knew that silence was a rare commodity, and when I managed to snatch a few minutes of it, I could daydream, pretend to be someone else somewhere else—and this was fun. But I couldn't do it if someone was bugging me. On days when my mother was at work, I would often send the kids outside to play and lock them out, just so I could have the house to myself for at least fifteen minutes. I loved pretending that none of them existed for a while, although after I finished with my fantasy world, it was reassuring to see them all there. I think I was grounded.

16   When Dorothy's house began to spin and spin and spin, I was curious as to where it was going to land. And to be honest, I didn't know little Dorothy was actually dreaming until she woke up and opened the door and everything was in color! It looked like Paradise to me. The foliage was almost an iridescent green, the water bluer than I'd ever seen in any of the lakes in Michigan. Of course, once I realized she was in fact dreaming, it occurred to me that this very well might be the only way to escape. To dream up another world. Create your own.

17   I had no clue that Dorothy was going to find trouble, though, even in her dreams. Hell, if I had dreamed up something like another world, it would've been a perfect one. I wouldn't have put myself in such a precarious situation. I'd have been able to go straight to the Wizard, no strings attached. First of all, that she walked was stupid to me; I would've asked one of those Munchkins for a ride. And I never bought into the idea of those slippers, but once I bought the whole idea, I accepted the fact that the girl was definitely lost and just wanted to get home. Personally, all I kept thinking was, if she could get rid of that Wicked Witch of the West, the Land of Oz wasn't such a bad place to be stuck in. It beat the farm in Kansas.

18   At the time, I truly wished I could spin away from my family and home and land someplace as beautiful and surreal as Oz—if only for a little while. All I wanted was to get a chance to see another side of the world, to be able to make comparisons, and then decide if it was worth coming back home.

19   What was really strange to me, after the Good Witch of the North tells Dorothy to just stay on the Yellow Brick Road to get to the Emerald City and find the Wizard so she can get home, was when Dorothy meets the Scarecrow, the Tin Man, and the Lion—all of whom were missing something I'd never even given any thought to. A brain? What did having one really mean? What would not having one mean? I had one, didn't I, because I did well in school. But because the Scarecrow couldn't make up his mind, thought of himself as a failure, it dawned on me that having a brain meant you had choices, you could make decisions and, as a result, make things happen. Yes, I thought, I had one, and I was going to use it. One day. And the Tin Man, who didn't have a heart. Not having one meant you were literally dead to me, and I never once thought of it as being the house of emotions (didn't know what emotions were), where feelings of jealousy, devotion, and sentiment lived. I'd never thought of what else a heart was good for except keeping you alive. But I did have feelings, because they were often hurt, and I was

envious of the white girls at my school who wore mohair sweaters and box-pleat skirts, who went skiing and tobogganing and yachting and spent summers in Quebec. Why didn't white girls have to straighten their hair? Why didn't their parents beat each other up? Why were they always so goddamn happy?

20   And courage. Oh, that was a big one. What did having it and not having it mean? I found out that it meant having guts and being afraid but doing whatever it was you set out to do anyway. Without courage, you couldn't do much of anything. I liked courage and assumed I would acquire it somehow. As a matter of fact, one day my mother *told* me to get her a cup of coffee, and even though my heart was pounding and I was afraid, I said to her pointblank, "Could you please say please?" She looked up at me out of the corner of her eye and said, "What?" So I repeated myself, feeling more powerful because she hadn't slapped me across the room already, and then something came over her and she looked at me and said, "Please." I smiled all the way to the kitchen, and from that point forward, I managed to get away with this kind of behavior until I left home when I was seventeen. My sisters and brother—to this day—don't know how I stand up to my mother, but I know. I decided not to be afraid or intimidated by her, and I wanted her to treat me like a friend, like a human being, instead of her slave.

21   I do believe that Oz also taught me much about friendship. I mean, the Tin Man, the Lion, and the Scarecrow hung in there for Dorothy, stuck their "necks" out and made sure she was protected, even risked their own "lives" for her. They told each other the truth. They trusted each other. All four of them had each other's best interests in mind. I believe it may have been a while before I actually felt this kind of sincerity in a friend, but really good friends aren't easy to come by, and when you find one, you hold on to them.

22   Okay. So Dorothy goes through hell before she gets back to Kansas. But the bottom line was, she made it. And what I remember feeling when she clicked those heels was that you have to have faith and be a believer, for real, or nothing will ever materialize. Simple as that. And not only in life but even in your dreams there's always going to be adversity, obstacles, knots, or some kind of bullshit you're going to have to deal with in order to get on with your life. Dorothy had a good heart and it was in the right place, which is why I supposed she won out over the evil witch. I've learned that one, too. That good *always* overcomes evil; maybe not immediately, but in the long run, it does. So I think I vowed when I was little to try to be a good person. An honest person. To care about others and not just myself. Not to be a selfish person, because my heart would be of no service if I used it only for myself. And I had to have the courage to see other people and myself as not being perfect (yes, I had a heart and a brain, but some other things would turn up missing, later), and I would have to learn to untie every knot that I encountered—some self-imposed, some not—in my life, and to believe that if I did the right things, I would never stray too far from my Yellow Brick Road.

23   I'm almost certain that I saw Oz annually for at least five or six years, but I don't remember how old I was when I stopped watching it. I do know that by the time my parents were divorced (I was thirteen), I couldn't sit through it again. I was a mature teen-ager and had finally reached the point where Dorothy got on

my nerves. Singing, dancing, and skipping damn near everywhere was so corny and utterly sentimental that even the Yellow Brick Road became sickening. I already knew what she was in for, and sometimes I rewrote the story in my head. I kept asking myself, what if she had just run away and kept going, maybe she would've ended up in Los Angeles with a promising singing career. What if it had turned out that she hadn't been dreaming, and the Wizard had given her an offer she couldn't refuse—say, for instance, he had asked her to stay on in the Emerald City, that she could visit the farm whenever she wanted to, but, get a clue, Dorothy, the Emerald City is what's happening; she could make new city friends and get a hobby and a boyfriend and free rent and never have to do chores . . .

24   I had to watch *The Wizard of Oz* again in order to write this, and my six-and-a-half-year-old son, Solomon, joined me. At first he kept asking me if something was wrong with the TV because it wasn't in color, but as he watched, he became mesmerized by the story. He usually squirms or slides to the floor and under a table or just leaves the room if something on TV bores him, which it usually does, except if he's watching Nickelodeon, a high-quality cable kiddie channel. His favorite shows, which he watches with real consistency, and, I think, actually goes through withdrawal if he can't see them for whatever reason, are "Inspector Gadget," "Looney Tunes," and "Mr. Ed." "Make the Grade," which is sort of a junior-high version of "Jeopardy," gives him some kind of thrill, even though he rarely knows any of the answers. And "Garfield" is a must on Saturday morning. There is hardly anything on TV that he watches that has any real, or at least plausible, drama to it, but you can't miss what you've never had.

25   The Wicked Witch intimidated the boy no end, and he was afraid of her. The Wizard was also a problem. So I explained—no, I just told him pointblank— "Don't worry, she'll get it in the end, Solomon, because she's bad. And the Wizard's a fake, and he's trying to sound like a tough guy, but he's a wus." That offered him some consolation, and even when the Witch melted he kind of looked at me with those *Home Alone* eyes and asked, "But where did she go, Mommy?" "She's history," I said. "Melted. Gone. Into the ground. Remember, this is pretend. It's not real. Real people don't melt. This is only TV," I said. And then he got that look in his eyes as if he'd remembered something.

26   Of course he had a nightmare that night and of course there was a witch in it, because I had actually left the sofa a few times during this last viewing to smoke a few cigarettes (the memory bank is a powerful place—I still remembered many details), put the dishes in the dishwasher, make a few phone calls, water the plants. Solomon sang, "We're off to see the Wizard" for the next few days because he said that was his favorite part, next to the Munchkins (who also showed up in his nightmare).

27   So, to tell the truth, I really didn't watch the whole movie again. I just couldn't. Probably because about thirty or so years ago little Dorothy had made a lasting impression on me, and this viewing felt like overkill. You only have to tell me, show me, once in order for me to get it. But even still, the movie itself taught me a few things that I still find challenging. That it's okay to be an idealist, that

you have to imagine something better and go for it. That you have to believe in *something*, and it's best to start with yourself and take it from there. At least give it a try. As corny as it may sound, sometimes I am afraid of what's around the corner, or what's not around the corner. But I look anyway. I believe that writing is one of my "corners"—an intersection, really; and when I'm confused or reluctant to look back, deeper, or ahead, I create my own Emerald Cities and force myself to take longer looks, because it is one sure way that I'm able to see.

28   Of course, I've fallen, tumbled, and been thrown over all kinds of bumps on my road, but it still looks yellow, although every once in a while there's still a loose brick. For the most part, though, it seems paved. Perhaps because that's the way I want to see it.

Questions for Discussion

1. Why did McMillan feel the need to "escape" as a child by watching TV in Port Huron? Do you feel that the kind of escape she describes is unhealthy? What does McMillan see as the relationship between escape, dreaming, and creativity?
2. What are the "knots" that McMillan refers to? How does her attitude toward them differ from the attitude of her family and her hometown friends?
3. Why did McMillan identify with Dorothy's relationship with her Aunt Em? Why was McMillan happy for Dorothy when she ran away in the film?
4. What did Oz and Dorothy's companions teach McMillan about thoughts, feelings, courage, friendship, and faith? If you saw this film as a child, did you find similar messages in it?
5. At what point did McMillan realize that she could no longer relate to the world of Oz? How did she rewrite the story in her head to make it more relevant? When McMillan views the film again with her young son, how does her son react to the show? Why were his responses different from her responses as a youngster?
6. How does McMillan conclude her reflections on the lessons she learned from Oz? What in particular has she learned from the film that will help her as a writer?

Ideas for Writing

1. Develop your journal writing into an essay in which you reflect as McMillan does on the impact on your current dreams and values of a movie you saw repeatedly in childhood. If possible, rent the film on video and view it again to see whether it still holds the same message for you now as it did in childhood.
2. Write an essay that presents your point of view on the impact of television watching on children.

❧ Frank Baum

The Magic Art of the Great Humbug, *from* The Wonderful Wizard of Oz

Frank Baum (1856–1919) was born into a large, affluent family; his father was active in the oil industry, in banking, and in real estate. As a child Baum loved reading fairy tales and developed an interest in the theater, acting, writing, and producing plays. Still he followed his father into business and enjoyed working as a traveling salesman, which he perceived as a form of acting. Baum's wife, Maud Gage, the daughter of an early leader of the feminist movement, introduced Baum to theosophy, a new religion that emphasized feminist beliefs, science, spiritual transformation, "mind cure" or positive thinking ideas, and magic—themes that came to underlie much of Baum's later writing. As a successful salesman in Chicago, caught up in the excitement of the new urban scene, with its emphasis on theater, consumerism, and advertising, he founded a magazine of advice for department store publicists, The Show Window, *where he also published some of his own fairy tales. After the success of* The Wonderful Wizard of Oz *in 1900, Baum moved to Los Angeles, where he lived luxuriously, writing more than 70 children's novels. Critic William Leach has said that Baum's writings celebrate the "gaudy secular spectacle of America's new commercial and urban abundance."*

JOURNAL

Write about an advertisement on TV or print media that you found dreamlike and "fake," and at the same time appealing.

1   The four travelers walked up to the great gate of the Emerald City and rang the bell. After ringing several times it was opened by the same Guardian of the Gate they had met before.

2   "What! are you back again?" he asked in surprise.

3   "Do you not see us?" answered the Scarecrow.

4   "But I thought you had gone to visit the Wicked Witch of the West."

5   "We did visit her," said the Scarecrow.

6   "And she let you go again?" asked the man in wonder.

7   "She could not help it, for she is melted," explained the Scarecrow.

8   "Melted! Well, that is good news, indeed," said the man. "Who melted her?"

9   "It was Dorothy," said the Lion gravely.

10   "Good gracious!" exclaimed the man, and he bowed very low indeed before her.

11   Then he led them into his little room and locked the spectacles from the great box on all their eyes, just as he had done before. Afterward they passed on through the gate into the Emerald City, and when the people heard from the Guardian of the Gate that they had melted the Wicked Witch of the West they all gathered around the travelers and followed them in a great crowd to the Palace of Oz.

12   The soldier with the green whiskers was still on guard before the door, but he let them in at once and they were again met by the beautiful green girl, who showed each of them to his old room at once, so they might rest until the Great Oz was ready to receive them.

13   The soldier had the news carried straight to Oz that Dorothy and the other travelers had come back again, after destroying the Wicked Witch; but Oz made no reply. They thought the Great Wizard would send for them at once, but he did not. They had no word from him the next day, nor the next, nor the next. The waiting was tiresome and wearing, and at last they grew vexed that Oz should treat them in so poor a fashion, after sending them to undergo hardships and slavery. So the Scarecrow at last asked the green girl to take another message to Oz, saying if he did not let them in to see him at once they would call the Winged Monkeys to help them, and find out whether he kept his promises or not. When the Wizard was given this message he was so frightened that he sent word for them to come to the Throne Room at four minutes after nine o'clock the next morning. He had once met the Winged Monkeys in the Land of the West, and he did not wish to meet them again.

14   The four travelers passed a sleepless night, each thinking of the gift Oz had promised to bestow upon him. Dorothy fell asleep only once, and then she dreamed she was in Kansas, where Aunt Em was telling her how glad she was to have her little girl at home again.

15   Promptly at nine o'clock the next morning the green-whiskered soldier came to them, and four minutes later they all went into the Throne Room of the Great Oz.

16   Of course each one of them expected to see the Wizard in the shape he had taken before, and all were greatly surprised when they looked about and saw no one at all in the room. They kept close to the door and closer to one another, for the stillness of the empty room was more dreadful than any of the forms they had seen Oz take.

17   Presently they heard a Voice, seeming to come from somewhere near the top of the great dome, and it said solemnly,

18   "I am Oz, the Great and Terrible. Why do you seek me?"

19   They looked again in every part of the room, and then, seeing no one, Dorothy asked,

20   "Where are you?"

21   "I am everywhere," answered the Voice, "but to the eyes of common mortals I am invisible. I will now seat myself upon my throne, that you may converse with me." Indeed, the Voice seemed just then to come straight from the throne itself; so they walked toward it and stood in a row while Dorothy said:

22   "We have come to claim our promise, O Oz."

23   "What promise?" asked Oz.

24   "You promised to send me back to Kansas when the Wicked Witch was destroyed," said the girl.

25   "You promised to give me brains," said the Scarecrow.

26   "And you promised to give me a heart," said the Tin Woodman.

27   "And you promised to give me courage," said the Cowardly Lion.

28   "Is the Wicked Witch really destroyed?" asked the Voice, and Dorothy thought it trembled a little.

29   "Yes," she answered, "I melted her with a bucket of water."

30   "Dear me," said the Voice; "how sudden! Well, come to me tomorrow, for I must have time to think it over."

31   "You've had plenty of time already," said the Tin Woodman angrily.

32   "We shan't wait a day longer," said the Scarecrow.

33   "You must keep your promises to us!" exclaimed Dorothy.

34   The Lion thought it might be as well to frighten the Wizard, so he gave a large, loud roar, which was so fierce and dreadful that Toto jumped away from him in alarm and tipped over the screen that stood in a corner. As it fell with a crash they looked that way, and the next moment all of them were filled with wonder. For they saw, standing in just the spot the screen had hidden, a little, old man, with a bald head and a wrinkled face, who seemed to be as much surprised as they were. The Tin Woodman, raising his axe, rushed toward the little man and cried out,

35   "Who are you?"

36   "I am Oz, the Great and Terrible," said the little man, in a trembling voice, "but don't strike me—please don't!—and I'll do anything you want me to."

37   Our friends looked at him in surprise and dismay.

38   "I thought Oz was a great Head," said Dorothy.

39   "I thought Oz was a lovely Lady," said the Scarecrow.

40   "And I thought Oz was a terrible Beast," said the Tin Woodman.

41   "And I thought Oz was a Ball of Fire," exclaimed the Lion.

42   "No; you are all wrong," said the little man meekly. "I have been making believe."

43   "Making believe!" cried Dorothy. "Are you not a great Wizard?"

44   "Hush, my dear," he said; "don't speak so loud, or you will be overheard—and I should be ruined. I'm supposed to be a great Wizard."

45   "And aren't you?" she asked.

46   "Not a bit of it, my dear; I'm just a common man."

47   "You're more than that," said the Scarecrow, in a grieved tone; "you're a humbug."

48   "Exactly so!" declared the little man, rubbing his hands together as if it pleased him; "I am a humbug."

49   "But this is terrible," said the Tin Woodman; "how shall I ever get my heart?"

50   "Or I my courage?" asked the Lion.

51   "Or I my brains?" wailed the Scarecrow, wiping the tears from his eyes with his coat-sleeve.

52 "My dear friends," said Oz, "I pray you not to speak of these little things. Think of me, and the terrible trouble I'm in at being found out."

53 "Doesn't anyone else know you're a humbug?" asked Dorothy.

54 "No one knows it but you four—and myself," replied Oz. "I have fooled everyone so long that I thought I should never be found out. It was a great mistake my ever letting you into the Throne Room. Usually I will not see even my subjects, and so they believe I am something terrible."

55 "But I don't understand," said Dorothy, in bewilderment. "How was it that you appeared to me as a great Head?"

56 "That was one of my tricks," answered Oz. "Step this way, please, and I will tell you all about it."

57 He led the way to a small chamber in the rear of the Throne Room, and they all followed him. He pointed to one corner, in which lay the Great Head, made out of many thicknesses of paper, and with a carefully painted face.

58 "This I hung from the ceiling by a wire," said Oz; "I stood behind the screen and pulled a thread to make the eyes move and the mouth open."

59 "But how about the voice?" she inquired.

60 "Oh, I am a ventriloquist," said the little man, "and I can throw the sound of my voice wherever I wish; so that you thought it was coming out of the Head. Here are the other things I used to deceive you." He showed the Scarecrow the dress and the mask he had worn when he seemed to be the lovely Lady; and the Tin Woodman saw that his Terrible Beast was nothing but a lot of skins, sewn together, with slats to keep their sides out. As for the Ball of Fire, the false Wizard had hung that also from the ceiling. It was really a ball of cotton, but when oil was poured upon it the ball burned fiercely.

61 "Really," said the Scarecrow, "you ought to be ashamed of yourself for being such a humbug."

62 "I am—I certainly am," answered the little man sorrowfully; "but it was the only thing I could do. Sit down, please, there are plenty of chairs, and I will tell you my story."

63 So they sat down and listened while he told the following tale:

64 "I was born in Omaha—"

65 "Why, that isn't very far from Kansas!" cried Dorothy.

66 "No; but it's farther from here," he said, shaking his head at her sadly. "When I grew up I became a ventriloquist, and at that I was very well trained by a great master. I can imitate any kind of a bird or beast." Here he mewed so like a kitten that Toto pricked up his ears and looked everywhere to see where she was. "After a time," continued Oz, "I was tired of that, and became a balloonist."

67 "What is that?" asked Dorothy.

68 "A man who goes up in a balloon on circus day, so as to draw a crowd of people together and get them to pay to see the circus," he explained.

69 "Oh," she said; "I know."

70 "Well, one day I went up in a balloon and the ropes got twisted, so that I couldn't come down again. It went way up above the clouds, so far that a current

of air struck it and carried it many, many miles away. For a day and a night I traveled through the air, and on the morning of the second day I awoke and found the balloon floating over a strange and beautiful country.

71   "It came down gradually, and I was not hurt a bit. But I found myself in the midst of a strange people, who, seeing me come from the clouds, thought I was a great Wizard. Of course I let them think so, because they were afraid of me, and promised to do anything I wished them to.

72   "Just to amuse myself, and keep the good people busy, I ordered them to build this City, and my palace; and they did it all willingly and well. Then I thought, as the country was so green and beautiful, I would call it the Emerald City, and to make the name fit better I put green spectacles on all the people, so that everything they saw was green."

73   "But isn't everything here green?" asked Dorothy.

74   "No more than in any other city," replied Oz; "but when you wear green spectacles, why of course everything you see looks green to you. The Emerald City was built a great many years ago, for I was a young man when the balloon brought me here, and I am a very old man now. But my people have worn green glasses on their eyes so long that most of them think it really is an Emerald City, and it certainly is a beautiful place, abounding in jewels and precious metals, and every good thing that is needed to make one happy. I have been good to the people, and they like me; but ever since this Palace was built I have shut myself up and would not see any of them.

75   "One of my greatest fears was the Witches, for while I had no magical powers at all I soon found out that the Witches were really able to do wonderful things. There were four of them in this country, and they ruled the people who live in the North and South and East and West. Fortunately, the Witches of the North and South were good, and I knew they would do me no harm; but the Witches of the East and West were terribly wicked, and had they not thought I was more powerful than they themselves, they would surely have destroyed me. As it was, I lived in deadly fear of them for many years; so you can imagine how pleased I was when I heard your house had fallen on the Wicked Witch of the East. When you came to me I was willing to promise anything if you would only do away with the other Witch; but, now that you have melted her, I am ashamed to say that I cannot keep my promises."

76   "I think you are a very bad man," said Dorothy.

77   "Oh, no, my dear; I'm really a very good man; but I'm a very bad Wizard, I must admit."

78   "Can't you give me brains?" asked the Scarecrow.

79   "You don't need them. You are learning something every day. A baby has brains, but it doesn't know much. Experience is the only thing that brings knowledge, and the longer you are on earth the more experience you are sure to get."

80   "That may all be true," said the Scarecrow, "but I shall be very unhappy unless you give me brains."

81   The false Wizard looked at him carefully.

82   "Well," he said, with a sigh, "I'm not much of a magician, as I said; but if you will come to me tomorrow morning, I will stuff your head with brains. I cannot tell you how to use them, however; you must find that out for yourself."

83   "Oh, thank you—thank you!" cried the Scarecrow. "I'll find a way to use them, never fear!"

84   "But how about my courage?" asked the Lion anxiously.

85   "You have plenty of courage, I am sure," answered Oz. "All you need is confidence in yourself. There is no living thing that is not afraid when it faces danger. True courage is in facing danger when you are afraid, and that kind of courage you have in plenty."

86   "Perhaps I have, but I'm scared just the same," said the Lion. "I shall really be very unhappy unless you give me the sort of courage that makes one forget he is afraid."

87   "Very well; I will give you that sort of courage tomorrow," replied Oz.

88   "How about my heart?" asked the Tin Woodman.

89   "Why, as for that," answered Oz, "I think you are wrong to want a heart. It makes most people unhappy. If you only knew it, you are in luck not to have a heart."

90   "That must be a matter of opinion," said the Tin Woodman. "For my part, I will bear all the unhappiness without a murmur, if you will give me the heart."

91   "Very well," answered Oz, meekly. "Come to me tomorrow and you shall have a heart. I have played Wizard for so many years that I may as well continue the part a little longer."

92   "And now," said Dorothy, "how am I going to get back to Kansas?"

93   "We shall have to think about that," replied the little man. "Give me two or three days to consider the matter and I'll try to find a way to carry you over the desert. In the meantime you shall all be treated as my guests, and while you live in the Palace my people will wait upon you and obey your slightest wish. There is only one thing I ask in return for my help—such as it is. You must keep my secret and tell no one I am a humbug."

94   They agreed to say nothing of what they had learned, and went back to their rooms in high spirits. Even Dorothy had hope that "The Great and Terrible Humbug," as she called him, would find a way to send her back to Kansas, and if he did that she was willing to forgive him everything.

95   Next morning the Scarecrow said to his friends:

96   "Congratulate me. I am going to Oz to get my brains at last. When I return I shall be as other men are."

97   "I have always liked you as you were," said Dorothy simply.

98   "It is kind of you to like a Scarecrow," he replied. "But surely you will think more of me when you hear the splendid thoughts my new brain is going to turn out." Then he said good-bye to them all in a cheerful voice and went to the Throne Room, where he rapped upon the door.

99   "Come in," said Oz.

100   The Scarecrow went in and found the little man sitting down by the window, engaged in deep thought.

101   "I have come for my brains," remarked the Scarecrow a little uneasily.

102   "Oh, yes; sit down in that chair, please," replied Oz. "You must excuse me for taking your head off, but I shall have to do it in order to put your brains in their proper place."

103   "That's all right," said the Scarecrow. "You are quite welcome to take my head off, as long as it will be a better one when you put it on again."

104   So the Wizard unfastened his head and emptied out the straw. Then he entered the back room and took up a measure of bran, which he mixed with a great many pins and needles. Having shaken them together thoroughly, he filled the top of the Scarecrow's head with the mixture and stuffed the rest of the space with straw, to hold it in place. When he had fastened the Scarecrow's head on his body again he said to him,

105   "Hereafter you will be a great man, for I have given you a lot of bran-new brains."

106   The Scarecrow was both pleased and proud at the fulfillment of his greatest wish, and having thanked Oz warmly he went back to his friends.

107   Dorothy looked at him curiously. His head was quite bulging out at the top with brains.

108   "How do you feel?" she asked.

109   "I feel wise, indeed," he answered earnestly. "When I get used to my brains I shall know everything."

110   "Why are those needles and pins sticking out of your head?" asked the Tin Woodman.

111   "That is proof that he is sharp," remarked the Lion.

112   "Well, I must go to Oz and get my heart," said the Woodman. So he walked to the Throne Room and knocked at the door.

113   "Come in," called Oz, and the Woodman entered and said,

114   "I have come for my heart."

115   "Very well," answered the little man. "But I shall have to cut a hole in your breast, so I can put your heart in the right place. I hope it won't hurt you."

116   "Oh, no," answered the Woodman. "I shall not feel it at all."

117   So Oz brought a pair of tinners' shears and cut a small, square hole in the left side of the Tin Woodman's breast. Then, going to a chest of drawers, he took out a pretty heart, made entirely of silk and stuffed with sawdust.

118   "Isn't it a beauty," he asked.

119   "It is, indeed!" replied the Woodman, who was greatly pleased. "But is it a kind heart?"

120   "Oh, very!" answered Oz. He put the heart in the Woodman's breast and then replaced the square of tin, soldering it neatly together where it had been cut.

121   "There," said he; "now you have a heart that any man might be proud of. I'm sorry I had to put a patch on your breast, but it really couldn't be helped."

122   "Never mind the patch," exclaimed the happy Woodman. "I am very grateful to you, and shall never forget your kindness."

123   "Don't speak of it," replied Oz.

124   Then the Tin Woodman went back to his friends, who wished him every joy on account of his good fortune.

125   The Lion now walked to the Throne Room and knocked at the door.

126   "Come in," said Oz.

127   "I have come for my courage," announced the Lion, entering the room.

128   "Very well," answered the little man; "I will get it for you."

129   He went to a cupboard and reaching up to a high shelf took down a square green bottle, the contents of which he poured into a green-gold dish, beautifully carved. Placing this before the Cowardly Lion, who sniffed at it as if he did not like it, the Wizard said,

130   "Drink."

131   "What is it?" asked the Lion.

132   "Well," answered Oz, "if it were inside of you, it would be courage. You know, of course, that courage is always inside one; so that this really cannot be called courage until you have swallowed it. Therefore I advise you to drink it as soon as possible."

133   The Lion hesitated no longer, but drank till the dish was empty.

134   "How do you feel now?" asked Oz.

135   "Full of courage," replied the Lion, who went joyfully back to his friends to tell them of his good fortune.

136   Oz, left to himself, smiled to think of his success in giving the Scarecrow and the Tin Woodman and the Lion exactly what they thought they wanted. "How can I help being a humbug," he said, "when all these people make me do things that everybody knows can't be done? It was easy to make the Scarecrow and the Lion and the Woodman happy, because they imagined I could do anything."

Questions for Discussion

1. Why does Oz keep Dorothy and her companions waiting for so long? How do they finally persuade him to allow them into the Throne Room? How do the visitors finally find out Oz's true identity?

2. What is the significance of each of the false identities or disguises that Oz uses: the great Head, the lovely Lady, the terrible Beast, the ball of Fire, and the voice that comes from an invisible entity who is "everywhere"? How do these disguises correspond to ways in which a god is typically revealed to the faithful?

3. When the Scarecrow accuses the Wizard of being a "humbug," or fraud, he doesn't seem insulted; instead, he admits it and "rub[s] his hands together as if it pleased him." What comment does the story seem to be making on the ethics of fakery and trickery such as the Wizard practices?

4. What is the significance of the Wizard's original vocation? How has his training as a circus performer and publicist prepared him for his current occupation and success?

5. The Wizard claims to be a "very good man; but . . . a very bad Wizard" and admits that he lacks the "real" magical powers of the four Witches. What does the story seem to suggest about the nature of magic? In what sense is what the Wizard does actual magic? Does the story imply that there is a distinction between magic and fakery?

6. Although the Wizard claims to be unable to grant Dorothy's companions their wishes, he manages to get them to *believe* that they have these qualities. How does he accomplish this feat, and what does his achievement suggest about the "real" nature of intelligence, love, and courage?

Ideas for Writing

1. Write an essay about modern advertising and mass entertainment in which you respond to the Wizard's final question, "How can I help being a humbug . . . when all these people make me do things that everyone knows can't be done?" Do you agree that advertisers and entertainers are simply filling the public's need to be fooled, to believe in dreams and magic? If the public really has such a need, is it unethical to attempt to fill it?

2. Discuss an aspect of modern media—perhaps even a particular television program, periodical, or advertising campaign—that you believe to be a "humbug," encouraging people to believe in something that simply isn't true. How much harm does this media program or promotion do to people?

 ## Gary Soto

El Radio

Gary Soto (b. 1952) was raised in the San Joaquin Valley of California by a large Spanish-speaking family of factory and field workers. When Soto began attending Fresno City College, he declared a major in geography, but reading modern poetry convinced Soto that he wanted to understand more about the power of language to capture universal feelings and intense experiences. He transferred to California State University at Fresno, where he studied poetry with Pulitzer Prize–winning poet Philip Levine. After graduating with honors, he continued his education at the University of California at Irvine, where he completed his M.F.A. in 1976. Soto has been teaching English and Chicano studies at the University of California at Berkeley since 1977. His first book of poetry, The Elements of San Joaquin *(1977), established his reputation as a poet; since then, Soto has won many awards for his poetry. He has also written several narrative collections and won the American Book Award in 1985 for his autobiographical vignettes in* Living Up The Street: Narrative Recollections. *His most recent collections include*

Small Faces *(1986) and the story collection* Local News *(1993), in which "El Radio" appears.*

What role did the media play in your dreams and fantasies when you were an adolescent?

1   At seven-fifteen in the evening, Patricia Ruiz's mother dabbed lipstick on her small, shapely mouth. Her father worked a red tie around his neck, swallowing twice so that his Adam's apple rode up and down like an elevator. At seven twenty-two, both were standing at the mirror in the bathroom, her mother rubbing Passion-scented lotion on her wrists and her father spraying Obsession in the cove of his neck.

2   They were in a rush to go to the opera, a recent interest Patricia couldn't understand. Only a year ago they were listening every Friday night to "The Slow-Low Show" of oldies-but-goodies, hosted by *El Tigre*. Now it was opera on Friday nights, and a new Lexus in the driveway, a sleek machine that replaced their '74 Monte Carlo.

3   "Lock all the doors, *mi'ja*," Patricia's mother said, swishing in her chiffon dress. To Patricia, her mother looked like a talking flower, for she was slim as a flower and a bouquet of wonderful smells rose up from her.

4   Her father came into the living room plucking lint from the sleeve of his jacket. Patricia thought her father was handsome: his trim mustache, the silver at his temples, his romantically sad-looking eyes. Her girlfriends said he resembled Richard Gere, especially when he was in a stylish suit, as he was now.

5   "Pat, I rented you a movie," her father said, pointing vaguely at the cassette on the coffee table. "We'll be home by ten-thirty, eleven at the latest."

6   From the couch, a *Seventeen* in her lap, Patricia watched her parents get ready for the evening. She thought they were cute, like a boyfriend and girlfriend brimming with puppy love.

7   "I'll be okay," she said. She got up from the couch and kissed them. Their delicious smells were pleasantly overwhelming.

8   As her parents hurried out the front door, Patricia hurried to the telephone in the kitchen. Her best friend, Melinda, who lived two blocks away, was waiting for her call.

9   "They're gone," she announced. "Come on over."

10   Patricia hung up and took down a can of frozen orange juice from the freezer. While she was mixing the juice, spanking the clods of frozen orange pulp with a paddlelike spoon until they broke apart, she snapped her fingers and said, "It's party time!" She remembered that "The Slow-Low Show" of oldies-but-goodies was on the air. She turned on the small radio on the windowsill and the stereo in the living room. *El Tigre*, the host of the program, was sending out the message, "Now this one goes out to Slinky from Mystery Girl in Tulare. And this goes to Johnny Y in Corcoran from *La Baby Tears*, who says, 'I'll be waiting for

you.' And we got special love coming from Yolanda to her old man, Raul, who says, 'Baby, I'm the real thing.' Yes, *gente*, the world turns with plenty of slow-low romance."

11   While *El Tigre* put on the record, "Let's Get It On," Patricia went to the kitchen to make popcorn. She got a bottle of vegetable oil from the cupboard and a pot from the oven. The oven's squeaky door grated on her nerves when it was opened or closed. She was pouring in a handful of kernels when Melinda pounded on the back door.

12   "Hey, *Ruca*," Melinda greeted her when Patricia unlatched the door. Melinda was a chubby classmate in eighth grade at Kings Canyon Junior High. She was wearing a short black dress and her lipstick was brownish red against a pale, pancaked face. Her eyelashes were dark and sticky with mascara.

13   "*Ruca*, yourself, *esa*," Patricia greeted, shaking the pot over the burner and its flower of bluish flames. The kernels were exploding into white popcorn.

14   Melinda turned up the radio and screamed, "Ay, my favorite." "Ninety-Six" was playing, and Melinda, standing at the counter, was pretending to play the keyboard. She lip-synched the words and bobbed her head to the beat. When the song ended, Melinda poured herself a glass of orange juice and asked her friend, "Patty, you ever count how many tears you cried?"

15   Patricia shook her head and started giggling.

16   "One time, when my mom wouldn't let me to go the Valentine's dance—the one last year when the homeboys from Sanger showed up—I cried exactly ninety-six tears. Just like the song."

17   "Get serious," Patricia said, her eyes glinting in disbelief. She poured the popcorn into a bowl, with just a pinch of salt because she heard a spoonful of salt was worse for your complexion than nine Milky Way candy bars devoured in an hour. "How can you count your tears?"

18   "I used my fingers."

19   "No way."

20   "*De veras*," Melinda argued. She clicked her fingernails against the counter, and the sound resembled the *click-click* of a poodle's nails on a linoleum floor.

21   The two of them took the popcorn and orange juice into the living room and cuddled up on the couch, careful not to spill. On the radio, *El Tigre* was whispering, "This one goes out from Marta to *El Güero*. And we got a late bulletin from Enrique to Patricia. Message is—"

22   "Hey, Patty, some guy's got eyes for you," Melinda said. Her eyes were shiny with excitement. She jumped up and boosted the volume of the stereo. "The message is," *El Tigre* continued, "'don't get fooled by plastic love.'"

23   "I like that," Melinda said.

24   "*Chale*. No way," Patricia said, trying to laugh it off. She got up and turned down the volume. "I don't know no Enrique."

25   "Enrique de la Madrid!" Melinda screamed. "Danny's brother."

26   "That little squirt? The *vato* just lost his baby teeth last week."

27   The girls laughed and started dancing separately to Mary Wells's song, "My Guy." They continued dancing, fingers snapping and bodies waving in slow mo-

tion when the song ended and was followed by Aretha Franklin's "I Heard It Through the Grapevine."

28   When that song faded to a thumping bass followed by a scratchy silence, they sat down on the couch, legs folded underneath them. There was a glow of happiness about them, a shine in their eyes. Patricia took a single popcorn and threw it in Melinda's mouth. Melinda threw a single popcorn at Patricia's mouth. It hit her in the eye, and they laughed and threw handfuls of popcorn at each other. They liked hanging out together. They liked that they could dance wildly and lip-synch nonsense lyrics without feeling stupid.

29   They became quiet when *El Tigre* cleared his voice and whispered, "From Fowler, we celebrate the first but not last anniversary of Susie and Manny. From us, *su familia*, steady love for that eternal couple. And check it out, real serious commotion from Softy, who says to his Lorena in Dinuba, 'Let's get back together.'"

30   When "Angel Baby" came on, the girls eased into the couch and nursed their orange juice and slowly chewed their popcorn. Their feelings were smoky. They synched the words, certain that the singer must have had a deep relationship. Patricia figured that the singer's boyfriend must have found another girl, and then lost that girl and joined the Army.

31   Melinda looked at Patricia, who looked at Melinda. Melinda asked, "Anyone ever call you Angel Baby?"

32   Patricia sat up and, giggling, said, "*Cállate*, Melinda, you're ruinin' the song." She thought for a second about Melinda's question. "No, no one's ever called me Angel Baby. But my dad calls me Sweetie."

33   "My dad calls me *La* Pumpkin."

34   "*Órale*. Your *papi*'s got it right," Patricia laughed. She bounced off the couch and, heading to the kitchen, asked, "You want more orange juice?"

35   "*Simón, esa*," Melinda said.

36   While Patricia was in the kitchen, Melinda spent her time at the mirror on the far wall, where Patricia's baby pictures hung, wrapped in the dust of years. She dabbed her lips with lipstick and picked up a picture. She looked at her friend and had to admit that she was a cute little thing.

37   When Jr. Walker and the All-Stars' "Shotgun" began its soulful blare, Melinda put down the picture and started chugging to the song, elbows churning at her side, singing, "You're a lousy, nogood, stinkin' Shot-gunnnnnnnn."

38   "Go, brown girl, go!" Patricia yelled when she came into the living room. She put down the glasses of orange juice and chugged along with Melinda, elbows flapping at her side like the wings of a wet chicken. They laughed and felt happy, and couldn't think of a better time. When the song ended, Patricia felt her cheek with the back of her hand. She was hot but feeling great. She took a drink of orange juice.

39   "Yeah, we're gonna have to come up with a name for you, *ruca*," Melinda said. She sized Patricia up, and, stroking her chin, said, "How 'bout *La Flaca*?"

40   "*Y tu, La* Pumpkin!" Patricia chided. She ran her hands down her hips. Yeah, I am skinny, she told herself, but at least I'm not a fat *mamacita!*

41 "*La Flaca!*"

42 "*La Pumpkin!*"

43 "*La Flaca!*"

44 "*La Pumpkin!*"

45 The girls laughed at their nicknames and threw popcorn at each other. Melinda then suggested that they call *El Tigre* and dedicate a song.

46 "*A quién?*" Patricia asked.

47 "Enrique de la Madrid," teased Melinda as she jumped over the couch and headed for the telephone in the hallway.

48 "*Chale!*" Patricia screamed, her heart pounding from the fear and delight. "I don't like that squirt."

49 "But he got eyes for you."

50 "You mean *you.*"

51 "*Pues no.* You mean *you!*"

52 Patricia pulled on Melinda's arm and Melinda pushed Patricia. Suddenly they were on the floor wrestling, both laughing and calling the other by her nickname. In the background, *El Tigre* was whispering, "Now stay cool, *y* stay in school."

53 When Melinda reached for the telephone, the receiver fell off the hook and corkscrewed on its cord. Even though her mouth was inches away and she had yet to dial the radio station, she was yelling, "*Esta ruca, se llama la Flaca de* Kings Canyon Junior High, wants to dedicate a song to her sleepy boyfriend. She wants—"

54 Patricia put her hand over Melinda's mouth and felt the smear of lipstick working into her palm. Melinda pulled Patricia's hair, lightly, and Patricia pulled on Melinda, not so lightly. They struggled and laughed, and finally Melinda said, "Okay, okay, you win."

55 They both sat up, breathing hard but feeling good. After catching her breath, Patricia said, "I'll call *El Tigre* and have him do a *dedica* to my parents."

56 "*Que idea!*"

57 Patricia dialed "El Radio," and immediately she got *El Tigre*, who said in a low, low-riding voice, "*Qué pasa? Cómo te llamas, esa?*"

58 Without thinking, Patricia said, "*La Flaca y mi carnala La* Pumpkin *del barrio de* South Fresno."

59 "*Y tu escuela?*"

60 "Roosevelt High," Patricia lied. She didn't want *El Tigre* to know that he was rapping with a junior high kid.

61 "And what oldie-but-goodie do you want me to spin for you? *Y tu dedica?*"

62 "I wanna hear 'Oh, Donna,' by Ritchie Valens." Patricia moved the telephone to her other ear, giving her time to think about the dedication. "And I . . . I want to dedicate the song to my parents, Jerry and Sylvia, I do love you, from your only but eternal daughter, Patricia."

63 "*Pues,* I'll get it on in a sec. Stay cool, *ruca,* and keep up the grades."

64 Patricia hung up, heart pounding. She had never been so nervous. She put the telephone back on the table.

65 "You did good. 'Oh, Donna' is my next favorite," Melinda said. Melinda got up slowly from the floor and went to the mirror to tease her hair back into shape. She

looked down at her hand and made a face. "Ay, Patty, you broke one of my fingernails."

66   Patricia felt her cheek. She was hot from wrestling and talking with *El Tigre*. The only other famous personality she had spoken to was Ronald McDonald when he came down in a helicopter at the McDonald's on Kings Canyon Boulevard. And Ronald was nothing like *El Tigre*; he only gave away french fries, not oldies-but-goodies.

67   "You ever been on TV?" Patricia asked. She was high about her voice carrying over all of Fresno on "The Slow-Low Show."

68   "Nah," Melinda said. She had her compact out and was retouching her face. "I was in the newspaper once."

69   "You were?"

70   "Yeah, it was when they reopened the pool at Roosevelt. I was first in line." She closed the compact and brought out her mascara. "The paper was hard up."

71   On the radio, the Supremes' "I Hear a Symphony" was playing, a song which prompted Melinda to ask, "So your dad and mom are at the symphony?"

72   "Opera," Patricia corrected.

73   "They like that stuff?"

74   "*Quién sabe?* I think they want to try something they don't know about."

75   "Shoot, if I had their car, I'd be cruisin' Blackstone," Melinda said. She began to fumble in her purse for her lipstick.

76   "But you don't have a license," Patricia said.

77   "*Pues*, I'll just put on some more makeup, and who can tell?"

78   "But you don't know how to drive."

79   "It's easy. Just put the stick on 'D,' and press the *cosita*."

80   "Yeah, but what happened when your brother took out your mom's car?"

81   "You comparin' me to my brother? The guy *es un tonto*." Melinda took a fingernail file from her purse and began to whittle down her broken fingernail. "Yeah, your dad's Lexus is sharp, but so was his Monte Carlo."

82   "Yeah, I don't know why he traded it in," Patricia reflected.

83   At that moment there was the jingling of keys at the front door. Melinda gave Patricia a frightened look. Patricia's eyes flashed to the spilled popcorn and the blaring stereo, then to the clock on the end table. It was only 9:35.

84   "It's either the cops or my parents," Patricia said.

85   "Same thing," Melinda said, as she started to rush to the kitchen in hopes of making it to the back door.

86   But it was too late. The door opened with a sigh and the two girls were staring at Patricia's shocked parents. Her father took the key from the door, and her mother looked around the room trying to assess the damage.

87   "What's been going on?" her mother snapped as she walked toward Patricia. For a moment, Patricia thought she was going to pinch her but she only stomped into the kitchen. "Are there any boys here?" she asked. Her voice was edged with anger.

88   "No, just me and Melinda."

89   Her mother sniffed the air for boys and cigarettes. She saw the popcorn spewed over the rug.

90   "I spilled the bowl, Mrs. Ruiz," Melinda volunteered as she and Patricia scrambled to pick up the popcorn. "I tripped."

91   "I can't leave you alone! Can't I trust you?"

92   "Mom, we were just listening to *El Tigre*."

93   Patricia's father was quiet and withdrawn. He undid his tie and turned down the stereo. He threw himself into his easy chair, feet up on the hassock.

94   "What's wrong?" Patricia asked her father. He seemed unusually quiet.

95   He turned his sad eyes to his daughter. "The car broke down. It's brand-new."

96   "Broke down!" Patricia shouted.

97   "Yes, *broke down*," her mother repeated. Turning to Melinda, she asked, "Does your mother know where you are?"

98   "Ah, sort of," Melinda lied, her face turned away from Patricia's mother. She hated lying to grown-ups, especially parents with bad tempers.

99   Patricia's mother gave Melinda a doubtful glare and muttered, "*mentirosas*, both of you." She wiped away a few loose kernels of popcorn from the couch and sat down, her high heels dropping off her feet like heavy petals from a branch.

100   "You mean you didn't get to the opera?" Patricia asked. Before her mother or father could answer, a quick-thinking Melinda raced to the stereo and turned up the volume. *El Tigre*, in his Slow-Low low-riding voice, was whispering, "I'm coming at you at nine thirty-nine, and I hope you're kicking back in the heart of *Aztlán*."

101   "Yes, and I might be kicking these low-class *cholas* in the behind," her mother spoke to the radio. Patricia could see that her mother was softening and that she and Melinda were out of danger.

102   "We got *una dedica*," *El Tigre* continued, "from Larry M. to Shy Girl in West Fresno, who says, 'I lost a good thing,' To Gina of Los Banos, 'Happy Birthday,' from her father and mother. And from *La Flaca* to her parents Jerry and Sylvia, I do love you, from your only but eternal daughter. *La Flaca* has asked for 'Oh, Donna,' *y pues*, why not?"

103   "That's me, Mom. *La Flaca!*" Patricia yelled.

104   "You?" her mother asked, giving her daughter a questioning look.

105   "Yeah. I'm *La Flaca* and Melinda's *La* Pumpkin."

106   "My dad calls me *La* Pumpkin." Melinda grinned.

107   Patricia's father laughed. He laughed long and hard until a single tear rolled from one of his eyes. "Did you hear these *cholas? La Flaca y La* Pumpkin." He got up and boosted the volume of the radio, which was playing, "Oh, Donna." He asked his daughter playfully, "How'd you know my first girlfriend was named Donna?"

108   Patricia's mother slapped his arm and said, "Ay, *hombre*. Now look at you with a broken-down Lexus."

109   "Dad, you should have kept the Monte Carlo," Patricia said, feeling truly out of danger.

110   "Yeah, you're right." He smiled wearily.

111   "Come on, Dad, let's dance," Patricia suggested.

112   "Let's party down!" Melinda yelled. She chugged off to the kitchen, lip synching the words to "Oh, Donna."

113   "The heck with the opera," he said after a moment of hesitation. "It's better with *El Tigre*." He took his daughter's hands in his and they danced, one-two, one-two, while her mother snapped her fingers to the beat. In the kitchen Melinda stood at the stove making a new batch of popcorn.

Questions for Discussion

1. What do Patricia's feelings about her parents and their evening at the opera reveal about her relationship with them?
2. Interpret Melinda and Patricia's party ritual: the food the girls prepare, their outfits, the radio station they play. How do their cultural values contrast with those of their parents?
3. What are the girls trying to understand about life through the lyrics of the songs they sing? Does the story suggest that these songs are preparing them for the adult world and for real romantic relationships?
4. Why do the girls finally call *El Tigre?* Which of the girls' remarks suggest they know that they are not yet adults and that they are aware of practicing to grow up?
5. When their parents return home, how does the song the girls have dedicated help to ease the disappointments of the parents' evening?
6. In what ways are the girls' dreams and the parents' dreams intertwined?

Ideas for Writing

1. Write an essay that discusses the relationship between Patricia and her parents. In what ways has Patricia been influenced by her parents? How has she been influenced by radio shows and music that she identifies with? In what ways is her behavior typical of a modern teenager?
2. Write a story about one or more teenage characters who shape their values in relationship to the music they hear on the radio.

   # Louise Erdrich

Dear John Wayne

Louise Erdrich (b. 1954) was raised in Wahlpeton, North Dakota, as a member of the Turtle Mountain Chippewa tribe. Her parents encouraged her to write, and her culture valued story telling. Erdrich attended Dartmouth College where she studied with Michael Dorris, a professor of anthropology and Native American cultures, whom she later married. She earned a B.A. from Dartmouth in 1976 and an M.F.A. in creative writing from Johns Hopkins University several years later. Before beginning her career as a writer, Erdrich worked as a poetry teacher at prisons and as an editor for the Circle, *a Boston Indian Council newspaper. She published her first collection of poetry,* Jacklight *in 1984. Her first novel* Love Medicine (1984, expanded edition 1993), which won the National Book*

Critics Circle Award, introduces many of the characters and clan histories that are developed in her later novels, The Beet Queen *(1986),* Tracks *(1988), and* The Bingo Palace *(1994). Louise Erdrich often works on her writing with her husband Michael Dorris; they collaborated on the novel* The Crown of Columbus *(1992). Her most recent work includes a memoir,* The Blue Jay's Dance *(1994), and a novel,* Tales of Burning Love *(1996). The poem that follows, "Dear John Wayne," is included in* Jacklight.

JOURNAL

Write about a film that influenced your view of a particular cultural, ethnic, or national group.

August and the drive-in picture is packed.
We lounge on the hood of the Pontiac
surrounded by the slow-burning spirals they sell
at the window, to vanquish the hordes of mosquitoes.
5 Nothing works. They break through the smoke-screen
   for blood.

Always the look-out spots the Indians first,
spread north to south, barring progress.
The Sioux, or Cheyenne, or some bunch
in spectacular columns, arranged like SAC missiles,
10 their feathers bristling in the meaningful sunset.

The drum breaks. There will be no parlance.
Only the arrows whining, a death-cloud of nerves
swarming down on the settlers
who die beautifully, tumbling like dust weeds
15 into the history that brought us all here
together: this wide screen beneath the sign of the bear.

The sky fills, acres of blue squint and eye
that the crowd cheers. His face moves over us,
a thick cloud of vengeance, pitted
20 like the land that was once flesh. Each rut,
each scar makes a promise: *It is*
not over, this fight, not as long as you resist.
Everything we see belongs to us.
A few laughing Indians fall over the hood
25 slipping in the hot spilled butter.
The eye sees a lot, John, but the heart is so blind.
How will you know what you own?
He smiles, a horizon of teeth
the credits reel over, and then the white fields
30 again blowing in the true-to-life dark.

The dark films over everything.
We get into the car
scratching our mosquito bites, speechless and small
as people are when the movie is done.
35 We are back in ourselves.

How can we help but keep hearing his voice,
the flip side of the sound-track, still playing:
Come on, boys, we've got them
where we want them, drunk, running.
40 *They will give us what we want, what we need:*
The heart is a strange wood inside of everything
we see, burning, doubling, splitting out of its skin.

Sheila Chanani

What struck me the most about the poem was the image of the author as a young girl staring at the smile of John Wayne. That smile is supposed to be the smile of a hero, the smile of an American icon. However, to the little girl it is also sinister and represents lies and a hatred that she cannot understand. As she sits quietly in the drive-in, she sees her people demeaned for the purpose of entertaining the masses. The hazy night represents the confusion of the girl who watches her history being cheapened and misrepresented. The menacing smile will stay in her head as she travels home remembering words that will impact her life forever.

Questions for Discussion

1. What is the significance of the setting of the poem: a drive-in movie in August, where "hordes of mosquitoes" attack Indian patrons?

2. How are the Native Americans characterized in the second stanza? How does Erdrich use ironic images and details to create a critique of the stereotypical attitudes of Native Americans that the film reflects? Are Native Americans characterized differently in contemporary films?

3. What image of the "history that brought us all here together" is presented in the poem? How would the Native Americans have told the film's story?

4. What is the impact of the huge close-up face and eye of John Wayne described in the fourth stanza? What attitude toward Native Americans does Wayne's face portray? Why is the poem addressed to John Wayne?

5. What criticisms of John Wayne's values and the values of the western film genre are made through the italicized lines in stanzas five and six? Who is speaking in these lines?

6. Who is describing the heart in these lines: "the heart is so blind. . . ." and "The heart is a strange wood. . . ."? Interpret the meaning of these lines.

Ideas for Writing

1. Write a critique of a particular film that you believe exploits racist stereotypes and could possibly influence the public negatively against a particular group of people.

2. Write about a film that you believe challenges stereotypes and presents a positive or original, revealing view of a group of people who have been stereotyped negatively.

  # Gish Jen

Challenging the Asian Illusion

Gish Jen was born in 1955 and grew up in the New York suburbs. Her parents had emigrated from China in the late 1940s, and therefore the American values Jen encountered in school were dramatically different from those she learned from her parents at home. Jen earned her B.A. at Harvard and then studied business at Stanford for one year. Jen worked as a teacher in China for a year and came back to finish her first novel, Typical American *(1991), which is drawn from her experiences growing up as an Asian American. Jen has also published stories in publications such as* The New Yorker *and the* Atlantic Monthly. *Her most recent novel is* Mona in the Promised Land *(1996). Gish Jen lives in Cambridge,*

Massachusetts, with her husband and son. In "Challenging the Asian Illusion"
she is critical of the way the media creates stereotypes of Asians.

JOURNAL

Discuss the representation of Asians and Asian Americans in the media.

1   For a very long time, when people talked about race, they talked about black America and white America. Where did that put Asian-Americans?

2   Spike Lee touches on the Asian-American dilemma in *Do the Right Thing* when the Korean grocer, afraid of having his business attacked by rioting blacks, yells: "I not white! I black! Like you! Same!"

3   Unlike the grocer, though, my family and I identified mostly with white America, which, looking back, was partly wishful thinking, partly racism and partly an acknowledgment that, whatever else we did face, at least we did not have to contend with the legacy of slavery.

4   Yet we were not white. We were somehow borderline; we did not quite belong. Now, not only has the number of Asian-Americans in this country doubled in the last decade, we are growing faster than any other ethnic group. How meaningful it will ultimately prove to lump the Hmong with the Filipinos with the Japanese remains to be seen. Still, to be perceived as a significant minority is a development for which I, at least, am grateful.

5   There is a sense that to be perceived at all, a minority group must be plagued with problems—a problem in itself, to be sure. But what about our problems— were they significant enough to warrant attention? Who cared, for instance, that we did not see ourselves reflected on movie screens? Until recently, it did not occur to most of us that the absence of Asian and Asian-American images was symptomatic of a more profound invisibility.

6   Today, though, it is shocking to behold how little represented we have been, and in how blatantly distorted a manner. There has been some progress now that more Asian-Americans like David Henry Hwang and Philip Kan Gotanda have begun to write for stage and screen: also, some recent Caucasian-directed television shows, including *Shannon's Deal* and *Davis Rules,* are breaking new ground.

7   For the most part, however, film, television and theater, from *Miss Saigon* to *Teen-Age Mutant Ninja Turtles,* have persisted in perpetuating stereotypes. Mostly this has been through the portrayal of Asian characters; Asian-Americans have rarely been represented at all.

8   This invisibility is essentially linked to the process by which fanciful ideas are superimposed onto real human beings. How are everyday Asians transformed into mysterious "Orientals," after all, if not by distance? Americans can be led to believe anything about people living in a far-off land, or even a distinctly unfamiliar place like Chinatown. It is less easy with a kid next door who plays hockey and air guitar.

9   Over the years, Asians have been the form onto which white writers have freely projected their fears and desires. That this is a form of colonialism goes almost without saying; it can happen only when the people whose images are appropriated are in no position to object.

10   For certainly anyone would object to being identified with a figure as heartlessly evil and preternaturally cunning as Fu Manchu, a brilliant but diabolical force set on taking over the world. The character's prototype was invented in 1916, in a climate of hysteria over the "threat" that Asian workers posed to native labor. We behold its likeness in figures like Odd Job in *Goldfinger* (1964); his influence can be seen in depictions of Chinatown as a den of iniquity in movies like *The Year of the Dragon* (1985) and *True Believer* (1988). *Chinatown* (1974) used it as a symbol of all that is rotten in the city of Los Angeles, despite the fact that no Chinese person had much to do with the evil turnings of the plot.

11   What fuels these images is xenophobia. In periods of heightened political tension, they tend to recur; in more secure times, they are replaced by more benign images. Charlie Chan for example, arose in 1926, shortly after the last of a series of laws restricting Chinese immigration had been passed and the "Yellow Peril" seemed to be over.

12   The benign images, however, are typically no more tied to reality than their malign counterparts; vilification is merely replaced by glorification. The aphorism-spouting Charlie Chan (played by Warner Oland, a white actor in yellowface) is godlike in his intelligence, the original Asian whiz kid; you would not be surprised to hear he had won a Westinghouse prize in his youth. More message than human being, he recalls the ever-smiling black mammy that proliferated during Reconstruction: Don't worry, he seems to say, no one's going to go making any trouble.

One Good Guy, But He's a Rat

13 In today's social climate of multi-culturalism, movies like *Rambo*, which made the Vietnamese out to be so much cannon fodder, seem to be behind us, at least temporarily. Instead, reflecting the American preoccupation with Japan, there is *Teen-Age Mutant Ninja Turtles*. Here the Japanese enemy gang leader is once again purely demonic and bestial, a hairless, barbaric figure who wears a metal claw for ornament. What gives the movie a more contemporary stamp is the fact that Master Splinter, the good-guy rodent leader of the Mutant Turtles, is also Japanese. It is as if Fu Manchu and Charlie Chan were cast into a single movie—seemingly presenting a balanced view of the Japanese as good and bad.

14   But the fact that the "good" Japanese is a rat means that slanty eyes belong to the bad guy. And as individuals the Japanese are still portrayed as sub- or superhuman, possessing fabulous abilities and arcane knowledge that center on (another contemporary twist) martial arts.

15   Is it a sign of a fitness-crazed age that this single aspect of Asian culture is so enthralling? So perennially popular are movies like *The Karate Kid* (1984) and this year's *Iron and Silk* that one begins to wonder whether Asian males pop out of the

womb doing mid-air gyrations. The audience marvels: How fantastic, these people! Meanwhile, the non-Asian roles are the more recognizably human ones.

16   Real humanity similarly eludes the Asian characters in the Broadway play *Miss Saigon*. As in *Teen-Age Mutant Ninja Turtles*, they are either simply evil or simply good, with the possible exception of the Engineer (Jonathan Pryce) who, loathsome as he is, seems more self-interested than evil. Half-white, he seems to be, correspondingly, halfway human. In contrast, Thuy, the major Vietnamese character, is portrayed as so inhuman that he would kill a child in cold blood. Is this what Communists do? Asians? When Kim (Lea Salonga), the heroine, shoots her erstwhile loyal fiancé, the audience applauds, feeling no more for him than for Rambo's victims. The subhuman brute has got what he deserved.

17   At the same time, the audience does feel, horribly, for Kim, who has been forced to pull the trigger and now must live with blood on her hands. What a fate for a paragon of virtue! She is Madame Butterfly unpinned from her specimen board and let loose to flutter around the room again: abandoned, virtuous, she waits faithfully for her white lover, only to discover that he has married. He returns for his son (it's always a son); she kills herself.

18   Isn't this a beautiful story? Annette Kolodny, a feminist critic, has observed that when the Western mind feels free to remake a place and people according to its liking, it conceives of that place and people as a woman. This has been nowhere so true as in the case of the "Orient," and correspondingly, no woman, it seems, has been portrayed as more exquisitely feminine than an Oriental.

19   Take any play in which both Oriental and Caucasian women appear—say, *South Pacific*—and it is immediately obvious which is more delicate, more willing to sacrifice for her man, more docile. Never mind that there are in the world real women who might object to having their image appropriated for such use.

20   But of course, women do object. I object, especially since the only possible end for this invented Butterfly is suicide. For how would the white characters go on with their lives?

21   It is an irony of stage history that a musical as conventional in its use of the Butterfly story should follow so closely on the heels of another play that turns the same narrative on its head. The 1988 Broadway play *M. Butterfly* offers not just the "beautiful story" itself, but also a white man who has been taken in by it. So enthralled is René Gallimard by the idea of his Butterfly, the projection of his own desire, that he forgets there is a real person—Song Liling, a man and a spy—upon which his notions are imposed.

22   Ultimately, *M. Butterfly* makes clear that for the "game" of Orientalism, there is a price to pay, not only by those whose images are appropriated, but by the appropriators.

23   Do stereotypes lurk even here? It might seem so, but would a stereotype wonder, as does Song Liling, whether he and Gallimard might not continue on together, even after the truth has been revealed. When Song asks, "What do I do now?" he conveys how helpless he is too, how powerless. This is a human being. That he should be is maybe not so surprising, given that he was invented by David Henry Hwang, an Asian-American.

One Step Forward: Spoof the Stereotype

24 Are Asian-American writers the only hope for new forms of characterization? Perhaps, when even directors as intelligent as Woody Allen portray Chinatown as having opium dens. In his most recent movie, *Alice*, Mr. Allen's recycling of an Asian sage is likewise problematic. Could he not have created a spoof of a sage—a character who winked at the stereotype even as he played it—without any damage to the plot?

25   Spoofing the stereotype was the strategy taken last spring in an episode of the now-cancelled television series *Shannon's Deal* that featured a pony-tailed Korean immigrant. Here were clear signs for hope: the immigrant at first appeared to be an all-knowing Charlie Chan, but turned out to be at once less and more. At moments way ahead of the investigator Shannon, he proved to be way behind at others; he knew all the aphorisms but had trouble passing the bar exam, and discussed his own tendency to drop pronouns.

26   Other signs of change include a jeans-wearing, face-making, poker-playing Japanese character in *Davis Rules*. Unexotic Mrs. Yamagami (Tamayo Otsuki) even shows a sense of humor, characterizing a coworker as "a rebel without a car." Similarly, in *Twin Peaks*, the figure of Jocelyn (Joan Chen), evil as she is, does not stand in contrast to the good, white characters the way a female Fu Manchu—a dragon lady—might. Neither, certainly, is she any Butterfly. She is, within the show's offbeat context, just one of the gang.

27   All these characters are heartening, since they are not simply unexamined projections onto the Asian race. Still, as might be expected, directors like Wayne Wang and playwrights like Philip Kan Gotanda are not only more likely to present Asian-Americans in their work, but to present Asian-Americans who are not of the immigrant generation. In Mr. Wang's movie *Dim Sum* (1987) and Mr. Gotanda's film *The Wash* (1988), Asian-Americans are presented in far greater complexity than is typical of the mainstream media; the characters seem more captured than constructed, more like flesh-and-blood than cartoons. This is partly a matter of their status as protagonists rather than peripheral figures.

28   And more images are needed if the few that exist now are not to become new stereotypes. Since the much publicized success of Connie Chung, for example, Asian-American anchorwomen have become a staple in films like *Year of the Dragon* and *Moscow on the Hudson*. With real-life repercussions: the San Francisco newscaster Emerald Yeh tells of an interview with CNN, during which she was more or less asked why she couldn't do her hair like Connie Chung's.

29   Ridiculous, right? And yet such is the power of image. We would not have to insist that images reflect life, except that all too often we ask life to reflect images.

Questions for Discussion

1. Gish Jen thinks that one of the first problems of Asian immigrants is their profound invisibility. Why does she believe that they are invisible, and why is their invisibility such a serious problem? Why, for example, have film, television, and theater chosen to portray Asians rather than Asian Americans? What other evidence do you see in the media and in

your community to support Jen's claim? Who is to "blame" for this misrepresentation?

2. Why does Jen argue that the maligned images of Asians in films from the 1916 Fu Manchu to their portrayals in films like *Chinatown* (1974) and *True Believer* (1988) are fueled by xenophobia? Explain why you agree or disagree with her.

3. How has the recent interest in multiculturalism affected the way that Asians and Asian Americans have been portrayed in the media? Why does Jen believe that the media's portrayals are still stereotypical? Do you think the media stereotypes Asian Americans? Why?

4. Jen implies that Asian American filmmakers are the ones who may be able to help humanize the image of Asian Americans in the media. Do you think this is the only way for the media to stop perpetuating stereotypes of Asian Americans? What other solutions might work?

5. How does Jen compare and contrast the stereotyping of her race to other minority races in this country?

6. "We would have to insist that images reflect life, except that all too often we ask life to reflect images." What are the implications of Jen's statement? How does this concluding statement reflect on the points she has made about the media's portrayal of Asian Americans in the body of her essay?

Ideas for Writing

1. Write an essay about a time when you realized that you held a stereotypical view of a person of another culture, race, or gender. Narrate the turning point in the situation and then explain why you think you had internalized the stereotype, how you were changed by your experience, and why you think people accept stereotypical attitudes toward others who are different from themselves.

2. Write an essay that presents your point of view on the way that Asian Americans are portrayed in the media. Refer to television programs, commercials, advertisements, and films that you have seen and thought about.

 # Umberto Eco

The City of Robots

Umberto Eco was born in 1932 in Alessandria, Italy, and earned his Ph.D. in 1954 from the University of Turin. Eco, who is currently a professor at the University of Bologna in Italy, has taught at universities all over the world. He is world-renowned for his study of semiotics, how cultures communicate through

signs, and is also considered an expert on logic, literature, aesthetics, cultural stud-
ies, and history. His first novel, The Name of the Rose *(1980), which became*
an international best seller, has been translated into over 20 languages and has
won several literary awards in Europe. In the following essay Eco reflects on the
role of the theme park in American culture.

Write about a visit to a theme park such as Disneyland, Marriott's Great America, or Seven Flags over Texas. What were your impressions of the theme park?
What did you learn about your own values and the values of American popular
culture from your visit?

1   In Europe, when people want to be amused, they go to a "house" of amusement
(whether a cinema, theater, or casino); sometimes a "park" is created, which
may seem a "city," but only metaphorically. In the United States, on the contrary,
as everyone knows, there exist amusement cities. Las Vegas is one example; it is
focused on gambling and entertainment, its architecture is totally artificial, and it
has been studied by Robert Venturi as a completely new phenomenon in city
planning, a "message" city, entirely made up of signs, not a city like the others,
which communicate in order to function, but rather a city that functions in order
to communicate. But Las Vegas is still a "real" city, and in a recent essay on Las
Vegas, Giovanni Brino showed how, though born as a place for gambling, it is
gradually being transformed into a residential city, a place of business, industry,
conventions. The theme of our trip—on the contrary—is the Absolute Fake; and
therefore we are interested only in absolutely fake cities. Disneyland (California)
and Disney World (Florida) are obviously the chief examples, but if they existed
alone they would represent a negligible exception. The fact is that the United
States is filled with cities that imitate a city, just as wax museums imitate painting
and the Venetian palazzos or Pompeiian villas imitate architecture. In particular
there are the "ghost towns," the Western cities of a century and more ago. Some
are reasonably authentic, and the restoration or preservation has been carried out
on an extant, "archeological" urban complex; but more interesting are those born
from nothing, out of pure imitative determination. They are "the real thing."

2   There is an embarrassment of riches to choose from: You can have fragments of
cities, as at Stone Mountain near Atlanta, where you take a trip on a nineteenth-
century train, witness an Indian raid, and see sheriffs at work, against the background of a fake Mount Rushmore. The Six Guns Territory, in Silver Springs, also
has train and sheriffs, a shot-out in the streets and French can-can in the saloon.
There is a series of ranchos and Mexican missions in Arizona; Tombstone with its
OK Corral, Old Tucson, Legend City near Phoenix. There is the Old South Bar-
b-Q Ranch at Clewison, Florida, and so on. If you venture beyond the myth of the
West, you have cities like the Magic Mountain in Valencia, California, or Santa

Claus Village, Polynesian gardens, pirate islands, Astroworlds like the one in Kirby, Texas, and the "wild" territories of the various Marinelands, as well as ecological cities, which we will discuss elsewhere.

3   There are also the ship imitations. In Florida, for example, between Tampa and St. Petersburg, you can board the *Bounty*, anchored at the edge of a Tahitian village, faithfully reconstructed according to the drawings preserved by the Royal Society in London, but with an eye also on the old film with Charles Laughton and Clark Gable. Many of the nautical instruments are of the period, some of the sailors are waxworks, one officer's shoes are those worn by the actor who played the part, the historical information on the various panels is credible, the voices that pervade the atmosphere come from the sound track of the movie. But we'll stick to the Western myth and take as a sample city the Knott's Berry Farm of Buena Park, Los Angeles.

4   Here the whole trick seems to be exposed; the surrounding city context and the iron fencing (as well as the admission ticket) warn us that we are entering not a real city but a toy city. But as we begin walking down the first streets, the studied illusion takes over. First of all, there is the realism of the reconstruction: the dusty stables, the sagging shops, the offices of the sheriff and the telegraph agent, the jail, the saloon are life size and executed with absolute fidelity; the old carriages are covered with dust, the Chinese laundry is dimly lit, all the buildings are more or less practical, and the shops are open, because Berry Farm, like Disneyland, blends the reality of trade with the play of fiction. And if the dry-goods store is fake nineteenth-century and the shopgirl is dressed like a John Ford heroine, the candies, the peanuts, the pseudo-Indian handicrafts are real and are sold for real dollars, just as the soft drinks, advertised with antique posters, are real, and the customer finds himself participating in the fantasy because of his own authenticity as a consumer; in other words, he is in the role of the cowboy or the gold-prospector who comes into town to be fleeced of all he has accumulated while out in the wilds.

5   Furthermore the levels of illusion are numerous, and this increases the hallucination—that is to say, the Chinese in the laundry or the prisoner in the jail are wax dummies, who exist, in realistic attitudes, in settings that are equally realistic, though you can't actually enter them; but you don't realize the room in question is a glass display case, because it looks as if you could, if you chose, open the door or climb through the window; and then the next room, say, which is both the general store and the justice of the peace's office, looks like a display case but is actually practical, and the justice of the peace, with his black alpaca jacket and his pistols at his hips, is an actual person who sells you his merchandise. It should be added that extras walk about the streets and periodically stage a furious gun battle, and when you realize that the average American visitor is wearing blue jeans not very different from the cowboys', many of the visitors become confused with the extras, increasing the theatricality of the whole. For example, the village school, reconstructed with hyperrealistic detail, has behind the desk a schoolmarm wearing a bonnet and an ample checked skirt, but the children on the benches are little passing visitors, and I heard one tourist ask his wife if the children were real or

"fake" (and you could sense his psychological readiness to consider them, at will, extras, dummies, or moving robots of the sort we will see in Disneyland).

6   Apparently ghost towns involve a different approach from that of wax museums or museums for copies of works of art. In the first nobody expects the wax Napoleon to be taken for real, but the hallucination serves to level the various historical periods and erase the distinction between historical reality and fantasy; in the case of the works of art what is culturally, if not psychologically, hallucinatory is the confusion between copy and original, and the fetishization of art as a sequence of famous subjects. In the ghost town, on the contrary, since the theatricality is explicit, the hallucination operates in making the visitors take part in the scene and thus become participants in that commercial fair that is apparently an element of the fiction but in fact represents the substantial aim of the whole imitative machine.

7   In an excellent essay on Disneyland as "degenerate utopia" ("a degenerate utopia is an ideology realized in the form of myth"), Louis Marin analyzed the structure of that nineteenth-century frontier city street that receives entering visitors and distributes them through the various sectors of the magic city. Disneyland's Main Street seems the first scene of the fiction whereas it is an extremely shrewd commercial reality. Main Street—like the whole city, for that matter—is presented as at once absolutely realistic and absolutely fantastic, and this is the advantage (in terms of artistic conception) of Disneyland over the other toy cities. The houses of Disneyland are full-size on the ground floor, and on a two-thirds scale on the floor above, so they give the impression of being inhabitable (and they are) but also of belonging to a fantastic past that we can grasp with our imagination. The Main Street façades are presented to us as toy houses and invite us to enter them, but their interior is always a disguised supermarket, where you buy obsessively, believing that you are still playing.

8   In this sense Disneyland is more hyperrealistic than the wax museum, precisely because the latter still tries to make us believe that what we are seeing reproduces reality absolutely, whereas Disneyland makes it clear that within its magic enclosure it is fantasy that is absolutely reproduced. The Palace of Living Arts presents its Venus de Milo as almost real, whereas Disneyland can permit itself to present its reconstructions as masterpieces of falsification, for what it sells is, indeed, goods, but genuine merchandise, not reproductions. What is falsified is our will to buy, which we take as real, and in this sense Disneyland is really the quintessence of consumer ideology.

9   But once the "total fake" is admitted, in order to be enjoyed it must seem totally real. So the Polynesian restaurant will have, in addition to a fairly authentic menu, Tahitian waitresses in costume, appropriate vegetation, rock walls with little cascades, and once you are inside nothing must lead you to suspect that outside there is anything but Polynesia. If, between two trees, there appears a stretch of river that belongs to another sector, Adventureland, then that section of stream is so designed that it would not be unrealistic to see in Tahiti, beyond the garden hedge, a river like this. And if in the wax museums wax is not flesh, in Disneyland, when rocks are involved, they are rock, and water is water, and a baobab a

baobab. When there is a fake—hippopotamus, dinosaur, sea serpent—it is not so much because it wouldn't be possible to have the real equivalent but because the public is meant to admire the perfection of the fake and its obedience to the program. In this sense Disneyland not only produces illusion, but—in confessing it—stimulates the desire for it: A real crocodile can be found in the zoo, and as a rule it is dozing or hiding, but Disneyland tells us that faked nature corresponds much more to our daydream demands. When, in the space of twenty-four hours, you go (as I did deliberately) from the fake New Orleans of Disneyland to the real one, and from the wild river of Adventureland to a trip on the Mississippi, where the captain of the paddle-wheel steamer says it is possible to see alligators on the banks of the river, and then you don't see any, you risk feeling homesick for Disneyland, where the wild animals don't have to be coaxed. Disneyland tells us that technology can give us more reality than nature can.

10   In this sense I believe the most typical phenomenon of this universe is not the more famous Fantasyland—an amusing carousel of fantastic journeys that take the visitor into the world of Peter Pan or Snow White, a wondrous machine whose fascination and lucid legitimacy it would be foolish to deny—but the Caribbean Pirates and the Haunted Mansion. The pirate show lasts a quarter of an hour (but you lose any sense of time, it could be ten minutes or thirty); you enter a series of caves, carried in boats over the surface of the water, you see first abandoned treasures, a captain's skeleton in a sumptuous bed of moldy brocade, pendent cobwebs, bodies of executed men devoured by ravens, while the skeleton addresses menacing admonitions to you. Then you navigate an inlet, passing through the crossfire of a galleon and the cannon of a fort, while the chief corsair shouts taunting challenges at the beleaguered garrison; then, as if along a river, you go by an invaded city which is being sacked, with the rape of the women, theft of jewels, torture of the mayor; the city burns like a match, drunken pirates sprawled on piles of kegs sing obscene songs; some completely out of their heads, shoot at the visitors; the scene degenerates, everything collapses in flames, slowly the last songs die away, you emerge into the sunlight. Everything you have seen was on human scale, the vault of the caves became confused with that of the sky, the boundary of this underground world was that of the universe and it was impossible to glimpse its limits. The pirates moved, danced, slept, popped their eyes, sniggered, drank—really. You realize that they are robots, but you remain dumbfounded by their verisimilitude. And, in fact, the "Audio-Animatronic" technique represented a great source of pride for Walt Disney, who had finally managed to achieve his own dream and reconstruct a fantasy world more real than reality, breaking down the wall of the second dimension, creating not a movie, which is illusion, but total theater, and not with anthropomorphized animals, but with human beings. In fact, Disney's robots are masterpieces of electronics; each was devised by observing the expressions of a real actor, then building models, then developing skeletons of absolute precision, authentic computers in human form, to be dressed in "flesh" and "skin" made by craftsmen, whose command of realism is incredible. Each robot obeys a program, can synchronize the movements of mouth and eyes with the words and sounds of the audio, repeating ad infinitum all day long his established

part (a sentence, one or two gestures) and the visitor, caught off guard by the succession of events, obliged to see several things at once, to left and right and straight ahead, has no time to look back and observe that the robot he has just seen is already repeating his eternal scenario.

11   The "Audio-Animatronic" technique is used in many other parts of Disneyland and also enlivens a review of presidents of the United States, but in the pirates' cave, more than anywhere else, it demonstrates all its miraculous efficacy. Humans could do no better, and would cost more, but the important thing is precisely the fact that these are not humans and we know they're not. The pleasure of imitation, as the ancients knew, is one of the most innate in the human spirit; but here we not only enjoy a perfect imitation, we also enjoy the conviction that imitation has reached its apex and afterwards reality will always be inferior to it.

12   Similar criteria underlie the journey through the cellars of the Haunted Mansion, which looks at first like a rundown country house, somewhere between Edgar Allan Poe and the cartoons of Charles Addams; but inside, it conceals the most complete array of witchcraft surprises that anyone could desire. You pass through an abandoned graveyard, where skeletal hands raise gravestones from below, you cross a hill enlivened by a witches' sabbath complete with spirits and beldams; then you move through a room with a table all laid and a group of transparent ghosts in nineteenth-century costume dancing while diaphanous guests, occasionally vanishing into thin air, enjoy the banquet of a barbaric sovereign. You are grazed by cobwebs, reflected in crystals on whose surface a greenish figure appears, behind your back; you encounter moving candelabra. . . . In no instance are these the cheap tricks of some tunnel of love; the involvement (always tempered by the humor of the inventions) is total. As in certain horror films, detachment is impossible; you are not witnessing another's horror, you are inside the horror through complete synesthesia; and if there is an earthquake the movie theater must also tremble.

13   I would say that these two attractions sum up the Disneyland philosophy more than the equally perfect models of the pirate ship, the river boat, and the sailing ship *Columbia*, all obviously in working order. And more than the Future section, with the science-fiction emotions it arouses (such as a flight to Mars experienced from inside a spacecraft, with all the effects of deceleration, loss of gravity, dizzying movement away from the earth, and so on). More than the models of rockets and atomic submarines, which prompted Marin to observe that whereas the fake Western cities, the fake New Orleans, the fake jungle provide life size duplicates of organic but historical or fantastic events, these are reduced-scale models of mechanical realities of today, and so, where something is incredible, the full-scale model prevails, and where it is credible, the reduction serves to make it attractive to the imagination. The Pirates and the Ghosts sum up all Disneyland, at least from the point of view of our trip, because they transform the whole city into an immense robot, the final realization of the dreams of the eighteenth-century mechanics who gave life to the Writer of Neuchâtel and the Chess-playing Turk of Baron von Kempelen.

14   Disneyland's precision and coherence are to some extent disturbed by the ambitions of Disney World in Florida. Built later, Disney World is a hundred fifty

times larger than Disneyland, and proudly presents itself not as a toy city but as the model of an urban agglomerate of the future. The structures that make up California's Disneyland form here only a marginal part of an immense complex of construction covering an area twice the size of Manhattan. The great monorail that takes you from the entrance to the Magic Kingdom (the Disneyland part proper) passes artificial bays and lagoons, a Swiss village, a Polynesian village, golf courses and tennis courts, an immense hotel: an area dedicated, in other words, to organized vacationing. So you reach the Magic Kingdom, your eyes already dazzled by so much science fiction that the sight of the high medieval castle (far more Gothic than Disneyland: a Strasbourg Cathedral, let's say, compared to a San Miniato) no longer stirs the imagination. Tomorrow, with its violence, has made the colors fade from the stories of Yesterday. In this respect Disneyland is much shrewder; it must be visited without anything to remind us of the future surrounding it. Marin has observed that, to enter it, the essential condition is to abandon your car in an endless parking lot and reach the boundary of the dream city by special little trains. And for a Californian, leaving his car means leaving his own humanity, consigning himself to another power, abandoning his own will.

15   An allegory of the consumer society, a place of absolute iconism, Disneyland is also a place of total passivity. Its visitors must agree to behave like its robots. Access to each attraction is regulated by a maze of metal railings which discourages any individual initiative. The number of visitors obviously sets the pace of the line; the officials of the dream, properly dressed in the uniforms suited to each specific attraction, not only admit the visitor to the threshold of the chosen sector, but, in successive phases, regulate his every move ("Now wait here please, go up now, sit down please, wait before standing up," always in a polite tone, impersonal, imperious, over the microphone). If the visitor pays this price, he can have not only "the real thing" but the abundance of the reconstructed truth. Like the Hearst Castle, Disneyland also has no transitional spaces; there is always something to see, the great voids of modern architecture and city planning are unknown here. If America is the country of the Guggenheim Museum or the new skyscrapers of Manhattan, then Disneyland is a curious exception and American intellectuals are quite right to refuse to go there. But if America is what we have seen in the course of our trip, then Disneyland is its Sistine Chapel, and the hyperrealists of the art galleries are only the timid voyeurs of an immense and continuous "found object."

Questions for Discussion

1. According to Eco, what is the distinction between an "amusement city," a "real" city, and a "total fake"? What examples does he give? Can you think of others?
2. How do "fake" cities blend and at times confuse "the reality of trade with the play of fiction"? What role do the "extras" play in this confusion?
3. In what sense does the author Louis Marin see Disneyland as a "degenerate utopia"? What ideology and what myth does Disneyland exploit?

4. Why is it so important for the spectators' enjoyment that the "total fake" appear to be "totally real" in each of Disneyland's dreamlike lands or "sectors"? How does this creation of the appearance of reality lead us to the impression that "technology can give us more reality than nature can"?

5. How do Eco's extensive descriptions of the Pirates of the Caribbean and the Haunted Mansion help to support and clarify the points he makes about pleasure, illusion, and seeming reality through robotic techniques in Disneyland?

6. According to Eco, how is California's Disneyland, with its smaller size and prohibition against cars, superior to Florida's huge, futuristic Disneyworld?

7. Why does Eco believe Disneyland to be an "allegory of the consumer society"? In what sense must the visitors "behave like its [Disneyland's] robots"?

Ideas for Writing

1. Write an essay in response to Eco's claim at the end of the essay that Disneyland, more so than other American architectural masterpieces and museums such as the Guggenheim, is America's "Sistine Chapel"— that is, a place of worship where our true national values are enshrined in a culturally appropriate artistic form.

2. Do some research into Walt Disney's goals for Disneyland. What were his values and cultural beliefs? Have these values been successfully realized in the final product, or, as Eco suggests, do values of passive consumerism seem more dominant? What values do you think Disneyland embodies?

 Terri Sevilla

"The Little Princess" and Me

Terri Sevilla, who grew up in a working-class suburb in Hayward, California, has recently returned to night school after working for a number of years. Sevilla paints, draws, and does photography. Her workplace at the Oakland airport is decorated with her photographs of her fellow workers, and, with a coauthor, she has written a self-published book, Fascinating Facts About the Golden Gate Bridge. *In the following essay she is responding to a question that asked her to write about a movie that changed her life, after reading Terry McMillan's essay on the Wizard of Oz. In her essay, Sevilla explores her lifelong fascination with the films of Shirley Temple.*

JOURNAL

Write about a character in a film or a movie star hero or heroine with whom you identified strongly as a young child. What needs were fulfilled in you through your identification with the star and the characters he or she played?

---

1   The earliest memories of my life start in the living room of my parent's house, beginning at about age four. This was the suburbs in the mid-fifties, and the boomerang shaped coffee table and cream-colored Naugahyde couch were among the austere, uncomfortable entities that formed a backdrop for the main attraction in my home, the television set. By the fifties, the popularity of television had begun to grow at a phenomenal rate, with families everywhere in America enjoying the adventure of "living color" programs such as *The Walt Disney Show* and *Bonanza*.

2   Television was not the mainstay of my entertainment, as I had developed a reverence for books and reading. However, almost by accident one day I stumbled upon the "Shirley Temple Theater," a regular children's program that featured re-runs of old black and white films by Shirley Temple which had entertained a generation of children before me. The fact that no one else in my family could tolerate watching these 90-minute adventures added to my enthusiasm and helped to validate these old films, for it was my view that whenever my family rejected something, it must certainly hold some value for me.

3   At this time I was in need of a vehicle that would help me to articulate my thoughts and feelings. I had searched through heroes among literary characters looking for my alter-ego, but none quite fit my needs. I was a little girl who desperately wanted to reclaim some of the personal power I felt I had already lost, as adults attempted to limit my freedom of behavior and association, keeping me away from the intellectual stimulation of the adult world and exiling me increasingly to the second-class paradise of my room.

4   One particular Shirley Temple movie seemed particularly to address my search for the heroic. In *The Little Princess* Shirley is Sarah Crew, daughter of Colonel Crew of the British Army. He is called to South Africa to fight in the war against the Boers, and Sarah must stay behind in Miss Minchin's School of Decorum for Girls. Sarah, who has the most powerful and wealthy parent of any of the girls, was also the most humane and down to earth student. Even as the spiteful and jealous schoolmates nickname her "The Little Princess," she is loving and generous to all. She befriends all of the people usually considered to be invisible by people of her station, such as the house servant from India, the orphan teacher (an old vaudevillian), and the young couple (the English teacher and the rider instructor) who have defied Miss Minchin by falling in love with one another.

5   The plot turns ugly when Sarah's father is listed as missing in action and Sarah is left a pauper. Immediately, life changes for my hero. She is relegated to a cold, dark attic to live with another orphan-waif, Becky. This part of the movie always moved me deeply, as it seemed to mirror my life, with the chaos and drama my family was experiencing as we slid into the trough of one of America's periodic recessions and endured innumerable family squabbles. As my family's idyllic life in the suburbs decayed and crumbled around our ears, I watched over and over again as Sarah carried her inner strength into the darkness of each new dilemma. In fact, as time went on she became ever more determined to withstand the many attempts at breaking her spirit with which the harsh world challenged her. Sarah would not only survive; she would also succeed in finding her father, whom she believed to be very much alive, despite all evidence to the contrary. This was the crux of the whole movie to me: Sarah was able to be successful in solving her seemingly insurmountable problems simply by being the sweet, intelligent, good-hearted little girl she was. Doors were opened for her and obstacles were easily overcome through her use of persuasion and her compellingly loving nature.

6   I remember feeling a surge of self-determination and personal power whenever I put myself into the role of Sarah Crew. I, too, had somehow developed into an intelligent and extremely kind-hearted little girl. I, too, loved all people and sought to relate to everyone I encountered. I, too, cherished the variety and textural differences of individuals. When little Sarah does succeed in finding her father, against all odds, and reclaims her happy life, I was convinced over and over again that she had a magical quality, a heroism that few others could see or even imagine. I understood and I "believed" in Sarah and her magic; therefore, I too should be able to reconstruct negative realities into positive dreams. Unfortunately, this was a movie and not the story of my life; I was neither Sarah Crew nor Shirley Temple.

7   As I reflect back on the lessons I derived from this film, I see them now as decidedly mixed. For one thing, no amount of precociousness or sweetness will budge a truly mean-spirited opponent. Adults can be erratic in their response to children's demands; some of them at certain times will appreciate what you offer them and understand your neediness, responding with genuine softness and caring, while at other times they will become threatened and uneasy, pushing you and your problems far away. While watching Sarah wade through her dramas and hard times, I began to see the serious limitations of most of the people around me. I couldn't rely on the adults in my life to be as the adults were in the movie. They simply were not going to wake up and respond to me and to my problems as they did to the endearing, plucky Sarah. But, like Sarah, I saw, and continue to see, the value and larger truth offered in *The Little Princess*. For me, that truth was the insight that we must take a stand about who we believe ourselves to be, and about what kind of people we want to become as adults. As with little Sarah's situation, there aren't any guarantees about what lies ahead. Goodness must be its own reward, not a means to an end.

8   So, here are the really hard questions I was left to answer: What kind of a person am I? Am I kind, generous and noble even if my father is missing in action

and I am a pauper? Am I sweet and giving and intelligent, even if my parents are alcoholics and abuse me? Does who I am depend on how others behave toward me? Am I strong enough and intelligent and brave enough to separate my choices about my character development from the negative, reactionary responses I sometimes receive when I simply try to be myself? Well, it hasn't been easy, but I always figured this: Sarah Crew was proof positive that someone else on this earth had thoughts similar to mine, and if Shirley Temple, in *The Little Princess*, could be the little girl I wanted to be, then so could I.

Questions for Discussion

1. What fascination did the Shirley Temple movies hold for Terri Sevilla when she was a young girl? Now as an adult, does she regard them differently from the way she responded to them as a child?

2. How did the difficulties experienced within Sevilla's family life in her early years help to motivate her positive responses to *The Little Princess*? Could Sevilla have provided more details about her family life, or do you know enough to understand her need for a hero like Sarah Crew?

3. Does the essay provide us with enough details from *The Little Princess* so that, if you had never seen a Shirley Temple film, you could understand the impact these films had on Sevilla? What other details might she have provided?

4. Compare the way Terri Sevilla describes her family life and her changing responses to *The Little Princess* with the way Terry McMillan describes her responses to *The Wizard of Oz*. What similar needs do the two films fulfill for both Sevilla and McMillan, despite their differences in social class and background? How are their responses to the fantasies created by the films different?

5. Do you agree with Sevilla's conclusion that child film heroes like Sarah Crew are basically positive influences in the lives of young people?

 ## Amanda Morgan

When Beauty Is the Beast

Amanda Morgan (b. 1975), a native Texan, remembers writing her first poem, "School Days," when she was four; writing is still the best way for her to develop self-understanding. Morgan who wrote this essay in her freshman year is now completing a Master's Degree in International Relations. She realizes that her interest in writing about the beauty myth is rooted in her experiences as a child training for the ballet; even then being thin was a prerequisite to success that was enforced by competition. At college Morgan sees the destructive impact of the mass fitness and dieting hysteria on many women's self-esteem. In researching and writing this paper, Morgan hoped to create a source of information to "loosen the ties that paralyze women in a contemporary corset: the ideal of thinness."

JOURNAL

Statistics suggest that more and more adolescents and college women are suffering from eating disorders. What do you think are the causes of this health problem? To what extent is the problem a community issue?

1   Headlines blare "Thin is in," and impossibly lean yet curvaceous models haunt commercials. They smile as if to say, "Go on a strict carrot diet, take 3 aerobics classes a day, and when you look like me . . . you'll be happy!" Unfortunately, most women will never be able to achieve the exclusive ideal that defines beauty in our society. Vegetables and stair master will only go so far; in the end, one's shape is more dependent upon genetics than self-control. Cultural standards of beauty promote body image ideals that are unachievable for most women, and thus detrimental to women's physical and psychological health.

2   All of the ways that a woman views her body, as beautiful, ugly, too fat, or too thin, combine to form her body image, which represents her perception of her physical appearance. Body image is an integral part of a woman's self-concept. The role of body image in the construction of self-confidence has significant implications, considering the importance of self-confidence in determining how people interact with others. Twenty-five to thirty-three percent of a person's sense of confidence is dependent upon body image (Lang 68). Since self-confidence often affects one's ability to communicate, express, and assert oneself, body image impacts all aspects of life from social relationships to occupational success. The significance of body image extends far beyond what a woman eats and wears.

3   Another cause of eating disorders in women is the social assumption that a woman's unhappiness is trivial compared to other modern social problems. A woman who worries about her appearance is considered vain; in fact, many believe that a woman who diets has a personality flaw. I've long suspected that many men don't hold much respect for dieting, or women who are obsessed with their weight. My suspicions were confirmed once on a dinner date. Usually, I drink diet coke, and have for so long that regular sodas taste much too sweet. However, as I was ordering my dinner, some inner urge compelled me to order a regular coke. After we ordered, my date made a big deal about my drink choice. Explaining that he didn't like to see women drink "those horrible tasting" diet sodas, he offered his approval of what he perceived to be my lack of concern over my weight. My date's focus on what I decided to eat is reflective of a double standard in society that constantly feeds women messages to change their body, often through weight loss, while at the same time being unwilling to witness their struggle to maintain a slender body image or to even acknowledge the legitimacy of their struggle.

4   While one's appearance may not be crucial in the grand scheme of life, feelings that arise from a negative body image can have serious long-term consequences. Besides low self-esteem, low levels of confidence, and depression, negative body image takes its physical tolls. Feelings of fatness often result in what the American Psychiatric Association refers to as "pathological eating behavior" or disordered eating (Strauman 946). In extreme cases of dieting, women can become anorexic, an eating disorder characterized by self-starvation, or bulimic, an eating disorder characterized by frequent and compulsive binge eating followed by purging (Rodin, *Body Traps* 36). These syndromes aren't always treated with the same seriousness given to other public health threats, despite the prevalence of fatalities. However, eating disorders are real problems and must be recognized as such, for real people die because of them. Statistics suggest that more American women die of anorexia in a period of twelve months than the total number of people who died from AIDS, from the beginning of the epidemic to 1988 (Wolfe 182).

5   While most women don't suffer to the extreme of becoming anorexic or bulimic, chronic dieting to lose weight has become an unfortunate societal norm. Despite wide-range acceptance of dieting as the solution to body dissatisfaction, dieting has been shown to be ineffective in permanent weight reduction, for all but 1% of women. Kelly Brownell, a psychologist and weight loss expert at Yale University, points out that "if one defines successful [dieting] as reaching ideal body weight and maintaining it for five years, a person is more likely to recover from almost any form of cancer than from obesity" (Rodin, *Body Traps* 167). For the 72% of American women who diet and the ever increasing numbers of men, the quest to mold a better body, while not ending in anorexia or bulimia, often leads to increased unhappiness and increased obesity (Rodin, *Body Traps* 166). Besides being ineffectual, dieting has serious physiological effects, including a suppressed metabolic rate, broken-down muscle tissue (which further decreases the body's calorie burning capacity), increased ability to store food as fat, and increased desire for high-fat foods. Dieting upsets the body's natural chemistry, thus supporting the weight problem it is supposed to remedy (Brainin-Rodriquez 1).

6   Since diets are often hard to maintain, many women end up in a cycle of alternating periods of dieting and nondieting. This inconsistent way of eating further confuses the body's chemistry, increasing the ease of weight gain (through more efficient use of food), and decreasing the body's ability to lose weight. This "yo-yo" dieting and subsequent weight fluctuation has also been correlated with an increased risk for heart disease (Rodin, *Body Traps* 187). If a person desperately desires to lose weight, the most long-term and healthy solution lies in a change of life-styles, a permanent commitment to health, consisting of a balanced but not restrictive low-fat diet and moderate exercise. However, a person must overcome a negative body image and learn to love himself/herself at any weight. Due to widespread failure of dieting efforts and the associated health risks, alleviating body dissatisfaction might be more successful through an emphasis on changing one's attitude rather than changing one's body.

7   In our culture, the decision to diet arises more often in response to a negative body image than a desire to improve health (Myers and Biocca 112). Women diet

to lose this weight that doesn't conform to the current beauty ideal, which praises a slim lower body. Most women store fat on their thighs, buttocks, and hips, areas which generally don't pose the risk of later health complications. In fact, this extra fatty tissue is natural and necessary for women's bodies to function properly. Fat is essential for menstruation, childbearing, nursing, and the production and storage of estrogen after menopause (Tavris 34). Many women diet to lose fat, when the fat itself doesn't put them at a medical risk.

8   Not only is dieting often the result of the psychological conflict that occurs when a person's actual body image doesn't compare favorably to her ideal body image, but is compounded with additional negative psychological effects as well, including stress, preoccupation with food, and depression (Tavris 35). Dieting is also seen by society as an indication or sign of an individual's self-control and will power. By correlating dieting with self-control, dieting takes on additional importance in a woman's identity, which can result in intense feelings of worthlessness and personal failure if the diet is broken. Women's "obsession" and dissatisfaction with their physiques have serious physical and psychological implications.

9   The fact that there are so many women afflicted by body dissatisfaction in America indicates that it is not just an individual, personal problem, but a societal issue derived from values in American or Western culture. Society must begin to recognize negative body image as a harmful disorder that deserves and requires treatment, rather than trivialize its significance by confusing it with vanity. Women are judging themselves against unrealistic standards of beauty presented through the media. "Every day women are flooded with portrayals of flawless models and actresses. Their beauty seems real and attainable and becomes the standard for attractiveness" (Lang 68). The standards of "beauty" that women strive to emulate are distorted and misleading. Magazine pictures, for example, have a hidden agenda; they manipulate women into believing that it is easy to look like the models when in fact models spend many hours with professional make-up artists and hair stylists before a shoot. Hundreds of pictures are taken from every angle, for each picture printed. Then the photo is airbrushed and sometimes literally cut with scissors to eliminate every minute flaw (Wolfe 83). The resulting faces and bodies that confront women are impossibly perfect; they only serve to lower women's self-esteem.

10   Fashion magazines play an intimate role in the lives of many women. I read *Seventeen* magazine from the time I was eleven years old to the middle of my high school career. From the time I spent pouring over the images and articles, I learned the secrets of womanhood, such as what a woman should look like, how a woman should dress, and how a woman must look, dress, and behave if she wishes to be competitive in the Great Boyfriend Quest. While deeply engrossed in a magazine, I experienced a feeling comparable to identifying with the heroine of a novel. For a brief period of time I could mentally become that model, imagining what it must feel like to be so beautiful—a method of vicariously feeling desirable. Then, of course, the advertisements and articles unveiled the secrets to the models' beauty, providing hope to transform that beautiful, confident feeling from a fantasy to reality. I've since learned that you can't buy happiness in a mascara bot-

tle. However, I have discovered that it is possible to purchase misery in the form of women's fashion magazines. Once I realized that they made me feel insufficient and undesirable, I quit reading them.

11   Not only are women comparing themselves to unrealistic ideals, they are judging themselves through fun house mirrors, focusing on imagined and magnified imperfections. "A recent study showed that 95 percent of women think they are heavier than they really are—by an average of 25 percent" (Rodin, "The New Meaning of Thin" 226). Women's resulting body images are thus as hopelessly distorted as the images presented to them in the media. The media not only emphasize to a woman the differences between her body and the "ideal," but serve to broaden the gap in her mind, as she distorts her *actual* figure into perceived ugliness. A study measuring the effect of television advertising and programming on body image distortions in young women found that a woman's perception of her body shape can be altered by watching even 30 minutes of TV broadcasting (Myers and Biocca 108).

12   The media's gender bias in the promotion of thinness is well documented, from television shows and their characters to magazine advertisements and articles, and might explain why women seem to be more vulnerable to body dissatisfaction than men. For example, 69.1% of female TV characters were rated thin compared to 17.5% of male characters, while only 5% of women characters were rated as heavy, compared to 25.5% of male characters (Tavris 32). While the media may not be the original or only promoters of this exaggerated standard of thinness for women, it is one of the most influential due to the popularity of television, movies, and magazines (Myers and Biocca 110).

13   Advertisers take advantage of women's need to appear beautiful. They specifically target and exploit women's feelings about their body image, successfully promoting a $33-billion-a-year diet industry, a $20-billion-a-year cosmetics industry, and a $300-million-a-year cosmetic surgery industry (Wolfe, 17). "Ads aimed at women work by lowering their self-esteem" (Wolfe 276). Ads make women feel like they must alter some aspect of themselves in order to be beautiful, and then present the magical remedy in the form of the advertised product. If ads didn't make women feel incomplete, women wouldn't have a need for the promoted product. Day in and day out, women are manipulated in ways that are ultimately disempowering and destructive, all in the name of money.

14   Media images become even more powerful as thinness comes to reflect more than mere aesthetic ideal; in today's culture thinness is a social virtue that reflects acceptable personality, behavioral, and life-style patterns. "For many, weight is a quick and concrete barometer by which to measure how well they are doing as women" (Rodin "The New Meaning of Thin," 224). Thinness has become a metaphor for success, and a status symbol associated with "the good life" (Myers and Biocca 111). Due to the perceived correlation between achievement and thinness, women in professions and higher education are especially vulnerable to the obsession with body weight and to eating disorders, which can arise from a negative body image (Tavris 32). For example, I met a young woman the summer

before her freshman year at University of Michigan who has struggled against bulimia since junior high school. In her environment, bulimia seemed to be as com-
municable as the bubonic plague. She reported that the administrators of her New
York City college preparatory school were forced to lock all women's bathrooms
during the lunch hour to prevent women from vomiting their lunches.

15   The shape of a woman's body is perceived as a visible statement to the world of
her success, assuming that a "good body" represents personality characteristics
such as discipline and willpower that would lead to success in other areas of her
life as well. By allowing thinness and weight control to represent self-control, we
are assuming that body shape is more malleable than it actually is. There is a tendency to disregard the medical fact that the female body is genetically programmed to store fat (Rodin "The New Meaning of Thin" 224). The fat that is
necessary for the proper functioning of a woman's body has become a symbol of an
unwillingness to strive toward self-improvement. "Americans become convinced
that weight reveals something desperately true about the person beneath the
pounds" (Schwartz 5).

16   The female body is often seen as a symbol whose meaning evolves with the
changing social standards. The beauty ideal by which we judge women is constantly in flux, from Twiggy's straight boyish figure, to the voluptuous curves of
Marilyn Monroe. For any culture, at any specific time, beauty requires a definition. This unstable definition is written in response to the historical and socioeconomic realities of the era. During the years in which motherhood and domes-
ticity are promoted, the beauty ideal leans toward voluptuous, full-breasted
women. Conversely, during ages in which women have entered the work force or
pursued educational opportunities, slender, strong, "boyish" figures are esteemed
(Tavris 30). The current "hybrid" ideal, valuing full breasts, narrow hips, and a
slim lower body, is a reflection of society's uncertainty with regard to the woman's
role within society, requiring women to be both career- and family-oriented
(Tavris 33).

17   America's willingness to "judge the book by the cover" and assume a correlation between personality characteristics and body shape is irrational, for the
beauty ideal is neither timeless or universal. Images of ideal beauty are "wholly socially constructed" (Ussher 38). However, there does seem to be a recurring trend
of a beauty ideal which rejects women's natural bodies, requiring barbaric, painful
and often deforming and debilitating alterations. For example, wealthy Chinese
women succumbed to "footbinding," which stunted foot growth, producing 3-
inch stubs for feet. Unable to walk without assistance, women achieved this feminine ideal at the expense of excruciating pain and handicap (Ussher 33). Female
circumcision is another example of an ideal that promotes the mutilation of
women's bodies to fit into a standard of feminine and sexual attractiveness
(Ussher 33).

18   This barbarism in the name of beauty is also prevalent in Western culture and
history. For instance, Victorian women wore corsets that forced their bodies into
exaggerated hourglass shapes, sometimes crushing and damaging internal organs.
Despite popular belief, modern day "liberated" women are not much better off

than their Victorian sisters. Though the corset has been abandoned, women are still "forcing their bodies into exaggeratedly slim shapes, or increasingly, into exaggeratedly voluptuous shapes" to fit societal ideas of beauty and fashion (Tavris 36). Women diet, exercise excessively, and even seek a surgeon's knife to conform to modern, Western ideals of sexual appeal. All these varied cultural practices "share the violent subjugation of women in the name of feminine beauty and enhancement of sexual desirability, permissible because of the ideology which defines a woman's worth through her attractiveness to men" (Ussher 33).

19   In the quest to overcome a negative body image, there are other aspects of one's life that are more malleable to permanent change than the actual flesh of one's physique. For instance a change in attitude may go a long way in contributing to the creation of a healthy body image. The body should be regarded in a respectful manner, and treated with equal respect by nourishing it with healthy food, moderate exercise, relaxation, and pleasure (Rodin, *Body Traps* 249). Developing strategies to avoid situations and people who contribute to feelings of personal negativism is also helpful. For example, if working out is painful and leaves one with feelings of inferiority because the "workout buddy" looks like spandex was created especially to display every perfect curve of her body, then one should find another activity to share with Ms. Spandex Queen (and another workout buddy!).

20   In the struggle to forge a positive body image, it is also important to guard against the careless acceptance of society's ideas as one's own. As long as women accept the external, narrow standards of beauty dictated by society, they will be subjected to feelings of failure and low self-esteem. Actress Rosanne Barr Arnold is a good example of a person who has chosen to accept her body, rather than strive to conform to externally socially constructed standards that for her may be genetically unreachable. Arnold is not only a role model in terms of her positive individual decisions, but in her attempt to change society's narrowly defined ideals by publicly challenging widespread, common attitudes toward the stereotypes associated with obesity and the importance placed upon thinness.

21   Individuals need to recognize that a person's human value is in no way correlated with external, socially constructed concepts of "beauty." Women must learn to be content with their own unique and innate beauty, and abandon the endless struggle to be beautiful according to the culturally prescribed definition. Once women learn to find beauty by looking inward instead of out, they will be more likely to find confidence and success.

WORKS CITED

Brainin-Rodriguez, Laura. "Dieting and You." Joint Nutrition Education Program by Stanford University Food Service and Cowell's Health Promotion Program Information Sheet.

Lang, Susan. "Shape Up Your Body Image." *New Woman* March 1933: 68–70.

Myers, Philip, and Frank Biocca. "The Elastic Body Image: The Effect of Television Advertising and Programming on Body Image Distortions in Young Women." *Journal of Communication*, 42.3 (1992): 108–133.

Rodin, Dr. Judith. *Body Traps*. New York: William Morrow Company, 1992.

———. "The New Meaning of Thin." *Glamour Magazine* May 1992: 224–227.

Schwartz, Hillel. *Never Satisfied*. New York: The Free Press, 1986.

Strauman, Timothy J. "Self-Discrepancies and Vulnerability to Body Dissatisfaction and Disordered Eating." *Journal of Personality and Social Psychology* 61 (1991): 946–956.

Tavris, Carol. *The Mismeasure of Women*. New York: Simon & Schuster, 1992.

Ussher, Jane M. *The Psychology of the Female Body*. New York: Routledge, 1989.

Wolfe, Naomi. *The Beauty Myth*. New York: Anchor Books, Doubleday, 1991.

Questions for Discussion

1. State Morgan's thesis in your own words.

2. List several examples of media images that perpetuate the myth that beautiful women are more desirable. Do these beauty myths affect you?

3. According to Morgan, in what ways do cultural standards of beauty affect a society and individuals within a society? Could you develop Morgan's argument? Explain why you agree or disagree with her point of view.

4. How much power do you think the media have in influencing individuals and social trends? For example, how powerful is the beauty myth? Develop your responses with evidence from your own experiences or observations.

5. How has the media's portrayal of women's social roles changed in the twentieth century? What new types of media portrayals would you like to see developed?

6. Was the essay convincing? Do you have any suggestions for ways to strengthen the argument?

Chapter Writing Topics

1. Many critics have commented that mass communications media often portray a biased or stereotyped image of minority groups, sometimes excluding certain groups altogether. Do research into the media coverage of one ethnic group and write up your conclusions in the form of a documented research essay.

2. Write a research paper that discusses the media's coverage and influence on the outcome of a significant event in your community, city, or state.

3. Write an essay that focuses on the ways that computers and the electronic environment have influenced your life or the life of someone close to you. Consider whether communication through computers and the World Wide Web are more positive than negative or more negative than positive.

4. Examine the current television schedule for programs that you think encourage imagination, creativity, and a concern for the inner life. Write an evaluative review of two or three such programs.

5. Write a research paper that addresses the impact of a particular mass medium or aspect of a medium on the values and self-concept of citizens in our society. Define and present examples of the problem, then suggest solutions such as legislation or citizen action. You could discuss such issues as children's TV programs, MTV, subliminal persuasion or

other forms of manipulative advertising, or excessive sex and violence in the media.

6. Write an essay that discusses the way that images of roles and behavior for women are created and reinforced by the mass media.

7. Write about a film that examines issues of advertising, propaganda, or mass media on the inner life of the individual. Watch the film and take notes on the dialogue and any other details that can be used to support the conclusions you draw; also read some critical responses to the film, both in popular journals and in specialized magazines that critique films. You might select a film from the following list:

Day of the Locust, Network, Broadcast News, 1984, Closet Land, The Kiss of the Spider Woman, The Celluloid Closet, Hoop Dreams, Pulp Fiction, To Die For, Johnny Mnemonic, Glengarry Glen Ross

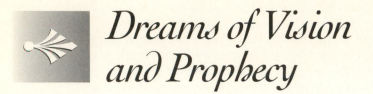

Dreams of Vision and Prophecy

9

Two gates there are that give passage to fleeting dreams; one is made of horn, one of ivory. The dreams that pass through sawn ivory are deceitful, bearing a message that will not be fulfilled; those that come through polished horn have truth behind them to be accomplished by people who see them.

HOMER
The Odyssey, Book XIX

I have a dream that my four little children will one day live in a nation where they will not be judged by the color of their skin, but by the content of their character.

MARTIN LUTHER KING, JR.
I Have a Dream

Holiness is a force, and like the others can be resisted. It was given, but I didn't want to see it, God or no God. It was as if God had said, "I am here, but not as you have known me. This is the look of silence and of loneliness unendurable: it too has always been mine, and now will be yours."

ANNIE DILLARD
A Field of Silence

Creativity, Problem Solving, and Synthesis

Creativity involves combining information and experience into a new form that solves problems and/or produces something that a person can take pride in, such as a piece of writing that is humanely and aesthetically satisfying, both to oneself and to others. While many people are inspired by the examples of creative visionaries in different fields and can learn from studying their techniques, creativity is fundamentally a generative rather than an imitative and technical process, a process of discovery that often originates in the unconscious mind. An open, receptive mental attitude encourages the initiation of the creative process.

Everyone is potentially creative; in fact, all people are creative for a part of each night when they dream, whether or not they are consciously aware of the process. As author John Steinbeck noted, a problem is often "resolved in the morning after the committee of sleep has worked it out." In waking life people are creative in a more conscious, directed manner, seeking solutions to problems in order to survive and to make their lives more comfortable and rewarding. For example, when you redecorate your room, look for a better job, or select a new course of study in school, you are working on creative solutions for the problems that you have recognized in your life.

Although it is true that everyone exercises some degree of creativity, it is equally true that most people have the potential to be far more creative in many aspects of their lives than they are currently. Writers, psychologists, and social scientists have identified patterns of behavior that are likely to block an individual's creativity. Understanding how these mental traps work may help you to find a way to release yourself from nonproductive behavior and to become more creative.

Habit Versus Risk

Habit and self-image can be major blocks to creativity. If your inner self-image is that of a person stuck in a round of repetitive daily tasks and rituals, it is unlikely that you will feel that you have the capacity to be creative. You may have come to believe that you really need to follow a ritualized pattern in performing your job, relating to people, or writing. This type of thinking also protects you from taking risks: the risk of an original expression of a feeling or situation, the risk of a controversial solution to a problem, the risk of not being understood by others.

Furthermore, creative risk-taking approaches to problem solving can be quite time-consuming. Many people convince themselves that they don't have the time to explore a new and creative approach, that it is more efficient to follow a method that has worked (or "sort of" worked) in the past. This inclination to play it safe and to be overly concerned with time management is typical of workers, managers, students, teachers, and writers who fear change and are wary of embarking on a new direction in their lives. Even if you see yourself as a non–risk-taking person, it is never too late to change; fantasizing about new approaches and thinking about alternatives is a positive first step toward finding creative solutions. Try to develop your alternative fantasies as do many of the writers in this chapter.

Reason Versus Intuition

You may be building another obstacle to uncovering your creativity if you value a linear, rational approach to handling problems to the extent that you ignore the imaginative, emotional, and intuitive side of the mind and the solutions that your imagination might suggest. Did you know that many landmark solutions to creative problems, both in the arts and in the sciences, were born in the unconscious mind and some specifically in dreams:

Descartes's philosophical system, the invention of the sewing machine needle, the pattern of the benzene ring, as well as the basic concepts for classic
works of literature such as Mary Shelley's *Frankenstein,* Samuel Taylor Coleridge's "Kubla Khan," and Robert Louis Stevenson's *The Strange Case of
Dr. Jekyll and Mr. Hyde.*

While we do not want you to think that all you have to do is to take a nap
and allow your problems to solve themselves or that if you sleep long enough
you will discover the seeds of great art and great ideas, we do encourage you
to look to your dream mind for ideas and feelings and to allow your unconscious mind to have time to process and integrate ideas that are being developed by your rational mind. For example, after you have finished the first
draft of a paper, go for a walk, or a swim, or listen to some music, or take a
nap. Let your unconscious mind have a chance to think about what you have
written. When you return to your first draft, you may find that your unconscious mind has sent you new ideas to work with or that you have a solution
to a problem in your paper that was concerning you.

Developing Self-Confidence: Learning to Trust Your Own Process as a Writer

Another barrier to the creative process can be built by an overeagerness to
please an authority such as a teacher. If you focus your energy on trying to
please your teacher at the expense of what you think or believe, an inner
conflict may keep you from writing your paper altogether. If you become
overreliant on your instructor's assignment and approval, you will not be developing your own working style and sense of independence, which every
writer must possess. Finally if you rush to produce a finished paper in one
draft, you will miss the excitement of discovery, the potential for personal involvement that is an essential part of the writing process; it is always preferable to relax and work within a writing project rather than to become overly
concerned with what it is supposed to be.

Evaluation and Application

The creative problem-solving process does include evaluation and application—but only after you give free expression to a range of imaginative solutions and ideas. Once you have finished the creative or generative part of
your writing project, you will want to think about whether or not you have
accomplished your goals. To evaluate your work you need to establish clear
standards so that you can compare your work with that of others. Always
try to formulate standards that are challenging and yet realistic.

Peer sharing can be a useful comparative and evaluative process that will
help you to create realistic standards for assessing your own writing in relationship to your classmates'. Through sharing your work as well as reading
and editing the work of your classmates, you will begin to develop realistic
standards for the style, structure, and content of your writing. Learn to ask

questions of yourself and of your peers. Develop criteria for evaluating papers as you go along. Soon you will find that you have established a vocabulary that allows you to talk about one anothers' papers and that you have defined some standards for effective writing.

Synthesis

Synthesis, the final step in the creative process, involves bringing a number of different ideas or solutions, which you may have considered separately, together to form an integrated solution. For example, if you are trying to decide on a method for presenting an essay on "How to Make Your Dreams Work for You," you will need to evaluate and then synthesize or integrate the different points of view of experts as well as your own on the subject of dream power. Synthesis is an excellent metaphor for the gathering and unifying of information from diverse sources that can produce a lively research paper such as Amanda Morgan's "When Beauty Is the Beast" in Chapter 8 or an imaginative story such as Ryan Wesley Bounds's "The New Enlightenment," which grew out of a year of campus discussions and much course work regarding controversial issues related to multiculturalism. In a sense, synthesis also defines the writing process itself, as writing involves bringing together a number of different skills to solve a variety of problems: engaging your reader's interest, persuading your reader, developing an overall structure and pattern, supporting your main ideas, and using language that is both appropriate and creative.

Writing is a rewarding activity that can help you to discover your own thoughts and feelings and to combine them in new ways. In performing any type of writing, you work through the stages and difficulties inherent in the creative process as a whole.

T H E M A T I C   I N T R O D U C T I O N

Prophetic dreams and visions provide valuable insights into the human spirit at its most creative, courageous, and hopeful. From ancient times to the present, people have discovered solutions to personal, aesthetic, social, and scientific problems as well as spiritual healing through paying heed to the messages from their unconscious minds and their dreams. The selections in this chapter present a variety of dreams of vision or prophecy from different cultures, generations, and social classes. We hope that reading and reflecting on these dreams and visions will help you develop insight into possible alternatives to the spiritual and social dilemmas we face today.

We begin with two poems that reflect on heaven. "The Tyger," William Blake's visionary poem, explores the double-sided nature of the human character and of creation itself. This poem urges us to think about what kind of God would make an intensely evil and yet compelling creature. In the second poem, "Heaven," by Cathy Song, the poem's speaker, a young mother, comments on her son's vision of heaven as China, the home of his ancestors.

The next selection also asks us to think about how we feel about our relationship to God and his intentions. Annie Dillard's "A Field of Silence" captures a moment of intense illumination; while living a life of solitude on a farm, she is taken by the power of God and the unknown. Finally Dillard must turn away from the intensity of her vision, yet she is changed by her insight. We hope that reading Dillard's reflection as well as the two poems that introduce this chapter will encourage you to think for a time about the world in its immensity, the world beyond the day-to-day routines and struggles that mark your rational journey.

What hopes do we have for our future? This is a question that all of us ask and that politicians, writers, and religious leaders often try to help us to answer through speculative or reflective writing and through direct calls to change: We see political values and the spiritual visions integrated in Black Elk's "The Great Vision." As a Sioux Indian medicine man, he writes of his vision of Native American solidarity and cultural renewal that became the cornerstone of his life, moving him to help his community change their destiny. The next reading, Martin Luther King's, "I Have a Dream," presents another kind of political and spiritual vision delivered in modern and biblical language to create a plea for a future free of racial injustice and exploitation: "[W]hen we allow freedom to ring, when we let it ring from every village and every hamlet, from every state and every city, we will be able to speed up that day when all of God's children, black men and white men, Jews and Gentiles, Protestants and Catholics, will be able to join hands and sing in the words of the old Negro spiritual: "'Free at last. Free at last. Thank God Almighty, we are free at last.'"

Following in the tradition of King's political and religious vision of the future, Terry Tempest Williams in "The Clan of One-Breasted Women" addresses another fundamental ethical issue: the morality of United States nuclear bomb testing in the Utah desert since the early 1970s, which continues to cause deaths from nuclear fallout. Williams sees women as the mothers of the earth who have a new responsibility: "The women couldn't bear it any longer. They were mothers. They had suffered labor pains but always under the promise of birth. The red hot pains beneath the desert promised death only, as each bomb became a stillborn. A contract had been made and broken between human beings and the land. A new contract was being drawn by the women, who understood the fate of the earth as their own."

Linda Hogan provides yet another perspective on our responsibility to the human community in her essay "The Voyagers." She explores the ways in which the Interstellar Record carried by the 1977 Voyagers reflects a collective and positive vision of our life here on earth: the Voyager becomes "a sacred space, a ritual enclosure that contains our dreaming the way a cathedral holds the bones of saints." And Hogan speculates about how the vision of our world sent into space for other human life on as yet unknown planets will be interpreted and about how our record can help us to see what is wrong with life on earth in the present. The next selection, a story, E. M. Forster's "The Other Side of the Hedge," presents a pastoral agrarian world that stands in contrast to the values of progress and the work ethic that propels those of us who accept life on the road as we know it in a capitalistic world.

We think that student writer Ivana Kim's dreams for the future will bring you inspiration as they combine her pragmatism and idealism in her essay. "Dreams as Conscious Visions." The second student selection, "The New Enlightenment," by Ryan Wesley Bounds, creates an ironic vision of a future "enlightened" society in which multiculturalism has become legally mandated.

Powerful writing is nurtured through connections: between the inner world of dreams and the imagination, between the world of experience and knowledge, between one's own feeling for and mastery of the conventions of language and written expression. As you gain more experience expressing and crafting your ideas about yourself, your world, and your hopes for the future, we hope that writing will become a vital and versatile means for expressing your visions.

William Blake

The Tyger

William Blake (1757–1827), who is now regarded as one of the greatest of the Romantic poets, was born in London and apprenticed at the age of fourteen to an engraver. Blake's engravings illustrated many popular books of his day as well as his own poems. Because his work was original and visionary, Blake was unable to get much of it published during his lifetime. In fact his hand-illustrated series of lyrical and epic poems, beginning with Songs of Innocence *(1789) and* Songs of Experience *(1794), which form one of the most strikingly original and independent bodies of work in the Western cultural tradition, were not published during his lifetime. Blake lived in poverty for the last twenty-five years of his life; his great contribution was not appreciated until after his death.*

JOURNAL

Describe and interpret an image that came to you in a dream or a nightmare, one that you consider creative and at the same time frightening.

Tyger! Tyger! burning bright
In the forests of the night,
What immortal hand or eye
Could frame thy fearful symmetry?

5 In what distant deeps or skies
Burnt the fire of thine eyes?
On what wings dare he aspire?
What the hand, dare seize the fire?

And what shoulder, & what art,
10 Could twist the sinews of thy heart?
And when thy heart began to beat,
What dread hand? & what dread feet?

What the hammer? what the chain?
In what furnace was thy brain?
15 What the anvil? what dread grasp
Dare its deadly terrors clasp?

When the stars threw down their spears,
And water'd heaven with their tears,
Did he smile his work to see?
20 Did he who made the lamb make thee?

Tyger! Tyger! burning bright
In the forests of the night,
What immortal hand or eye
Dare frame thy fearful symmetry?

Questions for Discussion

1. How and why is the tyger presented in the poem as an image in a nightmare? What other images are used to describe the tyger?
2. What is "fearful" about the tyger? Why does the speaker in the poem seem obsessed with the tyger?
3. What questions does the speaker pose about the tyger's origins and his creator? What are the implications of these questions?
4. What images are used to describe the possible tools that helped to create the tyger? What does each tool symbolize?
5. How are poetic effects such as rhyme, repeated vowel and consonant sounds, and patterns of rhythm used to intensify the fearful vision of the tyger?
6. What contrast is developed in the poem between the creator of the tyger and the maker of the lamb? Why is it difficult to imagine the same creator for both?

Ideas for Writing

1. Develop your journal entry into an essay in which you discuss the origins and implications of the dream-image described in the original entry. What does it reveal about your interests and creative process?
2. Write an interpretation of Blake's poem: How does the poem as a whole create or "frame" the tyger's "fearful symmetry," and what is revealed in the poem about the act of visionary creation?

 # Cathy Song

Heaven

Born in Hawaii in 1955 to a family that traced its origins to Korea and other parts of Asia, Cathy Song attended Wellesley College and Boston University, where she received an M.A. in creative writing. She has taught creative writing at a number of colleges in the United States and at the University of Hawaii. Her first book of poems, Picture Bride (1982), won the Yale Younger Poets Series. Her most recent book of poems, Frameless Windows, Squares of Light (1988), explores issues of family and multicultural heritage, as does the following poem, "Heaven," about a Chinese American boy who dreams of China as a promised land, in an ironic reversal of the dreams of many immigrants who travel to the United States.

JOURNAL

Explore your ideas of heaven or the afterlife. Did you believe more strongly in the afterlife as a child than you do now?

He thinks when we die we'll go to China.
Think of it—a Chinese heaven
where, except for his blond hair,
the part that belongs to his father,
5   everyone will look like him.
China, that blue flower on the map,
bluer than the sea
his hand must span like a bridge
to reach it.
10 An octave away.

I've never seen it.
It's as if I can't sing that far.
But look—
on the map, this black dot.
15 Here is where we live,
on the pancake plains
just east of the Rockies,
on the other side of the clouds.
A mile above the sea,
20 the air is so thin, you can starve on it.
No bamboo trees
but the alpine equivalent,
reedy aspen with light, fluttering leaves.
Did a boy in Guangzhou dream of this
25 as his last stop?

I've heard the trains at night
whistling past our yards,
what we've come to own,
the broken fences, the whiny dog, the rattletrap cars.
30 It's still the wild west,
mean and grubby,
the shootouts and fistfights in the back alley.
With my son the dreamer
and my daughter, who is too young to walk,
35 I've sat in this spot
and wondered why here?

Why in this short life,
this town, this creek they call a river?

He had never planned to stay,
40 the boy who helped to build
the railroads for a dollar a day.
He had always meant to go back.
When did he finally know
that each mile of track led him further away,
45 that he would die in his sleep,
dispossessed,
having seen Gold Mountain,
the icy wind tunneling through it,
these landlocked, makeshift ghost towns?

50 It must be in the blood,
this notion of returning.
It skipped two generations, lay fallow,
the garden an unmarked grave.
On a spring sweater day

55 it's as if we remember him.
I call to the children.
We can see the mountains
shimmering blue above the air.
If you look really hard
60 says my son the dreamer,
leaning out from the laundry's rigging,
the work shirts fluttering like sails,
you can see all the way to heaven.

Questions for Discussion

1. Why does the boy in the poem regard China as a "heaven"? Does his mother seem to share his feelings?
2. How does the mother describe the community where she and her family currently live? Does she seem happy there?
3. Who was the "boy in Guangzhou" (Canton, a seaport in southern China) to whom the mother refers? What was the boy's dream?
4. What is the importance of the image of the railroad in the poem? Why does the mother evoke the history of the Chinese American railroad laborers? How were their aspirations and dreams similar to and yet different from those of the mother and her son?

5. What is the significance of the imagery of "the laundry's rigging" and "work shirts fluttering like sails" in the last lines of the poem? What type of a "voyage" is suggested here?

Ideas for Writing

1. Interview older members of your family and ask them about their dream of the future and the afterlife. Write an essay in which you compare and contrast your own dreams of the future or afterlife with those of your older relatives. What did you learn about the origins of your own dreams about the future through learning more about the dreams of older family members?

2. Write an essay or poem about a country you have never visited that you imagined at one time as being "heavenly," as offering opportunities and values missing from your own society.

 Annie Dillard

A Field of Silence

See the headnote on Annie Dillard in Chapter 1. In her essay "A Field of Silence" (1978) Dillard explores a powerful vision she once had on a remote farm and reflects on the difficulty she has in accepting and sharing this kind of intense, visionary experience in a world that values rationality and scientific progress.

JOURNAL

Write about a moment on an ordinary day when you felt you were moving away from your familiar perception of reality and beginning to experience the world from a new perspective: as profoundly silent, vast, unified, in some sense different from "normal" experience.

1   There is a place called "the farm" where I lived once, in a time that was very lonely. Fortunately I was unconscious of my loneliness then, and felt it only deeply, bewildered, in the half-bright way that a puppy feels pain.

2   I loved the place, and still do. It was an ordinary farm, a calf-raising, haymaking farm, and very beautiful. Its flat, messy pastures ran along one side of the central portion of a quarter-mile road in the central part of an island, an island in Puget Sound, so that from the high end of the road you could look west toward the Pacific, to the Sound and its hundred islands, and from the other end—and from the farm—you could see east to the water between you and the mainland, and beyond it the mainland's mountains slicked smooth with snow.

3   I liked the clutter about the place, the way everything blossomed or seeded or rusted; I liked the hundred half-finished projects, the smells, and the way the animals always broke loose. It is calming to herd animals. Often a regular rodeo breaks out—two people and a clever cow can kill a morning—but still, it is calming. You laugh for a while, exhausted, and silence is restored; the beasts are back in their pastures, the fences not fixed but disguised as if they were fixed, ensuring the animals' temporary resignation; and a great calm descends, a lack of urgency, a sense of having to invent something to do until the next time you must run and chase cattle.

4   The farm seemed eternal in the crude way the earth does—extending, that is, a very long time. The farm was as old as earth, always there, as old as the island, the Platonic form of "farm," of human society itself and at large, a piece of land eaten and replenished a billion summers, a piece of land worked on, lived on, grown over, plowed under, and stitched again and again, with fingers or with leaves, in and out and into human life's thin weave. I lived there once.

5   I lived there once and I have seen, from behind the barn, the long roadside pastures heaped with silence. Behind the rooster, suddenly, I saw the silence heaped on the fields like trays. That day the green hayfields supported silence evenly sown; the fields bent just so under the even pressure of silence, bearing it, even, palming it aloft: cleared fields, part of a land, a planet, they did not buckle beneath the heel of silence, nor split up scattered to bits, but instead lay secret, disguised as time and matter as though that were nothing, ordinary—disguised as fields like those which bear the silence only because they are spread, and the silence spreads over them, great in size.

6   I do not want, I think, ever to see such a sight again. That there is loneliness here I had granted, in the abstract—but not, I thought, inside the light of God's presence, inside his sanction, and signed by his name.

7   I lived alone in the farmhouse and rented; the owners, Angus and Lynn, in their twenties, lived in another building just over the yard. I had been reading and restless for two or three days. It was morning. I had just read at breakfast an Updike story, "Packed Dirt, Churchgoing, A Dying Cat, A Traded Car," which moved me. I heard our own farmyard rooster and two or three roosters across the street screeching. I quit the house, hoping at heart to see Lynn or Angus, but immediately to watch our rooster as he crowed.

8   It was Saturday morning late in the summer, in early September, clear-aired and still. I climbed the barnyard fence between the poultry and the pastures; I watched the red rooster, and the rooster, reptilian, kept one alert and alien eye on me. He pulled his extravagant neck to its maximum length, hauled himself high on his legs, stretched his beak as if he were gagging, screamed, and blinked. It was a ruckus. The din came from everywhere, and only the most rigorous application of reason could persuade me that it proceeded in its entirety from this lone and maniac bird.

9   After a pause, the roosters across the street would start, answering the proclamation, or cranking out another round, arrhythmically, interrupting. In the same way there is no pattern nor sense to the massed stridulations of cicadas; their

skipped beats, enjambments, and failed alterations jangle your spirits, as though each of those thousand insects, each with identical feelings, were stubbornly deaf to the others, and loudly alone.

10   I shifted along the fence to see if Lynn or Angus was coming or going. To the rooster I said nothing, but only stared. And he stared at me: we were both careful to keep the wooden fence slat from our line of sight, so that this profiled eye and my two eyes could meet. From time to time I looked beyond the pastures to learn if anyone might be seen on the road.

11   When I was turned away in this manner, the silence gathered and struck me. It bashed me broadside from nowhere, as if I'd been hit by a plank. It dropped from the heavens above me like yard goods; ten acres of fallen, invisible sky choked the fields. The pastures on either side of the road turned green in a surrealistic fashion, monstrous, impeccable, as if they were holding their breath. The roosters stopped. All the things of the world—the fields and the fencing, the road, a parked orange truck—were stricken and self-conscious. A world pressed down on their surfaces, a world battered just within their surfaces, and that real world, so near to emerging, had got struck.

12   There was only silence. It was the silence of matter caught in the act and em-barrassed. There were no cells moving, and yet there were cells. I could see the shape of the land, how it lay holding silence. Its poise and its stillness were unen-durable, like the ring of the silence you hear in your skull when you're little and notice you're living, the ring which resumes later in life when you're sick.

13   There were flies buzzing over the dirt by the henhouse, moving in circles and buzzing, black dreams in chips off the one long dream, the dream of the regular world. But the silent fields were the real world, eternity's outpost in time, whose look I remembered but never like this, this God-blasted, paralyzed day. I felt my-self tall and vertical, in a blue shirt, self-conscious, and wishing to die. I heard the flies again; I looked at the rooster who was frozen looking at me.

14   Then at last I heard whistling, human whistling far on the air, and I was not able to bear it. I looked around, heartbroken; only at the big yellow Charolais farm far up the road was there motion—a woman, I think, dressed in pink, and pushing a wheelbarrow easily over the grass. It must have been she who was whistling and heaping on top of the silence those hollow notes of song. But the slow sound of the music—the beautiful sound of the music ringing the air like a stone bell—was isolate and detached. The notes spread into the general air and became the weightier part of silence, silence's last straw. The distant woman and her wheel-barrow were flat and detached, like mechanized and pink-painted properties for a stage. I stood in pieces, afraid I was unable to move. Something had unhinged the world. The houses and roadsides and pastures were buckling under the silence. Then a Labrador, black, loped up the distant driveway, fluid and cartoonlike, to-ward the pink woman. I had to try to turn away. Holiness is a force, and like the others can be resisted. It was given, but I didn't want to see it, God or no God. It was as if God had said, "I am here, but not as you have known me. This is the look of silence, and of loneliness unendurable: it too has always been mine, and now will be yours." I was not ready for a life of sorrow, sorrow deriving from knowledge I could just as well stop at the gate.

15   I turned away, willful, and the whole show vanished. The realness of things disassembled. The whistling became ordinary, familiar; the air above the fields released its pressure and the fields lay hooded as before. I myself could act. Looking to the rooster I whistled to him myself, softly, and some hens appeared at the chicken house window, greeted the day, and fluttered down.

16   Several months later, walking past the farm on the way to a volleyball game, I remarked to a friend, by way of information, "There are angels in those fields." Angels! That silence so grave and so stricken, that choked and unbearable green! I have rarely been so surprised at something I've said. Angels! What are angels! I had never thought of angels, in any way at all.

17   From that time I began to think of angels. I considered that sights such as I had seen of the silence must have been shared by the people who said they saw angels. I began to review the thing I had seen that morning. My impression now of those fields is of thousands of spirits—spirits trapped, perhaps, by my refusal to call them more fully, or by the paralysis of my own spirit at that time—thousands of spirits, angels in fact, almost discernible to the eye, and whirling. If pressed I would say they were three or four feet from the ground. Only their motion was clear (clockwise, if you insist); that, and their beauty unspeakable.

18   There are angels in those fields, and I presume, in all fields, and everywhere else. I would go to the lions for this conviction, to witness this fact. What all this means about perception, or language, or angels, or my own sanity, I have no idea.

Questions for Discussion

1. How does the "loneliness" Dillard experiences on the farm help to set the stage for her vision?
2. What causes Dillard's vision? Why does her vision end?
3. How does Dillard make the abstraction of "silence" concrete and alive? Why does she create such a vibrant image of the silence? How do you respond to her image?
4. Why is the stillness "unendurable"? What similes does Dillard use to express her concept? Why does she "try to turn away" from her vision? Why is her vision one of "sorrow"?
5. Why does Dillard reverse an accepted assumption by referring to the "regular world" as a "dream"? What does she mean by "regular" and "dream" in the context of her essay?
6. After having time to reflect, Dillard decides, "There are angels in those fields." How do you imagine the angels? Why is it significant that Dillard, usually so precise and perceptive, has "no idea" about the meaning of her vision and has difficulty talking about it? How do you interpret her vision?

Ideas for Writing

1. Write a reflective essay on a vision or an intense moment of insight you have had. Was it difficult for you to share this experience? Were you able to do so? In what form?

2. Write an essay in which you attempt to interpret Dillard's vision, based on what you know about her from reading this essay and "Aim for the Chopping Block" (Chapter 1). What does Dillard's vision reveal about her personality and values?

 ## Black Elk and John G. Neihardt

The Great Vision, from Black Elk Speaks

John G. Neihardt (1881–1973) was the Poet Laureate of Nebraska and a student of American Indian history and folklore. In the early 1930s he gained the trust of Black Elk, a visionary Sioux medicine man who was active in the Plains Indians Messiah Movement of the 1880s and a relative to Chief Crazy Horse. Black Elk Speaks (1932) retells the story of Black Elk's life and his vision quests. "The Great Vision" relates a vision Black Elk had as a child during a time of sickness. His vision of the revitalization of the Indian nation gave a purpose and direction to Black Elk's entire life and was an inspiration to his community.

JOURNAL

Write about a vision or dream you had in childhood that helped to shape the values and choices of your later life.

1   I entered the village, riding, with the four horse troops behind me—the blacks, the whites, the sorrels, and the buckskins; and the place was filled with moaning and with mourning for the dead. The wind was blowing from the south like fever, and when I looked around I saw that in nearly every tepee the women and the children and the men lay dying with the dead.

2   So I rode around the circle of the village, looking in upon the sick and dead, and I felt like crying as I rode. But when I looked behind me, all the women and the children and the men were getting up and coming forth with happy faces.

3   And a Voice said: "Behold, they have given you the center of the nation's hoop to make it live."

4   So I rode to the center of the village, with the horse troops in their quarters round about me, and there the people gathered. And the Voice said: "Give them now the flowering stick that they may flourish, and the sacred pipe that they may know the power that is peace, and the wing of the white giant that they may have endurance and face all winds with courage."

5   So I took the bright red stick and at the center of the nation's hoop I thrust it in the earth. As it touched the earth it leaped mightily in my hand and was a waga

chun, the rustling tree,* very tall and full of leafy branches and of all birds singing. And beneath it all the animals were mingling with the people like relatives and making happy cries. The women raised their tremolo of joy, and the men shouted all together: "Here we shall raise our children and be as little chickens under the mother sheo's† wing."

6   Then I heard the white wind blowing gently through the tree and singing there, and from the east the sacred pipe came flying on its eagle wings, and stopped before me there beneath the tree, spreading deep peace around it.

7   Then the daybreak star was rising, and a Voice said: "It shall be a relative to them; and who shall see it, shall see much more, for thence comes wisdom; and those who do not see it shall be dark." And all the people raised their faces to the east, and the star's light fell upon them, and all the dogs barked loudly and the horses whinnied.

8   Then when the many little voices ceased, the great Voice said: "Behold the circle of the nation's hoop, for it is holy, being endless, and thus all powers shall be one power in the people without end. Now they shall break camp and go forth upon the red road, and your Grandfathers shall walk with them." So the people broke camp and took the good road with the white wing on their faces, and the order of their going was like this:

9   First, the black horse riders with the cup of water; and the white horse riders with the white wing and the sacred herb; and the sorrel riders with the holy pipe; and the buckskins with the flowering stick. And after these the little children and the youths and maidens followed in a band.

10   Second, came the tribe's four chieftains, and their band was all young men and women.

11   Third, the nation's four advisers leading men and women neither young nor old.

12   Fourth, the old men hobbling with their canes and looking to the earth.

13   Fifth, old women hobbling with their canes and looking to the earth.

14   Sixth, myself all alone upon the bay with the bow and arrows that the First Grandfather gave me. But I was not the last; for when I looked behind me there were ghosts of people like a trailing fog as far as I could see—grandfathers of grandfathers and grandmothers of grandmothers without number. And over these a great Voice—the Voice that was the South—lived, and I could feel it silent.

15   And as we went the Voice behind me said: "Behold a good nation walking in a sacred manner in a good land!"

16   Then I looked up and saw that there were four ascents ahead, and these were generations I should know. Now we were on the first ascent, and all the land was green. And as the long line climbed, all the old men and women raised their hands, palms forward, to the far sky yonder and began to croon a song together, and the sky ahead was filled with clouds of baby faces.

---

*The cottonwood
†Prairie hen

17   When we came to the end of the first ascent we camped in the sacred circle as before, and in the center stood the holy tree, and still the land about us was all green.

18   Then we started on the second ascent, marching as before, and still the land was green, but it was getting steeper. And as I looked ahead, the people changed into elks and bison and all four-footed beings and even into fowls, all walking in a sacred manner on the good red road together. And I myself was a spotted eagle soaring over them. But just before we stopped to camp at the end of that ascent, all the marching animals grew restless and afraid that they were not what they had been, and began sending forth voices of trouble, calling to their chiefs. And when they camped at the end of that ascent, I looked down and saw that leaves were falling from the holy tree.

19   And the Voice said: "Behold your nation, and remember what your Six Grandfathers gave you, for thenceforth your people walk in difficulties."

20   Then the people broke camp again, and saw the black road before them towards where the sun goes down and black clouds coming yonder; and they did not want to go but could not stay. And as they walked the third ascent, all the animals and fowls that were the people ran here and there, for each one seemed to have his own little vision that he followed and his own rules; and all over the universe I could hear the winds at war like wild beasts fighting.*

21   And when we reached the summit of the third ascent and camped, the nation's hoop was broken like a ring of smoke that spreads and scatters and the holy tree seemed dying and all its birds were gone. And when I looked ahead I saw that the fourth ascent would be terrible.

22   Then when the people were getting ready to begin the fourth ascent, the Voice spoke like someone weeping, and it said: "Look there upon your nation." And when I looked down, the people were all changed back to human, and they were thin, their faces sharp, for they were starving. Their ponies were only hide and bones, and the holy tree was gone.

23   And as I looked and wept, I saw that there stood on the north side of the starving camp a sacred man who was painted red all over his body, and he held a spear as he walked into the center of the people, and there he lay down and rolled. And when he got up, it was a fat bison standing there, and where the bison stood a sacred herb sprang up right where the tree had been in the center of the nation's hoop. The herb grew and bore four blossoms on a single stem while I was looking—a blue,† a white, a scarlet, and a yellow—and the bright rays of these flashed to the heavens.

24   I know now what this meant, that the bison were the gift of a good spirit and were our strength, but we should lose them, and from the same good spirit we must find another strength. For the people all seemed better when the herb had grown and bloomed, and the horses raised their tails and neighed and pranced around, and I

---

*At this point Black Elk remarked: "I think we are near that place now, and I am afraid something very bad is going to happen all over the world." He cannot read and knows nothing of world affairs.
†Blue as well as black may be used to represent the power of the west.

could see a light breeze going from the north among the people like a ghost; and suddenly the flowering tree was there again at the center of the nation's hoop where the four-rayed herb had blossomed.

25   I was still the spotted eagle floating, and I could see that I was already in the fourth ascent and the people were camping yonder at the top of the third long rise. It was dark and terrible about me, for all the winds of the world were fighting. It was like rapid gun-fire and like whirling smoke, and like women and children wailing and like horses screaming all over the world.

26   I could see my people yonder running about, setting the smoke-flap poles and fastening down their tepees against the wind, for the storm cloud was coming on them very fast and black, and there were frightened swallows without number fleeing before the cloud.

27   Then a song of power came to me and I sang it there in the midst of that terrible place where I was. It went like this:

A good nation I will make live.
This the nation above has said.
They have given me the power to make over.

And when I had sung this, a Voice said: "To the four quarters you shall run for help, and nothing shall be strong before you. Behold him!"

28   Now I was on my bay horse again, because the horse is of the earth, and it was there my power would be used. And as I obeyed the Voice and looked, there was a horse all skin and bones yonder in the west, a faded brownish black. And a Voice there said: "Take this and make him over"; and it was the four-rayed herb that I was holding in my hand. So I rode above the poor horse in a circle, and as I did this I could hear the people yonder calling for spirit power, "A-hey! a-hey! a-hey! a-hey!" Then the poor horse neighed and rolled and got up, and he was a big, shiny, black stallion with dapples all over him and his mane about him like a cloud. He was the chief of all the horses; and when he snorted, it was a flash of lightning and his eyes were like the sunset star. He dashed to the west and neighed, and the west was filled with a dust of hoofs, and horses without number, shiny black, came plunging from the dust. Then he dashed toward the north and neighed, and to the east and to the south, and the dust clouds answered, giving forth their plunging horses without number—whites and sorrels and buckskins, fat, shiny, rejoicing in their fleetness and their strength. It was beautiful, but it was also terrible.

29   Then they all stopped short, rearing, and were standing in a great hoop about their black chief at the center, and were still. And as they stood, four virgins, more beautiful than women of the earth can be, came through the circle, dressed in scarlet, one from each of the four quarters, and stood about the great black stallion in their places; and one held the wooden cup of water, and one the white wing, and one the pipe, and one the nation's hoop. All the universe was silent, listening; and then the great black stallion raised his voice and sang. The song he sang was this:

"My horses, prancing they are coming.
My horses, neighing they are coming;
Prancing, they are coming.
All over the universe they come.
They will dance; may you behold them.   (4 times)

A horse nation, they will dance. May you behold them."   (4 times)

His voice was not loud, but it went all over the universe and filled it. There was nothing that did not hear, and it was more beautiful than anything can be. It was so beautiful that nothing anywhere could keep from dancing. The virgins danced, and all the circled horses. The leaves on the trees, the grasses on the hills and in the valleys, the waters in the creeks and in the rivers and the lakes, the four-legged and the two-legged and the wings of the air—all danced together to the music of the stallion's song.

30   And when I looked down upon my people yonder, the cloud passed over, blessing them with friendly rain, and stood in the east with a flaming rainbow over it.

31   Then all the horses went singing back to their places beyond the summit of the fourth ascent, and all things sang along with them as they walked.

32   And a Voice said: "All over the universe they have finished a day of happiness." And looking down, I saw that the whole wide circle of the day was beautiful and green, with all fruits growing and all things kind and happy.

33   Then a Voice said: "Behold this day, for it is yours to make. Now you shall stand upon the center of the earth to see, for there they are taking you."

34   I was still on my bay horse, and once more I felt the riders of the west, the north, the east, the south, behind me in formation, as before, and we were going east. I looked ahead and saw the mountains there with rocks and forests on them, and from the mountains flashed all colors upward to the heavens. Then I was standing on the highest mountain of them all, and round about beneath me was the whole hoop of the world.* And while I stood there I saw more than I can tell and I understood more than I saw; for I was seeing in a sacred manner the shapes of all things in the spirit, and the shape of all shapes as they must live together like one being. And I saw that the sacred hoop of my people was one of the many hoops that made one circle, wide as daylight and as starlight, and in the center grew one mighty flowering tree to shelter all the children of one mother and one father. And I saw that it was holy.

35   Then as I stood there, two men were coming from the east, head first like arrows flying, and between them rose the daybreak star. They came and gave a herb to me and said: "With this on earth you shall undertake anything and do it." It was the day-break-star herb, the herb of understanding, and they told me to drop it on the earth. I saw it falling far, and when it struck the earth it rooted and grew and flowered, four blossoms on one stem, a blue, a white, a scarlet, and a yellow; and the rays from these streamed upward to the heavens so that all creatures saw it and in no place was there darkness.

*Black Elk said the mountain he stood upon in his vision was Harney Peak in the Black Hills. "But anywhere is the center of the world," he added.

36   Then the Voice said: "Your Six Grandfathers—now you shall go back to them."

37   I had not noticed how I was dressed, until now, and I saw that I was painted red all over, and my joints were painted black, with white stripes between the joints. My bay had lightning stripes all over him, and his mane was cloud. And when I breathed, my breath was lightning.

38   Now two men were leading me, head first like arrows slanting upward—the two that brought me from the earth. And as I followed on the bay, they turned into four flocks of geese that flew in circles, one above each quarter, sending forth a sacred voice as they flew: Br-r-r-p, br-r-r-p, br-r-r-p, br-r-r-p!

39   Then I saw ahead the rainbow flaming above the tepee of the Six Grandfathers, built and roofed with cloud and sewed with thongs of lightning; and underneath it were all the wings of the air and under them the animals and men. All these were rejoicing, and thunder was like happy laughter.

40   As I rode in through the rainbow door, there were cheering voices from all over the universe, and I saw the Six Grandfathers sitting in a row, with their arms held toward me and their hands, palms out; and behind them in the cloud were faces thronging, without number, of the people yet to be.

41   "He has triumphed!" cried the six together, making thunder. And as I passed before them there, each gave again the gift that he had given me before—the cup of water and the bow and arrows, the power to make live and to destroy; the white wing of cleansing and the healing herb; the sacred pipe; the flowering stick. And each one spoke in turn from west to south, explaining what he gave as he had done before, and as each one spoke he melted down into the earth and rose again; and as each did this, I felt nearer to the earth.

42   Then the oldest of them all said: "Grandson, all over the universe you have seen. Now you shall go back with power to the place from whence you came, and it shall happen yonder that hundreds shall be sacred, hundreds shall be flames! Behold!"

43   I looked below and saw my people there, and all were well and happy except one, and he was lying like the dead—and that one was myself. Then the oldest Grandfather sang, and his song was like this:

"There is someone lying on earth in a sacred manner.
There is someone—on earth he lies.
In a sacred manner I have made him to walk."

44   Now the tepee, built and roofed with cloud, began to sway back and forth as in a wind, and the flaming rainbow door was growing dimmer. I could hear voices of all kinds crying from outside: "Eagle Wing Stretches is coming forth! Behold him!"

45   When I went through the door, the face of the day of earth was appearing with the daybreak star upon its forehead; and the sun leaped up and looked upon me, and I was going forth alone.

46   And as I walked alone, I heard the sun singing as it arose, and it sang like this:

"With visible face I am appearing.
In a sacred manner I appear.
For the greening earth a pleasantness I make.
The center of the nation's hoop I have made pleasant.
With visible face, behold me!
The four-leggeds and two-leggeds, I have made them to walk;
The wings of the air, I have made them to fly.
With visible face I appear.
My day, I have made it holy."

47   When the singing stopped, I was feeling lost and very lonely. Then a Voice
above me said: "Look back!" It was a spotted eagle that was hovering over and
spoke. I looked, and where the flaming rainbow tepee, built and roofed with
cloud, had been, I saw only the tall rock mountain at the center of the world.

48   I was all alone on a broad plain now with my feet upon the earth, alone but for
the spotted eagle guarding me. I could see my people's village far ahead, and I
walked very fast, for I was homesick now. Then I saw my own tepee, and inside I saw
my mother and my father, bending over a sick boy that was myself. And as I entered
the tepee, someone was saying: "The boy is coming to; you had better give him some
water."

49   Then I was sitting up; and I was sad because my mother and my father didn't
seem to know I had been so far away.

Questions for Discussion

1. What is the significance of the Nation's hoop, the flowering stick, the
   sacred pipe, and the giant wing? What importance do these symbols
   have in the American Indian culture and universally?

2. What are the "four ascents" that Black Elk and the Indian nation climb
   in the vision? Why are the ascents significant?

3. How would you interpret the images and symbols in each of the first
   three ascents: the holy tree, the people turned to animals, the broken
   hoop, and starving people?

4. Does the fourth ascent suggest a solution to the problems implied by
   the first three? What strengths of the Indian culture are implied
   through the images of the "sacred man . . . painted red," the black stallion, and the four virgins bearing the sacred symbols?

5. What is Black Elk's final vision at the peak of the fourth ascent? What
   force of unification does he find amongst humanity?

6. Why do the Grandfathers tell Black Elk to return "whence you came,"
   to the home of his parents?

Ideas for Writing

1. Write an essay in which you try to interpret Black Elk's vision in terms
   of the struggle of the Native Americans to reassert their cultural heritage after the coming of the white man.

2. Create your own vision of a future or an afterlife in which your people
   (friends, family, community) are strong and united. Try to use symbols
   that are especially meaningful to you and to your cultural heritage.

Martin Luther King, Jr.

I Have a Dream

Martin Luther King, Jr. (1928–1968), who came from a family of ministers, graduated from Morehouse University and received a Ph.D. in theology from Boston University. After graduation, King became a pastor and founded the Southern Christian Leadership Conference, developing the concept, derived from the teachings of Thoreau and Gandhi, of nonviolent civil disobedience resistance to obtain civil rights and an end to segregation. King won the Nobel Peace Prize in 1964 and wrote many speeches and essays on race and civil rights. "I Have a Dream," King's most famous speech, was originally delivered in 1963 in front of the Lincoln Memorial in Washington, D.C., before a crowd estimated at 300,000. Notice how King uses powerful language, images, and comparisons to express his idealistic dream of the future of America.

JOURNAL

Write about an idealistic dream that you have for the future of your country or your people.

1 I am happy to join with you today in what will go down in history as the greatest demonstration for freedom in the history of our nation.

2 Five score years ago, a great American, in whose symbolic shadow we stand today, signed the Emancipation Proclamation. This momentous decree came as a great beacon light of hope to millions of Negro slaves who had been seared in the flames of withering injustice. It came as a joyous daybreak to end the long night of their captivity.

3 But one hundred years later, the Negro still is not free; one hundred years later, the life of the Negro is still sadly crippled by the manacles of segregation and the chains of discrimination; one hundred years later, the Negro lives on a lonely island of poverty in the midst of a vast ocean of material prosperity; one hundred years later, the Negro is still languished in the corners of American society and finds himself in exile in his own land.

4 So we've come here today to dramatize a shameful condition. In a sense we've come to our nation's capital to cash a check. When the architects of our republic wrote the magnificent words of the Constitution and the Declaration of Independence, they were signing a promissory note to which every American was to fall heir. This note was the promise that all men, yes, black men as well as white men, would be guaranteed the unalienable rights of life, liberty, and the pursuit of happiness.

5 It is obvious today that America has defaulted on this promissory note in so far as her citizens of color are concerned. Instead of honoring this sacred obligation, America has given the Negro people a bad check, a check which has come back

marked "insufficient funds." But we refuse to believe that the bank of justice is bankrupt. We refuse to believe that there are insufficient funds in the great vaults of opportunity of this nation. And so we've come to cash this check, a check that will give us upon demand the riches of freedom and the security of justice.

6   We have also come to this hallowed spot to remind America of the fierce urgency of now. This is no time to engage in the luxury of cooling off or to take the tranquilizing drug of gradualism. Now is the time to make real the promises of democracy; now is the time to rise from the dark and desolate valley of segregation to the sunlit path of racial justice; now is the time to lift our nation from the quicksands of racial injustice to the solid rock of brotherhood; now is the time to make justice a reality for all of God's children. It would be fatal for the nation to overlook the urgency of the moment. This sweltering summer of the Negro's legitimate discontent will not pass until there is an invigorating autumn of freedom and equality.

7   Nineteen sixty-three is not an end, but a beginning. And those who hope that the Negro needed to blow off steam and will now be content, will have a rude awakening if the nation returns to business as usual. There will be neither rest nor tranquility in America until the Negro is granted his citizenship rights. The whirlwinds of revolt will continue to shake the foundations of our nation until the bright day of justice emerges.

8   But there is something that I must say to my people, who stand on the worn threshold which leads into the palace of justice. In the process of gaining our rightful place, we must not be guilty of wrongful deeds. Let us not seek to satisfy our thirst for freedom by drinking from the cup of bitterness and hatred. We must forever conduct our struggle on the high plain of dignity and discipline. We must not allow our creative protests to degenerate into physical violence. Again and again we must rise to the majestic heights of meeting physical force with soul force. The marvelous new militancy, which has engulfed the Negro community, must not lead us to a distrust of all white people. For many of our white brothers, as evidenced by their presence here today, have come to realize that their destiny is tied up with our destiny. And they have come to realize that their freedom is inextricably bound to our freedom. We cannot walk alone. And as we walk, we must make the pledge that we shall always march ahead. We cannot turn back.

9   There are those who are asking the devotees of Civil Rights, "When will you be satisfied?" We can never be satisfied as long as the Negro is the victim of the unspeakable horrors of police brutality; we can never be satisfied as long as our bodies, heavy with the fatigue of travel, cannot gain lodging in the motels of the highways and the hotels of the cities; we cannot be satisfied as long as the Negro's basic mobility is from a smaller ghetto to a larger one; we can never be satisfied as long as our children are stripped of their selfhood and robbed of their dignity by signs stating "For Whites Only"; we cannot be satisfied as long as the Negro in Mississippi cannot vote and a Negro in New York believes he has nothing for which to vote. No! No, we are not satisfied, and we will not be satisfied until "justice rolls down like waters and righteousness like a mighty stream."

10   I am not unmindful that some of you have come here out of great trials and tribulations. Some of you have come fresh from narrow jail cells. Some of you

have come from areas where your quest for freedom left you battered by the storms of persecution and staggered by the winds of police brutality. You have been the veterans of creative suffering. Continue to work with the faith that unearned suffering is redemptive. Go back to Mississippi. Go back to Alabama. Go back to South Carolina. Go back to Georgia. Go back to Louisiana. Go back to the slums and ghettos of our Northern cities, knowing that somehow this situation can and will be changed. Let us not wallow in the valley of despair.

11   I say to you today, my friends, so even though we face the difficulties of today and tomorrow, I still have a dream. It is a dream deeply rooted in the American dream. I have a dream that one day this nation will rise up and live out the true meaning of its creed, "We hold these truths to be self-evident, that all men are created equal." I have a dream that one day on the red hills of Georgia, sons of former slaves and the sons of former slave owners will be able to sit down together at the table of brotherhood. I have a dream that one day even the state of Mississippi, a state sweltering with the heat of injustice, sweltering with the heat of oppression, will be transformed into an oasis of freedom and justice. I have a dream that my four little children will one day live in a nation where they will not be judged by the color of their skin, but by the content of their character.

12   I HAVE A DREAM TODAY!

13   I have a dream that one day down in Alabama—with its vicious racists, with its Governor having his lips dripping with the words of interposition and nullification—one day right there in Alabama, little black boys and black girls will be able to join hands with little white boys and white girls as sisters and brothers.

14   I HAVE A DREAM TODAY!

15   I have a dream that one day every valley shall be exalted, and every hill and mountain shall be made low. The rough places will be plain and the crooked places will be made straight, "and the glory of the Lord shall be revealed, and all flesh shall see it together."

16   This is our hope. This is the faith that I go back to the South with. With this faith we will be able to hew out of the mountain of despair a stone of hope. With this faith we will be able to transform the jangling discords of our nation into a beautiful symphony of brother-hood. With this faith we will be able to work together, to pray together, to struggle together, to go to jail together, to stand up for freedom together, knowing that we will be free one day. And this will be the day. This will be the day when all of God's children will be able to sing with new meaning, "My country 'tis of thee, sweet land of liberty, of thee I sing. Land where my fathers died, land of the pilgrims' pride, from every mountainside, let freedom ring." And if America is to be a great nation, this must become true.

17   So let freedom ring from the prodigious hilltops of New Hampshire; let freedom ring from the mighty mountains of New York; let freedom ring from the heightening Alleghenies of Pennsylvania; let freedom ring from the snow-capped Rockies of Colorado; let freedom ring from the curvaceous slopes of California. But not only that. Let freedom ring from Stone Mountain of Georgia; let freedom ring from Lookout Mountain of Tennessee; let freedom ring from every hill and mole hill of Mississippi. "From every mountainside, let freedom ring." And when this happens, and when we allow freedom to ring, when we let it ring from every

village and every hamlet, from every state and every city, we will be able to speed up that day when all of God's children, black men and white men, Jews and Gentiles, Protestants and Catholics, will be able to join hands and sing in the words of the old Negro spiritual: "Free at last. Free at last. Thank God Almighty, we are free at last."

Questions for Discussion

1. What is the "dream" to which the title of the essay refers? What techniques or strategies does King use to define his dream? Is his definition effective? Why or why not?
2. What does King mean by his analogy of a "promissory note"? Is this an effective metaphor?
3. Who is the primary audience of King's speech, the "we" to whom he refers in paragraph 4, the "you" in paragraph 10? How does King try to appeal to the needs and concerns of this audience?
4. Who is the secondary audience for the speech, other than those to whom he refers as having "come to our nation's capital to cash a check"? What rhetorical strategies in the speech are designed to stretch its message beyond the immediate needs and expectations of the present audience and to appeal to other audiences?
5. What does King mean by "creative suffering" in paragraph 10? How does this expression reflect different aspects of his vision of nonviolent resistance?
6. How does King use repetition of images, phrases, and entire sentences to help convey his dream to his audience? Provide examples.

Ideas for Writing

1. Write an essay that discusses a dream that you have for your society. Express your dream in emotional and persuasive language and imagery that is designed to appeal to a specific audience that you understand well. Be clear about your intended audience before you begin to write.
2. Write a letter to King in response to his "dream" speech. If he were alive today, would he feel that parts of his dream had "come true"? What aspects of his dream still need to be accomplished?

 ## Terry Tempest Williams

The Clan of One-Breasted Women

Terry Tempest Williams works as a naturalist for the Utah Museum of Natural History and lives with her husband in the mountains outside of Salt Lake City. She is a well-respected nature writer; some of her better known published works in-

clude Pieces of White Shell *(1984)*, Coyote's Canyon *(1989)*, An Unspoken Hunger *(1994)*, *and* Desert Quartet *(1995)*. *"The Clan of One-Breasted
Women" is excerpted from* Refuge: An Unnatural History of Family and
Place *(1992)*. *As you read this selection think about how many aspects of your
lifestyle and health are being affected by misuse of the natural environment.*

<hr>

JOURNAL

Write about an event you have witnessed, learned about, or participated in
that involved a protest against some form of social injustice.

<hr>

1   I belong to a Clan of One-Breasted Women. My mother, my grandmothers, and
    six aunts have all had mastectomies. Seven are dead. The two who survive have
    just completed rounds of chemotherapy and radiation.

2   I've had my own problems: two biopsies for breast cancer and a small tumor be-
    tween my ribs diagnosed as a "borderline malignancy."

3   This is my family history.

4   Most statistics tell us breast cancer is genetic, hereditary, with rising percent-
    ages attached to fatty diets, childlessness, or becoming pregnant after thirty. What
    they don't say is living in Utah may be the greatest hazard of all.

5   We are a Mormon family with roots in Utah since 1847. The "word of wisdom"
    in my family aligned us with good foods—no coffee, no tea, tobacco, or alcohol.
    For the most part, our women were finished having their babies by the time they
    were thirty. And only one faced breast cancer prior to 1960. Traditionally, as a
    group of people, Mormons have a low rate of cancer.

6   Is our family a cultural anomaly? The truth is, we didn't think about it. Those
    who did, usually the men, simply said, "bad genes." The women's attitude was
    stoic. Cancer was part of life. On February 16, 1971, the eve of my mother's
    surgery, I accidentally picked up the telephone and overheard her ask my grand-
    mother what she could expect.

7   "Diane, it is one of the most spiritual experiences you will ever encounter."

8   I quietly put down the receiver.

9   Two days later, my father took my brothers and me to the hospital to visit her.
    She met us in the lobby in a wheelchair. No bandages were visible. I'll never for-
    get her radiance, the way she held herself in a purple velvet robe, and how she
    gathered us around her.

10 "Children, I am fine. I want you to know I felt the arms of God around me."

11 We believed her. My father cried. Our mother, his wife, was thirty-eight years
    old.

12 A little over a year after Mother's death, Dad and I were having dinner to-
    gether. He had just returned from St. George, where the Tempest Company was
    completing the gas lines that would service southern Utah. He spoke of his love
    for the country, the sandstoned landscape, bare-boned and beautiful. He had just

finished hiking the Kolob trail in Zion National Park. We got caught up in reminiscing, recalling with fondness our walk up Angel's Landing on his fiftieth birthday and the years our family had vacationed there.

13   Over dessert, I shared a recurring dream of mine. I told my father that for years, as long as I could remember, I saw this flash of light in the night in the desert—that this image had so permeated my being that I could not venture south without seeing it again, on the horizon, illuminating buttes and mesas.

14   "You did see it," he said.

15   "Saw what?"

16   "The bomb. The cloud. We were driving home from Riverside, California. You were sitting on Diane's lap. She was pregnant. In fact, I remember the day, September 7, 1957. We had just gotten out of the Service. We were driving north, past Las Vegas. It was an hour or so before dawn, when this explosion went off. We not only heard it, but felt it. I thought the oil tanker in front of us had blown up. We pulled over and suddenly, rising from the desert floor, we saw it, clearly, this golden-stemmed cloud, the mushroom. The sky seemed to vibrate with an eerie pink glow. Within a few minutes, a light ash was raining on the car."

17   I stared at my father.

18   "I thought you knew that," he said. "It was a common occurrence in the fifties."

19   It was at this moment that I realized the deceit I had been living under. Children growing up in the American Southwest, drinking contaminated milk from contaminated cows, even from the contaminated breasts of their mothers, my mother—members, years later, of the Clan of One-Breasted Women.

20   It is a well-known story in the Desert West, "The Day We Bombed Utah," or more accurately, the years we bombed Utah: above ground atomic testing in Nevada took place from January 27, 1951 through July 11, 1962. Not only were the winds blowing north covering "low-use segments of the population" with fallout and leaving sheep dead in their tracks, but the climate was right. The United States of the 1950s was red, white, and blue. The Korean War was raging. McCarthyism was rampant. Ike was it, and the cold war was hot. If you were against nuclear testing, you were for a communist regime.

21   Much has been written about this "American nuclear tragedy." Public health was secondary to national security. The Atomic Energy Commissioner, Thomas Murray, said, "Gentlemen, we must not let anything interfere with this series of tests, nothing."

22   Again and again, the American public was told by its government, in spite of burns, blisters, and nausea, "It has been found that the tests may be conducted with adequate assurance of safety under conditions prevailing at the bombing reservations." Assuaging public fears was simply a matter of public relations. "Your best action," an Atomic Energy Commission booklet read, "is not to be worried about fallout." A news release typical of the times stated, "We find no basis for concluding that harm to any individual has resulted from radioactive fallout."

23   On August 30, 1970, during Jimmy Carter's presidency, a suit was filed, *Irene Allen v. The United States of America*. Mrs. Allen's case was the first on an alpha-

betical list of twenty-four test cases, representative of nearly twelve hundred plaintiffs seeking compensation from the United States government for cancers caused by nuclear testing in Nevada.

24   Irene Allen lived in Hurricane, Utah. She was the mother of five children and had been widowed twice. Her first husband, with their two oldest boys, had watched the tests from the roof of the local high school. He died of leukemia in 1956. Her second husband died of pancreatic cancer in 1978.

25   In a town meeting conducted by Utah Senator Orrin Hatch, shortly before the suit was filed, Mrs. Allen said, "I am not blaming the government, I want you to know that, Senator Hatch. But I thought if my testimony could help in any way so this wouldn't happen again to any of the generations coming up after us . . . I am happy to be here this day to bear testimony of this."

26   God-fearing people. This is just one story in an anthology of thousands.

27   On May 10, 1984, Judge Bruce S. Jenkins handed down his opinion. Ten of the plaintiffs were awarded damages. It was the first time a federal court had determined that nuclear tests had been the cause of cancers. For the remaining fourteen test cases, the proof of causation was not sufficient. In spite of the split decision, it was considered a landmark ruling. It was not to remain so for long.

28   In April 1987, the Tenth Circuit Court of Appeals overturned Judge Jenkins's ruling on the ground that the United States was protected from suit by the legal doctrine of sovereign immunity, a centuries-old idea from England in the days of absolute monarchs.

29   In January 1988, the Supreme Court refused to review the Appeals Court decision. To our court system it does not matter whether the United States government was irresponsible, whether it lied to its citizens, or even that citizens died from the fallout of nuclear testing. What matters is that our government is immune: "The King can do no wrong."

30   In Mormon culture, authority is respected, obedience is revered, and independent thinking is not. I was taught as a young girl not to "make waves" or "rock the boat."

31   "Just let it go," Mother would say. "You know how you feel, that's what counts."

32   For many years, I have done just that—listened, observed, and quietly formed my own opinions, in a culture that rarely asks questions because it has all the answers. But one by one, I have watched the women in my family die common, heroic deaths. We sat in waiting rooms hoping for good news, but always receiving the bad. I cared for them, bathed their scarred bodies, and kept their secrets. I watched beautiful women become bald as Cytoxan, cisplatin, and Adriamycin were injected into their veins. I held their foreheads as they vomited green-black bile, and I shot them with morphine when the pain became inhuman. In the end, I witnessed their last peaceful breaths, becoming a midwife to the rebirth of their souls.

33   The price of obedience has become too high.

34   The fear and inability to question authority that ultimately killed rural communities in Utah during atmospheric testing of atomic weapons is the same fear I saw in my mother's body. Sheep. Dead sheep. The evidence is buried.

35   I cannot prove that my mother, Diane Dixon Tempest, or my grandmothers, Lettie Romney Dixon and Kathryn Blackett Tempest, along with my aunts developed cancer from nuclear fallout in Utah. But I can't prove they didn't.

36   My father's memory was correct. The September blast we drove through in 1957 was part of Operation Plumbbob, one of the most intensive series of bomb tests to be initiated. The flash of light in the night in the desert, which I had always thought was a dream, developed into a family nightmare. It took fourteen years, from 1957 to 1971, for cancer to manifest in my mother—the same time, Howard L. Andrews, an authority in radioactive fallout at the National Institutes of Health, says radiation cancer requires to become evident. The more I learn about what it means to be a "downwinder," the more questions I drown in.

37   What I do know, however, is that as a Mormon woman of the fifth-generation of Latter-day Saints, I must question everything, even if it means losing my faith, even if it means becoming a member of a border tribe among my own people. Tolerating blind obedience in the name of patriotism or religion ultimately takes our lives.

38   When the Atomic Energy Commission described the country north of the Nevada Test Site as "virtually uninhabited desert terrain," my family and the birds at Great Salt Lake were some of the "virtual uninhabitants."

39   One night, I dreamed women from all over the world circled a blazing fire in the desert. They spoke of change, how they hold the moon in their bellies and wax and wane with its phases. They mocked the presumption of even-tempered beings and made promises that they would never fear the witch inside themselves. The women danced wildly as sparks broke away from the flames and entered the night sky as stars.

40   And they sang a song given to them by Shoshone grandmothers:

Ah ne nah, nah	Consider the rabbits
nin nah nah—	How gently they walk on the earth—
ah ne nah, nah	Consider the rabbits
nin nah nah—	How gently they walk on the earth—
Nyaga mutzi	We remember them
oh ne nay—	We can walk gently also—
Nyaga mutzi	We remember them
oh ne nay—	We can walk gently also—

The women danced and drummed and sang for weeks, preparing themselves for what was to come. They would reclaim the desert for the sake of their children, for the sake of the land.

41   A few miles downwind from the fire circle, bombs were being tested. Rabbits felt the tremors. Their soft leather pads on paws and feet recognized the shaking sands, while the roots of mesquite and sage were smoldering. Rocks were hot from the inside out and dust devils hummed unnaturally. And each time there was another nuclear test, ravens watched the desert heave. Stretch marks appeared. The land was losing its muscle.

42   The women couldn't bear it any longer. They were mothers. They had suffered labor pains but always under the promise of birth. The red hot pains beneath the desert promised death only, as each bomb became a stillborn. A contract had been made and broken between human beings and the land. A new contract was being drawn by the women, who understood the fate of the earth as their own.

43   Under the cover of darkness, ten women slipped under a barbed-wire fence and entered the contaminated country. They were trespassing. They walked toward the town of Mercury, in moonlight, taking their cues from coyote, kit fox, antelope squirrel, and quail. They moved quietly and deliberately through the maze of Joshua trees. When a hint of daylight appeared they rested, drinking tea and sharing their rations of food. The women closed their eyes. The time had come to protest with the heart, that to deny one's genealogy with the earth was to commit treason against one's soul.

44   At dawn, the women draped themselves in mylar, wrapping long streamers of silver plastic around their arms to blow in the breeze. They wore clear masks, that became the faces of humanity. And when they arrived at the edge of Mercury, they carried all the butterflies of a summer day in their wombs. They paused to allow their courage to settle.

45   The town that forbids pregnant women and children to enter because of radiation risks was asleep. The women moved through the streets as winged messengers, twirling around each other in slow motion, peeking inside homes and watching the easy sleep of men and women. They were astonished by such stillness and periodically would utter a shrill note or low cry just to verify life.

46   The residents finally awoke to these strange apparitions. Some simply stared. Others called authorities, and in time, the women were apprehended by wary soldiers dressed in desert fatigues. They were taken to a white, square building on the other edge of Mercury. When asked who they were and why they were there, the women replied, "We are mothers and we have come to reclaim the desert for our children."

47   The soldiers arrested them. As the ten women were blindfolded and handcuffed, they began singing:

You can't forbid us everything
You can't forbid us to think—
You can't forbid our tears to flow
And you can't stop the songs that we sing.

The women continued to sing louder and louder, until they heard the voices of their sisters moving across the mesa:

Ah ne nah, nah
nin nah nah—
Ah ne nah, nah
nin nah nah—
Nyaga mutzi
oh ne nay—
Nyaga mutzi
oh ne nay—

"Call for reinforcements," one soldier said.

48   "We have," interrupted one woman, "we have—and you have no idea of our numbers."

49   I crossed the line at the Nevada Test Site and was arrested with nine other Utahns for trespassing on military lands. They are still conducting nuclear tests in the desert. Ours was an act of civil disobedience. But as I walked toward the town of Mercury, it was more than a gesture of peace. It was a gesture on behalf of the Clan of One-Breasted Women.

50   As one officer cinched the handcuffs around my wrists, another frisked my body. She found a pen and a pad of paper tucked inside my left boot.

51   "And these?" she asked sternly.

52   "Weapons," I replied.

53   Our eyes met. I smiled. She pulled the leg of my trousers back over my boot.

54   "Step forward, please," she said as she took my arm.

55   We were booked under an afternoon sun and bused to Tonopah, Nevada. It was a two-hour ride. This was familiar country. The Joshua trees standing their ground had been named by my ancestors, who believed they looked like prophets pointing west to the Promised Land. These were the same trees that bloomed each spring, flowers appearing like white flames in the Mojave. And I recalled a full moon in May, when Mother and I had walked among them, flushing out mourning doves and owls.

56   The bus stopped short of town. We were released.

57   The officials thought it was a cruel joke to leave us stranded in the desert with no way to get home. What they didn't realize was that we were home, soul-centered and strong, women who recognized the sweet smell of sage as fuel for our spirits.

Questions for Discussion

1. Why did the author's grandmother believe that a mastectomy is "one of the most spiritual experiences you will ever encounter"? Why do you think that the author's mother looks radiant after her mastectomy and tells her children, "I felt the arms of God around me"?

2. What is the meaning of Williams's recurring dream of a "flash of light" in the desert night? What real-world physical event does the dream recall? What are the long-term, hidden consequences of this event?

3. Why does Williams believe that "to deny one's genealogy with the earth was to commit treason against one's soul"? Why does Williams participate in the ritual protest in Mercury? Why are the protesters arrested for civil disobedience? With whose position are you in agreement?

4. What weapons does Williams have with her during the protest? Why do her weapons have more and less power than nuclear bombs that are being tested?

5. How does the officials' "cruel joke" on the protestors turn out differently from what they had expected? In what sense are the women victorious, despite the physical defeat of their protest?

6. What is Williams's purpose in writing this essay? Do you think that she would feel as her mother did if she were to develop breast cancer?

Ideas for Writing

1. Write your own script for an event designed to protest some social or environmental problem or injustice; if possible, stage your protest. Then write a report on its effect and reflect on its impact on the situation you were protesting and on your understanding of the social problem.
2. Develop your journal entry into an essay.

 # Linda Hogan

The Voyagers

Linda Hogan (b. 1947), who is a member of the Chickasaw tribe, was raised in Denver, Colorado. She completed her M.A. at the University of Colorado at Boulder in 1978. Hogan began her career teaching creative writing and Native American literature at the University of Colorado at Boulder and went on to teach poetry and literature in outreach programs in Colorado and Oklahoma. From 1982 to 1984 she was an assistant professor of English in the TRIBES program at Colorado Colleges Institute; she was an associate professor of American Indian Studies at the University of Minnesota from 1984 to 1989. Since then she has been an associate professor of English at the University of Colorado at Boulder. Hogan, "who has an eye for detail, and the Native American rituals and customs," has said, "My writing comes from and goes back to the community, both the human and the global community. I am interested in the deepest questions, those of spirit, of shelter, of growth and movement toward peace and liberation, inner and outer." Her most recent work includes The Big Woman: Stories *(1987),* Mean Spirit: A Novel *(1990),* Book of Medicines: Poems *(1993), and* Dwellings *(1995), in which "The Voyagers" appears*

JOURNAL

What dreams or fantasies do you have about space travel?

1   I remember one night, lying on the moist spring earth beside my mother. The fire of stars stretched away from us, and the mysterious darkness traveled without limit beyond where we lay on the turning earth. I could smell the damp new grass that night, but I could not touch or hold such black immensity that lived above our world, could not contain within myself even a small corner of the universe.

2   There seemed to be two kinds of people; earth people and those others, the sky people, who stumbled over pebbles while they walked around with their heads in clouds. Sky people loved different worlds than I loved; they looked at nests in treetops and followed the long white snake of vapor trails. But I was an earth person, and while I loved to gaze up at night and stars, I investigated the treasures at my feet, the veined wing of a dragonfly opening a delicate blue window to secrets of earth, a lusterless beetle that drank water thirstily from the tip of my finger and was transformed into sudden green and metallic brilliance. It was enough mystery

for me to ponder the bones inside our human flesh, bones that through some in-credible blueprint of life grow from a moment's sexual passion between a woman and a man, walk upright a short while, then walk themselves back to dust.

3   Years later, lost in the woods one New Year's eve, a friend found the way home by following the north star, and I began to think that learning the sky might be a practical thing. But it was the image of earth from out in space that gave me up-ward-gazing eyes. It was that same image that gave the sky people an anchor in the world, for it returned us to our planet in a new and loving way.

4   To dream of the universe is to know that we are small and brief as insects, born in a flash of rain and gone a moment later. We are delicate and our world is frag-ile. It was the transgression of Galileo to tell us that we were not the center of the universe, and now, even in our own time, the news of our small being here is treacherous enough that early in the space program, the photographs of Earth were classified as secret documents by the government. It was thought, and right-fully so, that the image of our small blue Earth would forever change how we see ourselves in context with the world we inhabit.

5   When we saw the deep blue and swirling white turbulence of our Earth re-flected back to us, says photographer Steven Meyers, we also saw "the visual evi-dence of creative and destructive forces moving around its surface, we saw for the first time the deep blackness of that which surrounds it, we sensed directly, and probably for the first time, our incredibly profound isolation, and the special fact of our being here." It was a world whose intricately linked-together ecosystem could not survive the continuing blows of exploitation.

6   In 1977, when the Voyagers were launched, one of these spacecraft carried the Interstellar Record, a hoped-for link between earth and space that is filled with the sounds and images of the world around us. It carries parts of our lives all the way out to the great Forever. It is destined to travel out of our vast solar system, out to the far, unexplored regions of space in hopes that somewhere, millions of years from now, someone will find it like a note sealed in a bottle carrying our his-tory across the black ocean of space. This message is intended for the year 8,000,000.

7   One greeting onboard from Western India says: "Greetings from a human be-ing of the Earth. Please contact." Another, from Eastern China, but resembling one that could have been sent by my own Chickasaw people, says: "Friends of space, how are you all? Have you eaten yet? Come visit us if you have time."

8   There is so much hope in those greetings, such sweetness. If found, these mes-sages will play our world to a world that's far away. They will sing out the strangely beautiful sounds of Earth, sounds that in all likelihood exist on no other planet in the universe. By the time the record is found, if ever, it is probable that the trum-peting bellows of elephants, the peaceful chirping of frogs and crickets, the wild dogs baying out from the golden needle and record, will be nothing more than a gone history of what once lived on this tiny planet in the curving tail of a spiral galaxy. The undeciphered language of whales will speak to a world not our own, to people who are not us. They will speak of what we value the most on our planet, things that in reality we are almost missing.

9   A small and perfect world is traveling there, with psalms journeying past Sat-

urn's icy rings, all our treasured life flying through darkness, going its way alone back through the universe. There is the recorded snapping of fire, the song of a river traveling the continent, the living wind passing through dry grasses, all the world that burns and pulses around us, even the comforting sound of a heartbeat taking us back to the first red house of our mothers' bodies, all that, floating through the universe.

10   The Voyager carries music. A Peruvian wedding song is waiting to be heard in the far, distant regions of space. The Navajo Night Chant travels through darkness like medicine for healing another broken world. Blind Willie Johnson's slide guitar and deep down blues are on that record, in night's long territory.

11   The visual records aboard the Voyager depict a nearly perfect world, showing us our place within the whole; in the image of a snow-covered forest, trees are so large that human figures standing at their base are almost invisible. In the corner of this image is a close-up of a snow crystal's elegant architecture of ice and air. Long-necked geese fly across another picture, a soaring eagle. Three dolphins, sun bright on their silver sides, leap from a great ocean wave. Beneath them are underwater blue reefs with a shimmering school of fish. It is an abundant, peaceful world, one where a man eats from a vine heavy with grapes, an old man walks through a field of white daisies, and children lovingly touch a globe in a classroom. To think that the precious images of what lives on earth beside us, the lives we share with earth, some endangered, are now tumbling through time and space, more permanent than we are, and speaking the sacred language of life that we ourselves have only just begun to remember.

12   We have sent a message that states what we most value here on earth; respect for all life and ways. It is a sealed world, a seed of what we may become. What an amazing document is flying above the clouds, holding Utopia. It is more magical and heavy with meaning than the cave paintings of Lascaux, more wise than the language of any holy book. These are images that could sustain us through any cold season of ice or hatred or pain.

13   In *Murmurs of Earth*, written by members of the committee who selected the images and recordings, the records themselves are described in a way that attests to their luminous quality of being: "They glisten, golden, in the sunlight, . . . encased in aluminum cocoons." It sounds as though, through some magical metamorphosis, this chrysalis of life will emerge in another part of infinity, will grow to a wholeness of its own, and return to us alive, full-winged, red, and brilliant.

14   There is so much hope there that it takes us away from the dark times of horror we live in, a time when the most cruel aspects of our natures have been revealed to us in regions of earth named Auschwitz, Hiroshima, My Lai, and Rwanda, a time when televised death is the primary amusement of our children, when our children are killing one another on the streets.

15   At second glance, this vision for a new civilization, by its very presence, shows us what is wrong with our world. Defining Utopia, we see what we could be now, on earth, at this time, and next to the images of a better world, that which is absent begins to cry out. The underside of our lives grows in proportion to what is denied. The darkness is made darker by the record of light. A screaming silence falls between the stars of space. Held inside that silence are the sounds of gunfire,

the wailings of grief and hunger, the last, extinct song of a bird. The dammed river goes dry, along with its valleys. Illnesses that plague our bodies live in this crack of absence. The broken link between us and the rest of our world grows too large, and the material of nightmares grows deeper while the promises for peace and equality are empty, are merely dreams without reality.

16   But how we want it, how we want that half-faced, one-sided God.

17   In earlier American days, when Catholic missions were being erected in Indian country, a European woman, who was one of the first white contacts for a northern tribe of people, showed sacred paintings to an Indian woman. The darker woman smiled when she saw a picture of Jesus and Mary encircled in their haloes of light. A picture of the three kings with their crowns and gifts held her interest. But when she saw a picture of the crucifixion, the Indian woman hurried away to warn others that these were dangerous people, people to fear, who did horrible things to one another. This picture is not carried by the Voyager, for fear we earth people would "look" cruel. There is no image of this man nailed to a cross, no saving violence. There are no political messages, no photographs of Hiroshima. This is to say that we know our own wrongdoings.

18   Nor is there a true biology of our species onboard because NASA officials vetoed the picture of a naked man and pregnant woman standing side by side, calling it "smut." They allowed only silhouettes to be sent, as if our own origins, the divine flux of creation that passes between a man and a woman, are unacceptable, something to hide. Even picture diagrams of the human organs, musculature, and skeletal system depict no sexual organs, and a photograph showing the birth of an infant portrays only the masked, gloved physician lifting the new life from a mass of sheets, the mother's body hidden. While we might ask if they could not have sent the carved stone gods and goddesses in acts of beautiful sexual intimacy on temple walls in India, this embarrassment about our own carriage of life and act of creative generation nevertheless reveals our feelings of physical vulnerability and discomfort with our own life force.

19   From an American Indian perspective, there are other problems here. Even the language used in the selection process bespeaks many of the failings of an entire system of thought and education. From this record, we learn about our relationships, not only with people, but with everything on earth. For example, a small gold-eyed frog seen in a human hand might have been a photograph that bridges species, a statement of our kinship with other lives on earth, but the hand is described, almost apologetically, as having "a dirty fingernail." Even the clay of creation has ceased to be the rich element from which life grows. I recall that the Chilean poet Pablo Neruda wrote "What can I say without touching the earth with my hands?" We must wonder what of value can ever be spoken from lives that are lived outside of life, without a love or respect for the land and other lives.

20   In *Murmurs of Earth*, one of the coauthors writes about hearing dolphins from his room, "breathing, playing with one another. Somehow," he says, "one had the feeling that they weren't just some sea creatures but some very witty and intelligent beings living in the next room." This revealing choice of words places us above and beyond the rest of the world, as though we have stepped out of our nat-

ural cycles in our very existence here on earth. And isn't our world full of those rooms? We inhabit only a small space in the house of life. In another is a field of corn. In one more is the jungle world of the macaw. Down the hall, a zebra is moving. Beneath the foundation is the world of snakes and the five beating hearts of the earthworm.

21   In so many ways, the underside of our lives is here. Even the metals used in the record tell a story about the spoils of inner earth, the laborers in the hot mines. Their sweat is in that record, hurtling away from our own galaxy.

22   What are the possibilities, we wonder, that our time capsule will be found? What is the possibility that there are lives other than our own in the universe? Our small galaxy, the way of the milk, the way of sustenance, is only one of billions of galaxies, but there is also the possibility that we are the only planet where life opens, blooms, is gone, and then turns over again. We hope this is not the case. We are so young we hardly know what it means to be a human being, to have natures that allow for war. We barely even know our human histories, so much having unraveled before our time, and while we know that our history creates us, we hope there is another place, another world we can fly to when ours is running out. We have come so far away from wisdom, a wisdom that is the heritage of all people, an old kind of knowing that respects a community of land, animals, plants, and other people as equal to ourselves. Where we know the meaning of relationship.

23   As individuals, we are not faring much better. We are young. We hardly know who we are. We face the search for ourselves alone. In spite of our search through the universe, we do not know our own personal journeys. We still wonder if the soul weighs half an ounce, if it goes into the sky at the time of our death, if it also reaches out, turning, through the universe.

24   But still, this innocent reaching out is a form of ceremony, as if the Voyager were a sacred space, a ritual enclosure that contains our dreaming the way a cathedral holds the bones of saints.

25   The people of earth are reaching out. We are having a collective vision. Like young women and men on a vision quest, we seek a way to live out the peace of the vision we have sent to the world of stars. We want to live as if there is no other place, as if we will always be here. We want to live with devotion to the world of waters and the universe of life that dwells above our thin roofs.

26   I remember that night with my mother, looking up at the black sky with its turning stars. It was a mystery, beautiful and distant. Her body I came from, but our common ancestor is the earth, and the ancestor of earth is space. That night we were small, my mother and I, and we were innocent. We were children of the universe. In the gas and dust of life, we are voyagers. Wait. Stop here a moment. Have you eaten? Come in. Eat.

Questions for Discussion

1. Hogan makes a distinction between sky people and earth people. Which of her own categories does she fit into? Which do you fit into? Why are her categories useful?

2. How does Hogan use detail and evidence to help you reflect on how the knowledge accumulated through the space program has affected the way that Americans see themselves?

3. What is included on the Interstellar Record for people who will be living in the year 8,000,000? Why is it so hopeful? Does thinking about the record encourage or inspire you to rethink your relationship to your community? In what ways?

4. Identify images and details that Hogan uses which give you a sense of visual space and perspective as well as of sound and feeling.

5. According to Hogan, what is wrong with the current definition of utopia? Do you agree or disagree with her? Why?

6. What does Hogan object to in the presentation of the *Murmurs of the Earth*? Discuss why you agree or disagree with her.

Ideas for Writing

1. Imagine that you are making the tape for the Voyager. Write an essay that describes the music you have selected and explains your choices. (You might want to actually make the tape and submit it with your essay.)

2. Hogan says, "We inhabit only a small space in the house of life." Draw a picture of the house of the world. Write an essay that discusses your picture—your home's structure and who inhabits the rooms.

3. Hogan believes, "We are having a collective vision. Like young men and women on a vision quest, we seek a way to live out the peace of the true vision we have sent to the world of stars." Write an essay in which you discuss why you see the space program as a collective vision.

 # E. M. Forster

The Other Side of the Hedge

E. M. Forster (1879–1970) was born in London and educated at Cambridge. Individualistic and liberal in his political views, Forster was a member of the Bloomsbury group, a distinguished coterie of writers and critics that included Virginia Woolf and Roger Frye. A prolific author of critical essays, stories, and social novels such as A Room with a View (1908) and Passage to India (1924), Forster wrote the utopian fantasy "The Other Side of the Hedge" (1903) during a transitional period in his early life, shortly after his graduation from Cambridge and after a trip to Greece and Italy. The story presents an alternative vision to competitive, technologically oriented modern lifestyles.

JOURNAL

Write about an experience, fantasy, or dream you have had in which you found yourself exhausted by your current lifestyle and imagined or ventured into an "alternate world" where you could relax and not be bothered by the pressures of competition.

1   My pedometer told me that I was twenty-five; and, though it is a shocking thing to stop walking, I was so tired that I sat down on a milestone to rest. People outstripped me, jeering as they did so, but I was too apathetic to feel resentful, and even when Miss Eliza Dimbleby, the great educationist, swept past, exhorting me to persevere, I only smiled and raised my hat.

2   At first I thought I was going to be like my brother, whom I had had to leave by the roadside a year or two round the corner. He had wasted his breath on singing, and his strength on helping others. But I had travelled more wisely, and now it was only the monotony of the highway that oppressed me—dust under foot and brown crackling hedges on either side, ever since I could remember.

3   And I had already dropped several things—indeed, the road behind was strewn with the things we all had dropped; and the white dust was settling down on them, so that already they looked no better than stones. My muscles were so weary that I could not even bear the weight of those things I still carried. I slid off the milestone into the road, and lay there prostrate, with my face to the great parched hedge, praying that I might give up.

4   A little puff of air revived me. It seemed to come from the hedge; and, when I opened my eyes, there was a glint of light through the tangle of boughs and dead leaves. The hedge could not be as thick as usual. In my weak, morbid state, I longed to force my way in, and see what was on the other side. No one was in sight, or I should not have dared to try. For we of the road do not admit in conversation that there is another side at all.

5   I yielded to the temptation, saying to myself that I would come back in a minute. The thorns scratched my face, and I had to use my arms as a shield, depending on my feet alone to push me forward. Halfway through I would have gone back, for in the passage all the things I was carrying were scraped off me, and my clothes were torn. But I was so wedged that return was impossible, and I had to wiggle blindly forward, expecting every moment that my strength would fail me, and that I should perish in the undergrowth.

6   Suddenly cold water closed round my head, and I seemed sinking down for ever. I had fallen out of the hedge into a deep pool. I rose to the surface at last, crying for help, and I heard someone on the opposite bank laugh and say: "Another!" And then I was twitched out and laid panting on the dry ground.

7   Even when the water was out of my eyes, I was still dazed, for I had never been in so large a space, nor seen such grass and sunshine. The blue sky was no longer a strip, and beneath it the earth had risen grandly into hills—clean, bare buttresses,

with beech trees in their folds, and meadows and clear pools at their feet. But the hills were not high, and there was in the landscape a sense of human occupation—so that one might have called it a park, or garden, if the words did not imply a certain triviality and constraint.

8   As soon as I got my breath, I turned to my rescuer and said:

9   "Where does this place lead to?"

10   "Nowhere, thank the Lord!" said he, and laughed. He was a man of fifty or sixty—just the kind of age we mistrust on the road—but there was no anxiety in his manner, and his voice was that of a boy of eighteen.

11   "But it must lead somewhere!" I cried, too much surprised at his answer to thank him for saving my life.

12   "He wants to know where it leads!" he shouted to some men on the hill side, and they laughed back, and waved their caps.

13   I noticed then that the pool into which I had fallen was really a moat which bent round to the left and to the right, and that the hedge followed it continually. The hedge was green on this side—its roots showed through the clear water, and fish swam about in them—and it was wreathed over with dog-roses and Traveller's Joy. But it was a barrier, and in a moment I lost all pleasure in the grass, the sky, the trees, the happy men and women, and realized that the place was but a prison, for all its beauty and extent.

14   We moved away from the boundary, and then followed a path almost parallel to it, across the meadows. I found it difficult walking, for I was always trying to out-distance my companion, and there was no advantage in doing this if the place led nowhere. I had never kept step with anyone since I left my brother.

15   I amused him by stopping suddenly and saying disconsolately, "This is perfectly terrible. One cannot advance: one cannot progress. Now we of the road—"

16   "Yes. I know."

17   "I was going to say, we advance continually."

18   "I know."

19   "We are always learning, expanding, developing. Why, even in my short life I have seen a great deal of advance—the Transvaal War, the Fiscal Question, Christian Science, Radium. Here for example—"

20   I took out my pedometer, but it still marked twenty-five, not a degree more.

21   "Oh, it's stopped! I meant to show you. It should have registered all the time I was walking with you. But it makes me only twenty-five."

22   "Many things don't work in here," he said. "One day a man brought in a Lee-Metford, and that wouldn't work."

23   "The laws of science are universal in their application. It must be the water in the moat that has injured the machinery. In normal conditions everything works. Science and the spirit of emulation—those are the forces that have made us what we are."

24   I had to break off and acknowledge the pleasant greetings of people whom we passed. Some of them were singing, some talking, some engaged in gardening, hay-making, or other rudimentary industries. They all seemed happy; and I might have been happy too, if I could have forgotten that the place led nowhere.

25   I was startled by a young man who came sprinting across our path, took a little fence in fine style, and went tearing over a ploughed field till he plunged into a lake, across which he began to swim. Here was true energy, and I exclaimed: "A cross-country race! Where are the others?"

26   "There are no others," my companion replied; and, later on, when we passed some long grass from which came the voice of a girl singing exquisitely to herself, he said again: "There are no others." I was bewildered at the waste in production, and murmured to myself, "What does it all mean?"

27   He said: "It means nothing but itself"—and he repeated the words slowly, as if I were a child.

28   "I understand," I said quietly, "but I do not agree. Every achievement is worthless unless it is a link in the chain of development. And I must not trespass on your kindness any longer. I must get back somehow to the road and have my pedometer mended."

29   "First, you must see the gates," he replied, "for we have gates, though we never use them."

30   I yielded politely, and before long we reached the moat again, at a point where it was spanned by a bridge. Over the bridge was a big gate, as white as ivory, which was fitted into a gap in the boundary hedge. The gate opened outwards, and I exclaimed in amazement, for from it ran a road—just such a road as I had left—dusty under foot, with brown crackling hedges on either side as far as the eye could reach.

31   "That's my road!" I cried.

32   He shut the gate and said: "But not your part of the road. It is through this gate that humanity went out countless ages ago, when it was first seized with the desire to walk."

33   I denied this, observing that the part of the road I myself had left was not more than two miles off. But with the obstinacy of his years he repeated: "It is the same road. This is the beginning, and though it seems to run straight away from us, it doubles so often, that it is never far from our boundary and sometimes touches it." He stooped down by the moat, and traced on its moist margin an absurd figure like a maze. As we walked back through the meadows, I tried to convince him of his mistake.

34   "The road sometimes doubles to be sure, but that is part of our discipline. Who can doubt that its general tendency is onward? To what goal we know not—it may be to some mountain where we shall touch the sky, it may be over precipices into the sea. But that it goes forward—who can doubt that? It is the thought of that that makes us strive to excel, each in his own way, and gives us an impetus which is lacking with you. Now that man who passed us—it's true that he ran well, and jumped well, and swam well; but we have men who can run better, and men who can jump better, and who can swim better. Specialization has produced results which would surprise you. Similarly, that girl—"

35   Here I interrupted myself to exclaim: "Good gracious me! I could have sworn it was Miss Eliza Dimbleby over there, with her feet in the fountain!"

36   He believed that it was.

37   "Impossible! I left her on the road, and she is due to lecture this evening at Tunbridge Wells. Why, her train leaves Cannon Street in—of course my watch has stopped like everything else. She is the last person to be here."

38   "People always are astonished at meeting each other. All kinds come through the hedge, and come at all times—when they are drawing ahead in the race, when they are lagging behind, when they are left for dead. I often stand near the boundary listening to the sounds of the road—you know what they are—and wonder if anyone will turn aside. It is my great happiness to help someone out of the moat, as I helped you. For our country fills up slowly, though it was meant for all mankind."

39   "Mankind have other aims," I said gently, for I thought him well-meaning; "and I must join them." I bade him good evening, for the sun was declining, and I wished to be on the road by nightfall. To my alarm, he caught hold of me, crying: "You are not to go yet!" I tried to shake him off, for we had no interests in common, and his civility was becoming irksome to me. But for all my struggles the tiresome old man would not let go; and, as wrestling is not my specialty, I was obliged to follow him.

40   It was true that I could have never found alone the place where I came in, and I hoped that, when I had seen the other sights about which he was worrying, he would take me back to it. But I was determined not to sleep in the country, for I mistrusted it, and the people too, for all their friendliness. Hungry though I was, I would not join them in their evening meals of milk and fruit, and, when they gave me flowers, I flung them away as soon as I could do so unobserved. Already they were lying down for the night like cattle—some out on the bare hillside, others in groups under the beeches. In the light of an orange sunset I hurried on with my unwelcome guide, dead tired, faint from want of food, but murmuring indomitably: "Give me life, with its struggles and victories, with its failures and hatreds, with its deep moral meaning and its unknown goal!"

41   At last we came to a place where the encircling moat was spanned by another bridge, and where another gate interrupted the line of the boundary hedge. It was different from the first gate; for it was half transparent like horn, and opened inwards. But through it, in the waning light, I saw again just such a road as I had left—monotonous, dusty, with brown crackling hedges on either side, as far as the eye could reach.

42   I was strangely disquieted at the sight, which seemed to deprive me of all self-control. A man was passing us, returning for the night to the hills, with a scythe over his shoulder and a can of some liquid in his hand. I forgot the destiny of our race. I forgot the road that lay before my eyes, and I sprang at him, wrenched the can out of his hand, and began to drink.

43   It was nothing stronger than beer, but in my exhausted state it overcome me in a moment. As in a dream, I saw the old man shut the gate, and heard him say: "This is where your road ends, and through this gate humanity—all that is left of it—will come in to us."

44   Though my senses were sinking into oblivion, they seemed to expand ere they reached it. They perceived the magic song of nightingales, and the odour of invisible hay, and stars piercing the fading sky. The man whose beer I had stolen lowered me down gently to sleep off its effects, and, as he did so, I saw that he was my brother.

Kris Hager

After reading "The Other Side of the Hedge," I discovered that the dominant visual image in my mind was that of the gates opening outward onto the road. As I read the story, the one intriguing question that continually interrupted my thoughts was: "Where do I fit in"?

My drawing is the direct result of the impact that one particular quote toward the end of the story had on me in providing the answer to that question. "This is where your road ends, and humanity—all that is left of it—will come in to us." According to my interpretation, the peaceful, friendly paradise that the narrator accidentally stumbled into is actually the ultimate goal of humanity, and the pinnacle of progress and civilization. Because I envision myself as a competitive, goal-oriented, and motivated individual, I consider myself still on the road, inching forward. My drawing represents the achievement of the goal of life, and the gates at the end of the road welcoming those of us from life's rocky road into a beautiful paradise. This exercise was definitely helpful in shaping my perception of the story.

Although freewriting, outlining, and brainstorming help to focus our attention on the plot, style, and purpose of the story, drawing shifts our attention toward the more sensory details. Not only do we see more clearly and vividly the imagery and visual details presented by the author, but we can also gain a deeper understanding of personal perspective. Each individual's mental picture of "The Other Side of the Hedge" depends on which concepts, expressions, or details had the greatest impact and the most influence. Drawing helped me find myself in this story as part of humanity struggling forward toward the gates to paradise.

Questions for Discussion

1. What type of person is the narrator? Do you like him? How does he feel about competition? What is his attitude toward his brother? Does he find pleasure in his life?

2. What is the meaning of the road and the runners on it? What does the hedge suggest? What does it hide from view?

3. What is suggested by the narrator's closing his eyes just before seeing the light through the hedge? What is the significance of the narrator's difficult passage through the hedge ("all the things I was carrying were scraped off me . . . I had to wiggle blindly forward")?

4. What are the main qualities of life on "the other side of the hedge"? How is the landscape different? In what type of activities do the citizens participate? How do they feel about progress and achievement?

5. What is your response to the narrator's initial reaction to the world on the other side of the hedge? Do you agree that this world is "but a prison" that "the place led nowhere"? Are the narrator's arguments about the advantages of the road convincing?

6. Who is the man with the scythe? What choice does the narrator make at the close of the story? Why? Do you find the ending of the story hopeful or disturbing?

Ideas for Writing

1. Write an extended comparison between your own vision of a relaxed, noncompetitive lifestyle and the other side of the hedge presented in Forster's story. How is your perspective on noncompetitiveness similar to and/or different from that of Forster's narrator? How much of your life do you feel should be spent in noncompetitive activities?

2. Based on evidence given in the story, write an essay in which you interpret the narrator's final gesture. Do you believe that the narrator has changed his perspective and that he will stay on the other side, or do you think he will return to life on the road? In your view, has he made the right decision?

 # Ivana Kim

Dreams as Conscious Visions

A freshman student from San Marino, California, when she wrote this essay, Ivana Kim is studying medicine at Harvard Medical School. Ivana Kim began the following essay, a definition of her own dream or personal vision of the future, by writing down all the ideas that came into her head when she thought about the con-

cept of the dream. She then "selected the best ideas and organized them," after which she "sat down and wrote the paper—very slowly." She typically writes her papers a few sentences at a time, doing most of her revision in her mind, and comments that "writing is work to me because I put so much thought into each sentence, but the satisfaction I feel when I finish a piece makes the work worthwhile."

JOURNAL

How do you see yourself ten years from now? What are you doing currently to attain your dreams of the future?

1   One day during Freshman English as we were discussing the idea of keeping dream journals, I said to myself, "How can I keep a dream journal? I don't remember any of my dreams. I'm not even sure if I do dream." However, I soon realized that I do indeed dream and that there are certain dreams I never forget. These are not dreams I have while I am sleeping; they are visions I create in my conscious mind, visions of what I want for my future. I believe our most important dreams are those we have when fully conscious. "Dream" in this sense of the word does not merely refer to images that appear to us in our sleep; it is something more specific. Our conscious dreams are expressions of our most meaningful desires, desires that are more significant to our futures than those hidden ones which psychologists such as Freud and Jung believe are expressed in our nocturnal dreams. We can act on our waking aspirations because we can understand the desires which are embodied in them; these wishes are concrete. Our conscious hopes do not need to be interpreted. Instead of leaving us mystified with only a vague idea of their messages, these dreams guide us and clearly point out the direction of our lives. Conscious dreams are hopeful visions of what we want to be, what we want to happen, what we want to do. Such dreams are not altogether realistic, but they help us set and achieve the goals that enable us to find fulfillment in life.

2   When Martin Luther King, Jr. said, "I have a dream," he was referring to this visionary type of dream. He wanted the United States to become a nation in which people would be judged "not by the color of their skin but by the content of their character." His greatest desire was to obtain freedom and justice for all. His dream was not completely realistic; it is not possible to erase prejudice totally from the minds of all citizens. However, this vision of an ideal America motivated King's actions, driving him to set smaller more realistic goals as a means of nearing the ideal. His dream was not a fleeting image which occurred in the darkness of night; it was a source of permanent inspiration. He said, "I *have* a dream. . . . I have a dream *today*." He didn't say, "I had a dream last night." King's words exemplify the meaning of the word "dream" as a conscious, idealistic, long-lived hope which gives direction to a person's life. Additionally, King's dream was not simply a personal dream; it sparked an enthusiasm that was contagious. His dream was shared by all of those involved in the civil rights movement, strengthening

them to endure pain and hardship in order to move closer to the fulfillment of their vision. Thus, a dream is not necessarily limited to an individual; many people can believe in the same dream.

3   Those who live in America share a common hope: the American Dream, which is a conscious vision of opportunity and success. The same idealistic belief that anything is possible through hard work motivates the average American, although specific ideas of success may differ among individuals. One person's dream might consist of finding a secure job, marrying an attractive person, buying a comfortable suburban house and a nice car, and having two children. Another person might long to live in a log cabin in the woods and open an outdoors school in order to teach people about nature. The common link between the two visions is both people's belief that they can attain what they dream if only they strive hard enough and take advantage of the opportunities America offers. Neither of these dreams includes realities such as paying taxes and bills, changing diapers, facing harsh weather and wild animals, or dealing with all the paperwork and problems of starting a school. Such mundane details are unnecessary in dreams. Dreams should *not* be totally realistic. When they become burdened with reality they are no longer inspirational and cease to be dreams. Our conscious dreams represent ideal situations consciously constructed and sustained to embody personal values and priorities, and therefore inspire us to work and to achieve.

4   We also have dreams that are purely personal. They do not have to be common to millions of people, like the American Dream, or to be so profound that they involve the entire nation, like King's. Every individual has a personal dream which gives meaning and direction to his or her life. I dream about becoming a doctor, of being called "Dr. Kim," doing rounds in a hospital, having the knowledge and skill to relieve pain and cure illness, feeling the emotional satisfaction that comes from such work. Although many others may share the same dream, I believe my vision is unique because it involves my own values and reasons for wanting to become a doctor and because I solely am sustaining it. I could choose to abandon this dream at any time, but I don't. It is my creation. As I continue to keep it before me, it influences the courses I select, the activities in which I choose to participate, the amount of time I study, and my general attitude toward academics. The dream I have for my career is one of my most important sources of motivation. I do not dream of the many years of study, sleepless nights, and other details of reality; I dream of the rewards and fulfillment in attaining something I so strongly desire. Thus, my personal dream is an image of my highest aspirations, which I sustain in my conscious mind to guide and inspire my choices and actions.

5   The word "dream" then, as defined through the preceding examples, means a vision of our hopes and desires which we purposefully retain in our minds to help direct our lives but which is not completely buried in reality. This definition gives dreams much more significance than one in which dreams are simply pictures we see in our sleep. To quote Walt Disney, "A dream is a wish your heart makes." A conscious dream is a wish somewhere in between a fantasy and a goal. Such aspirations are not as imaginary and unattainable as fantasies, but they are loftier and more idealistic than practical goals. They are the wishes of our conscious mind and heart which make us reach higher and grow.

Questions for Discussion

1. In what sense does Ivana Kim use the words "dream" and "vision"? Compare her definition to the definitions of other writers in this chapter.
2. Do you agree with the importance Ivana Kim places on "conscious dreaming," or do you think that the unconscious mind plays a larger part in formulating our dreams and aspirations than she believes?
3. Why does Ivana Kim think that conscious dreams should not concern themselves with the realistic, practical details necessary for their accomplishment? Do you agree with her?
4. Compare Ivana Kim's vision of the American Dream with that held by the speaker and her son in Cathy Song's "Heaven." Which view seems more realistic? Which dream coincides most with your own American Dream?

 ## Ryan Wesley Bounds

The New Enlightenment

Ryan Wesley Bounds, originally from Hermiston, Oregon, is intrigued by issues of psychology, law, and society. He was a freshman when he wrote the following essay for his composition class, responding to a question that asked students to "Create a negative or positive future utopian community, a model or flawed society based on some of the highest dreams and ideals of our culture or of your own ideals." In his essay, Bounds explores the concept of multiculturalism in the form of an imaginary future society dedicated to multiculturist ideals. Bounds went through a number of revisions, twice sharing the essay with his classmates, to find ways to make his utopic vision clearer.

JOURNAL

Write about a conflict you have had with a parent over an issue related to culture or tradition. Was the conflict resolved, and if so, how?

1 "I just don't understand why it is so hard for you to accept," sighed Banthas, "that I do not believe in them." He could see the anger in his father's face.

2 Mr. Fobi clenched his fist and pounded it on the table. "I do not see why you are being so difficult. What is there that is unbelievable? The gods inhabit every-

thing. Our lives are good because they will it to be. The gods cannot be seen or touched; their existence is not scientifically provable, nor disputable. You have to believe, Banthas, because you have no choice. Do not turn your back on them and on your family . . . do not abandon our ideals."

3   Banthas, a typical-looking Zambezian youth of twenty-third century America, leaned petulantly against the stark white wall of the family kitchen. His arms laid across the traditional leather vest, which he habitually wore foppishly unfastened, and his eyes rolled in exaggerated irritation. "Why do I have to believe in everything that you believe in to be a member of this family?"

4   "Banthas, a family is a people's most fundamental and sacred unit. It is so special because, like an entire culture, its members share the same attitudes and traditions. People in the same family are bound by common ideals. Didn't you learn the story of the young man who left his family and struck out over the dunes and the mountains? Don't you remember how he lost his confidence and his sense of himself because he lost contact with the ideas of his people? Cultural education should teach you that lesson, if no other." Banthas' father was becoming less angry, but in his anger's stead grew anxiety. He could not imagine what was compelling his oldest and (by Zambezian custom) most favored son to denounce the infinite wisdom of his forefathers.

5   Mr. Fobi, nevertheless, was certain of two things. First, something had gone terribly wrong with the educational and political system of the vast multicultural society of which his family was a member. Surely, Banthas had not nurtured this revulsion against his people's idols on his own; the Education Minister—currently a Mandarin Buddhist—had obviously not taken proper steps to ensure that Zambezian culture was portrayed with the esteem and appreciation it deserved. (Why would he? To expect that he would be as interested in Zambezian culture as in his own would be unreasonable, indeed.) Secondly, Mr. Fobi was certain that he could not allow his son to ignore the principles of his culture, of his family, and of his ancestors. Such indulgence would threaten the fragile foundation of the larger multicultural society and the very integrity of the proud Zambezian community. Surely, he thought, Banthas could be made to see that.

6   The following day, intent on investigating the precise cause of his son's alarming shift in attitudes, Mr. Fobi decided to spend his lunch hour viewing a part of Banthas' class at Public School #954, which every youth within five miles was required to attend. As Mr. Fobi strode through the crowded halls of the school, he was jostled by students of every earthly complexion, all wearing—quite nearly like badges of personal merit—the costume of their particular culture. It was beyond him how the Aleutian students could bear the oppressive Los Angeles heat in their heavy sealskin jackets, but, of course, he was not Aleutian. Amid a thousand other thoughts, Mr. Fobi could not help but marvel: "it is miraculous that all these young adults from different backgrounds can attend school, grow and work together, and yet so valiantly resist the temptation to hate each other . . . or to love each other." He was tremendously relieved that this emotionally neutral tolerance was possible.

7   The portion of the curriculum that Mr. Fobi saw was an exploration of man's

origin from the perspectives of the African cultures. As he feared, the Zambezian outlook was woefully misrepresented by the South African guest-lecturer, who was personally responsible for teaching all 75 of the acknowledged African cultures that day. Despite the best of intentions, the Zambezian perspective was portrayed as merely superstitious and irrational, and no explanation or poetic justification was provided for the belief system that had been passed down from father to son for three hundred generations. Most distressingly of all, the lecturer spent only half as long on the Zambezian view as he did on those of western and southern Africa (the latter two cultural regions were, in Mr. Fobi's view, mostly the same, anyway). "How," he despaired, "is Banthas supposed to appreciate and remain loyal to his own people, when their culture is so unfairly presented? It is no wonder he does not believe—no wonder that he embraces the godlessness of the western and southern peoples."

8   Mr. Fobi returned to the Regional Tribunal, where he worked as a judge. It was Mr. Fobi's particular duty to preside over the trial and sentencing of any fellow Zambezian who was charged with a crime, just as it was Mr. Andreassen's duty to dispense justice to his fellow Danes. The days of expecting a person to receive a fair trial from a judge of a different race or creed had vanished with the New Enlightenment. It was, in Mr. Fobi's day, unquestioned that a person should be judged and punished only within the context of his own cultural upbringing, since a person of a different race or creed could not hope to have a complete comprehension of someone from another culture, despite the best efforts of Cultural Education. This realization was the foundation of the new social system, and the pride of every modern thinker.

9   At the end of the day, Mr. Fobi returned home. He had been pondering the previous evening's conversation with Banthas, and decided that the best course would be to reveal to his son the danger that the young man's novel beliefs held for Zambezians and for the larger society. Mr. Fobi walked into the recreation room, where he found Banthas watching a French comedy on the wall-sized monitor. He addressed his son with an air of understanding and support, "Banthas, I have realized why it is that you do no believe what your mother and I see as the truth. By the shortsighted design of that Mandarin Minister of Education" (his voice assumed a subtle sneer), "Zambezian ideals have been shown as silly and as unimportant. You see value being placed elsewhere, on other African cultures and the Chinese cultures. It must confuse you, I understand that." Mr. Fobi held his breath, waiting for the response he knew to be forthcoming.

10   "Father, I do admit to being confused, but I cannot force myself to believe all that you and mother believe. What difference does it make anyway?

11   "It makes all the difference in the world, Banthas. For the same reason that a Zambezian can never marry a person of Greek or Cambodian descent, you must not surrender the ideals of your people. To do so would hasten the dissolution of our proud and independent culture, and, as the gods would have it, nothing is worse than to lose one's ancestral culture." Mr. Fobi sighed and continued: "Before the New Enlightenment, everyone thought as you did. Premium value was placed on personal success in a society dominated by one cul-

ture. Myopic policies and lust for personal indulgence brought many great cultures to their destruction as they melted into the traditions of the dominant people. But, with the New Enlightenment, these cultures were rediscovered and their value finally appreciated. The education that you receive and the laws on which I rule reflect our society's commitment never to allow another culture's destruction. Culture is no longer merely man's expression of himself, but the end of man's actions."

12   "Father, I know all about the New Enlightenment," Banthas insisted, "but what does this have to do with me?"

13   Mr. Fobi was quick to respond. "Banthas, it means that you will learn to believe in the gods. It means that you will go to the temple with your mother and me. It means that you will not watch any more of these ludicrous French comedies—for they obviously steer your mind in the wrong direction. If you, Banthas, are allowed to abandon the righteous ideals of the Zambezian people, then all who are educated incorrectly by our required schools will abandon them, as well. Our culture—our people—would be no more. All this because you presumed to express your beliefs instead of those of your parents and your neighbors."

14   Banthas rested his head on his hand as he sat in his chair. He reached up and turned off the monitor, and the image of the laughing Frenchman faded from sight. He turned and watched the stern figure of his father as it marched silently from the darkened room.

15   Banthas sat for at least a quarter of an hour in the empty room, ruminating over his situation and the unfortunate but unequivocal signs of dementia he perceived in his father. Then, possessed by nothing but his will to do things his own way, Banthas went to his room to perform, perhaps for the last time, what had become his favorite self-indulgence. He locked the door to his room and quietly, oh so quietly, played a recording of an English rock band (whose music was the very antithesis of Zambezian pipe music). With swift and furtive movements, though he knew the door was locked, Banthas shed the brown leather outfit which was the hallmark of the proper Zambezian and donned a pair of faded denim jeans and a plain white t-shirt. After admiring his appearance in the mirror, he left his room, sneaked out of the house, and headed resolutely toward the center of the metropolis to pretend—if just for a day—that he was not Zambezian, after all.

Questions for Discussion

1. A utopian fiction is a kind of argument for a vision of the world, a vision that coincides with or is critical of the utopia or "distopia" presented in the story. Does Bounds argue either for or against Zambezian society in his story? Provide examples of scenes, comments, and encounters within the story that could be considered as positive or negative arguments.

2. Mr. Fobi is relieved to observe that the youths in Public School #954 neither love nor hate each other. Why does he think it is good that the students do not love their peers? How do you respond to his reasoning here?

3. Do Mr. Fobi's fears that Zambezian culture would disintegrate if Ban-thas pursued his own ideas seem valid, or simply a reflection of the rigidity of his ideals and insecurities?

4. Do you think that it is possible for every group of people in a society to be treated fairly, to receive the same benefits as any other group? Would the "New Enlightenment" be a beneficial revolution for America?

5. Ryan Wesley Bounds's first draft for this essay was rather abstract and generalized in its description of Zambezian society and its institutions. He revised it to make it more physical and concrete, so that readers could become more involved and identify more strongly with the characters. Give examples of Bounds's attempts to make his vision more physical and tangible. Do you think he was successful, or would more concrete details improve the story?

Chapter Writing Topics

1. In essay or story form create a utopian community based on some of the highest dreams and ideals of American culture, of a particular cultural group within America, or of your own ideals. Conclude with an explanation of the choices you made in setting up your utopian world, and an analysis of the potentially negative aspects of your utopia as well as ideas for how you might handle the problems.

2. Create your own vision or speculation about the future as do King, Black Elk, and Dillard.

3. Develop an ideal program for educating today's children to be citizens of the future. What emphasis would you put on science and technology? How would you introduce dreams, myths, and imaginative literature? How would you present history, social science, and politics? What books would you assign, and why? Discuss several particular projects that you might have your students complete to give your readers a sense of how you would teach.

4. Write an essay in which you propose an ideal social and educational program for the writer, drawing on both your own ideas and on ideas presented throughout this text. Also describe the community or setting that would help the writer to flourish.

5. The "future visions" of many of the ethnic and cultural groups in the United States vary greatly due to their histories and prior successes or failures in attaining the "American Dream." Compare the future visions of two different ethnic groups represented in this chapter or elsewhere in the text—Asian Americans, African Americans, Native Americans, Hispanic Americans. Discuss the historical origins of the dreams of each group and the confidence or pessimism that each currently has for attaining the dream.

6. After thinking about Annie Dillard's "A Field of Silence," Black Elk's "The Great Vision," and the other discussions of the power of visions in

this chapter, write about a visionary experience that you have had. When you are finished narrating the experience, present your interpretation of its meaning and impact on your life.

7. Many films have been made that attempt to provide visions of possible futures. Select and view a film that presents a vision of the future; then discuss the vision: Does it seem probable in a literal or symbolic way? Why? You might select a film from the following list:

Metropolis, 2001: A Space Odyssey, Brazil, Blade Runner, Terminator 1 & 2, Dreams (Kurosawa), Handmaids' Tale, Strange Days, The Last Wave

CREDITS

Maya Angelou, "The Angel of the Candy Counter," from *I Know Why the Caged Bird Sings*. Copyright © 1969 by Maya Angelou. Reprinted by permission of Random House, Inc.

Julie Apodaca, "Gay Marriage: Why the Resistance?" Reprinted by permission of the author.

Margaret Atwood, "Reading Blind." Written as an introduction to *The Best American Short Stories 1989*, published in the United States by Houghton Mifflin, edited by Margaret Atwood and Shannon Ravenel. It is herewith reprinted with permission of the author.

Bruno Bettelheim, "Fairytales and the Existential Predicament," from *The Uses of Enchantment: The Meaning and Importance of Fairytales*. Copyright © 1975, 1976 by Bruno Bettelheim. Reprinted by permission of Alfred A. Knopf, Inc.

Eavan Boland, "The Source," from *In a Time of Violence*. Copyright © 1994 by Eavan Boland. Reprinted by permission of W. W. Norton & Company, Inc.

Jorges Luis Borges, "The Book of Sand," from *The Book of Sand*, translated by Norman Thomas di Giovanni. Translation copyright © 1971, 1975, 1976, 1977 by Emece Editores, S. A., and Norman Thomas di Giovanni. Used by permission of Dutton Signet, a division of Penguin Books USA Inc.

Ryan Bounds, "The New Enlightenment." Reprinted by permission of the author.

Elizabeth Bowen, "Out of a Book," from *Collected Impressions*. Copyright © 1946 by Elizabeth Bowen. Reproduced by permission of Curtis Brown Ltd., Literary Executors of the Estate of Elizabeth Bowen.

Joseph Campbell, "The Four Functions of Mythology," from *Myths, Dreams and Religion*. Copyright © 1970 by the Society for Arts, Religion, and Contemporary Culture.

Joyce Chang, "Drive Becarefully." Reprinted by permission of the author.

John Cheever, "The Enormous Radio," from *The Enormous Radio and Other Stories*. Copyright © 1953, 1981 by John Cheever. Reprinted by permission of The Wylie Agency, Inc.

Judith Ortiz Cofer, "The Other," from *Reaching for the Mainland and Selected New Poems*. Copyright © 1995 and reprinted by permission of Bilingual Press.

Judith Ortiz Cofer, "Silent Dancing." Reprinted with permission from the publisher of *Silent Dancing: A Partial Remembrance of a Puerto Rican Childhood*. (Houston: Arte Publico Press-University of Houston, 1990).

Rosa Contreras, "On Not Being a Girl." Reprinted by permission of the author.

Annie Dillard, "Aim for the Chopping Block." Excerpt to be titled, "Aim for the

INDEX